American Legal History

American Legal History
Cases and Materials

KERMIT L. HALL   WILLIAM M. WIECEK
PAUL FINKELMAN

New York   Oxford
OXFORD UNIVERSITY PRESS
1991

Oxford University Press

Oxford   New York   Toronto
Delhi   Bombay   Calcutta   Madras   Karachi
Petaling Jaya   Singapore   Hong Kong   Tokyo
Nairobi   Dar es Salaam   Cape Town
Melbourne   Auckland

and associated companies in
Berlin   Ibadan

Published by Oxford University Press, Inc.,
200 Madison Avenue, New York, New York 10016

Oxford is a registered trademark of Oxford University Press

Library of Congress Cataloging-in-Publication Data
Hall, Kermit.
American legal history : cases and materials / Kermit L. Hall,
William M. Wiecek, Paul Finkelman.
p.   cm.   Includes bibliographical references and index.
ISBN 0-19-505907-7. — ISBN 0-19-505908-5 (pbk.)
1. Law—United States—History and criticism.   I. Wiecek, William M., 1938 –.
II. Finkelman, Paul, 1949–.   III. Title.
KF352.A7H35   1991
349.73—dc20   [347.3]   90-39128

1 3 5 7 9 8 6 4 2

Printed in the United States of America
on acid-free paper

To our teachers
Paul L. Murphy, Stanley I. Kutler,
Stanley N. Katz
and to
Harold M. Hyman,
who has taught us all

Preface

Just two decades ago, American legal history was a new field. Only a few law schools and even fewer history departments offered courses in the history of private law and legal institutions on anything like a regular basis. When law was studied in its historical context, the emphasis was on public law generally and the work of the Supreme Court specifically. Courses in either constitutional history or, in political science departments and law schools, its twin, constitutional law, were the closest brush that most undergraduates and law students had with the nation's legal past. The history of American law was, at best, a reprise on major Supreme Court cases and the justices that delivered them. Today, however, American legal history, if not a fully mature field, is at least growing up fast. Thanks in part to a more eclectic approach to legal education in law schools and to the impact of social history on the undergraduate history curriculum, American legal history is now taught at almost every law school and in a good number of history departments. And it is increasingly taught with an eye to merging rather than separating themes of private and public law development.

This book is designed to serve undergraduate as well as graduate courses in departments of history and political science while fitting comfortably in legal history courses taught in law schools. We have, for example, made a particular effort to meet the needs of instructors and students, whatever their academic discipline, by including extensive headnotes that locate documents in their historical context. But this format is only one way in which this book differs from conventional law school casebooks and traditional documentary collections used in history and political science courses. We have excluded perplexing questions and small-change note cases that overwhelm many law school casebooks. We have, instead, provided excerpts of cases that are longer than those typically found in documentary collections. Finally, we have used materials from secondary sources, such as articles from law reviews and journals, only sparingly. Our goal is to let the documents of legal history speak for themselves. At the same time, we take an expansive view of American legal culture, so much so that we have included materials not usually found in casebooks, such as speeches, government reports, and works of philosophy. These kinds of documents, we believe, help to fit legal change with social, economic, and political developments. In short, our approach is one that stresses the tension inherent in our legal system between law as a technical subject with its own internal logic and law as a scheme of social choice responsive to a host of political, social, and economic pressures.

We have chosen documents that illustrate important developments in legal history or that exemplify a particular direction of legal change. This approach reflects the reality of legal history. Legal change is often marked not by a great case and a great precedent, but by a series of incremental developments that gradually lead to a new consensus within the legal community and often society as a whole. In this way, legal history at the state level is not like the history of the federal Constitution, where a change of justices on the United States Supreme Court has resulted in dramatic changes in constitutional law.

We, of course, recognize that the federal government, whether through the Supreme Court, Congress, or the presidency, has been a powerful engine of legal change. But we also believe that an important ingredient in our legal history has been the changed importance of each within our legal system. For example, the nineteenth-century Supreme Court often ratified legal developments that had begun at the state level; the early-twentieth-century Court often stymied legal change; and the post–Depression era Supreme Court has often been in the vanguard of legal change. Since the Civil War, the nature of American federalism has shifted from a state-oriented system to one centered on the national government. In the past fifty years, the Supreme Court and Congress have done much to promote social change through the law. Indeed, when one views the history of American law, as we do, as the unfolding of social choices through the legal process, then the modern High Court and its justices, as well as Congress, take on considerable importance. For these reasons, our later chapters have far more material dealing with the national government—the Court, Congress, and even the presidency—than do the earlier ones.

Throughout this book, we have sought to provide opportunities to understand the interaction of public and private law developments. We believe, on balance, that the traditional distinction between legal and constitutional history has been often misleading, invariably artificial, and frequently irrelevant. Public and private law are best viewed as reciprocal and reinforcing phenomena. Changes in private and public law evolved from decisions by state courts and the lower federal courts, as well as from laws passed by state legislatures. Because these changes took place within the American federal system, legal developments were necessarily incremental, local, and seldom simultaneous throughout the country. Nevertheless, legal change did spread, usually reaching most, if not all, states. Many of these changes were also part of our constitutional history. To illustrate: the steamboat monopoly granted to Robert R. Livingston and Robert Fulton in New York, which had the blessing of that state's highest court, and the subsequent development of the Erie Canal in New York were probably as important to the growth of American commerce, and the development of the Constitution's commerce clause, as Chief Justice Marshall's landmark opinion in *Gibbons* v. *Ogden* (1824). In some areas of law, such as torts, state legislative policy-making and state court decisions have always predominated. In the modern era, however, in areas such as civil liberties and civil rights, decisions by the Supreme Court have not only initiated new paths in the law, but instantly nationalized them as well. Desegregation, reapportionment, and the legal recognition of personal autonomy and a right to privacy are well-known examples of the impact of the nation's highest court on law and public policy. They have also been, of course, highly controversial, since Americans have disagreed not only about the substance of these changes, but whether the Court's role in bringing them about has been appropriate.

We have combined the organizational principles of both history and law in this volume. Most law school casebooks are arranged topically, as is most legal education itself. This topical approach is even true for the study of constitutional law, which is the most historical course of the traditional law school curriculum. Historical studies, however, are usually organized chronologically to show change over time. We have embraced this approach, not only because we have, after all, fashioned a book of history, but also because we believe that the best way to understand the important changes in American law is to appreciate the constancy of much of our legal culture from its English origins to the present. Our goal is to display legal developments in their historical context.

While we have organized the book chronologically, we have also retained thematic and topical coherence. Thus many subjects—such as torts, property, the law of race relations, marriage and the family, and contracts—reappear throughout the volume. Slavery, for example, was a fact of life for millions of Americans from the seventeenth century to 1865. Something on the law of slavery is found in each of the first four chapters, while Chapters 5, 8, and 10 have materials on race relations and the law since emancipation. Similarly, material on the law of family relations and children is discussed in Chapters 1, 5, 7, and 10. This arrangement makes it possible to follow legal developments in many fields over the course of three and a half centuries. The organization of this book, therefore, reflects our abiding belief that legal history can contribute to both an undergraduate's study of the American past and law student's grasp of the legal system.

We hope that this casebook will serve for years, perhaps decades, in the teaching of American legal history. With that in mind, we look forward to the suggestions, criticisms, and comments of our colleagues who use this book. Many have already helped us in the creation of this book. Library staffs at the University of Florida and its College of Law, Syracuse University College of Law, Brooklyn Law School, and the reference and interlibrary loan staffs of SUNY Binghamton have cheerfully helped us find and procure documents. The staffs of the University of Pittsburgh Law Library, Albany Law School Library, and Broome County Supreme Court Library were generous with their time and resources.

Research assistants and clerical staff have shared the more mundane aspects of documentary collection and editing. At Florida, we were helped by Steven Prescott, Eric Rise, Elizabeth Monroe, and Steve Noll; at Syracuse, by Colleen Grzeskowiak, Bill Karchner, and Valerie Cross; at Brooklyn, by Degna P. Levister, Elayna Nacci, and Jordan Tamagni. Cassie Dix, Joyce Phillips, Rebecca McKnight, and Danny Payne, all of the University of Florida, contributed their word-processing talents. A special debt is owed to Nita Melton and Nancy Schmit, of the Copy Center at the University of Florida's College of Law, for the good humor and patient professionalism they displayed.

We also wish to thank a variety of colleagues and friends whose help was essential to the making of this book. They include John Arthur, Gordon Bakken,

Michal Belknap, George Butler, Robert Cottrol, Jim Ely, Stephen Gottlieb, John Johnson, Judy Lauer, Jelica Nikolic, Jenni Parrish, Judith Schafer, and Jamil Zainaldin. Our colleagues and spouses have patiently borne the sacrifices of time forced on them.

Nancy Lane, of Oxford University Press, threw her enthusiastic support behind this project at an early stage. She has become a valued friend of legal history over the years. Irene Pavitt, also of Oxford, was a model of professionalism in moving the manuscript into the production process.

The dedication of this book acknowledges our teachers, the proverbial giants on whose shoulders we attempt to stand. American legal history owes an incalculable debt to their wisdom and teaching. The three of us are the richer for their friendship, encouragement, and good counsel.

Gainesville, Fla.   K.L.H.
Syracuse, N.Y.   W.M.W.
Brooklyn, N.Y.   P.F.
August 1990

Abbreviated Contents

Contents

American Legal History

1

Law in the Morning of America: The Beginnings of American Law, to 1760

An interplay between inherited legal culture and the New World environment molded law in early America. The legal historian George Lee Haskins has referred to this as a combination of "tradition and design."[1] Out of this interplay emerged a new synthesis, a distinctly American legal culture. This chapter surveys these two different sources of American law, inherited culture and indigenous environment, and explores the ways in which they blended.

English inhabitants of the mainland colonies, even those who were born in the New World, did not think of themselves as "Americans" until late in the eighteenth century. Rather, they considered themselves English people who happened to be living outside the realm for a time. They therefore regarded themselves as heirs of the English constitutional tradition and, especially, of those parts of it that guaranteed individual liberty.

English Protestant religious thought emphasized both the individual and the community. It thus laid a foundation for the prominent place of individualism in American law, lending American legal institutions, both public and private, a strong bent toward protecting the rights of the individual. At the same time, the communitarian element of Protestant theology suggested a role for law in protecting the community. American law has never been exclusively individualistic in its emphasis, particularly in the early period when English Americans felt themselves beset on all sides by hostile peoples: Catholic Spaniards to the south, Catholic French to the north, Indians everywhere, and enslaved Africans in their midst. This feeling produced a fortress mentality that relied on law to fortify the community.

The New World environment forced changes on this inherited legal culture. Although Americans thought of themselves as English people, the very act of creating new societies provided both the opportunity and the necessity for inventing or adapting legal institutions appropriate to the New World environment. For example, legal institutions that supported the established church in England, such as canon law and its courts, were unsuited to the religiously heterogeneous societies of America, particularly in the middle colonies. The emergence of religious toleration in the colonies was an adaptation to conditions unique to the New World.

Americans had an opportunity to create a legal order entirely anew, rather than having to crawl out from underneath centuries of custom and tradition that provide the basis for inherited legal systems. Americans selected out of the English heritage only those legal elements that suited their needs. Rhode Island's 1663 charter, for example, limited conformity to English laws only to those suited to the "nature and constitution of the place and people there."[2] In his *Commentaries on the Constitution*, first published in 1833, Justice Joseph Story summed up this tradition. The colonists

> did not carry over with them all the laws of England when they migrated hither, for many of them must, from the nature of the case, be wholly inapplicable to their situation, and inconsistent with their comfort and property. . . . [T]hey carry with them all the laws applicable to their situation, and not repugnant to the local and political circumstances, in which they are placed.[3]

Americans created their legal order in a spirit of eclectic opportunism, drawing from various sources of law and devising new rules of law when they found nothing suitable in existing systems.

Thus free to choose from English and foreign laws or to invent new legal concepts, Americans were less constrained than their English compeers in molding laws to fit their society's needs. Consequently, American law was easier to reform and more instrumentalist in its development than British law.

Americans did not develop their laws unthinkingly or reflexively. On the contrary, they displayed a remarkable sophistication in thinking about the governance of their societies. Drawing freely on varied sources of political thought, from the Bible and justice-of-the-peace manuals at the beginning of the seventeenth century to the writings of Montesquieu, James Harrington, and John Locke, by the eve of the Revolution, Americans evolved a political philosophy to support the choices they made about the directions of their legal development. Eventually, they reaffirmed their commitment to the English common law as the foundation of their legal order, but it was the common law stripped of unsuitable doctrines. Americans regarded the common law as a guarantor of personal liberty, not merely as a quarry of private law. Thus conceived, the common law became a foundation of republican liberty after the American Revolution.

Early American law contained within itself the basis of the legal and constitutional order of the post-Revolutionary states and nation. During the first century of English settlement, American law incorporated some essentials of what we today call the rule of law, including concepts of higher law, limited government, due process of law, and consent as the basis of legal obligation. Much of later American constitutionalism was anticipated and recapitulated in early legal development. Law, as historian Arthur Bestor has observed, has a configurative effect: it molds people and the way they think as much as it is molded by them.[4] So it was with law in America's morning. We have become the people that we are today because of the laws that we adopted in the early English settlements.

The English Heritage

The beginnings of American law trace back to landmarks of English constitutional development. The earliest and most revered of these was Magna Charta.

Magna Charta
1215

Chapter 39 of Magna Charta is the source of modern procedural and substantive due process. Its law-of-the-land phrasing appears in many of the early American state constitutions and, together with the cognate concept of due process, is at the core of modern concepts of limited government.

39.   No freeman shall be captured or imprisoned or disseised or outlawed or exiled or in any way destroyed, nor will we go against him or send against him, except by lawful judgment of his peers or by the law of the land.

Note: Due Process and the Law of the Land

Two parliamentary enactments of the late Middle Ages supplemented chapter 39 by extending the benefits of Magna Charta beyond the nobility to all subjects of the realm. The first provided that "every Man may be free to sue for and defend his Right in our Courts and elsewhere, according to the Law" (20 Edw. III, c. 4 [1346]). The second introduced the phrase "due process of law" for the first time into English law: "no Man, of what Estate or Condition that he be, shall be put out of Land or Tenement, nor taken, nor imprisoned, nor put to Death, without being brought in answer by due Process of Law" (28 Edw. III, c. 3 [1354]). American courts in the nineteenth and twentieth centuries were to hold that the phrases "law of the land" and "due process of law" were equivalent.

Note: The Glorious Revolution

England's constitutional struggles in the seventeenth century shaped Americans' image of themselves and of their legal order. In a conflict lasting the better part of that century, the Stuart monarchs insisted that the king was superior to the laws and was himself the lawgiver; in the words of Lord Chancellor Ellesmere in *Calvin's Case* (1608), "the monarch is the law; the king is the law speaking." Opposed to these absolutist pretensions was an idea originally expressed by Henry de Bracton in the thirteenth century: the king is under God and under the law. Sir Edward Coke, Chief Justice of the Court of Common Pleas in the early seventeenth century, warmly promoted this idea.

Tensions developed between the Stuart monarchs and successive Parliaments over constitutional questions involving the raising of taxes. The Crown's growing need for revenue to finance foreign campaigns and to subdue the rebellious Scots confronted the stubborn determination of parliamentarians (like John Pym) to establish parliamentary prerogatives and inhibit the king's attempts to govern without the consent of Parliament. The resulting struggles degenerated into the Civil War of 1642 to 1649 between royalist and parliamentary forces, which resulted in the complete triumph of the latter. The victors tried King Charles I for treason against Parliament and beheaded him in 1649.

Then ensued a unique period in English history, the republican Commonwealth, known as the Protectorate after the accession of Oliver Cromwell as Protector in 1653. Puritan theological and political belief enjoyed a short-lived ascendancy during the Commonwealth, while more radical and democratic ideas surfaced. Constitutional turbulence was not suppressed until Charles II, son of Charles I, was restored to the throne in 1660.

The Restoration did not resolve underlying constitutional conflicts, however. The Habeas Corpus Act of 1679 provided a statutory basis for issuance of that guaranty of the subject's liberty, but a more comprehensive resolution of the threat posed by royal pretensions was still needed. Supporters of parliamentary power (now called Whigs) were dismayed when Charles's brother, James II, succeeded him to the throne in 1685, for James, a Roman Catholic, attempted to remove disabilities that Parliament had imposed on Roman Catholics and Dissenters. This seemed to threaten the Protestant succession. In 1688, facing unified resistance, James fled the kingdom, and Parliament offered the throne to his Protestant daughter Mary and her husband, William, Prince of Orange. The Glorious Revolution finally settled the constitutional struggles of the seventeenth century, secured the Protestant Reformation, and buried absolutist pretensions. Many of these results were explicitly ratified by Parliament in the Bill of Rights of 1689.

Note: The *Case of the Seven Bishops* (1688)

The *Case of the Seven Bishops* (1688) demonstrated the reality of the continuing threat posed by Stuart absolutism, as well as popular resistance to it, in a state trial involving constitutional questions of the right to petition and seditious libel. To ease restrictions on Roman Catholics and Dissenters, James II proclaimed the Declaration of Indulgence in 1687 and ordered that it be read in all churches of the realm. Seven Anglican bishops sent a private petition to the king asking to be relieved from the requirement, partly because of the threat it posed to the security of the Reformation and the place of the established church, and partly because they believed it to be an unconstitutional exercise by the king of the power of dispensation (that is, the king was taking it upon himself, without any constitutional warrant, to disregard a law, a pretension that Parliament had declared illegal in 1662 and 1672). Papacy and absolutism once again took center stage as constitutional questions, but in the *Case of the Seven Bishops* they were complicated by two other constitutional issues: the right of subjects to petition the king, and the reach of the common-law crime of seditious libel as a means of suppressing political opposition. In the trial of the bishops, the Chief Justice of Kings Bench instructed the jury that "anything that shall disturb the government or make mischief and a stir among the people" constitutes seditious libel. His colleague Justice Allybone elaborated this position:

> I think, in the first place, that no man can take upon him to write against the actual exercise of the government unless he have leave from the government, but he makes a libel, be what he writes true or false. . . . Then, I lay down this for my next position: that no private man can take upon him to write concerning the government at all. For what has any private man to do with the government, if his interest be not stirred or shaken? . . . When I intrude myself into other men's business that does not concern my particular interest, I am a libeller. . . . Now then, let us consider further, whether, if I will take upon me to contradict the government, any specious pretence that I shall put

upon it shall . . . give it a better denomination. And truly I think it is the worse because it comes in a better dress . . . ; so that, whether it be in the form of a supplication or an address or a petition, if it be what it ought not to be, let us call it by its true name . . . —it is a libel. . . . Then, gentlemen, consider what this petition is. This is a petition relating to something that was done and ordered by the government. Whether the reasons of the petition be true or false, I will not examine that now; nor will I examine the prerogative of the crown; but only take notice that this relates to the acts of the government. . . . And shall or ought anybody to come and impeach that as illegal which the government has done? Truly, in my opinion, I do not think he should or ought; for by this rule may every act of the government be shaken when there is not a parliament . . . sitting.

But two of the judges disagreed with this view, and the jury acquitted the bishops, to wild popular acclaim. Whigs shortly thereafter invited William and Mary to accept the English throne. The popular and political vindication of the bishops did not resolve any of the issues raised in their case, though. These included the following: Do subjects have a right to petition the king or Parliament, and, if so, may any conditions be imposed on that right? Can persons be criminally prosecuted for criticizing the government or its policies? Is truth a defense in a prosecution for seditious libel? How far may a jury disregard the instructions of a court in a criminal prosecution? Can the jury determine for itself whether a law should be disregarded on the grounds that it is unconstitutional? Many of these were raised a generation later in the colony of New York in *Zenger's Case* (1735), excerpted later in this chapter.

The English Bill of Rights
1689

This document, the first fruits of the Glorious Revolution, set forth the liberties of the subject that the parliamentary party had struggled for most of the seventeenth century to affirm against Stuart absolutism. It was a direct forerunner of the American Bill of Rights, which was adopted a century later.

And thereupon the said lords spiritual and temporal, and commons, pursuant to their respective letters and elections, being now assembled in a full and free representative of this nation, taking into their most serious consideration the best means for attaining the ends aforesaid, do in the first place (as their ancestors in like case have usually done) for the vindicating and asserting their ancient rights and liberties, declare:

1. That the pretended power of suspending laws, or the execution of laws, by regal authority, without consent of parliament, is illegal.

2. That the pretended power of dispensing of laws, or the execution of laws, by regal authority, as it hath been assumed and exercised of late, is illegal.

3. That the commission for erecting the late court of commissioners for ecclesiastical causes, and all other commissions and courts of like nature are illegal and pernicious.

4. That levying money for or to the use of the crown, by pretence of prerogative, without grant of parliament, for longer time, or in other manner than the same is or shall be granted, is illegal.

5. That it is the right of the subjects to petition the King, and all committ-
ments and prosecutions for such petitioning are illegal.

6. That the raising or keeping a standing army within the kingdom in time of
peace, unless it is with consent of parliament, is against law.

7. That the subjects which are protestants, may have arms for their defence
suitable to their conditions, and as allowed by law.

8. That election of members of parliament ought to be free.

9. That the freedom of speech, and debates or proceedings in parliament,
ought not to be impeached or questioned in any court or place out of parliament.

10. The excessive bail ought not to be required, nor excessive fines imposed;
nor cruel and unusual punishments inflicted. . . .

*   *   *

13. And that for redress of all grievances, and for the amending strengthening
and preserving of the laws, parliaments ought to be held frequently. . . .

JOHN LOCKE
"Of Civil Government"
1690

*John Locke, writing during the Glorious Revolution, summed up the principles
for which the Whigs contended, providing a basis for modern theories of liberal
government. A century later, Americans of the Revolutionary generation, familiar with his writings, regarded them as a synopsis of the constitutional principles
vindicated in the Glorious Revolution. Although other writers, notably Baron de
Montesquieu, were more influential and more frequently cited in American Revolutionary debates, Locke's eloquent summation of liberal constitutional principles seemed to hold up to Americans a mirror of the ideas of their own
Revolution.*

Man being born, as has been proved, with a Title to perfect Freedom, and an
uncontrouled enjoyment of all the Rights and Priviledges of the Law of Nature,
equally with any other Man, or Number of Men in the World, hath by Nature a
Power, not only to preserve his Property, that is, his Life, Liberty and Estate,
against the Injuries and Attempts of other Men; but to judge of, and punish the
breaches of that Law in others, as he is perswaded the Offence deserves. . . .

Whenever, therefore, any number of men are so united into one society as to quit
every one his executive power of the law of nature and to resign it to the public,
there and there only is a political or civil society. And this is done wherever any
number of men, in the state of nature, enter into society to make one people, one
body politic, under one supreme government, or else when any one joins himself to,
and incorporates with any government already made; for thereby he authorizes the
society or, which is all one, the legislative thereof to make laws for him as the
public good of the society shall require, to the execution whereof his own assistance, as to his own decrees, is due. And this puts men out of a state of nature into
that of a commonwealth by setting up a judge on early, with authority to determine

all the controversies and redress the injuries that may happen to any member of the commonwealth, which judge is the legislative or magistrates appointed by it. . . .

Men being, as has been said, by nature all free, equal, and independent, no one can be put out of this estate and subjected to the political power of another without his own consent. The only way whereby any one divests himself of his natural liberty and puts on the bonds of civil society is by agreeing with other men to join and unite into a community for their comfortable, safe, and peaceable living one amongst another, in a secure enjoyment of their properties and a greater security against any that are not of it. This any number of men may do, because it injures not the freedom of the rest; they are left as they were in the liberty of the state of nature. When any number of men have so consented to make one community or government, they are thereby presently incorporated and make one body politic wherein the majority have a right to act and conclude the rest. . . .

The great and chief end, therefore, of men's uniting into commonwealths and putting themselves under government is the preservation of their property. To which in the state of nature there are many things wanting.

First there wants an established, settled, known law, received and allowed by common consent to be the standard of right and wrong and the common measure to decide all controversies between them; for though the law of nature be plain and intelligible to all rational creatures, yet men, being biased by their interests as well as ignorant for want of studying it, are not apt to allow of it as a law binding to them in the application of it to their particular cases.

Secondly, in the state of nature there wants a known and indifferent judge with authority to determine all differences according to the established law; for every one in that state being both judge and executioner of the law of nature, men being partial to themselves, passion and revenge is very apt to carry them too far and with too much heat in their own cases, as well as negligence and unconcernedness to make them too remiss in other men's.

Thirdly, in the state of nature there often wants power to go back and support the sentence when right, and to give it due execution. They who by any injustice offend will seldom fail, where they are able, by force, to make good their injustice; such resistance many times makes the punishment dangerous and frequently destructive to those who attempt it.

*   *   *

But though Men when they enter into Society, give up the Equality, Liberty, and Executive Power they had in the State of Nature, into the hands of the Society, to be so far disposed of by the Legislative, as the good of the Society shall require; yet it being only with an intention in every one the better to preserve himself his Liberty and Property; (For no rational Creature can be supposed to change his condition with an intention to be worse) the power of the Society, or Legislative constituted by them, can never be suppos'd to extend farther than the common good; but is obliged to secure every ones Property by providing against those three defects above-mentioned, that made the State of Nature so unsafe and uneasie. And so whoever has the Legislative or Supream Power of any Common-wealth, is bound to govern by establish'd standing Laws, promulgated and known to the People, and not by Extemporary Decrees; by indifferent and upright Judges, who are to decide Controversies by those Laws; and to employ the force of the Community at home, only in the Execution of such Laws, or abroad to prevent or redress Foreign Injuries, and secure the Community from Inroads and Invasion. And all this to be directed to no end, but the Peace, Safety, and publick good of the People.

*   *   *

These are the bounds which the trust that is put in them by the society and the law of God and nature have set to the legislative power of every commonwealth, in all forms of government:

First, they are to govern by promulgated established laws, not to be varied in particular cases, but to have one rule for rich and poor, for the favorite at court and the countryman at plough.

Secondly, these laws ought to be designed for no other end ultimately but the good of the people.

Thirdly, they must not raise taxes on the property of the people without the consent of the people, given by themselves or their deputies. And this properly concerns only such governments where the legislative is always in being, or at least where the people have not reserved any part of the legislative to deputies to be from time to time chosen by themselves.

Though in a Constituted Commonwealth, standing upon its own Basis, and acting according to its own Nature, that is, acting for the preservation of the Community, there can be but one Supream Power, which is the Legislative, to which all the rest are and must be subordinate, yet the Legislative being only a Fiduciary Power to act for certain ends, there remains still in the People a Supream Power to remove or alter the Legislative, when they find the Legislative act contrary to the trust reposed in them. For all Power given with trust for the attaining an end, being limited by that end, whenever that end is manifestly neglected, or opposed, the trust must necessarily be forfeited, and the Power devolve into the hands of those that gave it, who may place it anew where they shall think best for their safety and security. . . .

The Beginnings of Constitutionalism in America

Throughout American experience, the polestar of public law has been the concept of "constitutionalism," a vague and comprehensive catchword embracing the ideals of limited government, the rule of law, and the various structural devices that achieve the substantive content of republican government in America. The origins of constitutionalism long predated the Republic. They derived partly from the way that we think about the sources of law, and partly from the way that Americans structured the goverments of their societies. Compact theory and practice, as exemplified in the Mayflower Compact of 1620, was a basic element of constitutionalism. So was representative government, a logical derivative of social covenants.

One of the constitutional dichotomies that fueled the Glorious Revolution both in the mother country and in the colonies was the conflict between governmental power and individual liberty. Americans confronted this dualism from the outset, especially in Massachusetts. John Winthrop, a founder and longtime leader of the Bay Colony, addressed the issue before any English settlers landed, when in his lay sermon aboard the ship *Arbella* in 1629 he coined the endlessly captivating image of America as a "city upon a hill." Winthrop emphasized the primacy of community over individual interests. Roger Williams, a voice of heterodoxy in the Bay Colony, espoused an altogether different approach to governance, condemning government efforts to coerce belief. Between them, Winthrop and Williams defined the polar opposites of power and liberty that have remained constants throughout our political history. Finally, that remarkable early codification, the Laws and Liberties of Massachusetts (1648), provided a sophisticated official affirmation of the sources of governmental authority.

Constitutionalism also derived from the structuring of colonial government, which took different forms. The covenants of Plymouth embodied compact theory in its purest form. A variant was the liberal and democratic order established in Rhode Island under the influence of Roger Williams. Emigration to the New World languished during the disorders of the English Civil War and Protectorate, but resumed vigorously after the Restoration. The charters and compacts of the Restoration period embody many innovations in the forms and principles of government. For example, the bizarre and abortive experiments in John Locke's Fundamental Constitutions of Carolina, the liberal and democratizing approaches of William Penn in his Frames of Government for Pennsylvania, and the do-it-yourself innovations in guarantees for personal liberty in New York's Charter of Libertyes (1683): all attest to the robust experimentation in a constitutional form of government that characterized America's first century.

The Mayflower Compact
1620

This brief constitutive document demonstrates how powerfully the paradigm of compact influenced the earliest settlers of New England. It also represented an effort by the Pilgrim leadership of the Plymouth Colony to control the non-Pilgrim gentiles in their midst, who had their own notions about freedom in the New World. In either capacity, it may justly be considered America's first constitution.

In the Name of God, Amen. We, whose names are underwritten, the Loyal Subjects of our dread Sovereign Lord King James, by the Grace of God, of Great Britain, France, and Ireland, King, Defender of the Faith, &c. Having undertaken for the Glory of God, and Advancement of the Christian Faith, and the Honour of our King and Country, a Voyage to plant the first Colony in northern Parts of Virginia; Do by these Presents, solemnly and mutually, in the Presence of God and one another covenant and combine ourselves together into a civil Body Politick, for our better Ordering and Preservation, and Furtherance of the Ends aforesaid: And by Virtue hereof do enact, constitute, and frame, such just and equal Laws, Ordinances, Acts, Constitutions, and Offices, from time to time, as shall be thought most meet and convenient for the general good of the Colony; unto which we promise all due Submission and Obedience.

JOHN WINTHROP
"A Model of Christian Charity"
1629

At the beginning of colonization in the early seventeenth century, English settlers aspired to an organic unity in the societies they were creating. One basis of this hope was the social compact, or covenant, uniting all members of a society through the bond of an agreement that constituted them a body politic. This thinking was particularly congenial to Puritan emigrants, for whom covenant already occupied a central place in their ecclesiology. From the organic bond created by compact flowed a utopian vision of America as a "city upon a hill." John Winthrop drew these themes together in his shipboard sermon on the Arbella *in 1629, in a masterly fusion of theological and secular concepts blazing with the inner vision of prophecy.*

For the work we have in hand, it is by mutual consent through a special overruling providence and a more than an ordinary approbation of the churches of Christ, to seek out a place of cohabitation and consortship, under a due form of government both civil and ecclesiastical. In such cases as this, the care of the public must oversway all private respects by which not only conscience but mere civil policy doth bind us; for it is a true rule that particular estates cannot subsist in the ruin of the public.

*   *   *

Thus stands the cause between God and us: we are entered into covenant with Him for this work; we have taken out a commission, the Lord hath given us leave to draw our own articles. We have professed to enterprise these actions upon these and these ends; we have hereupon besought Him of favor and blessing. Now if the Lord shall please to hear us and bring us in peace to the place we desire, then hath He ratified this covenant and sealed our Commission [and] will expect a strict performance of the articles contained in it. But if we shall neglect the observation of these articles which are the ends we have propounded, and dissembling with our God, shall fall to embrace this present world and prosecute our carnal intentions, seeking great things for ourselves and our posterity, the Lord will surely break out in wrath against us, be revenged of such a perjured people, and make us know the price of the breach of such a covenant.

Now the only way to avoid this shipwreck and to provide for our posterity is to follow the counsel of Micah: to do justly, to love mercy, to walk humbly with our God. For this end, we must be knit together in this work as one man. We must entertain each other in brotherly affection; we must be willing to abridge ourselves of our superfluities for the supply of others' necessities; we must uphold a familiar commerce together in all meekness, gentleness, patience and liberality. We must delight in each other, make others' conditions our own, rejoice together, mourn together, labor and suffer together: always having before our eyes our commission and community in the work, our community as members of the same body. So shall we keep the unity of the spirit in the bond of peace, the Lord will be our God and delight to dwell among us, as His own people, and will command a blessing upon us in all our ways.

*   *   *

For we must consider that we shall be as a city upon a hill, the eyes of all people are upon us. So that if we shall deal falsely with our God in this work we have undertaken, and so cause him to withdraw His present help from us, we shall be made a story and a by-word through the world.

ROGER WILLIAMS
"The Bloudy Tenent of Persecution"
1644

The unity demanded by Winthrop dissolved quickly, first in the commercial southern colonies, and then, within a generation, in the more homogeneous theocracies of New England. In the realm of political theory, a principal enemy of that unity was the tension between the need for powerful government and the demand for individual liberty.

Roger Williams was certainly not typical of his time and place, and his call for religious freedom should not be taken as representative of American thought in the seventeenth century. Yet Williams prefigures later trends in American thinking about public law, particularly the relationship between church and state in a secular, pluralistic society. He was ahead of his time in his ideas about popular sovereignty.

. . . All Civill States with their Officers of justice in their respective constitutions and administrations are proved essentially Civill, and therefore not Judges, Governours or Defendours of the Spiritual or Christian state and Worship.

Sixthly, It is the will and command of God that (since the comming of his Sonne the Lord Jesus) a permission of the most Paganish, Jewish, Turkish, or Antichristian consciences and worships, bee granted to all men in all Nations and Countries: and they are onely to bee fought against with that Sword which is only (in Soule matters) able to conquer, to wit, the Sword of Gods Spirit, the Word of God.

*   *   *

Eighthly, God requireth not an uniformity of Religion to be inacted and inforced in any civil state, which inforced uniformity (sooner or later) is the greatest occasion of civill Warre, ravishing of conscience, persecution of Christ Jesus in his servents, and of the hypocrisie and destruction of millions of souls.

Ninthly, In holding an inforced uniformity of Religion in a Civill State, wee must necessarily disclaime our desires and hopes of the Jewes conversion to Christ.

Tenthly, An inforced uniformity of Religion throughout a Nation or civill State, confounds the Civill and Religious, denies the principles of Christianity and civility, and that Jesus Christ is come in the Flesh.

Eleventhly, the Permission of other consciences and worships then a state professeth, only can (according to God) procure a firme and lasting peace, (good assurance being taken according to the wisedome of the civill state for uniformity of civill obedience from all sorts).

Twelfthly, lastly, true civility and Christianity may both flourish in a state or Kingdome, notwithstanding the permission of divers and contrary consciences, either of Jew or Gentile.

. . . [T]he proper meanes whereby the Civill Power may and should attaine its end, are onely Political, and principally these Five.

First the erecting and establishing what forme of Civill Government may seeme in wisedome most meet, according to generall rules of the Word, and state of the people.

Secondly, the making, publishing, and establishing of wholesome Civil Laws, not only such as concern Civill Justice, but also the free passage of true Religion: for, outward Civill Peace ariseth and is maintained from them both, from the latter as well as the former:

Civill peace cannot stand intire, where Religion is corrupted, . . . And yet such Lawes, though conversant about Religion, may still be counted Civill Lawes, as on the contrary, an Oath doth still remaine Religious, though conversant about Civill matters.

Thirdly, Election and appointment of Civill officers, to see execution of those Lawes.

Fourthly, Civill Punishments and Rewards, of Trangressors and Observers of these Lawes.

Fifthly, Taking up Armes against the Enemies of Civill Peace.

*   *   *

So that the Magistrates, as Magistrates, have no power of setting up the Forme of Church Government, electing Church officers, punishing with Church censures, but to see that the Church doth her duty herein. And on the other side, the Churches as Churches, have no power (though as members of the Commonweale they may have power) of erecting or altering formes of Civill Government, electing of Civill officers, inflicting Civill punishments (no, not on persons excommunicate) as by deposing Magistrates from their Civill Authoritie, or withdrawing the hearts of the people against them, to their Lawes, no more then to discharge wives, or children, or servants, from due obedience to their husbands, parents, or masters: or by taking up armes against their Magistrates, though he persecute them for Conscience: for though members of Churches who are publique officers also of the Civill State, may suppresse by force the violent of Usurpers, as Jehoiada did Athaliah, yet this they doe not as members of the Church, but as officers of the Civill State.

*   *   *

First, whereas they say, that the Civill Power may erect and establish what forme of civill Government may seem in wisdom most meet, I acknowledge the proposition to be most true, both in itself, and also considered with the end of it, that a civill Government is an Ordinance of God, to conserve the civill peace of people so farre as concernes their Bodes and Goods, as formerly hath been said.

But from this Grant I infer, (as before hath been touched) that the Soveraigne, originall, and foundation of civill power lies in the people, (whom they must needs meane by the civill power distinct from the Government set up.) And if so, that a

People may erect and establish what forme of Government seemes to them most meete for their civill condition: It is evident that such Governments as are by them erected and established, have no more power, nor for no longer time, then the civill power or people consenting and agreeing shall betrust them with. This is cleere not only in Reason, but in the experience of all commonweales, where the people are not deprived of their naturall freedome by the power of Tyrants.

The Laws and Liberties of Massachusetts
1648

This justification for the origins of government would be a significant document in any age. But considering that it was penned less than thirty years after the founding of the Massachusetts Bay Colony, its sophistication and maturity are extraordinary. Seldom has a legislative drafting committee composed so cogent a statement of political philosophy, encompassing the ideals of the community and an articulate theory of imputed consent.

To Our Beloved Brethren and Neighbours
the Inhabitants of the Massachusetts, the Governour, Assistants
and Deputies assembled in the Generall Court of that
Jurisdiction with grace and peace in our
Lord Jesus Christ

So soon as God had set up Politicall Government among his people Israel hee gave them a body of lawes for judgment both in civil and criminal causes. These were brief and fundamental principles, yet withall so full and comprehensive as out of them clear deductions were to be drawne to all particular cases in future times. For a Common-wealth without lawes is like a Ship without rigging and steeradge. Nor is it sufficient to have principles or fundamentalls, but these are to be drawn out into so many of their deductions as the time and conditions of that people may have use of. And it is very unsafe & injurious to the body of the people to put them to learn their duty and libertie from generall rules, nor is it enough to have lawes except they be also just. Therefore among other priviledges which the Lord bestowed upon his peculiar people, these he calls them specially to consider of, that God was neerer to them and their lawes were more righteous then other nations. God was sayd to be amongst them or neer to them because of his Ordinances established by himselfe, and their lawes righteous because himselfe was their Law-giver: yet in the comparison are implyed two things, first that other nations had something of Gods presence amongst them. Secondly that there was also somewhat of equitie in their lawes, for it pleased the Father (upon the Covenant of Redemption with his Son) to restore so much of his Image to lost man as whereby all nations are disposed to worship God, and to advance righteousness: . . . They did by nature the things contained in the law of God. But the nations corrupting his Ordinances (both of Religion, and Justice) God withdrew his presence from them proportionably whereby they vvere given up to abominable lusts. . . . Wheras if they had vvalked

according to that light & lavv of nature they might have been preserved from such
moral evils and might have injoyed common blessing in all their natural and civil
Ordinances: now, if it might have been so with the nations who were so much
strangers to the Covenant of Grace, what advantage have they who have interests in
this Covenant, and may injoye the special presence of God in the puritie and native
simplicitie of all his Ordinances by which he is so neer to his owne people. This
hath been no small priviledge, and advantage to us New-England that our Churches,
and civil State have been planted and growne up (like two vvines) together like that
of Israel in the vvilderness by which we were put in minde (and had opportunity put
into our hands) not only to gather our Churches, and set up the Ordinances of Christ
Jesus in them according to the Apostolick patterne by such lights as the Lord
graciously afforded us: but also withall to frame our civil Politie, and lawes according to the rules of his most holy word whereby each do help and strengthen other
(the Churches the civil Authoritie, and the Civil Authoritie the Churches) and so
both prosper the better without such emulation, and contention for priviledges or
priority as have proved the misery (if not ruine) of both in other places.

*   *   *

These Lawes which were made successively in divers former years, we have
reduced under several heads in an alphabeticall method, that so they might the more
readilye be found . . . wherin (upon every occasion) you might readily see the rule
which you ought to walke by.

*   *   *

You have called us from among the rest of our Bretheren and given us power to
make the lawes: we must now call upon you to see them executed: remembring that
old & true proverb, The execution of the law is the life of the law. If one sort of you
viz: non-Freemen should object that you had no hand in calling us to this worke, and
therfore think yourselvs not bound to obedience &c. Wee answer that a subsequent,
or implicit consent is of like force in this case, as an express precedent power: for in
puting your persons and estates into the protection and way of subsistance held forth
and exercised within this Jursidiction, you doe tacitly submit to this Government
and to all the wholesome lawes thereof[.]

*   *   *

If any of you meet with some law that seemes not to tend to your particular
benefit, you must consider that lawes are made with respect to the whole people,
and not to each particular person: and obedience to them must be yielded with
respect to the common welfare, not to thy private advantage, and as thou yeildest
obedience to the law for common good, but to thy disadvantage: so another must
observe some other law for thy good, though to his own damage; thus must we be
content to bear one anothers burden and so fullfill the Law of Christ.

That distinction which is put between the Lawes of God and the lawes of men,
becomes a snare to many as it is mis-applyed in the ordering of their obedience to
civil Authoritie; for when the Authoritie is of God and that in way of an Ordinance . . . and when the administration of it is according to deductions, and rules
gathered from the word of God, and the clear light of nature in civil nations, surely
there is no humane law that tendeth to common good (according to those principles)
but the same is mediately a law of God, and that in way of an Ordinance which all
are to submit unto and that for conscience sake. . . .

Forasmuch as the free fruition of such Liberties, Immunities, priviledges as humanitie, civilitie & christianity call for as due to everie man in his place, & proportion, without impeachment & infringement hath ever been, & ever will be the tranquility & stability of Churches & Comon-wealths; & the deniall or deprivall thereof the disturbance, if not ruine of both:

It is therefore ordered by this Court, & Authority thereof, That no mans life shall be taken away; no mans honour or good name shall be stayned; no mans person shall be arrested, restrained, bannished, dismembered nor any wayes punished; no man shall be deprived of his wife or children; no mans goods or estate shal be taken away from him; nor any wayes indamaged under colour of Law or countenance of Authoritie unless it be by the vertue or equity of some expresse law of the Country warranting the same established by a General Court & sufficiently published; or in case of the defect of a law in any particular case by the word of God. And in capital cases, or cases concerning dismembring or banishment according to that word to be judged by the General Court.

The Rhode Island Patent
1643

Because the English Civil War had already begun, this Patent was issued by Parliament, not the king. It accordingly has several remarkably advanced features: the settlers themselves constituted the corporation and were endowed with full powers of self-government; the principle of majoritarianism was explicitly recognized; and the Patent was issued on the application of the settlers, who were then free to set up any "Form of Civil Government" that suited them. These progressive features were appropriate to this settlement of "the otherwise-minded," as they were later known. Because the Patent did not provide for appointment of the governor by the Crown, proprietor, or company in England, Rhode Island (like Connecticut) became an autonomous quasi-commonwealth, called "the licentious republic" by its more conservative neighbors.

And whereas there is a Tract of Land in the Continent of America aforesaid, called by the Name of the Narraganset Bay; . . .

And whereas the said English, have represented their Desire to the said Earl, and Commissioners to have their hopeful beginnings approved and confirmed by granting unto them a free Charter of Civil Incorporation and Government: that they may order and govern their Plantation in such a Manner as to maintain Justice and peace, both among themselves and towards all Men with whom they shall have to do. . . .

[We] Do by the Authority of the aforesaid Ordinance of the Lords and Commons give, grant and confirm to the aforesaid Inhabitants of the Towns of Providence, Portsmouth and Newport, a free and absolute Charter of Incorporation to be known by the Name of the Incorporation of Providence Plantations, in the Narraganset-Bay, in New-England.—Together with full Power and Authority to rule themselves, and such others as shall hereafter inhabit within any Part of the said Tract of land, by such a Form of Civil Government, as by voluntary consent of all, or the greater Part of them, they shall find most suitable to their Estate and Condition: and, for that End, to make and ordain such Civil Laws and Constitutions, and to inflict such punishments upon Transgressors, and for Execution therefor so to place, and displace Officers of Justice, as they, or the greater Part of them, shall by free Consent agree unto. Provided nevertheless, that the said Laws, Constitutions, and Punishments, for the Civil Government of the said Plantations be conformable to the Laws of England so far as the Nature and Constitution of the place will admit.

Note: The Post-Restoration Charters

The upheavals of the Civil War and Commonwealth temporarily halted both emigration from England and the process of chartering colonies. With the return of domestic peace in 1660, both resumed vigorously. The charters issued after the Restoration display a more educated grasp of New World conditions and a more sophisticated understanding of how to structure government there. The excerpts below illustrate three widely variant forms that American experimentation in government-making took. The first charter, the fantastic Fundamental Constitutions of Carolina penned by John Locke, has an almost science-fiction air about it. The second charter, William Penn's Frame of Government (1682 draft) is a more realistic yet liberal attempt by a much different kind of proprietor to provide a paternalistic constitution. The third charter, which was abrogated by yet another kind of proprietor (the Duke of York) and hence never went into effect, shows that demands for self-government and protection of the rights of subjects were not confined to benevolent proprietors, but were prevalent among the colonists themselves.

The Fundamental Constitutions of Carolina
1669

The Fundamental Constitutions of Carolina were an exotic charter, far outside the mainstream of American constitutional development. Yet they remain interesting to us for several reasons. The hierarchy of landed, hereditary nobility could never have been transplanted to the mainland colonies, but it suggested a proprietary attitude far removed from that of William Penn. Securities for slavery sat cheek-by-jowl with guarantees of religious freedom and civil liberty. Lawyers were barred. All versions of the Fundamental Constitutions were drafted by John Locke, then in the service of one of the proprietors, the Earl of Shaftesbury; the one excerpted here dates from 1669.

Our sovereign Lord The King having, out of his Royal Grace and Bounty, granted unto us the Province of Carolina, with all the Royalties, Proprieties, Jurisdictions, and Privileges of a County Palatine, as large and ample as the County Palatine of Durham, with other great Privileges; for the better settlement of the Government of the said Place, and establishing the Interest of the Lords Proprietor with Equality, and without Confusion; and that the Government of this Province may be made most agreeable to the Monarchy under which we live, and of which this Province is a part; and that we may avoid erecting a numerous Democracy: we the Lords and Proprietors of the Province aforesaid, have agreed to this following Form of Government, to be perpetually established amongst us, unto which we do oblige our selves, our Heirs and Successors, in the most binding ways that can be devised.

1.   The eldest of the Lords Proprietors shall be Palatine; and upon the Decease of the Palatine, the eldest of the seven surviving Proprietors shall always succeed him.

*   *   *

3.   The whole Province shall be divided into Counties; each County shall consist of eight Seigniories, eight Baronies, and four Precincts; each Precinct shall consist of six Colonies.

*   *   *

9.   There shall be just as many Landgraves as there are Counties, and twice as many Caciques, and no more. These shall be the hereditary Nobility of the Province, and, by right of their Dignity, be Members of Parliament. Each Landgrave shall have four Baronies, and each Cacique two Baronies, hereditarily and unalterably annexed to and settled upon the said dignity. . . .

*   *   *

71.   There shall be a Parliament, consisting of the Proprietors, or their Deputies, the Landgraves and Caciques, and one Freeholder out of every Precinct, to be chosen by the Freeholders of the said Precinct respectively. They shall Sit all together in one Room, and have every Member one vote. . . .

*   *   *

97.   But since the Natives of that Place, who will be concerned in our Plantation, are utterly Strangers to Christianity, whose Idolatry, Ignorance, or Mistake gives us no right to expel or use them ill; and those who remove from other Parts to Plant there will unavoidably be of different Opinions concerning Matters of Religion, the liberty whereof they will expect to have allowed them, and it will not be reasonable for us, on this account, to keep them out; that Civil Peace may be maintained amidst the diversity of Opinions, and our Agreement and Compact with all Men may be duly and faithfully observed, the violations whereof, upon what pretence soever, cannot be without great offence to Almighty God, and great scandal to the true Religion, which we profess; and also, that Jews, Heathens, and other Dissenters from the purity of Christian Religion may not be scared and kept at a distance from it, but, by having an opportunity of acquainting themselves with the truth and reasonableness of its Doctrines, and the peaceableness and inoffensiveness of its Professors, may, by good usage and persuasion, and all those convincing Methods of gentleness and meekness suitable to the Rules and Design of the Gospel, be won over to embrace and unfeignedly receive the Truth: Therefore, any seven or more Persons agreeing in any religion, shall constitute a church or profession, to which they shall give some name, to distinguish it from others. . . .

*   *   *

107.   Since Charity obliges us to wish well to the Souls of all Men and Religion ought to alter nothing any Man's Civil Estate or Right, it shall be lawful for Slaves, as well as others, to Enter themselves and be of what church or Profession

any of them shall think best, and thereof be as fully Members as any Freeman. But yet, no Slave shall hereby be exempted from that Civil Dominion his Master has over him, but be in all other things in the same State and Condition he was in before. . . .

*   *   *

110.   Every Freeman of Carolina shall have absolute Power and Authority over his Negro Slaves, of what Opinion or Religion soever.

WILLIAM PENN
First Frame of Government
1682

William Penn's preface to the Frame of Government that he provided for Pennsylvania in 1682 not only displayed his benign spirit but also contained several ideas congenial to Americans in the ensuing century, such as the concept of balancing forces in government and the central place of popular virtue in sustaining the constitutions of free governments.

I know what is said by the several admirers of monarchy, aristocracy and democracy, which are the rule of one, a few, and many, and are the three common ideas of government, when men discourse on the subject. But I chuse to solve the controversy with this small distinction, and it belongs to all three: Any government is free to the people under it (whatever be the frame) where the laws rule, and the people are a party to those laws, and more than this is tyranny, oligarchy, or confusion. . . .

*   *   *

Governments, like clocks, go from the motion men give them; and as governments are made and moved by men, so by them they are ruined too. Wherefore governments rather depend upon men, than men upon governments. Let men bee good, and the government cannot be bad; if it be ill, they will cure it. But, if men be bad, let the government be never so good, they will endeavor to warp and spoil it to their turn.

I know some say, let us have good laws, and no matter for the men that execute them: but let them consider, that though good laws do well, good men do better: for good laws may want good men, and be abolished or evaded by ill men: but good men will never want good laws, nor suffer ill ones. It is true, good laws have some awe upon ill ministers, but that is where they have not power to escape or abolish them, and the people are generally wise and good: but a loose and depraved people (which is the question) love laws and an administration like themselves. That, therefore, which makes a good constitution, must keep it, viz: men of wisdom and virtue, qualities, that because they descend not with worldly inheritances, must be carefully propagated by a virtuous education of youth; for which after ages will owe more to the care and prudence of founders, and the successive magistracy, than to their parents, for their private patrimonies. . . .

*   *   *

But, next to the power of necessity (which is a solicitor, that will take no denial) this induced me to a compliance, that we have (with reverence to God, and good conscience to men) to the best of our skill contrived and composed to the frame and laws of this government, to the great end of all government, viz: To support power in reverence with the people and to secure the people from the abuse of power; that they may be free by their just obedience, and the magistrates honourable, for their administration: for liberty without obedience is confusion, and obedience without liberty is slavery. To carry this evenness is partly owing to the constitution, and partly to the magistracy: where either of these fail, government will be subject to convulsions; but where both are wanting, it must be totally subverted; then where both meet, the government is like to endure. Which I humbly pray and hope God will please to make the lot of this Pensilvania. Amen.

WILLIAM PENN

The New-York Charter of Libertyes
1683

The Charter of Libertyes contained liberal guarantees for the liberty of the subject, significantly including those most basic elements of the ancient constitution—Magna Charta's chapter 39, and the petit and grand juries. Note too these forward-looking provisions: a primitive homestead exemption, the forerunner of the Third Amendment, and the security of dower. The provision for religious toleration was inevitable in a province as heterogeneous as New York; the only surprise is that religious establishments survived at all, albeit in an enfeebled state. This statute ("Charter" is a misnomer) never became law; it was vetoed by the king. But it is suggestive of innate liberal inclinations that were released by the Glorious Revolution in the colonies.

For the better Establishing the Government of this province of New Yorke and that Justice and Right may be Equally done to all persons within the same
Bee It Enacted by The Governour Councell and Representatives now in Generall Assembly mett and assembled and by the authority of the same.
That the Supreme Legislative Authority under his Majesty and Royall Highnesse James Duke of Yorke Albany &c Lord Proprietor of the said province shall forever be and reside in a Governour, Councell, and the people mett in Generall Assembly.
That The Exercise of the Chiefe Magistracy and Administracon of the Government over the said province shall bee in the said Governour assisted by a Councell with whose advice and Consent or with at least four of them he is to rule and Governe the same according to the Lawes thereof. . . .

*   *   *

That Noe freeman shall be taken and imprisoned or be disseized of his ffreehold or Libertye or ffree Customes or be outlawed or Exiled or any other ways destroyed nor shall be passed upon adjudged or condemned But by the Lawfull Judgment of his peers and by the Law of this province. Justice nor Right shall be neither sold denied or deferred to any man within this province.
That Noe aid, Tax, Tallage, Assessment, Custome, Loane, Benevolence or Imposicon whatsoever shall be layed assessed imposed or levyed on any of his Majestyes Subjects within this province or their Estates upon any manner of Colour

or pretence but by the act and Consent of the Governour Councell and Representatives of that people in Generall Assembly mett and Assembled.

That noe Man of what Estate or Condicon soever shall be putt out of his Lands or Tenements, nor taken, nor imprisoned, nor disherited, nor banished nor any wayes distroyed without being brought to Answere by due Course of Law.

That a ffreeman shall not be amerced for a small fault, but after the manner of his fault and for a great fault after the Greatness thereof Saveing to him his freehold, And a husbandman saveing to him his Wainage and a merchant likewise saveing to him his merchandize. And none of the said Amerciaments shall be assessed but by the oath of twelve honest and Lawfull men of the Vicinage provided the faults and misdemeanours be not in Contempt of Courts of Judicature.

All Tryalls shall be by the verdict of twelve men, and as neer as may be peers or Equalls And of the neighbourhood and in the County Shire or Division where the fact Shall arise or grow Whether the Same be by Indictment Informacon Declaracon or otherwise against the person Offender or Defendant.

That In all Cases Capitall or Criminall there shall be a grand Inquest who shall first present the offence and then twelve men of the neighborhood to try the Offender who after his plea to the Indictment shall be allowed his reasonable Challenges.

That In all Cases whatsoever Bayle by sufficient Suretyes shall be allowed and taken unless for treason or felony plainly and specially Expressed and menconed in the Warrant of Committment provided Always that nothing herein contained shall Extend to discharge out of prison upon bayle any person taken in Execucon for debts or otherwise legally sentenced by the Judgment of any of the Courts of Record within the province.

That Noe ffreeman shall be compelled to receive any Marriners or Souldiers into his house and there suffere them to Sojourne against their willes provided Always it be not in time of Actuall Warr within this province.

That Noe Commissions for proceeding by Marshall Law against any of his Majestyes Subjects within this province shall issue forth to any person or persons whatsoever Least by Colour of them any of his Majestyes Subjects bee destroyed or putt to death Except all such officers persons and Soldiers in pay throughout the Government. . . .

*   *   *

That Noe Estate of a feme Covert shall be sold or conveyed But by Deed acknowledged by her in Some Court of Record the Woman being secretly Examined if She doth it freely without threats or Compulsion of her husband.

*   *   *

That a Widdow after the death of her husband shall have her Dower And shall and may tarry in the Chiefe house of her husband forty dayes after the death of her husband within which forty days her Dower shall be assigned her And for her Dower shall be assigned unto her the third part of all the Lands of her husband dureing Coverture, Except she were endowed of Lesse before Marriage. . . .

*   *   *

That Noe person or persons which professe ffaith in God by Jesus Christ Shall at any time be any wayes molested punished disquited or called in Question for any

Difference in opinion or Matter of Religious Concernment, who doe not actually disturb the Civill peace of the province, But that all and Every such person or persons may from time to time and at all times freely have and fully enjoy his or their Judgments or Consciencyes in matters of Religion throughout all the province, they behaving themselves peaceably and quietly and not useing this Liberty to Lycentiousnesse nor to the civill Injury or outward disturbance of others. . . .

The Sources of Law in America

American lawyers today like to think that the common law was the only body of English law that Americans drew on for their own law, that it was adopted early in the period of English settlement, and that its reception was both inevitable and non-controversial. Each of these assumptions is wrong.

More than half a century ago, the legal historian Julius Goebel speculated that it would have been unlikely that the settlers of New England would have replicated the common law—"as absurd as to expect that they would establish a religious system on the principles of the Anglican Church."[5] Rather, he suggested, in creating their new legal order they would have drawn on the body of law most familiar to them: English local and customary law of the sort found in the borough custumals and in the practice of the manorial and county courts. Subsequent scholarship has confirmed Goebel's conjecture. The result was a heterogeneous body of law, "a layman's version of English legal institutions," Daniel Boorstin called it.[6]

In New York during the proprietary period (1664–1684), an overlaid system of at least four separate bodies of law and judicial systems prevailed: Roman-Dutch civil law; the "Bible codes" of the Connecticut immigrants in Westchester County and on Long Island, reaffirmed in the Duke's Laws of 1665; the laws enforced in the manorial courts on Long Island and up the Hudson River valley; and the common law, which achieved full suzerainty in the legal reforms of 1691. But until it did, the common law met vigorous competition from its rivals. A Dutch resident of Dutchess County contumaciously proclaimed that he "Valued no English law no more than a Turd."[7]

American law was composed in unequal parts of vaguely and inaccurately remembered fragments of common law, local law, and Mosaic law (in New England and on Long Island). To further complicate the picture, the colonies borrowed from one another's laws extensively, yet with great selectivity, choosing only those elements of law suited to their local conditions.

The English common law was a part of American law, of course, however imperfectly it may have been understood and received before 1700. So were parliamentary statutes enacted before the settlement of a particular colony. Subsequent statutes were not part of a colony's laws unless explicitly made applicable to it. New England presents a special case, however. Alhough the common law was eventually received there after the American Revolution, Massachusetts resisted the extension of English law before the 1690s. John Winthrop insolently proclaimed that "our allegiance binds us not the laws of England any longer than while we live in England, for the laws of the Parliament of England reach no further, nor do the king's writs under the great seal go any further."⁸ In 1678, the General Court of Massachusetts-Bay objected to the Navigation Acts, insisting that "the lawes of England are bounded within the fower [four] seas, and doe not reach America."⁹ John Adams, writing in 1776 as "Novanglus," reiterated that viewpoint: "Our ancestors were entitled to the common law of England when they emigrated; that is, to just so much of it as they pleased to adopt, and no more. They were not bound or obliged to submit to it, unless they chose."¹⁰

Note: Reception of the Common Law

The common law was eventually received in all American jurisdictions, including refractory New England, by the nineteenth century. The beginnings of reception may be found in the charters to companies and proprietors granted by the Stuart monarchs in the early seventeenth century. Most of these charters insisted that any laws enacted by the colonists for their own governance must conform to the legal culture of the mother country. The 1632 Charter to the Massachusetts-Bay Company contained a formulation that expressed both kinds of constraints: the General Court of the Company was authorized to enact laws "So, nevertheless, that the Laws aforesaid be consonant to Reason, and be not repugnant or contrary, but (so far as conveniently may be) agreeable to the Laws, Statutes, Customs, and Rights of this Our Kingdom of England."¹¹

Such provisions were the first step on the road to the reception of the common law in America, as well as to the transference of English libertarian traditions, such as the principles derived from Magna Charta. Viewed by the Crown at the time as a means of controlling distant settlements, the conformity clauses came to be seen by Americans in the next century as an assurance that the settlers enjoyed the same rights and liberties as English people who had never left the realm.

William Blackstone on Reception
1765

Long before Americans began to think seriously about the transit of English law, English judges and lawyers had begun to work out the bases of a theory of reception of their legal systems. This was not surprising, since the English had become active colonizers in the sixteenth century and had had to confront the practical problems of legal administration for places like Ireland even earlier. After a century of development, the English theory of reception was summed up by William Blackstone, the magisterial commentator on English laws, in 1765.

Besides these adjacent islands, our more distant plantations in America, and elsewhere, are also in some respect subject to the English laws. Plantations or colonies, in distant countries, are either such where the lands are claimed by right of occupancy only by finding them desert and uncultivated, and peopling them from the mother-country; or where, when already cultivated, they have been either gained by conquest, or ceded to us by treaties. And both these rights are founded upon the law of nature, or at least upon that of nations. But there is a difference between these two species of colonies, with respect to the laws by which they are bound. For it hath been held that if an uninhabited country be discovered and planted by English subjects, all the English laws then in being, which are the birthright of every subject, are immediately there in force. But this must be understood with very many and very great restrictions. Such colonists carry with them only so much of the English law as is applicable to their own situation and the condition of an infant colony; such, for instance, as the general rules of inheritance, and of protection from personal injuries. The artificial refinements and distinctions incident to the property of a great and commercial people, the laws of police and revenue, (such especially as are enforced by penalties,) the mode of maintenance for the established clergy, the jurisdiction of spiritual courts, and a multitude of other provisions, are neither necessary nor convenient for them, and therefore are not in force. What shall be admitted and what rejected, at what times, and under what restrictions, must, in case of dispute, be decided in the first instance by their own provincial judicature, subject to the revision and control of the king in council: the whole of their constitution being also liable to be new-modelled and reformed by the general superintending power of the legislature in the mother-country. But in conquered or ceded countries, that have already laws of their own, the king may indeed alter and change those laws; but till he does actually change them, the ancient laws of the country remain, unless such as are against the law of God, as in the case of an infidel country. Our American plantations are principally of this latter sort, being obtained in the last century either by right of conquest and driving out the natives (with what natural justice I shall not at present inquire), or by treaties. And therefore the common law of England, as such, has no allowance or authority there; they being no part of the mother-country, but distinct (though dependent) dominions. They are subject, however, to the control of the parliament; though (like Ireland, Man, and the rest) not bound by any acts of parliament, unless particularly named. . . .

Giddings v. Brown
1657

The process of reception of English law may be glimpsed in this precocious opinion in a case involving a challenge to a compelled assessment, levied to support the maintenance of a town's minister. This opinion demonstrates that ideas we associate with the nineteenth century, such as rudimentary forms of substantive due process and the rule of law, were current in the seventeenth century. Judge Symonds's opinion emphasizes the primacy of fundamental law, seen in both a religious and a secular sense.

[Court of Assistants for Essex County, Massachusetts, per Samuel Symonds, Assistant:]

I understand this to be about a fundamentall law, and that a fundamentall law properly so called. It is such a law as that God and nature have given to a people. So that it is in the trust of their governors in highest place and others, to preserve, but not in their power to take away from them. Of which sort are these, viz.

1. Election of the supreame governours.

2. That every subject shall and may enjoy what he hath a civell right or title unto, soe as it cannot be taken from him by way of gift or loan, to the use or to be made the right or property of another man, without his owne free consent.

3. That such lawes (though called libertyes) yet more properly they may be called rights, and in this sense this may be added as a third fundamentall law, ...

First, This may be given as a reason, that it is against a fundamentall law in nature to be compelled to pay that which others doe give. For then no man hath any certaynty or right to what he hath, if it be in the power of others (by pretence of authority or without) to give it away (when in their prudence they conceive it to be for the benefit of the owner soe to doe) without his owne consent.

Secondly, This to me is some strengthening to induce my apprehension in this case, viz. That not withstanding in England, it cannot be denied, but that mens estates were sometymes unduly taken from them: Some by force, some by fraud, some by sinister wresting of evidence, yea, and sometimes of law itselfe as about knighthood-money, shipmoney, &c. yet I dare say, if search be made into histories, lawyers bookes of reports, records &c. it cannot be made to appeare that in the most exorbitant times any man hath had his estate taken from him as by the gift of others, under colour of lawe, or countenance of authority. Noe, noe, lawyers would have blushed to have given such a construction of lawes; and suddenly their faces would have waxed pale. For the Kinge would have beene too wise to have owned the plea. And what would all wise men have said for such taking away the greatest outward right or liberty from them? For it may be understood, that benevolencies, incouraging gratuities, leaves, or privy seales, were not required by law, or by pretence of lawe, but desired as by favour. However they were obtained by illegall and tyranicall meanes, as was apprehended. . . .

     *   *   *

See Sir Henry Finch, recorder of London, in his first booke of lawe, page 74, having ended his rules about native fundamentall lawes, he saith in the next page, Therefore lawes positive doe lose their force and are noe lawes at all, which are directly contrary to the former viz. native or fundamentall.

     *   *   *

But now to answer some objections that may be made to the case in hande.

Objection.   Suppose it be true what is expressed, and granted that he were a strange man that should deny the same in the generall: Yet, notwithstanding, it hindereth not that a towne (when and as often as they thinke good, in their prudence) may doe it for good ends, and soe (in speciall cases) it may lawfully be done in the particular, upon the lawe made page the 9th, that every inhabitant shall contribute to all charges in church and commonwealth (whereof he doth or may receive a benefitt) else he shall be strayned.

Answer.   I conceive that it is an extreame dishonour cast upon the generall court, to make such a construction of their positive laws as doth infringe the fundamentall law of mine and thine: for it must needs be voyd, if it should indeed be necessarily construed against the right or liberty of the subject. But the law in its true sense is good.

The Zenger Trial
1735

An apt illustration of the enduring consequences of the Glorious Revolution is provided by the 1735 trial of John Peter Zenger for seditious libel in New York. The arguments of Philadelphia attorney Andrew Hamilton (no relation to Alexander Hamilton) drew on several themes of continuing significance in American public law. His emphasis on the differing social and economic bases of law in America and the mother country was pertinent for the reception of the common law. His concluding peroration, which at first glance seems to be empty and exaggerated rhetoric, was in fact an extrapolation of legal arguments in their broader ideological significance.

Mr. Hamilton.   May it please Your Honor; I agree with Mr. Attorney, that government is a sacred thing, but I differ very widely from him when he would insinuate that the just complaints of a number of men who suffer under a bad administration is libeling that administration.

*   *   *

What strange doctrine is it to press everything for law here which is so in England? I believe we should not think it a favor, at present at least, to establish this practice. In England, so great a regard and reverence is had to the judges, that if any man strikes another in Westminster Hall while the judges are sitting, he shall lose his right hand and forfeit his land and goods for so doing. And though the judges here claim all the powers and authorities within this government that a Court of King's Bench has in England, yet I believe Mr. Attorney will scarcely say that such a punishment could be legally inflicted on a man for committing such an offense in the presence of the judges sitting any court within the Province of New York. The reason is obvious; a quarrel or riot in New York cannot possibly be attended with those dangerous consequences that it might in Westminster Hall; nor (I hope) will it be alleged that any misbehavior to a governor in the plantations will, or ought to be, judged of or punished as a like undutifulness would be to our Sovereign. From all which, I hope Mr. Attorney will not think it proper to apply his law cases (to support the cause of his Governor) which have only been judged where the King's safety or honor was concerned. It will not be denied but that a freeholder in the Province of New York has as good a right to the sole and separate use of his lands as a freeholder in England, who has a right to bring an action of trespass against his neighbor for suffering his horse or cow to come and feed upon his land, or eat his corn, whether enclosed or not enclosed; and yet I believe it would be looked upon as a strange attempt for one man here to bring an action against another, whose cattle and horses feed upon his grounds not enclosed, or indeed for eating and treading down his corn, if that were not enclosed. Numberless are the instances of this kind that might be given, to show that what is good law at one time and in one place is not so at another time and in another place; so that I think the law seems to expect that in these parts of the world men should take care, by a good fence, to preserve their property from the injury of unruly beasts. And perhaps there may be as good reason why men should take the same care to make an honest and upright conduct a fence and security against the injury of unruly tongues.

*   *   *

Mr. Chief Justice.   You cannot be admitted, Mr. Hamilton, to give the truth of a libel in evidence. A libel is not to be justified; for it is nevertheless a libel that is true.

Mr. Hamilton.   I am sorry the Court has so soon resolved upon that piece of law; I expected first to have been heard to that point. I have not in all my reading met with an authority that says we cannot be admitted to give the truth in evidence upon an information for a libel.

Mr. Chief Justice.   The law is clear, that you cannot justify a libel.

*   *   *

Mr. Chief Justice.   Mr. Hamilton, the court is of opinion, you ought not to be permitted to prove the facts in the papers: These are the words of the book, "It is far from being a justification of a libel, that the contents thereof are true, or that the person upon whom it is made had a bad reputation, since the greater appearance there is of truth in any malicious invective, so much the more provoking it is."

Mr. Hamilton.   These are Star Chamber cases, and I was in hopes that practice had been dead with the Court.

Mr. Chief Justice.   Mr. Hamilton, the Court have delivered their opinion, and we expect you will use us with good manners; you are not to be permitted to argue against the opinion of the Court.

Mr. Hamilton.   With submission, I have seen the practice in very great courts, and never heard it deemed unmannerly to—

Mr. Chief Justice.   After the Court have declared their opinion, it is not good manners to insist upon a point in which you are overruled.

Mr. Hamilton.   I will say no more at this time; the Court I see is against us in this point; and that I hope I may be allowed to say.

*   *   *

Mr. Chief Justice.   No, Mr. Hamilton; the jury may find that Zenger printed and published those papers, and leave it to the Court to judge whether they are libelous; you know this is very common; it is in the nature of a special verdict, where the jury leave the matter of law to the Court.

Mr. Hamilton.   I know, may it please Your Honor, the jury may do so; but I do likewise know they may do otherwise. I know they have the right beyond all dispute to determine both the law and the fact, and where they do not doubt of the law, they ought to do so. This leaving it to the judgment of the Court whether the words are libelous or not in effect renders juries useless (to say no worse) in many cases; but this I shall have occasion to speak to by and by; and I will with the Court's leave proceed to examine the inconveniences that must inevitably arise from the doctrines Mr. Attorney has laid down: and I observe in support of this prosecution, he has frequently repeated the words taken from the case of Libel. Famosis in 5.Co. This is indeed the leading case, and to which almost all the other cases upon the subject of libels do refer; and I must insist that upon saying that according as this case seems to be understood by the Court and Mr. Attorney, it is not law at this day: For though I own it to be base and unworthy to scandalize any man, yet I think it is even villainous to scandalize a person of public character, and I will go so far into Mr. Attorney's doctrine as to agree that if the faults, mistakes, nay even the vices of such a person be private and personal, and don't affect the peace of the public, or the liberty or property of our neighbor, it is unmanly and unmannerly to expose them either by word or writing. But when a ruler of people brings his personal failings, but much more his vices, into his administration, and the people find themselves affected by them, either in their liberties or properties, that will alter the case mightily, and all the high things that are said in favor of rulers, and of dignities, and upon the side of power, will not be able to stop people's mouths when they feel themselves oppressed, I mean in a free government. It is true in times past it was a crime to speak truth, and in that terrible Court of Star Chamber, many worthy and brave men suffered for so doing; and yet even in that Court and in those bad times, a great and good man durst say, what I hope will not be taken amiss of me to say in the place, to wit, The practice of informations for libels is a sword in the hands of a wicked king and an arrant coward to cut down and destroy the innocent; the one cannot because of his high station, and the other dares not because of his want of courage, revenge himself in another manner.

*   *   *

But to conclude; the question before the Court and you gentlemen of the jury is not of small nor private concern, it is not the cause of a poor printer, nor of New York alone, which you are now trying: No! It may in its consequence affect every freeman that lives under a British government on the main of America. It is the best cause.

Law and Colonial Society

Law permeated the lives and institutions of early Americans, just as it does in our society today. It regulated their behavior and their social relations, even the most intimate, in ways that we would find unacceptable in our time. Women, children, and other persons who did not enjoy full legal and political capacity labored under disabilities imposed by law. In addition, the spirit of paternalism permeated such laws. Blacks, both slaves and free, were much more severely regulated, and almost nothing of a benign paternalist nature can be found in the early laws of slavery and race. In the more hierarchical society of early America, law attempted to police the boundaries between the classes with far greater rigor than it does in our time.

The criminal law of colonial America served numerous purposes, as it still does. Among these were economic regulation, maintenance of order (especially for purposes of encouraging economic growth), policing morality, and, above all, social control. When thinking about criminal law in America before the Civil War, it is necessary to remember that prisons were nonexistent before independence; jails or lockups were often little more than some convenient attic, basement, or even cave; police forces existed only in the form of a rural constabulary and a rudimentary watch force in some cities; and law enforcement was much more a private citizen's responsibility than it is today.

Marriage, Women, and the Family

William Blackstone on Women in the Eyes of the Law 1765

Blackstone summed up the legal status of married women at common law in his passages on the husband–wife relationship, which the lawyers of the time called "coverture." (Blackstone himself explains the etymology of this "law-french" word in the following passages.) Like the law of slavery, the legal subordination of women strikes the late-twentieth-century mind as shocking; yet Blackstone and his contemporaries regarded it as part of the natural order of things—indeed, a consequence of natural law.

By marriage, the husband and wife are one person in law: that is, the very being or legal existence of the woman is suspended during the marriage, or at least is incorporated and consolidated into that of the husband: under whose wing, protection, and cover, she performs everything; and is therefore called in our law-french a femme covert; . . . [she] is said to be covert-baron, or under the protection and influence of her husband, her baron, or lord; and her condition during her marriage is called her coverture. Upon this principle, of an union of person in husband and wife, depend almost all the legal rights, duties and disabilities, that either of them acquire by the marriage. I speak not at present of the rights of property, but of such as are merely personal.

*   *   *

If the wife be injured in her person or property, she can bring no action for redress without her husband's concurrence, and in his name, as well as her owne: neither can she be sued, without making the husband a defendant. . . .

*   *   *

But though our law in general considers man and wife as one person, yet there are some instances in which she is separately considered; as inferior to him, and acting by his compulsion. And therefore all deeds executed and acts done, by her, during her coverture, are void, or at least voidable; except it be a fine, or the like matter of record, in which case she must be solely and secretly examined, to learn if her act be voluntary. She cannot by will devise lands to her husband, unless under special circumstances; for at the time of making it she is supposed to be under his coercion. And in some felonies, and other inferior crimes, committed by her, through constraint of her husband, the law excuses her: but this extends not to treason or murder.

The husband also (by the old law) might give his wife moderate correction. For as he is to answer for her misbehaviour, the law thought it reasonable to intrust him with this power of restraining her, by domestic chastisement, in the same moderation that a man is allowed to correct his servants or children; for whom the master or parent is also liable in some cases to answer. But this power of correction was confined within reasonable bounds, and the husband was prohibited from using any violence to his wife. . . . The civil law gave the husband the same, or a larger authority over his wife. . . . But, with us, in the politer reign of Charles the Second, this power of correction began to be doubted: and a wife may now have security of the peace against her husband; or in return, a husband against his wife. Yet the lower rank of people, who were always fond of the old common law, still claim and exert their ancient privilege: and the courts of law still permit a husband to restrain a wife of her liberty, in case of any gross misbehaviour.

These are the chief legal effects of marriage during the coverture; upon which we may observe, that even the disabilities, which the wife lies under, are for the most part intended for her protection and benefit. So great a favorite is the female sex of the laws of England.

Note: Women and the Law in the Colonial Era

In the light of modern scholarship, Blackstone's generalizations may be too broad, even facile, as applied to the American colonies. American law concerning the rights and status of women before independence was much more diverse than Blackstone's summation would suggest—which is to be expected, since he was writing on the law of the mother country and seldom deigned to take notice of colonial law.

Historians today are divided on the question of how well married American women fared under the law, compared with their English sisters. Richard B. Morris's pioneering work, *Studies in the History of American Law*, originally published in 1930, presented a benign, optimistic view of women's condition.

> The new legal rights which married women acquired to a greater or lesser degree throughout the colonies evolved out of the revised concept of the institution of marriage which resulted from the Protestant Revolution and out of the different economic and social conditions of colonial America. . . . (1) The courts clearly recognized the right of both the husband and the wife to the consortium of the other spouse, and to that end enjoined compulsory cohabitation upon couples whose mutual indifference had led to their separation, and ordered wife-deserters to return home. (2) The courts throughout the colonies took practical steps to compel recreant husbands to support their wives and children, and, in the south, an action for alimony independent of the suit for judicial separation was frequently brought. (3) The married woman was protected from the personal abuse, the cruelty, and the improper conduct exercised toward her by her husband. This attitude of humane paternalism over marriage was without precedent at common law. . . .
>
> These frequent testimonial practices, in which little or no deference was shown to restrictions existing under the common-law system, render the additional service of illustrating the extent to which the married woman in the American colonies had achieved emancipation in the law.[12]

But seventeenth- and eighteenth-century American society was too complex for such generalizations to sustain validity outside a specific time and place. Recent work, specifically focusing on the question of women's legal status from the seventeenth through the nineteenth centuries, has been skeptical of claims for a liberalized legal status of women. Marylynn Salmon's study *Women and the Law of Property in*

Early America reached the following conclusions, suggesting that Blackstone's generalizations came closer to describing the reality of colonial practice than Morris thought.

My inquiry into the property rights of American women revealed above all else a picture of their enforced dependence, both before and after the Revolution. Single women functioned on a legal par with men in property rights (although they did not enjoy the political rights associated with property ownership in early American society), but wives exercised only a truncated proprietary capacity. No colony or state allowed married women, or femes coverts, as lawmakers termed them, the legal ability to act independently with regard to property. Only under certain circumstances, at particular times, in precise ways, could a wife exercise even limited control over the family estate, including what she contributed to it. Under property law, the male head of household held the power to manage his own property as well as his wife's.[13]

There is considerable, although scattered, evidence to support Morris's view. One example is a 1718 Pennsylvania statute conferring the special legal status of "feme-sole traders" on married women who conducted businesses during their husband's extended absence. The act recited the reasons for its necessity, before enumerating the specially conferred legal capacities enjoyed by the women to whom it applied.

An Act Concerning Feme-Sole Traders.

Whereas it often happens that mariners and others, whose circumstances as well as vocations oblige them to go to sea, leave their wives in a way of shop-keeping: and such of them as are industrious, and take due care to pay the merchants they gain so much credit with, as to be well supplied with shop-goods from time to time, whereby they get a competent maintenance for themselves and children, and have been enabled to discharge considerable debts left unpaid by their husbands at their going away; but some of those husbands, having so far lost sight of their duty to their wives and tender children, that their affections are turned to those, who, in all probability, will put them upon measures, not only to waste what they may get abroad, but misapply such effects as they leave in this province: For preventing whereof, and to the end that the estates belonging to such absent husbands may be secured for the maintenance of their wives and children, and that the goods and effects which such wives acquire, or are entrusted to sell in their husband's absence, may be preserved for satisfying of those who so entrust them, That where any mariners or others are gone, or hereafter shall go, to sea, leaving their wives at shop-keeping, or to work for their livelihood at any other trade in this province, all such wives shall be deemed adjudged and taken, and are hereby declared to be, as feme-sole traders, and shall have ability, and are by this act enabled, to sue and be sued, plead and be impleaded, at law, in any court or courts of this province, during their husbands' natural lives, without naming their husbands in such suits, pleas or actions: And when judgments are given against such wives for any debts contracted, or sums of money due from them, since their husbands left them, executions shall be awarded against the goods and chattels in the possession of such wives, or in the hands or possession of others in trust for them.[14]

A letter to the editor—the editor in this case being none other than John Peter Zenger—from a group of New York women hinted at underlying economic circumstances that provided the necessary social and economic preconditions for some liberalization of women's status.

Mr. Zenger,

We, the widdows of this city, have had a Meeting, and as our case is something Deplorable, we beg you will give it Place in your Weekly Journal, that we may be Relieved, it is as follows.

We are the House keepers, Pay our Taxes, carry on Trade, and most of us are she Merchants, and as we in some measure contribute to the Support of Government, we ought to be Intitled to some of the Sweets of it; but we find ourselves entirely neglected, while the Husbands that live in our Neighborhood are daily invited to Dine at Court; we have the Vanity to think we can be full as Entertaining, and make as brave a Defence in Case of an Invasion and Perhaps not turn Taile as soon as some of them.[15]

Note: Children, Apprenticeship, Education

The local governments of colonial America intervened drastically into the internal affairs of families, supervising the welfare of children and, in cases of suspected neglect, placing them with masters in a system known as binding-out. American legislation on the subject derived from the Elizabethan Poor Law of 1601.[16] The system of apprenticeship was widely used both as a means of providing for orphaned children and for training children up to a trade. Naturally, almost all the children bound out were of poor parents; the more affluent were able to make their own arrangements. In this sense, apprenticeship served as an instrument of social control. It was also a means of providing for some rudimentary but compulsory education. New England was unusual in even considering, much less aspiring to, universal public education.

Virginia Apprenticeship Statute
1646

Whereas sundry laws and statutes by act of parliament established, have with great wisdome ordained, for the better educating of youth in honest and profitable trades and manufactures, as also to avoyd sloath and idleness wherewith such young children are easily corrupted, as also for reliefe of such parents whose poverty extends not give them breeding, That the justices of the peace should at their discretion, bind out children to tradesmen or husbandmen to be brought up in some good and lawfull calling, And whereas God almighty, among many his other blessings, hath vouchsafed increase of children to this collony, who now are multiplied to a considerable number, who if instructed in good and lawfull trades may much improve the honor and reputation of the country, and noe lesse their owne good and theire parents comfort: But forasmuch as for the most part the parents, either through fond indulgence or perverse obstinacy, are most averse and unwilling to parte with theire children, Be it therefore inacted by authoritie of this Grand Assembly, according to the aforesayd laudable custom in the kingdom of England, That the commissioners of the several countyes respectively do, at their discretion, make choice of two children in each county of the age of eight or seven years at the least, either male or female, which are to be sent up to James Citty between this and June next to be imployed in the public flax houses under such master and mistresse as shall be there appointed, In carding, knitting and spinning &c. And that the said children be furnished from the said county with sixe barrells of corne, two coverletts, or one rugg and one blankett: One bed, one wooden bowle or tray, two pewter spoons, a sow shote of six months old, two laying hens, with convenient apparell both linen and woollen, with hose and shooes. And for the better provision of howseing for the said children, It is inacted, That there be two houses built by the first of April next of forty foot long apiece with good and substantial timber, The houses to be twenty foot broad apiece, eight foot high in the pitche and a stack of brick chimneys standing in the midst of each house, and that they be lofted with sawne boards and made with convenient partitions, And it is further thought fitt that the commissioners have caution not to take up any children but from such parents who by reason of their poverty are disabled to maintaine and educate them.

Children's Education in Plymouth
1685

Forasmuch as the good Education of Children and Youth is of singular use and benefit to any Commonwealth; and whereas many Parents and Masters either through an over respect to their own Occasions and Business, or not duely considering the good of their Children and Servants, have too much neglected their duties in their Education whilst they are young and capable of Learning.

It is Ordered: That the Select men of every Town, shall have a vigilant Eye from time to time over their Brethen and Neighbours, to see that all Parents and Masters do duely endeavour by themselves or others to teach their Children and Servants as they grow capable, so much Learning as through the blessing of God they may attain; at least to be able duely to read the Scriptures, and other profitable Books Printed in the English Tongue; and the knowledge of the Capital Laws; and in some competent measure, the main Grounds and Principles of Christian Religion, necessary to Salvation; by causing them to learn some orthodox Catechisime without book, or otherwayes instructing them, as they may be able to give a due answer to such plain and ordinary questions as may by them or others be propounded to them concerning the same. And further that all Parents and Masters do breed and bring up their Children and Apprentices in some honest lawful Calling and Imployment, that may be profitable for themselves and the Country. And if after Warning and Admonition given by any of the Select Men unto such Parents or Masters, they shall still remain negligent in their duty, in any of the particulars aforementioned, whereby Children or Servants may be in danger to grow Barbarous, Rude and Stubborn, and so to prove Pests instead of Blessings to the Country; That then a Fine of ten shillings shall be Levyed on the Goods of such Negligent Parent or Master to the Towns use, except extream poverty call for a Mitigation of the Fine. And if in three Months after that, there be no due care taken, and continued for the Education of such Children and Apprentices as aforesaid, then a Fine of twenty shillings to be Levyed on such Delinquents to the Towns use; except as aforesaid. And lastly, if in three Months after that their be no Reformation of the said Neglect, then the Select Men, with the Advice of two Magistrates shall put such Children to Apprentice;

Boyes till they come to twenty one, and Girls eighteen years of Age, where they may be Educated according to the Rules of this Order.

Slavery

Note: Slavery and Race in Early America

The origins of slavery in America are murky. About all that can be said with certainty of the historical record for the years before 1690 is this: (1) Blacks were brought involuntarily to the mainland, either directly from Africa or via the island colonies, at first in small numbers, then in an increasing flood after the Restoration. (2) English settlers from the start were conscious of differences between themselves and the Africans, although they defined this difference not in terms of race, as we do today—black and white—but in terms of culture and religion—Englishmen or Christians versus savages or pagans. Race consciousness as we know it in modern times was not present at the beginning but developed later. (3) Blacks before 1660 usually began their life in America in some sort of unfree status, but they were often able to become free in one way or another and then to enjoy some of the benefits of freedom, such as property ownership. (4) There was an appreciable deterioration in the legal status of blacks as the seventeenth century wore on, culminating in the adoption of full-blown slave codes in the colony of (South) Carolina in the 1690s.

The Germantown Protest Against Slavery
1688

This is the first known public objection to slaveholding and the slave trade in the British mainland colonies of North America. It was adopted by a group of German Mennonite settlers in Pennsylvania and foreshadowed ideas concerning slavery that were to become dominant among the Quakers during the eighteenth century. While wholly moral and religious in content, the Germantown Protest came to have legal and constitutional implications, demonstrating Americans' facility in translating extralegal concerns into constitutional discourse.

These are the reasons why we are against the traffic of men-body, as followeth: Is there any that would be done or handled at this manner? viz., to be sold or made a slave for all the time of his life? How fearful and faint-hearted are many at sea, when they see a strange vessel, being afraid it should be a Turk and they should be taken, and sold for slaves into Turkey. Now, what is this better done, than Turks do? Yea, rather it is worse for them, which say they are Christians: for we hear that the most part of such negers are brought hither against their will and consent, and that many of them are stolen. Now, though they are black, we cannot conceive there is more liberty to have them slaves as it is to have other white ones. There is a saying, that we should do to all men like as we will be done ourselves; making no difference of what generation, descent, or colour they are. And those who steal or rob men, and those who buy or purchase them are they not all alike? Here is liberty of conscience, which is right and reasonable: here ought to be likewise liberty of the body except of evil-doers, which is another case. But to bring men thither, or to rob and sell them against their will, we stand against. In Europe there are many oppressed for conscience sake: and here there are those oppressed which are of a black colour. And we who know that men must not committ adultery—some do committ adultery in others, separating wives from their husbands and giving them to others: and some sell the children of these poor creatures to other men. Ah! do consider well this thing, you who do it, if you would be done at this manner—and if it is done according to Christianity! You surpass Holland and Germany in this thing. This makes an ill report in all those countries of Europe, where they hear of [it], that the Quakers do here handel men as they handel there the cattle. And for that reason some have no mind or inclination to come hither. And who shall maintain this your cause, or plead for it? Truly, we cannot do so, except you shall inform us better hereof, viz.: that Christians have liberty to practice these things. Pray, what thing in the world can be done worse towards us, than if men should rob or steal us away, and sell us for slaves to strange countries; separating husbands from their wives and children. Being now this is not done in the manner we would be done; therefore, we contradict, and are against this traffic of men-body. And we who profess that it is not lawful to steal, must, likewise, avoid to purchase such things as are stolen, but rather help to stop this robbing and stealing, if possible. And such men ought to be delivered out of the hands of the robbers, and set free as in Europe. Then is Pennsylvania to have a good report, instead, it hath now a bad one, for this sake, in other countries; Especially whereas the Europeans are desirous to know in what manner the Quakers do rule in their province: and most of them do look upon us with an envious eye. But if this is done well, what shall we say is done evil?

If once these slaves (which they say are so wicked and stubborn men,) should join themselves—fight for their freedom, and handel their masters and mistresses, as they did handel them before; will these masters and mistresses take the sword at hand and war against these poor slaves, like, as we are able to believe, some will not refuse to do? Or have these poor negers not as much right to fight for their freedom, as you have to keep them slaves?

Now consider well this thing, if it is good or bad. And in case you find it to be good to handel these blacks in that manner, we desire and require you hereby lovingly that you may inform us herein, which at this time never was done, viz., that Christians have such a liberty to do so. To the end we shall be satisfied on this point, and satisfy likewise our good friends and acquaintances in our native country, to whom it is a terror, or fearful thing, that men should be handelled so in Pennsylvania.

South Carolina Slave Code
1740

This codification of statutory laws relating to slaves was the most comprehensive of the pre-Revolutionary period. Its provisions established the fundamental characteristics of slavery in the mainland colonies and set forth a comprehensive regulation of blacks' and whites' behavior in a slave society. The substance of this code permeated the laws of the slave states until the Civil War.

An Act for the better Ordering and Governing [of] Negroes and other Slaves in this Province

Whereas in his majesty's plantations in America, slavery has been introduced and allowed; and the people commonly called negroes, Indians, mulatos and mestizos have [been] deemed absolute slaves, and the subjects of property in the hands of particular persons the extent of whose power over slaves ought to be settled and limited by positive laws so that the slaves may be kept in due subjection and obedience, and the owners and other persons having the care and government of slaves, may be restrained from exercising too great rigour and cruelty over them; and that the public peace and order of this Province may be preserved:

Be it enacted, that all negroes, Indians (free Indians in amity with this government, and negroes, mulatos and mestizos who are now free excepted) mulatos or mestizos who now are or shall hereafter be in this Province, and all their issue and offspring born or to be born, shall be and they are hereby declared to be and remain for ever herafter absolute slaves, and shall follow the condition of the mother; and shall be deemed, . . . taken, reputed and adjudged in law to be chattels personal in the hands of their owners and possessors and their executors, administrators and assigns to all intents, constructions and purposes whatsoever, Provided that if any negro Indian mulato, or mestizo shall claim his or her freedom, it shall and may be lawful for such negro, Indian, mulato, or mestizo, or any person or persons whatsoever, on his or her behalf to apply to the justices of his Majesty's court of common pleas by petition or motion, either during the sitting of the said court, or before any of the justices of the same court at any time in the vacation. And the said court or any of the justices thereof, shall and they are hereby fully impowered to admit any person so applying, to be guardian for any negro, Indian, mulato or mestizo, claiming his, her or their freedom, and such guardians shall be enabled, intitled and capable in law to bring an action of trespass, in the nature of ravishment of ward against any person who shall claim property in, or who shall be in possession of any such negro, Indian, mulato or mestizo.

*　　　*　　　*

Provided that in any action or suit to be brought in pursuance of the direction of this act the burthen of the proof shall lay upon the plaintiff, and it shall be always presumed, that every negro, Indian, mulato, and mestizo, is a slave unless the contrary can be made appear (the Indians in amity with this government excepted) in which case the burden of the proof shall lie on the defendant.

*　　　*　　　*

III.   And for the better keeping slaves in due order and subjection: be it further enacted that no person whatsoever, shall permit or suffer any slave under his or their care or management, and who lives, or is employed in Charlestown, or any other town in this Province to go out of the limits of the said town, or any such slave, who lives in the country to go out of the plantation to which such slave belongs, or in which plantation such slave is usually employed, without a letter subscribed and directed, or a ticket in the words following. . . .

*　　　*　　　*

V.   If any slave who shall be out of the house or plantation where such slave shall live or shall be usually employed, or without some white person in company with such slave, shall refuse to submit or to undergo the examination of any white person, it shall be lawful for any such white Person to pursue, apprehend and moderately correct such slave; and if such slave shall assault and strike such white person, such slave may be lawfully killed.

*　　　*　　　*

IX.   And whereas natural justice forbids, that any person of what condition soever should be condemned unheard, and the order of civil government requires that for the due and equal administration of justice, some convenient method and form of trial should be established, Be it therefore enacted, that all crimes and offences which shall be committed by slaves in this Province and for which capital punishment shall or lawfully may be inflicted, shall be heard, examined, tried, adjudged, and finally determined by any 2 justices assigned to keep the peace, and any number of freeholders not less than 3 or more than 5 in the county where the offence shall be committed and can be most conveniently assembled; either of which justices, on complaint made or information received of any such offence committed by a slave, shall commit the offender to the safe custody of the constable of the parish where such offence shall be committed, and shall without delay by warrant under his hand and seal, call to his assistance, and request any one of the nearest justices of the peace to associate with him; and shall by the same warrant summon such a number of the neighbouring freeholders as aforesaid, to assemble and meet together with the said justices, at a certain day and place not exceeding 3 days after the apprehending of such slave or slaves: and the justices and freeholders being so assembled, shall cause the slave accused or charged, to be brought before them, and shall hear the accusations which shall be brought against such slave, and his or her defence, and shall proceed to the examination of witnesses, and other evidence, and finally hear and determine the matter brought before them, in the most summary and expeditious manner; and in case the offender shall be convicted of any crime for which by law the offender ought to suffer death, the said justices shall give judgment, and award and cause execution of their sentence to be done, by inflicting such manner of death, and at such time as the said justices, by and with the consent of the freeholders shall direct, and which they shall judge will be most effectual to deter others from offending in the like manner.

*　　　*　　　*

[XVI.]   Be it therefore enacted, that the several crimes and offences herein-after particularly enumerated, are hereby declared to be felony without the benefit of the clergy, That is to say, If any slave, free negro, mulatto, Indian, or mestizo, shall willfully and maliciously burn or destroy any stack of rice, corn or other grain, of the product, growth or manufacture of this Province; or shall willfully and maliciously set fire to, burn or destroy any tar kiln, barrels of pitch, tar, turpentine or rosin, or any other of the goods or commodities of the growth, produce or manufacture of this Province; or shall feloniously steal, take or carry away any slave, being the property of another, with intent to carry such slave out of this Province; or shall willfully and maliciously poison, or administer any poison to any person, free man, woman, servant or slave; every such slave, free negro, mulatto, Indian (except as before excepted) and mestizo, shall suffer death as a felon.

XVII.   Any slave who shall be guilty of homicide of any sort, upon any white person, except by misadventure or in defence of his master or other person under whose care and government such slave shall be, shall upon conviction thereof as aforesaid, suffer death. And every slave who shall raise or attempt to raise an insurrection in this Province, or shall endeavor to delude or entice any slave to run away and leave this Province; every such slave and slaves, and his and their accomplices, aiders and abettors, shall upon conviction as aforesaid suffer death. Provided always, That it shall and may be lawful to and for the justices who shall pronounce sentence against such slaves, and by and with the advice and consent of the freeholders as aforesaid, if several slaves shall receive sentence at one time, to mitigate and alter the sentence of any slave other than such as shall be convicted of the homicide of a white person, who they shall think may deserve mercy, and may inflict such corporal punishment (other than death) on any such slave, as they in their discretion shall think fit, any thing herein contained to the contrary thereof in any wise notwithstanding. Provided, That one or more of the said slaves who shall be convicted of the crimes or offences aforesaid, where several are concerned, shall be executed for example, to deter others from offending in the like kind.

*   *   *

XXXIII.   And whereas several owners of slaves do suffer their slaves to go and work where they please, upon condition of paying to their owners certain sums of money agreed upon between the owner and slave; which practice occasioned such slaves to pilfer and steal to raise money for their owners, as well as to maintain themselves in drunkenness and evil courses; for prevention of which practices for the future, Be it enacted, that no owner, master or mistress of any slave, after the passing of this act, shall permit or suffer any of his, her or their slaves to go and work out of their respective houses or families, without a ticket in writing under pain of forfeiting the sum of current money, for every such offence.

*   *   *

XXXVI.   And for that as it is absolutely necessary to the safety of this Province, that all due care be taken to restrain the wanderings and meetings of negroes and other slaves, at all times, and more especially on Saturday nights, Sundays and other holidays, and the using and carrying wooden swords, and other mischievous and dangerous weapons, or using and keeping of drums, horns, or other loud instruments, which may call together or give sign or notice to one another of their wicked designs and purposes; and that all masters, overseers and others may be enjoined diligently and carefully to prevent the same, Be it enacted, that it shall be lawfull for all masters, overseers and other persons whomsoever, to apprehend and take up any negro or other slave that shall be found out of the plantation of his or their master or owner, at any time, especially on Saturday nights, Sundays or other holidays, not being on lawful business, and with a letter from their master or a ticket, or not having a white person with them, and the said negro or other slave or slaves correct by a moderate whipping.

XXXVII.   And whereas cruelty is not only highly unbecoming those who profess themselves Christians, but is odious in the eyes of all men who have any sense of virtue or humanity; therefore to restrain and prevent barbarity being exercised toward slaves, Be it enacted, That if any person or persons whosoever, shall willfully murder his own slave, or the slave of another person, every such person shall upon conviction thereof, forfeit and pay the sum of £700 current money, and shall be rendered, and is hereby declared altogether and forever incapable of holding, exercising, enjoying or receiving the profits of any office, place or employment civil or military within this Province: . . . And if any person shall on a sudden heat or passion, or by undue correction, kill his own slave or the slave of any person, he shall forfeit the sum of £350 current money, And in case any person or person shall wilfully cut out the tongue, put out the eye, castrate or cruelly scald, burn, or deprive any slave of any limb or member, or shall inflict any other cruel punishment, other than by whipping or beating with a horsewhip, cow-skin, switch or small stick, or by putting irons on, or confining or imprisoning such slave; every such person shall for every such offence, forfeit the sum of £100 current money.

XXXVIII.   That in case any person in this Province, who shall be owner, or who shall have the care government or charge of any slave, or slaves, shall deny, neglect or refuse to allow such slave or slaves under his or her charge, sufficient cloathing, covering or food, it shall and may be lawfull for any person or persons, on behalf of such slave or slaves, to make complaint to the next neighbouring justice in the parish where such slave or slaves live, or are usually employed; and if there shall be no justice in the parish, then to the next justice in nearest parish: and the said justice shall summons the party against whom such complaint shall be made, and shall enquire of, hear and determine the same: and if the said justice shall find the said complaint to be true, or that such person will not exculpate or clear himself from the charge, by his or her own oath, which such person shall be at liberty to do in all cases where positive proof is not given of the offence, such justice shall and may make such orders upon the same for the relief of such slave or slaves, as he in his discretion shall think fit, and shall and may let and impose a fine or penalty on any person who shall offend in the premises, in any sum not exceeding £20 current money, for each offence.

*   *   *

XLIV.   And whereas many owners of slaves, and others who have the care, management and overseeing of slaves, do confine them so closely to hard labour; that they have not sufficient time for natural rest—Be it therefore enacted, That if any owner of slaves, or other person who shall have the care, management, or overseeing of any slaves, shall work or put any such slave or slaves to labour, more than 15 hours in 24 hours, from the 25th day of March to the 25th day of September, or more than 14 hours in 24 hours, from the 25th day of September to the 25th day of March; every such person shall forfeit any sum not exceeding or under £20, nor under £5 current money, for every time he, she or they shall offend herein, at the discretion of the justice before whom the complaint shall be made.

XLV.   And whereas the having of slaves taught to write, or suffering them to be employed in writing, may be attended with great inconveniences; Be it enacted, that all and every person and persons whatsoever, who shall hereafter teach, or cause any slave or slaves to be taught to write, or shall use or employ any slave as a scribe in any manner of writing whatsoever, hereafter taught to write; every such person and persons shall, for every such offence, forfeit the sum of £100 cuurrent money.

The New York "Negro Plot"
1741

In 1741, a time of heightened tensions among English colonists because of the mother country's involvement in a war against Spain (the so-called War of Jenkins' Ear, 1739–1742), some white inhabitants of New York City were convulsed by a spasm of fear that enslaved blacks of the city, guided by Spanish agents (including the inevitable but fictitious Jesuit priest), were about to rise up in insurrection, torch the city, slaughter the whites, and rape white women, all this as prelude to some eventual Spanish attack. Spurred on by the increasingly extravagant, not to say mad, revelations of a white servant girl, white New Yorkers resorted to law to try the supposed insurrectionists of both races. By the time the chief witness's disclosures crossed the line into lunacy, thirteen slaves had been burned at the stake, eighteen hanged (plus two white confederates), and seventy transported to various non-English colonies. Many level-headed contemporaries scoffed at the idea that there was any plot at all. So Daniel Horsmanden, a judge of the Supreme Court of Judicature who presided at the trials, compiled a record of the hearing to convince the skeptics. The following excerpts, the charge to the grand jury investigating events and the grand jury's return, reveal the public mind at the earliest and therefore least hysterical stage.

Mr. Justice Philipse gave the charge to the grand jury, as followeth:
Gentlemen of the grand jury,

It is not without some concern, that I am obliged at this time to be more particular in your charge than for many preceding terms there hath been occasion. The many frights and terrors which the good people of this city have of late been put into, by repeated and unusual fires, and burning of houses, give us too much room to suspect, that some of them at least, did not proceed from mere chance, or common accidents; but on the contrary, from the premeditated malice and wicked pursuits of evil and designing persons; and therefore, it greatly behoves us to use our utmost diligence, by all lawful ways and means, to discover the contrivers and perpetrators of such daring and flagitious undertakings: that, upon conviction, they may receive condign punishment; for although we have the happiness of living under a government which exceeds all others in the excellency of its constitution and laws, yet if those to whom the execution of them (which my lord Coke calls the life and soul of the law) is committed, do not exert themselves in a conscientious discharge of their respective duties, such laws which were intended for a terror to the evil-doer, and a protection to the good, will become a dead letter, and our most excellent constitution turned into anarchy and confusion; every one practising what he listeth, and doing what shall seem good in his own eyes: to prevent which, it is the duty of all grand juries to inquire into the conduct and behaviour of the people in their respective counties; and if, upon examination, they find any to have transgressed the laws of the land, to present them, that so they may by the court be put upon their trial, and then either to be discharged or punished according to their demerits.

I am told there are several prisoners now in jail, who have been committed by the city magistrates, upon suspicion of having been concerned in some of the late fires; and others, who under pretence of assisting the unhappy sufferers, by saving their goods from the flames, for stealing, or receiving them. This indeed, is adding affliction to the afflicted, and is a very great aggravation of such crime, and therefore deserves a narrow inquiry: that so the exemplary punishment of the guilty (if any such should be so found) may deter others from committing the like villainies; for this kind of stealing, I think, has not been often practised among us.

Gentlemen,

Arson, or the malicious and voluntary burning, not only a mansion house, but also any other house, and the out buildings, or barns, and stables adjoining thereto, by night or by day, is felony at common law; and if any part of the house be burned, the offender is guilty of felony, notwithstanding the fire afterwards be put out, or go out of itself.

This crime is of so shocking a nature, that if we have any in this city, who, having been guilty thereof, should escape, who can say he is safe, or tell where it will end?

Gentlemen,

Another Thing which I cannot omit recommending to your serious and diligent inquiry, is to find out and present all such persons who sell rum, and other strong liquor to negroes. It must be obvious to every one, that there are too many of them in this city who, under pretence of selling what they call a penny dram to a negro, will sell to him as many quarts or gallons of rum, as he can steal money or goods to pay for.

How this notion of its being lawful to sell a penny dram, or a pennyworth of rum to a slave, without the consent or direction of his master, has prevailed, I know not; but this I am sure of, that there is not only no such law, but that the doing of it is directly contrary to an act of the assembly now in force, for the better regulating of slaves. The many fatal consequences flowing from this prevailing and wicked practice, are so notorious, and so nearly concern us all, that one would be almost surprised, to think there should be a necessity for a court to recommend a suppressing of such pernicious houses: thus much in particular; now in general.

My charge, gentlemen, further is, to present all conspiracies, combinations, and other offences, from treasons down to trespasses; and in your inquiries, the oath you, and each of you have just now taken will, I am persuaded, be your guide, and I pray God to direct and assist you in the discharge of your duty.

*   *   *

This evidence of a conspiracy, not only to burn the city, but also destroy and murder the people, was most astonishing to the grand jury, and that any white people should become so abandoned as to confederate with slaves in such an execrable and detestable purpose, could not but be very amazing to every one that heard it; what could scarce be credited; but that the several fires had been occasioned by some combination of villains, was, at the time of them naturally to be collected from the manner and circumstances attending them.

White Indentured Servitude
1761

Black slaves were not the only unfree people in colonial America. Many whites, too, were held in an unfree status known as indentured servitude. Comparison of slavery with servitude suggests at first glance that the latter was less oppressive. Servants served for only a term of years (usually four to seven); slaves remained slaves for life. The status of servants did not extend to their children (except to babies born to servant girls, and that for only a limited period); slave mothers passed on slave status to their children. Statutory law required that servants be taught to read; it forbade teaching slaves their letters. But servitude was in practice a less benign institution than it might appear. Social historians estimate that only one in ten white indentured servants survived to become a property-owning free person; the rest died in servitude or, if they survived, emerged as day laborers or hired farmhands. Thus the adult servant was usually closer in status to a slave than he or she was to a juvenile apprentice. The following document, a selection from an eighteenth-century justice-of-the-peace manual for the province of South Carolina, recapitulates the statutory basis of servitude.

Servants

Where any person or persons are imported into this province without being under indenture or contract, and are unable or unwilling to pay for their passages, it shall be lawful for the importer or importers of such person or persons, before any one of his Majesty's justices of the peace within this province, to take an indenture or indentures executed under the hand and seal of such person or persons, in consideration of such passage money, to serve the said importer or his assigns five years, from the arrival of such person or persons in this province, if he or she at the time of such arrival is of the age of sixteen years or upwards; and to serve until the age of twenty-one years, if such person or persons, at his or her arrival is under the age of sixteen years; which indenture or indentures shall be as binding and effectual in law as if the same had been executed before the arrival of such person or persons in this province. . . .

If any servant or servants shall lay violent hands on, beat or strike his, her or their master, mistress or overseer, and be convicted thereof by confession, or evidence of his fellow servant or otherwise, before any two justices of the peace in this province, the said justices are required and authorized to order such servant to serve his or her master or mistress, or their assigns, without any wages, for any time not exceeding six months after his or her time by indenture or otherwise is expired, or to order such corporal punishment to be inflicted on such servant, by the hands of a constable or some other white person, not exceeding twenty-one stripes, as the said justices shall in their discretion think fitting, according to the nature of the crime.

Any servant or servants unlawfully absenting from his, her or their master, mistress or overseer, shall for every such day's absence serve a week, and so in proportion for a longer or shorter time, provided the whole servitude for such absence does not exceed two years, over and above the time any such servant was to serve by indenture or otherwise, and shall also satisfy his, her or their master or mistress for all such charges as shall be laid out and expended for taking up, whipping and bringing home such servant, by a further and additional servitude, provided the whole time of such additional servitude does not exceed one year after the expiration of the first servitude.

* * *

Every master or mistress shall provide and allow his or her servant or servants, sufficient diet, cloathing and lodging, and shall not exceed the bounds of moderation in correcting them beyond the merit of their offences; and it is lawful for any servant, upon any master or mistress, or overseer, by order or consent of any such master or mistress denying and not providing sufficient meat, drink, lodging and cloathing, or who shall unreasonably burthen them beyond their strength with labour, or debar them of their necessary rest and sleep, or excessively beat or abuse them to repair to any one of his Majesty's justices, there to make his, her or their complaint. And if the said justice shall find by lawful proof that the said servant's complaint is just, he is impowered and required, under the penalty of Five Pounds proclamation-money, by warrant under his hand and seal directed to the next constable, to levy and distrain the goods and chattels of such master or mistress, any sum not exceeding Four Pounds proclamation-money, to be disposed of for the use of the poor of the parish where such offence is committed. And for the second offence, any two justices of the peace are authorised and required, under the penalty of Five Pounds proclamation-money each, by instrument in writing under their hands and seals, to make an order directed to any constable to sell and dispose of the remaining time of service of such servant to any other white person, for such money as can be got for the same, to be paid to the church-wardens of the parish where the offence is committed, for the use of the poor.

* * *

No servant or servants whatsoever shall travel by land or water above two miles from the place of his, her or their residence, without a note under the hand of his, her or their master or mistress, or overseer, expressing a permission for such servants so travelling. And if such servant or servants be found two miles from the place of his or their residence, they shall be deemed and taken as fugitive servants, and shall suffer such penalties and punishments as are provided against run-away servants.

* * *

In all cases where a man is punishable by a fine, a servant shall receive corporal punishment; (that is to say) for every Twenty Shillings proclamation-money fine nine lashes, and so many such several punishments as there are pounds severally included in the fine. Provided the whole doth not exceed thirty-nine lashes.

*   *   *

Every man-servant shall, at the expiration of his servitude, have allowed and given to him, one new hat, a good coat and breeches, either of jersey or broad cloth, two new shirts of coarse white linen, one new pair of shoes and stockings. And all women servants, at the expiration of their servitude, shall have allowed and given them, a waistcoat and petticoat of new half thicks or coarse plains, two new shifts of white linen, a new pair of shoes and stockings, a blue apron, and two caps of white linen.

Colonial Welfare Systems

An Act for the Relief of the Poor
1741

The British colonies attempted to provide supplementary and residual systems for relief of the poor, disabled, and infirm. Primary responsibility for the disabled rested on their families; where there were no near relatives available to foot the bill, care of the poor and infirm rested with the towns.

Colonial laws were modeled on the Poor Laws of the reign of Elizabeth I. First enacted in 1598 and then reenacted in definitive form in 1601, the English Poor Laws provided for appointment of overseers of the poor in every parish. These officers had comprehensive authority to bind out the children of the poor as apprentices, as well as those adults "married or unmarried as, having no means to maintain them, use no ordinary and daily trade of life to get their living by." They were empowered to raise taxes in money and in kind (flax, wool, iron, etc.), to build "convenient houses of dwelling for the said impotent poor," and in general to operate a parish-based welfare system vaguely resembling modern workfare experiments.[17] The colonies were content either to imitate the Elizabethan legislation or to elaborate on it, as in the following 1742 Delaware statute.

For the Prevention of straggling and indigent Persons from coming into and being chargeable to the Inhabitants, and for the better Relief of the Poor of this Government; Be It Enacted . . .

That the Constables and Overseers of the Poor in each Hundred within the several Counties of this Government, shall and are hereby required to make diligent Inspection and Enquiry in their respective Districts after all vagrant, poor and impotent Persons coming into the same in order to settle or otherwise; and if any such shall be found as aforesaid, such Overseer or Constable shall and is hereby required to make Report thereof to the next Justice of the Peace of the said County; and the said Justice shall and is hereby required, by Warrant under his Hand and Seal, to cause such vagrant, poor or impotent Persons to be apprehended, and brought before him or some other Justice of the Peace of the same County; and if it

appear to the Justice before whom such Person is or shall be brought, that such
Person is likely to become chargeable as aforesaid, such Justice shall and is hereby
required to order such vagrant, poor or impotent Person, if able to travel, immediately to depart the County, or to give sufficient Security to indemnify the County,
as herein after mentioned; and upon Refusal or Neglect of such vagrant, poor or
impotent Person to depart or give Security as aforesaid, it shall and may be lawful to
and for any Two Justices of the Peace of the same County, to cause every such
Person so refusing or neglecting, to be publickly whipp'd at the common Whipping-
Post, with any Number of Lashes not exceeding Fifteen, and the same Punishment
to be repeated every Day, or so often as he or she shall not be depart the same as
aforesaid.

*   *   *

. . . [T]he Father and Grandfather, Mother and Grandmother, being of sufficient
Ability, shall at their own Charges relieve and maintain their poor, blind, lame and
impotent Children and Grand-children, as the Justices of the Peace at their General
Court of Quarter-Sessions shall order and direct; and the Children and Grand-
children, being of Ability, shall, by such Order of the Justices as aforesaid, at their
own Charges relieve and maintain their Fathers and Mothers, Grand-fathers and
Grand-mothers, not having any Estate, nor being of Ability to work; upon Pain of
forfeiting Forty Shillings for every Month they or any of them shall fail therein, to
be levied monthly, together with Costs, by Distress and Sale of the Goods and
Chattels of such Father, Mother, Grandfather, Grandmother, Child or Children
respectively, by Warrant under the Hands and Seals of any Two Justices of the Peace
of the same County, and paid to the Treasurer for the Use of the Poor of the same
County.

*   *   *

Every poor Person, whose Name shall stand on the List of any of the Counties of
this Government as one of the Poor of the said County, shall on the Right Sleeve, or
on the Back of his or her upper Garment, in an open and visible Manner, wear such
Badge or Mark as herein after is mentioned and expressed, That is to say, A large
Roman or Capital P, together with the first Letter of the Name of the County
whereof such poor Person is an Inhabitant, cut either in Red or Blue Cloath, as by
the Overseers of the Poor of the Hundred wherein such poor Persons doth reside,
shall be directed and appointed.

Note: Colonial Workfare

There was nothing gentle or humane about the colonial poor laws by the standards of
the late twentieth century. Over all of them hung the odor of moral disapproval. At
times these laws approached the criminalization of poverty. A Massachusetts statute
of 1646 provided

> Every township, or such as are deputed to order the prudentials thereof, shall have
> power to present to the Quarter Courte all idle & unprofitable persons, & all children,
> who are not diligently implied [employed] by their parents, which Courte shall have
> power to dispose of them, for their owne welfare & improvement of the common
> good.[18]

Class Legislation and Sumptuary Laws

Note: Class and Status in Early America

The English settlers saw no reason to question the stratification of their society, even in the New World. God ordained that "in all times some must be rich, some poor, some high and eminent in power and dignity, others mean and in subjection," John Winthrop declared in his 1629 shipboard sermon.[19] The Cambridge Platform of 1648 required the elders of the churches "to see that none in the church live inordinately, out of rank and place."[20] To accomplish this end, the elites of all the colonies tried to regulate the wages, dress, and recreation of the lower classes as a means of disciplining their behavior and attitudes. Massachusetts-Bay magistrates frowned on high wages, which only encouraged "vaine and idle waste of much precious tyme."[21] Responding to the crisis of King Philip's War in 1675, Massachusetts enacted the "Provoking Evils" laws, which prohibited excessive wages, with punishment for only the worker, not the master.[22] Even more annoying to the elites were the social pretensions of the lower orders, whereby persons of "meane condition, educations and callings" should presume to "take upon them the garbe of Gentlemen." Consequently, the Massachusetts General Court attempted to punish those who dressed "exceeding the quality and condition of their Persons and Estate."[23] Legislation over the years prohibited various sorts of finery and ostentation to the common people: lace, buttons, "silke or tiffany hoodes," long hair on men, silks, girdles, hatbands, silver and gold thread, slashed sleeves, short sleeves, needlework caps, ruffs, and beaver hats. All who violated the dress code "shalbe looked at as contemnors of authority, & regardless of the publike weale."[24] But Massachusetts-Bay magistrates readily discharged ladies from prosecution for violation of the laws when it was proved that their husbands had a net worth of £200 and another lady "upon testimony of her being brought up above the ordinary rank."[25] Virginia hit on a clever enforcement device: it permitted tax assessments "according to his apparell, if he be married, according to his owne & his wives, or either of their apparell."[26] The Old Dominion reenacted an English benchmark of meanness when it prohibited seven occupational categories or groups of the lower classes—farmers, sailors, fishermen, craftsmen, laborers, apprentices, and servants—from playing at "Bear-baiting, Bull-baiting, Bowling, Cards, Cock-fighting, Coits, Dice, Foot-ball, Nine-pins, Tennis."[27]

Yet the sumptuary laws of New England largely went unenforced. They had to be reenacted recurrently because existing legislation was universally disregarded. It was one thing to denounce extravagant dress for the poor; it was something else altogether to make such prohibitions stick. The statutes therefore are gauges of ruling-class attitudes only and not of actual behavior (except in a negative way). Their proliferation attests only to universal disregard and nonenforcement. This problem was endemic to all other kinds of morals legislation.[28]

If unseemly ostentation in dress was offensive in the poorer classes, it was obnoxious in slaves. South Carolina legislators found it necessary to include a special sumptuary law in the 1740 slave code because "many of the slaves in the Province wear clothes much above the condition of slaves." With absurd specificity, the statute obliged masters to prohibit their slaves from wearing "any sort of apparel whatsoever, finer, other, or of greater value than negro cloth, duffils, kerseys, osnabrings, blue linen, check linen or coarse garlix, or callicoes, checked cottons, or Scotch plaids."[29]

Democracy and Deference

The Incident of the Roxbury Carters
1705

An incident reported by Massachusetts Governor Joseph Dudley in 1705 suggests that democratic impulses may have been breaking through the crust of social constraint, changing the social matrix from which laws emerged. Dudley's version must be read with a great deal of skepticism: it is unlikely that the event occurred just as he described it. Yet this vignette of the stubborn, almost insolent, egalitarianism of the farmers confronting the social pretensions of an unpopular governor provides a glimpse of a social order churning from below.

Roxbury 23 Janu: 1705.

Revered and Dear Sir,—That you may not be imposed upon I have conveyed to you my memorial to the Judges referring to the ingures offered mee upon the road, which I desire you will communicate to the ministers of your circle whose good opinion I desire to mayntain, and have not in the matter by any means forfeited.

I am Sir Your humble servant

J. Dudley.

The Governour informs the Queen's Justices of her majestys Superior Court that on friday, the seventh of December last past, he took his Journey from Roxbury towards newhampshire and the Province of mayn for her majestys immediate service there: and for the ease of the Guards had directed them to attend him the next morning at Rumney house, and had not proceeded above a mile from home before he mett two Carts in the Road loaden with wood, of which the Carters were, as he is since informed, Winchester and Trobridge.

The Charet wherein the Governour was, had three sitters and three servants depending, with trunks and portmantles for the journey, drawn by four horses one very unruly, and was attended only at that instant by Mr. William Dudley, the Governours son.

When the Governour saw the carts approaching, he directed his son to bid them give him the way, having a Difficult drift, with four horses and a tender Charet so heavy loaden, not fit to break the way. Who accordingly did Ride up and told them the Governour was there, and they must give way: immediately upon it, the second Carter came up to the first, to his assistance, leaving his own cart, and one of them says aloud, he would not goe out of the way for the Governour: whereupon the Govr came out of the Charet and told Winchester he must give way to the Charet. Winchester answered boldly, without any other words, "I am as good flesh and blood as you; I will not give way; you may goe out of the way:" and came towards the Governour.

Whereupon the Governour drew his sword, to secure himself and command the

Road, and went forward; yet without either saying or intending to hurt the carters, or once pointing or passing at them; but justly supposing they would obey and give him the way; and again commanded them to give way. Winchester answered that he was a Christian and would not give way: and as the Governour came towards him, he advanced and at len[g]th layd hold on the Gov.r and broke the sword in his hand. Very soon after came a justice of peace, and sent the Carters to prison. The Justices are further informed that during this talk with the carters, the Gov.r demanded their names, which they would not say, Trobridg particularly saying he was well known, nor did they once in the Govrs hearing or sight pull of their hatts or say they would go out of the way, or any word to excuse the matter, but absolutely stood upon it, as above is sayd; and once, being two of them, one on each side of the fore-horse, laboured and put forward to drive upon and over the Governour.

And this is averred upon the honour of the Governour.

J. Dudley.

Law and the Colonial Economy

Throughout the seventeenth century, the mainland colonies attempted to control their economies extensively, regulating prices, wages, and the quality of output. Early in the seventeenth century, the colonies sought to re-create the British system of regulating wages and labor. These efforts at wage control drew on the models of the English Statute of Labourers (1351) and the Statute of Artificers (1563). But wage control was doomed to failure for two reasons: workers were scarce, and they were mobile. In the end, the market persistently drove wages through the statutory ceilings, and the legislature could only respond, with a growing sense of futility, with yet another (and inevitably unsuccessful) attempt at capping them.

Wage regulation was not the only kind of economic regulation tried by the colonies. Early in the seventeenth century, Massachusetts attempted to reenact the English assize of bread. All colonies regulated weights and measures. In those colonies that exported a valuable staple, principally tobacco in the Chesapeake, colonial authorities vigilantly controlled the grades and quality of the export. Virginia planters reluctantly accepted the wisdom of this effort in the early eighteenth century. New England regulated the manufacture of barrels and the cooperage trade generally. All colonies offered bounties, either for the killing of pestiferous wildlife or for the manufacture of valuable products like potash. Some examples of such forms of economic regulation, quality control, and subsidization follow.

The Laws and Liberties of Massachusetts
1648

Cask & Cooper

It is ordered by this Court and authoritie thereof, that all cask used for any liquor, fish, or other commoditie to be put to sale shall be of London assize, and that fit persons shal be appointed from time to time in all places needfull, to gage all such vessels or cask & such as shal be found of due assize shal be marked with the

Gagers marks, & no other who shal have for his paines four pence for every tun, & so proportionably. And every County court or any one Magistrate upon notice given them shall appoint such Gagers to view the said cask, & to see that they be right, & of sound & wel seasoned timber, & that everie Cooper have a distinct brand-mark on his own cask, upon payn of forfeiture of twenty shilling in either case, & so proportionably for lesser vessels.

The Laws of South Carolina
1734

For Encouragement to introduce into this Collony the Art of making Potash, Be it Enacted by the Authority aforesaid, That any Person now residing in this Province, or who shall hereafter come into the same, shall within Ten Years after the Ratification of this Act instruct the Inhabitants of this Collony in making Potash, (that is such as are willing to undertake the same) in such Manner that the said Commodity be made fit for the Market in Great-Britain, that such Persons shall receive Forty Shillings per Ton out of the publick Treasury of this Province for the first Five Hundred Tons that shall be entered or ship'd on board any Ship or Vessel sailing out of any Ports in this part of the Province, and the Receiver for the time being is hereby required to pay Forty Shillings aforesaid, for every Ton of Potash that is ship'd on board any Vessel sailing out of this Collony.

In this Province the Number of the Inhabitants being few for so great Extent of Land, the erecting of Mills of all kinds, and other Mechanick Engines, will greatly improve the Country itself and its Trade and Navigation: Be it therefore Enacted by the Authority aforsaid, That whatsoever Person or Persons shall after the Ratification of this Act erect a Mill, to saw with the Wind or Water, so as to bring the same to compleate Perfection, as in Holland or in any other Countries, he or they shall have the Privilege of erecting Wind or Water Sawmills in part of this Province exclusive of all others, for the Term of Eight Years, after the first Sawmill begins to Work, and if any other Person or Persons erect or cause to be erected in this Collony, any Wind or Water Sawmills within the Term of Eight years after the time aforesaid, without the Consent and Licence of those who erects the first, he shall forfeit the Sum of One Thousand Pounds, to be recovered for the Use of those to whom this Privilege exclusive of others doth belong.

Early Criminal Law

In early America, criminal law served several distinct objectives. Most fundamentally, it was one of the principal means of keeping the peace—the most basic purpose of criminal law in any society. This objective took on a special urgency in colonial America because the English settlers who framed and administered criminal law considered their societies to be beset by constant peril from three sources: the physical environment, external enemies, and internal foes (Indians, blacks, and others ethnically or religiously distinct). These pressures sometimes induced a state of mind close to mass paranoia, as in the case of the rumored slave insurrections known as the 1712 and 1741 "Negro Plots" in New York.

An important means of keeping the peace was identifying and protecting group identity by policing deviant behavior. Sociologists such as Emile Durkheim, Kai Erikson, and Harold Garfinkel have stressed the importance of societies determining what behavior is acceptable and what is threatening, constantly redefining boundaries between the two. In Erikson's vivid figure, "morality and immorality meet at the public scaffold, and it is during this meeting that the line between them is drawn."[30]

But criminal law also served purposes other than the constabulary one. To a greater extent than today, criminal law was an adjunct to economic regulation, a convenient means of enforcing the pervasive regulatory apparatus of the seventeenth and eighteenth centuries. In this capacity, it promoted economic development in the specie-starved, investment-hungry economies of colonial America. Particularly in the New England colonies (except, as always, Rhode Island), criminal law was used to punish sin and other transgressions of the moral order, at least before independence. Criminal law was also a means of social control, imposing fines, whipping, banishment, and forms of public degradation (the stocks, for example, or branding), by which the ruling classes policed the behavior of those inferior to them on social and economic scales.

The Salem Witch Trials
1692

The most notorious criminal trials of colonial America occurred during the summer of 1692, when over 150 women and men of Salem, Massachusetts, were accused of witchcraft. Nineteen were hanged as witches, and one man was pressed to death for refusing to plead. One of these victims was George Burroughs, a former minister. Some of the evidence and testimony against him appears below.

The community hysteria that produced the prosecutions abated because of efforts by laymen like Thomas Brattle and clergy like Increase Mather, who condemned the trial court's reliance on what was called "spectral evidence" — that is, the testimony of the afflicted about supernatural apparitions. The second excerpt is from a tract published by Mather's son, the already-prominent divine Cotton Mather, that recommended a more cautious approach to evidentiary problems. Neither Mather père nor fils doubted the reality of witchcraft and the actual presence of evil spirits among humans; but both, especially the elder, were troubled by the loose evidentiary standards that characterized the witchcraft trials in the specially convened Court of Oyer and Terminer.

The witchcraft frenzy in Massachusetts ended as abruptly as it had begun. By the autumn of 1692, many persons outside Salem began to have doubts about the persecutions. The court was discharged, and the remaining accused were freed. The General Court (the legislative body of the colony) later enacted a resolution expressing its regret to the survivors of the condemned.

The Examination of Geo: Burroughs 9 May, 1692.

. . . [Burroughs] denied that his house [at] Casco was haunted, yet he owned there were Toads. He denied that he made his wife swear, that she could not write to his father Ruck without his approbation of her letter to her Father. He owned that none of his children, but the eldest was Baptized The above was in private none of the Bewitched being present, At his entry into the Room many (if not all the Bewitched) were grievously tortured.

1. Sus. Sheldon testified that Burroughs' two wives appeared in their winding sheets, and said that man killed them.

He was bid to look upon Sus. Sheldon.

He looked back and knocked down all (or most), of the afflicted who stood behind him.

2. Mary Lewis' deposition going to be read and he looked upon her and she fell into a dreadful and tedious fit,

3. Mary Walcott

4. Eliz Hubbard   Testimony going to be read
   Susan Sheldon   and they all fell into fits

Being asked what he thought of these things. He answered it was an amazing and humbling Providence, but he understood nothing of it and he said (some of you may observe, that) when they begin to name my name, they cannot name it.

Ann Putnam junior   Testified that his 2 wives &
Susan Sheldon   2 children were destroyed
                     by him.

The Bewitched were so tortured that Authority ordered them to be taken away some of them.

*   *   *

View of Body of Geo. Burroughs

We whose names are under written received an order from the sheriff for to search the bodies of George Burroughs and George Jacobs we find nothing upon the body of the above said burroughs but what is natural, but upon the body of George Jacobs we find 3 teats which according to the best of our Judgments we think is not natural for we run a pin through 2 of them and he was not sensible of it, one of them being within his mouth upon the Inside of his right cheek and 2nd upon his right shoulder blade an[d] a 3rd upon his right hip.

*   *   *

Ann Putnam v. *Geo Burroughs*

The Deposition of Ann putnam who testifieth and saith that on 20th of April 1692 at evening she saw the Apparition of a minister at which she was grievously affrighted and cried out oh dreadful: dreadful here is a minister com[e], what are Ministers witches to: whence com[e] you and What is your name for I will complain of you though you be A minister: if you be a wizard: and immediately i was tortured by him being Racked and almost choked by him: and he tempted me to write in his book which I Refused with loud out cries and said I would not write in his book though he tore me all to pieces but told him that it was a dreadful thing: that he which was a Minister that should teach children to fear God should com[e] to persuade poor creatures to give their souls to the devil: Oh, dreadful, dreadful, tell me your name that I may know who you are: then again he tortured me and urged me to write in his book: which I Refused: and then presently he told me that his name was George Burroughs and that he had had three wives: and that he had bewitched the Two first of them to death; and that he killed Mistress Lawson because she was unwilling to go from the village and also killed Mr. Lawson's child because he went to the eastward with Sir Edmon[d Andros] and preached so to the soldiers and that he had bewitched a great many soldiers to death at the eastward when Sir Edmon was there, and that he had made Abigail Hobbs a witch and several witches more: and he has continued ever since; by times tempting me to write in his book and grievously torturing me by beating pinching and almost choking me several times a day and he also told me that he was above a witch he was a conjurer.

Jurat in Curia.

Ann Putnam v. Geo. Burroughs

The deposition of Ann putnam who testifieth and saith that on the 3th of may, 1692, at evening I saw the Apparition of Mr. George Burroughs who grievously tortured me and urged me to write in his book which I refused then he told me that his Two first wives would appear to me presently and tell me a great many lies but I should not believe them, then Immediately appeared to me the form of Two women in winding sheets and napkins about their heads, at which I was greatly affrighted, and they turned their faces towards Mr. Burroughs and looked very red and angry and told him that he had been a cruel man to them, and that their blood did cry vengeance against him: and also told him that they should be clothed with white Robes in heaven, when he should be cast into hell, and immediately he vanished away, and as soon as he was gone the Two women turned their faces towards me and looked as pale as a white wall: and told me that they were Mr. Burroughs Two first wives and that he had murdered them; and one told me that she was his first wife and he stabbed her under the left Arm and put a piece of ceiling wax on the wound and she pulled aside the winding sheet, and showed me the place and also told me that she was in the house Mr parris now lived where it was done, and the other told me that Mr. Burroughs and that wife which he hath now killed her in the vessel as she was coming to see her friends because they would have one another; and they both charged me that I should tell these things to the Magistrates before Mr Burroughs face and if he did now own them they did not know but they should appear there: this morning, also Mistress Lawson and her daughter Ann appeared to me whom I knew, and told me that Mr. Burroughs murdered them, this morning also appeared to me another woman in a winding sheet and told me that she was goodman Fuller's first wife and Mr. Burroughs killed her because there was some difference between her husband and him, also on the 9th may during the time of his examination he did most grievously torment and afflict mary Walcott mercy lewin Eliz. Hubbard and Abigail williams by pinching pricking and choking them. . . .

COTTON MATHER
The Wonders of the Invisible World
1693

Quaere, Whether if God would have us to proceed any further than bare Enquiry upon what Report there may come against any Man, from the World of Spirits, he will not by his Providence at the same time have brought into our hands, these more evident and sensible things, whereupon a man is to be esteemed a Criminal. But I will venture to say this further, that it will be safe to account the Names as well as the Lives of our Neighbors; two considerable things to be brought under a Judicial Process, until it be found by Humane Observations that the Peace of Mankind is thereby disturbed. We are Humane Creatures, and we are safe while we say, they must be Humane Witnesses, who also have in the particular Act of Seeing, or Hearing, which enables them to be Witnesses, had no more than Humane Assistances that are to turn the Scale when Laws are to be executed.

I was going to make one Venture more; that is, to offer some safe Rules, for the finding out of the Witches, which are at this day our accursed Troublers: but this were a Venture too Presumptuous and Icarian for me to make; I leave that unto those Excellent and Judicious Persons, with whom I am not worthy to be numbered: All that I shall do, shall be to lay before my Readers, a brief Synopsis of what has been written on that Subject, by a Triumvirate of as Eminent Persons as have ever handled it. I will begin with,

An Abstract of Mr. Perkins's Way for the Discovery of Witches

I.   There are Presumptions, which do at least probably and conjecturally note one to be a Witch.
These give occasion to Examine, yet they are no sufficient Causes of Conviction.

II.   If any Man or Woman be notoriously defamed for a Witch, this yields a strong Suspicion. Yet the Judge ought carefully to look, that the Report be made by Men of Honesty and Credit.

III.   If a Fellow-Witch, or Magician, give Testimony of any Person to be a Witch; this method is not sufficient for Condemnation; but it is a fit Presumption to cause a straight Examination.

IV.   If after Cursing there follow Death, or at least some mischief: for Witches are wont to practice their mischievous Facts by Cursing and Banning: This also is a sufficient matter of Examination, tho' not of Conviction.

V.   If after Enmity, Quarrelling, or Threatening, a present mischief does follow: that also is a great Presumption.

VI.   If the Party suspected be the Son or Daughter, the man-servant or maid-servant, the Familiar Friend, near Neighbor, or old Companion, of a known and convicted Witch; this may be likewise a Presumption; for Witchcraft is an Art that may be learned, and conveyed from man to man.

VII.   Some add this for a Presumption: If the Party suspected be found to have the Devil's mark; for it is commonly thought, when the Devil makes his covenant with them, he always leaves his mark behind them, whereby he knows them for his own:—a mark whereof no evident Reason in Nature can be given.

VIII.   Lastly, If the party examined be Unconstant, or contrary to himself, in his deliberate Answers, it argueth a Guilty Conscience, which stops the freedom of Utterance. And yet there are causes of Astonishment, which may befal the Good, as well as the Bad.

IX.   But then there is a Conviction, discovering the Witch, which must proceed from just and sufficient proofs, and not from bare presumptions.

X.   Scratching of the suspected party, and Recovery thereupon, with several other such weak Proofs; as also, the fleeting [floating] of the suspected Party, thrown upon the Water; these Proofs are so far from being sufficient, that some of them are, after a sort, practices of Witchcraft.

XI.   The Testimony of some Wizzard, tho' offering to shew the Witches Face in a Glass: This, I grant, may be a good Presumption, to cause a strait Examination; but a sufficient Proof of Conviction it cannot be. If the Devil tell the Grand Jury, that the person in question is a Witch, and offers withal to confirm the same by Oath, should the Inquest receive his Oath or Accusation to condemn the man? Assuredly no. And yet, that is as much as the Testimony of another Wizzard, who only by the Devil's help reveals the Witch.

XII.   If any man, being dangerously sick, and like to dy, upon Suspicion, will take it on his Oath, that such an one hath bewitched him, it is an Allegation of the same nature, which may move the Judge to examine the Party, but it is of no moment for Conviction.

XIII.   Among the sufficient means of Conviction, the first is, the free and voluntary Confession of the Crime, made by the party suspected and accused, after Examination. I say not, that a bare confession is sufficient, but a Confession after due Examination, taken upon pregnant presumptions. What needs now more witness or further Enquiry?

XIV.   There is a second sufficient Conviction, by the Testimony of two Witnesses, of good and honest Report, avouching before the Magistrate, upon their own Knowledge, the two things: either that the party accused hath made a League with the Devil, or hath done some known practices of witchcraft. And, all Arguments that do necessarily prove either of these, being brought by two sufficient Witnesses, are of force fully to convince the party suspected.

XV.   If it can be proved, that the party suspected hath called upon the Devil, or desired his Help, this is a pregnant proof of a League formerly made between them.

XVI.   If it can be proved, that the party hath entertained a Familiar Spirit, and had Conference with it, in the likeness of some visible Creatures; here is Evidence of Witchcraft.

XVII.   If the witnesses affirm upon Oath, that the suspected person hath done any action or work which necessarily infers a Covenant made, as, that he hath used Enchantments, divined things before they come to pass, and that peremptorily, raised Tempests, caused the Form of a dead man to appear; it proveth sufficiently, that he or she is a Witch. . . .

2

Law in a Republican Revolution
1760–1815

The American Revolution had a more profound effect on the development of law than any other event in American experience. Even the upheaval of the Civil War and Reconstruction, which re-created our constitutional order, was not as far-reaching in its influence. In the years between 1760 and 1776, Americans achieved more than national independence, and between 1775 and 1783 they did more than wage a war of national liberation. In these years, the British mainland colonies became republican states, while Americans implemented republicanism as a working system in their state governments. Throughout, ideology and law played decisive roles, driving and at the same time constraining the course of revolutionary political development.

After independence, Americans combined republican ideology and practical experience to create a national government, first as a loose confederation that managed to see them through the American War of Independence, and then as a national republic that was itself a state having sufficient powers of governance. One of the essential characteristics of that national government was a judiciary fully competent to enforce its laws and protect national policy against state particularism.

Without being conscious of it, Americans and Britons had been drifting apart in their understanding of their shared constitutional heritage. The bases for differences between them had existed from the time of the earliest seventeenth-century settlements, but those divisive potentials remained latent through the course of what historians call "The Great War for Empire," the century-long struggle between Britain and France for dominance on the European continent, in North America, and in Asia. In 1763, that struggle concluded triumphantly for Great Britain, which then turned to two long-neglected problems in colonial affairs: tightening up colonial administration and increasing the revenue from the colonies.

When confronted with these policy innovations, Americans continued to think along the lines disclosed in Chapter 1. That is, they regarded themselves as English people, entitled to all the rights of their fellow-subjects still resident within the realm, plus certain rights peculiar to their situation. When challenged on a particular belief, such as the autonomy of colonial government, they would rethink the implications of something they had long taken for granted, and this forced reconsideration would then lead them to an extension of their original position.

Americans thus discovered their most important revolutionary concept—popular sovereignty. At the outset of the American Revolution, no one in the colonies entertained any idea of disavowing loyalty to the Crown or of locating sovereign authority in the people themselves. Americans came to that belief slowly between 1760 and 1776. They repeatedly and sincerely insisted on their fealty to the Crown, through the Declaration and Resolves of the First Continental Congress (1774). But Whig-minded Americans gradually came to see that Parliament's claim of full legislative power over the colonies, coupled with the British theory of virtual representation, was incompatible with their rights as colonists, especially self-government.

After independence, Americans evolved a coherent republican ideology—that is, a political philosophy that protected individual and collective rights, specified the sources of those rights, identified dangers to them, and, in a teleological sense, provided a vision of America's destiny. Americans blended their heritage as English people with their actual experience in colonial governance for the preceding 150 years to produce a political philosophy based on the most revolutionary idea about government the world has yet known: the people are capable of governing themselves, without the superintendence of king, nobility, church, party, or tyrant.

Americans promptly put republicanism to practical use in structuring their state governments. Not surprisingly, they discovered that they were not of one mind about the meaning of republicanism. Their beliefs and hopes sorted themselves out along a spectrum, with conservative and radical poles. The radical-minded were inclined to a pure democracy, in which government would be as closely in the hands of the people as the circumstances of time, space, and technology would permit. This vision was realized in the Pennsylvania Constitution of 1776, with its array of democratic features tying the day-to-day operations of government immediately to the people. Conservatives condemned such experiments, fearing that popular majorities in direct control of government would threaten property rights and the stability of society. They propounded a different vision of popular sovereignty, one in which structures of government would distance the people from the actual exercise of power.

Americans at first had less success in creating a national government than they had experienced in establishing state governments, principally because they had accumulated over a century of experience in provincial governance, whereas their attempts at transcolonial integration (the New England Confederation of 1643, the Albany Plan of Union of 1754) had been failures. The Articles of Confederation, drafted in 1776 but not ratified until 178l, created a loose confederacy that had some characteristics of a true government, but eventually proved incapable of serving as a vehicle for long-term peacetime governance of the nation. The Framers' success in establishing a national government under the Constitution of 1787 has impressed later generations as superhuman, given the sectional divisions and particularist antagonisms that had to be overcome. In accomplishing this, the Framers produced an impressive body of political theory that enriched republican thought.

In the first decade of its operation, the new national government established precedents that became elements of American constitutionalism scarcely less significant than the Constitution itself. But the sectional and policy conflicts of the first decade also spawned competing theories about the nature of the Union. Located in the doctrines of Alexander Hamilton, John Marshall, Joseph Story, and Daniel Webster, a conservative and nationalistic vision extolled the power of the national government as a unifying force overriding the local self-interest of state public policy. The other vision was propounded by Thomas Jefferson, James Madison in the Virginia Resolutions, and a claque of Virginia political theorists and jurists, most prominently Judge Spencer Roane. They emphasized the primacy of the states as embodiments of popular sovereignty, and squinted suspiciously at national power. The conflict between these competing visions, given practical relevance by the expansion of slavery, dominated political debate in the United States until the Civil War. Although the nationalist vision eventually triumphed, the state-power theory left a lingering suspicion of national power.

The American Revolution

A 1750 election-day sermon delivered in Boston by the Reverend Jonathan Mayhew demonstrated just how provincial Americans had become in the development of their political life. James Otis, Jr., of Massachusetts attempted to identify American rights in the 1760s, but he could not escape the ambivalence of the early American position, defending colonial liberties while retaining loyalty to the British system. Perceiving the chasm that separated them from the Americans, the British articulated their own position, officially in the Declaratory Act of 1766 and unofficially in William Blackstone's *Commentaries*. The relentless erosion of relations between Great Britain and its colonies was signaled in 1774 by the Declaration and Resolves of the First Continental Congress, which set forth the essential American constitutional position. In 1776, Thomas Jefferson's Declaration of Independence cut the final emotional and ideological ties binding the former American colonies to the British Empire.

JONATHAN MAYHEW
"Unlimited Submission and Non-resistance to the Higher Powers"
1750

Starting from a shared fund of political theory in the early eighteenth century, British and American thinking about constitutional issues diverged, without either mother country or colonies being aware of how far apart from each other they were growing. A good example of this divergence was provided in an election sermon delivered by the Massachusetts Congregational minister Jonathan Mayhew in 1750, a decade before overt stirring of revolutionary sentiment. Taking as his text an admonition of St. Paul, "Let every soul be subject unto the higher powers. . . . the powers that be are ordained of God" (Romans 13:1), Mayhew stood the apostle on his head.

Common tyrants and public oppressors are not entitled to obedience from their subjects by virtue of anything here laid down by the inspired apostle.

I now add, further, that the apostle's argument is so far from proving it to be the duty of people to obey and submit to such rulers as act in contradiction to the public good, and so to the design of their office, that it proves the direct contrary. For, please to observe, that if the end of all civil government be the good of society; if this be the thing that is aimed at in constituting civil rulers; and if the motive and argument for submission to government be taken from the apparent usefulness of civil authority,—it follows, that when no such good end can be answered by submission, there remains no argument or motive to enforce it; and if, instead of this good end's being brought about by submission, a contrary end is brought about, and the ruin and misery of society effected by it, here is a plain and positive reason against submission in all such cases, should they ever happen. And therefore, in such cases, a regard to the public welfare ought to make us withhold from our rulers that obedience and submission which it would otherwise be our duty to render to them. . . .

Note: Litigation and the Coming of the Revolution

John Peter Zenger's case was the earliest example of a process that promoted the Revolution. A case would come before local courts, growing out of a local political controversy, such as Zenger's criticism of the administration of royal Governor William Cosby. The attorney representing one of the parties appealed to the jury in terms that appear to us, on their face, to be empty rhetoric. But the rhetorical appeal couched an articulation of a fundamental constitutional belief cherished by Americans (e.g., truth as a defense in a prosecution for seditious libel). This doctrinal advance thereupon became embedded in American belief as a constitutional principle.

This process was often repeated during the American Revolution. In the *Writs of Assistance Case* of 1761 in Massachusetts, a young attorney, James Otis, Jr., denounced the Crown's resort to general writs used in investigations of smuggling. After condemning such writs in uncompromising terms, Otis declaimed:

> But had this writ been in any book whatever, it would have been illegal. All precedents are under the control of the principles of law. . . . No Acts of Parliament can establish such a writ; though it should be made in the very words of the petition, it would be void. An act against the constitution is void.

John Adams, who was present at Otis's argument, later noted in his Diary that "then and there the brat Independence was born."

In the "Parson's Cause" of 1763 (sometimes known as the *Two-Penny Act Case*), Patrick Henry made an even more dramatic leap from rhetorical appeal to constitutional principle. He argued that a Virginia statute regulating the pay of clergy of the established church, which had the effect of diminishing the curates' salaries, was a good law that contributed to the welfare of the people, and that its disallowance by King George III consequently violated the compact between king and people. By such action, the king degenerated into a tyrant and forfeited the right to his subjects' obedience. The attorney-general, aghast, leapt up to object: "The gentleman speaks treason!" Nonetheless, the jury endorsed Henry's argument and returned only a nominal verdict for the plaintiff-clergyman.

JAMES OTIS
"The Rights of the British Colonies"
1764

This disjointed essay, frequently self-contradictory and at times approaching incoherence, reflects the confusion in the minds of Americans generally in 1764. Otis mirrored the ambivalence of Americans in the early stages of the Revolution. On one hand, they considered themselves British subjects and appealed to the British constitution as a barrier to arbitrary power. On the other hand, they claimed rights inconsistent with the allegiance they professed, claims that their British fellow-subjects found incomprehensible and revolutionary.

I affirm that government is founded on the necessity of our natures and that an original supreme, sovereign, absolute, and uncontrollable earthly power must exist in and preside over every society, from whose final decisions there can be no appeal but directly to Heaven. It is therfore originally and ultimately in the people. I say this supreme absolute power is originally and ultimately in the people; and they never did in fact freely, nor can they rightfully make an absolute, unlimited renunciation of this divine right. It is ever in the nature of the thing given in trust and on a condition the performance of which no mortal can dispense with, namely, that the person or persons on whom the sovereignty is conferred by the people shall incessantly consult their good.

        *   *   *

I also lay it down as one of the first principles from whence I intend to deduce the civil rights of the British colonies, that all of them are subject to and dependent on Great Britain and that therefore as over subordinate governments the Parliament of Great Britain has an undoubted power and lawful authority to make acts for the general good that by naming them shall and ought to be equally binding as upon the subjects of Great Britain within the realm. This principle, I presume, will be readily granted on the other side of the Atlantic. It has been practised upon for twenty years to my knowledge, in the province of Massachusetts Bay and I have ever received it that it has been so from the beginning in this and the sister provinces through the continent.

I am aware some will think it is time for me to retreat, after having expressed the power of the British Parliament in quite so strong terms. But 'tis from and under this very power and its acts, and from the common Law, that the political and civil rights of the colonists are derived; and upon those grand pillars of liberty shall my defense be rested. No act of Parliament can deprive them of the liberties of such, unless any will contend that an act of Parliament can make slaves not only of one but two millions of the commonwealth. And if so, why not of the whole? I freely own that I can find nothing in the laws of my country that would justify the Parliament in making one slave, nor did they ever professedly undertake to make one.

        *   *   *

Every British subject born on the continent of America or in any other of the British dominions is by the law of God and nature, by the common law, and by act of Parliament (exclusive of all charters from the crown) entitled to all the natural, essential, inherent, and inseparable rights of our fellow subjects in Great Britain. Among those rights are the following, which it is humbly conceived no man or body of men, not excepting the Parliament, justly, equitably, and consistently with their own rights and the constitution can take away.

*   *   *

These are their bounds, which by God and nature are fixed; hitherto have they a right to come, and no further.

1.   To govern by stated laws.
2.   Those laws should have no other end ultimately but the good of the people.
3.   Taxes are not to be laid on the people but by their consent in person or by deputation.

*   *   *

That the colonists, black and white, born here are freeborn British subjects, and entitled to all the essential civil rights of such is a truth not only manifest from the provincial charters, from the principles of the common law, and acts of Parliament, but from the British constitution, which was re-established at the [Glorious] Revolution with a professed design to secure the liberties of all the subjects to all generations.

*   *   *

The power of Parliament is uncontrollable but by themselves, and we must obey. They only can repeal their own acts. There would be an end of all government if one or a number of subjects or subordinate provinces should take upon them so far to judge of the justice of an act of Parliament as to refuse obedience to it. If there was nothing else to restrain such a step, prudence ought to do it, for forceably resisting the Parliament and the King's laws is high treason. Therefore let the Parliament lay what burdens they please on us, we must, it is our duty to submit and patiently bear them till they will be pleased to relieve us. And 'tis to be presumed the wisdom and justice of that august assembly always will afford us relief by repealing such acts as through mistake or other human infirmities have been suffered to pass, if they can be convinced that their proceedings are not constitutional or not for the common good.

*   *   *

To say the Parliament is absolute and arbitrary is a contradiction. The Parliament cannot make 2 and 2, 5: omnipotency cannot do. The supreme power in a state is jus dicere only: jus dare strictly speaking, belongs alone to GOD.[1] Parliaments are in all cases to declare what is for the good of the whole; but it is not the declaration of Parliament that makes it so. There must be in every instance a higher authority, viz., GOD. Should an act of Parliament be against any of his natural laws, which are immutably true, their declaration would be contrary to eternal truth, equity, and justice, and consequently void: and so it would be adjudged by the Parliament itself when convinced of their mistake.

William Blackstone on the Imperial Constitution
1765

Sir William Blackstone (1723–1780) was the first Vinerian Professor of Law at Oxford, where he introduced courses on English law. His lectures, published in

1765 as Commentaries on the Laws of England, *have stood for two centuries as the classic exposition of English law. The passages reprinted below on reception of the common law and parliamentary power represented the core of orthodoxy in the English view of the imperial constitution. In this outlook, there was obviously little room for accommodating the American position. Thus from the outset of the Revolution, the two sides were irreconcilable.*

[O]ur more distant plantations in America, and elsewhere, are also in some respects subject to the English laws. Plantations or colonies, in distant countries, are either such where the lands are claimed by right of occupancy only by finding them desert and uncultivated, and peopling them from the mother-country; or where, when already cultivated, they have been either gained by conquest, or ceded to us by treaties. And both these rights are founded upon the law of nature, or at least upon that of nations. But there is a difference between these two species of colonies, with respect to the laws by which they are bound. For it hath been held that if an uninhabited country be discovered and planted by English subjects, all the English laws then in being, which are the birthright of every subject, are immediately there in force. But this must be understood with very many and very great restrictions. Such colonists carry with them only so much of the English law as is applicable to their own situation and the condition of an infant colony; such, for instance, as the general rules of inheritance, and of protection from personal injuries. The artificial refinements and distinctions incident to the property of a great and commercial people, the laws of police and revenue, (such especially as are enforced by penalties,) the mode of maintenance for the established clergy, the jurisdiction of spiritual courts, and a multitude of other provisions, are neither necessary nor convenient for them, and therefore are not in force. What shall be admitted and what rejected, at what times, and under what restrictions, must, in case of dispute, be decided in the first instance by their own provincial judicature, subject to the revision and control of the king in council: the whole of their constitution being also liable to be new-modelled and reformed by the general superintending power of the legislature in the mother-country. But in conquered or ceded countries, that have already laws of their own, the king may indeed alter and change those laws; but till he does actually change them, the ancient laws of the country remain, unless such as are against the law of God, as in the case of an infidel country. Our American plantations are principally of this latter sort, being obtained in the last century either by right of conquest and driving out the natives (with what natural justice I shall not at present inquire), or by treaties. And therefore the common law of England, as such, has no allowance or authority there; they being no part of the mother-country, but distinct (though dependent) dominions. They are subject, however, to the control of the parliament; though (like Ireland, Man, and the rest) not bound by any acts of parliament, unless particularly named.

*   *   *

III.   We are next to examine the laws and customs relating to parliment, thus united together and considered as one aggregate body.

The power and jurisdiction of parliament, says sir Edward Coke, is so transcendent and absolute, that it cannot be confined, either for causes or persons, within any bounds. It has sovereign and uncontrollable authority in the making, confirming, enlarging, restraining, abrogating, repealing, reviving, and expounding of laws, concerning matters of all possible denominations, ecclesiastical, or temporal, civil, military, maritime, or criminal: this being the place where that absolute despotic power, which must in all governments reside somewhere, is intrusted by the constitution of these kingdoms.

*   *   *

It must be owned that Mr. Locke and other theoretical writers, have held, that "there remains still inherent in the people a supreme power to remove or alter the legislative, when they find the legislative act countrary to the trust reposed in them; for when such trust is abused, it is thereby forfeited, and devolves to those who gave it." But, however just this conclusion may be in the theory, we cannot practically adopt it, nor take any legal steps for carrying it into execution under any dispensation of government at present actually existing. For this devolution of power, to the people at large, includes in it a dissolution of the whole form of government established by that people; reduces all the members to their original state of equality; and, by annihilating the sovereign power, repeals all positive laws whatsoever before enacted. No human laws will therefore suppose a case, which at once must destroy all law, and compel men to build afresh upon a new foundation; nor will they make provision for so desperate an event, as must render all legal provisions ineffectual. So long therefore as the English constitution lasts, we may venture to affirm, that the power of parliament is absolute and without control.

The Declaratory Act
1766

This statute was the official British response to American arguments on the limits of Parliament's authority over the colonies.

An act for the better securing the dependency of his Majesty's dominions in America upon the crown and parliament of Great Britain.

Whereas several of the houses of representatives in his Majesty's colonies and plantations in America, have of late, against law, claimed to themselves, or to the general assemblies of the same, the sole and exclusive right of imposing duties and taxes upon his Majesty's subjects in the said colonies and plantations; and have, in pursuance of such claim, passed certain votes, resolutions, and orders, derogatory to the legislative authority of parliament, and inconsistent with the dependency of the said colonies and plantations upon the crown of Great Britian: may it therefore please your most excellent Majesty, that it may be declared; and be it declared by the King's most excellent majesty, by and with the advice and consent of the lords spiritual and temporal, and commons, in this present parliament assembled, and by the authority of the same, that the said colonies and plantations in America have been, are, and of right ought to be, subordinate unto, and dependent upon the imperial crown and parliament of Great Britain; and that the King's majesty, by and with the advice and consent of the lords spiritual and temporal, and commons of Great Britain, in parliament assembled, had, hath, and of right ought to have, full power and authority to make laws and statutes of sufficient force and validity to bind the colonies and people of America, subjects of the crown of Great Britain, in all cases whatsoever.

The Declaration and Resolves of the Continental Congress
1774

The Declaration and Resolves of 1774 set forth the essential American constitutional position. But differences had by now gone too far for Parliament to temporize further with what it had come to regard as treasonable constitutional experimentation. What seemed obvious and equitable to Americans appeared irrational and seditious to the British.

That the inhabitants of the English colonies in North-America, by the immutable laws of nature, the principles of the English constitution, and the several charters or compacts, have the following Rights:

Resolved, 1. That they are entitled to life, liberty and property: and they have never ceded to any foreign power whatever, a right to dispose of either without their consent.

Resolved, 2. That our ancestors, who first settled these colonies, were at the time of their emigration from the mother country, entitled to all the rights, liberties, and immunities of free and natural-born subjects, within the realm of England.

Resolved, 3. That by such emigration they by no means forfeited, surrendered, or lost any of those rights, but that they were, and their descendants now are, entitled to the exercise and enjoyment of all such of them, as their local and other circumstances enable them to exercise and enjoy.

Resolved, 4. That the foundation of English liberty, and of all free government, is a right in the people to participate in their legislative council and as the English colonists are not represented, and from their local and other circumstances, cannot properly be represented in the British parliament, they are entitled to a free and exclusive power of legislation in their several provincial legislatures, where their right of representation can alone be preserved, in all cases of taxation and internal policy, subject only to the negative of their sovereign, in such manner as has been heretofore used and accustomed; But, from the necessity of the case, and a regard to the mutual interest of both countries, we cheerfully consent to the operation of such acts of the British parliament as are bona fide, restrained to the regulation of external commerce, for the purpose of securing the commercial advantages of the whole empire to the mother country, and the commercial benefits of its respective members; excluding every idea of taxation internal or external, for raising a revenue on the subjects, in America, without their consent.

Resolved, 5. That the respective colonies are entitled to the common law of

England, and more especially to the great and inestimable privilege of being tried by their peers of the vicinage, according to the course of that law.

Resolved, 6. That they are entitled to the benefit of such of the English statutes, as existed at the time of their colonization; and which they have, by experience, respectively found to be applicable to their several local and other circumstances.

TOM PAINE
Common Sense
1776

Even after the shooting war began in 1775, most Americans longed for a reconciliation of some sort with the mother country. It was left to the brilliant propaganda of Tom Paine to sever the final remaining psychological and constitutional link with Britain—the individual's sense of personal loyalty to the king, the "royal brute" and the "crowned ruffian," as Paine called him.

This is supposing the present race of kings in the world to have had an honorable origin; whereas it is more than probable, that, could we take off the dark covering of antiquity and trace them to their first rise, we should find the first of them nothing better than the principal ruffian of some restless gang; whose savage manners or preeminence in subtility obtained him the title of chief among plunderers: and who by increasing in power and extending his depredations, overawed the quiet and defenceless to purchase their safety by frequent contributions. . . .

     *   *   *

England since the conquest hath known some few good monarchs, but groaned beneath a much larger number of bad ones; yet no man in his senses can say that their claim under William the Conqueror is a very honorable one. A French bastard landing with an armed banditti and establishing himself king of England against the consent of the natives is in plain terms a very paltry rascally original. It certainly hath no divinity in it. However it is needless to spend much time in exposing the folly of herditary rights: if there were any so weak as to believe it, let them promiscuously worship the ass and the lion, and welcome. I shall neither copy their humility, nor disturb their devotion. . . . The plain truth is, that the antiquity of English monarchy will not bear looking into.

     *   *   *

In England a king hath little more to do than to make war and give away places; which, in plain terms, is to empoverish the nation and set it together by the ears. A pretty business indeed for a man to be allowed eight hundred thousand sterling a year for, and worshipped into the bargain! Of more worth is one honest man to society, and in the sight of God, than all the crowned ruffians that ever lived.

     *   *   *

But where, say some, is the king of America? I'll tell you, he reigns above, and doth not make havoc of mankind like the royal brute of Great Britain. Yet that we may not appear to be defective even in earthly honors, let a day be solemnly set apart for proclaiming the charter; let it be brought forth placed on the divine law, the Word of God; let a crown be placed thereon, by which the world may know, that so far as we approve of monarchy, that in America the law is king. For as in absolute governments the king is law, so in free countries the law ought to be king; and there ought to be no other. But lest any ill use should afterwards arise, let the crown at the conclusion of the ceremony be demolished, and scattered among the people whose right it is.

The Declaration of Independence
1776

Thomas Jefferson's great masterpiece of political theory and propaganda divides into two sections. The first is a brilliantly succinct restatement of liberal political theory, as previously articulated by John Locke and others. The second section is an extended indictment of the misdeeds of King George III. It served the essential function of severing Americans' psychological loyalty and allegiance to the king. (All Whig Americans by this time had rejected Parliament's legislative authority over the colonies.)

The unanimous Declaration of the thirteen
United States of America.

When in the course of human events, it becomes necessary for one people to dissolve the political bands which have connected them with another, and to assume, among the Powers of the earth, the separate and equal station to which the Laws of Nature and of Nature's God entitle them, a decent respect to the opinions of mankind requires that they should declare the causes which impel them to the separation.

We hold these truths to be self-evident, that all men are created equal, that they are endowed by their Creator with certain unalienable Rights, that among these, are Life, Liberty, and the pursuit of Happiness. That, to secure these rights, Governments are instituted among Men, deriving their just Powers from the consent of the governed. That, whenever any form of Government becomes destructive of these ends, it is the Right of the People to alter or to abolish it, and to institute new Government, laying its foundation on such Principles, and organizing its Powers in such form, as to them shall seem most likely to effect their Safety and Happiness. Prudence, indeed, will dictate that Governments long established should not be changed for light and transient causes; and, accordingly, all experience hath shewn, that mankind are more disposed to suffer, while evils are sufferable, than to right themselves by abolishing the forms to which they are accustomed. But, when a long train of abuses and usurpations, pursuing invariably the same Object, evinces a design to reduce them under absolute Despotism, it is their right, it is their duty, to throw off such Government, and to provide new Guards for their future Security. Such has been the patient sufferance of these Colonies; and such is now the necessity which constrains them to alter their former Systems of Government. The history of the present King of Great Britain is a history of repeated injuries and usurpations, all having in direct object the establishment of an absolute Tyranny over these States. To prove this, let Facts be submitted to a candid world.

He has refused his Assent to Laws, the most wholesome and necessary for the public good.

He has forbidden his Governors to pass Laws of immediate and pressing importance, unless suspended in their operation till his Assent should be obtained; and when so suspended, he has utterly neglected to attend to them.

He has refused to pass other Laws for the accommodation of large districts of people, unless those people would relinquish the right of Representation in the Legislature, a right inestimable to them and formidable to tyrants only.

           *   *   *

He has made Judges dependent on his Will alone, for the tenure of their offices, and the amount and payment of their salaries.

He has erected a multitude of New Offices, and sent hither swarms of Officers to harass our People, and eat out their substance.

He has kept among us, in times of peace, Standing Armies without the Consent of our legislature.

He has affected to render the Military independent of and superior to the Civil Power.

He has combined with others to subject us to a jurisdiction foreign to our constitution, and unacknowledged by our laws; giving his Assent to their Acts of pretended Legislation:

For quartering large bodies of armed troops among us:

For protecting them, by a mock Trial, from Punishment for any Murders which they should commit on the Inhabitants of these States:

For cutting off our Trade with all parts of the world:

For imposing taxes on us without our Consent:

For depriving us in many cases, of the benefits of Trial by jury:

For transporting us beyond Seas to be tried for pretended offences:

For abolishing the free System of English Laws in a neighbouring Province, establishing therein an Arbitrary government, and enlarging its Boundaries so as to render it at once an example and fit instrument for introducing the same absolute rule into these Colonies:

For taking away our Charters, abolishing our most valuable Laws, and altering fundamentally the Forms of our Governments:

For suspending our own Legislatures, and declaring themselves invested with Power to legislate for us in all cases whatsoever.

He has abdicated Government here, by declaring us out of his Protection and waging War against us.

He has plundered our seas, ravaged our Coasts, burnt our towns, and destroyed the lives of our people.

He is at this time transporting large armies of foreign mercenaries to compleat the works of death, desolation, and tyranny, already begun with circumstances of Cruelty & perfidy scarcely paralleled in the most barbarous ages, and totally unworthy the Head of a civilized nation.

He has constrained our fellow Citizens taken Captive on the high seas to bear Arms against their Country, to become the executioners of their friends and Brethren, or to fall themselves by their Hands.

He has excited domestic insurrections amongst us, and has endeavoured to bring on the inhabitants of our frontiers, the merciless Indian savages, whose known rule of warfare, is an undistinguished destruction of all ages, sexes, and conditions. In every stage of these Oppressions We have Petitioned for Redress in the most humble terms: Our repeated Petitions have been answered only by repeated injury. A Prince, whose character is thus marked by every act which may define a Tyrant, is unfit to be the ruler of a free people.

Nor have We been wanting in attention to our British brethren. We have warned them from time to time of attempts by their legislature to extend an unwarrantable jurisdiction over us. We have reminded them of the circumstances of our emigration and settlement here. We have appealed to their native justice and magnanimity, and we have conjured them by the ties of our common kindred to disavow these usurpations, which, would inevitably interrupt our connections and correspondence. They too must have been deaf to the voice of justice and of consanguinity. We must, therefore, acquiesce in the necessity, which denounces our Separation, and hold them, as we hold the rest of mankind, Enemies in War, in Peace Friends.

We, therefore, the Representatives of the United States of America, in General Congress, Assembled, appealing to the Supreme Judge of the world for the rectitude of our intentions, do, in the Name, and by Authority of the good People of these Colonies, solemnly publish and declare, That these United Colonies are, and of Right ought to be free and independent states; that they are Absolved from all Allegiance to the British Crown, and that all political connection between them and the State of Great Britian, is and ought to be totally dissolved; and that as Free and Independent States, they have full Power to levy War, conclude Peace, contract Alliances, establish Commerce, and to do all other Acts and Things which Independent States may of right do. And for the support of this Declaration, with a firm reliance on the Protection of Divine Providence, we mutually pledge to each other our Lives, our Fortunes, and our sacred Honor.

Republican State Constitutionalism

The American Revolution was the hothouse in which republican ideology was nurtured. Independence provided Americans the opportunity of applying republican principles to create actual mechanisms of state governance. The first vehicles for incorporating these tenets into actual governments were the state constitutions, drafted by the state legislatures between 1776 and 1790. Reflecting a continuum of republican thought, these constitutions ranged themselves along a radical to conservative spectrum, with Pennsylvania's 1776 Constitution embodying the democratic sentiments expressed in the anonymous radical pamphlet *The People the Best Governors*. By contrast, the constitution that the people of Massachusetts eventually ratified in 1790 exemplified the conservative republicanism of John Adams, who warned of the dangers of too immediate and powerful popular control over the actual workings of government.

The early state constitutions often contained some law-reform mandates. Other reform projects were undertaken by the legislatures or by individual reformers like

Thomas Jefferson. These law-reform efforts encompassed both private law, like the abolition of primogeniture and entail in Virginia, and public law issues, such as religious disestablishment or the abolition or melioration of slavery. Disestablishment proved to be easy, but abolition foundered on the racism prevalent among white Americans. Nevertheless, the Confederation Congress, in its last great accomplishment, banned slavery from the Northwest Territory while extending republicanism and religious liberty to the region.

The Virginia Declaration of Rights
1776

The Virginia Declaration of Rights, drafted by George Mason, served as a prototype for many subsequent Bills of Rights in state constitutions. The obscure phrase of Section 1, "when they enter into a state of society," was inserted by the Virginia legislature to prevent the language of freedom and equality from being applied to slaves. Otherwise, the declaration is a précis of republican theory at the apex of the Revolution.

A declaration of rights made by the representatives of the good people of Virginia, assembled in full and free convention; which rights do pertain to them and their posterity, as the basis and foundation of government.

Section 1.   That all men are by nature equally free and independent, and have certain inherent rights, of which, when they enter into a state of society, they cannot, by any compact, deprive or divest their posterity; namely, the enjoyment of life and liberty, with the means of acquiring and possessing property, and pursuing and obtaining happiness and safety.

Sec. 2.   That all power is vested in, and consequently derived from, the people; that magistrates are their trustees and servants, and at all times amenable to them.

Sec. 3.   That government is, or ought to be, instituted for the common benefit, protection, and security of the people, or community; of all the various modes and forms of government, that is best which is capable of producing the greatest degree of happiness and safety, and is most effectually secured against the danger of maladministration; and that, when any government shall be found inadequate or contrary to these purposes, a majority of the community hath an indubitable, inalienable, and indefeasible right to reform, alter, or abolish it, in such manner as shall be judged most conducive to the public weal.

Sec. 4.   That no man, or set of men, are entitled to exclusive or separate emoluments or privileges from the community, but in consideration of public services; which, not being descendible, neither ought the offices of magistrate, legislator, or judge to be hereditary.

Sec. 5.   That the legislative and executive powers of the State should be separate and distinct from the judiciary; and that the members of the two first may be restrained from oppression, by feeling and participating in the burdens of the people, they should, at fixed periods, be reduced to a private station, returning into that body from which they were originally taken, and the vacancies be supplied by frequent, certain and regular elections, in which all, or any part of the former members, to be again eligible, or ineligible, as the law shall direct.

Sec. 6.   That elections of members to serve as representatives of the people, in assembly, ought to be free; and that all men, having sufficient evidence of permanent common interest with, and attachment to the community, have the right of suffrage, and cannot be taxed or deprived of their property for public uses, without their own consent, or that of their representatives so elected, nor bound by any law to which they have not, in like manner, assembled, for the public good.

Sec. 7.   That all power of suspending laws, or the execution of laws, by any authority, without consent of the representatives of the people, is injurious to their rights, and ought not to be exercised.

Sec. 8.   That in all capital or criminal prosecutions a man hath a right to demand the cause and nature of his accusation, to be confronted with the accusers and witnesses, to call for evidence in his favor, and to a speedy trial by an impartial jury of twelve men of his vicinage, without whose unanimous consent he cannot be found guilty; nor can he be compelled to give evidence against himself; that no man be deprived of his liberty, except by the law of the land or the judgment of his peers.

Sec. 9.   That excessive bail ought not to be required, nor excessive fines imposed, nor cruel and unusual punishments inflicted.

Sec. 10.   That general warrants, whereby an officer or messenger may be commanded to search suspected places without evidence of a fact committed, or to seize any person or persons not named, or whose offence is not particularly described and supported by evidence, are grievous and oppressive, and ought not to be granted.

Sec. 11.   That in controversies respecting property, and in suits between man and man, the ancient trial by jury is preferable to any other, and ought to be held sacred.

Sec. 12.   That the freedom of the press is one of the great bulwarks of liberty, and can never be restrained but by despotic governments.

Sec. 13.   That a well-regulated militia, composed of the body of the people, trained to arms, is the proper, natural, and safe defence of a free State; that standing armies, in time of peace, should be avoided, as dangerous to liberty; and that in all cases the military should be under strict subordination to, and governed by, the civil power.

Sec. 14.   That the people have a right to uniform government; and, therefore, that no government separate from, or independent of the government of Virginia, ought to be erected or established within the limits thereof.

Sec. 15.   That no free government, or the blessings of liberty, can be preserved to any people, but by a firm adherence to justice, moderation, temperance, frugality, and virtue, and by frequent recurrence to fundamental principles.

Sec. 16.   That religion, or the duty which we owe to our Creator, and the manner of discharging it, can be directed only by reason and conviction, not by force or violence; and therefore all men are equally entitled to the free exercise of religion, according to the dictates of conscience; and that it is the mutual duty of all to practise Christian forbearance, love, and charity towards each other.

The People the Best Governors
1776

The anonymous and well-read author of this pamphlet, probably a New En-
glander, advocated a number of radical ideas that aimed at a single objective:
enhancing the role of the people in their own government. To this end, he would
shorten as much as possible the leash of representation, removing all mechanisms
of government that tended to transfer control of governmental power farther from
the people.

God gave mankind freedom by nature, made every man equal to his neighbor, and
has virtually enjoined them to govern themselves by their own laws. . . . The
people best know their own wants and necessities, and therefore are best able to rule
themselves. . . . That I might help in some measure to eradicate the notion of
arbitrary power, heretofore drank in, and to establish the liberties of the people of
this country upon a more generous footing, is the design of the following impartial
work, now dedicated by the Author to the honest farmer and citizen.

The just power of a free people respects first the making and secondly the
executing of laws. The liberties of people are chiefly, I may say entirely guarded by
having the controul of these two branches in their own hands.

*   *   *

The question now that closes the whole arises, what it is that ought to be the
qualification of a representative. In answer, we observe that fear is the principle of a
despotic, honour of a kingly, and virtue is the principle of a republican government.
Social virtue and knowledge, I say then is the best and only necessary qualification
of the person before us. But it will be said that an estate of two hundred, four
hundred pounds, or some other sum is essential. So sure as we make interest
necessary in this case, as sure we root out virtue; and what will then become of the
genuine principle of freedom? This notion of an estate has the directest tendency to
set up the avaricious over the heads of the poor, though the latter are ever so
virtuous. Let it not be said in future generations that money was made by the
founders of the American States an essential qualification in the rulers of a free
people.

*   *   *

Lastly, let every government have an equal weight in the general congress, and
let the representatives of the respective states be chosen by the people annually by
ballot in their stated town meetings; the votes to be carried in and published at the
appointed election as with respect to a governor, council, &c., in manner aforesaid;
and the assemblies of the respective states may have power to instruct the said
representatives from time to time as they shall think proper. It appears that the forms
of government that have hitherto been proposed since the breach with Great Britain,
by the friends of the American States, have been rather too arbitrary. The people are
now contending for freedom; and would to God they might not only obtain, but
likewise keep it in their own hands. I own myself a friend to a popular government;
have freely submitted my reasons upon it. And although the plan here proposed

might not ever [have] been adopted as yet, nevertheless those as free have alone secured the liberties of former ages, and a just notion of them has guarded the people against the sly insinuations and proposals of those of a more arbitrary turn, whose schemes have a tendency to deprive mankind of their natural rights.

Note: The Pennsylvania Constitution of 1776

Of all the thirteen new states (plus Vermont, for the time being an independent republic), none came closer to achieving the radical vision of *The People the Best Governors* than Pennsylvania. In its 1776 Constitution, it incorporated a number of democratic innovations, including a unicameral legislature (an inheritance of the colonial period, when Pennsylvania had the only legislature of that sort on the mainland). The new constitution also added the following devices: taxpayer suffrage, an annual ballot, requirements that the doors of the assembly always be open and that its deliberations and votes be printed weekly, septennial reapportionment, mandatory rotation in office, a collegial executive that could act only as a body (in place of a unitary governor), judges who were elected every seven years and were removable by the legislature for "misbehaviour," abolition of imprisonment for debt, mandated penal reform, compulsory public education, and a septennial Council of Censors that was to determine whether the constitution had been observed.

Unfortunately for the cause of democracy, the 1776 Constitution was widely unpopular throughout its sixteen-year life, due in some measure to the fact that its supporters virtually disfranchised opponents of the constitution by means of an unacceptable oath. In what some historians consider a counterrevolution, Pennsylvanians opposed to the constitution managed to annul it in 1790, replacing it with a document that conformed more closely to those of other states.

Somerset v. Stewart
Lofft 1, 98 Eng. Rep. 499 (K.B. 1772)

Somerset *v.* Stewart *was the foundation of all subsequent legal debate over slavery in the United States. It exercised a profound influence on the law of slavery in America, passing as it did into the common law of the states after independence. It is significant for both its condemnation of the nature of slavery and its assertion that the slave law of a foreign state does not control the law of the forum state.*

James Somerset, a slave in Virginia and Massachusetts, accompanied his master to England. Once there, he ran off to freedom, but was caught and consigned to a ship captain to be sold in Jamaica. The great British abolitionist Granville Sharp obtained a writ of habeas corpus from Lord Mansfield, Chief Justice of King's Bench, to inquire into the cause of Somerset's detention. Mansfield's opinion, although it did not abolish slavery in England (as Sharp hoped it would), did articulate principles that dominated all later controversies about slavery.

[T]he only question before us is, whether the cause on the return is sufficient? If it is, the negro must be remanded; if it is not, he must be discharged. Accordingly, the return states, that the slave departed and refused to serve; whereupon he was kept, to be sold abroad. So high an act of dominion must be recognized by the law of the country where it is used. The power of a master over his slave has been extremely different, in different countries. The state of slavery is of such a nature, that it is incapable of being introduced on any reasons, moral or political; but only positive law, which preserves its force long after the reasons, occasion, and time itself from whence it was created, is erased from memory: it's so odious, that nothing can be suffered to support it, but positive law. Whatever inconveniences, therefore, may follow from a decision, I cannot say this case is allowed or approved by the law of England; and therefore the black must be discharged.

The Pennsylvania Gradual Abolition Act
1780

This far-sighted statute reflected one of the first domestic social consequences of the American Revolution. Its rhetorical preamble was not cynically self-serving, as the detailed provisions that follow for protecting the freedom of former slaves attest. However, the provisions for apprenticeship of children born to slaves approximated the cost of raising the children. The statute in its criminal-law provisions also began the long and tortured progression toward equality of all races before the law.

An Act for the gradual abolition of slavery.

Section 1. . . . We esteem it a peculiar blessing granted to us, that we are enabled this day to add one more step to universal civilization, by removing as much as possible the sorrows of those who have lived in undeserved bondage, and from which, by the assumed authority of the kings of Great Britain, no effectual, legal relief could be obtained. Weaned by a long course of experience from those narrow prejudices and partialities we had imbibed, we find our hearts enlarged with kindness and benevolence towards men of all conditions and nations; and we conceive ourselves at this particular period extraordinarily called upon, by the blessings which we have received, to manifest the sincerity of our profession, and to give a substantial proof of our gratitude.

                                 *   *   *

    Sect. 3.   Be it enacted, . . . That all persons, as well Negroes and Mulattoes as who shall be born within this state from and after the passing of this act, shall not be deemed and considered as servants for life, or slaves; and that all servitude for life, or slavery of children, in consequence of the slavery of their mothers, in the case of all children born within this state, from and after the passing of this act as aforesaid, shall be, and hereby is utterly taken away, extinguished and for ever abolished.

Sect. 4[.]   Provided always, and be it further enacted by the authority aforesaid, That every Negro and Mulatto child born within this state after the passing of this act as aforesaid (who would, in case this act had not been made, have been born a servant for years, or life, or a slave) shall be deemed to be and shall be by virtue of this act the servant of such person or his or her assigns, who would in such case have been entitled to the service of such child, until such child shall attain unto the age of twenty eight years, in the manner and on the conditions whereon servants bound by indenture for four years are or may be retained and holden[.]

*   *   *

Sect. 7[.]   And be it further enacted by the authority aforesaid, That the offences and crimes of Negroes and Mulattoes, as well slaves and servants as freemen, shall be enquired of, adjudged, corrected and punished in like manner as the offences and crimes of the other inhabitants of this state are and shall be enquired of, adjudged, corrected, and punished, and not otherwise, except that a slave shall not be admitted to bear witness against a freeman.

The Virginia Statute for Religious Freedom
1786

When Thomas Jefferson composed his own epitaph, he commemorated himself for three things: the Declaration of Independence, the creation of the University of Virginia, and the authorship of this statute. Its preamble is a long-winded compendium of the author's liberal opinions. In a nation as heterogeneous as America, a disestablishment policy was necessarily the wave of the future; religious tests and establishments were moribund after independence. But in Virginia, they always had been, and this statute did not radically derange the existing order of things.

An act for establishing religious freedom

I.   Whereas Almighty God hath created the mind free; that all attempts to influence it by temporal punishments or burthens, or by civil incapacitations, tend only to beget habits of hypocrisy and meanness; and are a departure from the plan of the Holy author of our religion, who being Lord both of body and mind, yet chose not to propagate it by coercions on either, as was in his Almighty power to do; that the impious presumption of legislators and rulers, civil as well as ecclesiastical, who being themselves but fallible and uninspired men, have assumed dominion over the faith of others, setting up their own opinions and modes of thinking as the only true and infallible, and as such endeavouring to impose upon others, hath established and maintained false religions over the greatest part of the world, and through all time; that to compel a man to furnish contributions of money for the propagation of opinions which he disbelieves, is sinful and tyrannical; that even the forcing him to support this or that teacher of his own religious persuasion, is depriving him of the comfortable liberty of giving his contributions to the particular pastor, whose morals he would make his pattern, and whose powers he feels most persuasive to righteousness, and is withdrawing from the ministry those temporary rewards, which proceeding from an approbation of their personal conduct are an additional incitement to earnest and unremitting labours for the instruction of mankind; that our civil rights have no dependence on our religious opinions, any more than our opinions in physics and geometry; and therefore the proscribing any citizen as unworthy the public confidence by laying upon him an incapacity of being called to offices of trust and emolument, unless he profess or renounce this or that religious opinion, is depriving him injuriously of those privilges and advantages to which in common with his fellow-citizens he has a natural right; that it tends only to corrupt the principles of that religion it is meant to encourage, by bribing with a monopoly of worldly honours and emoluments, those who will externally profess and conform to it; that though indeed these are criminal who do not withstand such temptation, yet neither are those innocent who lay the bait in their way; that to suffer the civil magistrate to intrude his powers into the field of opinion, and to restrain the profession or propagation of principles on supposition of their ill tendency, is a dangerous fallacy, which at once destroys all religious liberty, because he being of course judge of that tendency will make his opinions the rule of judgment, and approve or condemn the sentiments of others only as they shall square with or differ from his own; that it is time enough for the rightful purposes of civil government, for its officers to interfere when principles break out into overt acts against peace and good order; and finally, that truth is great and will prevail if left to herself, that she is the proper and sufficient antagonist to error, and has nothing to fear from the conflict, unless by human interposition disarmed of her natural weapons, free argument and debate, errors ceasing to be dangerous when it is permitted freely to contradict them.

II.   Be it enacted by the General Assembly, That no man shall be compelled to frequent or support any religious worship, place, or ministry whatsoever, nor shall be enforced, restrained, molested, or burthened in his body or goods, nor shall otherwise suffer on account of his religious opinions or belief; but that all men shall be free to profess, and by argument to maintain, their opinion in matters of religion, and that the same shall in no wise diminish, enlarge, or affect their civil capacities.

III.   And though we well know that this assembly elected by the people for the ordinary purposes of legislation only, have no power to restrain the acts of succeeding assemblies, constituted with the powers equal to our own, and that therefore to declare this act to be irrevocable would be of no effect in law; yet we are free to declare, and do declare, that the rights hereby asserted are of the natural rights of mankind, and that if any act shall be hereafter passed to repeal the present, or to narrow its operation, such act will be an infringement of natural right.

THOMAS JEFFERSON
Notes on the State of Virginia
1785

One of the most important effects of the Revolution was its stimulation of long-standing movements for the reform of both public and private law. Thomas

Jefferson was more prominent in such efforts than others, having drafted several proposed constitutions for his state and having actively participated in the enactment of statutes embodying law-reform goals, such as the 1786 Statute for Religious Freedom. In 1785, he published a conspectus of the physical and social characteristics of Virginia, Notes on the State of Virginia, *in which he summarized post-independence efforts at law reform.*

This constitution [of Virginia] was formed when we were new and unexperienced in the science of government. It was the first, too, which was formed in the whole United States. No wonder then that time and trial have discovered very capital defects in it.

1.   The majority of the men in the State, who pay and fight for its support, are unrepresented in the legislature, the roll of freeholders entitled to vote not including generally the half of those on the roll of the militia, or of the tax-gatherers.

2.   Among those who share the representation, the shares are very unequal. Thus the county of Warwick, with only one hundred fighting men, has an equal representation with the county of Loudon, which has one thousand seven hundred and forty-six. So that every man in Warwick has as much influence in the government as seventeen men in Loudon.

*   *   *

3.   The senate is, by its constitution, too homogeneous with the house of delegates. Being chosen by the same electors, at the same time, and out of the same subjects, the choice falls of course on men of the same description. The purpose of establishing different houses of legislation is to introduce the influence of different interests or different principles.

*   *   *

4.   All the powers of government, legislative, executive, and judiciary, result to the legislative body. The concentrating [of] these in the same hands is precisely the definition of despotic government. It will be no alleviation that these powers will be exercised by a plurality of hands, and not by a single one. One hundred and seventy-three despots would surely be as oppressive as one. Let those who doubt it turn their eyes on the republic of Venice. As little will it avail us that they are chosen by ourselves. An elective despotism was not the government we fought for, but one which should not only be founded on free principles, but in which the powers of government should be so divided and balanced among several bodies of magistracy, as that no one could transcend their legal limits, without being effectually checked and restrained by the others.

*   *   *

5.   That the ordinary legislature may alter the constitution itself.

*   *   *

Many of the laws which were in force during the monarchy being relative merely to that form of government, or inculcating principles inconsistent with republicanism, the first assembly which met after the establishment of the commonwealth appointed a committee to revise the whole code, to reduce it into proper form and volume, and report it to the assembly. This work has been executed by three gentlemen, and reported; but probably will not be taken up till a restoration of peace shall leave to the legislature leisure to go through such a work.

The plan of the revisal was this. The common law of England, by which is meant, that part of the English law which was anterior to the date of the oldest statutes extant, is made the basis of the work. It was thought dangerous to attempt to reduce it to a text; it was therefore left to be collected from the usual monuments of it. Necessary alterations in that, and so much of the whole body of the British statutes, and of acts of assembly, as were thought proper to be retained, were digested into one hundred and twenty-six new acts, in which simplicity of style was aimed at, as far as was safe. The following are the most remarkable alterations proposed:

To change the rules of descent, so as that the lands of any person dying intestate shall be divisible equally among all his children, or other representatives, in equal degree.

To make slaves distributable among the next of kin, as other movables.

To have all public expenses, whether of the general treasury, or of a parish or county, (as for the maintenance of the poor, building bridges, court-houses, etc.,) supplied by assessment on the citizens, in proportion to their property.

To hire undertakers for keeping the public roads in repair, and indemnify individuals through whose lands new roads shall be opened.

To define with precision the rules whereby aliens should become citizens, and citizens make themselves aliens.

To establish religious freedom on the broadest bottom.

To emancipate all slaves born after the passing [of] the act.

[Here follow Jefferson's extensive, ambivalent, and tortured musings on slavery and race, wherein he called for the gradual abolition of slavery in the Old Dominion, followed by the immediate expulsion of free blacks. His meditations on the inferiority of blacks, as he saw it, were anthropological, yet reflected the racism universal among whites of his time.]

*　　*　　*

The revised code further proposes to proportion crimes and punishments.

Pardon and privilege of clergy are proposed to be abolished; but if the verdict be against the defendant, the court in their discretion may allow a new trial. No attainder to cause a corruption of blood, or forfeiture of dower. Slaves guilty of offences punishable in others by labor, to be transported to Africa, or elsewhere, as the circumstances of the time admit, there to be continued in slavery. A rigorous regimen proposed for those condemned to labor.

Another object of the revisal is, to diffuse knowledge more generally through the mass of the people. This bill proposes to lay off every county into small districts of five or six miles square, called hundreds, and in each of them to establish a school, for teaching, reading, writing, and arithmetic. The tutor to be supported by the hundred, and every person in it entitled to send their children three years gratis, and as much longer as they please, paying for it. These schools to be under a visitor who is annually to choose the boy of best genius in the school, of those whose parents are too poor to give them further education, and to send him forward to one of the grammar schools, of which twenty are proposed to be erected in different parts of the country, for teaching, Greek, Latin, Geography, and the higher branches of numerical arithmetic. Of the boys thus sent in one year, trial is to be made at the grammar schools one or two years, and the best genius of the whole selected, and continued six years, and the residue dismissed. By this means twenty of the best geniuses will be raked from the rubbish annually, and be instructed, at the public expense, so far as the grammar schools go. At the end of six years instruction, one half are to be discontinued (from among whom the grammar schools will probably be supplied with future masters); and the other half, who are to be chosen for the superiority of their parts and disposition, are to be sent and continued three years in the study of such sciences as they shall choose, at William and Mary college, the plan of which is proposed to be enlarged, as will be hereafter explained, and extended to all the useful sciences. The ultimate result of the whole scheme of education would be the teaching all the children of the State reading, writing, and common arithmetic; turning out ten annually, of superior genius, well taught in Greek, Latin, Geography, and the higher branches of arithmetic; turning out ten others annually, of still superior parts, who, to those branches of learning, shall have added such of the sciences as their genius shall have led them to; the furnishing to the wealthier part of the people convenient schools at which their children may be educated at their own expense. The general objects of this law are to provide an education adapted to the years, to the capacity, and the condition of every one, and directed to their freedom and happiness.

The Northwest Ordinance
1787

Second only to the preservation of independence and the successful prosecution of the war, the Northwest Ordinance was the most notable achievement of the Confederation Congresses. It rejected the policy of colonial status for American territories, laying the basis for equality of status among all the American states. It also projected principles of liberal government into the new territories and excluded slavery north of the Ohio River.

Sec. 5.　The governor and judges, or a majority of them, shall adopt and publish in the district such laws of the original States, criminal and civil, as may be necessary, and best suited to the circumstances of the district, and report them to Congress from time to time, which laws shall be in force in the district until the organization of the general assembly therein, unless disapproved of by Congress; but afterwards the legislature shall have authority to alter them as they shall think fit.

*　　　*　　　*

Sec. 9.　So soon as there shall be five thousand free male inhabitants, of full age, in the district, upon giving proof thereof to the governor, they shall receive authority, with time and place, to elect representatives from their counties and townships, to represent them in the general assembly: Provided, That for every five hundred free male inhabitants there shall be one representative, and so on, progressively, with the number of free male inhabitants, shall the right of representation increase, until the number of representatives shall amount to twenty-five; after which the number and proportion of representatives shall be regulated by the legislature.

Sec. 13.　And for extending the fundamental principles of civil and religious liberty, which form the basis whereon these republics, their laws and constitutions, are erected; to fix and establish those principles as the basis of all laws, constitutions, and governments, which forever hereafter shall be formed in the said territory; to provide, also, for the establishment of States, and permanent government therein, and for their admission to a share in the Federal councils on an equal footing with the original States, at as early periods as may be consistent with the general interest:

Sec. 14. It is hereby ordained and declared, by the authority aforesaid, that the following articles shall be considered as articles of compact, between the original States and the people and States in the said territory, and forever remain unalterable, unless by common consent, to wit:

Article I

No person, demeaning himself in a peaceable and orderly manner, shall ever be molested on account of his mode of worship, or religious sentiments, in the said territory.

Article II

The inhabitants of the said territory shall always be entitled to the benefits of the writs of habeas corpus, and of the trial by jury; of a proportionate representation of the people in the legislature, and of judicial proceedings according to the course of the common law. All persons shall be bailable, unless for capital offences, where the proof shall be evident, or the presumption great. All fines shall be moderate; and no cruel or unusual punishment shall be inflicted. No man shall be deprived of his liberty or property, but by the judgment of his peers, or the law of the land, and should the public exigencies make it necessary, for the common preservation, to take any person's property, or to demand his particular services, full compensation shall be made for the same. And, in the just preservation of rights and property, it is understood and declared, that no law ought ever to be made or have force in the said territory, that shall, in any manner whatever, interfere with or affect private contracts, or engagements, bona fide, and without fraud previously formed.

Article III

Religion, morality, and knowledge being necessary to good government and the happiness of mankind, schools and the means of education shall forever be encouraged. The utmost good faith shall always be observed towards the Indians; their lands and property shall never be taken away from them without their consent; and in their property, rights, and liberty they never shall be invaded or disturbed unless in just and lawful wars authorized by Congress; but laws founded in justice and humanity shall, from time to time, be made, for preventing wrongs being done to them, and for preserving peace and friendship with them.

*   *   *

Article VI

There shall be neither slavery nor involuntary servitude in the said territory, otherwise than in the punishment of crimes, whereof the party shall have been duly
convicted: Provided always, That any person escaping into the same, from whom
labor or service is lawfully claimed in any one of the original States, such fugitive
may be lawfully reclaimed, and conveyed to the person claiming his or her labor or
service as aforesaid.

Republican National Constitutionalism

The first revolution in government occurred at the state level, but it was just as
necessary to adapt republican principles to structuring a national government. The
Articles of Confederation, ratified in 1781, provided the beginning of such a government, in the form of a federation having some attributes of national authority. Under
its authority, the Confederation Congress successfully waged war, conducted di-
plomacy, and carried on essential governmental functions, including providing government for the territories under the Northwest Ordinance. But such success did not
appease the discontents of nationalist leaders like James Madison, who sought to
replace the Confederation with a more vigorous national authority.

The Philadelphia Convention of 1787 successfully resolved most of the conflicts
among the states and sections, and Madison managed to capture much of the debate
there in notes he transcribed each evening. Historiographic controversy continues,
though, on what precisely the Convention did accomplish and what it left undone or
fatally compromised.

Modern historians are not the only ones skeptical of the achievements of the
Convention; opponents of ratification, called antifederalists, raised an array of both
serious and captious criticisms of the Constitution of 1787. Madison and Alexander
Hamilton rebutted these brilliantly in *The Federalist Papers* of 1787 to 1788, the
former developing his synthesis of republican theory and federations in Number l0,
and the latter anticipating judicial review as a consequence of the same republican
theory in Number 78.

The Articles of Confederation
1781

*America's first national constitution was a hybrid document. It clearly estab-
lished a federation rather than a nation, and numerous provisions prevented the
emergence of full nationhood, especially the "expressly delegated" clause of
Article II. Yet a nation existed embryonically within its provisions; it was clearly
more than a league organized for defense. Historians have long disputed the
Articles' prospects for evolving into a permanent national charter.*

Articles of Confederation and perpetual Union between the states of Newhampshire,
Massachusetts-bay, Rhodeisland and Providence Plantations, Connecticut, New-

York, New-Jersey, Pennsylvania, Delaware, Maryland, Virginia, North-Carolina, South-Carolina and Georgia.

*　　　*　　　*

Article II.　Each state retains its sovereignty, freedom, and independence, and every Power, Jurisdiction and right, which is not by the confederation expressly delegated to the United States, in Congress assembled.

Article III.　The said states hereby severally enter into a firm league of friendship with each other, for their common defence, the security of their Liberties, and their mutual and general welfare, binding themselves to assist each other, against all force offered to, or attacks made upon them, or any of them, on account of religion, sovereignty, trade, or any other pretence whatever.

*　　　*　　　*

Article V.　For the more convenient management of the general interests of the united states, delegates shall be annually appointed in such manner as the legislature of each state shall direct, to meet in Congress on the first Monday in November, in every year, with a power reserved in each state, to recall its delegates, or any of them, at any time within the year, and to send others in their stead, for the remainder of the Year.

In determining questions in the united states in Congress assembled, each state shall have one vote.

*　　　*　　　*

Article VIII.　All charges of war, and all other expences that shall be incurred for the common defence or general welfare, and allowed by the united states in congress assembled, shall be defrayed out of a common treasury, which shall be supplied by the several states in proportion to the value of all land within each state, granted to or surveyed for any Person, as such land and the buildings and improvements thereon shall be estimated according to such mode as the united states in congress assembled, shall from time to time direct and appoint.

The Philadelphia Convention
1787

James Madison took detailed notes of the debates at the Philadelphia Convention, while participating in those debates more actively than all but a handful of his colleagues. The following excerpts present the highly nationalistic Randolph Plan (actually drafted by Madison) and the ensuing debate that focused on the problem of the representation of states in the new Congress. In the course of that debate, Madison, James Wilson, and George Mason made penetrating observations on democracy, interest-group politics, and federalism.

The Randolph or Virginia Plan
May 29, 1787

[Virginia Governor Edmund Randolph] then commented on the difficulty of the crisis, and the necessity of preventing the fulfillment of the prophecies of the American downfall.

He observed that in revising the federal system we ought to inquire 1. into the properties, which such a government ought to possess, 2. the defects of the confederation, 3. the danger of our situation & 4. the remedy.

1. The Character of such a government ought to secure 1. against foreign invasion: 2. against dissensions between members of the Union, or seditions in particular states: 3. to procure to the several States various blessings, of which an isolated situation was incapable: 4. to be able to defend itself against incroachment: & 5. to be paramount to the state constitutions.

*   *   *

He then proceeded to enumerate the defects: 1. that the confederation produced no security against foreign invasion; congress not being permitted to prevent a war nor to support it by their own authority—Of this he cited many examples; most of which tended to shew, that they could not cause infractions of treaties or of the law of nations, to be punished: that particular states might by their conduct provoke war without controul; and that neither militia nor draughts being fit for defence on such occasions, inlistments only could be successful, and these could not be executed without money. 2. that the foederal government could not check the quarrels between states, nor a rebellion in any, not having constitutional power nor means to interpose according to the exigency:

3. that there were many advantages, which the U.S. might acquire, which were not attainable under the confederation—such as a productive impost—counteraction of the commercial regulations of other nations—pushing of commerce ad libitum—etc.etc.

4. that the foederal government could not defend itself against the incroachments from the states.

5. that it was not even paramount to the state constitutions, ratified, as it was in ma[n]y of the states.

3. He next reviewed the danger of our situation, appealed to the sense of the best friends of the U.S.—the prospect of anarchy from the laxity of government every where; and to other considerations.

4. He then proceeded to the remedy; the basis of which he said must be the republican principle.

He proposed as conformable to his ideas the following resolutions, which he explained one by one. . . .

1. Resolved that the Articles of Confederation ought to be so corrected & enlarged as to accomplish the objects proposed by their institution; namely, "common defence, security of liberty, and general welfare."

2. Resolved therefore that the rights of suffrage in the National Legislature ought to be proportioned to the Quotas of contribution, or to the number of free inhabitants, as the one or the other rule may seem best in different cases.

3. Resolved that the National Legislature ought to consist of two branches.

4. Resolved that the members of the first branch of the National Legislature ought to be elected by the people of the several States every   for the term of   [.]

*   *   *

5. Resolved that the members of the second branch of the National Legislature

ought to be elected by those of the first, out of a proper number of persons nominated by the individual Legislatures[.]

*   *   *

6. Resolved that each branch ought to possess the right of originating Acts; that the National Legislature ought to be empowered to enjoy the Legislative Rights vested in Congress by the Confederation & moreover to legislate in all cases to which the separate States are incompetent, or in which the harmony of the United States may be interrupted by the exercise of individual Legislation; to negative all laws passed by the several States, contravening in the opinion of the National Legislature the articles of Union; and to call forth the force of the Union against any member of the Union failing to fulfill its duty under the articles thereof.

7. Resolved that a National Executive be instituted; to be chosen by the National Legislature for the term of   years, to receive punctually at stated times, a fixed compensation for the services rendered, in which no increase or diminution shall be made so as to affect the Magistracy, existing at the time of increase or diminution, and to be ineligible a second time; and that besides a general authority to execute the National laws, it ought to enjoy the Executive rights vested in Congress by the Confederation.

8. Resolved that the Executive and a convenient number of the National Judiciary, ought to compose a Council of revision with authority to examine every act of the National Legislature before it shall operate, & every act of a particular Legislature before a Negative thereon shall be final; and that the dissent of the said Council shall amount to a rejection, unless the Act of the National Legislature be again passed, or that of a particular Legislature be again negatived by   of the members of each branch.

9. Resolved that a National Judiciary be established to consist of one or more supreme tribunals, and of inferior tribunals to be chosen by the National Legislature, to hold their offices during good behaviour; and to receive punctually at stated times fixed compensation for their services, in which no increase or diminution shall be made so as to affect the persons actually in office at the time of such increase or diminution; that the jurisdiction of the inferior tribunals shall be to hear & determine in the first instance, and of the supreme tribunal to hear and determine in the dernier resort, all piracies & felonies on the high seas, captures from an enemy, cases in which foreigners or citizens of other States applying to such jurisdictions may be interested, or which respect the collection of the National revenue; impeachments of any National officers, and questions which may involve the national peace and harmony.

*   *   *

Mr. Wilson. He wished for vigor in the Government, but he wished that vigorous authority to flow immediately from the legitimate source of all authority. The Government ought to possess not only first the force, but secondly the mind or sense of the people at large. The Legislature ought to be the most exact transcript of the whole Society. Representation is made necessary only because it is impossible for the people to act collectively. The opposition was to be expected he said from the Governments, not from the Citizens of the States. The latter had parted as was observed (by Mr. King) with all the necessary powers; and it was immaterial to them, by whom they were exercised, if well exercised. The State officers were to be the losers of power. The people he supposed would be rather more attached to the national Government than to the State Governments as being more important in itself, and more flattering to their pride. There is no danger of improper elections if made by large districts. Bad elections proceed from the smallness of the districts which give an opportunity to bad men to intrigue themselves into office.

* * *

Colonel Mason. Under the existing Confederacy, Congress represent the States not the people of the States; their acts operate on the States, not on the individuals. The case will be changed in the new plan of Government. The people will be represented; they ought therefore to choose the Representatives. The requisites in actual representation are that the Representatives should sympathize with their constituents; should think as they think, & feel as they feel; and that for these purposes should even be residents among them. Much he said had been alleged against democratic elections. He admitted that much might be said; but it was to be considered that no Government was free from imperfections & evils; and that improper elections in many instances, were inseparable from Republican Governments. But compare these with the advantage of this Form in favor of the rights of the people, in favor of human nature. He was persuaded there was a better chance for proper elections by the people, if divided into large districts, than by the State Legislatures.

The Paterson or Small States Plan
June 15, 1787

Mr. Paterson, said as he had on a former occasion given his sentiments on the plan proposed by Mr. Randolph he would now avoiding repetition as much as possible give his reasons in favor of that proposed by himself. He preferred it because it accorded 1. with the powers of the Convention, 2. with the sentiments of the people. If the confederacy was radically wrong, let us return to our States, and obtain larger powers, not assume them of ourselves.

* * *

. . . If the sovereignty of the States is to be maintained, the Representatives must be drawn immediately from the States, not from the people: and we have no power to vary the idea of equal sovereignty. The only expedient that will cure the difficulty, is that of throwing the States into Hotchpot.

* * *

Mr. Wilson entered into a contrast of the principal points of the two plans so far he said as there had been time to examine the one last proposed. These points were 1. in the Virginia plan there are two & in some degree three branches in the Legislature: in the plan from N.J. there is to be a single legislature only—2. Representation of the people at large is the basis of the one:—the State Legislatures, the pillars of the other—3. proportional representation prevails in one:—equality of suffrage in the other—4. A single Executive Magistrate is at the head of the one:—a plurality is held out in the other.—5. in the one the majority of the people of the

U.S. must prevail:—in the other a minority may prevail. 6. the National Legislature is to make laws in all cases to which the separate States are incompetent &—:—in place of this Congress are to have additional power in a few cases only—7. A negative on the laws of the States:—in place of this coertion to be substituted—8. The Executive to be removable on impeachment & conviction;—in one plan: in the other to be removeable at the instance of majority of the Executives of the States— 9. Revision of the laws provided for in one:—no such check in the other—10. inferior national tribunals in one:—none such in the other. 11. In the one jurisdiction of National tribunals to extend etc.—; an appellate jurisdiction only allowed in the other. 12. Here the jurisdiction is to extend to all cases affecting the National peace & harmony: there, a few cases only are marked out. 13. finally the ratification is in this way to be by the people themselves:—in that by the legislative authorities according to the thirteenth article of Confederation.

Antifederalist Critiques of the Constitution: Elbridge Gerry's Report on the Constitution as Printed in *Massachusetts Centinel* November 3, 1787

Although a Massachusetts delegate to the Philadelphia Convention and an advocate of a strong national government there, Elbridge Gerry, a republican Patriot and statesman of the Confederation Congress, eventually opposed ratification on the grounds that the document subordinated the states. Such inconsistency was characteristic of Gerry's later career, but the views expressed in the following report faithfully express and recapitulate one strand of antifederalist thought.

New-York, 18th October, 1787.

Gentlemen,

I have the honour to inclose, pursuant to my commission, the constitution proposed by the federal Convention.

To this system I gave my dissent, and shall submit my objections to the honourable Legislature.

It was painful for me, on a subject of such national importance, to differ from the respectable members who signed the constitution: But conceiving as I did, that the liberties of America were not secured by the system, it was my duty to oppose it.—

My principal objections to the plan, are, that there is no adequate provision for a representation of the people—that they have no security for the right of election— that some of the powers of the Legislature are ambiguous, and others indefinite and dangerous—that the Executive is blended with and will have undue influence over the Legislature—that the judicial department will be oppressive—that treaties of the highest importance may be formed by the President with the advice of two thirds of a quorum of the Senate—and that the system is without security of a bill of rights. These are objections which are not local, but apply equally to all the States.

As the Convention was called for "the sole and express purpose of revising the Articles of Confederation, and reporting to Congress and the several Legislatures such alterations and provisions as shall render the Federal Constitution adequate to the exigencies of government and the preservation of the union," I did not conceive that these powers extended to the formation of the plan proposed, but the Convention being of a different opinion, I acquiesced in it, being fully convinced that to preserve the union, an efficient government was indispensibly necessary: and that it would be difficult to make proper amendments to the articles of Confederation.

The Constitution proposed has few, if any federal features, but is rather a system of national government: Nevertheless, in many respects I think it has great merit, and by proper amendments, may be adapted to the "exigencies of government," and preservation of liberty.

The question on this plan involves others of the highest importance—1st. Whether there shall be a dissolution of the federal government? 2dly. Whether the several State Governments shall be so altered, as in effect to be dissolved? and 3dly, Whether in lieu of the federal and State Governments, the national Constitution now proposed shall be substituted without amendment? Never perhaps were a people called on to decide a question of greater magnitude—Should the citizens of America adopt the plan as it now stands, their liberties may be lost: Or should they reject it altogether Anarchy may ensue. It is evident therefore, that they should not be precipitate in their decisions; that the subject should be well understood, lest they should refuse to support the government, after having hastily accepted it.

If those who are in favor of the Constitution, as well as those who are against it, should preserve moderation, their discussions may afford much information and finally direct to an happy issue.

It may be urged by some, that an implicit confidence should be placed in the Convention: But, however respectable the members may be who signed the Constitution, it must be admitted, that a free people are the proper guardians of their rights and liberties—that the greatest men may err—and that their errours are sometimes, of the greatest magnitude.

Others may suppose, that the Constitution may be safely adopted, because therein provision is made to amend it: But cannot this object be better attained before a ratification, than after it? And should a free people adopt a form of Government, under conviction that it wants amendment?

And some may conceive, that if the plan is not accepted by the people, they will not unite in another: But surely whilst they have the power to amend, they are not under the necessity of rejecting it.

*   *   *

I shall only add, that as the welfare of the union requires a better Constitution than the Confederation, I shall think it my duty as a citizen of Massachusetts, to support that which shall be finally adopted, sincerely hoping it will secure the liberty and happiness of America. . . .

E. Gerry

Federalist, Number 10
1787

James Madison's first contribution as "Publius" is the most frequently quoted of the Federalist *essays. It is a masterly summation of the premises of what has come to be called, in the twentieth century, interest-group pluralism. It also presented the heart of modern "liberal" (as contrasted with "republican") thought. Madison used the contrast between republics and democracies to great effect.*

Among the numerous advantages promised by a well constructed Union, none deserve to be more accurately developed than its tendency to break and control the violence of faction. The friend of popular governments, never finds himself so much alarmed for their character and fate, as when he contemplates their propensity to this dangerous vice. He will not fail therefore to set a due value on any plan which, without violating the principles to which he is attached, provides a proper cure to it. The instability, injustice and confusion introduced into the public councils, have in truth been the mortal diseases under which popular governments have every where perished; as they continue to be the favorite and fruitful topics from which the adversaries to liberty derive their most specious declamations. The valuable improvements made by the American Constitutions on the popular models, both ancient and modern, cannot certainly be too much admired; but it would be an unwarrantable partiality, to contend that they have as effectually obviated the danger on this side as was wished and expected. Complaints are every where heard from our most considerate and virtuous citizens, equally the friends of public and private faith, and of public and personal liberty; that our governments are too unstable; that the public good is disregarded in the conflicts of rival parties; and that measures are too often decided, not according to the rules of justice, and the rights of the minor party; but by the superior force of an interested and over-bearing majority. However anxiously we may wish that these complaints had no foundation, the evidence of known facts will not permit us to deny that they are in some degree true. It will be found indeed, on a candid review of our situation, that some of the distresses under which we labor, have been erroneously charged on the operation of our governments; but it will be found, at the same time, that other causes will not alone account for many of our heaviest misfortunes; and particularly, for the prevailing and increasing distrust of public engagements, and alarm for private rights, which are echoed from one end of the continent to the other. These must be chiefly, if not wholly, effects of the unsteadiness and injustice, with which a factious spirit has tainted our public administrations.

By a faction I understand a number of citizens, whether amounting to a majority or minority of the whole, who are united and actuated by some common impulse of passion, or of interest, adverse to the rights of other citizens, or to the permanent and aggregate interest of the community.

*   *   *

As long as the reason of man continues fallible, and he is at liberty to exercise it, different opinions will be formed. As long as the connection subsists between his reason and his self-love, his opinions and passions will have a reciprocal influence on each other; and the former will be objects to which the latter will attach themselves. The diversity in the faculties of men from which the rights of property originate, is not less an insuperable obstacle to a uniformity of interests. The protection of these faculties is the first object of Government. From the protection of different and unequal faculties of acquiring property, the possession of different degrees and kinds of property immediately results; and from the influence of these on the sentiments and views of the respective proprietors, ensues a division of the society into different interests and parties.

The latent causes of faction are thus sown in the nature of man; and we see them every where brought into different degrees of activity, according to the different circumstances of civil society. A zeal for different opinions concerning religion, concerning Government and many other points, as well of speculation as of practice; and attachment to different leaders ambitiously contending for pre-eminence and power; or to persons of other descriptions whose fortunes have been interesting to the human passions, have in turn divided mankind into parties, inflamed them with mutual animosity, and rendered them much more disposed to vex and oppress each other, than to co-operate for their common good. So strong is this propensity of mankind to fall into mutual animosities, that where no substantial occasion presents itself, the most frivolous and fanciful distinctions have been sufficient to kindle their unfriendly passions, and excite their most violent conflicts. But the most common and durable source of factions, has been the various and unequal distribution of property. Those who hold, and those who are without property, have ever formed distinct interests in society. Those who are creditors, and those who are debtors, fall under a like discrimination. A landed interest, a manufacturing interest, a mercantile interest, a monied interest, with many lesser interests, grow up of necessity in civilized nations, and divide them into different classes, actuated by different sentiments and views. The regulation of these various and interfering interests forms the principal task of modern Legislation, and involves the spirit of party and faction in the necessary and ordinary operations of Government.

* * *

The inference to which we are brought, is, that the causes of faction cannot be removed; and that relief is only to be sought in the means of controlling its effects.

If a faction consists of less than a majority, relief is supplied by the republican principle, which enables the majority to defeat its sinister views by regular vote: It may clog the administration, it may convulse the society; but it will be unable to execute and mask its violence under the forms of the Constitution. When a majority is included in a faction, the form of popular government on the other hand enables it to sacrifice to its ruling passion or interest, both the public good and the rights of other citizens. To secure the public good, and private rights, against the danger of such a faction, and at the same time to preserve the spirit and the form of popular government, is then the great object to which our enquiries are directed: Let me add that it is the great desideratum, by which alone this form of government can be rescued from the opprobrium under which it has so long labored, and be recommended to the esteem and adoption of mankind.

By what means is this object attainable? Evidently by one of two only. Either the existence of the same passion or interest in a majority at the same time, must be prevented; or the majority, having such co-existent passion or interest, must be rendered, by their number and local situation, unable to concert and carry into effect schemes of oppression. If the impulse and the opportunity be suffered to coincide, we well know that neither moral nor religious motives can be relied on as an adequate control. They are not found to be such on the injustice and violence of individuals, and lose their efficacy in proportion to the number combined together; that is, in proportion as their efficacy becomes needful.

From this view of the subject, it may be concluded, that a pure Democracy, by which I mean, a Society, consisting of a small number of citizens, who assemble and administer the Government in person, can admit of no cure for the mischiefs of faction. A common passion or interest will, in almost every case, be felt by a majority of the whole; a communication and concert results from the form of Government itself; and there is nothing to check the inducements to sacrifice the weaker party, or an obnoxious individual. Hence it is, that such Democracies have ever been spectacles of turbulence and contention; have ever been found incompatible with personal security, or the rights of property; and have in general been as short in their lives, as they have been violent in their deaths. Theoretic politicians, who have patronized this species of Government, have erroneously supposed, that by reducing mankind to a perfect equality in their political rights, they would, at the same time, be perfectly equalized and assimilated in their possessions, their opinions, and their passions.

A Republic, by which I mean a Government in which the scheme of representation takes place, opens a different prospect, and promises the cure for which we are seeking. Let us examine the points in which it varies from pure Democracy, and we shall comprehend both the nature of the cure, and the efficacy which it must derive from the Union.

The two great points of difference between a Democracy and a Republic are, first, the delegation of the Government, in the latter, to a small number of citizens elected by the rest: secondly, the greater number of citizens, and greater sphere of country, over which the latter may be extended.

The effect of the first difference is, on the one hand to refine and enlarge the public views, by passing them through the medium of a chosen body of citizens, whose wisdom may best discern the true interest of their country, and whose patriotism and love of justice, will be least likely to sacrifice it to temporary or partial considerations. Under such a regulation, it may well happen that the public voice pronounced by the representatives of the people, will be more consonant to the public good, than if pronounced by the people themselves convened for the purpose. On the other hand, the effect may be inverted. Men of factious tempers, of local prejudices, or of sinister designs, may by intrigue, by corruption or by other means, first obtain the suffrages, and then betray the interests of the people. The question resulting is, whether small or extensive Republics are most favorable to the election of proper guardians of the public weal: and it is clearly decided in favor of the latter by two obvious considerations.

In the first place it is to be remarked that however small the Republic may be, the Representatives must be raised to a certain number, in order to guard against the cabals of a few; and that however large it may be, they must be limited to a certain number, in order to guard against the confusion of a multitude. Hence the number of Representatives in the two cases, not being in proportion to that of the Constituents, and being proportionally greatest in the small Republic, it follows, that if the proportion of fit characters, be not less, in the large than in the small Republic, the former will present a greater option, and consequently a greater possibility of a fit choice.

In the next place, as each Representative will be chosen by a greater number of citizens in the large than in the small Republic, it will be more difficult for unworthy candidates to practise with success the vicious arts, by which elections are too often carried; and the suffrages of the people being more free, will be more likely to centre on men who possess the most attractive merit, and the most diffusive and established characters.

*   *   *

The other point of difference is, the greater number of citizens and extent of territory which may be brought within the compass of Republican, than of Democratic Government; and it is this circumstance principally which renders factious combinations less to be dreaded in the former, than in the latter. The smaller the society, the fewer probably will be the distinct parties and interests composing it; the fewer the distinct parties and interests, the more frequently will a majority be found of the same party; and the smaller the number of individuals composing a majority, and the smaller the compass within which they are placed, the more easily will they concert and execute their plans of oppression. Extend the sphere, and you take in a greater variety of parties and interests; you make it less probable that a majority of the whole will have a common motive to invade the rights of other citizens; or if such a common motive exists, it will be more difficult for all who feel it to discover their own strength, and to act in unison with each other.

Federalist, Number 78
1788

Number 78 is the first of Alexander Hamilton's great essays on the judiciary. Here he candidly laid out a defense of judicial review, an extraordinarily bold move at the time. Judicial review had been broached in a few states by 1788, but it was nowhere widely accepted as legitimate or desirable. Hamilton, unlike Madison, had the gift of writing aphoristically, and this essay contains some of his most memorable phrases.

According to the plan of the convention, all the judges who may be appointed by the United States are to hold their offices during good behaviour, which is conformable to the most approved of the state constitutions; and among the rest, to that of this state. Its propriety having been drawn into question by the adversaries of that plan, is no light symptom of the rage for objection which disorders their imaginations and judgments. The standard of good behaviour for the continuance in office of the judicial magistracy is certainly one of the most valuable of the modern improvements in the practice of government. In a monarchy it is an excellent barrier to the depotism of the prince: In a republic it is a no less excellent barrier to the encroachments and oppressions of the representative body. And it is the best expedient which can be devised in any government, to secure a steady, upright and impartial administration of the laws.

Whoever attentively considers the different departments of power must perceive, that in a government in which they are separated from each other, the judiciary, from the nature of its functions, will always be the least dangerous to the political rights of the constitution; because it will be least in a capacity to annoy or injure them. The executive not only dispenses the honors, but holds the sword of the community. The legislature not only commands the purse, but prescribes the rules by which the duties and rights of every citizen are to be regulated. The judiciary on the contrary has no influence over either the sword or the purse, no direction either of the strength or of the wealth of the society, and can take no active resolution whatever. It may truly be said to have neither Force nor Will, but merely judgment; and must ultimately depend upon the aid of the executive arm even for the efficacy of its judgments.

This simple view of the matter suggests several important consequences. It proves incontestibly that the judiciary is beyond comparison the weakest of the three departments of power; that it can never attack with success either of the other two; and that all possible care is requisite to enable it to defend itself against their attacks. It equally proves, that though individual oppression may now and then proceed from the courts of justice, the general liberty of the people can never be endangered from that quarter: I mean, so long as the judiciary remains truly distinct from both the legislative and executive. For I agree that "there is no liberty, if the power of judging be not separated from the legislative and executive powers." And it proves, in the last place, that as liberty can have nothing to fear from the judiciary alone, but would have everything to fear from its union with either of the other departments; that as all the effects of such an union must ensue from a dependence of the former on the latter, notwithstanding a nominal and apparent separation; that as from the natural feebleness of the judiciary, it is in continual jeopardy of being overpowered, awed or influenced by its coordinate branches; and that as nothing can contribute so much to its firmness and independence, as permanency in office, this quality may therefore be justly regarded as an indispensable ingredient in its constitution; and in a great measure as the citadel of the public justice and the public security.

The complete independence of the courts of justice is peculiarly essential in a limited constitution. By a limited constitution I understand one which contains certain specified exceptions to the legislative authority; such for instance as that it shall pass no bills of attainder, no ex post facto laws, and the like. Limitations of this kind can be preserved in practice no other way than through the medium of the courts of justice; whose duty it must be to declare all acts contrary to the manifest tenor of the constitution void. Without this, all the reservations of particular rights or privileges would amount to nothing.

Some perplexity respecting the right of the courts to pronounce legislative acts void, because contrary to the constitution, has arisen from an imagination that the doctrine would imply a superiority of the judiciary to the legislative power. It is urged that the authority which can declare the acts of another void, must necessarily be superior to the one whose acts may be declared void. As this doctrine is of great importance in all the American constitutions, a brief discussion of the grounds on which it rests cannot be unacceptable.

There is no position which depends on clearer principles, than that every act of a delegated authority, contrary to the tenor of the commission under which it is exercised, is void. No legislative act therefore contrary to the constitution can be valid. To deny this would be to affirm that the deputy is greater than his principal;

that the servant is above his master; that the representatives of the people are superior to the people themselves; that men acting by virtue of powers may do not only what their powers do not authorise, but what they forbid.

If it be said that the legislative body are themselves the constitutional judges of their own powers, and that the construction they put upon them is conclusive upon the other departments, it may be answered, that this cannot be the natural presumption, where it is not to be collected from any particular provisions in the constitution. It is not otherwise to be supposed that the constitution could intend to enable the representatives of the people to substitute their will to that of their constituents. It is far more rational to suppose that the courts were designed to be an intermediate body between the people and the legislature, in order, among other things, to keep the latter within the limits assigned to their authority. The interpretation of the laws is the proper and peculiar province of the courts. A constitution is in fact, and must be, regarded by the judges as a fundamental law. It therefore belongs to them to ascertain its meaning as well as the meaning of any particular act proceeding from the legislative body. If there should happen to be an irreconcileable variance between the two, that which has the superior obligation and validity ought of course to be preferred; or in other words, the constitution ought to be preferred to the statute, the intention of the people to the intention of their agents.

Nor does this conclusion by any means suppose a superiority of the judicial to the legislative power. It only supposes that the power of the people is superior to both; and that where the will of the legislature declared in its statutes, stands in opposition to that of the people declared in the constitution, the judges ought to be governed by the latter, rather than the former. They ought to regulate their decisions by the fundamental laws, rather than by those which are not fundamental.

This exercise of judicial discretion in determining between two contradictory laws, is exemplified in a familiar instance. It not uncommonly happens, that there are two statutes existing at one time, clashing in whole or in part with each other, and neither of them containing any repealing clause or expression. In such a case, it is the province of the courts to liquidate and fix their meaning and operation; so far as they can by any fair construction be reconciled to each other; reason and law conspire to dictate that this should be done. Where this is impracticable, it becomes a matter of necessity to give effect to one, in exclusion of the other. The rule which has obtained in the courts for determining their relative validity is that the last in order of time shall be preferred to the first. But this is mere rule of construction, not derived from any positive law, but from the nature and reason of the thing. It is a rule not enjoined upon the courts by legislative provision, but adopted by themselves, as consonant to truth and propriety, for the direction of their conduct as interpreters of the law. They thought it reasonable, that between the interfering acts of an equal authority, that which was the last indication of its will, should have the preference.

But in regard to the interfering acts of a superior and subordinate authority, of an original and derivative power, the nature and reason of the thing indicate the converse of that rule as proper to be followed. They teach us that the prior act of a superior ought to be preferred to the subsequent act of an inferior and subordinate authority; and that, accordingly, whenever a particular statute contravenes the constitution, it will be the duty of the judicial tribunals to adhere to the latter, and disregard the former.

It can be of no weight to say, that the courts on the pretense of a repugnancy, may substitute their own pleasure to the constitutional intentions of the legislature. This might as well happen in the case of two contradictory statutes; or it might as well happen in every adjudication upon any single statute. The courts must declare the sense of the law; and if they should be disposed to exercise will instead of judgment, the consequence would equally be the substitution of their pleasure to that of the legislative body. The observation, if it proved anything, would prove that there ought to be no judges distinct from that body.

If then the courts of justice are to be considered as the bulwarks of a limited constitution against legislative encroachments, this consideration will afford a strong argument for the permanent tenure of judicial offices, since nothing will contribute so much as this to that independent spirit in the judges, which must be essential to the faithful performance of so arduous a duty.

This independence of the judges is equally requisite to guard the constitution and the rights of individuals from the effects of those ill humours which the arts of designing men, or the influence of particular conjunctures, sometimes disseminate among the people themselves, and which, though they speedily give place to better information and more deliberate reflection, have a tendency in the mean time to occasion dangerous innovations in the government, and serious oppressions of the minor party in the community. Though I trust the friends of the proposed constitution will never concur with its enemies in questioning that fundamental principle of republican government, which admits the right of people to alter or abolish the established constitution whenever they find it inconsistent with their happiness; yet it is not to be inferred from this principle, that the representatives of the people, whenever a momentary inclination happens to lay hold of a majority of their constituents incompatible with the provisions in the existing constitution, would on that account be justifiable in a violation of those provisions; or that the courts would be under a greater obligation to connive at infractions in this shape, than when they had proceeded wholly from the cabals of the representative body. Until the people have by some solemn and authoritative act annulled or changed the established form, it is binding upon themselves collectively, as well as individually; and no presumption, or even knowledge of their sentiments, can warrant their representatives in a departure from it, prior to such an act.

The New Republic

Ratification of the Constitution marked the beginning, not the end, of controversy over the new government's powers, particularly those that involved conflict with state authority. Continuing sectional controversy, plus the outbreak of the French Revolution and the resumption of world war between England and France, led to the emergence of parties espousing differing constitutional programs. These divisions cut across all issues coming before the new national government. Hamilton and Madison debated presidential power in the Helvidius–Pacificus essays of 1793. Political unrest throughout the 1790s raised recurrent questions of national authority. The Whiskey Rebellion provided the first major test of the nation's ability to suppress resistance to its laws. In his Farewell Address of 1796, President George Washington laid down principles governing the conduct of both domestic and foreign policy that reflected the conservative republicanism of his principal adviser, Alexander Hamilton. The outbreak of the undeclared naval war between France and America in 1798 led to Federalist enactment of the Alien and Sedition Acts, which in turn produced a series of prosecutions for seditious libel. Madison and Jefferson articulated an alternative theory of national power under the Constitution in the momentous Virginia and Kentucky Resolutions of 1798 and 1799, arguing for the unconstitutionality of the Alien and Sedition Acts, and of prosecutions under them.

The Bill of Rights
1791

Antifederalists, such as Elbridge Gerry, objected to the Constitution as it came from the Philadelphia Convention because it contained few guarantees for personal liberty and insufficient restraints on governmental power. To secure ratification in critical states like Virginia, Federalists had to promise that they would propose such guarantees as amendments to the Constitution. Under the leadership of James Madison in the House of Representatives, they promptly redeemed this promise. Twelve amendments were proposed in 1789; ten were ratified by 1791, and those ten are known today as the Bill of Rights. They are a somewhat more concise catalogue of individual liberties than comparable Declarations of Rights in most state constitutions of the period.

The Bill of Rights appears in the Appendix, and accordingly is not reprinted here (see pp. 574–576).

Hamilton versus Madison on Presidential Power
1793

This classic confrontation between Alexander Hamilton, writing under the pen name "Pacificus," and James Madison, writing as "Helvidius," was an important early exploration of presidential power in the conduct of foreign and military affairs. Hamilton contended for a general, interstitial, and residual executive power: the president can do anything he is not explicitly forbidden to do. Madison, relying on a separation-of-powers theory, rejected his antagonist's ample concept of presidential power in favor of one by which the president is narrowly bounded by the Constitution, particularly by grants of power to Congress. The dichotomy these two men exposed is more pertinent than ever today.

[Hamilton:]

The second Article of the Constitution of the UStates, section 1st, established this general Proposition, That "The Executive Power shall be vested in a President of the United States of America."

The same article in a succeeding Section proceeds to designate particular cases of Executive Power. It declares among other things that the President shall be Commander in Chief of the army and navy of the UStates and of the Militia of the several states when called into the actual service of the UStates, that he shall have power by and with the advice of the senate to make treaties; that it shall be his duty to receive ambassadors and other public Ministers and to take care that the laws be faithfully executed.

It would not consist with the rules of sound construction to consider this enumeration of particular authorities as derogating from the more comprehensive grant contained in the general clause, further than as it may be coupled with express restrictions or qualifications; as in regard to the cooperation of the Senate in the appointment of Officers and the making of treaties; which are qualifications of the general executive powers of appointing officers and making treaties: Because the difficulty of a complete and perfect specification of all the cases of Executive authority would naturally dictate the use of general terms—and would render it improbable that a specification of certain particulars was designed as a substitute for those terms, when antecedently used. The different mode of expression employed in the constitution in regard to the two powers the Legislative and the Executive serves to confirm this inference. In the article which grants the legislative powers of the Government the expressions are—"All Legislative powers herein granted shall be vested in a Congress of the UStates;" in that which grants the Executive Power the expressions are, as already quoted "The Executive Power shall be vested in a President of the UStates of America."

The enumeration ought rather therefore to be considered as intended by way of greater caution, to specify and regulate the principal articles implied in the definition of Executive Power; leaving the rest to flow from the general grant of that power, interpreted in conformity to other parts [of] the constitution and to the principles of free government.

The general doctrine then of our constitution is, that the Executive Power of the Nation is vested in the President; subject only to the exceptions and qualifications which are expressed in the instrument.

[Madison:]

The basis of [Hamilton's] reasoning is, we perceive, the extraordinary doctrine, that the powers of making war and treaties, are in their nature executive; and therefore comprehended in the general grant of executive power, where not specially and strictly excepted out of the grant.

* * *

If we consult for a moment, the nature and operation of the two powers to declare war and make treaties, it will be impossible not to see that they can never fall within a proper definition of executive powers. The natural province of the executive magistrate is to execute laws, as that of the legislature is to make laws. All his acts therefore, properly executive, must pre-suppose the existence of the laws to be executed. A treaty is not an execution of laws; it does not pre-suppose the existence of laws. It is, on the contrary, to have itself the force of a law, and to be carried into execution, like all other laws, by the executive magistrate. To say then that the power of making treaties which are confessedly laws, belongs naturally to the department which is to execute the laws, is to say, that the executive department naturally includes a legislative power. In theory, this is an absurdity—in practice a tyranny.

The power to declare war is subject to similar reasoning. A declaration that there shall be war, is not an execution of laws: it does not suppose pre-existing laws to be executed: it is not in any respect, an act merely executive. It is, on the contrary, one of the most deliberative acts that can be performed; and when performed, has the effect of repealing all the laws operating in a state of peace, so far as they are inconsistent with a state of war: and of enacting as a rule for the executive, a new code adapted to the relation between the society and its foreign enemy. In like manner a conclusion of peace annuls all the laws peculiar to a state of war, and revives the general laws incident to a state of peace.

These remarks will be strengthened by adding that treaties, particularly treaties of peace, have sometimes the effect of changing not only the external laws of the society, but operate also on the internal code, which is purely municipal, and to which the legislative authority of the country is of itself competent and compleat.

From this view of the subject it must be evident, that although the executive may be a convenient organ of preliminary communications with foreign governments, on the subjects of treaty or war; and the proper agent for carrying into execution the final determinations of the competent authority; yet it can have no pretensions from the nature of the powers in question compared with the nature of the executive trust, to that essential agency which gives validity to such determinations. It must be further evident that, if these powers be not in their nature purely legislative, they partake so much more of that, than of any other quality, that under a constitution leaving them to result to their most natural department, the legislature would be without a rival in its claim.

Another important inference to be noted is, that the powers of making war and treaty being substantially of a legislative, not an executive nature, the rule of interpreting exceptions strictly, must narrow instead of enlarging executive pretensions on those subjects.

GEORGE WASHINGTON
Farewell Address
1796

George Washington's Farewell Address is usually recalled for the foreign policy advice (no entangling alliances) contained in its latter section. But its ghost-author, Alexander Hamilton, considered the conservative homily on domestic affairs that preceded the foreign policy section to be at least equally important. In several eloquent passages, Hamilton restated the precepts of conservative republicanism first voiced by John Adams twenty years earlier, enlightened by the experience of two decades of self-government.

This government, the offspring of your own choice, uninfluenced and unawed; adopted upon full investigation and mature deliberation; completely free in its principles; in the distribution of its powers uniting security with energy, and containing within itself provision for its own amendment, has a just claim to your confidence and your support. Respect for its authority, compliance with its laws, acquiescence in its measures, are duties enjoined by the fundamental maxims of true liberty. The basis of our political system is the right of the people to make and to alter their constitutions of government. But the constitution which at any time exists, until changed by an explicit and authentic act of the whole people, is sacredly obligatory upon all. The very idea of the power and the right of the people to establish government, presupposes the duty of every individual to obey the established government.

All obstructions to the execution of the laws, all combinations and associations, under whatever plausible character, with the real design to direct, control, counteract, or awe the regular deliberations and action of the constituted authorities, are destructive of this fundamental principle, and of fatal tendency. They serve to organize faction; to give it an artificial and extraordinary force; to put in the place of the delegated will of the nation, the will of party, often a small, but artful and enterprising minority of the community; and according to the alternate triumphs of different parties, to make the public administration the mirror of the ill concerted and incongruous projects of faction, rather than the organ of consistent and wholesome plans, digested by common councils, and modified by mutual interests.

Towards the preservation of your government, and the permanency of your present happy state, it is requisite not only that you steadily discountenance irregular opposition to its acknowledged authority, but also that you resist with care the spirit of innovation upon its principles, however specious the pretext. One method of assault may be to affect in the forms of the constitution alterations which will impair the energy of the system, and thus to undermine what cannot be directly overthrown. In all the changes to which you may be invited, remember that time and habit are at least as neccessary to fix the true character of governments, as of other human institutions; that experience is the surest standard by which to test the real tendency of the existing constitutions of a country; that facility in changes upon the credit of mere hypothesis and opinion, exposes to perpetual change, from the endless variety of hypothesis and opinion; and remember especially, that from the efficient management of your common interests, in a country so extensive as ours a government of as much vigor as is consistent with the perfect security of liberty, is indispensable. Liberty itself will find in such a government, with powers properly distributed and adjusted, its surest guardian. It is, indeed, little else than a name, where the government is too feeble to withstand the enterprises of faction, to confine each member of society within the limits prescribed by the laws, and to maintain all in the secure and tranquil enjoyment of the rights of person and property.

The Sedition Act
1798

Taken with the Alien Acts enacted in the same year, this statute was part of a package of measures by which the Federalists harassed the Jeffersonian Republicans after the outbreak of the naval quasi-war with France. The statute enacted

the common law of seditious libel. Although modern opinion considers it fla-
grantly unconstitutional, the Sedition Act was in its time actually a progressive
measure in some respects, especially in making truth a defense and the jury the
judge of both fact and law. It expired of its own force, but not before numerous
prosecutions under it vexed the Federalists' opponents. The statute went a long
way toward making legitimate political opposition a criminal offense.

Sec. 2.   And be it further enacted, That if any person shall write, print, utter or
publish, or shall cause or procure to be written, printed, uttered, or published, or
shall knowingly and willingly assist or aid in writing, printing, uttering or publishing any false, scandalous and malicious writing or writings against the government
of the United States, or either house of the Congress of the United States, or the
President of the United States, with intent to defame the said government, or either
house of the said Congress, or the said President, or to bring them, into contempt or
disrepute; or to excite against them, or either or any of them, the hatred of the good
people of the United States, or to stir up sedition within the United States, or to
excite any unlawful combinations therein, for opposing or resisting any law of the
United States, or any act of the President of the United States, done in pursuance of
any such law, or of the powers in him vested by the constitution of the United
States, or to resist, oppose, or defeat, any such law or act, or to aid, encourage or
abet any hostile designs or any foreign nation against the United States, their people
or government, then such person, being thereof convicted before any court of the
United States having jurisdiction thereof, shall be punished by a fine not exceeding
two thousand dollars, and by imprisonment not exceeding two years.

Sec. 3.   And be it further enacted and declared, That if any person shall be
prosecuted under this act, for the writing or publishing any libel aforesaid, it shall
be lawful for the defendant, upon the trial of the cause, to give in evidence in his
defence, the truth of the matter contained in the publication charged as libel. And
the jury who shall try the cause, shall have a right to determine the law and the fact,
under the direction of the court, as in other cases.

Sec. 4.   And be it further enacted, That this act shall continue and be in force
until the third day of March, one thousand eight hundred and one, and no longer[.]

The Virginia and Kentucky Resolutions
1798–1799

If the Constitution of 1787 implicitly embodied a nationalist outlook on govern-
ment, the Virginia and Kentucky Resolutions expressed what might be considered
a state-sovereignty counter-Constitution. James Madison contributed to both tra-
ditions, being the father of both the Constitution and the counter-Constitution. In
any event, the Resolutions provided the constitutional foundation of all later
anticonsolidationist thought, and were the ancestors of nullification and seces-
sion. Contrast the vision of Union they embody with the vision of John Marshall
from 1810 through 1824 to see the polarity that dominated constitutional con-
troversy until it was resolved by the Civil War.

THOMAS JEFFERSON
Kentucky Resolution
November 10, 1798

1.   Resolved, That the several states composing the United States of America are not united on the principle of unlimited submission to their general government; but that, by compact, under the style and title of a Constitution for the United States, and of amendments thereto, they constituted a general government for special purposes, delegated to that government certain definite powers, reserving, each state to itself, the residuary mass of right to their own self-government; and that whensover the general government assumes undelegated powers, its acts are un-authoritative, void, and no force; that to this compact each state acceded as a state, and is an integral party; that this government, created by this compact, was not made the exclusive or final judge of the extent of the powers delegated to itself, since that would have made its discretion, and not the Constitution, the measure of its powers; but that, as in all other cases of compact among parties having no common judge, each party has an equal right to judge for itself, as well of infractions as the mode and measure of redress.

2.   Resolved, That the Constitution of the United States having delegated to Congress a power to punish treason, counterfeiting the securities and current coin of the United States, piracies and felonies committed on the high seas, and offences against the laws of nations, and no other crimes whatever; and it being true, as a general principle, and one of the amendments to the Constitution having also declared "that the powers not delegated to the United States by the Constitution, nor prohibited by it to the states, are reserved to the states respectively, or to the people,"—therefore, also, the [Sedition Act] (and all other their acts which assume to create, define, or punish crimes other than those enumerated in the Constitution,) are altogether void, and of no force; and that the power to create, define, and punish, such other crimes is reserved, and of right appertains, solely and exclusively, to the respective states, each within its own territory.

3.   Resolved, That it is true, as a general principle, and is also expressly declared by one of the amendments to the Constitution, that "the powers not delegated to the United States by the Constitution, nor prohibited by it to the states, are reserved to the states respectively, or to the people;" and that, no power over the freedom of religion, freedom of speech, or freedom of the press, being delegated to the United States by the Constitution, nor prohibited by it to the states, all lawful powers respecting the same did of right remain, and were reserved to the states, or to the people; . . . . That therefore the act of the Congress of the United States, passed on the 14th of July, 1798, entitled "An Act in Addition to the Act entitled 'An Act for the Punishment of certain Crimes against the United States,'" which does abridge the freedom of the press, is not law, but is altogether void, and of no force.

*   *   *

7.   Resolved, That the construction applied by the general government [of the necessary-and-proper clause] goes to the destruction of all the limits prescribed to

their power by the Constitution; that words meant by that instrument to be subsidiary only to the execution of the limited powers, ought not to be so construed as
themselves to give unlimited powers, nor a part so to be taken as to destroy the
whole residue of the instrument[.]

*   *   *

In questions of power, then, let no more be said of confidence in man, but bind
him down from mischief by the chains of the Constitution. That this commonwealth
does therefore call on its co-states for an expression of their sentiments on the acts
concerning aliens, and for the punishment of certain crimes herein before specified,
plainly declaring whether these acts are or are not authorized by the federal compact. And it doubts not that their sense will be so announced as to prove their
attachment to limited government, whether general or particular, and that the rights
and liberties of their co-states will be exposed to no dangers by remaining embarked
on a common bottom with their own; but they will concur with this commonwealth
in considering the said acts as so palpably against the Constitution as to amount to
an undisguised declaration, that the compact is not meant to be the measure of the
powers of the general government, but that it will proceed in the exercise over these
states of all powers whatsoever. That they will view this as seizing the rights of the
states, and consolidating them in the hands of the general government, with a power
assumed to bind the states, not merely in cases made federal, but in all cases
whatsoever, by laws made not with their consent, but by others against their consent; that this would be to surrender the form of government we have chosen, and
live under one deriving its powers from its own will, and not from our authority; and
that the co-states, recurring to their natural rights not made federal, will concur in
declaring these void and of no force, and will each unite with this commonwealth in
requesting their repeal at the next session of Congress.

JAMES MADISON
Virginia Resolution
December 21, 1798

That this Assembly doth explicitly and peremptorily declare, that it views the
powers of the federal government as resulting from the compact to which the states
are parties, as limited by the plain sense and intention of the instrument constituting
that compact, as no further valid than they are authorized by the grants enumerated
in that compact; and that, in case of a deliberate, palpable, and dangerous exercise
of other powers, not granted by the said compact, the states, who are parties thereto,
have the right, and are in duty bound, to interpose, for arresting the progress of the
evil, and for maintaining, within their respective limits, the authorities, rights and
liberties, appertaining to them.

That the General Assembly doth also express its deep regret, that a spirit has, in
sundry instances, been manifested by the federal government to enlarge it powers
by forced constructions of the constitutional charter which defines them; and that
indications have appeared of a design to expound certain general phrases (which,
having been copied from the very limited grant of powers in the former Articles of
Confederation, were the less liable to be misconstrued) so as to destroy the meaning

and effect of the particular enumeration which necessarily explains and limits the general phrases, and so as to consolidate the states, by degrees, into one sovereignty, the obvious tendency and inevitable result of which would be, to transform the present republican system of the United States into an absolute, or, at best, a mixed monarchy.

THOMAS JEFFERSON
Kentucky Resolution
November 14, 1799

Resolved, That this commonwealth considers the federal Union, upon the terms and for the purposes specified in the late compact, conducive to the liberty and happiness of the several states: That it does now unequivocally declare its attachment to the Union, and to that compact, agreeably to its obvious and real intention, and will be among the last to seek its dissolution: That, if those who administer the general government be permitted to transgress the limits fixed by that compact, by a total disregard to the special delegations of power therein contained, an annihilation of the state governments, and the creation, upon their ruins, of a general consolidated government, will be the inevitable consequence: That the principle and construction, contended for by sundry of the state legislatures, that the general government is the exclusive judge of the extent of the powers delegated to it, stop not short of despotism—since the discretion of those who administer the government, and not the Constitution, would be the measure of their powers: That the several states who formed that instrument, being sovereign and independent, have the unquestionable right to judge of the infraction; and, That a nullification, by those sovereignties, of all unauthorized acts done under color of that instrument, is the rightful remedy: That this commonwealth does, under the most deliberate reconsideration declare, that the said Alien and Sedition Laws, are in their opinion, palpable violations of the said Constitution; and however cheerfully it may be disposed to surrender its opinion to a majority of its sister states, in matters of ordinary or doubtful policy, yet, in momentous regulations like the present, which so vitally wound the best rights of the citizen, it would consider a silent acquiescence as highly criminal: That, although this commonwealth, as a party to the federal compact, will bow to the laws of the Union, yet it does, at the same time, declare, that it will not now, or ever hereafter, cease to oppose, in a constitutional manner, every attempt, at what quarter soever offered, to violate that compact: And finally, in order that no pretext or arguments may be drawn from a supposed acquiescence, on the part of this commonwealth, in the constitutionality of those laws, and be thereby used as precedents for similar future violations of the federal compact, this commonwealth now enter against them in solemn Protest.

THOMAS JEFFERSON
First Inaugural Address
1801

This statesmanlike address was remarkable for its conciliatory approach to its author's inveterate and embittered political enemies. Considering that Jefferson regarded his election as "the Revolution of 1800," as he called it, his claim that Americans were now all Federalists and all Republicans was not so much naive as reassuring. In this address, Jefferson succinctly stated the ideals of his administration in phrases that could have served throughout the nineteenth century as a program for a Republic blessed by abundance and untroubled by external enemies.

During the contest of opinion through which we have passed the animation of discussions and of exertions has sometimes worn an aspect which might impose on strangers unused to think freely and to speak and to write what they think; but this being now decided by the voice of the nation, announced according to the rules of the Constitution, all will, of course, arrange themselves under the will of the law, and unite in common efforts for the common good. All, too, will bear in mind this sacred principle, that though the will of the majority is in all cases to prevail, that will to be rightful must be reasonable; that the minority possesses their equal rights, which equal law must protect, and to violate would be oppression. Let us, then, fellow-citizens, unite with one heart and one mind. Let us restore to social intercourse that harmony and affection without which liberty and even life itself are but dreary things. And let us reflect that, having banished from our land that religious intolerance under which mankind so long bled and suffered, we have yet gained little if we countenance a political intolerance as despotic, as wicked, and capable of as bitter and bloody persecutions. During the throes and convulsions of the ancient world, during the agonizing spasms of infuriated man, seeking through blood and slaughter his long-lost liberty, it was not wonderful that the agitation of the billows should reach even this distant and peaceful shore; that this should be more felt and feared by some and less by others, and should divide opinions as to measures of safety. But every difference of opinion is not a difference of principle. We have called by different names brethren of the same principle. We are all Republicans, we are all Federalists. If there be any among us who would wish to dissolve this Union or to change its republican form, let them stand undisturbed as monuments of the safety which error of opinion may be tolerated where reason is left free to combat it. I know, indeed, that some honest men fear that a republican government can not be strong, that this Government is not strong enough; but would the honest patriot, in the full tide of successful experiment, abandon a government which has so far kept us free and firm on the theoretic and visionary fear that this Government, the world's best hope, may by possibility want energy to preserve itself? I trust not. I believe this, on the contrary, the strongest Government on earth. I believe it the only one where every man, at the call of the law, would fly to the standard of the law, and would meet invasions of the public order as his own personal concern. Sometimes it is said that man can not be trusted with the government of himself. Can he, then, be trusted with the government of others? Or have we found angels in the forms of kings to govern him? Let history answer this question.

*   *   *

About to enter, fellow-citizens, on the exercise of duties which comprehend everything dear and valuable to you, it is proper you should understand what I deem the essential principles of our Government and consequently those which ought to shape its Administration. I will compress them within the narrowest compass they will bear, stating the general principle, but not all its limitations. Equal and exact justice to all men, of whatever state or persuasion, religious or political; peace, commerce, and honest friendship with all nations, entangling alliances with none; the support of the State governments in all their rights, as the most competent administrations for our domestic concerns and the surest bulwarks against anti-republican tendencies; the preservation of the General Government in its whole constitutional vigor, as the sheet anchor of our peace at home and safety abroad; a jealous care of the right of election by the people—a mild and safe corrective of abuses which are lopped by the sword of revolution where peaceable remedies are unprovided; absolute acquiescence to the decisions of the majority, the vital principle of republics, from which is no appeal but to force, the vital principle and immediate parent of despotism; a well-disciplined militia, our best reliance in peace and for the first moments of war, till regulars may relieve them; the supremacy of the civil over the military authority; economy in the public expense, that labor may be lightly burthened; the honest payment of our debts and sacred preservation of the public faith; encouragement of agriculture, and of commerce as its handmaid; the diffusion of information and arraignment of all abuses at the bar of the public reason; freedom of religion; freedom of the press, and freedom of person under the protection of the habeas corpus, and trial by juries impartially selected. These principles form the brightest constellation which has gone before us and guided our steps through an age of revolution and reformation. The wisdom of our sages and blood of our heroes have been devoted to their attainment. They should be the creed of our political faith, the text of civic instruction, the touchstone by which to try the services of those we trust; and should we wander from them in moments of error or of alarm, let us hasten to retrace our steps and to regain the road which alone leads to peace, liberty, and safety.

Courts and Judges in the New Nation

From the outset, courts played a prominent role in both state and national governments. The scope of that role remained unclear, however, at both the federal and state levels. The inability of the Philadelphia Convention to establish a clear place for lower federal courts was emblematic of controversies surrounding the national judiciary. The so-called Madisonian Compromise, by which Congress was given power to create lower federal courts but was not required to do so, merely passed the insoluble political controversy from the Convention to the new government. Congress partially resolved the problem by creating lower federal courts in the Judiciary Act of 1789, but it, too, compromised on their role. Congress gave the new national judiciary less than all the jurisdiction authorized by the Constitution's Article III, and it provided that state substantive law would furnish the rules of decision for cases that came to federal courts because the parties were citizens of different states.

In its first decade, the United States Supreme Court handed down a number of important decisions. None had a more lasting influence than *Calder* v. *Bull* (1798), which embedded the doctrine of higher law into American law. The proponent of that idea, Justice Samuel Chase, proved to be an intemperate and partisan Federalist off and on the bench. When they came to power, Jeffersonian Republicans, who regarded Chase as an epitome of Federalist reaction entrenched on the bench after its rejection at the polls, attempted to impeach him. The failure of that impeachment effort signaled the permanence, if not the invulnerability, of federal judicial power.

Federalist jurists like Chief Justices John Jay and John Marshall succeeded in ensconcing their vision of the rule of law in the Constitution. In order for Chief Justice Marshall to establish courts as ultimate guardians of the rule of law, he had to elevate Alexander Hamilton's views in *The Federalist,* Number 78, to the status of constitutional dogma. The 1803 case of *Marbury* v. *Madison* provided Marshall with an opportunity to do just that, asserting the doctrine of judicial review: the power of courts to hold a statute or an action of the executive branch unconstitutional and accordingly to refuse to give it effect.

The Judiciary Act
1789

In 1911, Justice Henry B. Brown hailed this statute as "the most important and the most satisfactory Act ever passed by Congress." For once, the hyperbole is justified. Over time, the statute proved to be the keystone in the arch of the federal union. Yet in its time it was a compromise measure, and its Section 34 made a considerable concession to the supporters of state judicial power, who feared that the federal courts would overshadow the state courts. Both Sections 25 and 34 remain central to the evolution of federal judicial power.

Sec. 25. And be it further enacted, That a final judgment or decree in any suit, in the highest court of law or equity of a State in which a decision in the suit could be had, where is drawn in question the validity of a treaty or statute of, or an authority exercised under the United States, and the decision is against their validity; or where is drawn in question the validity of a statute of, or an authority exercised under any State, on the ground of their being repugnant to the constitution, treaties or laws of the United States, and the decision is in favour of such their validity, or where is drawn in question the construction of any clause of the constitution, or of a treaty, or statute of, or commission held under the United States, and the decision is against the title, right, privilege or exemption specially set up or claimed by either party, under such clause of the said constitution, treaty, statute, or commission, may be reexamined and reversed or affirmed in the Supreme Court of the United States upon a writ of error, . . . and the proceeding upon the reversal shall also be the same, except that the Supreme Court, instead of remanding the cause for a final decision as before provided, may at their discretion, if the cause shall have been once remanded before, proceed to a final decision of the same, and award execution. But no other error shall be assigned or regarded as a ground of reversal in any case as aforesaid, than such as appears on the face of the record, and immediately respects the before mentioned questions of validity or construction of the said constitution, treaties, statutes, commissions, or authorities in dispute.

*   *   *

Sec. 34.   And be it further enacted, That the laws of the several states, except where the constitution, treaties or statutes of the United States shall otherwise require or provide, shall be regarded as rules of decision in trials at common law in the courts of the United States in cases where they apply.

Jefferson versus Hamilton
on the Bank of the United States
1791

In 1791, Secretary of the Treasury Alexander Hamilton proposed that Congress grant a corporate charter to the Bank of the United States. The Bank would be a depository for public revenues and act as the government's central financial institution, regulating currency and lending money to the national treasury. But it would also be a private corporation, with profits going to its stockholders.

President Washington had doubts about the constitutionality of the Bank bill because nothing in the Constitution explicitly authorized Congress to charter corporations. So he requested the members of his cabinet to render advisory opinions on the constitutional question. The opinions submitted by Secretary of State Jefferson and Secretary of the Treasury Hamilton set forth two opposing ways of interpreting the Constitution, loosely called in our day strict versus loose construction. John Marshall virtually plagiarized Hamilton's argument for his opinion in McCulloch v. Maryland *(1819), upholding the constitutionality of the Second Bank of the United States and rejecting Jefferson's narrow interpretive approach.*

[Jefferson:]

I consider the foundation of the Constitution is laid on this ground: That "all powers not delegated to the United States, by the Constitution, nor prohibited by it to the States, are reserved to the States or to the people." . . . To take a single step beyond the boundaries thus specially drawn around the powers of Congress, is to take possession of a boundless field of power, no longer susceptible of any definition.

The incorporation of a bank, and the powers assumed by this bill, have not, in my opinion, been delegated to the United States, by the Constitution.

1.   They are not among the powers specially enumerated. . . .

II.   Nor are they within either of the general phrases, which are the two following:—

1.   To lay taxes to provide for the general welfare of the United States, that is to say, "to lay taxes for the purpose of providing for the general welfare." For the laying of taxes is the power, and the general welfare the purpose for which the power is to be exercised. They are not to lay taxes ad libitum for any purpose they

please; but only to pay the debts or provide for the welfare of the Union. In like manner, they are not to do anything they please to provide for the general welfare, but only to lay taxes for that purpose. To consider the latter phrase, not as describing the purpose of the first, but as giving a distinct and independent power to do any act they please, which might be for the good of the Union, would render all the preceding and subsequent enumerations of power completely useless.

It would reduce the whole instrument to a single phrase, that of instituting a Congress with power to do whatever would be for the good of the United States; and, as they would be the sole judges of the good or evil, it would be also a power to do whatever evil they please.

*   *   *

2.   The second general phrase is, "to make all laws necessary and proper for carrying into execution the enumerated powers." But they can all be carried into execution without a bank. A bank therefore is not necessary, and consequently not authorized by this phrase.

It has been urged that a bank will give great facility or convenience in the collection of taxes. Suppose this were true: yet the Constitution allows only the means which are "necessary" not those which are merely "convenient" for effecting the enumerated powers. If such a latitude of construction be allowed to this phrase as to give any non-enumerated power, it will go to every one, for there is not one which ingenuity may not torture into convenience in some instance or other, to some one of so long a list of enumerated powers. It would swallow up all the delegated powers, and reduce the whole to one power, as before observed. Therefore it was that the Constitution restrained them to the necessary means, that is to say, to those means without which the grant or power would be nugatory.

[Hamilton:]

It is not denied that there are implied, as well as express powers, and that the former are as effectually delegated as the latter. And for the sake of accuracy it shall be mentioned, that there is another class of powers, which may be properly denominated resulting powers.

*   *   *

It is conceded, that implied powers are to be considered as delegated equally with express ones.

Then it follows, that as a power of erecting a corporation may as well be implied as any other thing; it may as well be employed as an instrument or means of carrying into execution any of the specified powers, as any other instrument or means whatever. The only question must be, in this as in every other case, whether the means to be employed, or in this instance the corporation to be erected, has a natural relation to any of the acknowledged objects or lawful ends of the government.

*   *   *

To this mode of reasoning respecting the right of employing all the means requisite to the execution of the specified powers of the Government, it is objected that none but necessary & proper means are to be employed, & the Secretary of

State [Jefferson] maintains, that no means are to be considered as necessary, but those without which the grant of the power would be nugatory.

* * *

All the arguments therefore against the constitutionality of the bill derived from the accidental existence of certain State-banks: institutions which happen to exist to day, & for aught that concerns the government of the United States, may disappear tomorrow, must not only be rejected as fallacious, but must be viewed as demonstrative, that there is a radical source of error in the reasoning.

It is essential to the being of the National government, that so erroneous a conception of the meaning of the word necessary, should be exploded.

It is certain, that neither the grammatical, nor popular sense of the term requires that construction. According to both, necessary often means no more than needful, requisite, incidental, useful, or conducive to. It is a common mode of expression to say, that it is necessary for a government or a person to do this or that thing, when nothing more is intended or understood, than that the interests of the government or person require, or will be promoted, by the doing of this or that thing. The imagination can be at no loss for exemplifications of the use of the word in this sense.

And it is the true one in which it is to be understood as used in [the] constitution. The whole turn of the clause containing it, indicates, that it was the intent of the convention, by that clause to give a liberal latitude to the exercise of the specified powers.

* * *

The truth is that difficulties on this point are inherent in the nature of the foederal constitution. They result inevitably from a division of the legislative power. The consequence of this division is, that there will be cases clearly within the power of the National Government; others clearly without its power; and a third class, which will leave room for controversy & difference of opinion, & concerning which a reasonable latitude of judgment must be allowed.

But the doctrine which is contended for is not chargeable with the consequence imputed to it. It does not affirm that the National government is sovereign in all respects, but that it is sovereign to a certain extent: that is, to the extent of the objects of its specified powers.

It leaves therefore a criterion of what is constitutional, and of what is not so. This criterion is the end to which the measure relates as a mean. If the end be clearly comprehended within any of the specified powers, & if the measure have an obvious relation to that end, and is not forbidden by any particular provision of the constitution—it may safely be deemed to come within the compass of the national authority.

Calder v. Bull
3 Dall. (3 U.S.) 386 (1798)

Justice Samuel Chase's opinion in this case is the clearest and most definitive expression of higher-law doctrine to emanate from the United States Supreme Court. But opinions in the pre-Marshall era were delivered seriatim, so it was not necessarily of more binding precedential authority than Justice James Iredell's, which expressed diametrically contrasting views. Nevertheless, the eminent twentieth-century constitutional authority Edward S. Corwin thought that Chase's opinion expounded what he called "the basic doctrine of American constitutional law."

[Chase:]

I cannot subscribe to the omnipotence of a state legislature, or that it is absolute and without control; although its authority should not be expressly restrained by the constitution, or fundamental law of the state. The people of the United States erected their constitutions or forms of government, to establish justice, to promote the general welfare, to secure the blessings of liberty, and to protect their persons and property from violence. The purposes for which men enter into society will determine the nature and terms of the social compact; and as they are the foundation of the legislative power, they will decide what are the proper objects of it. The nature, and ends of legislative power will limit the exercise of it. This fundamental principle flows from the very nature of our free republican governments, that no man should be compelled to do what the laws do not require; nor to refrain from acts which the laws permit. There are acts which the federal, or state legislature cannot do, without exceeding their authority. There are certain vital principles in our free republican governments, which will determine and overrule an apparent and flagrant abuse of legislative power; as to authorize manifest injustice by positive law; or to take away that security for personal liberty, or private property, for the protection whereof the government was established. An act of the legislature (for I cannot call it a law), contrary to the great first principles of the social compact, cannot be considered a rightful exercise of legislative authority. The obligation of a law, in governments established on express compact, and on republican principles, must be determined by the nature of the power on which it is founded.

A few instances will suffice to explain what I mean. A law that punished a citizen for an innocent action, or, in other words, for an act, which, when done, was in violation of no existing law; a law that destroys or impairs the lawful private contracts of citizens; a law that makes a man a judge in his own cause; or a law that takes property from A. and gives it to B.; it is against all reason and justice, for a people to intrust a legislature with such powers; and therefore, it cannot be presumed that they have done it. The genius, the nature and the spirit of our state governments, amount to a prohibition of such acts of legislation; and the general principles of law and reason forbid them. The legislature may enjoin, permit, forbid and punish; they may declare new crimes; and establish rules of conduct for all its citizens in future cases; they may command what is right, and prohibit what is wrong; but they cannot change innocence into guilt; or punish innocence as a crime; or violate the right of an antecedent lawful private contract; or the right of private property. To maintain that our federal, or state legislature possesses such powers, if they had not been expressly restrained, would, in my opinion, be a political heresy, altogether inadmissible in our free republican governments.

[Iredell:]

If, then, a government, composed of legislative, executive and judicial departments, were established, by a constitution which imposed no limits on the legislative power, the consequence would inevitably be, that whatever the legislative power chose to enact, would be lawfully enacted, and the judicial power could never interpose to pronounce it void. It is true, that some speculative jurists have held, that a legislative act against natural justice must, in itself, be void; but I cannot think that, under such a government any court of justice would possess a power to declare it so.

*   *   *

In order, therefore, to guard against so great an evil, it has been the policy of all the American states, which have, individually, framed their state constitutions, since the revolution, and the people of the United States, when they framed the federal constitution, to define with precision the objects of the legislative power; and to restrain its exercise within marked and settled boundaries. If any act of Congress, or of the legislature of a state, violates those constitutional provisions, it is unquestionably void; though, I admit, that as the authority to declare it void is of a delicate and awful nature, the court will never resort to that authority, but in a clear and urgent case. If, on the other hand, the legislature of the Union, or the legislature of any member of the Union, shall pass a law, within the general scope of their constitutional power, the court cannot pronounce it to be void, merely because it is, in their judgment, contrary to the principles of natural justice. The ideas of natural justice are regulated by no fixed standard: the ablest and the purest men have differed upon the subject; and all that the court could properly say, in such an event, would be, that the legislature (possessed of an equal right of opinion) had passed an act which, in the opinion of the judges, was inconsistent with the abstract principles of natural justice.

Marbury v. *Madison*
1 Cranch (5 U.S.) 137 (1803)

The principle of judicial review had been asserted and in some states established before 1803. The North Carolina case of Bayard v. *Singleton (1787) was the first to do so explicitly, but numerous cases before and after 1787 asserted the power implicitly. Thus it is incorrect to think of* Marbury *as being the first case to establish the power. But if not first in time, it is certainly the most important of any.*

In his discursive and prolix opinion, Marshall broached the doctrine of political questions, to be developed by his successor Roger Taney in Luther v. Borden *(1849). He implicitly chastised President Jefferson and Secretary of State Madison for having committed an illegal act, yet by declining jurisdiction left himself invulnerable to executive retaliation (and it is uncertain which Jefferson felt more keenly: Marshall's rebuke or the frustration of not being able to disregard it).*

But far greater than any of this are the last few pages of the opinion, where

*Marshall asserted the power of judicial review and attempted to show its inev-
itability on the basis of fundamental principles. Yet his reasoning was both
vulnerable and ambiguous on its central point. Is the power of judicial review
merely an incident of the Court's ordinary function of deciding cases—and in
doing so, choosing between conflicting laws? Or did Marshall assert here some
special and extraordinary power for the Court, a unique function entrusted to it
of superintending the separation of powers and the proper operation of the
Constitution? Finally, the pivotal point of Marshall's reasoning is his assertion
that the Constitution is law; all else follows from this one basic proposition.*

In the order in which the court has viewed this subject, the following questions have
been considered and decided.

    1st.   Has the applicant a right to the commission he demands?

    2dly.   If he has a right, and that right has been violated, do the laws of his
country afford him a remedy?

    3dly.   If they do afford him a remedy, is it a mandamus issuing from this court?

*   *   *

    Mr. Marbury, then, since his commission was signed by the president, and
sealed by the secretary of state, was appointed. . . .

    To withhold his commission, therefore, is an act deemed by the court not
warranted by law, but violative of a vested legal right.

    This brings us to the second inquiry; which is,

    2dly.   If he has a right, and that right has been violated, do the laws of his
country afford him a remedy?

    The very essence of civil liberty certainly consists in the right of every individu-
al to claim the protection of the laws, whenever he receives an injury. One of the
first duties of government is to afford that protection.

*   *   *

    Is the act of delivering or withholding a commission to be considered as a mere
political act, belonging to the executive department alone, for the performance of
which entire confidence is placed by our constitution in the supreme executive; and
for any misconduct respecting which, the injured individual has no remedy?

*   *   *

    It is not believed that any person whatever would attempt to maintain such a
proposition.

    It follows, then, that the question, whether the legality of an act of the head of a
department be examinable in a court of justice or not, must always depend on the
nature of that act.

*   *   *

    By the constitution of the United States, the president is invested with certain
important political powers, in the exercise of which he is to use his own discretion,
and is accountable only to his country in his political character and to his own
conscience. To aid him in the performance of these duties, he is authorized to
appoint certain officers, who act by his authority, and in conformity with his orders.

    In such cases, their acts are his acts; and whatever opinion may be entertained of
the manner in which executive discretion may be used, still there exists, and can

exist, no power to control that discretion. The subjects are political. They respect the nation, not individual rights, and being intrusted to the executive, the decision of the executive is conclusive.

*   *   *

The conclusion from this reasoning is, that where the heads of departments are the political or confidential agents of the executive, merely to execute the will of the president, or rather to act in cases in which the executive possesses a constitutional or legal discretion, nothing can be more perfectly clear than their acts are only politically examinable. But where a specific duty is assigned by law, and individual rights depend upon the performance of that duty, it seems equally clear that the individual who considers himself injured, has a right to resort to the laws of his country for a remedy.

*   *   *

It is, then, the opinion of the court,

1st.   That by signing the commission of Mr. Marbury, the President of the United States appointed him a justice of peace for the county of Washington, in the district of Columbia; and that the seal of the United States, affixed thereto by the secretary of state, is conclusive testimony of the verity of the signature, and of the completion of the appointment; and that the appointment conferred on him a legal right to the office for the space of five years.

2dly.   That, having this legal title to the office, he has a consequent right to the commission; a refusal to deliver which is a plain violation of that right, for which the laws of his country afford him a remedy.

It remains to be inquired whether,

3dly.   He is entitled to the remedy for which he applies.

*   *   *

This, then, is a plain case for a mandamus, either to deliver the commission, or a copy of it from the record; and it only remains to be inquired,

Whether it can issue from this court.

*   *   *

When an instrument organizing fundamentally a judicial system, divides it into one supreme, and so many inferior courts as the legislature may ordain and establish; then enumerates its powers, and proceeds so far to distribute them, as to define the jurisdiction of the supreme court by declaring the cases in which it shall take original jurisdiction, and that in others it shall take appellate jurisdiction; the plain import of the words seems to be, that in one class of cases its jurisdiction is original, and not appellate; in the other it is appellate, and not original. If any other construction would render the clause inoperative, that is an additional reason for rejecting such other construction, and for adhering to their obvious meanings.

To enable this court, then, to issue a mandamus, it must be shown to be an exercise of appellate jurisdiction, or to be necessary to enable them to exercise appellate jurisdiction. It is the essential criterion of appellate jurisdiction, that it revises and corrects the proceedings in a cause already instituted, and does not create that cause. Although, therefore, a mandamus may be directed to courts, yet to issue such a writ to an officer for the delivery of a paper, is in effect the same as to sustain an original action for that paper, and, therefore, seems not to belong to appellate, but to original jurisdiction. Neither is it necessary in such case as this, to enable the court to exercise its appellate jurisdiction.

The authority, therefore, given to the supreme court, by the act establishing the judicial courts of the United States, to issue writs of mandamus to public officers, appears not to be warranted by the constitution; and it becomes necessary to inquire whether a jurisdiction so conferred can be exercised.

The question, whether an act, repugnant to the constitution, can become the law of the land, is a question deeply interesting to the United States; but, happily, not of an intricacy proportioned to its interest. It seems only necessary to recognise certain principles, supposed to have been long and well established, to decide it.

That the people have an original right to establish, for their future government, such principles as, in their opinion, shall most conduce to their own happiness is the basis on which their whole American fabric has been erected. The exercise of this original right is a very great exertion; nor can it, nor ought it, to be frequently repeated. The principles, therefore, so established are deemed fundamental. And as the authority from which they proceed is supreme, and can seldom act, they are designed to be permanent.

This original and supreme will organizes the government, and assigns to different departments their respective powers. It may either stop here, or establish certain limits not to be transcended by those departments.

The government of the United States is of the latter description. The powers of the legislature are defined and limited; and that those limits may not be mistaken, or forgotten, the constitution is written. To what purpose are powers limited, and to what purpose is that limitation committed to writing, if these limits may, at any time, be passed by those intended to be restrained? The distinction between a government with limited powers is abolished, if those limits do not confine the persons on whom they are imposed, and if acts prohibited and acts allowed, are of equal obligation. It is a proposition too plain to be contested, that the constitution controls any legislative act repugnant to it; or, that the legislature may alter the constitution by an ordinary act.

Between these alternatives there is no middle ground. The constitution is either a superior paramount law, unchangeable by ordinary means, or it is on a level with ordinary legislative acts, and, like other acts, is alterable when the legislature shall please to alter it.

If the former part of the alternative be true, then a legislative act contrary to the constitution is not law: if the latter part be true, then written constitutions are absurd attempts, on the part of the people, to limit a power in its own nature illimitable.

Certainly all those who have framed constitutions contemplate them as forming the fundamental and paramount law of the nation, and, consequently, the theory of every such government must be, that an act of the legislature, repugnant to the constitution, is void.

This theory is essentially attached to a written constitution, and, is consequently, to be considered, by this court, as one of the fundamental principles of our society. It is not therefore to be lost sight of in the further consideration of this subject.

If an act of the legislature, repugnant to the constitution is void, does it, notwithstanding its validity, bind the courts, and oblige them to give it effect? Or, in other words, though it be not law, does it constitute a rule as operative as if it was a law? This would be to overthrow in fact what was established in theory; and would seem at first view, an absurdity too gross to be insisted on. It shall, however, receive a more attentive consideration.

It is emphatically the province and duty of the judicial department to say what the law is. Those who apply the rule to particular cases, must of necessity expound and interpret that rule. If two laws conflict with each other, the courts must decide on the operation of each.

So if a law be in opposition to the constitution; if both the law and the constitution apply to a particular case, so that the court must either decide that case conformably to the law, disregarding the constitution; or conformably to the constitution, disregarding the law; the court must determine which of these conflicting rules governs the case. This is of the very essence of judicial duty.

If, then, the courts are to regard the constitution, and the constitution is superior to any ordinary act of the legislature, the constitution, and not such ordinary act, must govern the case to which they both apply.

Those, then, who controvert the principle that the constitution is to be considered, in court, as a paramount law, are reduced to the necessity of maintaining that courts must close their eyes on the constitution, and see only the law. This doctrine would subvert the very foundation of all written constitutions. It would declare that an act which, according to the principles and theory of our government, is entirely void, is yet, in practice, completely obligatory. It would declare that if the legislature shall do what is expressly forbidden, such act, notwithstanding the express prohibition, is in reality effectual. It would be giving to the legislature a practical and real omnipotence, with the same breath which professes to restrict their powers within narrow limits. It is prescribing limits, and declaring that those limits may be passed at pleasure.

*   *   *

It is also not entirely unworthy of observation, that in declaring what shall be the supreme law of the land, the constitution itself is first mentioned; and not the laws of the United States generally, but those only which shall be made in pursuance of the constitution, have that rank.

Thus, the particular phraseology of the constitution of the United States confirms and strengthens the principle, supposed to be essential to all written constitutions, that a law repugnant to the constitution is void; and that courts, as well as other departments, are bound by that instrument.

3

The Active State and the Mixed Economy 1812–1860

The Golden Age of American Law

The period from 1787 to 1861 has been called the "golden age" of American law. Scholarship on the era describes it as "the creative period," "the transformation" of law, and "the Americanization" of the law. Well before the current resurgence in American legal history, Roscoe Pound called this the "formative era of American law." Historian Daniel J. Boorstin argues that it was an era of "creative outbursts" in "legal history."[1]

In this period, the United States Supreme Court was the most prominent judicial body in the nation, and many of its decisions shaped both public and private law. However, collectively the state courts had far greater influence on the development of law. The federal courts had limited jurisdiction, while the state courts determined most issues of private law. Chief Justice Lemuel Shaw of Massachusetts and Chancellor James Kent of New York were particularly influential, but a host of other state judges also contributed to legal developments.

Treatise writers were also important to legal developments. Before the Civil War, access to law was limited; there was no national reporter system. Reports from other states were also difficult to acquire. Rhode Island and Georgia did not even report their supreme court decisions until 1828 and 1845. South Carolina had no unified courts of equity and law; thus reports for that state were divided. For a time, New York and North Carolina also published separate equity reports. Statutes were even more difficult to find. Most lawyers and judges relied on treatise writers, who ascertained the state of the law and provided voluminous citations to state, federal, and English cases. William Wetmore Story's *Treatise on the Law of Contracts* (1844), for example, cited over 3,500 cases. Story was the son of the greatest treatise writer of the age, Justice Joseph Story, whose various *Commentaries* on Agency, Bailments, Conflicts, Equity, Promissory Notes, and the Constitution made him "a one-man West Publication Company."[2] James Kent's four-volume *Commentaries on American Law* went through twelve editions between 1830 and 1873. These and more specialized treatises, such as Joseph Angell's *A Treatise on the Law of Watercourses* (five editions before 1854) and Francis Hilliard's *The Law of Torts and Private Wrongs*

(1859), helped create a national legal system by giving Americans access to the growing number of reported cases, the various printed codes, and statutes. Treatises and commentaries enabled state judges from throughout the country to cite one another.

The growth of American law also mirrored changes in technology, commerce, and settlement. Steamboats, railroads, and water-powered mills revolutionized the economy as the new technology changed everything it touched. Workplaces became increasingly dangerous and impersonal, while machines gradually replaced skilled artisans. These changes led to litigation involving injured workers and labor unions.

Business organizations became increasingly complex. Large factories, steamboats, and railroads required unprecedented capital formation. Initially, economic development depended on government intervention through public works projects (such as the Erie Canal), through monopolies (such as the New York steamboat franchise), or through special charters (such as that given to the First and Second Banks of the United States). Economic development depended on government intervention to protect or support particular industries and entrepreneurs. Supporters of these distributive governmental activities argued that the people of the state and the nation benefited from technological and economic developments. Chief Justice James Kent of New York applauded the steamboat monopoly because "under its auspices the experiment of navigating boats by steam has been made and crowned with triumphant success." Through such successes, the stockholders of the Bank and the owners of the steamboat monopoly—men of prominence, wealth, and political connection—benefited from the actions of the government.

Opponents of monopolies saw little justice in such distributive governmental supports, which they argued were gifts to special interests at the expense of the taxpayers. President Andrew Jackson thought government should "shower its favors alike on the high and the low, the rich and poor" and not give special benefits to powerful individuals. Competitors of state-supported monopolies argued that special charters and grants hurt consumers. Advocates of laissez faire, they insisted that the law of the marketplace rather than laws of Congress or state legislatures would bring about lower prices and better service.

By the mid-1830s, governments were moving away from direct involvement in the economy. Their place was taken by thousands of newly organized corporations. In the nineteenth century, Americans remade the corporation into a dynamic legal tool that enabled investors to pool their resources for rapid capital formation. This economic development led to an explosion in contract law. In 1765 William Blackstone's influential *Commentaries on the Laws of England* devoted only about 40 pages, out of nearly 2,000, to contracts. But as changing national and international markets affected the price of goods and labor, agreements among corporations and individuals grew increasingly complex. By 1850 contracts had become the dominant field of American private law. This expanded contract law jettisoned old ideas of equity, fairness, and reasonableness. New measures of damages, based on expectations and changing values of goods, emerged. A meeting of the minds of two contractors replaced the paternalistic concept that a contract was a fair exchange of goods or labor for money. The doctrine of *caveat emptor* replaced the idea that "a sound price warrants a sound commodity."

Similar changes swept tort law. In 1776 torts was almost unknown as a field. As late as 1835, Francis Hilliard's *The Elements of Law; Being a Comprehensive Summary of American Jurisprudence* barely recognized the existence of tort law. However, tort law developed so rapidly that by 1859 Hilliard published a two-volume treatise on the subject, *The Law of Torts and Private Wrongs*, with citations to over 5,000 cases. Railroads, steamboats, mills, and urbanization were the great engines driving this revolution in tort law. By the end of the Civil War, courts were beginning to conclude that an insurance policy rather than a lawsuit was the proper way for a society to allocate the costs of accidents due to technological change.

Not all changes in the law were welcome. Southern states frequently rejected the application of certain tort rules to slaves. Louisiana, continuing its civil law heritage, likewise rejected the concept of caveat emptor. In the West, a distinctly American law of water arose, to take into account differences of climate and topology.

Changing attitudes toward government intervention in the economy also affected economic growth and legal development. Before 1830, the federal government chartered a national bank, established protective tariffs, and built roads. But after 1835, the national government retreated from active participation in the economy, and, with a few exceptions, left stimulation, promotion, and regulation to the states.

The states took various positions on economic development. New York led the way with the nation's most dramatic, ambitious, expensive, and ultimately successful internal improvement program—the Erie Canal and its system of feeder canals. Some states subsidized corporations, while others specifically prohibited subsidies. Most states gave mills, factories, and railroads the right to take land through eminent domain proceedings. Some states prohibited liquor sales on moral grounds. Mississippi prohibited the importation of slaves for sale, not on moral grounds, but in a futile attempt to limit the outflow of money from the state. The northern states ended slavery outright, and in the process destroyed the value of vast amounts of property.

The history of the nineteenth century demonstrates that the legal system facilitated the development of the economy. Legal historians disagree about the merits of this development. James Willard Hurst argues that "the central purpose of our legal order, [is] that law exists for the benefit of people and not people for the benefit of law." Hurst places particular emphasis on legislators who passed new laws that facilitated "the release of creative energies." Morton J. Horwitz, on the contrary, emphasizes "common law judges . . . play[ing] a central role in directing the course of social change."[3] Hurst sees this release of energies helping the common people of America; Horwitz finds a more narrowly directed "instrumentalism" that aided entrepreneurs and stockholders at the expense of poorer people.

The differences between Hurst and Horwitz illustrate some of the questions raised by the development of law in mid-nineteenth-century America. The debates among today's scholars reflect similar discussions among pre–Civil War legislators, jurists, lawyers, and theorists. These debates over economic and legal policy were also affected by political questions that embraced not only the economy of the nation, but also the emerging sectional conflicts over slavery and the nature of the national Union itself. The important issues of slavery and the Union are dealt with in Chapter 4 of this book. Nevertheless, these public law questions should be kept in mind as we consider how the state and national governments affected the development of the economy and of private law in the nineteenth century.

Commerce, Legislative Promotion, and Law in the New Republic

From the end of the War of 1812 until the Civil War, private investors and the government were partners in the development of the economy. State courts and legislatures were often more important than individual entrepreneurs in stimulating commercial expansion and economic growth. The states encouraged new industries in a variety of ways, including subsidies, monopolies, enabling acts, and charters. States were particularly interested in expanding their transportation networks. Even before steam technology was perfected, New York granted monopolies to stimulate regular steamboat service in the state.

The New York Steamboat Monopoly and the Federal Commerce Power

New York's steamboat monopoly is a classic example of state economic intervention. In 1798 New York gave Robert R. Livingston an exclusive fourteen-year franchise to operate a steamboat "within the" state. In 1803 Livingston and Robert Fulton launched the nation's first steamboat. New York then granted Livingston and Fulton a new twenty-year franchise. In April 1808, when Livingston and Fulton finally began operating regular steamboat service between Albany and New York City, the legislature rewarded them by extending the monopoly until 1838 if they were able to put three more boats into operation. Anyone competing with the monopoly, in violation of this charter, "would forfeit" their "boats and vessels" and "engines."

Sometime after April 1808, James Van Ingen began to operate a steamboat between New York City and Albany, "in contravention of" Livingston's grant. In September 1811, Livingston and Fulton filed a bill in Chancery, asking that Van Ingen be enjoined from operating his steamboat in New York waters without their permission. On November 18, Chancellor John Lansing refused to grant Livingston and Fulton the injunction. In his opinion, Lansing wrote:

> Suppose this grant valid; if the legislature of this state could make an exclusive grant of that nature, could they not have extended it to vessels impelled *by the winds* or *by oars*, and to vessels of every other description, capable of floating? If they cannot, where is the line of distinction to be drawn between what has been granted, and what is unsusceptible of grant? If carried to this extent, would it not be an abridgement of common rights? Could it comport with the constitutional provision, that the citizens of all the states are to have like privileges and immunities with the citizens of the several states? With whom are they to be ranked? With the class who hold exclusive rights in the state, or with the excluded class of citizens? If the most favored citizens are not to give the test, what proportion of the collective number of the citizens of this state are to constitute it? If a numerical calculation is to be admitted, are a tenth, a hundredth or a thousandth part to afford such test? Would it consist with the intent of the constitution of the *United States*, that any portion of the citizens of an individual state, described by their age, their occupations, or estates, should have the exclusive right of using the navigable waters of such state? Can the constitution be so constructed as to give rights to the citizens of all the states, superior to the rights of that state in which they are to be exercised? Or was the second section of the fourth article intended to secure equal rights to all? And should the grant in this case partake of the nature of a contract, could its consideration be legally carved out of the *jus publicum* of the citizens of the *United States*?

Livingston v. Van Ingen
9 Johns. (N.Y.) 507 (1812)

After losing in Chancery Court, Livingston and Fulton appealed to the New York Court for the Trial of Impeachments and the Correction of Errors, which unanimously reversed Chancellor Lansing's decision and issued the injunction against Van Ingen.

Kent, Ch. J. The great point in this cause is, whether the several acts of the legislature which have been passed in favor of the appellants, are to be regarded as constitutional and binding.

In the first place, the presumption must be admitted to be extremely strong in favor of their validity. The act in the year 1798 was peculiarly calculated to awaken attention, as it was the first act that was passed upon the subject, after the adoption of the federal constitution, and it would naturally lead to a consideration of the power of the state to make such a grant. That act was, therefore, a legislative exposition given to the powers of the state governments, and there were circumstances existing at the time, which gave that exposition singular weight and importance. It was a new and original grant to one of the appellants, encouraging him, by the pledge of an exclusive privilege for twenty years, to engage, according to the language of the preamble to the statute, in the "uncertainty and hazard of a very expensive experiment." The legislature must have been clearly satisfied of their competency to make this pledge, or they acted with deception and injustice towards the individual on whose account it was made. There were members in that legislature, as well as in all the other departments of the government, who had been deeply concerned in the study of the constitution of the United States, and who were masters of all the critical discussions which had attended the interesting progress of its adoption. Several of them had been members of the state convention, and this was particularly the case with the exalted character, who at that time was chief magistrate of this state, (Mr. [John] Jay,) and who was distinguished, as well in the council of revision, as elsewhere, for the scrupulous care and profound attention with which he examined every question of a constitutional nature.

If they are void, it must be because the people of this state have alienated to the government of the United States their whole original power over the subject matter of the grant. No one can entertain a doubt of a competent power existing in the legislature, prior to the adoption of the federal constitution. The capacity to grant separate and exclusive privileges appertains to every sovereign authority. It is a necessary attribute of every independent government. All our bank charters, turnpike, canal and bridge companies, ferries, markets, &c. are grants of exclusive privileges for beneficial public purposes. These grants may possibly be inexpedient or unwise, but that has nothing to do with the question of constitutional right. In the present case, the grant to the appellants took away no vested right. It interfered with no man's property. It left every citizen to enjoy all the rights of navigation, and all the use of the waters of this state which he before enjoyed. There was, then, no injustice, no violation of first principles, in a grant to the appellants, for a limited time, of the exclusive benefit of their own hazardous and expensive experiments.

The first impression upon every unprejudiced mind would be, that there was justice and policy in the grant. Clearly, then, it is valid, unless the power to make it be taken away by the constitution of the United States.

1. As to the power to regulate commerce. This power is not, in express terms, exclusive, and the only prohibition upon the states is, that they shall not enter into any treaty or compact with each other, or with a foreign power, nor lay any duty on tonnage, or on imports or exports, except what may be necessary for executing their inspection laws. Upon the principles above laid down, the states are under no other constitutional restriction, and are, consequently, left in possession of a vast field of commercial regulation; all the internal commerce of the state by land and water remains entirely, and I may say exclusively, within the scope of its original sovereignty. The congressional power relates to external not to internal commerce, and it is confined to the regulation of that commerce. . . .

The states are under no other restrictions than those expressly specified in the constitution, and such regulations as the national government may, by treaty, and by laws, from time to time, prescribe. Subject to these restrictions, I contend, that the states are at liberty to make their own commercial regulations. There can be no other safe or practicable rule of conduct, and this, as I have already shown, is the true constitutional rule arising from the nature of our federal system. This does away all color for the suggestion that the steam-boat grant is illegal and void under this clause in the constitution. It comes not within any prohibition upon the states, and it interferes with no existing regulation. Whenever the case shall arise of an exercise of power by congress which shall be directly repugnant and destructive to the use and enjoyment of the appellants' grant, it would fall under the cognizance of the federal courts, and they would, of course, take care that the laws of the union are duly supported. I must confess, however, that I can hardly conceive of such a case, because I do not, at present, perceive any power which congress can lawfully carry to that extent. But when there is no existing regulation which interferes with the grant, nor any pretence of a constitutional interdict, it would be extraordinary for us to adjudge it void, on the mere contingency of a collision with some future exercise of congressional power. Such a doctrine is a monstrous heresy. It would go, in a great degree, to annihilate the legislative power of the states. . . .

The grant to the appellants may, then, be considered as taken subject to such future commercial regulations as congress may lawfully prescribe. Congress, indeed, has not any direct jurisdiction over our interior commerce or waters. Hudson river is the property of the people of this state, and the legislature have the same jurisdiction over it that they have over the land, or over any of our rivers or lakes. They may, in their sound discretion, regulate and control, enlarge or abridge the use of its waters, and they are in the habitual exercise of that sovereign right. . . .

What has been the uniform, practical construction of this power? Let us examine the code of our statute laws. Our turnpike roads, our toll-bridges, the exclusive grant to run stage-wagons, our laws relating to paupers from other states, our Sunday laws, our rights of ferriage over navigable rivers and lakes, our auction licenses, our licenses to retail spirituous liquors, the laws to restrain hawkers and peddlers; what are all these provisions but regulations of internal commerce, affecting as well the intercourse between the citizens of this and other states, as between our own citizens? So we also exercise, to a considerable degree, a concurrent power with congress in the regulation of external commerce. What are our inspection laws relative to the staple commodities of this state, which prohibit the exportation, except upon certain conditions, of flour, of salt provisions, of certain articles of lumber, and of pot and pearl ashes, but regulations of external commerce? Our health and quarantine laws, and the laws prohibiting the importation of slaves, are striking examples of the same kind.

Are we prepared to say, in the face of all these regulations, which form such a mass of evidence of the uniform construction of our powers, that a special privilege for the exclusive navigation by a steam-boat upon our waters, is void, because it may, by possibility, and in the course of events, interfere with the power granted to congress to regulate commerce? Nothing, in my opinion, would be more preposterous and extravagant. Which of our existing regulations may not equally interfere with the power of congress? It is said that a steamboat may become the vehicle of foreign commerce; and, it is asked, can then the entry of them into this state, or the use of them within it, be prohibited? I answer yes, equally as we may prohibit the entry or use of slaves, or of pernicious animals, or an obscene book, or infectious goods, or any thing else that the legislature shall deem noxious or inconvenient. Our quarantine laws amount to an occlusion of the port of New-York from a portion of foreign commerce, for several months in the year; and the mayor is even authorized under those laws to stop all commercial intercourse with the ports of any neighboring state.

The grant of 1798, was made to Chancellor Livingston, as "the possessor of a mode of applying the steam engine to propel a boat on new and advantageous principles." This power to encourage the importation of improvements, by the grant of an exclusive enjoyment, for a limited period, is extremely useful, and the English nation have long perceived and felt its beneficial effects. This will appear by a cursory view of the law of that country. The creation of monopolies was anciently claimed and exercised as a branch of the royal prerogative.

. . . [T]he uniform opinion, in England . . . has been that imported improvements, no less than original inventions ought to be encouraged by patent. And can we for a moment suppose that such a power does not exist in the several states? We have seen that it does not belong to congress, and if it does not reside in the states, it resides nowhere, and is wholly extinguished. This would be leaving the states in a condition of singular and contemptible imbecility. The power is important in itself, and may be most beneficially exercised for the encouragement of the arts; and if well and judiciously exerted, it may ameliorate the condition of society, by enriching and adorning the country with useful and elegant improvements. This ground is clear of any constitutional difficulty, and renders the argument in favor of the validity of the statutes perfectly conclusive. And permit me here to add, that I think the power has been wisely applied, in the instance before us, to the creation of the privilege now in controversy. Under its auspices the experiment of navigating boats by steam has been made, and crowned with triumphant success. Every lover of the arts, every patron of useful improvement, every friend to his country's honor, has beheld this success with pleasure and admiration. From this single source the improvement is progressively extending to all the navigable waters of the United

States, and it promises to become a great public blessing, by giving astonishing facility, despatch and safety, not only to travelling, but to the internal commerce of this country. It is difficult to consider even the known results of the undertaking, without feeling a sentiment of good will and gratitude towards the individuals by whom they have been procured, and who have carried on their experiment with patient industry, at great expense, under repeated disappointments, and while constantly exposed to be held up, as dreaming projectors, to the whips and scorns of time. So far from charging the authors of the grant with being rash and inconsiderate, or from wishing to curtail the appellants of their liberal recompense, I think the prize has been dearly earned and fairly won, and that the statutes bear the stamp of an enlightened and munificent spirit.

I am accordingly of opinion . . . that an injunction be awarded.

Note: The Mix of Economics, Politics, and Law

Besides the constitutional issues, *Livingston* v. *Van Ingen* raised questions about how the economy ought to be organized. Supporters of exclusive franchises argued that technological change was expensive and risky, and that grants such as the steamboat monopoly encouraged entrepreneurs to take risks and make investments that would benefit the entire society. Opponents argued that the franchise was a special privilege, granted to those with money and power.

This case also had political overtones. Lansing had been a leading antifederalist in 1787, while Livingston had been one of New York's most vocal federalists. Both Livingston and Lansing later allied themselves with Jefferson, but relations between the two were strained. James Kent, however, was an unabashed federalist who disagreed with Lansing on almost all political and economic issues.

Article I, Section 8, of the Constitution gave Congress power to regulate commerce among the states, with foreign nations, and with Indians. In *The Federalist*, Number 42, James Madison argued that this clause would prevent "unceasing animosities" over commerce that would "terminate in serious interruptions of the public tranquility." *Gibbons* v. *Ogden* illustrates the interstate rivalries and hostility that Madison feared.

Gibbons v. Ogden
9 Wheat. (22 U.S.) 1 (1824)

In 1815 Aaron Ogden, a former governor of New Jersey, purchased from the owners of the Livingston–Fulton franchise the right to operate a steamboat from New York City to Elizabethtown, New Jersey. In 1819 Ogden sued his former partner, Thomas Gibbons, for infringing on his franchise rights by independently operating a steamboat service between New York and New Jersey. This case raised a critical federal issue. Gibbons argued that his federal coasting license entitled him to operate his boats anywhere in the United States. In upholding the right of New York to grant a steamboat monopoly, Chancellor Kent rejected this argument. In Gibbons v. Ogden, *17 Johns. (N.Y.) 488 (1820), New York's highest court affirmed Kent's ruling. Gibbons appealed to the United States Supreme*

Court. By this time, New Jersey and Connecticut had adopted laws retaliating against New York ships. Although docketed in 1820, the case was not finally decided until 1824, when Chief Justice Marshall rejected the New York monopoly with his crucial interpretation of the commerce clause.

Mr. Chief Justice Marshall. . . .

The appellant contends that this decree [the injunction against Gibbons] is erroneous, because the laws which purport to give the exclusive privilege it sustains, are repugnant to the constitution and laws of the United States.

They are said to be repugnant—

1st.   To that clause in the constitution which authorizes Congress to regulate commerce.

The words are, "Congress shall have power to regulate commerce with foreign nations, and among the several States, and with the Indian tribes."

The subject to be regulated is commerce. . . . The counsel for the appellee would limit it to traffic, to buying and selling, or the interchange of commodities, and do not admit that it comprehends navigation. This would restrict a general term, applicable to many objects, to one of its significations. Commerce, undoubtedly, is traffic, but it is something more: it is intercourse. It describes the commercial intercourse between nations, and parts of nations, in all its branches, and is regulated by prescribing rules for carrying on that intercourse. The mind can scarcely conceive a system for regulating commerce between nations, which shall be silent on the admission of the vessels of the one nation into the ports of the other, and be confined to prescribing rules for the conduct of individuals, in the actual employment of buying and selling, or of barter.

If commerce does not include navigation, the government of the Union has no direct power over that subject, and can make no law prescribing what shall constitute American vessels, or requiring that they shall be navigated by American seamen. Yet this power has been exercised from the commencement of the government, has been exercised with the consent of all, and has been understood by all to be a commercial regulation. All America understands, and has uniformly understood, the word "commerce," to comprehend navigation. It was so understood, and must have been so understood, when the constitution was framed. The power over commerce, including navigation, was one of the primary objects for which the people of America adopted their government, and must have been contemplated in forming it. The convention must have used the word in that sense, because all have understood it in that sense; and the attempt to restrict it comes too late.

The word used in the constitution, then, comprehends, and has been always understood to comprehend, navigation within its meaning; and a power to regulate navigation, is as expressly granted, as if that term had been added to the word "commerce."

The subject to which the power is next applied, is to commerce "among the several States." The word "among" means intermingled with. . . . Commerce among the States, cannot stop at the external boundary line of each State, but may be introduced into the interior.

It is not intended to say that these words comprehend that commerce, which is completely internal, which is carried on between man and man in a State, or between different parts of the same State, and which does not extend to or affect other States. Such a power would be inconvenient, and is certainly unnecessary.

Comprehensive as the word "among" is, it may very properly be restricted to that commerce which concerns more States than one. The phrase is not one which would probably have been selected to indicate the completely interior traffic of a State, because it is not an apt phrase for that purpose. . . . The completely internal commerce of a State, then, may be considered as reserved for the State itself.

But, in regulating commerce with foreign nations, the power of Congress does not stop at jurisdictional lines of the several States. It would be a very useless power, if it could not pass those lines. The commerce of the United States with foreign nations, is that of the whole United States. Every district has a right to participate in it. The deep streams which penetrate our country in every direction, pass through the interior of almost every State in the Union, and furnish the means of exercising this right. If Congress has the power to regulate it, that power must be exercised whenever the subject exists. If it exists within the States, if a foreign voyage may commence or terminate at a port within a State, then the power of Congress may be exercised within a State.

This principle is, if possible, still more clear, when applied to commerce "among the several States." They either join each other, in which case they are separated by a mathematical line, or they are remote from each other, in which case other States lie between them. What is commerce "among" them; and how is it to be conducted? Can a trading expedition between two adjoining States, commence and terminate outside of each? And if the trading intercourse be between two States remote from each other, must it not commence in one, terminate in the other, and probably pass through a third? Commerce among the States must, of necessity, be commerce with the States. . . . We are now arrived at the inquiry—What is this power?

It is the power to regulate; that is, to prescribe the rule by which commerce is to be governed. This power, like all others vested in Congress, is complete in itself, may be exercised to its utmost extent, and acknowledges no limitations, other than are prescribed in the constitution. These are expressed in plain terms, and do not affect the questions which arise in this case. . . . [T]he sovereignty of Congress, though limited to specified objects, is plenary as to those objects, the power over commerce with foreign nations, and among the several States, is vested in Congress as absolutely as it would be in a single government, having in its constitution the same restrictions on the exercise of the power as are found in the constitution of the United States. The wisdom and the discretion of Congress, their identity with the people, and the influence which their constituents possess at elections, are, in this, as in many other instances, as that, for example, of declaring war, the sole restraints on which they have relied, to secure them from its abuse. They are the restraints on which the people must often rely solely, in all representative governments.

The power of Congress, then, comprehends navigation, within the limits of every State in the Union; so far as that navigation may be, in any manner, connected with "commerce with foreign nations, or among the several States, or with the Indian tribes." It may, of consequence, pass the jurisdictional line of New York, and act upon the very waters to which the prohibition now under consideration applies.

But it has been urged that, although the power of Congress to regulate commerce . . . have no other limits than are prescribed in the constitution, yet the States may severally exercise the same power, within their respective jurisdictions. In support of this argument, it is said, that they possessed it as an inseparable attribute of sovereignty, before the formation of the constitution, and still retain it, except so far as they have surrendered it by that instrument; that this principle results from the nature of the government, and is secured by the tenth amendment; that an affirmative grant of power is not exclusive, unless in its own nature it be such that the continued exercise of it by the former possessor is inconsistent with the grant, and that this is not of that description.

The grant of the power to lay and collect taxes is like the power to regulate commerce, made in general terms, and has never been understood to interfere with the exercise of the same power by the States; and hence . . . has been applied to the question under consideration. But the two grants are not . . . similar in their terms or their nature. Although many of the powers formerly exercised by the States, are transferred to the government of the Union, yet the State governments remain, and constitute a most important part of our system. The power of taxation is indispensable to their existence, and is a power which . . . is capable of residing in, and being exercised by, different authorities at the same time. We are accustomed to see it placed, for different purposes, in different heads. Taxation . . . is not incompatible with a power in another to take what is necessary for other purposes. Congress is authorized to lay and collect taxes, &c. to pay the debts, and provide for the common defence and general welfare of the United States. This does not interfere with the power of the States to tax for the support of their own governments; nor is the exercise of that power by the States an exercise of any portion of the power that is granted to the United States. . . . But, when a State proceeds to regulate commerce with foreign nations, or among the several States, it is exercising the very power that is granted to Congress, and is doing the very thing which Congress is authorized to do. There is no analogy, then, between the power of taxation and the power of regulating commerce.

. . . The sole question is, can a State regulate commerce with foreign nations and among the States, while Congress is regulating it?

*   *   *

. . . In argument . . . it has been contended that if a law, passed by a state in the exercise of its acknowledged sovereignty, comes into conflict with a law passed by Congress in pursuance of the constitution, they affect the subject, and each other, like equal opposing powers.

But the framers of our constitution foresaw this state of things, and provided for it, by declaring the supremacy not only of itself, but of the laws made in pursuance of it. The nullity of any act, inconsistent with the constitution, is produced by the declaration that the constitution is the supreme law. . . . In every case the act of Congress or the treaty, is supreme; and the law of the state, though not enacted, in the exercise of powers not controverted, must yield to it.

In pursuing this inquiry at the bar, it has been said that the constitution does not confer the right of intercourse between state and state. That right derives its source from those laws whose authority is acknowledged by civilized man throughout the world. This is true. The constitution found it an existing right, and gave to Congress the power to regulate it. In the exercise of this power, Congress has passed "an act for enrolling or licensing ships or vessels to be employed in the coasting trade and fisheries, and for regulating the same." The counsel for the respondent contend, that this act does not give the right to sail from port to port, but confines itself to regulating a pre-existing right, so far only as to confer certain privileges on enrolled and licensed vessels in its exercise.

　　　　　*　　　*　　　*

This act demonstrates the opinion of Congress, that steam boats may be enrolled and licensed, in common with vessels using sails. They are, of course, entitled to the same privileges, and can no more be restrained from navigating waters, and entering ports which are free to such vessels, than if they were wafted on their voyage by the winds, instead of being propelled by the agency of fire. The one element may be as legitimately used as the other, for every commercial purpose authorized by the laws of the Union; and the act of a State inhibiting the use of either to any vessel having a license under the act of Congress comes, we think, in direct collision with that act.

Note: The Effect of *Gibbons*

Marshall's opinion was generally greeted with praise. Most Americans believed that the transportation monopolies hindered economic growth and led to unnecessary interstate conflicts. Within two weeks after the decision, a ship from Connecticut arrived in New York harbor. This was the end of interstate rivalries and retaliation over shipping monopolies. Within a year, the New York court struck down the Livingston monopoly for shipping solely within the state. *Gibbons* is the most important commerce clause case in Supreme Court history. All subsequent nineteenth-century commerce clause cases (and many twentieth-century ones) were, to a great extent, merely commentary on *Gibbons*.

The Second Bank of the United States

In 1791, Secretary of the Treasury Alexander Hamilton proposed that Congress charter the Bank of the United States, which would be a depository for public funds and serve as the government's central financial institution, regulating currency and lending money to the national treasury. The Bank would also be a private corporation whose stockholders would share the profits. The Bank raised fundamental questions of distributive justice. Should the government give public support to a private enterprise in such a way that some would benefit and others might be harmed? Or should the government avoid such economic activity, even if the commerce of the entire nation suffered? These continued as political and legal issues for the next forty years.

Hamilton believed that the Bank was vital for economic development and that it would make the young nation prosperous, vigorous, and glorious. He argued that the Bank was constitutionally permissible, under the necessary and proper clause of Article I. Congressman James Madison and Secretary of State Thomas Jefferson opposed the Bank because it would aid business interests and argued that Congress lacked the power to grant corporate charters. After considering these arguments, President Washington signed the bill granting the Bank a twenty-year charter. In 1811, Congress refused to recharter the Bank, in part on constitutional grounds similar to those used by Jefferson and Madison in 1791.

In 1816, in the aftermath of the War of 1812, Congress rechartered the Bank as the Second Bank of the United States. President Madison now believed the constitutional question was "precluded . . . by repeated circumstances of the validity of such an institution in acts of the legislative, executive, and judicial branches, of the Government . . . [and] a concurrence of the general will of the nation."

Private investors held 80 percent of the Second Bank's stock and elected twenty directors. The federal government owned the remaining stock, and the president appointed five directors. The Bank's notes were legal tender for payment of debts and federal taxes and functioned as the only national currency. Congress guaranteed it would not charter any competing banks. The charter regulated the types of loans the Bank could make, required that the Bank make reports to the Secretary of the Treasury, made the Bank's records available to congressional committees, and stipulated that the Bank maintain branch offices throughout the nation. The charter also required the Bank to pay the United States government $1.5 million.

By 1818, much of the Bank's support had evaporated, especially in the South and the West. The Bank's monopoly seemed undemocratic, and some of its speculative investments and a few fraudulent activities by some Bank officials led to local opposition. The Bank's tight credit policies were constricting the economy, gradually pushing the nation toward the Panic of 1819. In this atmosphere, two states prohibited the Bank outright, while six others taxed the Bank's operations.

McCulloch v. Maryland
4 Wheat. (17 U.S.) 316 (1819)

Maryland imposed a tax of $15,000 on all banks operating in the state that were not chartered by the state. Only the Bank of the United States fit this description. The Bank's cashier at the Baltimore branch, James McCulloch, refused to pay the tax. The Maryland Supreme Court upheld the tax, and McCulloch appealed to the United States Supreme Court.

Mr. Chief Justice Marshall delivered the opinion of the Court.

In the case now to be determined, the defendant, a sovereign State, denies the obligation of a law enacted by the legislature of the Union, and the plaintiff, on his part, contests the validity of an act which has been passed by the legislature of that State. The constitution of our country, in its most interesting and vital parts, is to be considered; the conflicting powers of the government of the Union and of its members, as marked in that constitution, are to be discussed; and an opinion given, which may essentially influence the great operations of the government.

The first question made in the cause is, has Congress power to incorporate a bank?

It has been truly said, that this can scarcely be considered as an open question. . . . The principle now contested was introduced at a very early period of our history, has been recognized by many successive legislatures, and has been acted upon by the judicial department, in cases of peculiar delicacy, as a law of undoubted obligation.

*　　　*　　　*

In discussing this question, the counsel for the State of Maryland have deemed it of some importance, in the construction of the constitution, to consider that instrument not as emanating from the people, but as the act of sovereign and independent States. The powers of the general government, it has been said, are delegated by the States, who alone are truly sovereign; and must be exercised in subordination to the States, who alone possess supreme dominion.

It would be difficult to sustain this proposition. The Convention which framed the constitution was indeed elected by the State legislatures. But the instrument, when it came from their hands, was a mere proposal, without obligation. . . . It was reported to the then existing Congress of the United States, with a request that it might "be submitted to a Convention of Delegates, chosen in each State by the people thereof, under the recommendation of its Legislature, for their assent and ratification." This mode of proceeding was adopted; and by the Convention, by Congress, and by the State Legislatures, the instrument was submitted to the people. They acted upon it in the only manner in which they can act safely, effectively, and wisely, on such a subject, by assembling in Convention.

From these Conventions the constitution derives its whole authority. The government proceeds directly from the people; is "ordained and established" in the name of the people; and is declared to be ordained, "in order to form a more perfect union, establish justice, ensure domestic tranquility, and the blessings of liberty to themselves and to their posterity." The assent of the States, in their sovereign capacity, is implied in calling a Convention, and thus submitting that instrument to the people. But the people were at perfect liberty to accept or reject it; and their act was final. It required not the affirmance, and could not be negatived, by the State governments. The constitution, when thus adopted, was of complete obligation, and bound the State sovereignties.

The government of the Union, then . . . is, emphatically, and truly, a government of the people. In form and in substance it emanates from them. Its powers are granted by them, and are to be exercised directly on them, and for their benefit.

This government is acknowledged by all to be one of enumerated powers. The principle, that it can exercise only the powers granted to it . . . is now universally admitted. But the question respecting the extent of the powers actually granted, is perpetually arising, and will probably continue to arise, as long as our system shall exist.

*　　　*　　　*

If any one proposition could command the universal assent of mankind, we might expect it would be this—that the government of the Union, though limited in its powers, is supreme within its sphere of action. This would seem to result necessarily from its nature. It is the government of all; its powers are delegated by all; it represents all, and acts for all. The nation, on those subjects on which it can act, must necessarily bind its component parts. But this question is not left to mere reason: the people have, in express terms, decided it, by saying, "this constitution, and the laws of the United States, which shall be made in pursuance thereof," "shall be the supreme law of the land," and by requiring that the members of the State legislatures, and the officers of the executive and judicial departments of the States, shall take the oath of fidelity to it.

The government of the United States, then, though limited in its powers, is supreme; and its laws, when made in pursuance of the constitution, form the supreme law of the land, "any thing in the constitution or laws of any State to the contrary notwithstanding."

Among the enumerated powers, we do not find that of establishing a bank or creating a corporation. But there is no phrase in the instrument which, like the articles of confederation, excludes incidental or implied powers; and which requires that every thing granted shall be expressly and minutely described. Even the 10th amendment, which was framed for the purpose of quieting the excessive jealousies which had been excited, omits the word "expressly," and declares only that the powers "not delegated to the United States, nor prohibited to the States, are reserved to the States or to the people;" thus leaving the question, whether the particular power which may become the subject of contest has been delegated to the one government, or prohibited to the other, to depend on a fair construction of the whole instrument. The men who drew and adopted this amendment had experienced the embarrassments resulting from the insertion of this word in the articles of confederation, and probably omitted it to avoid those embarrassments. A constitution, to contain an accurate detail of all the subdivisions of which its great powers will admit, and of all the means by which they may be carried into execution, would partake of the prolixity of a legal code, and could scarcely be embraced by the human mind. It would probably never be understood by the public. Its nature, therefore, requires, that only its great outlines should be marked, its important objects designated, and the minor ingredients which compose those objects be deduced from the nature of the objects themselves. That this idea was entertained by the framers of the American constitution, is not only to be inferred from the nature of the instrument, but from the language. Why else were some of the limitations, found in the ninth section of the 1st article, introduced? It is also, in some degree, warranted by their having omitted to use any restrictive term which might prevent its receiving a fair and just interpretation. In considering this question, then we must never forget, that it is a *constitution* we are expounding.

Although, among the enumerated powers of government, we do not find the word "bank" or "incorporation," we find the great powers to lay and collect taxes; to borrow money; to regulate commerce; to declare and conduct a war; and to raise and support armies and navies. The sword and the purse, all the external relations, and no inconsiderable portion of the industry of the nation, are intrusted to its government. It can never be pretended that these vast powers draw after them others of inferior importance, merely because they are inferior. Such an idea can never be advanced. But it may with great reason be contended, that a government, entrusted with such ample powers, on the due execution of which the happiness and prosperity of the nation so vitally depends, must also be entrusted with ample means for their execution. The power being given, it is the interest of the nation to facilitate its execution. . . . Throughout this vast republic, revenue is to be collected and expended, armies are to be marched and supported. The exigencies of the nation may require that the treasure raised in the north should be transported to the south, that raised in the east conveyed to the west, or that this order should be reversed. Is that construction of the constitution to be preferred which would render these operations difficult, hazardous, and expensive? Can we adopt that construction, (unless the words imperiously require it,) which would impute to the framers of that instrument, when granting these powers for the public good, the intention of impeding their exercise by withholding a choice of means? If, indeed, such be the mandate of the constitution, we have only to obey; but that instrument does not profess to enumerate the means by which the powers it confers may be executed; nor does it prohibit the creation of a corporation, if the existence of such a being be essential to the beneficial exercise of those powers. It is, then, the subject of fair inquiry, how far such means may be employed.

     *   *   *

 The creation of a corporation, it is said, appertains to sovereignty. This is admitted. . . . In America, the powers of sovereignty are divided between the government of the Union, and those of the States. They are each sovereign with respect to the objects committed to the other. . . . The power of creating a corporation, though appertaining to sovereignty, is not, like the power of making a war, or levying taxes, or of regulating commerce, a great substantive and independent power. . . . It is never the end for which other powers are exercised, but a means by which other objects are accomplished. . . . No sufficient reason is, therefore, perceived, why it may not pass as incidental to those powers which are expressly given, if it be a direct mode of executing them.

 But the constitution of the United States has not left the right of Congress to employ the necessary means, for the execution of the powers conferred on the government, to general reasoning. To its enumeration of powers is added that of making "all laws which shall be necessary and proper, for carrying into execution the foregoing powers, and all other powers vested by this constitution, in the government of the United States, or in any department thereof."

     *   *   *

 . . . The subject is the execution of those great powers on which the welfare of a nation essentially depends. It must have been the intention of those who gave these powers, to insure, as far as human prudence could insure, their beneficial execution. This could not be done by confiding the choice of means to such narrow limits as not to leave it in the power of Congress to adopt any which might be appropriate, and which were conducive to the end. This provision is made in a constitution intended to endure for the ages to come, and consequently, to be adapted to the various *crises* of human affairs. To have prescribed the means by which government should, in all future time, execute its powers, would have been to change, entirely, the character of the instrument, and give it the properties of a legal code. It would have been an unwise attempt to provide, by immutable rules, for exigencies which, if foreseen at all, must have been seen dimly, and which can be best provided for as they occur. To have declared that the best means shall not be used, but that those alone without which the power given would be nugatory, would have been to deprive the legislature of the capacity to avail itself of experience, to exercise its reason, and to accommodate its legislation to circumstances. If we apply this principle of construction to any of the powers of the government, we shall find it so pernicious in its operation that we shall be compelled to discard it. . . .

*   *   *

In ascertaining the sense in which the word "necessary" is used in this clause of the constitution, we may derive some aid from that with which it is associated. Congress shall have power "to make all laws which shall be necessary and proper to carry into execution" the powers of the government. If the word "necessary" was used in that strict and rigorous sense for which the counsel for the State of Maryland contend, it would be an extraordinary departure from the usual course of the human mind, as exhibited in composition, to add a word, the only possible effect of which is to qualify that strict and rigorous meaning; to present to the mind the idea of some choice of means of legislation not straitened and compressed within the narrow limits for which gentlemen contend.

But the argument which most conclusively demonstrates the error of the construction contended for by the counsel for the State of Maryland, is founded on the intention of the Convention, as manifested in the whole clause. . . . That it might employ those which, in its judgement, would most advantageously effect the object to be accomplished. That any means adapted to the end, any means which tended directly to the execution of the constitutional powers of the government, were in themselves constitutional. This clause, as constructed by the State of Maryland, would abridge, and almost annihilate this useful and necessary right of the legislature to select its means. That this could not be intended, is . . . too apparent for controversy. We think so for the following reasons:

1st.   The clause is placed among the powers of Congress, not among the limitations on those powers.

2nd.   Its terms purport to enlarge, not to diminish the powers vested in the government. It purports to be an additional power, not a restriction on those already granted. No reason has been, or can be assigned for this concealing an intention to narrow the discretion of the national legislature under words which purport to enlarge it. The framers of the constitution wished its adoption, and well knew that it would be endangered by its strength, not by its weakness.

. . . If no other motive for its insertion can be suggested, a sufficient one is found in the desire to remove all doubts respecting the right to legislate on that vast mass of incidental powers which must be involved in the constitution, if that instrument be not a splendid bauble.

We admit, as all must admit, that the powers of the government are limited, and that its limits are not to be transcended. But we think the sound construction of the constitution must allow to the national legislature that discretion, with respect to the means by which the powers it confers are to be carried into execution, which will enable that body to perform the high duties assigned to it, in the manner most beneficial to the people. Let the end be legitimate, let it be within the scope of the constitution, and all means which are appropriate, which are plainly adapted to that end, which are not prohibited, but consist with the letter and spirit of the constitution, are constitutional.

*   *   *

It being the opinion of the Court, that the act incorporating the bank is constitutional; and that the power of establishing a branch in the State of Maryland might be properly exercised by the bank itself, we proceed to inquire—

2. Whether the State of Maryland may, without violating the constitution, tax that branch?

That the power to tax involves the power to destroy; that the power to destroy may defeat and render useless the power to create; that there is a plain repugnance, in conferring on one government a power to control the constitutional measures of another, which other, with respect to those very measures, is declared to be supreme over that which exerts the control, are propositions not to be denied. But all inconsistencies are to be reconciled by the magic of the word CONFIDENCE. Taxation, it is said, does not necessarily and unavoidably destroy. To carry it to the excess of destruction would be an abuse, to presume which, would banish that confidence which is essential to all government.

But is this a case of confidence? Would the people of any one State trust those of another with a power to control the most insignificant operations of their State government? We know they would not. Why, then, should we suppose that the people of any one State should be willing to trust those of another with a power to control the operations of a government to which they have confided their most important and most valuable interests? In the legislature of the Union alone, are all represented. The legislature of the Union alone, therefore, can be trusted by the people with the power of controlling measures which concern all, in the confidence that it will not be abused. This, then, is not a case of confidence, and we must consider it as it really is.

If the States may tax one instrument, employed by the government in the execution of its powers, they may tax any and every other instrument. They may tax the mail; they may tax the mint; they may tax patent rights; they may tax the papers of the custom-house; they may tax judicial process; they may tax all the means employed by the government, to an excess which would defeat all the ends of government. This was not intended by the American people. They did not design to make their government dependent on the States.

The Court has bestowed on this subject its most deliberate consideration. The result is a conviction that the States have no power, by taxation or other-wise, to retard, impede, burden, or in any manner control, the operations of the constitutional laws enacted by Congress to carry into execution the powers vested in the general government. This is, we think, the unavoidable consequence of that supremacy which the constitution has declared.

We are unanimously of opinion, that the law passed by the legislature of Maryland, imposing a tax on the Bank of the United States, is unconstitutional and void.

Note: A Court Opinion as Political Theory

Next to *Marbury* v. *Madison, McCulloch* was Chief Justice John Marshall's most important decision. The power of the reasoning, the strength of the argument, and the overall vision of the national government make this Marshall's "greatest" opinion. But was this thirty-seven-page opinion (remarkably long for the era) a work of law or of political theory? Marshall cited no cases at all. *The Federalist,* congressional debates, the Articles of Confederation, and the Constitution are the only external sources he noted. Marshall argued that the framers intended to write a Constitution that would "endure for ages to come." He interpreted the intentions from the text, and argued that the text was open-ended so that the Constitution could grow and develop over time. The opinion has shaped most subsequent American constitutional and political history because of Marshall's expansive interpretation of the necessary and proper clause.

ANDREW JACKSON
Veto Message
July 10, 1832

In June 1832, Congress extended the charter of the Bank. Friends of the Bank believed President Andrew Jackson would sign the bill because it had passed by large margins in both houses. But the Bank's supporters miscalculated. Jackson despised the Second Bank of the United States, which he blamed for causing the Panic of 1819, in which Jackson personally lost money. Jackson, the nation's first western president, also saw the Bank as the symbol of eastern power and privilege. He also objected to the fact that the Bank was controlled by only a few hundred American stockholders and that nearly one-quarter of the stock was owned by foreigners. Furthermore, he thought the bill would enrich these already wealthy people at the expense of the nation. Finally, Jackson disliked monopolies, and thought they should rarely be granted because their profits ultimately came "directly or indirectly out of the earnings of the American people." Having established the impolicy of the Bank in the first part of his veto message, Jackson turned to its constitutionality.

It is maintained by the advocates of the bank that its constitutionality in all its features ought to be considered as settled by precedent and by the decision of the Supreme Court. To this conclusion I can not assent. Mere precedent is a dangerous source of authority, and should not be regarded as deciding questions of constitutional power except where the acquiescence of the people and the States can be considered as well settled. So far from this being the case on this subject, an argument against the bank might be based on precedent. One Congress, in 1791, decided in favor of a bank; another, in 1811, decided against it. One Congress, in 1815, decided against a bank; another, in 1816, decided in its favor. Prior to the present Congress, therefore, the precedents drawn from that source were equal. If we resort to the States, the expressions of legislative, judicial, and executive opinions against the bank have been probably to those in its favor as 4 to 1. There is nothing in precedent, therefore, which, if its authority were admitted, ought to weigh in favor of the act before me.

If the opinion of the Supreme Court covered the whole ground of this act, it ought not to control the coordinate authorities of this Government. The Congress, the Executive, and the Court must each for itself be guided by its own opinion of the Constitution. Each public officer who takes an oath to support the Constitution swears that he will support it as he understands it, and not as it is understood by others. It is as much the duty of the House of Representatives, of the Senate, and of the President to decide upon the constitutionality of any bill or resolution . . . as it is of the supreme judges. . . . The opinion of the judges has no more authority over Congress than the opinion of Congress has over the judges, and on that point the President is independent of both. The authority of the Supreme Court must not, therefore, be permitted to control the Congress or the Executive when acting in their legislative capacities, but to have only such influence as the force of their reasoning may deserve.

It is to be regretted that the rich and powerful too often bend the acts of government to their selfish purposes. Distinctions in society will always exist under every just government. Equality of talents, of education, or of wealth can not be produced by human institutions. In the full enjoyment of the gifts of Heaven and the fruits of superior industry, economy, and virtue, every man is equally entitled to protection by law; but when the laws undertake to add to these natural and just advantages artificial distinctions, to grant titles, gratuities, and exclusive privileges, to make the rich richer and the potent more powerful, the humble members of society—the farmers, mechanics, and laborers—who have neither the time nor the means of securing like favors to themselves, have a right to complain of the injustice of their Government. There are no necessary evils in government. Its evils exist only in its abuses. If it would confine itself to equal protection, and, as Heaven does its rains, shower its favors alike on the high and the low, the rich and the poor, it would be an unqualified blessing. In the act before me there seems to be a wide and unnecessary departure from these just principles.

Nor is our Government to be maintained or our Union preserved by invasions of the rights and powers of the several States. In thus attempting to make our General Government strong we make it weak. Its true strength consists in leaving individuals and States as much as possible to themselves—in making itself felt, not in its power, but in its beneficence; not in its control, but in its protection; not in binding the States more closely to the center, but leaving each to move unobstructed in its proper orbit.

Experience should teach us wisdom. Most of the difficulties our Government now encounters and most of the dangers which impend over our Union have sprung from an abandonment of the legitimate objects of Government by our national legislation, and the adoption of such principles as are embodied in this act. Many of our rich men have not been content with equal protection and equal benefits, but have besought us to make them richer by act of Congress. By attempting to gratify their desires we have in the results of our legislation arrayed section against section, interest against interest, and man against man, in a fearful commotion which threatens to shake the foundations of our Union. It is time to pause in our career to review our principles, and if possible revive that devoted patriotism and spirit of compromise which distinguished the sages of the Revolution and the fathers of our Union. We can at least take a stand against all new grants of monopolies and exclusive privileges, against any prostitution of our Government to the advancement of the few at the expense of the many.

Note: Jacksonian Economics

This veto illustrates the hostility of Jackson and his followers to government intervention in the economy and to the privileged rich. After the veto, he ordered the removal of all government deposits in the Bank. Two Secretaries of the Treasury refused to remove the deposits because they feared that such an act would destroy the economy. Jackson finally appointed Roger B. Taney to the post, and he removed the deposits. In 1832, Jackson was reelected, campaigning against the "monster bank." Jackson rewarded Taney by appointing him Chief Justice of the United States. Shortly after Jackson left office, the Panic of 1837 broke out, dooming his successor, Martin Van Buren. With a few exceptions, Jackson's veto also ended any active role for the antebellum federal government in the nation's economy.

After the War of 1812, there was widespread support for federal aid to economic development. John C. Calhoun's "Bonus Bill" (1817) provided funds for internal improvements from money paid to the government by the Second Bank of the United States. President Madison vetoed this bill on constitutional grounds. President Monroe supported "the systematic and fostering care of the government for our manufacturers," but agreed with Madison that the Constitution prohibited federal funding of internal improvements. Monroe asked for a constitutional amendment to change this situation. No amendment was adopted, and in 1830 Andrew Jackson vetoed the Maysville Road Bill, asserting that because the road would be built entirely within one state (Kentucky) Congress had no power to fund it. This veto was also a slap at Jackson's Whig rival, Kentuckian Henry Clay. Jackson signed the Cumberland Road Bill in 1830, but that ended his support for internal improvements. In 1832, Jackson vetoed the rechartering of the Second Bank of the United States.

Note: A Federal Common Law

In *United States* v. *Hudson and Goodwin* (1812) and *United States* v. *Coolidge* (1816), the Supreme Court held that there was no federal common law of crimes and that prosecutions in federal court had to be based on a federal statute. However, in *Swift* v. *Tyson* (1842), a unanimous Supreme Court held that for civil litigation there was a federal common law, and federal district judges could develop their own rules, independent of state decisions and laws, consistent with final review by the Supreme Court. This resulted in a nationalization of commercial common-law jurisprudence at a time when access to state decisions was often difficult. For this reason, *Swift* is usually regarded as a "lawyer's" case.

Swift illustrates the connection between legal rules and nineteenth-century economic growth. In his opinion, Justice Joseph Story pointed out that without this rule almost all interstate transactions would be uncertain. In an age when private bank notes and bills of exchange functioned in the absence of a national currency, predictability and uniformity of commercial and legal rules were vital to the nation's economy. Even some Jacksonian states'-rights jurists, such as Roger B. Taney and Peter V. Daniel, joined Story because they understood that economic development and growth required consistent rules for commercial transactions. Nevertheless, Story's decision must also be seen as part of the ongoing tension between supporters of a strong federal judiciary and supporters of states' rights. The outcome was consistent with Story's lifelong goal of strengthening the federal courts and nationalizing law. *Swift* dovetails with Story's opinion in the same Court term in *Prigg* v. *Pennsylvania* (1842), which created a common-law right of recaption in fugitive slave cases (see Chapter 4).

Note: Canals, Internal Improvements, and the States

In the first half of the nineteenth century, the states led the development of the nation's transportation network. State activism included direct state construction of, investment in, and subsidies to canals, turnpikes, and railroads. State commissions established to promote economic development also simplified incorporation proceedings, expedited eminent domain condemnations, and aided the growth of transportation networks as well as water-powered manufacturing. New York's Erie Canal was the most dramatic, and most profitable, example of direct state involvement in internal development. Canal revenue more than made up for the cost of construction while helping to make New York the richest state in the nation. In 1825, after the canal opened but before its final completion, Governor DeWitt Clinton bragged to his legislature:

> For almost all useful purposes, the city of Detroit, will . . . be brought within a hundred miles of the city of Albany. Already have we witnessed the creative power of these communications, in the flourishing villages which have sprung up or been extended; in the increase of our towns; and, above all, in the prosperity of the city of New York . . . it is highly probable that in fifteen years its population will be doubled, and that in less than thirty years it will be the third city in point of numbers, in the civilized world, and the second, if not the first, in commerce.

Clinton's predictions proved basically correct. Other states, like Pennsylvania and Ohio, also built elaborate, although less successful, canal systems.

The background of the Erie Canal illustrates the necessity of government intervention in the construction of canals. As early as 1792, New York chartered (and invested in) two private canal companies. One quickly collapsed. The other barely survived. This experience showed that private enterprise could not raise sufficient capital to build and operate a large canal system. In 1808, the Secretary of the Treasury advocated federal support for canals. In anticipation of federal funds, New York surveyed a canal route from the Hudson River to Lake Erie. In 1810, the state appointed a Canal Commission, which concluded that private investment was insufficient to build a canal across New York. The next year, the legislature appointed DeWitt Clinton and Gouverneur Morris to lobby Congress for canal funding. A bill on this subject died in a House committee. After the War of 1812, Congress supported internal improvements, but Madison's 1817 veto of Calhoun's "Bonus Bill" made it clear that any canal in New York would have to be funded by the state.

Opponents of New York's canal program feared higher taxes. Party politics, not laissez-faire ideology, also led to opposition. Martin Van Buren and other Democrats opposed the canal because they did not want DeWitt Clinton to get credit for the project. Nevertheless, in 1816 the legislature appointed Clinton as head of a new

Canal Commission. In 1817, construction of the canal began. That same year, Clinton became governor. He was also governor in 1825, when the canal was completed.

State Constitutions and the Active State

Most of the state constitutions written between 1776 and 1803 said little about economic development. This left the question entirely in the hands of the state legislatures. Post-Revolutionary state governments regulated industries, granted charters to companies, and created monopolies. Some states gave direct cash subsidies to some industries or invested directly in private corporations. Even when such investments were honestly made and carefully managed, much of the public objected to this use of tax dollars, which enriched individual stockholders through the infusion of public money into private business.

Grants of monopolies to steamboat companies, bridges, and other enterprises also led to public opposition. Finally, the whole process of creating corporations came under public scrutiny. Without general incorporation laws, entrepreneurs were forced to seek legislative charters for their new companies. This process was time-consuming, expensive, and subject to political abuse. Equally important, some Americans disliked the whole idea of corporations, which limited the liabilities of investors and allowed irresponsible corporate owners and managers to avoid the costs of their negligence or mismanagement.

During the nation's second wave of state constitution making, from about 1820 to 1860, many constitutions severely restricted state involvement in the economy through provisions limiting state investment, state debt, and corporations.

Ohio Constitution
1851

Ohio's 1803 Constitution had no limitations on state expenditures or state intervention in the economy. However, the 1851 Constitution, like many of the state constitutions of the late antebellum period, severely limited state economic activity.

Article VIII
Public Debt and Public Works

Section 1.   The State may contract debts to supply casual deficits or failures in revenues, or to meet expenses not otherwise provided for; but the aggregate amount of such debts, direct or contingent . . . shall never exceed seven hundred and fifty thousand dollars; and the money, arising from the creation of such debts, shall be applied to the purpose for which it was obtained, or to repay the debts so contracted, and to no other purpose whatever.

Section 2.   In addition to the above limited power, the State may contract debts to repel invasion, suppress insurrection, defend the State in war, or to redeem the present outstanding indebtedness of the State; but the money, arising from the contracting of such debts, shall be applied to the purpose for which it was raised, or to repay such debts, and to no other purpose whatever; and all debts, incurred to redeem the present outstanding indebtedness of the State shall be so contracted as to be payable by the sinking fund, hereinafter provided for, as the same shall accumulate.

Section 3.   Except the debts above specified . . . [in] this article, no debt whatever shall hereafter be created by or on behalf of the State.

Section 4.   The credit of the State shall not, in any manner be given or loaned to, or in aid of, any individual association or corporation whatever; nor shall the State ever hereafter become a joint owner, or stockholder, in any company or association in this State, or elsewhere, formed for any purpose whatever.

Section 5.   The State shall never assume the debts of any county, city, town, or township, or of any corporation whatever, unless such debt shall have been created to repel invasion, suppress insurrection, or defend the State in war.

Section 6.   The General Assembly shall never authorize any county, city, town, or township, by vote of its citizens, or otherwise, to become a stockholder in any joint stock company, corporation, or association whatever; or to raise money for, or loan its credit to, or in aid of, any such company, corporation, or association.

*   *   *

Article XII
Finance and Taxation

*   *   *

Section 3.   The general assembly shall provide, by law, for taxing the notes and bills discounted or purchased, moneys loaned, and all other property, effects, or dues . . . of all banks, now existing or hereafter created, and of all bankers, so that all property employed in banking shall always bear a burden of taxation equal to that imposed on the property of individuals.

*   *   *

Section 6.   The State shall never contract any debt for purposes of internal improvement.

Article XIII
Corporations

Section 1.   The general assembly shall pass no special act conferring corporate powers.

Section 2.   Corporations may be formed under general laws; but all such laws may, from time to time, be altered or repealed.

Section 3.   Dues from corporations shall be secured by such individual liability of the stockholders, and other means, as may be prescribed by law; but, in all cases, each stockholder shall be liable, over and above the stock by him or her owned, and any amount unpaid thereon, to a further sum at least equal in amount to such stock.

Section 4.   The property of corporations, now existing or hereafter created, shall forever be subject to taxation, the same as the property of individuals.

Section 5.   No right of way shall be appropriated to the use of any corporation, until full compensation therefor shall be first made in money, or first secured by a deposit of money, to the owner, irrespective of any benefit from any improvement proposed by such corporation; which compensation shall be ascertained by a jury of twelve men, in a court of record, as shall be prescribed by law.

*   *   *

Section 7.   No act of the general assembly, authorizing associations with banking powers, shall take effect, until it shall be submitted to the people, at the general election next succeeding the passage thereof, and be approved by a majority of all the electors voting at such election.

Mississippi Constitution
1817

Like Ohio, Mississippi was a new western state on a developing frontier. Mississippi entered the Union thirteen years after Ohio, and some provisions of its first constitution reflect the political issues of America after the War of 1812. The 1832 Constitution also reflects the changing nature of the economy, as well as other important socioeconomic influences on the state.

Article VI
General Provisions

Section 9.   No bank shall be incorporated by the legislature without the reservation of a right to subscribe for, in behalf of the State, at least one-fourth part of the capital stock thereof, and the appointment of a proportion of the directors equal to the stock subscribed for.

*   *   *

Section 17.   Divorces from the bonds of matrimony shall not be granted, but in cases provided for by law, by suit in chancery; Provided, That no decree for such divorce shall have effect until the same shall be sanctioned by two-thirds of both branches of the general assembly.

Mississippi Constitution
1832

Article VII
General Provisions

Section 8.   No money from the treasury shall be appropriated to objects of internal improvement, unless the bill for that purpose be passed by two-thirds of both branches of the legislature. . . .

Section 9.   No law shall ever be passed to raise a loan of money upon the credit of the State, or to pledge the faith of the State, for the redemption of any loan or debt, unless such law be proposed in the senate or house of representatives, and be agreed to by a majority of the members of each house, and entered on the journals with the yeas and nays taken thereon, and be referred to the next succeeding legislature, and published for three months previous to the next regular election, in three newspapers of this State; and unless a majority of each branch of the legislature, so elected, after such publication, shall agree to and pass such a law; and in such case the yeas and nays shall be taken and entered on the journals of each house. . . .

*   *   *

Slaves

Section 1.   The legislature shall have no power to pass laws for the emancipation of slaves without the consent of the owners, unless where the slave shall have rendered to the State some distinguished service; in which case the owner shall be paid a full equivalent for the slave so emancipated. They shall have no power to prevent emigrants to this State from bringing with them such persons as are deemed slaves by the laws of any one of the United States, so long as any person of the same age or description shall be continued in slavery by the laws of this State: Provided, That such person or slave be the bona-fide property of such immigrants: And provided also, That laws may be passed to prohibit the introduction into this State of slaves who may have committed high crimes in other States. They shall have power to pass laws to permit the owners of slaves to emancipate them, saving the rights of creditors, and preventing them from becoming a public charge. They shall have full power to oblige the owners of slaves to treat them with humanity; to provide for them necessary clothing and provisions; to abstain from all injuries to them, extending to life or limb; and, in case of their neglect or refusal to comply with the directions of such laws, to have such slave or slaves sold for the benefit of the owner or owners.

Section 2.   The introduction of slaves into this State as merchandise, or for sale, shall be prohibited from and after the first day of May, eighteen hundred and thirty-three: Provided, That the actual settler or settlers shall not be prohibited from purchasing slaves in any State in this Union, and bringing them into this State for their own individual use, until the year eighteen hundred and forty-five.

Substantive Law and Economic Growth

The developing economy of the nineteenth century led to dramatic changes in the substantive law of the United States. Some decisions of the United States Supreme Court interpreting the commerce clause and the contracts clause of the Constitution were particularly important to economic development. As noted earlier, in *Gibbons* v. *Ogden* (1824) the Supreme Court used the commerce clause to strike down the steamboat monopoly that the New York courts had upheld in *Livingston* v. *Van Ingen* (1812).

Despite the importance of major federal cases, most of the substantive legal changes of the period came from the state courts. Property law and water law changed dramatically as English common-law rules dating from the Middle Ages seemed increasingly irrelevant to American conditions. Corporations increased in number, and a new field of law emerged. Tort law, virtually an unknown field before the Revolution, became a mainstay of litigation by 1860.

Nineteenth-century courts fashioned law to fit changing circumstances resulting from new technologies, industries, and business methods. Contract law, which evolved to fit the exigencies of world markets, placed new burdens on both consumers and businessmen through the rise of caveat emptor. Cases involving property and corporations often pitted older industries and technologies against newer ones, usually aiding the growth of new industries and the replacement of old ones. Even when the newer corporations lost a case, the precedents set were often helpful to the general growth of corporations. Thus in *Dartmouth College* v. *Woodward* (1819), the court sided with an older corporation but created a precedent that affected the vested rights of all new corporations.

More dramatic than suits between corporations were cases involving individuals who asked the courts to protect them from the more powerful economic entities they encountered. Initially, no American court recognized the right of workers to strike or bargain collectively. In *Commonwealth* v. *Hunt* (1842), Chief Justice Lemuel Shaw of the Massachusetts Supreme Judicial Court ruled that labor unions were not illegal conspiracies per se. This limited victory was not labor's "emancipation proclamation," as some historians have hailed it, but under it a few antebellum laborers, mostly skilled workers, were able to unionize and improve their working conditions and wages.

Workers were even less successful in protecting themselves from unsafe working conditions. In *Farwell* v. *Boston and Worcester Railroad* (1842), Chief Justice Shaw drastically limited the opportunity for injured workers to recover for job-related injuries. Thus the workers, not the investors, would bear the often tragic human costs of industrialization.

Courts were only slightly more sympathetic to shippers, passengers, and innocent bystanders harmed by the dangerous machines of nineteenth-century industrialization. Antebellum courts generally limited the liabilities of industries and placed the costs of industrial accidents on individuals. Courts denied bereaved plaintiffs the right to sue for the "wrongful death" of their relatives. Courts limited or barred recovery by victims of accidents through the adoption of the doctrine of contributory negligence. Courts also limited the liabilities of common carriers for lost goods, holding that property owners could not always sue industrial actors who negligently damaged their property. Insurance, not lawsuits, was the appropriate defense for property in the dangerous world of industrializing America.

The Advent of the Corporation

William Blackstone defined corporations as "artificial persons, who may maintain a perpetual succession, and enjoy a kind of legal immortality."[4] Before 1800, corporations usually created such institutions as colleges, hospitals, and, most common of all, governmental entities. New York City, for example, is a corporation. A few government-sponsored economic initiatives were also incorporated, such as the Virginia Company, which settled Jamestown in 1607, and the Royal Africa Company, which had a monopoly over English participation in the African slave trade. Private business, such as banks and insurance companies, were the least common corporations. In 1780, the United States had fewer than 20 business corporations. Forty years later, the nation boasted more than 1,800 corporations, engaged in transportation, commerce, finance, and manufacturing.

Incorporation offered three important advantages. First, corporations do not end with the death of their owners, but can exist beyond the life of any single individual or group of individuals. This advantage made them useful for creating government entities, like cities, and charitable operations, like hospitals or schools. The effects of this are obvious for businesses. Unlike a sole proprietorship or a partnership, a business corporation can continue long after its founders have died or retired. The second key aspect of a corporation is the limited liability it usually places on the stockholders. Each member of a partnership can be held personally liable for all debts that the partnership might incur. But in a corporation, a stockholder's liability is usually limited to his or her actual investment. Finally, a corporation facilitated the pooling of capital to raise the enormous sums necessary to build new forms of manufacturing, commerce, and transportation. Investors could place their funds with corporate directors, without having to worry about the day-to-day operations of the business. This allowed for rapid economic development in the nineteenth century.

During the early national period, corporations were viewed as monopolistic and partial to the rich. They were fundamentally antirepublican. Nevertheless, many Republicans recognized their value. Thus in *Currie's Administrator* v. *The Mutual Assurance Society* (Va., 1809), Judge Spencer Roane, a staunch Jeffersonian and a vigilant opponent of privilege, conceded that "those artificial persons are rendered necessary in the law from the inconvenience, if not impracticability of keeping alive the rights of associated bodies, by devolving them on one series of individuals after another."

The realization that corporations were a useful necessity led to their expanded use, even though they had antirepublican tendencies. State legislatures gradually democratized the incorporation process through "general incorporation laws," which allowed the creation of new corporations without special legislative acts. This is an example of what legal historian James Willard Hurst has called the use of law to facilitate "the release of creative energies."[5] This solution, while answering the republican critique of corporations as monopolies, led to a new problem: the proliferation of corporations and the subsequent concentration of wealth and power in the hands of these fictitious persons. Moreover, critics considered such bodies to be "soulless." Corporations were, after all, not human beings, but legal fictions whose sole reason for existence was the profit of stockholders who were themselves often removed from the operation of the business.

Dartmouth College v. *Woodward*
4 Wheat. (17 U.S.) 518 (1819)

In 1769, Dr. Eleazar Wheelock received a royal charter creating Dartmouth College, with a self-perpetuating board of trustees. This charter allowed Wheelock to appoint his own successor, unless the choice was "disapproved by the *trustees." Ten years later, Wheelock's son John became the college's second president. In 1816, the trustees removed the autocratic John Wheelock. The state legislature then amended the 1769 charter by creating "Dartmouth University," with a board of trustees and overseers favorable to Wheelock. In 1817, the old trustees operated Dartmouth College, with ninety-five students, while the new trustees operated Dartmouth University, with only fourteen students. Meanwhile, the old college trustees hired Daniel Webster (an alumnus) to sue William Woodward (the treasurer of the new Dartmouth University) for possession of the records, seal, and charter, as well as for $50,000 in damages. The case would determine the validity of the 1816 law, modifying the original corporate charter. The college trustees lost before the New Hampshire Supreme Court, but appealed to the United States Supreme Court. There Webster argued that the amendment of the corporate charter was actually a "law impairing the obligation of contracts," which violated Article I, Section 10, of the United States Constitution.*

The opinion of the Court was delivered by Mr. Chief Justice Marshall.

*   *   *

. . . The single question now to be considered is, do the acts [creating Dartmouth University] to which the verdict refers violate the constitution of the United States?

This Court can be insensible neither to the magnitude nor delicacy of this question. The validity of a legislative act is to be examined; and the opinion of the highest law tribunal of a State is to be revised: . . . On more than one occasion, this Court has expressed the cautious circumspection with which it approaches the consideration of such questions; and has declared, that, in no doubtful case, would it pronounce a legislative act to be contrary to the constitution. But the American people have said, in the constitution of the United States, that "no State shall pass any . . . law impairing the obligation of contracts." In the same instrument they also said, "that the judicial power shall extend to all cases in law and equity arising under the constitution." On the judges of this Court, then, is imposed the high and solemn duty of protecting, from even legislative violation, those contracts which the constitution of our country has placed beyond legislative control; and, however irksome the task may be, this is a duty from which we dare not shrink.

The title of the plaintiffs originates in a charter dated . . . 1769, incorporating twelve persons [as] . . . "The Trustees of Dartmouth College," granting to them and their successors the usual corporate privileges and powers, and authorizing the trustees, who are to govern the college, to fill up all vacancies which may be created in their own body.

The defendant claims under three acts of the legislature of New-Hampshire, the most material of which was passed on the 27th of June, 1816, and is entitled, "an act to amend the charter, and enlarge and improve the corporation of Dartmouth College."

*   *   *

It can require no argument to prove, that the circumstances of this case constitute a contract. An application is made to the crown for a charter to incorporate a religious and literary institution. In the application, it is stated that large contributions have been made for the object, which will be conferred on the corporation, as soon as it shall be created. The charter is granted, and on its faith the property is conveyed. Surely in this transaction every ingredient of a complete and legitimate contract is to be found.

The points for consideration are,

1. Is this contract protected by the constitution of the United States?
2. Is it impaired by the acts under which the defendant holds?

. . . This is the point on which the cause essentially depends. If the act of incorporation be a grant of political power, if it create a civil institution to be employed in the administration of the government, or if the funds of the college be public property, or if the State of New Hampshire, as a government, be alone interested in its transactions, the subject is one in which the legislature of the State may act according to its own judgement, unrestrained by any limitation of its power imposed by the constitution of the United States.

But if this be a private eleemosynary institution, endowed with a capacity to take property for objects unconnected with government, whose funds are bestowed by individuals on the faith of the charter . . . there may be more difficulty in the case, although neither the persons who have made these stipulations, nor those for whose benefit they were made, should be parties to the cause. Those who are no longer interested in the property, may yet retain such an interest in the preservation of their own arrangements, as to have a right to insist that those arrangements shall be held sacred . . . the trustees [may be] . . . so completely their representatives in the eye of the law, as to stand in their place, not only as respects the government of the college, but also as respects the maintenance of the college charter.

*   *   *

[Here Marshall discussed Dartmouth's history, demonstrating that its funds "consisted entirely of private donations" solicited by Dr. Eleazar Wheelock and that the "charter of incorporation was granted at his instance." Marshall concluded, "It is then an eleemosynary, and, as far as respects its funds, a private corporation." Marshall noted that "education is an object of national concern and a proper subject of legislation" and that governments could create colleges. But, he asked, was Dartmouth a government-created "institution"?]

Whence, then, can be derived the idea, that Dartmouth College has become a public institution, and its trustees public officers, exercising powers conferred by the public for public objects? Not from the source whence its funds were drawn; for its foundation is purely private and eleemosynary—Not from the application of those funds; for money may be given for education, and the persons receiving it do not, by being employed in the education of youth, become members of the civil government. Is it from the act of incorporation? Let this . . . be considered.

A corporation is an artificial being, invisible, intangible, and existing only in contemplation of law. Being the mere creature of law, it possesses only those properties which the charter of its creation confers upon it, either expressly, or as incidental to its very existence. These are such as are supposed best calculated to effect the object for which it was created. Among the most important are immortality; and if the expression be allowed, individuality; properties, by which a perpetual succession of many persons are considered as the same, and may act as a single individual. They enable a corporation to manage its own affairs, and to hold property without the perplexing intricacies, the hazardous and endless necessity, of perpetual conveyances for the purpose of transmitting it from hand to hand. It is chiefly for the purpose of clothing bodies of men, in succession, with these qualities and capacities, that corporations were invented, and are in use. By these means, a perpetual succession of individuals are capable of acting for the promotion of the particular object, like one immortal being. But this being does not share in the civil government of the country, unless that be the purpose for which it was created. Its immortality no more confers on it political power, or a political character, than immortality would confer such power or character on a natural person. It is no more a State instrument, than a natural person exercising the same powers would be. . . . Because the government has given it the power to take and to hold property in a particular form, and for particular purposes, has the government a consequent right substantially to change that form, or to vary the purposes to which the property is to be applied? This principle has never been asserted or recognized, and is supported by no authority. Can it derive aid from reason?

The objects for which a corporation is created are universally such as the government wishes to promote. They are deemed beneficial to the country; and this benefit constituted the consideration, and, in most cases, the sole consideration of the grant. In most eleemosynary institutions, the object would be difficult, perhaps unattainable, without the aid of a charter of incorporation. Charitable, or public spirited individuals, desirous of making permanent appropriations for charitable or other useful purposes . . . apply to the government, state their beneficial object, and offer to advance the money necessary for its accomplishment, provided the government will confer on the instrument which is to execute their designs the capacity to execute them. . . . The benefit to the public is considered as an ample compensation for the faculty it confers, and the corporation is created. If the advantages to the public constitute a full compensation for the faculty it gives, there can be no reason for exacting a further compensation, by claiming a right to exercise over this artificial being a power which changes its nature, and touches the fund, for the security and application of which it was created. There can be no reason for implying in a charter, given for a valuable consideration, a power which is not only not expressed, but is in direct contradiction to its express stipulations.

*   *   *

From this review of the charter, it appears, that Dartmouth College is an eleemosynary institution, incorporated for the purpose of perpetuating the application of the bounty of the donors, to the specified objects of that bounty; that its trustees or governors were originally named by the founder, and invested with the power of perpetuating themselves; that they are not public officers, nor is it a civil institution, participating in the administration of government; but a charity school, or a seminary of education, incorporated for the preservation of its property, and the perpetual application of that property to the objects of its creation.

*   *   *

This is plainly a contract to which the donors, the trustees, and the crown, (to whose rights and obligations New Hampshire succeeds,) were the original parties. It is a contract made on a valuable consideration. It is a contract for the security and disposition of property. It is a contract, on the faith of which, real and personal estate has been conveyed to the corporation. It is then a contract within the letter of the constitution, and within its spirit also. . . .

*   *   *

The opinion of the Court, after mature deliberation, is, that this is a contract, the obligation of which cannot be impaired, without violating the constitution of the United States. This opinion appears to us to be equally supported by reason, and by the former decisions of this Court.

. . . We next proceed to the inquiry, whether its obligation has been impaired by those acts of the legislature of New Hampshire. . . .

From the review of this charter, which has been taken, it appears, that the whole power of governing the college, of appointing and removing tutors, of fixing their salaries, of directing the course of study to be pursued by the students, and of filling up vacancies created in their own body, was vested in the [twelve] trustees. . . .

*   *   *

It has been already stated, that the act "to amend the charter . . . " increases the number of trustees to twenty-one, gives the appointment of the additional members to the executive of the State, and creates a board of overseers, to consist of twenty-five persons, of whom twenty-one are also appointed by the executive of New-Hampshire, who have power to inspect and control the most important acts of the trustees.

. . . The whole power of governing the college is transferred from trustees appointed according to the will of the founder, expressed in the charter, to the executive of New Hampshire. The management and application of the funds of this eleemosynary institution, which are placed by the donors in the hands of trustees named in the charter, and empowered to perpetuate themselves, are placed by this act under the control of the government of the State. The will of the State is substituted for the will of the donors, in every essential operation of the college. This is not an immaterial change. The founders of the college contracted, not merely for the perpetual application of the funds which they gave, to the objects for which those funds were given; they contracted also, to secure that application by the constitution of the corporation. They contracted for a system, which should, as far as human foresight can provide, retain forever the government of the literary institution they had formed, in the hands of persons approved by themselves. This system is totally changed.

*   *   *

It results from this opinion, that the acts of the legislature of New Hampshire, which are stated in the special verdict found in this cause, are repugnant to the constitution of the United States; and that the judgement . . . ought to have been for the plaintiffs. The judgement of the State Court must, therefore, be reversed.

Note: The Politics of the *Dartmouth College* Case

The Republican governor and state legislature viewed the old college as a bastion of Federalism tainted by a "royal" charter and wanted to democratize Dartmouth by making it a state institution. Thus, in part, this case must be placed in the context of the decline of New England Federalism and the rise of Jeffersonian Republicanism.

By interpreting a corporate charter to be a contract between the corporation owners or trustees and the state, Chief Justice Marshall laid out the constitutional protections and limitations that corporations would come to rely on for the rest of the nineteenth century and well into the twentieth.

Charles River Bridge Company *v. Warren Bridge Company* 11 Pet. (36 U.S.) 420 (1837)

By acts of 1785 and 1792, the Massachusetts legislature gave the Charles River Bridge Company a seventy-year charter to operate a toll bridge between Charlestown and Boston. In 1828, the legislature chartered the Warren Bridge Company to construct a second bridge, which would revert to the state as a toll-free bridge in six years or less. The proprietors of the Charles River Bridge sought an injunction against the new bridge, arguing that their charter constituted an exclusive contract with the state, that the new bridge charter violated that contract, and that a free bridge would destroy the value of their charter, which had almost thirty more years to run. Although brought to the United States Supreme Court under the contracts clause of the Constitution, this case illustrates how new technologies and new corporations affected nineteenth-century economic and legal development. Put simply, the case asked if a state could create new corporations that might compete with or destroy the vested interests of existing corporations.

Mr. Chief Justice Taney delivered the opinion of the court.

The questions involved in this case are of the gravest character, and the Court have given to them the most anxious and deliberate consideration. The value of the right claimed by the plaintiffs is large in amount; and many persons may no doubt be seriously affected in their pecuniary interests by any decision which the court may pronounce; and the questions which have been raised as to the power of the several states, in relation to the corporations they chartered, are pregnant with important consequences; not only to the individuals who are concerned in the corporate franchises, but to the communities in which they exist. . . .

*   *   *

The plaintiffs in error insist, mainly, upon two grounds: 1st. That by virtue of the grant of 1650, Harvard College was entitled, in perpetuity, to the right of keeping a ferry between Charlestown and Boston; that this right was exclusive; and that the legislature had not the power to establish another ferry on the same line of travel, because it would infringe the rights of the college; and that these rights, upon the erection of the bridge in the place of the ferry, under the charter of 1785, were transferred to, and became vested in "the proprietors of the Charles river bridge;" and . . . by virtue of this transfer of the ferry right, the rights of the bridge company were as exclusive in that line of travel, as the rights of the ferry. 2nd. That independently of the ferry right, the acts of the legislature of Massachusetts of 1785, and 1792 . . . necessarily implied that the legislature would not authorize another bridge, and especially a free one, by the side of this, and placed in the same line of travel, whereby the franchise granted to the "proprietors of the Charles River Bridge" should be rendered of no value; and the plaintiffs in error contend, that the grant of the ferry to the college, and of the charter to the proprietors of the bridge, are both contracts on the part of the state; and that the law authorizing the erection of the Warren bridge in 1828, impairs the obligation of one or both of these contracts.

*   *   *

But upon what ground can the plaintiffs in error contend that the ferry rights of the college have been transferred to the proprietors of the bridge? . . . It is not suggested that there ever was, in point of fact, a deed of conveyance executed by the college to the bridge company. . . . The petition to the legislature, in 1785, on which the charter was granted, does not suggest an assignment, nor any agreement or consent on the part of the college; and the petitioners do not appear to have regarded the wishes of that institution, as by any means necessary to ensure their success. . . . The legislature, in granting the charter . . . acted on the principles assumed by the petitioners. The preamble recites that the bridge "will be of great public utility;" and that is the only reason they assign, for passing the law which incorporated this company. . . . The ferry, with all its privileges was intended to be for ever at an end, and a compensation in money was given in lieu of it. The college acquiesced in this arrangement, and there is proof, in the record, that it was all done with their consent. Can a deed of assignment to the bridge company which would keep alive the ferry rights in their hands, be presumed under such circumstances? . . .

*   *   *

Neither can the extent of the pre-existing ferry right, whatever it may have been, have any influence upon the construction of the written charter for the bridge. It does not, by any means, follow, that because the legislative power in Massachusetts, in 1650, may have granted to a justly favored seminary of learning, the exclusive right of ferry between Boston and Charlestown, they would, in 1785, give the same extensive privilege to another corporation, who were about to erect a bridge in the same place. The fact that such a right was granted to the college, cannot . . . be used to extend the privileges of the bridge company beyond what the words of the charter naturally and legally import . . . and as the franchise of the ferry, and that of the bridge, are different in their nature, and were each established by separate grants, which have no words to connect the privileges of the one with the privileges of the other; there is no rule of legal interpretation, which would authorize the court to associate these grants together, and to infer that any privilege was intended to be given to the bridge company, merely because it had been conferred on the ferry. The charter to the bridge is a written instrument which must speak for itself, and be interpreted by its own terms.

*   *   *

. . . [T]he case most analogous to this, and in which the question came more directly before the court, is . . . *Providence Bank* v. *Billings* [1830]. . . . In that case, it appeared that the legislature of Rhode Island had chartered the bank, in the usual form of such acts of incorporation. The charter contained no stipulation on the part of the state, that it would not impose a tax on the bank, nor any reservation of the right to do so. It was silent on this point. Afterwards, a law was passed, imposing a tax on all banks in the state; and the right to impose this tax was resisted by the Providence Bank, upon the ground, that if the state could impose a tax, it might tax so heavily as to render the franchise of no value, and destroy the institution; that the charter was a contract, and that a power which may in effect destroy the charter is inconsistent with it, and is impliedly renounced by granting it. But the court said that the taxing power was of vital importance, and essential to the existence of government; and that the relinquishment of such a power is never to be assumed. . . . The case now before the court is, in principle, precisely the same. It is a charter from a state. The act of incorporation is silent in relation to the contested power. The argument in favor of the proprietors of the Charles river bridge, is the same, almost in words, with that used by the Providence Bank; that is, that the power claimed by the state, if it exists, may be so used as to destroy the value of the franchise they have granted to the corporation. The argument must receive the same answer. . . .

It may, perhaps, be said, that in the case of The Providence Bank, this court were speaking of the taxing power; which is of vital importance to the very existence of every government. But the object and end of all government is to promote the happiness and prosperity of the community by which it is established; and it can never be assumed, that the government intended to diminish its power of accomplishing the end for which it was created. And in a country like ours, free, active, and enterprising, continually advancing in numbers and wealth; new channels of communication are daily found necessary, both for travel and trade; and are essential to the comfort, convenience, and prosperity of the people. A state ought never to be presumed to surrender this power, because, like the taxing power, the whole community have an interest in preserving it undiminished. And when a corporation alleges, that a state has surrendered for seventy years, its power of improvement and public accommodation, in a great and important line of travel, along which a vast number of citizens must daily pass; the community have a right to insist, in the language of this court above quoted, "that its abandonment ought not to be presumed, in a case, in which the deliberate purpose of the state to abandon it does not appear." The continued existence of a government would be of no great value, if by implications and presumptions, it was disarmed of the powers necessary to accomplish the ends of its creation; and the functions it was designed to perform, transferred to the hands of privileged corporations. . . . No one will question that the interests of the great body of the people of the state, would, in this instance, be affected by the surrender of this great line of travel to a single corporation, with the right to exact toll, and exclude competition for seventy years. While the rights of private property are sacredly guarded, we must not forget that the community also have rights, and that the happiness and well being of every citizen depends on their faithful preservation.

*   *   *

The . . . Warren bridge . . . does not interrupt the passage over the Charles river bridge, nor make the way to it or from it less convenient. None of the faculties or franchises granted to that corporation, have been revoked by the legislature; and its right to take the tolls granted by the charter remains unaltered. In short, all the franchises and rights of property enumerated in the charter, and there mentioned to have been granted to it, remain unimpaired. But its income is destroyed by the Warren bridge; which, being free, draws off the passengers and property which would have gone over it, and renders their franchise of no value. This is the gist of the complaint. For it is not pretended, that the erection of the Warren bridge would have done them any injury, or in any degree affected their right of property; if it had not diminished the amount of their tolls. In order then to entitle themselves to relief, it is necessary to show, that the legislature contracted not to do the act of which they complain; and that they impaired, or in other words, violated that contract by the erection of the Warren bridge.

The inquiry then is, does the charter contain such a contract on the part of the state? Is there any such stipulation to be found in that instrument? It must be admitted on all hands, that there is none—no words that even relate to another bridge, or to the diminution of their tolls, or to the line of travel. If a contract on that subject can be gathered from the charter, it must be by implication. . . . Can such an agreement be implied? The rule of construction before stated is an answer to the question. In charters of this description, no rights are taken from the public, or given to the corporation, beyond those which the words of the charter, by their natural and proper construction, purport to convey. There are no words which import such a contract as the plaintiffs in error contend for, and none can be implied; and the same answer must be given to them that was given by this court to the Providence Bank. The whole community are interested in this inquiry, and they have a right to require that the power of promoting their comfort and convenience, and of advancing the public propriety, by providing safe, convenient, and cheap ways for the transportation of produce, and the purposes of travel, shall not be construed to have been surrendered or diminished by the state; unless it shall appear by plain words, that it was intended to be done.

*   *   *

Indeed, the practice and usage of almost every state in the Union, old enough to have commenced the work of internal improvement, is opposed to the doctrine contended for on the part of the plaintiffs in error. Turnpike roads have been made in succession, on the same line of travel; the later ones interfering materially with the profits of the first. These corporations have, in some instances, been utterly ruined by the introduction of newer and better modes of transportation. . . . In some cases, rail roads have rendered the turnpike roads on the same line of travel so entirely useless, that the franchise of the turnpike corporation is not worth preserving. Yet in none of these cases have the corporation supposed that their privileges were invaded, or any contract violated on the part of the state. . . .

And what would be the fruits of this doctrine of implied contracts on the part of the states, and of property in a line of travel by a corporation, if it should now be sanctioned by this court? To what results would it lead us? If it is to be found in the charter to this bridge, the same process of reasoning must discover it, in the various acts which have been passed, within the last forty years, for turn-pike companies. And what is to be the extent of the privileges of exclusion on the different sides of the road? The counsel who have so ably argued this case, have not attempted to define it by any certain boundaries. How far must the new improvement be distant from the old one? How near may you approach without invading its rights in the privileged line? If this court should establish the principles now contended for, what is to become of the numerous rail roads established on the same line of travel with turnpike companies; and which have rendered the franchises of the turnpike corporations of no value? Let it once be understood that such charters carry with them these implied contracts, and give this unknown and undefined property in a line of traveling; and you will soon find the old turnpike corporations awakening from their sleep, and calling upon this court to put down the improvements which have taken their place. The millions of property which have been invested in rail roads and canals, upon lines of travel which had been before occupied by turnpike corporations, will be put in jeopardy. We shall be thrown back to the improvements of the last century, and obliged to stand still, until the claims of the old turnpike corporations shall be satisfied; and they shall consent to permit these states to avail themselves of the lights of modern science, and to partake of the benefit of those improvements which are now adding to the wealth and prosperity, and the convenience and comfort, of every other part of the civilized world. Nor is this all. This court will find itself compelled to fix, by some arbitrary rule, the width of this new kind of property in a line of travel; for if such a right of property exists, we have no lights to guide us in marking out its extent, unless, indeed, we resort to the old feudal grants, and to the exclusive rights of ferries, by prescription, between towns; and are prepared to decide that when a turnpike road from one town to another, had been made, no rail road or canal, between these two points, could afterwards be established. This court are not prepared to sanction principles which must lead to such results.

Note: The Limited Liability of Stockholders

Vose v. *Grant* (Mass., 1819) and *Spear* v. *Grant* (Mass., 1819) endorsed the principle that stockholders are not personally liable for the actions of a company. Grant owned stock in a bank incorporated by the Massachusetts legislature in 1804. Vose and Spear held notes issued by the bank. An act of 1812 terminated the charters of all banks in the state, but required that the banks remain in operation until 1816, in order to pay off their notes, settle their accounts, and disburse remaining funds among the stockholders.

In 1813, the shareholders divided 75 percent of the capital among themselves, believing that the remaining capital was sufficient to pay off all outstanding notes. This was a miscalculation, and subsequently the bank failed to meet its obligations. Vose and Spear sued Grant, alleging that as a shareholder he was not entitled to his disbursement until all other obligations had been redeemed.

In *Vose,* the court asserted that "the stockholders are not liable to an action on account of a mistaken opinion, or vote, expressed or given at a legal meeting." The court concluded that "every holder of a bank note ought to understand that he holds only the promise of an individual to pay him the sum expressed in it. That individual is a corporation; a creature of the legislature. It may die, or become insolvent, like any other person." In *Spear,* Chief Justice Parker asserted that a bank note "cannot be the basis of an implied promise by the stockholders individually." Otherwise, "a stockholder, wholly innocent and ignorant of the mismanagement, which has brought the bank into discredit, might be ruined by reason of owning a single share in the stock of the corporation." In both cases, the court implied that equity proceedings might force the stockholders to disgorge their disbursements, to be divided among the noteholders. But without evidence of fraud, there was no common-law action "by which any one creditor can compel any one stockholder to pay him the amount of his stock."

Labor in an Industrializing Society

Antebellum labor law focused on two major issues: the right of workers to organize unions and take collective action, and the liability of employers for accidents to workers.

Traditionally, strikes, boycotts, and other collective action by labor organizations were considered illegal conspiracies. Between 1787 and 1842, there were seventeen labor-conspiracy trials. Nine involved shoemakers or bootmakers, known as cordwainers. The *Philadelphia Cordwainers Case* (1806) was the first major American labor-conspiracy trial. The Philadelphia cordwainers struck to protest the rise of retail shoe stores and mass-produced footwear. In 1809, there was a similar strike and conspiracy trial in New York. Both strikes were broken, the unions destroyed, and the labor organizers convicted and fined.

Safety was also important to workers. Industrialization, with its steamboats, railroads, and factories, was extremely hazardous. Before the industrial revolution, accidents were fewer and the common law assumed that an employer would provide a safe workplace and, "at his peril, employ servants who are skillful and careful."[6] These old common-law ideas made both greater sense and no sense at all in the emerging industrial society. They made greater sense because the workplace was more dangerous. In large factories or on railroads and steamboats, workers no longer knew many of their fellow employees and could not judge if they were careful. Many workers did not even know their ultimate employer, and they increasingly had less input into the safety of their workplace. Thus holding the employer liable for all injuries made sense from the workers' perspective.

Employers had a different view. They could no longer supervise all their workers or the company property at any given time. No one from management could ride on every train, making sure the crew followed all safety rules. Thus owners preferred rules limiting their liability for industrial accidents. In what was perhaps the most instrumental decision in his career, Chief Justice Shaw furthered the interests of industrialists in the Bay State, in holding that a railroad was not liable for the injuries to an engineer caused by a negligent "fellow servant" of the corporation. The result was that workers would be unable to recover for on-the-job injuries. Thus the cost of industrial injuries would be born by those least able to afford it—the workers and their families. Not until the adoption of workers' compensation schemes in the twentieth century would this change.

Note: The Traditional Theory of Labor Conspiracy

In *People* v. *Fisher* (1835), the New York Supreme Court upheld the indictment of journeyman bootmakers for conspiracy to prevent others from working and for "unlawfully and unjustly" intending to extort "large and exorbitant sums" from employers. The indictment noted that a shoemaker named Pennock, who had worked for a lower wage, was fired when other journeymen refused to work for anyone who employed Pennock. The court found that a "conspiracy" to raise wages would undermine the social and economic fabric of the country:

> It is important to the best interests of society that the price of labor be left to regulate itself, or rather be limited by the demand for it. Combinations and confederacies to enhance or reduce the prices of labor, or of any articles of trade or commerce, are injurious. They may be oppressive, by compelling the public to give more for an article of necessity or of convenience than it is worth; or on the other hand, of compelling the labor of the mechanic for less than its value. Without . . . improper interference . . . the price of labor or the wages of mechanics will be regulated by the demand for the manufactured article, and the value of that which is paid for it; but the right does not exist either to enhance the price of the article, or the wages of the mechanic, by any forced and artificial means. The man who owns an article of trade or commerce is not obliged to sell it for any particular price, nor is the mechanic, obliged by law to labor for any particular price. He may say that he will not make coarse boots for less than one dollar per pair, *but he has no right to say that no other mechanic shall make them for less*. The cloth merchant may say that he will not sell his goods for less than so much per yard, but has no right to say that any other merchant shall not sell for a less price. . . . All combinations therefore to effect such an object are injurious, not only to the individual particularly oppressed, but to the public at large.

In this case, the court found that "an industrious man was driven out of employment by the unlawful measures pursued by the defendants," which injured the community "by diminishing the quantity of productive labor, and of internal trade." The court continued:

> Competition is the life of trade. If the defendants cannot make coarse boots for less than one dollar per pair, let them refuse to do so; but let them not directly or indirectly undertake to say that others shall not do the work for a less price. It may be that Pennock, from greater industry or greater skill, made more profit by making boots at seventy-five cents per pair than the defendants at a dollar. He had a right to work for what he pleased. His employer had a right to employ him for such price as they could agree upon. The interference of the defendants was unlawful; its tendency is not only to individual oppression, but to public inconvenience and embarrassment."

Commonwealth v. *Hunt*
4 Met. (45 Mass.) 111 (1842)

The defendants, members of the Boston Journeymen Bootmakers' Society, refused to work for any employer who hired nonunion journeymen. When their employer, Isaac Wait, hired Jeremiah Horne, a nonunion journeyman, the defendants threatened to quit. Unwilling to lose all his employees, Wait fired Horne. District Attorney Samuel D. Parker, a Whig known for his opposition to labor organizers, abolitionists, and other reformers, prosecuted the union members for conspiracy. Robert Rantoul, a leading Jacksonian Democrat, defended Hunt, the president of the union. A jury of "gentlemen" took only twenty minutes to convict the workers, but the Massachusetts Supreme Judicial Court reversed the conviction.

[Chief Justice Shaw] . . . [W]e are of the opinion, that as a general description, though perhaps not a precise and accurate definition, a conspiracy must be a combination of two or more persons, by some concerted action, to accomplish some criminal or unlawful purpose, or to accomplish some purpose, not in itself criminal or unlawful, by criminal or unlawful means. . . .

* * *

The first count set forth, that the defendants, with diverse others unknown, on the day and at the place named, being workmen, and journeymen, in the art and occupation of bootmakers, unlawfully, perniciously and deceitfully designing and intending to continue, keep up, form, and unite themselves, into an unlawful club, society and combination, and make unlawful by-laws, rules and orders among themselves, and thereby govern themselves and other workmen, in the said art, and unlawfully and unjustly to extort great sums of money by means thereof, did unlawfully assemble and meet together, and being so assembled, did unjustly and corruptly conspire, combine, confederate and agree together, that none of them should thereafter, and that none of them would, work for any master or person whatsoever, in the said art, mystery and occupation, who should employ any workman or journeyman, or other person, in the said art, who was not a member of said club, society or combination, after notice given him to discharge such workman, from the employ of such master; to the great damage and oppression, &c.

* * *

Stripped then of these introductory recitals and alleged injurious consequencs, and of the qualifying epithets attached to the facts, the averment is this: that the defendants and others formed themselves into a society, and agreed not to work for any person, who should employ any journeyman or other person, not a member of such society. . . .

The manifest intent of the association is, to induce all those engaged in the same occupation to become members of it. Such a purpose is not unlawful. It would give them a power which might be exerted for useful and honorable purposes, or for dangerous and pernicious ones. If the latter were the real and actual object, and susceptible of proof, it should have been specially charged. Such an association might be used to afford each other assistance in times of poverty, sickness and distress; or to raise their intellectual, moral and social condition; or to make improvement in their art; or for other proper purposes. Or the association might be designed for purposes of oppression and injustice. But in order to charge all those, who become members of an association, with the guilt of a criminal conspiracy, it must be averred and proved that the actual, if not the avowed object of the association, was criminal. . . .

Nor can we perceive that the objects of this association, whatever they may have been were to be attained by criminal means. The means which they proposed to employ, as averred in this count, and which, as we are now to presume, were established by the proof, were, that they would not work for a person, who, after due notice, should employ a journeyman not a member of their society. Supposing the object of the association to be laudable and lawful, or at least not unlawful, are these means criminal? The case supposes that these persons are not bound by contract, but free to work for whom they please, or not to work, if they so prefer. In this state of things, we cannot perceive, that it is criminal for men to agree together to exercise their own acknowledged rights. . . . One way to test this is, to consider the effect of such an agreement, where the object of the association is acknowledged on all hands to be a laudable one. Suppose a class of workmen, impressed with the manifold evils of intemperance, should agree with each other not to work in a shop with any one who used it, or not to work for an employer, who should, after notice, employ a journeyman who habitually used it. The consequences might be the same. A workman, who should still persist in the use of ardent spirit, would find it more difficult to get employment; a master employing such an one might, at times, experience inconvenience in his work, in losing the services of a skilful but intemperate workman. Still . . . that as the object would be lawful, and the means not unlawful, such an agreement could not be pronounced a criminal conspiracy.

From this count in the indictment, we do not understand that the agreement was, that the defendants would refuse to work for an employer, to whom they were bound by contract for a certain time, in violation of that contract; nor that they would insist that an employer should discharge a workman engaged by contract for a certain time, in violation of such contract. It is perfectly consistent with every thing stated in this count, that the effect of the agreement was, that when they were free to act, they would not engage with an employer, or continue in his employment, if such employer, when free to act, should engage with a workman, or continue a workman in his employment, not a member of the association. If a large number of men . . . should combine together to violate their contract, and quit their employment together, it would present a very different question. Suppose a farmer, employing a large number of men, engaged for the year, at fair monthly wages, and suppose that just at the moment that his crops were ready to harvest, they should all combine to quit his service, unless he would advance their wages, at a time when other laborers could not be obtained. It would surely be a conspiracy to do an unlawful act, though of such a character, that if done by an individual, it would lay the foundation of a civil action only, and not of a criminal prosecution. It would be a case very different from that stated in this court.

The second count . . . alleges that the defendants . . . did assemble, conspire, confederate and agree together, not to work for any master of person who should employ any workman not being a member of . . . the Boston Journeymen Bootmaker's Society . . . and that by means of said conspiracy they did compel one Isaac B. Wait, a master cordwainer, to turn out of his employ one Jeremiah Horne, a journeyman boot-maker, &c. in evil example, &c. So far as the averment of a conspiracy is concerned, all the remarks made in reference to the first count are equally applicable to this. It is simply an averment of an agreement amongst themselves not to work for a person, who should employ any person not a member of a certain association. It sets forth no illegal or criminal purpose to be accomplished, nor any illegal or criminal means to be adopted for the accomplishment of any purpose. It was an agreement, as to the manner in which they would exercise an acknowledged right to contract with others for their labor. It does not aver a conspiracy or even an intention to raise their wages; and it appears by the bill of exceptions, that the case was not put upon the footing of a conspiracy to raise their wages. Such an agreement, as set forth in this count, would be perfectly justifiable. . . .

*   *   *

The third count, reciting a wicked and unlawful intent to impoverish one Jeremiah Horne . . . charges the defendants . . . with an unlawful conspiracy, by wrongful and indirect means, to impoverish said Horne and to deprive and hinder him, from his said art and trade and getting his support thereby, and that, in pursuance of said unlawful combination, they did . . . impoverish him.

If the fact of depriving Jeremiah Horne of the profits of his business, by whatever means it might be done, would be unlawful and criminal, a combination to compass that object would be an unlawful conspiracy, and it would be unnecessary to state the means. . . .

Suppose a baker in a small village had the exclusive custom of his neighborhood, and was making large profits by the sale of his bread. Supposing a number of those neighbors, believing the price of his bread too high, should propose to him to reduce his prices, or if he did not, that they would introduce another baker; and on his refusal, such other baker should, under their encouragement, set up a rival establishment, and sell his bread at lower prices; the effect would be to diminish the profit of the former baker, and to the same extent to impoverish him. And it might be said and proved, that the purpose of the associates was to diminish his profits, and thus impoverish him, though the ultimate and laudable object of the combination was to reduce the cost of bread to themselves and their neighbors. The same thing may be said of all competition in every branch of trade and industry; and yet it is through that competition, that the best interests of trade and industry are promoted. It is scarcely necessary to allude to the familiar instances of opposition lines of conveyance, rival hotels, and the thousand other instances, where each strives to gain custom to himself, by ingenious improvements, by increased industry, and by all the means by which he may lessen the price of commodities, and thereby diminish the profits of others.

We think, therefore, that associations may be entered into, the object of which is to adopt measures that may have a tendency to impoverish another, that is, to diminish his gains and profits, and yet so far from being criminal or unlawful, the object may be highly meritorious and public spirited. The legality of such an association will therefore depend upon the means to be used for its accomplishment. If it is to be carried into effect by fair or honorable and lawful means, it is, to say the least, innocent; if by falsehood or force, it may be stamped with the character of conspiracy. . . .

*   *   *

One case was cited, which was supposed to be much in point, and which is certainly deserving of great respect. The People v. Fisher. . . . was a conspiracy by journeymen to raise their wages, and it was decided to be a violation of the statutes, making it criminal to commit any act injurious to trade or commerce. It has, therefore, an indirect application only to the present case.

*   *   *

. . . [L]ooking solely at the indictment, disregarding the qualifying epithets, recitals and immaterial allegations, and confining ourselves to facts so averred as to be capable of being traversed and put in issue, we cannot perceive that it charges a criminal conspiracy punishable by law. The exceptions must, therefore, be sustained, and the judgment arrested.

Note: The Fellow Servant Rule

The fellow servant rule precluded a worker from suing an employer for job-related injuries caused by the negligence of another worker, or "fellow servant." Instead, the injured worker was forced to sue the negligent fellow servant, who in all probability was judgment proof. The rule was first announced in England, in *Priestly* v. *Fowler* (1837). Four years later, a divided South Carolina Supreme Court adopted the rule in *Murray* v. *South Carolina Rail Road* (1841), with the most distinguished member of the court, John Belton O'Neall, dissenting. Chief Justice Lemuel Shaw's enthusiastic embrace of the rule three years later paved the way for its spread to most states.

Farwell v. *The Boston and Worcester Railroad Co.*
4 Met. (45 Mass.) 49 (1842)

Farwell was an engineer for the Boston and Worcester Railroad. In 1837, his train derailed because a switchman—another employee, or fellow servant—failed to correctly move a track. In the accident, "the wheels of one of said cars passed over the right hand of the plaintiff, crushing and destroying the same."

Shaw, C. J. This is an action of new impression in our courts, and involves a principle of great importance. It presents a case, where two persons are in the service and employment of one company, whose business it is to construct and maintain a rail road, and to employ their trains of cars to carry persons and merchandise for hire. They are appointed and employed by the same company to perform separate duties and services, all tending to the accomplishment of one and the same purpose—that of the safe and rapid transmission of the trains; . . . The question is, whether, for damages sustained by one of the persons so employed, by means of the carelessness and negligence of another, the party injured has a remedy against the common employer. It is an argument against such an action, though certainly not a decisive one, that no such action has before been maintained.

It is laid down by Blackstone, that if a servant, by his negligence, does any damage to a stranger, the master shall be answerable for his neglect. But the damage must be done while he is actually employed in the master's service; otherwise, the servant shall answer for his own misbehavior. . . . This rule is obviously founded on the great principle of social duty, that every man, in the management of his own affairs, whether by himself or by his agents or servants, shall so conduct them as not to injure another; and if he does not, and another thereby sustains damage, he shall answer for it. If done by a servant, in the course of his employment, and acting within the scope of his authority, it is considered, in contemplation of law, so far the act of the master, that the latter shall be answerable *civiliter*. . . . The maxim *respondeat superior* is adopted in that case, from general considerations of policy and security.

But this does not apply to the case of a servant bringing his action against his own employer to recover damages for an injury arising in the course of that employment, where all such risks and perils as the employer and the servant respectively intend to assume and bear may be regulated by the express or implied contract between them, and which, in contemplation of law, must be presumed to be thus regulated.

The same view seems to have been taken by the learned counsel for the plaintiff in the argument; and it was conceded, that the claim could not be placed on the principle indicated by the maxim *respondeat superior*, which binds the master to indemnify a stranger for the damage caused by the careless, negligent or unskilful act of his servant in the conduct of his affairs. The claim, therefore, is placed, and must be maintained . . . on the ground of contract. . . . It would be an implied promise, arising from the duty of the master to be responsible to each person employed by him, in the conduct of every branch of business, where two or more persons are employed, to pay for all damage occasioned by the negligence of every other person employed in the same service. If such a duty were established by law—like that of a common carrier, to stand to all losses of goods not caused by the act of God or of a public enemy . . . it would be a rule of frequent and familiar occurrence, and its existence and application with all its qualifications and restrictions, would be settled by judicial precedents. But we are of opinion that no such rule has been established, and the authorities, as far as they go, are opposed to the principle. *Priestly* v. *Fowler, Murray* v. *South Carolina Rail Road Company*. The general rule, resulting from considerations as well of justice as of policy, is that he who engages in the employment of another for the performance of specified duties and services, for compensation, takes upon himself the natural and ordinary risks and perils incident to the performance of such services, and in legal presumption, the compensation is adjusted accordingly. And we are not aware of any principle which should except the perils arising from the carelessness and negligence of those who are in the same employment. These are perils which the servant is as likely to know, and against which he can as effectually guard, as the master. They are perils incident to the service, and which can be as distinctly foreseen and provided for in the rate of compensation as any others. To say that the master shall be responsible because the damage is caused by his agents, is assuming the very point which remains to be proved. They are his agents to some extent, and for some purposes; but whether he is responsible, in a particular case, for their negligence, is not decided by the single fact that they are, for some purposes, his agents. . . .

*   *   *

[Here Shaw examined the legal obligations of common carriers and innkeepers to protect freight, passengers, and guests, concluding they are held] . . . to the strictest responsibility for care, vigilance, and skill, on the part of themselves and all persons employed by them, and they are paid accordingly. The rule is founded on the expediency of throwing the risk upon those who can best guard against it.

We are of opinion that these considerations apply strongly to the case in question. Where several persons are employed in the conduct of one common enterprise or undertaking, and the safety of each depends much on the care and skill with which each other shall perform his appropriate duty, each is an observer of the conduct of the others, can give notice of any misconduct, incapacity or neglect of duty, and leave the service, if the common employer will not take such precautions, and employ such agents as the safety of the whole party may require. By these means, the safety of each will be much more effectually secured, than could be done by a resort to the common employer for indemnity in case of loss by the negligence of each other. Regarding it in this light, it is the ordinary case of one sustaining an injury in the course of his own employment, in which he must bear the loss himself, or seek his remedy, if he have any, against the actual wrong-doer.

In applying these principles to the present case, it appears that the plaintiff was employed by the defendants as an engineer, at the rate of wages usually paid in that employment, being a higher rate than the plaintiff had before received as a machinist. It was a voluntary undertaking on his part, with a full knowledge of the risks incident to the employment; and the loss was sustained by means of an ordinary casualty, caused by the negligence of another servant of the company. Under these circumstances, the loss must be deemed to be the result of a pure accident, like those to which all men, in all employments, and at all times, are more or less exposed; and like similar losses from accidental causes, it must rest where it first fell, unless the plaintiff has a remedy against the person actually in default; of which we give no opinion.

It was strongly pressed in the argument, that although this might be so, where two or more servants are employed in the same department of duty, where each can exert some influence over the conduct of the other, and thus to some extent provide for his own security; yet that it could not apply where two or more are employed in different departments of duty, at a distance from each other, and where one in no degree control or influence the conduct of another. But we think this is founded upon a supposed distinction, on which it would be extremely difficult to establish a practical rule. When the object to be accomplished is one and the same, when the employers are the same, and the several persons employed derive their authority and their compensation from the same source, it would be extremely difficult to distinguish, what constitutes one department and what a distinct department of duty. . . . If it were made to depend upon the nearness or distance of the persons from each other, the question would immediately arise, how near or how distant must they be, to be in the same or different departments. In a blacksmith's shop, persons working in the same building, at different fires, may be quite independent of each other, though only a few feet distant. In a ropewalk, several may be at work on the same piece of cordage, at the same time, at many hundred feet distant from each other, and beyond the reach of sight and voice, and yet acting together.

Besides, it appears to us, that the argument rests upon an assumed principle of responsibility which does not exist. The master . . . is not exempt from liability, because the servant has better means of providing for his safety, when he is employed in immediate connexion with those from whose negligence he might suffer; but because the *implied contract* of the master does not extend to indemnify the servant against the negligence of any one but himself; and he is not liable in tort, as for the negligence of his servant, because the person suffering does not stand towards him in the relation of a stranger, but is one whose rights are regulated by contract express or implied. The exemption of the master, therefore, from liability for the negligence of a fellow servant, does not depend exclusively upon the consideration, that the servant has better means to provide for his own safety, but upon other grounds. Hence the separation of the employment into different departments cannot create that liability, when it does not arise from express or implied contract, or from a responsibility created by law to third persons, and strangers, for the negligence of a servant.

Note: Chief Justice Shaw and Labor

Since the fellow servant rule involved personal injury, it might easily be categorized as a subspecies of tort law. Or, since the rule, as laid out by Chief Justice Shaw, also involved labor contracts, it might be considered a development in contract law. However, its most dramatic effect was on American workers injured on the job, and hence was a development in labor law. Embedded in Shaw's opinion is also the concept of "assumption of risk" applied to workers who take dangerous jobs.

Shaw's biographer, historian Leonard W. Levy, described *Commonwealth* v. *Hunt* as "the Magna Charta of American trade-unionism, for it removed the stigma of criminality from labor organizations."[7] Like the Magna Charta, however, the decision had little actual affect on the lot of working people in America. Shortly after the Civil War, lawyers, judges, and employers found other methods, most notably the labor injunction, to stifle labor organizations. Scholars have often wondered why in the same term of the Supreme Judicial Court, Shaw wrote the apparently prolabor decision in *Commonwealth* v. *Hunt*, and the apparently antilabor decision in *Farwell* v. *Boston and Worcester Railroad Co.* Can the two decisions be reconciled? Consider the kind of positive collective action that Shaw postulates in *Hunt*. Is such action similar to what he expects from workers in *Farwell*?

Note: Fellow Servants and Slaves

Most southern states refused to apply the fellow servant rule to slaves. In *Louisville and Nashville Railroad Co.* v. *Yandell* (1856), the Kentucky court wrote: "Whatever may be the wisdom and policy of this rule of law, when applied to free persons . . . we do not hesitate to reject its application to the present case, in which a slave was an employee." The court found that a slave could not be a fellow servant because

> [a] slave may not, with impunity, remind and urge a free white person, who is a co-employee, to a discharge of his duties, or reprimand him for his carelessness and neglect; nor may he, with impunity, desert his post at discretion when danger is impending, nor quit his employment on account of the unskillfulness, bad management, inattention, or neglect of others of the crew. Whatever may be the danger by reason of any of these causes, he must stand to his post, though destruction of life or limb may never be so imminent. He is fettered by the stern bonds of slavery—necessity is upon him, and he must hold on to his employment. Slaves, to be sure, are rational beings but without the power of obeying, at pleasure, the dictates of their reason and judgment.

Property

In describing traditional English property law, Blackstone asserted that "occupancy," which was "the taking possession of those things, which before belonged to nobody," was "the true ground and foundation of all property." This primitive concept of property, Blackstone noted, was modified by such legal actions as contract, forfeiture, bankruptcy, succession, marriage, and, most important of all, the royal prerogative, which gave the monarch title to all land "found without any owner."[8]

By the time of the American Revolution, "real property law had become the victim of too many able minds refining too many distinctions for too long. It was of almost incredible complexity; cynics like Oliver Cromwell called it an ungodly jumble. It had become a mystery, unintelligible except to experts."[9] This nearly incomprehensible system of land tenure and ownership—based on feudal tenancies, conveyances, deeds, the doctrine of estates, and common-law precedents—supported the social reality that most land in England was in the hands of a very small number of people and that often this land was not actually owned by any single individual, but was part of an "estate." The concept of an estate was described in the sixteenth century in *Walsingham's Case*:

> The land itself is one thing and the estate in land is another thing: for an estate in the land is a time in the land, or land for a time: and there are diversities of estates, which are no more than diversities of time; for he who hath a fee simple in the land has a time in the land without end, or land for a time without end; and he who has land in tail has a time in land, or the land for a time, as he has issue of his body; and he who has an estate in land for life has no time in it longer than his own life; and so of one who has an estate in land for the life of another, or for years.[10]

Unlike England, America lacked a feudal history and had an abundance of "land found without owner," since white Americans rarely recognized that Native Americans occupied and owned land. Furthermore, after 1776 Americans had no king to claim a prerogative right. Thus in the United States, important aspects of English property law was irrelevant. What America needed was a dynamic and flexible property law. To accommodate the American experience, some changes in property law developed in the colonial period. The most dramatic change was the enslavement of human beings and their conversion to chattel or real estate. In the wake of the Revolution, most of the states dispensed with entail for land ownership and primogeniture for intestate succession. One of the few restrictions on the land to survive the Revolution was dower rights for widows. Nineteenth-century courts and legislatures facilitated the growth of the economy by the abandonment of useless and counterproductive common-law rules. The rejection of implied monopolies, as described in the *Charles River Bridge Company* case, shows how antebellum judges favored dynamic economic growth over vested property rights. The proliferation of eminent domain laws, and their support by courts, facilitated the taking of private property for the construction of mill dams, roads, canals, and railroads. By mid-century, a "man's home" was no longer "his castle" if it stood along the route of a proposed railroad. The circumstances of the West especially affected water and mineral law, as well as the law of real property. Yet, despite these changes, migrating Americans usually carried with them eastern notions of property and private ownership.

Van Ness v. *Pacard*
2 Pet. (27 U.S.) 137 (1829)

Pacard erected a building on land rented from Van Ness. Before the lease expired, Pacard removed the building. Van Ness sued for trespass, under the common-law rule that structures built on leased land became part of that land, and could not be removed by the renter when the lease expired. In upholding a lower court decision in favor of Pacard, Justice Joseph Story explained that much of English property law was often irrelevant in America.

The general rule of the common law certainly is, that whatever is once annexed to the freehold becomes part of it, and cannot afterwards be removed, except by him who is entitled to the inheritance. . . .

The common law of England is not to be taken in all respects to be that of America. Our ancestors brought with them its general principles, and claimed it as their birthright; but they brought with them and adopted only that portion which was applicable to their situation. There could be little or no reason for doubting, that the general doctrine as to things annexed to the freehold, so far as it respects heirs and executors, was adopted by them. . . . But, between landlord and tenant, it is not so clear that the rigid rule of the common law, . . . was so applicable to their situation, as to give rise to necessary presumption in its favour. The country was a wilderness, and the universal policy was to procure its cultivation and improvement. The owner of the soil, as well as the public, had every motive to encourage the tenant to devote himself to agriculture, and to favour any erections which should aid this result; yet, in the comparative poverty of the country, what tenant could afford to erect fixtures of much expense or value, if he was to lose his whole interest therein by the very act of erection? His cabin or log-hut, however necessary for any improvement of the soil would cease to be his the moment it was finished. It might, therefore deserve consideration, whether, in case the doctrine were not previously adopted in a state by some authoritative practice of adjudication, it ought to be assumed by this Court as part of the jurisprudence of such state, upon the mere footing of its existence to the common law.

Note: Eminent Domain

Eminent domain allows the taking of land, without the consent of the owner, by the government or by a private party, under certain circumstances. This process requires a formal condemnation of property, followed by a payment for the value of the property. Eminent domain was vital to the development of roads, railroads, and factories in the nineteenth century.

Parham v. *The Justices of Decatur County*
9 Ga. 341 (1851)

Parham objected to the taking of his land for the construction of a road. This case allowed Judge Eugenius Nisbet of the Georgia Supreme Court to explain the theory behind eminent domain.

. . . It is very clear, that the Legislature may take the property of a citizen for purposes of public necessity or public utility. All grants of land are in subordination to the eminent domain which remains in the State; and from the necessities of the social compact, they are subject to this condition. The sovereign authority of the States, acting through the Legislature, is bound to protect and defend the States, and to promote the public happiness and prosperity of the people; and the Legislature is to judge when the public necessity or public utility requires the appropriation of the property of the citizen. I need not enlarge on these propositions—they are the law of this Court, more than once promulgated. Nor do we deny, that a highway is a work of public utility. It is necessary to commerce and intercourse. Nothing can be more conducive to the social well-being and commercial prosperity of a State, than roads. It were pagan and aboriginal not to have them. Our doctrine farther is, however, that the property of the citizen cannot be taken for any purpose of public utility or convenience, unless the law which appropriates it, makes provision for a just compensation to the proprietor. This is true at Common Law . . . recognized and affirmed by *Magna Charta*, and it is true by the special ordainment of the Constitution of the United States.

*   *   *

The general doctrine, that private property cannot be taken for public use, without compensation, has been more than once held here. The question, it is true, has come before us, except in one instance, in the construction of rail road charters, or bridge or ferry grants. The principle is the same in this case. Whether the property of a citizen can be taken at all or not, depends upon the use or necessity which requires it. The principle upon which the right of way for a rail road has been sustained is, that the rail road is of public utility, and, therefore, when property is taken for that object, it is taken for public use. So, in the case of a public road, the ground of the rightful assumption is public use. If, in the former case, compensation must be made, as we have held, so in the latter case. I see no difference, so far as the principle is concerned, between a common highway and a rail road. . . .

Note: *Barron* v. *Baltimore,* 7 Pet. 243 (1833)

Not all property destroyed by industrial development was taken through eminent domain. When public works improvements lowered the water level of the Baltimore harbor, ships could no longer reach Barron's wharf, leaving it "of little or no value." Barron sued the city for this "taking" of his property, and a county court awarded him $4,500. The Maryland Court of Appeals reversed this judgment because the state constitution had no just compensation provision. On appeal to the United States Supreme Court, Barron argued that he was entitled to compensation under the Fifth Amendment to the Constitution.

In dismissing the case for want of jurisdiction, Chief Justice Marshall concluded that "the fifth amendment must be understood as restraining the power of the general government, not as applicable to the States." Marshall asserted that the state constitutions were designed to protect the rights and liberties of the people from state action.

Barron illustrates the willingness of states to ignore vested interests in promoting economic development and the reluctance of the Supreme Court to interfere with the states on this issue. *Barron* is most important, however, for ensuring that the Bill of

Rights would not be applicable to the states before the Civil War. Some abolitionists and Republicans argued that *Barron* was incorrectly decided and that the Bill of Rights did limit state action. This minority position came into its own after the Civil War began, and the Fourteenth Amendment was written in part to apply the Bill of Rights to the states. Not until *Gitlow* v. *New York* (1925), however, would the Supreme Court begin to accept this result of the Civil War.

JOSEPH ANGELL
A Treatise on the Law of Watercourses
1854

While the steam engine revolutionized transportation, an expanded use of dams and water power changed the nature of manufacturing. The following selection from Joseph Angell's treatise illustrates the important connection between eminent domain law and water law in the nineteenth century.

Sec. 466.   As a general rule, it must undoubtedly rest in the discretion and wisdom of the legislature to determine when public uses require the assumption and appropriation of private property; although the question is one not without embarrassment, as the line of demarcation between a use that is public, and one that is strictly private, is not to be drawn without much consideration. It has been said by a learned Judge [Chief Justice Shaw], that "it is difficult, perhaps impossible, to lay down any general rule, that would precisely define the power of the government, in the exercise of the acknowledged right of eminent domain; it must be large and liberal, so as to meet the public exigencies, and it must be so limited and restrained, as to secure effectually the rights of the citizen; and it must depend, in some instances, upon the nature of the exigencies as they arise, and the circumstances of particular cases." One thing is incontrovertible, and that is, that the necessities of the public for the use to which the property is to be appropriated must exist as *the basis* upon which the right is founded. Where private property, therefore, is wanted merely for *ornamental* purposes, this right cannot be exercised, as the purpose must be *useful*.

Sec. 467.   Although it rests with the wisdom of the legislature to determine what is a "public use," and also the necessity for taking the property of an individual for that purpose; yet the right of eminent domain does not authorize the government, even for a full compensation, *to take the property of one citizen and transfer it to another*, when the public is not interested in the transfer. The possession and exertion of such a power would be incompatible with the nature and very object of all government; for, it being admitted, that a chief end for which government is instituted, is, that every man may enjoy his own; it follows, necessarily, that the rightful exercise of a power by the government of taking arbitrarily from any man what is his own, for the purpose of giving it to another, would subvert the very foundation principle upon which the government was organized. . . . [New York's] Chief Justice Savage . . . says, that, "the constitution, by authorizing appropriation of private property to public use, impliedly declares, that for any other use, private property shall not be taken from one and applied to the private use of another." It is in violation, he says, of natural right; and if it is not in violation of the *letter* of the constitution, it is of its spirit. . . . As has been declared by a learned Judge in Virginia, "Liberty itself consists essentially, as well as in the security of private property, as of the persons of individuals; and this security of private property is one of the primary objects of civil government, which our ancestors, in framing our Constitution, intended to secure to themselves and their posterity, effectually, and forever."

*   *   *

Sec. 476.   The constitutionality of the legislative power of taking private property depends upon the provision for a just indemnity; so that a statute incorporating a company to take private property without the consent of the owner, to promote any work for the public benefit, and making *no* provision for his indemnity, is unconstitutional and void. Thus the erection of a dam across a navigable water by an individual, under the authority of a statute of New Jersey, providing no remedy to the owner of a meadow overflowed by means of the dam, was held to be an injury for which the owner had his action for damages.

*   *   *

Sec. 479.   The Supreme Court of the State of New York, . . . say: "The Legislature of this State, it is believed, has never exercised the right of eminent domain in favor of mills of any kind. . . ." But nothing can be more clear, than that legislative acts of this character and for such object essentially promote the good of a community in its progress from a wilderness to cultivation, as was the case with the North American Colonies . . . when . . . the support of grist-mills and saw-mills was a measure of even vital necessity; and they were consequently encouraged in every possible manner. Mill-sites were, in some instances, appropriated from common lands, by the votes of their proprietors; and mills were often exempted from taxation. . . . In many instances they were erected in parts of the country still covered by the primitive forests, and where the extent of the flowing, and even the owners of the lands, were unknown. Even at the present day in . . . Georgia, the legislature have provided, that whoever will build a grist-mill on land so circumstanced, shall be entitled to the grant of an extensive tract of land, and whoever will build a saw-mill, to a grant of a much more extensive tract.

*   *   *

Sec. 484.   The effect of the statutes authorizing the flowing of land not belonging to the mill-owner, and providing a mode for estimating and recovering compensation therefor, take away . . . the right which the land-owner *prima facie* possesses of removing from his land a nuisance. For the same reason the only judicial remedy of the land-owner is the one prescribed by the statute, which is substituted for the action on the case. This was so expressly held in Massachusetts, . . . [that] the acts authorizing flowing, made expressly to relieve mill-owners from the difficulties and disputes to which they were before subject . . . [took] away the action at Common Law; an action which might be renewed for every new injury, and so harass the owner of a mill with continual lawsuits. . . .

Note: Water Rights in the East

Like England, the eastern United States was blessed with abundant water resources, which allowed for industrialization through the building of mills and dams. The problem of mill dams flooding adjacent lands was dealt with through mill dam acts, eminent domain law, and judicially determined compensation to landowners. Mills competing for the same water raised a more complex problem. The placement of water wheels by an upstream mill might flood out a mill downstream. Similarly, if a mill downstream raised the height of its dam, it might force water to back up into a mill farther upstream and disrupt the water's flow.

Cary v. Daniels
8 Met. (Mass.) 466 (1844)

In 1837, James Wilson owned two mills, known as the upper mill and lower mill, and a dam, known as the middle dam. The middle dam was conveniently located so that when water behind it backed up into the water wheels of the upper mill, the operators of that mill could easily walk to the middle dam and open the waste gate, to lower the water level between the two mills and prevent the interference with the upper mill. In 1837, Wilson sold the upper mill to Cary. Later that year, a flood destroyed the middle dam. Daniels bought the lower mill in 1838 and built a new, larger dam farther downstream. This dam was too far from Cary's mill to allow him to easily open the waste gates when the water began to back up. Furthermore, the new dam was higher and thus more frequently caused the river to back up into Cary's mill, disrupting its operation. Cary sued Daniels, arguing that he had a right to the unobstructed use of his mill, and that Daniels was obligated to allow him to open the new dam when necessary for the operation of his own mill. Chief Justice Shaw delivered the opinion of the court.

. . . The complaint is, that the lower dam is so raised as to set back the water and obstruct the free use of the plaintiff's water wheels.

Two questions were made at the trial. 1. Whether, as contended for by the plaintiff, he is not entitled, as against the defendant, to a free and unobstructed use of the stream below his mill, including a right to have the water run off as low as it would run in its natural bed. . . .

On the first point, we are of opinion that the claim cannot be maintained.

It is agreed on all hands, that the owner of a parcel of land, through which a stream of water flows, has a right to the use and enjoyment of the benefits to be derived therefrom, as it passes through his own land; but as this right is common to all through whose lands it flows, it follows that no one can wholly destroy or divert it; so as to prevent the water from coming to the proprietor below; nor can a lower proprietor wholly obstruct it, so as to throw it back upon the mills or lands of the proprietor above. We, of course, now speak of rights at common law, independent of any modification thereof by statute. But one of the beneficial uses of a watercourse, and in this country one of the most important, is its application to the working of mills and machinery; a use profitable to the owner, and beneficial to the public. It is therefore held, that each proprietor is entitled to such use of the stream, so far as it is reasonable, conformable to the usages and wants of the community, and having regard to the progress of improvement in hydraulic works, and not inconsistent with a like reasonable use by the other proprietors of land, on the same stream, above and below. This last limitation of the right must be taken with one qualification, growing out of the nature of the case. The usefulness of water for mill purposes depends as well on its fall as its volume. But the fall depends upon the grade of the land over which it runs. The descent may be rapid, in which case there may be fall enough for mill sites at short distances; or the descent may be so gradual as only to admit of mills at considerable distances. In the latter case, the erection of a mill on one proprietor's land may raise and set the water back to such a distance as to prevent the proprietor above from having sufficient fall to erect a mill on his land. It seems to follow, as a necessary consequence from these principles, that in such case, the proprietor who first erects his dam for such a purpose has a right to maintain it, as against the proprietors above and below; and to this extent, prior occupancy gives a prior title to such use. It is a profitable, beneficial, and reasonable use, and therefore one which he has a right to make. If it necessarily occupy so much of the fall as to prevent the proprietor above from placing a dam and mill on his land, it is *damnum absque injuria* [loss without injury]. For the same reason, the proprietor below cannot erect a dam in such a manner as to raise the water and obstruct the wheels of the first occupant. He had an equal right with the proprietor below to a reasonable use of the stream; he had made only a reasonable use of it; his appropriation to that extent, being justifiable and prior in time, necessarily prevents the proprietor below from raising the water, without interfering with a rightful use already made; and it is therefore not an injury to him. Such appears to be the nature and extent of the prior and exclusive right, which one proprietor acquires by a prior reasonable appropriation of the use of the water and its fall; and it results, not from any originally superior legal right, but from a legitimate exercise of his own common right, the effect of which is, de facto, to supersede and prevent a like use by other proprietors originally having the same common right. It is, in this respect, like the right in common, which any individual has, to use a highway; whilst one is reasonably exercising his own right, by a temporary occupation of a particular part of the street with his carriage or team, another cannot occupy the same place at the same time.

*   *   *

So the proprietor above may, in like manner, make any reasonable uses of the stream and fall of water which he can do consistently with the previous appropriation of the proprietor below. If, with a view of gaining an advantage to his mill, in low stages of water, which may occur perhaps during the greatest part of the year, he places his mill so low that, in high stages of water, the dam below will throw back water on his wheels, he may do so if he choose, because he thereby does no injury to any other proprietor. But if he sustains a damage from such back water, it is a damage resulting from no wrong done by the lower proprietor who had previously established his dam, and it is an inconvenience to which he subjects his mill for the sake of greater advantages; and he has no cause to complain.

*   *   *

The next claim of the plaintiff's is this; that he had a right, founded upon the usage and practice of his grantors, to open the waste gates of the middle dam, and thereby relieve his own mill from back water; and that the defendant, by taking down the middle dam, and erecting a new dam further down the stream, had either prevented him from the exercise of this right, or rendered the exercise of it more onerous and expensive. The court are of opinion, that this claim cannot be sustained. At the time of the practice relied on, the grantors were owners of both mills, and might favor one at the expense of the other, as the exigencies of their business might require, or at their own mere pleasure. But no right could be founded on such practice; because it was not adverse. When the estates were severed, and the rights of the respective proprietors became adverse, they stood upon the same footing as if no such usage had existed. The damages, therefore, which were given by the jury, for the violation of this supposed right, must be deducted from the verdict. . . .

But, for the reasons already given, the court are of opinion, that the defendant had no right to erect his new dam higher than his old one, so as to appropriate an increased portion of the stream to his own use, and thereby set back water upon the mill wheels of the plaintiff. The jury having found that he had so raised his dam, to the injury of the plaintiff, and assessed damages therefor separately, we think the verdict must be amended, so as to stand as a verdict for the latter sum only, and that judgment be rendered thereon for the plaintiff.

Note: Water Rights in the West

Cary v. *Daniels* illustrates the limitations on water use where water was abundant, population relatively dense, and settlement long-standing. In England and the East, the common law of water developed over many years to protect all users of a particular stream or river. Simply stated, under the common law people were free to use the water flowing by their property, as long as they did not diminish the water available to persons farther downstream or unreasonably disrupt the flow downstream and adversely affect users and landowners upstream. This rule, modified by eminent domain law and statutes protecting mill dams, was workable and sensible where streams, ponds, lakes, and rivers were common and rainfall was adequate for most crops. However, much of the common law of water and property was useless in the West, where the average annual rainfall of 16 inches was less than half that in the East. For example, abundant water resources meant that irrigation was virtually unknown in the East and in England. Thus Westerners had to develop statutes and a new common law to facilitate irrigation and other uses of water unknown in the East. The common law of water rights in the West was based on the concept of "reasonable use."

WALTER PRESCOTT WEBB
The Great Plains
1931

Drawing on Charles S. Kinney, Law of Irrigation and Water Rights and the Arid Region Doctrine of Appropriation of Waters *(1912), historian Webb described how a western law of water emerged.*

The custom or practice that came in to supplement or entirely displace the common law of riparian rights was that of prior appropriation for beneficial use, which practice Kinney has named the "Arid Region Doctrine of appropriation."

The Arid Region Doctrine of appropriation may be defined as that doctrine or rule of law which has grown up in this Western portion of our country, governing the use of water of the natural streams and other bodies, by its appropriation for any useful or beneficial purpose, based upon the physical necessities of the case; and, whereby for the purpose of applying the water to some beneficial use, the water must be diverted from its natural channels, and, in contradistinction to the strict construction of the common law of riparian rights, the place of use may be on either riparian or nonriparian lands, and the right based on priority. In fact, this doctrine is in derogation of the common law, and as said in an early California case, it is "without judicial or legislative precedent, either in our own country or in that from which we have borrowed our jurisprudence."

This doctrine is distinguished by the following characteristics:

1. It had its origin west of the hundredth meridian, and was and is unknown to the humid portion of the country.

2. It permits the use of water for beneficial or useful purposes as distinguished from the reasonable use of the modified common law.

3. It permits the diversion of water from the stream regardless of the diminution of the stream.

4. The water may be used either on riparian or on nonriparian lands. According to the common law all the land not immediately adjacent to the stream would have been left high and dry, but under the arid-region doctrine the reclamation of this land became possible.

5. The arid-region doctrine denies the equality among users so steadfastly maintained by the common law of riparian rights. It grants to the first appropriator an exclusive right and to later appropriators rights conditioned upon the prior rights of those who have gone before.

6. Under the common law a riparian owner's rights, though not inalienable, remain his without any specific act of commission or omission on his part—his by virtue of ownership of the land. He does not forfeit the right if he does not use it. Under the arid-region doctrine, on the contrary, the continuation of the privilege or right depends upon beneficial use combined with prior appropriation. Not to use the water, for example, is to forfeit it.

Irwin v. Phillips, et al.
5 Cal. 140 (1855)

Irwin v. Phillips *illustrates the rules or western water rights. Matthew Irwin, a California miner, diverted a stream from its natural course to his mining operation. Robert Phillips and others later began mining farther downstream, and found that they lacked sufficient water for their operation. Thus they began to "trench on" Irwin's dam, in an attempt to divert the water back into the original streambed. Irwin won a suit for trespass at the trial level, and Phillips appealed to the California Supreme Court, raising the question: Did the common law of England and the eastern United States apply to California? If it did, then Irwin had no right to divert water from its natural course. Phillips supported this position by citations to numerous cases from Massachusetts, New York, and Britain, and to American and English treatises, including Angell's* Watercourses. *Irwin argued that a substantially new law had developed in California, which allowed a first user to take as much water as he needed. This case illustrates the difficulties of allocating a scarce resource—water—according to common-law rules developed where the resource was plentiful. The case also illustrates nicely Oliver Wendell Holmes's assertion that the life of the law has not been logic, but has been "experience."*

Heydenfeldt, J. . . .

. . . The proposition to be settled is whether the owner of a canal in the mineral region of this State, constructed for the purpose of supplying water to miners, has the right to divert the water of a stream from its natural channel, as against the claims of those who, subsequent to the diversion, take up lands along the banks of the stream, for the purpose of mining. It must be premised that it is admitted on all sides that the mining claims in controversy, and the lands through which the stream runs and through which the canal passes, are a part of the public domain, to which there is no claim of private proprietorship; and that the miners have the right to dig for gold on the public lands. . . .

It is insisted by the appellants [Phillips] that in this case the common law doctrine must be invoked, which prescribes that a water course must be allowed to flow in its natural channel. But upon an examination of the authorities which support that doctrine, it will be found to rest upon the fact of the individual rights of landed proprietors upon the stream, the principle being both at the civil and common law that the owner of lands on the banks of a water course owns to the middle of the stream, and has the right in virtue of his proprietorship to the use of the water in its pure and natural condition. In this case the lands are the property either of the State or the United States. . . . It is certain that at the common law the diversion of water courses could only be complained of by riparian owners, who were deprived of the use, or those claiming directly under them. Can the appellants assert their present claim as tenants at will? To solve this question it must be kept in mind that their tenancy is of their own creation, their tenements of their own selection, and subsequent, in point of time, to the diversion of the stream. They had the right to mine where they pleased throughout an extensive region, and they selected the bank of a stream from which the water had been already turned, for the purpose of supplying the mines at another point.

Courts are bound to take notice of the political and social condition of the country which they judicially rule. In this State the larger part of the territory consists of mineral lands, nearly the whole of which are the property of the public. No right or intent of disposition of these lands has been shown either by the United States or the State governments, and . . . a system has been permitted to grow up by the voluntary action and assent of the population, whose free and unrestrained occupation of the mineral region has been tacitly assented to by the one government, and heartily encouraged by the expressed legislative policy of the other. If there are, as must be admitted, many things connected with this system, which are crude and undigested, and subject to fluctuation and dispute, there are still some which a universal sense of necessity and propriety have so firmly fixed as that they have come to be looked upon as having the force and effect of *res judicata*. Among these the most important are the rights of miners to be protected in the possession of their selected localities, and the rights of those who, by prior appropriation, have taken the waters from their natural beds, and by costly artificial works have conducted them for miles over mountains and ravines, to supply the necessities of gold diggers, and without which the most important interests of the mineral region would remain without development. So fully recognized have become these rights, that without any specific legislation conferring or confirming them, they are alluded to and spoken of in various acts of the Legislature in the same manner as if they were rights which had been vested by the most distinct expression of the will of the law makers; as for instance, in the Revenue Act "canals and water races" are declared to be property subject to taxation, and this when there was none other in the State than such as were devoted to the use of mining. . . . This simply goes to prove . . . that however much the policy of the State, as indicated by her legislation, has conferred the privilege to work the mines, it has equally conferred the right to divert the streams from their natural channels, and as these two rights stand upon an equal footing, when they conflict, they must be decided by the fact of priority, upon the maxim of equity, *qui prior est in tempore, potior est in jure* [he who is prior in time is better in right]. The miner who selects a piece of ground to work, must take it as he finds it, subject to prior rights, which have an equal equity, on account of an equal recognition from the sovereign power. If it is upon a stream, the waters of which have not been taken from their bed, they cannot be taken to his prejudice; but if they have been already diverted, and for as high and legitimate a purpose as the one he seeks to accomplish, he has no right to complain, no right to interfere with the prior occupation of his neighbor, and must abide the disadvantages of his own selection.

It follows from this opinion that the judgment of the Court below was substantially correct . . . and it is therefore affirmed.

Note: Law and Westward Migration

Most Americans have an image of "the West" as lawless and violent. While there is some basis for this view, there is another side to western migration. In his innovative study *Law for the Elephant: Property and Social Behavior on the Overland Trail* (1980), John Phillip Reid argues that Americans moving west brought with them both a respect for the law and a rudimentary knowledge of the law. He demonstrates that without lawyers, judges, or courts, the western settlers implemented such legal concepts as property, contract, and partnership. Reid finds that "except for definitions of possession and rules governing exclusive control of minerals, water, and open range, the law of the east was the law of the west. The concept of private property remained largely inviolable, even when conditions were trying and people desperate." Reid notes that

> few emigrants traveling the overland trail to the Pacific coast could have explained the meaning of "words of purchase" or fee simple absolute, yet all understood and a vast

majority respected the legal principles vesting in their individual exclusive enjoyment of property lawfully possessed. . . . [T]hey respected the rights of property owners much as if still back east in the midst of plenty. By respect of their neighbor and their neighbor's property they were, more often than not, adhering to a morality of law.

The Growth of Contract Law in the Nineteenth Century

The nineteenth century "was the golden age of contract law."[11] An almost unknown field in 1800, by 1860 it dominated American law. Examination of the legal treatises reveals this sudden development of contract law. In 1765, Blackstone devoted an entire volume of *Commentaries on the Laws of England* to property, but only a few pages to contracts. William Wetmore Story's 1844 contract treatise was over 400 pages long and cited more than 3,500 English and American cases. Three years later, he published a revised and expanded edition. In the 1850s, Theophilus Parsons published three editions of his two-volume *The Law of Contracts*.

Nineteenth-century law retained common-law notions that contracts with children, drunkards, and married women might be void because of the legal incompetence of the parties. Generally, slaves and southern free blacks were not allowed to make contracts. However, industrialization and the rise of national and international markets led to dramatic changes in other aspects of contract law.

Before the nineteenth century, a legally enforceable contract had to be fair; the exchange of money for goods or services had to be reasonable, under the theory that a "sound price warrants a sound commodity." By the 1840s, this was no longer true. Story's treatise noted that a contract required only "mutual assent of the parties" and a "valuable consideration," which he defined as "a legal consideration emanating from some injury or inconvenience to the one party, or some benefit to the other party." Courts no longer cared if the exchange of consideration was fair. "It is not necessary," Story noted, "that the consideration and promise should be equivalents in actual value, for it would be impossible, ever precisely to determine, whether in a given case the consideration was adequate, without a psychological investigation into the motives of the parties." Antebellum courts demanded only that

> each party to a contract may exercise his own discretion, as to the adequacy of consideration; and if the agreement be made bona fide, it matters not how insignificant the benefit may apparently be to the promisor, or how slight the inconvenience or damage appear to be to the promisee.

Story's explanation reveals much about the attitudes that mid-nineteenth-century capitalism fostered. Story declared that "if no contracts were good, but those, which were apparently of equal benefit to both parties, probably very few contracts, which are made, would be legally valid."[12] In other words, the law of the nineteenth century recognized and supported the belief that unfair bargains were necessary for the commercial and industrial development of the day. The maker of sharp bargains, the shrewd businessman, was legally protected unless there was "evidence of fraud or imposition."[13]

Morton Horwitz has noted that in the nineteenth century

> judges and jurists finally reject[ed] the longstanding belief that the justification of contractual obligation is derived from the inherent justice or fairness of an exchange. In its

place, they asserted for the first time that the source of the obligation of contract is the convergence of the wills of the contracting parties.[14]

In such a world, those with the most knowledge and greatest economic power tended to dictate the terms of contracts. Thus contract law generally favored sellers over buyers and employers over laborers and served as an instrument that aided the industrial and commercial entrepreneurs of the nineteenth century. This led to the "triumph of contract" over property, tort, and equity, as the law came "to ratify those forms of inequality that the market system produced."[15]

Seixas and Seixas v. *Woods*
2 Cai. R. (N.Y.) 48 (1804)

The Seixases purchased from Woods what he alleged was valuable brazilletto wood but was actually almost worthless peachum wood. Woods had purchased this shipment from a third party, without inspecting it, and, similarly, the Seixases bought the shipment without examining it. When the Seixases discovered the error, they sought to return the shipment to Woods, who refused to accept it or give a refund. The Seixases did not allege fraud by Woods, merely that he had improperly labeled his goods and had sold them as something they were not. Judges Smith Thompson and James Kent spoke for the New York Supreme Court, in finding for Woods on the grounds that there was no implied warranty and thus the buyers should have relied on caveat emptor.

Thompson, J. . . .

From the facts . . . it appears there was no *express warranty* by the defendant, or any *fraud* in the sale. The wood was sold and purchased as *brazilletto* wood, and a fair price for such wood paid, when in fact the wood was of a different quality, and of little or no value. The plaintiff's agent, who made the purchase, saw the wood when unloaded and delivered, and did not discover or know that it was of a different quality from that described in the bills of parcels; neither did the defendant, who was only consignee of this cargo, know that the wood was not *brazilletto*. The question then arises, whether there was an implied warranty, so as to afford redress to the plaintiffs, or whether the maxim *caveat emptor* must be applied to them. From an examination of the decisions in courts of common law, I can find no case where an action has been sustained under similar circumstances: an express warranty, or some fraud in the sale, are deemed indispensably necessary to be shown. . . . I see no injustice or inconvenience resulting from this doctrine, but, on the contrary, think it is best calculated to excite that caution and attention which all prudent men ought to observe in making their contracts. I . . . [find for] the defendant. . . .

Kent, J. . . . That without a warranty by the seller, or fraud on his part, the buyer must stand to all losses arising from latent defects, and that there is no instance in the *English* law of a contrary rule being laid down. The civil law, and the law of those countries which have adopted the civil as their common law, is more rigorous towards the seller, and make him responsible in every case for a latent defect . . . and, if the question was *res integra* in our law, I confess I should be overcome by the reasoning of the *Civilians*. And yet the rule of the common law has been well and elegantly vindicated . . . as most happily reconciling the claims of convenience with the duties of good faith. It requires the *purchaser* to apply his attention to those particulars which may be supposed within the reach of his observation and judgment, and the vendor to communicate those particulars and defects which cannot be supposed to be immediately within the reach of such attention. And even against his want of vigilance, the purchaser may provide, by requiring the vendor expressly to warrant the article. The mentioning the wood as *brazilletto* wood, in the bill of parcels, and in the advertisement some days previous to the sale, did not amount to a warranty to the plaintiffs. To make an affirmation at the time of the sale, a warranty, it must appear by evidence to be so intended, and not to have been a mere matter of judgment and opinion, and of which the defendant had no particular knowledge. Here it is admitted the defendant was equally ignorant with the plaintiffs, and could have had no such intention.

McFarland v. *Newman*
Watts (Pa.) 55 (1839)

McFarland *v.* Newman *shows the further advance of caveat emptor. Newman purchased McFarland's colt, which turned out to have "an incurable disease called glanders." At trial, Newman proved that the horse had "exhibited . . . symptoms all the time McFarland had him (a period of ten or eleven months)" but that at the sale McFarland declared the horse had been ill for only a few days and was suffering from "the ordinary distemper to which colts are subject." The jury awarded Newman $75 based on McFarland's "alleged warranty," and McFarland appealed.*

Gibson, C.J. . . . The civil law maxim is, doubtless, that a sound article is warranted by a sound price; but the common-law courts started with the doctrine that though the sale of a chattel is followed by an implied warranty of title, and a right of action *ex delicto* [out of the fault] for wilful misrepresentation of the quality; yet that maxim *caveat emptor*, disposes of all beside. Thus was the common law originally settled; and the current of decision ran smooth and clear in the channel thus marked out for it, from the days of the year books, till within a few years past, when it suddenly became turgid and agitated; and . . . it finally ran wild. The judges, in pursuit of a phantom in the guise of a principle of impracticable policy and questionable morality, broke away from the common law, not, however, by adopting the civil law principle of implied warranty as to soundness, but by laying hold on the vendor's commendation of his commodity, and not at first as absolutely constituting an express warranty, but as evidence of it. I say the policy of this principle is impracticable, because the operations of commerce are such as to require that the rules for its regulation admit of as few occasions for reclamation as possible; and I say its morality is questionable, because I am unable to discern anything immoral in the bona fide sale of an article represented to be exactly that as which the vendor had purchased it. It is to be remembered that I am speaking of the sale of a thing accepted by the vendee after opportunity had to inspect and test it, and not of a sale of which he was necessarily compelled by the circumstances to deal on the faith of the vendor's description; nor yet a sale on the concoction of which he was over-reached by misrepresentation or trick. . . .

*   *   *

As the case goes back to another jury, it is proper to intimate the principle on which a correct decision of it must depend. Though to constitute a warranty requires no particular form of words, the naked averment of a fact is neither a warranty itself, nor evidence of it. In connection with other circumstances, it certainly may be taken into consideration; but the jury must be satisfied from the whole that the vendor actually, and not constructively, consented to be bound for the truth of his representation. Should he have used expressions fairly importing a willingness to be thus bound, it would furnish a reason to infer that he had intentionally induced the vendee to treat on that basis; but a naked affirmation is not to be dealt with as a warranty, merely because the vendee had gratuitously relied on it; for not to have exacted a direct engagement, had he desired to buy on the vendor's judgment, must be accounted an instance of folly. Testing the vendor's responsibility by these principles, justice will be done without driving him into the toils of an imaginary contract.

Judgment reversed, and a *venire de novo* awarded.

Icar v. *Suares*
7 La. 517 (1835)

Because of its civil-law heritage, Louisiana completely rejected the concept of caveat emptor. Instead, the state required the vendor to disclose all known defects. A dissatisfied purchaser could file an action of redhibition, to rescind a sale if defects were not disclosed. The redhibition laws stemmed from Roman law concerning the sale of slaves, and in Louisiana this applied to the sale of slaves and other property. Icar initiated this redhibitory action to annul the sale of Kate, a slave, and recover his purchase price and other costs, on the ground that Kate had "the redhibitory vices of craziness and running away."

BULLARD, J., delivered the opinion of the court.

The plaintiff seeks to be relieved from a contract, by which he purchased from the defendant a recently imported slave, on account of two redhibitory vices, to wit: the habit of running away and madness. Judgment was rendered in his favor, and the defendant appealed.

The case turns altogether on matters of fact. We doubt whether the evidence establishes the habit of running away previous to the sale, but the opinion we have formed on the second ground, renders it unnecessary to give any positive opinion on the first.

It is contended that Kate was not crazy, but only stupid, and that stupidity is not madness, but on the contrary an apparent defect, against which the defendant did not warrant. . . . The code enumerates madness (folie) among the absolute vices of slaves, which give rise to the action of redhibition. Whether the subject of this action is idiotick . . . we [do not] consider it material, inasmuch as the code has declared, that a sale may be avoided on account of any vice or defect, which renders the thing absolutely useless, or its use so inconvenient and imperfect, that it must be supposed the buyer would not have purchased with a knowledge of the vice. La. Code. art. 2496.

We are satisfied from the evidence in the record . . . the slave in question was wholly, and perhaps worse than useless.

It is, therefore, ordered, adjudged and decreed, that the judgment of the District Court be affirmed, with costs.

Seymour v. Delancey, et al.
3 Cow. (N.Y.) 445 (1824)

Thomas Ellison contracted to give Seymour two farms for a one-third interest in a group of lots in the village of Newburgh, New York. The exchange of land was never carried out, and Seymour sued Ellison's heirs, the Delanceys, to require specific performance of the contract. In Seymour v. Delancey, et al., *6 Johns. Ch. (N.Y.) 222 (1822), Chancellor James Kent refused to order specific performance of the contract. Kent found that "at the date of the agreement, the village lots were not worth half the value of the country farms." Kent then asserted that*

there is a very great weight of authority against enforcing a contract, where the consideration is so inadequate as to render it a hard bargain, and an unequal and an unreasonable bargain; the argument is exceedingly strong against it in such cases, when it is considered that if equity acts at all, it must act ex vigore, *and carry the contract into execution, with unmitigated severity.*

Kent concluded

that inadequacy of price may, of itself, and without fraud or other ingredient, be sufficient to stay the application of the power of this Court to enforce a specific performance of a private contract to sell land. . . . In the present case, the inadequacy is so great as to give the character of hardship, unreasonableness and inequality to the contract, and to render it discreet and proper, under the established principles of the Court, to refuse to decree a specific performance. . . .

Seymour appealed to the New York Court for the Trial of Impeachments and the Correction of Errors. This unique body consisted of the entire New York State Senate, the justices of the New York Supreme Court, the chancellor, and the lieutenant governor. Chief Justice John Savage and nine senators voted to uphold Kent's decree. But Senator John Sudam wrote for the majority, which voted to reverse Kent.

. . . [I]t cannot be sustained, in my opinion, that *mere inequality* in value, which is not so gross as to strike the moral feeling of an indifferent man, would be sufficient to warrant the Chancellor in withholding a decree for specific performance. I admit that the exercise of the power, in a Court of Chancery, to enforce the specific performance of contracts for the sale or the exchange of land, rests in the sound discretion of the Court: but this is a sound legal discretion; and not the exercise of an arbitrary power, interfering with the contracts of individuals, and sporting with their vested rights. I also admit, that the party claiming the specific performance must present a case *fair*, *just* and *reasonable*; that the contract must be founded on *adequate consideration*; and that it must be free from *fraud, misrepresentation, deceit,* or *surprise*.

To determine whether, in fact, the agreement for exchange was hard, unequal, and disproportionate, and whether it was free from *fraud, surprise, &c.*, it will be necessary to examine, with as much brevity as possible, the history of this transaction.

*   *   *

[Here Senator Sudam pointed out that before agreeing to trade the farms for the one-third interest in the village lots, Ellison had purchased the other two-thirds interest in the lots from Seymour's relatives. Sudam continued:] . . . It is also in evidence that Ellison, during the summer, resided in New Windsor, in the county of Orange, adjoining the village of Newburgh, and that he was well acquainted with the property of the appellant, proposed to be exchanged for his two farms. It also appears that Ellison had a favorable opinion of Newburgh as a business place; and he may have been influenced by the consideration, that property there would rise in value, in consequence of the expected establishment of a navy yard.

*   *   *

The whole presents a very strong case, and one in which the contract should be carried into effect, unless some controlling rule of decision in our Equity Courts shall require the contrary.

There can be no doubt, from a review of the evidence, that Ellison made his bargain, well knowing all the facts in relation to the Newburgh lots, as well as his farms proposed to be exchanged for them. . . . It could not be pretended, that after a purchase of two-thirds of the whole property, he had never examined the premises, or that he had not ascertained the situation and comparative value of the Newburgh lots; for it is admitted by all parties, that at the time of the purchase from Drake Seymour, and his agreeing to purchase of S. S. Seymour, he was not incompetent to transact business of any kind. Immediately after this, the negotiation for the one-third of the appellant's lots commenced. . . . There is, therefore, no pretence, in my opinion, that Ellison was not fully acquainted with the premises, proposed to be exchanged with him, by the appellant. . . . He was in a situation deliberately to form his opinion, and unquestionably he did do so, as to the value of the Newburgh lots; and from his previous purchases, he must have ascertained their value, to his own satisfaction. Under the advice of his agent, he knew the value of the property to be conveyed by him to the appellant. We must take it, then, that Ellison deliberately, and with his eyes open, entered into the contract which the appellant now seeks to enforce by a decree of a Court of Equity.

I am, therefore, of opinion, from a review of the whole evidence, that this contract was, at the time the negotiation was first entered into, and at the time the articles were executed by Seymour and Ellison, certain fair and just, in all its parts.

The next question which presents itself to the consideration of the Court is, whether the contract between the appellant and Ellison is so *hard, unreasonable, or unequal*, that this Court will not aid to enforce it.

In reviewing this part of the case, it will be the duty of the Court to investigate the evidence as to the value of the Newburgh lots, and the farms to be exchanged for them. Should they arrive at the conclusion that *mere inadequacy in value, where there is no fraud, misrepresentation, imposition, or concealment of facts, is of itself sufficient to avoid the contract*, it will save a great deal of the labor and investigation which might otherwise be required. I admit, however, that where the inadequacy of price in a contract is so flagrant and palpable as to convince a man at the first blush, that one of the contracting parties had been imposed on by some false pretense, such a contract ought not to be enforced by this, or any other Court of Equity. It is not to be denied, that it is the settled doctrine of the Court of Chancery, that it will not carry into effect, specifically, a contract where the inadequacy of price amounts to conclusive evidence of fraud. . . .

*   *   *

I cannot assent to the doctrine, that inadequacy of price may, of itself and without fraud or other ingredient, be sufficient to stay the application of the power of a Court of Chancery, to enforce a specific performance of a private contract to sell land.

To establish this doctrine in the state of New York, would, to my mind, be sanctioning a principle, which would lead to very injurious results. Every member of this Court must be well aware how much property is held by contract; that purchases are constantly made upon speculation; that the value of real estate is fluctuating; and that there, most generally, exists an honest difference of opinion in regard to any bargain, as to its being a beneficial one, or not. To say, when all is fair, and the parties deal on equal terms, that a Court of Equity will not interfere, does not appear to me to be supported by authority . . . and unless I am bound down by some rigid rule of law, I, for one cannot consent to its introduction into our equity code.

*   *   *

There may be such inadequacy of price as, of itself, to be an evidence of fraud. But wherever this does not exist, and resort is had to the testimony of witnesses, and they differ in their valuation, as in the present case, the contract should be executed. . . .

The cause must therefore be remitted to the Court of Chancery, that the Chancellor may direct a Master to inquire whether the appellant can give to the respondents a clear and unincumbered title to the Newburgh lots; and if he can, a decree for a specific performance, according to the contract, must be entered against the respondents.

Note: Contracts and the Emerging Speculative Economy

Senator Sudam's opinion notes that "purchases are constantly made upon speculation." This statement anticipates a modern marketplace, based on securities, speculative contracts, and other kinds of risky investments. Sudam's opinion supports such an economic environment, but at the expense of those who might enter into blatantly unfair bargains out of ignorance.

Note: Contracts and the Federal Constitution

In antebellum America, contracts was the only area of substantive civil law with a major federal component. Article I, Section 10, of the Constitution prohibited states from "impairing the obligations of contracts." Both the *Dartmouth College* and *Charles River Bridge* cases reached the Court under the contracts clause. The first major contracts clause case was *Fletcher* v. *Peck*, 6 Cranch (U.S.) 87 (1810), which stemmed from one of America's greatest political scandals, the Yazoo Land Fraud.

In January, 1795, the Georgia legislature sold 35 million acres near the Yazoo River to four land companies for a paltry $500,000, less than 1½ cents an acre. Many members of the 1795 legislature held stock in the land companies, as did various state and federal officeholders. In 1796, a new legislature rescinded this sale, burned all records of the purchase, but did not return the $500,000 purchase price.

Fletcher v. *Peck* was a collusive suit brought to test the 1796 repeal. Peck, of Massachusetts, a holder of land under the 1795 law, sold 15,000 acres to Fletcher, of New Hampshire. Fletcher then sued Peck, arguing that the 1796 law rescinding the original grant prevented Peck from giving him good title to the land. Chief Justice Marshall, speaking for the Supreme Court, declared that the 1796 law was unconstitutional because the 1795 law was "in its nature a contract," and "absolute rights" had "been vested under that contract" and a repeal of the law could not "devest those rights." The Chief Justice admitted that "corruption" might "contaminate the very source of legislation or that impure motive" might "contribute to the passage of a law." But he rejected the idea that "the validity of a law depends upon the motives of its framers." Ignoring the notoriety of the land fraud, Marshall said of the Yazoo purchaser:

> He has paid his money for a title good at law; he is innocent, whatever may be the guilt
> of others, and equity will not subject him to the penalties attached to that guilt. All titles
> would be insecure, and the intercourse between man and man would be very seriously
> obstructed, if this principle be overturned.

This case provided constitutional precedent for protecting vested rights, but did not solve the questions surrounding the Yazoo land titles. In 1814, Congress indemnified all Yazoo landholders with a $5 million buyout. This was a political solution to what was from the beginning a political problem.

The Evolution of Modern Tort Law

The lack of a recognizable system of tort is one of the major differences between liability law before 1800 and after about 1850. The term "tort" appears only once in the index of Blackstone's *Commentaries on the Laws of England*. Book 3 of Blackstone, *Of Private Wrongs*, is "primarily devoted to English civil procedure: the jurisdictional allocations among the courts and the procedures for litigating them."[16] Blackstone did not discuss torts because the substance of the common law of wrongs was almost nonexistent before the mid-nineteenth century.

Before the nineteenth century, a variety of private wrongs—such as assault, libel, and trespass—were dealt with as separate legal actions. Under the writ system, courts "identified a residual category of noncriminal wrongs not arising out of contract,"[17] which were litigated under the old common-law writ system as "trespass" or "trespass on the case" (often called "case"). At this time "'torts' was not an autonomous branch of law," but was, as Oliver Wendell Holmes, Jr., noted in 1871, "a collection of unrelated writs."[18] Suits for harms that we would now call torts were not categorized as such, nor did lawyers use such modern legal concepts as "negligence," "duty," and "fault." At that time, "negligence" and "breach of duty" usually referred to the failure to perform the requirements of a contract or the failure of a government official to perform his function as established by common law or statute. Indeed, "perhaps the most important eighteenth century of line of cases in which negligence was a factor involved both common law and statutory actions against sheriffs for taking insufficient bond or for allowing imprisoned debtors to escape."[19]

In the mid-nineteenth century, the law of torts rapidly changed. Francis Hilliard's treatise *The Elements of Law* (1835) had only 7 minor references to tort law; however, in 1859 his two-volume, 1,200 page *The Law of Torts* contained citations to over 5,000 cases. This phenomenal growth in tort law resulted from two quite different— although ultimately interrelated—changes in Anglo-American society.

By mid-century, the old common-law system of writs and pleadings began to collapse because it could no longer efficiently serve the needs of the expanding legal system and a dynamic economy. The writ system was too slow and cumbersome. Technical pleadings, rather than the substance of a case, too often determined outcomes. The demise of the writ system ended the archaic distinctions between "trespass" and "trespass on the case," allowed for the substitution of more meaningful terminology, and forced lawyers and judges to think more systematically and categorically.

The end of the writ system did not, by itself, lead to either an explosion in tort law or doctrinal change. Both evolved with a changing economy. Industrialization led to more accidents and harms—more torts. The new machines of the nineteenth century—especially railroads and steamboats—all too frequently injured or killed bystanders, passengers, and operators. The old writ system was simply incapable of handling the exploding number and variety of suits caused by industrial mishaps. Moreover, these torts increasingly took place between strangers. In an earlier age, community relationships might have allowed for the compensation for losses without resort to law. But in the bustling and impersonal world of the railroad, the factory, and the city, courts provided the only forum for compensating accident victims. Out of these increasingly frequent accidents the modern law of torts emerged with its elements of fault, negligence, duty, and proximate causation.

The emerging tort law made tortfeasors generally liable for the harms they caused others. However, four rules evolved that undermined the likelihood of injured parties recovering damages. "Contributory negligence" prevented an injured person from winning damages if the defendant could prove that even a small part of the accident was caused by the injured party. The rule against "wrongful death" suits prevented the families of persons killed in accidents from recovering damages. The fellow servant rule (presented as part of the labor law section of this chapter) prevented most workers from recovering damages for job-related injuries. Finally, courts refused to hold tortfeasors responsible for damages resulting from "remote causation." These rules tended to aid the new nineteenth-century industries, especially the emerging railroads and steamboat companies.

Spencer v. Campbell
9 Watts & Serg. (Pa.) 32 (1845)

Campbell took his grain to the Spencers' mill, where a defective steam boiler exploded, killing Campbell's horse. Campbell sued in "trespass on the case," asserting that the Spencers had a duty to "use safe and convenient machinery" in their business and that "in disregard to this duty they procured a defective steam-boiler, and well knowing it to be defective used it." Campbell also argued that the Spencers "negligently managed their engine." The Spencers argued that they had purchased the boiler from one Meixsell, a reputable machinist, that they were not experts in this technology, and that they could not be held responsible for a manufacturer's defects. The presiding judge charged the jury in the following manner.

WOODWARD (President).—There is little ground to doubt the legal duty that was upon the defendants to provide reasonably sufficient and safe machinery for carrying on their business. This duty is on men in every branch of business, when they ask people to risk life and property in their hands and for their profit. The transporter of passengers or property . . . is required to have all the means and appliances necessary for a safe accomplishment of the work in hand; the innkeeper is bound to provide safe and convenient house-room for his guests and stabling for horses; and the rule applies with peculiar force to manufacturers and mechanics whose occupation brings customers . . . into the immediate vicinity of their machinery.

But whilst the defendants do not deny the alleged defectiveness of their steam-boiler, nor controvert the general principle of law applicable to all machinery, they seek to excuse themselves from liability in this case on the ground that being themselves unacquainted with steam engines, they applied to an experienced machinist for a competent and good engine for their grist mill, paid him a sound price, and received a machine which he represented to be safe and sufficient for their purposes; that he put it up for them, and instructed them in the use of it, and that they never applied all the power to the boiler which he assured them they might with safety put on; and that, until the explosion occurred, they did not know that the boiler was defective. The plaintiff charges them with "well knowing" the defective character of the boiler; and the negligence which constitutes the tort in this case depends on this question of knowledge. It is well known now and admitted that the boiler was defective; but did the defendants know this whilst they were using it? If they did, it was the grossest negligence in them to continue to use the boiler; if they did not, the plaintiff cannot recover on the first count of his declaration. . . .

*   *   *

If the jury should find it necessary thus to impute knowledge of the defectiveness of the engine to the defendants, they are not to be excused on account of any false security into which the representations of Meixsell, the machinist, may have betrayed them. They employed him at their own risk; they took his advice at their peril. Their customers never trusted in Meixsell; their confidence was in the Spencers. As between one of those customers and the Spencers, the opinions and assurances of Meixsell become unimportant. If the defendants chose to make his opinions the rule of their conduct in opposition to the testimony of their own senses, they have no right to visit the consequences of their folly on their innocent customers. The public repaired to their mill on the presumption that they employed all the precautions and care in conducting their business that men of ordinary prudence do commonly employ, and they were bound to know that the faith and confidence of their customers were in them, rather than in some irresponsible and unknown individual whose advice they had sought and obtained. Meixsell was undoubtedly false to the defendants, but this is their misfortune. They cannot transfer it to another innocent party who was a stranger to all that occurred between Meixsell and the defendants. They brought on the misfortune, and must therefore bear it.

     *   *   *

[Under this charge the jury found for Campbell, and the Spencers appealed to the Pennsylvania Supreme Court. Chief Justice John Bannister Gibson upheld the jury verdict.]

     *   *   *

. . . The only material inquiry, in the case before us, regards the nature and extent of the defendant's responsibility to their customers. It is true that the judge put the responsibility of a carrier or an innkeeper as illustration, not of the degree of diligence required but of the duty which the law imposed on him to provide all the means and appliances necessary for a safe accomplishment of his business; but he put the question on the true ground as a conclusion from the whole, that of ordinary care and skill. As the defendants were bound to use reasonable diligence to ascertain the quality of their machinery in regard to safety, they were answerable certainly for gross negligence of which there was evidence. They were warned of the danger not only to others, but by their own eyes; yet they preferred to rely on the assurances of the manufacturer; and the judge was right in charging that "if they chose to make his opinion the rule of their conduct in opposition to the evidence of their own senses, they had no right to visit the consequences of their folly on their customers." To work the engine under an extraordinary head of steam, though the boiler-head had been perceptibly sprung at the lowest pressure, was an act of rashness; and it is to be remembered that they were bound, not only to use due care, but to possess a competent share of skill on the principle by which the law implies an agreement to that effect on the part of every one who undertakes to perform a business, an office, or a duty. . . . [Here Chief Justice Gibson discussed the negligent operation of the boiler, implying that because it was defective, the Spencers used it negligently.] It is not to be doubted, then, that the disaster which ensued is one which he was bound to prevent, and for which all are answerable.

Judgment affirmed.

Brown v. Kendall
6 Cush. (60 Mass.) 292 (1850)

In attempting to separate their fighting dogs with a stick, Kendall accidentally hit Brown, injuring his eye.

SHAW, C.J. This is an action of trespass, *vi et armis*, brought by George Brown against George K. Kendall, assault and battery; . . . .

The facts set forth in the bill of exceptions preclude the supposition, that the blow . . . was intentional. The whole case proceeds on the assumption, that the damage sustained by the plaintiff . . . was inadvertent and unintentional; and the case involves the question how far, and under what qualifications, the party by whose unconscious act the damage was done is responsible for it. We use the term "unintentional" rather than involuntary, because in some of the cases, it is stated, that the act of holding and using weapon or instrument, the movement of which is the immediate cause of hurt to another, is a voluntary act, although its particular effect in hitting and hurting another is not within the purpose or intention of the party doing the act.

*   *   *

We think . . . that the plaintiff must come prepared with evidence to show either that the *intention* was unlawful, or that the defendant was *in fault*; for if the injury was unavoidable, and the conduct of the defendant was free from blame, he will not be liable. . . . If, in the prosecution of a lawful act, a casualty purely accidental arises, no action can be supported for an injury arising therefrom. . . . In applying these rules to the present case, we can perceive no reason why the instructions asked for by the defendant ought not to have been given; to this effect, that if both plaintiff and defendant at the time of the blow were using ordinary care, and the plaintiff was not, or if at that time, both the plaintiff and defendant were not using ordinary care, then the plaintiff could not recover.

In using this term, ordinary care, it may be proper to state, that what constitutes ordinary care will vary with the circumstances of cases. In general, it means that kind and degree of care, which prudent and cautious men would use, such as is required by the exigency of the case, and such as is necessary to guard against probable danger. A man, who should have occasion to discharge a gun, on an open and extensive marsh, or in a forest, would be required to use less circumspection and care, than if he were to do the same thing in an inhabited town, village, or city. To make an accident, or casualty, or as the law sometimes states it, inevitable accident, it must be such an accident as the defendant could not have avoided by the use of the kind and degree of care necessary to the exigency, and in the circumstances in which he was placed.

We are not aware of any circumstances in this case, requiring a distinction between acts which it was lawful and proper to do, and acts of legal duty. There are cases, undoubtedly, in which officers are bound to act under process, for the legality of which they are not responsible, and perhaps some others in which this distinction would be important. We can have no doubt that the act of the defendant in attempting to part the fighting dogs, one of which was his own, and for the injurious acts of which he might be responsible, was a lawful and proper act, which he might do by proper and safe means. If then, in doing this act, using due care and all proper precautions necessary to the exigency of the case, to avoid hurt to others, in raising his stick for that purpose, he accidentally hit the plaintiff in his eye, and wounded him, this was the result of pure accident, or was involuntary and unavoidable, and therefore the action would not lie. Or if the defendant was chargeable with some negligence, we think the plaintiff cannot recover without showing that the damage was caused wholly by the act of the defendant, and that the plaintiff's own negligence did not contribute as an efficient cause to produce it.

The court instructed the jury, that if it was not a necessary act, and the defendant was not in duty bound to part the dogs, but might with propriety interfere or not as he chose, the defendant was responsible for the consequences of the blow, unless it appeared that he was in the exercise of extraordinary care, so that the accident was inevitable, using the word not in a strict but a popular sense. This is to be taken in connection with the charge afterwards given, that if the jury believed, that the act of interference in the fight was unnecessary, (that is, as before explained, not a duty incumbent on the defendant,) then the burden of proving extraordinary care on the part of the defendant, or want of ordinary care on the part of the plaintiff, was on the defendant.

The court are of opinion that these directions were not conformable to law. If the act of hitting the plaintiff was unintentional, on the part of the defendant, and done in the doing of a lawful act, then the defendant was not liable, unless it was done in the want of exercise of due care, adapted to the exigency of the case, and therefore such want of due care became part of the plaintiff's case, and the burden of proof was on the plaintiff to establish it. . . .

. . . . [W]e are of opinion, that the other part of the charge, that the burden of proof was on the defendant, was incorrect. Those facts which are essential to enable the plaintiff to recover, he takes the burden of proving. The evidence may be offered by the plaintiff or by the defendant; the question of due care, or want of care, may be essentially connected with the main facts, and arise from the same proof; but the effect of the rule, as to the burden of proof, is this, that when the proof is all in, and before the jury . . . if it appears that the defendant was doing a lawful act, and unintentionally hit and hurt the plaintiff, then unless it also appears to the satisfaction of the jury, that the defendant is chargeable with some fault, negligence, carelessness, or want of prudence, the plaintiff . . . is not entitled to recover.

New trial ordered.

Note: The Emergence of Negligence

Brown v. *Kendall* is central to the development of tort law. Charles Gregory, echoing an earlier assessment by Oliver Wendell Holmes, asserts that Chief Justice Shaw's opinion was a "marked departure from the past," which led to "the establishment of a consistent theory of liability for unintentionally caused harm." Morton Horwitz argues that scholars have given "an exaggerated significance" to the case, but he does accept the argument that before the 1850s "negligence" did not apply in tort actions and that all actions for trespass were based on strict liability.[20] Whoever is right in this debate, *Brown* v. *Kendall* is an important case, as either a major new precedent or the best summary of the law as it already had developed.

In addition to articulating the need to establish negligence to win a tort suit, Shaw clearly stated the doctrine of "contributory negligence." Under this theory, an injured party cannot recover from a negligent tortfeasor if the injured party was even slightly responsible for the accident. In articulating a theory of contributory negligence, Shaw gave a great boon to America's industries. For the rest of the nineteenth century, and well into the twentieth, railroads and other industries often avoided paying tort damages because of the doctrine of contributory negligence.

Note: Toward the Future

The proliferation of accidents in an increasingly impersonal world of large cities, new technologies, and dangerous industries led to changes in behavior that went beyond using courts to recompense the injured for their losses. By 1866, the courts in New York believed that insurance against accidental damages was no longer a luxury; it was a standard and accepted practice in an age when remote causation led to damages where there was no clear tortfeasor who might be sued.

Ryan v. New York Central Railroad Co.
35 N.Y. 210 (1866)

This case illustrates how the courts began to deal with the kinds of catastrophic accidents that could develop because of industrialization. Ryan's house was destroyed by a fire, which was initially caused by a New York Central Railroad train. The fire spread to Ryan's house from other buildings. Ryan sued the railroad, on the grounds that it had caused the original fire. The court ruled that Ryan could not recover from the railroad and, in the process, suggested that the future road to protection from liability lay in insurance, not law suits. The court, of course, was both right and wrong about how the future would play out in this area of law in industrial America.

HUNT, J. On the 15th day of July, 1854, in the city of Syracuse, the defendant, by the careless management . . . of one of its engines, set fire to its woodshed, and a large quantity of wood therein. The plaintiff's house, situated at a distance of one hundred and thirty feet from the shed, soon took fire from the heat and sparks, and was entirely consumed, notwithstanding diligent efforts were made to save it. . . .

The question may be thus stated: A house in a populous city takes fire, through the negligence of the owner or his servant; the flames extend to and destroy an adjacent building: Is the owner of the first building liable to the second owner for the damage sustained by such burning?

It is a general principle that every person is liable for the consequences for his own acts. He is thus liable in damages for the proximate results of his own acts, but not for remote damages. It is not easy at all times to determine what are proximate and what are remote damages. In Thomas v. Winchester . . . JUDGE RUGGLES defines the damages for which a party is liable, as those which are the natural or necessary consequences of his acts. Thus, the owner of a loaded gun, who puts it in the hands of a child, by whose indiscretion it is discharged, is liable for the injury sustained by a third person from such discharge. . . . The injury is a natural and ordinary result of the folly of placing a loaded gun in the hands of one ignorant of the manner of using it, and incapable of appreciating its effects. The owner of a horse and cart, who leaves them unattended in the street, is liable for an injury done to a person or his property, by the running away of the horse. . . . for the same reason. The injury is the natural result of the negligence. If the party thus injured had, however, by the delay or confinement from his injury, been prevented from completing a valuable contract, from which he expected to make large profits, he could not recover such expected profits from the negligent party, in the cases supposed. Such damages would not be the necessary or natural consequences, nor the results ordinarily to be anticipated, from the negligence committed.

. . . So if an engineer upon a steamboat or locomotive, in passing the house of A., so carelessly manages its machinery that the coals and sparks from its fires fall upon and consume the house of A., the railroad company or the steamboat proprietors are liable to pay the value of the property thus destroyed.

. . . Thus far the law is settled and the principle is apparent. If, however, the fire communicates from the house of A. to that of B., and that is destroyed, is the negligent party liable for his loss? And if it spreads thence to the house of C., and thence to the house of D., and thence consecutively through the other houses, until it reaches and consumes the house of Z., is the party liable to pay the damages sustained by these twenty-four sufferers? The counsel for the plaintiff does not distinctly claim this, and I think it would not be seriously insisted that the sufferers could recover in such case. Where, then, is the principle upon which A. recovers and Z. fails?

*   *   *

[I] place my opinion upon the ground that, in the one case, to wit, the destruction of the building upon which the sparks were thrown by the negligent act of the party sought to be charged, the result was to have been anticipated the moment the fire was communicated to the building; that its destruction was the ordinary and natural result of its being fired. In the second, third or twenty-fourth case, as supposed, the destruction of the building was not a natural and expected result of the first firing. That a building upon which sparks and cinders fall should be destroyed or seriously injured must be expected, but that the fire should spread and other buildings be consumed, is not a necessary or an usual result. That it is possible, and that it is not unfrequent, cannot be denied. The result, however, depends, not upon any necessity of a further communication of the fire, but upon a concurrence of accidental circumstances, such as the degree of the heat, the state of the atmosphere, the condition and materials of the adjoining structures and the direction of the wind. These are accidental and varying circumstances. The party has no control over them, and is not responsible for their effects.

My opinion, therefore, is, that this action cannot be sustained, for the reason that the damages incurred are not the immediate but the remote result of the negligence of the defendants. The immediate result was the destruction of their own wood and sheds; beyond that, it was remote.

*   *   *

To sustain such a claim as the present . . . would subject to a liability against which no prudence could guard, and to meet which no private fortune would be adequate. Nearly all fires are caused by negligence, in its extended sense. In a country where wood, coal, gas and oils are universally used, where men are crowded into cities and villages, where servants are employed, and where children find their home in all houses, it is impossible that the most vigilant prudence should guard against the occurrence of accidental or negligent fires. A man may insure his own house or his own furniture, but he cannot insure his neighbor's building or furniture, for the reason that he has no interest in them. To hold that the owner must not only meet his own loss by fire, but that he must guarantee the security of his neighbors on both sides . . . would be to create a liability which would be the destruction of all civilized society. No community could long exist, under the operation of such a principle. In a commercial country, each man, to some extent, runs the hazard of his neighbor's conduct, and each, by insurance against such hazards, is enabled to obtain a reasonable security against loss. To neglect such precaution, and to call upon his neighbor, on whose premises a fire originated, to indemnify him instead, would be to award a punishment quite beyond the offense committed. It is to be considered, also, that if the negligent party is liable to the owner of a remote building thus consumed, he would also be liable to the insurance companies who should pay losses to such remote owners. The principle of subrogation would entitle the companies to the benefit of every claim held by the party to whom a loss should be paid.

In deciding this case, I have examined the authorities cited from the Year Books, and have not overlooked the English statutes on the subject, or the English decisions extending back for many years. It will not be useful further to refer to these authorities, and it will be impossible to reconcile some of them with the view I have taken.

The remoteness of the damage, in my judgment, forms the true rule on which the question should be decided, and which prohibits a recovery by the plaintiff in this case.

Note: Wrongful Death and Tort Law

The most bizarre development in nineteenth-century American tort law was the conclusion that there could be no tort action if the injured person died. In *Carey* v. *Berkshire Railroad* and *Skinner* v. *Housatonic Railroad*, 1 Cush. (Mass.) 475 (1848), the Massachusetts Supreme Judicial Court ruled against an action for wrongful death. As Chief Justice Shaw's biographer concluded, "the common law as construed by the Shaw Court made it costly for carriers to scratch but cheap to kill, particularly if the killing were instantaneous." This ruling survived the Civil War. In the 1870s, a "dead victim's survivors could only seek retribution through a criminal indictment, because the common law provided no civil remedy for wrongful death."[21] In 1883, the Massachusetts legislature allowed survivors to sue for wrongful death of their relatives killed in accidents. This law, however, did not apply to workers killed on the job. Their employers remained immune from suit under the fellow servant rule until an 1887 statute allowed such suits. Only gradually did other states overrule, through statutes, the common law development that prevented tort suits for wrongful death.

4

Slavery, the Civil War, and Reconstruction

From 1787 until the Civil War, the constitutional status of the states within the Union remained unresolved. The Constitution created a federal union with powers shared by the states and the national government, and with uncertain jurisdictional boundaries between these entities. The Constitution placed certain obligations on the states, but did not clearly indicate how those obligations were to be met or the role of the federal government in enforcing them. Although the Framers of the Constitution presumed that interstate comity would be voluntarily observed, the antebellum Constitution offered few mechanisms for settling interstate disputes when such cooperation was not forthcoming.

From 1787 until the end of the Civil War, slavery was central to conflicts both among the states and between the states and the national government. Even when not immediately on the agenda, slavery lurked in the background of most legal and constitutional wrangling. The Nullification Crisis of 1832, for example, was over a tariff. But much of South Carolina's general discomfort stemmed from the fear of slave revolts, a decline in the price of cotton, and the rejuvenated abolitionist movement.

The Constitution explicitly recognized slavery in five places, referring to slaves as "other Persons" and "Person[s] held to Service or Labour." Slavery influenced at least ten other clauses.

Under the Constitution, Congress lacked power to interfere with slavery in the states. By 1804, the North had either ended slavery outright or passed gradual abolition acts. Southern free blacks were pariahs, living perilously between slavery and freedom. Ninety percent of the nation's blacks were slaves, subject to the whims of their masters and the rules set out by southern courts and legislatures. They were property, to be bought, sold, inherited, and seized for debts. Short of murder and mutilation, their masters could generally treat them as they wished.

While the Constitution left the states free to regulate the status of slaves within their borders, the federal government had some jurisdiction over slavery. Congress prohibited the African slave trade in 1808, although enforcement was lax until 1861. The question of slavery in the territories led to federal laws, political debates, and *the* case of the era—*Dred Scott* v. *Sandford*. The problem of fugitive slaves led to debates, legal cases, and riots. Southerners argued that the Constitution protected their rights to reclaim fugitive slaves; some Northerners responded that "a higher law" compelled them to protect the freedom of those who sought to escape bondage.

Among the reasons for leaving the Union that Southerners offered in 1861 was the failure of Northerners to cooperate in the rendition of fugitive slaves.

Although the Constitution was the "supreme law of the land," antebellum state officials jealously resisted assertions of power by the federal government. By 1861, almost every state had, at some point, asserted its "sovereignty" and claimed the right to resist or nullify federal law, or even to secede from the Union. Antebellum federal officials were cautious about treading too heavily on the prerogatives of the states.

Despite general deference to the states, early on the United States Supreme Court asserted its power to declare state laws unconstitutional. States complained, sometimes resisted, and occasionally ignored mandates from the federal courts. State officials disregarded the ruling in *Worcester* v. *Georgia* (1832) that Georgia had no authority over certain Indians; in *Ableman* v. *Booth* (1859), the Wisconsin Supreme Court declared the federal Fugitive Slave Law of 1850 to be unconstitutional and then refused to comply with the United States Supreme Court's request for a copy of the record of the state proceedings; South Carolina officials ignored Justice William Johnson's opinion in *Elkison* v. *Deliesseline* (1823) that the state's Negro Seamen's Act was unconstitutional. Despite Johnson's opinion, six other southern states adopted almost identical legislation. Court decisions were not the only federal actions that states opposed. South Carolina declared a tariff to be null and void within its jurisdiction. Although the state backed down in the face of overwhelming federal power, nullification remained part of the nation's political and legal lexicon until the Civil War.

More dangerous than nullification was the claim that a state could leave the Union at will. If such a right existed, the Union was little more than a voluntary association. The dispute over the right to secede turned on differing theories of the Union. In the 1820s and 1830s, John Quincy Adams and Daniel Webster laid out the theory of a "perpetual Union," which Lincoln used in 1861 as part of his constitutional arguments against secession. Lincoln believed that the Constitution and the nation were created by the people, and the Union formed a perpetual contract that no state could break without the consent of the American people.

The alternative view argued that the Union was a compact of sovereign states. During the Sedition Act Crisis of 1798, Thomas Jefferson and James Madison endorsed this theory but did not advocate secession. Between the late 1820s and his death in 1850, South Carolina's John C. Calhoun refined the compact theory into an argument for state sovereignty, nullification, and secession. Calhoun argued that the states had created a national government with limited powers, and that if the national government exceeded its powers by threatening the rights and privileges of the states, the states were free to leave the Union.

The Civil War was partially a war over competing theories of constitutional government. During the war, theory and practice merged. The legal and intellectual arguments for a strong central government, a perpetual Union, and national supremacy that were used to oppose secession also helped create the ideological support for strengthening the national government, as well as consolidating enormous power in the hands of the president. Such centralization of power helped win the war. These theories also carried over to three new constitutional amendments, which fundamentally changed the nature of the Union.

Support for states' rights did not totally disappear with the end of the war. Andrew Johnson combined a states'-rights ideology with racism to frustrate congressional attempts to protect and enhance black freedom. The Supreme Court remained uncomfortable with the nationalization of power brought about by the war. For the rest of the century, the Court rejected many of the changes mandated by the Civil War Amendments and the statutes enacted to implement them. Tragically, the postwar Justices were unable to escape their own past and see that the Civil War and the new amendments had thoroughly altered the relationship of the states to the national government.

Black Americans suffered most from the Court's failure to appreciate the revolution in constitutional law brought about by the Civil War. Decisions in the *Slaughterhouse Cases* (1873), the *Civil Rights Cases* (1883), and numerous other cases undermined Congress's attempts to protect the rights that blacks had won during and immediately after the war. The Court failed to see how the war, the new federalism it produced, and the three new constitutional amendments had permanently altered race relations. The Court's failure to acknowledge and support the new federal structure in order to protect former slaves is ironic because as Lincoln recognized in his second inaugural, "All knew" that slavery "was somehow the cause of the war" and that only its eradication justified the horrors of the war itself. Tragically, the postwar Court made decisions affecting black rights as though nothing significant had occurred between 1861 and 1870, ignoring that the whole nature of the Constitution and the political system had changed because of the war against slavery.

The Civil War destroyed forever the once commonly accepted theory of state sovereignty. Federal supremacy was secured, not by legal theory and doctrine, but by the unanswerable arguments set forth by Generals Grant and Sherman. Appomattox signaled the end of state sovereignty and the viability of secession. The war also ended the debate over slavery by destroying the institution. Legally and rhetorically, Lincoln was the great emancipator. Practically, the title must be shared with the Union Army, which brought freedom to 3 million slaves through the force of arms. Among those under arms were nearly 200,000 blacks, many of whom had only recently been slaves.

While the Civil War ended arguments over state sovereignty, a rejuvenated states'-rights doctrine emerged from the ashes of the Confederacy. Southerners no longer claimed that their state laws were supreme; instead, they persuaded Congress and the Supreme Court that race relations was a local problem which the federal government should ignore. Blacks found that slavery had been replaced with a new kind of oppression, which took the form of segregation, separate and *unequal* access to public schools and other facilities, and a kind of economic bondage in the form of debt peonage. In the nineteenth century, blacks gained their freedom, but the promise of the Civil War Amendments remained unredeemed.

Slavery and State Law

At its height, the South's "peculiar institution" directly involved about 385,000 masters and some 3.5 million slaves worth over $1 billion. Indirectly, most white Southerners and more than 250,000 free blacks in the South were also affected by this system of bondage.

As property, slaves were bought and sold and were the objects of suits in tort, contract, property, and insurance law. As human beings, slaves could be prosecuted for crimes or be victims of crimes. For white lawmakers, slaves were an alien race to be controlled by the state and exploited by their masters, and a form of property to be protected from white strangers who might harm them. Jurists and legislators struggled with slaves' dual status as both property and persons.

Race and the Law of Negro Slavery

Slavery violated the tenets of American liberty and democracy. Nevertheless, it was an integral part of the economy of half the nation. Southerners justified slavery as an economic necessity and argued that American slavery was consistent with natural law because the system, unlike its counterpart in ancient or medieval Europe, was racially based. Southerners contended that blacks were racially inferior, and, therefore, enslaving them was not only legitimate, but a positive good for blacks as well as whites.

THOMAS R. R. COBB
An Inquiry into the Law of Negro Slavery
1858

Cobb was the reporter for the Georgia Supreme Court (1849–1857), a professor at the Lumpkin School of Law in Athens, and the man most responsible for drafting the Confederate Constitution. As a brigadier general in the Confederate Army, he was killed in action at Fredericksburg in 1862. Cobb was the only Southerner to write a treatise on slave law. Here he mixes racist theories with legal argument as he summarizes the rationales used by lawyers and judges to defend slavery.

18. . . . [W]e recognize in the negro a man, endowed with reason, will, and accountability, and in order to justify his subjection we must inquire of his intellectual and moral nature, and must be satisfied that its development is thereby promoted. If this be true, if the physical, intellectual, and moral development of the African race are promoted by a state of slavery, and their happiness secured to a greater extent than if left at liberty then their enslavement is consistent with the law of nature, and violative of none of its provisions. Is the negro's own happiness thereby best promoted? Is he therein most useful to his fellowman? Is he thereby more surely led to the discharge of his duty to God?

*   *   *

20. *First* then is the inquiry as to the physical adaptation of the negro to a state of servitude. His black color peculiarly fits him for the endurance of the heat of long-continued summers. The arched leg and receding heel seem to indicate a natural preparation for strength and endurance. The absence of nervous irritability gives to him a complete exemption from those inflammatory diseases so destructive

in hot and damp atmospheres, and hence the remarkable fact, that the ravages of that scourge of the tropics, the yellow fever, never reach the negro race. . . .

* * *

22.   *Second*. The mental inferiority of the negro has been often asserted and never successfully denied. An inviting field for digression is offered here, in the much-mooted question of the unity of the human race. It is unnecessary for our purposes to enter these lists. The law deals with men and things as they are, and whether the negro was originally a different species, or is a degeneration of the same, is a matter indifferent in the inquiry as to his proper status in his present condition. We deal with him as we find him, and according to the measure of his capacity, it is our duty to cultivate and improve him. . . .

* * *

31.   The prominent defect in the mental organization of the negro, is a want of judgment. He forms no definite idea of effects from causes. He cannot comprehend, so as to execute the simplest orders, unless they refresh his memory as to some previous knowledge. He is imitative, sometimes eminently so, but his mind is never inventive or suggestive. Improvement never enters into his imagination. . . . This mental defect, connected with the indolence and want of foresight of the negro, is the secret of his degradation. The imitative faculty makes the negro a good musician, yet he never originates a single air, nor invents a musical instrument. . . .

32.   Our next inquiry is as to the moral character of the negro. . . . The degraded situation of the barbarous tribes of Africa is well attested by every observer. So debased is their condition generally, that their humanity has been even doubted. . . .

* * *

69.   As all the negroes introduced into America were brought as slaves, the black color of the race raises the presumption of slavery, contrary to the principles of the common law, which would presume freedom until the contrary is shown. This presumption is extended, in most of the States, to mulattoes or persons of mixed blood, casting upon them the onus of proving a free maternal ancestor. . . .

70.   The issue and descendants of slaves, in the maternal line, are slaves. The rule, *partus sequitur ventrem*, has been adopted in all the States. The reason of this rule, as given by the civilians, was . . . "From principles of justice, the offspring, the increase of the womb, belongs to the master of the womb." This rule has been almost universal among those nations recognizing slavery. . . .

* * *

86.   Of the three great absolute rights guaranteed to every citizen by the common law, viz., the right of personal security, the right of personal liberty, and the right of private property, the slave, in a state of pure or absolute slavery, is totally deprived, being, as to life, liberty, and property, under the absolute and uncontrolled dominion of his master . . . however, no such state of slavery exists in these States. . . . [Because] modified is the slavery here, partly by natural law, partly by express enactment, and more effectually by the influence of civilization and Christian enlightenment . . . [producing] many of those protecting barriers, the denial of whose existence would shock an enlightened public sense.

87.   Statute law has done much to relieve the slave from this absolute dominion

[of the master]. . . . In all of the slaveholding States, the homicide of a slave is held to be murder. . . . Nor has the legislation of the States stopped at the protection of their lives, but the security of limbs and the general comfort of the body are, in most of the States, amply provided for, various penalties being inflicted on masters for their cruel treatment. . . .

The Power of the Master over the Slave

By the late antebellum period, the South universally accepted the idea that the law should punish strangers who harmed or killed slaves. Less certain was how a master's conduct might be limited by the law. The cases in this section confront three key issues involving a master's rights over the slave: whether a master had the right to punish a slave, whether a master could kill a slave, and whether a master had the right to free a slave.

State v. *Mann*
2 Dev. (N.C.) 263 (1829)

Elizabeth Jones rented her slave, Lydia, to John Mann. When Mann attempted to chastise Lydia for some "minor offence," she "ran off" and Mann shot her in the back. There was no allegation that Lydia was attempting to escape from bondage, only that she was attempting to avoid a beating. Jones procured Mann's indictment and conviction for battery, which Mann appealed. In his opinion of the court, Judge Thomas Ruffin conceded that a stranger could be indicted for battery on a slave. Ruffin also found that Jones had a right to sue Mann for any damages to Lydia "upon the general doctrine of bailment." But in the context of the criminal law, Ruffin equated the renter (Mann) with an owner and thus outlined the right of a master to punish a slave, and the right of the state to interfere with the master–slave relationship. Ruffin explored whether the state could interfere with an owner's treatment of his or her own slaves.

Ruffin, Judge—A Judge cannot but lament when such cases as the present are brought into judgment. It is impossible that the reasons on which they go can be appreciated, but where institutions similar to our own, exist and are thoroughly understood. The struggle, too, in the Judge's own breast between the feeling of the man, and the duty of the magistrate is a severe one, presenting strong temptation to put aside such questions, if it be possible. It is useless however, to complain of things inherent in our political state. And it is criminal in a Court to avoid any responsibility which the laws impose. With whatever reluctance therefore it is done the Court is compelled to express an opinion upon the extent of the dominion of the master over the slave in North-Carolina.

The indictment charges a battery on *Lydia*, a slave of *Elizabeth Jones*. . . . The enquiry here is whether a cruel and unreasonable battery on a slave, by the hirer, is indictable. . . . [Here Ruffin asserted that in a criminal case the hirer should be treated as though he were the owner of the slave.] [U]pon the general question, whether the owner is answerable *criminaliter* for a battery upon his own slave, or other exercise of authority or force not forbidden by statute, the Court entertains but little doubt.—That he is so liable, has never yet been decided; nor, as far as is known, been hitherto contended. There have been no prosecutions of the sort. The established habits and uniform practice of the country in this respect, is the best evidence of the portion of power, deemed by the whole community, requisite to the preservation of the master's dominion. . . . [A]rguments drawn from the well established principles which confer and restrain the authority of the parent over the child, the tutor over the pupil, the master over the apprentice, have been pressed on us. The Court does not recognize their application. There is no likeness between the cases. They are in opposition to each other, and there is an impassable gulf between them. The difference is that which exists between freedom and slavery—and a greater cannot be imagined. In the one, the end in view is the happiness of the youth, born to equal rights with that governor, on whom the duty devolves of training the young to usefulness, in a station which he is afterwards to assume among freemen. To such an end, and with such a subject, moral and intellectual instruction seem the natural means; and for the most part, they are found to suffice. Moderate force is superadded, only to make the others effectual. If that fail, it is better to leave the party to his own headstrong passions, and the ultimate correction of the law, than to allow it to be immoderately inflicted by a private person. With slavery it is far otherwise. The end is the profit of the master, his security and the public safety; the subject, one doomed in his own person, and his posterity, to live without knowledge, and without the capacity to make any thing his own, and to toil that another may reap the fruits. What moral considerations shall be addressed to such a being to convince him what it is impossible but that the most stupid must feel and know can never be true—that he is thus to labor upon a principle of natural duty, or for the sake of his own personal happiness, such services can only be expected from one who has no will of his own, who surrenders his will in implicit obedience to that of another. Such obedience is the consequence only of uncontrolled authority over the body. There is nothing else which can operate to produce the effect. The power of the master must be absolute, to render the submission of the slave perfect. I most freely confess my sense of the harshness of this proposition. I feel it as deeply as any man can. And as a principle of moral right, every person in his retirement must repudiate it. But in the actual condition of things, it must be so.—There is no remedy. This discipline belongs to the state of slavery. They cannot be disunited, without abrogating at once the rights of the master, and absolving the slave from his subjection. It constitutes the curse of slavery to both the bond and free portions of our population. But it is inherent in the relation of master and slave.

That there may be particular instances of cruelty and deliberate barbarity, where, in conscience the law might properly interfere, is most probable. The difficulty is to determine, where a Court may properly begin. Merely in the abstract it may well be asked, which power of the master accords with right. The answer will probably sweep away all of them. But we cannot look at the matter in that light. The truth is, that we are forbidden to enter upon a train of general reasoning on the subject. We cannot allow the right of the master to be brought into discussion in the Courts of Justice. The slave, to remain a slave, must be made sensible, that there is no appeal from his master; that his power is in no instance, usurped; but is conferred by the laws of man at least, if not by the law of God. The danger would be great indeed, if the tribunals of justice should be called on to graduate the punishment appropriate to every temper, and every dereliction of menial duty. No man can anticipate the many and aggravated provocations of the master, which the slave would be constantly stimulated by his own passions, or the instigation of others to give; or the consequent wrath of the master prompting him to bloody vengeance, upon the turbulent traitor—a vengeance generally practised with impunity by reason of its privacy. The Court therefore disclaims the power of changing the relation, in which these parts of our people stand to each other.

We are happy to see, that there is daily less and less occasion for the interposition of the Courts. The protection already afforded by several statutes, that all-powerful motive, the private interest of the owner, the benevolence towards each other, seated in the hearts of those who have been born and bred together, the frowns and deep execrations of the community upon the barbarian, who is guilty of excessive and brutal cruelty to his unprotected slave, all combined, have produced a mildness of treatment, and attention to the comforts of the unfortunate class of slaves, greatly mitigating the rigors of servitude, and ameliorating the condition of the slaves. The same causes are operating, and will continue to operate with increased action, until the disparity in numbers between the whites and blacks, shall have rendered the latter in no degree dangerous to the former, when the police now existing may be further relaxed. This result, greatly to be desired, may be much more rationally expected from the events above alluded to, and now in progress, than from any rash expositions of abstract truths, by a Judiciary tainted with a false and fanatical philanthropy, seeking to redress an acknowledged evil, by means still more wicked and appalling than even that evil.

I repeat, that I would gladly have avoided this ungrateful question. But being brought to it, the Court is compelled to declare, that while slavery exists amongst us in its present state, or until it shall seem fit to the Legislature to interpose express enactments to the contrary, it will be imperative duty of the Judges to recognize the full dominion of the owner over the slave, except where the exercise of it is forbidden by statute. And this we do upon the ground, that this dominion is essential to the value of slaves as property, to the security of the master, and the public tranquility, greatly dependent upon their subordination; and in fine, as most effectually securing the general protection and comfort of the slaves themselves.

Per Curiam—Let the judgment below be reversed, and judgment entered for the Defendant.

Note: Harriet Beecher Stowe on Southern Judges

The author of this opinion, Judge Thomas Ruffin, is generally considered to be one of the finest antebellum southern jurists. In her *Key to Uncle Tom's Cabin,* Harriet Beecher Stowe concluded: "No one can read this decision, so fine and clear in its expression, so dignified and solemn in its earnestness, and so dreadful in its results, without feeling at once a deep respect of the man [Ruffin] and the horror of the system."

Stowe referred to the next case as the "Ne Plus Ultra of Legal Humanity." "Nobody," she wrote, "could willingly read" this indictment "twice." She noted that Souther was sentenced to only five years in jail and, afterward, could buy "as many more negroes as he chooses."

Souther v. Commonwealth
7 Gratt. (Va.) 672 (1851)

Simeon Souther was indicted for murdering his own slave.

The count charged that on the first day of September 1849, the prisoner tied his negro slave Sam, with ropes about his wrists, neck, body, legs, and ankles, to a tree. That whilst so tied, the prisoner first whipped the slave with switches. That he next beat and cobbed the slave with a shingle, and compelled two of his slaves, a man and a woman, also to cob the deceased with the shingle. That whilst the deceased was so tied to the tree, the prisoner did strike, knock, kick, stamp, and beat him, upon various parts of his head, face and body; that he applied fire to his body, back, sides belly, groins and privy parts; that he then washed his body, & c., with warm water, in which pods of red pepper had been put and steeped, and he compelled his two slaves aforesaid, also to wash him with this same preparation of warm water and red pepper. . . . [Then] the prisoner untied the deceased from the tree, in such way as to throw him with violence to the ground, and he then and there did knock, kick, stamp, and beat the deceased upon his head, temples, and various parts of his body. That the prisoner then had the deceased carried into a shed room of his house, and there he compelled one of his slaves in his presence, to confine the deceased's feet in stocks . . . and to tie a rope about the neck of the deceased, and fasten it to a bed post in the room, there by strangling, choking and suffocating the deceased. And that whilst the deceased was thus made fast in stocks as aforesaid, the prisoner did kick, knock, stamp, and beat him, upon his head, face, breast, belly, sides, back, and body. And he again compelled his two slaves to apply fire to the body of the deceased whilst he was so made fast as aforesaid. And . . . from these various modes of punishment and torture, the slave Sam then and there died. It appeared that the prisoner commenced the punishment of the deceased in the morning, and that it was continued throughout the day; and that the deceased died in the presence of the prisoner and one of his slaves and one of the witnesses, whilst the punishment was still progressing.

Field, J. . . . The prisoner was indicted and convicted of murder in the second degree, in the Circuit court of Hanover at its April term last past, and was sentenced to the penitentiary for five years, the period of time ascertained by the jury. . . .

. . . It is believed that the records of criminal jurisprudence do not contain a case of more atrocious and wicked cruelty than was presented upon the trial of Souther; and yet it has been gravely and earnestly contended here by his counsel, that his offence amounts to manslaughter only.

It has been contended by the counsel of the prisoner, that a man cannot be indicted and prosecuted for the cruel and excessive whipping of his own slave. That it is lawful for the master to chastise his slave; and that if death ensues from such chastisement, unless it was intended to produce death, it is like the case of homicide, which is committed by a man in the performance of a lawful act, which is manslaughter only. It has been decided by this Court . . . that the owner of a slave, for the malicious, cruel and excessive beating of his own slave, cannot be indicted; yet it by no means follows when such malicious, cruel and excessive beating results in death though not intended and premeditated, that the beating is to be regarded as lawful, for the purpose of reducing the crime to manslaughter, when the whipping is inflicted for the sole purpose of chastisement. It is the policy of the law in respect to the relation of master and slave, and for the sake of securing proper subordination and obedience on the part of the slave, to protect the master from prosecution in all such cases, even if the whipping and punishment be malicious, cruel and excessive. But in so inflicting punishment for the sake of punishment, the owner of the slave acts at his peril; and if death ensues in consequence of such punishment, the relation of master and slave affords no ground of excuse or palliation. The principles of the common law in relation to homicide, apply to his case, without qualification or exception; and according to those principles, the act of the prisoner, in the case under consideration, amounted to murder. Upon this point we are unanimous. [The court affirmed Souther's five-year sentence.]

Mitchell v. Wells
35 Miss. 235 (1859)

In 1846, Edward Wells emancipated his slave (and also his daughter by a slave mistress) Nancy Wells in Ohio. Wells then returned to Mississippi, where he subsequently died, bequeathing $3,000 and other property to Nancy. Wells's executor, William Mitchell, refused to give Nancy her legacy, arguing that she was a slave. A chancery court awarded Nancy her estate, and Mitchell appealed to Mississippi's highest court, which examined whether Nancy's emancipation in Ohio affected her status in Mississippi. The two opinions excerpted here illustrate the connections between slavery and politics in the late antebellum period. They also illustrate the dilemma faced by slave societies between interfering with the actions of masters, as Justice William Harris's majority opinion urges, and conceding that the right of masters to control their property was the essence of slavery, as Justice Alexander Handy's dissent argues. This case reached the Mississippi court two years after the United States Supreme Court ruled in Dred Scott v. Sandford *that blacks were not citizens of the United States.*

[Handy, J.] [It is] . . . the obvious policy of the State on the subject of emancipation, as declared by her latest legislation, as well as by her settled conviction, that the interests of both races are best promoted by the institution of slavery as it exists amongst us, and most seriously prejudiced by either manumission in the Union, or colonization elsewhere.

I think it demonstrable, both upon principle and the weight of authority, that a slave, once domiciliated as such, in this State, can acquire no right, civil or political, within her limits, by manumission elsewhere. That manumission and citizenship, elsewhere conferred, cannot, even upon principles of comity, under our laws and policy, vest any right here.

* * *

Mississippi came into the Union under this Federal Constitution as a member of this political family, to be associated on terms of political equality, comity, or courtesy with the white race, who alone by that compact had a right to be thus associated. She came into the Union, not only recognizing the institution of slavery as her best policy, but forbidding the legislature from passing laws for the emancipation of slaves except by the consent of the owner. She came into the Union with this institution, not only sanctioned, provided for, and protected by her own Constitution, by the direct act and recognition of the other States of the Union, and by the express provisions of that same Constitution which had originally excluded the African race from the privileges of citizenship, but with a right to full protection, under that instrument, both for the enjoyment of her property in slaves, and against the degradation of political companionship, association, and equality with them in the future. Her climate, soil, and productions, and the pursuits of her people, their habits, manners, and opinions, all combine not only to sanction the wisdom, humanity, and policy of the system thus established by her organic law and fostered by her early legislation, but they require slave labor.

It was declared in the convention that framed the Federal Constitution, by some of their delegates, that Georgia and South Carolina would become barren wastes without slave labor, and so important did they deem it to their prosperity, that they openly announced that these States would not become parties to the Union if the slave trade should be prohibited.

. . . [In Mississippi] as early as 1822, emancipation, except for some distinguished service, and even then proven to and sanctioned by the legislature, was prohibited.

* * *

. . . [A]s late as February, 1857, the legislature of this State declared that "It shall not be lawful for any person, either by deed, will, or other conveyance, directly or in trust, . . . to make any disposition of any slave or slaves, for the purpose or with the intent to emancipate such slave or slaves in this State, or to provide that such slaves be removed to be emancipated elsewhere. . . ."

* * *

I cannot therefore doubt, in view of the whole subject, that it *now* is and *ever has been*, the policy of Mississippi to protect, preserve, and perpetuate the institution of slavery as it exists amongst us, and to prevent emancipation generally of Mississippi slaves.

* * *

A slave once domiciliated here, *during the continuance of that domicile* has no such rights [to inherit property]. If the appellee possess them at all, then she must have derived them from the law of her new domicile. That law, *proprio vigore*, has no extra-territorial operation, and could vest no right in the appellee *here*, except by the comity or consent of the State of Mississippi. She stands before the authorities of this State with no vested right, [and] . . . is entitled, therefore, to such *rights only*, as are not inconsistent with our laws or policy. . . . By our law she had neither capacity to sue, nor take, nor hold property, originally, before she left this State. The law of her new domicile confirming such rights in Ohio, are limited to that domicile, and cannot be made to extend over us without our consent, as she can have no *vested right* to claim or demand a mere favor, *a gratuity dependent at all times on the will of the donor*; when that favor or courtesy is withheld by the State, her right must cease with it, in obedience to the *will of the sovereign . . .* irrespective of rights acquired in another State.

[Here Harris quoted from Chief Justice Taney's opinion in *Dred Scott* v. *Sandford* that blacks were not citizens of the United States under the Constitution, but were, at the Founding, "considered a subordinate and inferior class of beings, . . . and whether emancipated or not, yet remained subject to their authority, and had no rights or privileges but such as those who held the power and the Government might choose to grant them."]

*   *   *

. . . I wholly dissent from the application of the doctrine of "comity" to cases like this. "Comity" forbids that a sister State of this confederacy should seek to introduce into the family of States, as equals or associates, a caste of different color, and of acknowledged inferiority, who, though existing among us at the time of our compact of Union, were excluded from the sisterhood by common consent.

*   *   *

No people are bound, or ought to enforce or hold valid, *in their courts of justice*, any contract which is injurious to their public rights, or offends their morals, or contravenes their policy, or violates a public law. [Citing James Kent]

*   *   *

The State of Ohio, forgetful of her constitutional obligations to the whole race, and afflicted with a *negro-mania*, which inclines her to *descend*, rather than elevate herself in the scale of humanity, chooses to take to her embrace, as citizens, the neglected race, who by common consent of the States united, were regarded, at the formation of our government, as an inferior caste, incapable of the blessings of free government, and occupying, in the order of nature, an intermediate state between the irrational animal and the white man.

In violation of good faith, as well as of the guarantees of the Constitution, efforts are made to destroy the rights of property in this race, which, at the time of the adoption of that instrument, was in servitude, in all or nearly all the States originally parties to the compact of Union. Mississippi and other States, under the firm conviction that the relation of master and slave . . . is mutually productive of the happiness and best interests of both, continues the institution, and desires to perpetuate it. She is unwilling to extend to the slave race freedom and equality of rights, or to elevate them into political association with the family of States.

Ohio persists; and not only so introduces slaves into her own political organization, but her citizens extend encouragement and inducement to the removal of slaves from Mississippi into the limits of Ohio; and then, in violation of the laws and policy of Mississippi, and in violation of the laws of the United States in relation to the rendition of fugitive slaves, introduces them into her limits as citizens.

Looking at the transaction in the light of comity, courtesy, founded on mutual respect and mutual good-will, regarding it as a question of neighborly politeness and good breeding, or in the more intimate relation of constitutional brotherhood, in which the advocates of this doctrine of comity choose to place it, and it seems to me that comity is terminated by Ohio, in the very act of degrading herself and her sister States, by the offensive association, and that the rights of Mississippi are outraged, when Ohio ministers to emancipation and the abolition of our institution of slavery, by such unkind, disrespectful, lawless interference with our local rights.

But when I am told that Ohio has not only the right thus to degrade and disgrace herself, and wrong us, but also, that she has the right to force her new associates into the Mississippi branch of the American family, to claim and exercise rights *here*, which our laws have always denied to this inferior race, and that Mississippi is bound to yield obedience to such demand, I am at a loss to understand upon what *principle* of law or reason, of courtesy or justice, such claim can be founded.

Suppose that Ohio, still further afflicted with her peculiar philanthropy, should determine to descend another grade in the scale of *her peculiar* humanity, and claim to confer citizenship on the chimpanzee or the ourang-outang (the most respectable of the monkey tribe), are we to be told that "comity" will require of the States not thus demented, to forget their own policy and self-respect, and lower their own citizens and institutions in the scale of being, to meet the necessities of the mongrel race thus attempted to be introduced into the family of sisters in this confederacy?

Ohio, by allowing the manumission of defendant in error in her jurisdiction, and conferring rights of citizenship *there*, contrary to the known policy of Mississippi, can neither confer freedom on a Mississippi slave, nor the right to acquire, hold, sue for, nor enjoy property in Mississippi.

Let the decree be reversed. . . .

[Justice Alexander Handy dissented.]

* * *

It is said that the violation by the non-slaveholding States, of the constitutional rights of the Southern States, in harboring our fugitive slaves . . . deprives them of all claim to international comity in reference to the rights of their free negroes who may seek to assert rights in our courts.

But this sacred duty,—to respect and enforce the rights of residents of other States, secured to them by the laws of those States,—can never be destroyed, whilst the confederacy continues, by the fact that the State under which the right is claimed, has been recreant to her obligations to the compact which binds the States together. If their courts of justice have been prostituted to the purposes of fanaticism and lawlessness, that is no reason why we should descend from our elevated position, which should be superior to such influences, follow their unworthy example, and make this court the medium of propagating our political theories upon the same subject. Whilst the confederacy continues, we cannot justify ourselves as a State in violating its spirit and principles, because other States have . . . been false to their duties and obligations. It may justify us in dissolving the compact, but not in violating our obligations under it whilst it continues.

* * *

The fundamental and controlling idea upon which property in slaves rests is, the *right of absolute disposition*; and this is paramount to any question as to how, or in whose behalf, the right shall be exercised. That right, so far as it refers to the disposition of the person of the slave, is unlimited, except as it is restricted by regulations of positive law. The restrictive policy, as declared by this State, is limited to emancipation of slaves in this State, to take effect here or elsewhere. But it does not extend to removal out of this State and emancipation there, and could not, for want of power to carry out any such policy. It would be contrary to all reason and principle for us to attempt to establish any law or policy prohibiting the owner in this State from removing his slave to England or India, and manumitting him there to reside there; and for the same reason, we have none interdicting the removal to Ohio for manumission and residence there. Our abstract opinions are, that such a course is impolitic; but such opinions have not been established *as a policy*. Our policy, *as a State*, has no reference whatever to free negroes out of the State, except to prevent them from coming to this State and residing here. It is based upon the same principle as all our domestic policy; having reference to our own internal welfare and protection, and to the promotion of the morality and happiness of society. . . . So our domestic policy has been strongly against banking in this State; yet no one would contend that a foreign bank might not sue in this State upon any legal right acquired in another State. These things, though contrary to a policy of a domestic character, contemplated by our laws, are not within their prohibition, because our laws have reference solely to the prevention of the mischiefs within this State.

Note: The *Somerset* Precedent in America

Before the 1830s, most southern states had recognized the right of masters to free their slaves in the North as well as the power of the free states to emancipate any slaves voluntarily brought into the North. *Mitchell* v. *Wells* was the last of a number of southern decisions rejecting the notion, dating from *Somerset* v. *Stewart* (1772), that slaves could gain freedom by being brought to a free state.

Slavery and the Constitution

Slavery was the most divisive constitutional issue in pre–Civil War America. A federal republic that was, in Lincoln's words, "half slave and half free" required accommodations and compromises over slavery. Indeed, much of the debate at the Constitutional Convention centered on slavery in the new nation.

In 1788, during the ratification struggle, General Charles Cotesworth Pinckney told the South Carolina legislature that

> we have a security that the general government can never emancipate them, for no such authority is granted, and it is admitted on all hands, that the general government has no powers but what are expressly granted by the constitution; and that all rights not expressed were reserved by the several states.

Mainstream nineteenth-century constitutional interpretation accepted this understanding that the national government had no power over slavery in the states where it existed. However, federal jurisdiction arose over (1) the African slave trade and the regulation of the interstate commerce in slaves, (2) the return of fugitive slaves, (3) slavery in the federal territories and District of Columbia, (4) the admission of new slave states into the Union, and (5) the interstate transit or sojourn of slaves through or in free states.

The Constitution prohibited any federal interference with the African slave trade until 1808, when Congress prohibited the importation of slaves and declared the African trade to be piracy. Enforcement of the laws prohibiting the trade was lax, and not until Lincoln's administration did the government seek the death penalty for a slave trader. While important for the development of admiralty law and international law, the cases on the slave trade had relatively little impact on domestic slavery or domestic legal developments. Their indifferent enforcement, however, illustrates the extent to which slaveowners and their northern "doughface" sympathizers controlled Congress, the judiciary, and the executive branch before the Civil War. In the 1850s, some proslavery extremists wanted to reopen the slave trade, but most Southerners rejected this idea. In 1861, the Confederate Constitution banned the African slave trade.

Although most antebellum lawyers and lawmakers would have conceded that Congress had the *power* to regulate the interstate slave trade, legislation on the subject was politically unthinkable because it would have threatened the Union. Commerce clause cases, such as *Gibbons* v. *Ogden*, recognized the special status of slaves in the general regulation of commerce. It is possible to see the influence of slavery, directly or indirectly, in almost every commerce clause case from 1820 to 1861.

The issues of fugitive slaves, slavery in the federal territories, and slave transit led to divisive debates in state legislatures and Congress, and before state and federal courts. Ultimately, these issues were decided not by constitutional arguments and ballots, but by battlefield tactics and bullets.

The Problem of Fugitive Slaves

The fugitive slave clause's wording and its placement in Article IV, Section 2, of the Constitution suggest that the Framers did not anticipate a federal law to enforce it. However, in 1793 Congress spelled out procedures for the return of fugitive slaves. The 1793 act allowed masters or their agents who captured runaways to bring them to any magistrate, state or federal, to obtain a "certificate of removal," authorizing the claimants to take the runaway slaves out of the states where they were found, and back to the state where the slaves owed service. By this time, all the New England states and Pennsylvania either had abolished slavery outright or were in the process of gradually eliminating it. By 1804, New York and New Jersey had joined this "first emancipation." These changes in northern law meant that in more than half the nation a presumption of servitude, based on race, no longer existed. The Fugitive Slave Law of 1793, with its lax evidentiary standards, gravely threatened the growing northern free black population. To prevent kidnapping, many free states passed "personal liberty laws," which supplemented the requirements of the federal law. In

1842, Pennsylvania's law led to the first United States Supreme Court decision on fugitive slaves.

Prigg v. Pennsylvania
16 Pet. (41 U.S.) 539 (1842)

In 1837 Edward Prigg, a professional slave catcher, seized Margaret Morgan, a runaway slave living in Pennsylvania. Prigg applied to a justice of the peace for certificates of removal under the federal law of 1793 and Pennsylvania's personal liberty law of 1826, which had higher evidentiary requirements than the federal law. The justice refused Prigg's request; so without any legal authority, Prigg removed Morgan and her children, including one conceived and born in Pennsylvania. Convicted of kidnapping under the 1826 law, Prigg appealed to the United States Supreme Court. At issue was the constitutionality of both the federal law of 1793 and the Pennsylvania law of 1826.

Mr. Justice Story delivered the opinion of the Court.

*   *   *

. . . Historically, it is well known, that the object of [the fugitive slave] clause was to secure to the citizens of the slaveholding states the complete right and title of ownership in their slaves, as property, in every state in the Union into which they might escape from the state where they were held in servitude. The full recognition of this right and title was indispensable to the security of this species of property in all the slaveholding states; and indeed, was so vital to the preservation of their domestic interests and institutions, that it cannot be doubted that it constituted a fundamental article, without the adoption of which the Union could not have been formed. Its true design was to guard against the doctrines and principles prevalent in the non-slaveholding states, by preventing them from intermeddling with, or obstructing, or abolishing the rights of the owners of slaves.

. . . [I]f the Constitution had not contained this clause, every non-slaveholding state in the Union would have been at liberty to . . . free all runaway slaves coming within its limits, and to have given them entire immunity and protection against the claims of their masters; a course which would have created the most bitter animosities, and engendered perpetual strife between the different states. The clause was, therefore, of the last importance to the safety and security of the southern states; and could not have been surrendered by them without endangering their whole property in slaves. The clause was accordingly adopted into the Constitution by the unanimous consent of the framers of it; a proof at once of its intrinsic and practical necessity.

The clause manifestly contemplates the existence of a positive, unqualified right on the part of the owner of the slave, which no state law or regulation can in any way qualify, regulate, control, or restrain. The slave is not to be discharged from service or labour, in consequence of any state law or regulation. Now, certainly . . . any state law or state regulation, which interrupts, limits, delays, or postpones the right of the owner to the immediate possession of the slave, and the immediate command of his service and labour, operates, pro tanto, a discharge of the slave therefrom. . . .

We have said that the clause contains a positive and unqualified recognition of the right of the owner in the slave, unaffected by any state law or regulation whatsoever. . . . If this be so, then all the incidents to that right attach also; the owner must, therefore, have the right to seize and repossess the slave, which the local laws of his own state confer upon him as property. . . . Upon this ground we have not the slightest hesitation in holding that, under and in virtue of the Constitution, the owner of a slave is clothed with entire authority, in every state in the Union, to seize and recapture his slave, whenever he can do it without any breach of the peace, or any illegal violence. In this sense, and to this extent this clause of the Constitution may properly be said to execute itself; and to require no aid from legislation, state or national.

*   *   *

If, therefore, the clause of the Constitution had stopped at the mere recognition of the right, without providing or contemplating any means by which it might be established and enforced in cases where it did not execute itself, it is plain that it would have, in a great variety of cases, a delusive and empty annunciation.

. . . [The slaveowners] require the aid of legislation to protect the right, to enforce the delivery, and to secure the subsequent possession of the slave. If, indeed, the Constitution guarantees the right, and if it requires the delivery upon the claim of the owner, (as cannot well be doubted,) the natural inference certainly is, that the national government is clothed with the appropriate authority and functions to enforce it. The fundamental principle applicable to all cases of this sort, would seem to be, that where the end is required, the means are given; and where the duty is enjoined, the ability to perform it is contemplated to exist on the part of the functionaries to whom it is entrusted. The clause is found in the national Constitution, and not in that of any state. It does not point out any state functionaries, or any state action to carry its provisions into effect. The states cannot, therefore, be compelled to enforce them; and it might well be deemed an unconstitutional exercise of the power of interpretation, to insist that the states are bound to provide means to carry into effect the duties of the national government, nowhere delegated or intrusted to them by the Constitution. On the contrary, the natural, if not the necessary conclusion is, that the national government, in the absence of all positive provisions to the contrary, is bound, through its own proper departments, legislative, judicial, or executive, as the case may require, to carry into effect all the rights and duties imposed upon it by the Constitution. . . .

Congress has taken this very view of the power and duty of the national government. . . . The result of their deliberations, was the passage of the act of the 12th of February, 1793. . . .

*   *   *

. . . We hold the [Fugitive Slave] act to be clearly constitutional in all its leading provisions, and, indeed, with the exception of that part which confers authority upon state magistrates, to be free from reasonable doubt and difficulty upon the grounds already stated. As to the authority so conferred upon state magistrates, while a difference of opinion . . . may exist still on the point, in different states, whether state magistrates are bound to act under it; none is entertained by this Court that state magistrates may, if they choose, exercise that authority, unless prohibited by state legislation.

The remaining question is, whether the power of legislation upon this subject is exclusive in the national government. . . . In our opinion it is exclusive. . . .

It is scarcely conceivable that the slaveholding states would have been satisfied with leaving to the legislation of the non-slaveholding states, a power of regulation, in the absence of that of Congress, which would or might practically amount to a power to destroy the rights of the owner. If the argument, therefore, of a concurrent power in the states to act upon the subject-matter in the absence of legislation by Congress, be well founded; then, if Congress had never acted at all . . . there would be a resulting authority in each of the states to regulate the whole subject as its pleasure; and to dole out its own remedial justice, or withhold it at its pleasure and according to its own views of policy and expediency. Surely such a state of things never could have been intended, under such a solemn guarantee of right and duty. On the other hand, construe the right of legislation as exclusive in Congress, and every evil, and every danger vanishes. The right and the duty are then co-extensive and uniform in remedy and operation throughout the whole Union. The owner has the same security, and the same remedial justice, and the same exemption from state regulation and control, through however many states he may pass with his fugitive slave in his possession, in transitu, to his own domicile. . . .

These are some of the reasons . . . upon which we hold the power of legislation on this subject to be exclusive in Congress. To guard, however, against any possible misconstruction of our views, it is proper to state, that we are by no means to be understood in any manner whatsoever to doubt or to interfere with the police power belonging to the states in virtue of their general sovereignty. That police power extends over all subjects within the territorial limits of the states; and has never been conceded to the United States. It is wholly distinguishable from the right and duty secured by the provision now under consideration. . . . We entertain no doubt whatsoever, that the states, in virtue of their general police power, possess full jurisdiction to arrest and restrain in runaway slaves, and remove them from their borders, and otherwise to secure themselves against their depredations and evil example, as they certainly may do in cases of idlers, vagabonds, and paupers. The rights of the owners of fugitive slaves are in no just sense interfered with, or regulated by such a course; and in many cases, the operations of this police power, although designed essentially for . . . the protection, safety, and peace of the state, may essentially promote and aid the interests of the owners. But such regulations can never be permitted to interfere with or to obstruct the just rights of the owner to reclaim his slave, derived from the Constitution of the United States; or with the remedies prescribed by Congress to aid and enforce the same.

Upon these grounds, we are of opinion that the act of Pennsylvania . . . is unconstitutional. . . .

[Chief Justice Taney concurred with the result in *Prigg*, but objected to Story's assertions that state officials could not be required to enforce the federal law. Taney also misconstrued Story's opinion to mean that the states were prohibited from adopting legislation to aid in the return of fugitive slaves.]

The opinion of the Court maintains that the power over this subject is so exclusively vested in Congress, that since the adoption of the Constitution, no state can pass any law in relation to it. In other words the state authorities are prohibited from interfering for the purpose of protecting the right of the master and aiding him in the recovery of his property. I think the states are not prohibited; and that, on the contrary, it is enjoined upon them as a duty to protect and support the owner when he is endeavouring to obtain possession of his property found within their respective territories.

*   *   *

Indeed, if the state authorities are absolved from all obligation to protect this right, and may stand by and see it violated without an effort to defend it, the act of Congress of 1793 scarcely deserves the name of a remedy . . . [because the law would] depend altogether for its execution upon the officers of the United States named in it. And the master must take the fugitive, after he has seized him, before a judge of the District or Circuit Court, residing in the state, and exhibit his proofs, and procure from the judge his certificate of ownership, in order to obtain the protection in removing his property which this act of Congress professes to give.

Now, in many of the states there is but one district judge, and there are only nine states which have judges of the Supreme Court residing within them. The fugitive will frequently be found by his owner in a place very distant from the residence of either of these judges; and would certainly be removed beyond his reach, before a warrant could be procured from the judge to arrest him, even if the act of Congress authorized such a warrant. But it does not authorize the judge to issue a warrant to arrest the fugitive; but evidently relied on the state authorities to protect the owner in making the seizure. . . . It is only necessary to state the provisions of this law in order to show how ineffectual and delusive is the remedy provided by Congress, if state authority is forbidden to come to its aid.

Note: *Prigg* and the Use of History

In *Prigg*, Justice Story characterized the fugitive slave clause as "a fundamental article, without the adoption of which the Union could not have been formed." The history of the clause undermined this argument. Late in the Constitutional Convention, South Carolina's Pierce Butler proposed a clause to "require fugitive slaves and servants to be delivered up like criminals." James Wilson objected that this "obliged the Executive of the State to do it, at the public expense." Roger Sherman sarcastically added that there was "no more propriety in the public seizing and surrendering a slave or servant, than a horse." In the face of this opposition, Butler withdrew his proposal. The next day, without any further debate or even a recorded vote, the delegates adopted what became the fugitive slave clause.

Note: *Prigg* and Its Aftermath

Justice Story's opinion did not in fact prohibit state enforcement of the 1793 law. Nevertheless, in the 1840s some northern jurists refused to hear fugitive slave cases, claiming that the Supreme Court's decision precluded them from taking jurisdiction. Various states adopted new personal liberty laws that removed state support for enforcement of the 1793 law. A Massachusetts act of 1843, for example, prohibited any state official, including sheriffs and judges, from participating in the return of a fugitive slave under the law of 1793, and denied slavecatchers access to public jails and other facilities.

The new personal liberty laws led to southern demands for a more stringent federal law. The Fugitive Slave Law of 1850 authorized the appointment of a federal commissioner in every county of the United States who could issue certificates of removal for fugitive slaves and call for aid from federal marshals, the military, and "bystanders, or *posse comitatus*." People interfering in the enforcement of the law could be jailed for up to six months and fined up to $1,000. An alleged fugitive could be seized on minimal evidence and brought before the commissioner, who issued the arrest warrant for a summary and juryless proceeding. At this hearing, the alleged fugitive was prohibited from testifying on his own behalf. A successful claimant was required to pay the federal commissioner a fee of $10, but if the commissioner decided against the claimant the fee was only $5. Congress justified this differential because the commissioner had more paperwork if he found in favor of the claimant; but to many Northerners, this seemed like a blatant attempt at bribery.

Reaction to the 1850 law took many forms. Many blacks, free and fugitive, living in the North fled to Canada. In a number of northern cities, blacks and their white allies formed self-defense groups. While most fugitive slave seizures ended in successful renditions, riots and rescues in Massachusetts, Pennsylvania, New York, Ohio, Illinois, and Wisconsin gave Americans the impression that the law was not being enforced. These incidents made national headlines, as alleged fugitive slaves avoided the clutches of federal officers, while an occasional slaveowner or policeman lost his life.

Note: Northern States'-Rights Arguments

In January 1855, a federal court convicted Sherman Booth for having rescued a fugitive slave, but less than two weeks later the Wisconsin Supreme Court declared the 1850 Fugitive Slave Law unconstitutional and released Booth from federal custody. Federal Marshal Stephen Ableman's appeal of the state court decision was delayed for three years because the Wisconsin court refused to send a record of the case to the United States Supreme Court. Chief Justice Taney's opinion for a unanimous court in *Ableman* v. *Booth*, 21 How. (U.S.) 506 (1859), upheld the 1850 law and asserted that no state could interfere with the rendition process or question the power of federal officers to arrest people under the law.

Slavery, the Territories, and Interstate Comity

The issue of slavery in the territories first emerged when Missouri sought to enter the Union as a slave state. Northerners argued that Missouri was north and west of the Ohio River and thus should be free under the Northwest Ordinance. The ensuing debate led to the Compromise of 1820, also called the Missouri Compromise, which brought Missouri into the Union as a slave state, but barred slavery from those territories north of the southern boundary of Missouri.

The acquisition of land during the Mexican War reopened the question of slavery in the territories. In 1846, northern congressmen tried to keep slavery out of all the territories acquired from Mexico through the Wilmot Proviso, but the proposal died in the Senate. Southerners, meanwhile, demanded the right to take their slaves into all the federal territories, even those free under the Compromise of 1820.

Political deadlock ended with the Compromise of 1850, which brought California into the Union as a free state, prohibited the public sale of slaves in the District of Columbia, led to the passage of the new Fugitive Slave Law, and opened some of the new territories to slavery. In 1854, the Kansas-Nebraska Act allowed slavery into some territories previously closed to slavery under the Missouri Compromise of 1820. The Kansas-Nebraska Act led to the formation of the Republican party, which was dedicated to stopping the spread of slavery in the territories.

Dred Scott v. Sandford
19 How. (60 U.S.) 393 (1857)

As the slave of John Emerson, an Army surgeon, Dred Scott lived on military bases in Illinois and at Fort Snelling (present-day Minnesota), an area that was free under the Missouri Compromise. In 1850, after Emerson's death, a St. Louis court, following Missouri precedents dating from 1824, held that Dred Scott had become free while living in nonslave jurisdictions and remained free, despite his return to Missouri. The Missouri Supreme Court reversed this result. Reflecting the proslavery ideology of the South, the Missouri court, in Scott v. Emerson, *15 Mo. 576 (1852), disavowed the old precedents:*

> *Times are not as they were when the former decisions on this subject were made. Since then not only individuals but States have been possessed of a dark and fell spirit in relation to slavery, whose gratification is sought in the pursuit of measures, whose inevitable consequence must be the overthrow and destruction of our government. Under such circumstances it does not behoove the State of Missouri to show the least countenance to any measure which might gratify this spirit.*

By this time, Emerson's widow had remarried and no longer claimed ownership of Dred Scott and his family. Scott's new owner was Mrs. Emerson's brother, John F. A. Sanford, a New Yorker. This allowed Scott to sue Sanford under diversity jurisdiction.[1] Sanford argued in a plea in abatement that as a black, Scott could not be a citizen of the United States. United States District Judge Robert W. Wells denied this plea, ruling that if Scott was free, then he was a citizen, for purposes of diversity jurisdiction. If he was not free, then his standing to sue was moot. On the merits of the case, Wells then ruled that Scott's status was legitimately determined by the Missouri Supreme Court, and upheld his enslavement. Scott then appealed to the United States Supreme Court. In his opinion, Chief Justice Roger B. Taney resolved two issues: the status of blacks, slave or free, under the Constitution, and the power of Congress to regulate slavery in the territories.

Mr. Chief Justice TANEY delivered the opinion of the court.

        *   *   *

The question is simply this: Can a negro, whose ancestors were imported into this country, and sold as slaves, become a member of the political community formed and brought into existence by the Constitution of the United States, and as such become entitled to all the rights, and privileges, and immunities, guaranteed by that instrument to the citizen? One of which rights is the privilege of suing in a court of the United States in the cases specified in the Constitution.

        *   *   *

The words "people of the United States" and "citizens" are synonymous terms, and mean the same thing. They both describe the political body who, according to our republican institutions, form the sovereignty, and who hold the power and conduct the Government through their representatives . . . The question before us is, whether the class of persons described in the plea in abatement compose a portion of this people, and are constituent members of the sovereignty? We think they are not, and that they are not included, and were not intended to be included, under the word "citizen" in the Constitution, and can therefore claim none of the rights and privileges which that instrument provides for and secure to citizens of the United States. On the contrary, they were at that time [1787] considered as a subordinate and inferior class of beings, who had been subjugated by the dominant race, and, whether emancipated or not, yet remained subject to their authority, and had no rights or privileges but such as those who held the power and the Government might choose to grant them.

It is not the province of the court to decide upon the justice or injustice, the policy or impolicy, of these laws. The decision of that question belonged to the political or law-making power; to those who formed the sovereignty and framed the Constitution. . . .

In discussing this question, we must not confound the rights of citizenship which a State may confer within its own limits, and the rights of citizenship as a member of the Union. It does not by any means follow, because he has all the rights and privileges of a citizen of a State, that he must be a citizen of the United States. . . . The Constitution has conferred on Congress the right to establish an uniform rule of naturalization, and this right is evidently exclusive, and has always been held by this court to be so. Consequently, no State, since the adoption of the Constitution, can by naturalizing an alien invest him with the rights and privileges secured to a citizen of a State under the Federal Government. . . .

        *   *   *

The question then arises, whether the provisions of the Constitution, in relation to the personal rights and privileges to which the citizen of a State should be entitled, embraced the Negro African race, at that time in this country, or who might afterwards be imported, who had then or should afterwards be made free in any State; and to put it in the power of a single State to make him a citizen of the United States, and endue him with the full rights of citizenship in every other State without their consent? Does the Constitution of the United States act upon him whenever he shall be made free under the laws of a State, and raised there to the rank of a citizen, and immediately clothe him with all the privileges of a citizen in every other State, and in its own courts?

The court think the affirmative of these propositions cannot be maintained. And if it cannot, the plaintiff in error could not be a citizen of the State of Missouri, within the meaning of the Constitution of the United States, and, consequently, was not entitled to sue in its courts.

*   *   *

In the opinion of the court, the legislation and histories of the times, and the language used in the Declaration of Independence, show, that neither the class of persons who had been imported as slaves, nor their descendants, whether they had become free or not, were then acknowledged as a part of the people, nor intended to be included in the general words used in that memorable instrument.

*   *   *

They had for more than a century before been regarded as beings of an inferior order, and altogether unfit to associate with the white race, either in social or political relations; and so far inferior, that they had no rights which the white man was bound to respect; and that the negro might justly and lawfully be reduced to slavery for his benefit. He was bought and sold, and treated as an ordinary article of merchandise and traffic, whenever a profit could be made by it. This opinion was at that time fixed and universal in the civilized portion of the white race. It was regarded as an axiom in morals as well as in politics, which no one thought of disputing, or supposed to be open to dispute; and men in every grade and position in society daily and habitually acted upon it in their private pursuits, as well as in matters of public concern, without doubting for a moment the correctness of this opinion.

*   *   *

. . . And, accordingly, a negro of the African race was regarded by them as an article of property, and held, and bought and sold as such, in every one of the thirteen colonies which united in the Declaration of Independence, and afterwards formed the Constitution of the United States. . . .

*   *   *

This state of public opinion had undergone no change when the Constitution was adopted, as is equally evident from its provisions and language.

*   *   *

. . . It is obvious that they [blacks] were not even in the minds of the framers of the Constitution when they were conferring special rights and privileges upon the citizens of the States. . . .

[Taney then discussed statutes and cases from various states, North and South, arguing that these precedents illustrated "the entire repudiation of the African Race."]

*   *   *

The legislation of the States therefore shows, in a manner not to be mistaken, the inferior and subject condition of that race at the time the Constitution was adopted, and long afterwards, throughout the thirteen States . . . and it is hardly consistent with the respect due to these States, to suppose that they regarded at that time, as fellow-citizens and members of the sovereignty, a class of beings whom they had thus stigmatized. . . . It cannot be supposed that they intended to secure to them rights, and privileges, and rank, in the new political body throughout the Union, which every one of them denied within the limits of its own dominion. More especially, it cannot be believed that the large slaveholding States regarded them as included in the word citizens, or would have consented to a Constitution which might compel them to receive them in that character from another State. For if they were so received, and entitled to the privileges and immunities of citizens, it would exempt them from the operation of the special laws and from the police regulations which they considered to be necessary for their own safety. It would give to persons of the negro race, who were recognized as citizens in any one State of the Union, the right to enter every other State whenever they pleased, singly or in companies, without pass or passport, and without obstruction, to sojourn there as long as they pleased, to go where they pleased at every hour of the day or night without molestation, unless they committed some violation of law for which a white man would be punished; and it would give them the full liberty of speech public and in private upon all subjects upon which its own citizens might speak; to hold public meetings upon political affairs, and to keep and carry arms wherever they went. And all of this would be done in the face of the subject race of the same color, both free and slaves, and inevitably producing discontent and insubordination among them, and endangering the peace and safety of the State.

It is impossible, it would seem, to believe that the great men of the slaveholding States, who took so large a share in framing the Constitution of the United States, and exercised so much influence in procuring its adoption, could have been so forgetful or regardless of their own safety and the safety of those who trusted and confided in them.

*   *   *

No one, we presume, supposes that any change in public opinion or feeling, in relation to this unfortunate race, in the civilized nations of Europe or in this country, should induce the Court to give to the words of the Constitution a more liberal construction in their favor than they were intended to bear when the instrument was framed and adopted. Such an argument would be altogether inadmissible in any tribunal called on to interpret it. If any of its provisions are deemed unjust, [the Constitution] . . . may be amended; but while it remains unaltered, it must be construed now as it was understood at the time of its adoption. It is not only the same in words, but the same in meaning, and delegates the same powers to the Government, and reserves and secures the same rights and privileges to the citizen; and as long as it continues to exist in its present form, it speaks not only in the same words, but with the same meaning and intent with which it spoke when it came from the hands of its framers, and was voted on and adopted by the people of the United States. Any other rule of construction would abrogate the judicial character of this court, and make it the mere reflex of the popular opinion or passion of the day. This court was not created by the Constitution for such purposes. Higher and graver trusts have been confided to it, and it must not falter in the path of duty.

*   *   *

. . . [Thus] the court is of opinion that, upon the facts stated in the plea in abatement, Dred Scott was not a citizen of Missouri within the meaning of the Constitution of the United States, and not entitled as such to sue in its courts. . . .

*   *   *

The act of Congress, upon which the plaintiff relies [to claim his freedom], declares that slavery and involuntary servitude, except as a punishment for crime, shall be forever prohibited in all that part of the territory ceded by France, under the name of Louisiana, which lies north of thirty-six degrees thirty minutes north latitude, and not included within the limits of Missouri. And the difficulty which meets us at the threshold of this part of the inquiry is, whether Congress was authorized to pass this law under any of the powers granted to it by the Constitution; for if the authority is not given by that instrument, it is the duty of this court to declare it void and inoperative, and incapable of conferring freedom upon any one who is held as a slave under the laws of any one of the States.

The counsel for the plaintiff has laid much stress upon that article in the Constitution which confers on Congress the power "to dispose of and make all needful rules and regulations respecting the territory or other property belonging to the United States;" but, in the judgment of the court, that provision has no bearing on the present controversy, and the power there given . . . was intended to be confined, to the territory which at that time belonged to, or was claimed by, the United States, and was within their boundaries as settled by the treaty with Great Britain, and can have no influence upon a territory afterwards acquired from a foreign Government. It was a special provision for a known and particular territory, and to meet a present emergency, and nothing more.

* * *

[Taney then discussed the power of Congress to acquire new territories for the United States.]

There is certainly no power given by the Constitution to the Federal Government to establish or maintain colonies bordering on the United States or at a distance, to be ruled and governed at its own pleasure; nor to enlarge its territorial limits in any way, except by the admission of new States. That power is plainly given. . . . But no power is given to acquire a Territory to be held and governed permanently in that character.

* * *

. . . [I]t may be safely assumed that citizens of the United States who migrate to a Territory belonging to the people of the United States, cannot be ruled as mere colonists, dependent upon the will of the General Government, and to be governed by any laws it may think proper to impose. The principle upon which our Governments rest, and upon which alone they continue to exist, is the union of States, sovereign and independent within their own limits in their internal and domestic concerns, and bound together as one people by a General Government, possessing certain enumerated and restricted powers, delegated to it by the people of the several States, and exercising supreme authority within the scope of the powers granted to it. . . . A power, therefore, in the General Government to obtain and hold colonies and dependent territories, over which they might legislate without restriction, would be inconsistent with its own existence in its present form. Whatever it acquires, it acquires for the benefit of the people of the several States who created it. It is their trustee acting for them, and charged with the duty of promoting the interests of the whole people of the Union in the exercise of the powers specifically granted.

* * *

But the power of Congress over the person or property of a citizen can never be a mere discretionary power under our Constitution and form of Government. The powers of the Government and the rights and privileges of the citizens are regulated and plainly defined by the Constitution itself. . . . The Territory being a part of the United States, the Government and the citizen both enter it under the authority of the Constitution, with their respective rights defined and marked out; and the Federal Government can exercise no power over his person or property, beyond what that instrument confers, nor lawfully deny any right which it has reserved.

A reference to a few of the provisions of the Constitution will illustrate this proposition.

For example, no one, we presume, will contend that Congress can make any law in a Territory respecting the establishment of religion, or the free exercise thereof, or abridging the freedom of speech or of the press, or the right of the people of the Territory peaceably to assemble, and to petition the Government for the redress of grievances.

*   *   *

These powers, and others, in relation to rights of person, . . . are, in express and positive terms, denied to the General Government; and the rights of private property have been guarded with equal care. Thus the rights of property are united with the rights of person, and placed on the same ground by the fifth amendment to the Constitution, which provides that no person shall be deprived of life, liberty, and property, without due process of law. And an act of Congress which deprives a citizen of the United States of his liberty or property, merely because he came himself or brought his property into a particular Territory of the United States, and who had committed no offense against the laws, could hardly be dignified with the name of due process of law.

*   *   *

Now, as we have already said . . . the right of property in a slave is distinctly and expressly affirmed in the Constitution. The right to traffic in it, like an ordinary article of merchandise and property, was guarantied to the citizens of the United States, in every State that might desire it, for twenty years. And the Government in express terms is pledged to protect it in all future time, if the slave escapes from his owner. This is done in plain words—too plain to be misunderstood. And no word can be found in the Constitution which gives Congress a greater power over slave property, or which entitles property of that kind to less protection than property of any other description. The only power conferred is the power coupled with the duty of guarding and protecting the owner in his rights.

Upon these considerations, it is the opinion of the court that the act of Congress which prohibited a citizen from holding and owning property of this kind in the territory of the United States . . . is not warranted by the Constitution, and is therefore void; and that neither Dred Scott himself, nor any of his family, were made free by being carried into this territory; even if they had been carried there by the owner, with the intention of becoming a permanent resident.

*   *   *

Note: The Reaction to *Dred Scott*

The unabashedly proslavery Chief Justice hoped that his magisterial, fifty-four-page opinion would finally settle, in the South's favor, the controversy over slavery in the territories, determine forever the status of blacks in America, and help destroy the new Republican party. His opinion had the opposite effect, in part because, as historian Don Fehrenbacher has written, "Taney's opinion, carefully read, proved to be a work of unmitigated partisanship, polemical in spirit though judicial in its language, and more like an ultimatum than a formula for sectional accommodation. Peace on Taney's terms resembled the peace implicit in a demand for unconditional surrender."[2]

In a sixty-nine-page dissent opinion, Justice Benjamin R. Curtis of Massachusetts took Taney to task at almost every point. Curtis argued that United States citizenship preceded the Constitution, that free blacks had been citizens of at least five states before 1787, and thus they had also been citizens of the United States at the time the Constitution was adopted. Curtis also argued that under a "reasonable interpretation of the language of the Constitution" Congress had the power to regulate slavery in the federal territories. This dissent heartened Northerners like Horace Greeley, who wrote that Taney's decision was "atrocious," "wicked," "abominable," "false," and built on "shallow sophistries" and "detestable hypocrisy." The *Chicago Tribune*, reflecting the shock and horror of many Northerners, wrote, "We scarcely know how to express our detestation of its inhuman dicta, or to fathom the wicked consequences which may flow from it."

One of the potential "wicked consequences" of the case was broadly hinted at by Justice Samuel Nelson, a New York Democrat, who noted in his concurrence that "except as restrained by the Federal Constitution," the states had "complete and absolute power over the subject" of slavery. This may have referred to only the fugitive slave clause. But Republicans saw a darker side to Nelson's opinion, especially because the Justice also noted there was some question about the

> right of the master with his slave, of transit into or through a free State, on business or commercial pursuits, or in the exercise of a federal right, or the discharge of a federal duty, being a citizen of the United States. . . . This question depends upon different considerations and principles from the one in hand, and turns upon the rights and privileges secured to a common citizen of the republic, under the Constitution of the United States. When that question arises, we shall be prepared to decide it.

ABRAHAM LINCOLN
"House Divided" Speech
June 16, 1858

After being nominated for the United States Senate, Abraham Lincoln gave his famous "House Divided" speech to the Illinois Republican Convention. Lincoln accused his opponent, Stephen A. Douglas, of being part of a conspiracy to open up all the territories to slavery and to even force slavery on the North. The key elements of this conspiracy were the Kansas-Nebraska Act of 1854 and the Dred Scott *decision. The Kansas-Nebraska Act allowed slavery in some territory from which it had been prohibited under the Missouri Compromise. Douglas accomplished this through "popular sovereignty," which allowed the people of a territory to decide for themselves if they wanted slavery. Lincoln believed that the 1854 act and popular sovereignty were preludes to the* Dred Scott *decision, which opened up all the territories to slavery. Lincoln feared that another* Dred Scott *decision would legalize slavery in the North.*

"A house divided against itself cannot stand."

I believe this government cannot endure, permanently half *slave* and half *free.*

I do not expect the Union to be *dissolved*—I do not expect the house to *fall*—but I *do* expect it will cease to be divided.

It will become *all* one thing, or *all* the other.

Either the *opponents* of slavery, will arrest the further spread of it, and place it where the public mind shall rest in the belief that it is in course of ultimate extinction; or its *advocates* will push it forward, till it shall become alike lawful in *all* the states, *old* as well as *new*—*North* as well as *South.*

Have we no *tendency* to the latter condition?

Let any one who doubts, carefully contemplate that now almost complete legal combination—piece of *machinery* so to speak—compounded of the Nebraska doctrine, and the Dred Scott decision. . . .

*   *   *

. . . [The Kansas-Nebraska Act] opened all the national territory to slavery. . . . This . . . had been provided for . . . in the notable argument of "*squatter sovereignty,*" otherwise called "*sacred right of self government,*" which latter phrase, though expressive of the only rightful basis of any government, was so perverted in this attempted use of it as to amount to just this: That if any *one* man, choose to enslave *another*, no *third* man shall be allowed to object.

*   *   *

While the Nebraska Bill was passing through Congress, a law case, involving the question of a negro's freedom . . . was passing through the U.S. Circuit Court for the District of Missouri; and both Nebraska Bill and law suit were brought to a decision in the same month of May, 1854. The Negro's name was "Dred Scott". . . .

*   *   *

[The points decided by the *Dred Scott* decision include] that whether the holding a negro in actual slavery in a free state, makes him free, as against the holder, the United States courts will not decide, but will leave to be decided by the courts of any slave state the negro may be forced into by the master.

This point is made, not to be pressed immediately . . . [that] the logical conclusion that what Dred Scott's master might lawfully do with Dred Scott, in the free state Illinois, every other master may lawfully do with any other *one*, or one *thousand* slaves, in Illinois, or in any other free state.

*   *   *

While the opinion of . . . Chief Justice Taney, in the Dred Scott case . . . expressly declare[s] that the Constitution of the United States neither permits congress nor a territorial legislature to exclude slavery from any United States territory, . . . [Taney] *omit*[s] to declare whether or not the same constitution permits a *state*, or the people of a state, to exclude it.

Possibly, this was a mere omission; but who can be quite sure. . . .

The nearest approach to the point of declaring the power of a state over slavery, is made by Judge Nelson. He approaches it more than once, using the precise idea, and *almost* the language too, of the Nebraska Act. On one occasion his exact language is, "except in cases where the power is restrained by the Constitution of the United States, the law of the State is supreme over the subject of slavery within its jurisdiction."

In what *cases* the power of the *states* is so restrained by the U.S. Constitution, is left an *open* question, precisely as the same question, as to the restraint on the power of the *territories* was left open in the Nebraska Act. Put *that* and *that* together, and we have another nice little niche, which we may, ere long, see filled with another Supreme Court decision, declaring that the Constitution of the United States does not permit a *state* to exclude slavery from its limits.

*   *   *

Such a decision is all that slavery now lacks of being alike lawful in all the states.

Welcome or unwelcome, such decision *is* probably coming, and will soon be upon us, unless the power of the present political dynasty shall be met and overthrown.

We shall *lie down* pleasantly dreaming that the people of Missouri are on the verge of making their state *free*; and we shall *awake* to the *reality*, instead, that the Supreme Court has made *Illinois* a *slave* state.

Note: The Next *Dred Scott* Decision

The next *Dred Scott* case that Lincoln feared was already making its way through the courts. *Lemmon v. The People* (N.Y., 1860) was the last of a line of cases that began with the English case *Somerset v. Stewart* (1772). In *Somerset*, Lord Chief Justice Mansfield of the Court of King's Bench held that a slave could not forcibly be removed from England. Somerset's counsel, William Davy, provided a metaphor for England and other free jurisdictions, declaring that "the air of England . . . is too pure for a slave to breathe in." In *Commonwealth v. Aves* (1836), Chief Justice Lemuel Shaw applied the principles of *Somerset*, holding that slavery was a creature of municipal law and no laws of Massachusetts would justify the enslavement of anyone except fugitive slaves. Thus Med, a six-year-old slave girl, was free because her owner voluntarily took her into Massachusetts.

In 1852, the Lemmons, who were from Virginia, traveled to New York City to change ships for direct steamboat passage to New Orleans. Although they planned to be in New York for only a day or two, a judge freed their eight slaves. New York businessmen raised money to recompense the Lemmons for the value of their slaves, but the state of Virginia appealed the case. In *Lemmon v. The People*, the New York Court of Appeals held that all slaves (except fugitives) became free the moment they entered the state. Citing *Somerset* and *Aves*, the court argued that

> every sovereign State has a right to determine by its laws the condition of all persons who may at any time be within its jurisdiction; to exclude therefrom those whose introduction would contravene its policy, or to declare the conditions upon which they may be received, and. . . . Each State, has, moreover, the right to enact such rules as it may see fit respecting the title to property. . . .

The court emphatically denied that "a citizen carries with him, into every State into which he may go, the legal institutions of the one in which he was born."

In dissent, Judge Thomas W. Clerke rhetorically asked:

> Is it consistent with this purpose of perfect union, and of perfect and unrestricted intercourse, that property which the citizen of one State brings into another State, for the purpose of passing through it to a State where he intends to take up his residence, shall be confiscated in the State through which he is passing, or shall be declared no property . . . ?

Clerke believed that the decision was "wanton aggression" for "mere propagandism." Clerke warned that under international law the act of New York "would be a valid cause" of war.

Later that year, South Carolina referred to *Lemmon* as one of its reasons for seceding. It is likely that the Taney Court would have overturned this decision, but before that could happen, the national compact fell apart.

Secession and Constitutional Theory

Throughout his presidential campaign, Lincoln reiterated that the federal government could not interfere with slavery in the states where it already existed. Lincoln also indicated that although he thought the Fugitive Slave Law might be unjust, he was prepared to enforce it as he would any other federal law.

Proslavery ideologues ignored such statements and focused on Lincoln's opposition to slavery in the territories and to the admission to the Union of any new slave states. Shortly after Lincoln's election, South Carolina elected a convention that unanimously endorsed secession.

South Carolina justified secession by arguing that Lincoln's "opinions and purposes" were "hostile to slavery." The theory behind secession developed from the nullification controversy of 1832 to 1833 and from John C. Calhoun's notion that the states were sovereign members of a compact and could withdraw from the compact at will. At that time, President Andrew Jackson responded with the Proclamation to the People of South Carolina, declaring that he would execute the laws, as he was sworn to do. Jackson warned the South Carolinians that "a forcible opposition could alone prevent the execution of the laws" and that "disunion by armed force is treason." In response to Jackson's proclamation, South Carolina adopted a series of resolutions, including one which asserted

> that each state of the Union has the right, whenever it may deem such a course necessary for the preservation of its liberties or vital interests, to secede peaceably from the Union, and that there is no constitutional power in the general government, much less in the executive department, of that government, to retain by force such state in the Union.

In 1860, South Carolina revived this theory.

President James Buchanan rejected this theory and agreed with Republicans that secession was illegal. But as a states'-rights Democrat (with strong southern sympathies), Buchanan also took no steps to stop secession. He believed that the federal government lacked the power to interfere with the states, even if they left the Union.

The Supreme Court supported this position in *Kentucky* v. *Dennison* (1861) by refusing to order Ohio to return a fugitive who was wanted for having helped a slave escape from Kentucky. Although he had no sympathy for the Ohio governor for protecting someone whom Kentucky regarded as a slave stealer, Chief Justice Taney concluded that the criminal extradition clause of the Constitution "is left to depend on the fidelity of the State Executive to the compact entered into with the other States when it adopted the Constitution" and that there was "no power delegated to the General Government . . . to use any coercive means to compel" a state governor to act. Delivered just before the Civil War began, Taney's opinion was obviously meant to deny Lincoln the power to coerce states back into the Union.

Upon taking office, Lincoln declared that the Union was "perpetual" and took actions to resupply Union troops stationed along the south Atlantic coast. Rather than allow Fort Sumter to be resupplied, Charleston authorities fired on it. For the next four years, the theory of secession was tested in a trial by battle. When the Civil War ended, all but one of the defeated Confederate states renounced secession; South Carolina, defiant to the end, merely repealed its Ordinance of Secession.

Declaration of the Immediate Causes Which Induce and Justify the Secession of South Carolina
December 24, 1860

Between the election of Lincoln in November 1860 and his inauguration in March 1861, seven states adopted ordinances of secession and declared they were no longer members of the Union. After the Civil War began, four more states left the Union. Immediately after Lincoln's election, South Carolina resurrected the popularly elected convention, previously used in the Nullification Crisis of 1832 to 1833, to consider secession. On December 24, this convention voted to leave the Union.

We hold that the Government . . . established [by the Constitution] is subject to the . . . fundamental principle, namely: the law of compact. We maintain that in every compact between two or more parties, the obligation is mutual; that the failure of one of the contracting parties to perform a material part of the agreement, entirely releases the obligation of the other; and that where no arbiter is provided, each party is remitted to his own judgment to determine the fact of failure, with all its consequences.

In the present case, that fact is established with certainty. We assert that fourteen of the States have deliberately refused, for years past, to fulfill their constitutional obligations, and we refer to their own Statutes for the proof.

The Constitution of the United States, in its fourth Article, provides as follows:

"No person held to service or labor in one State, under the laws thereof, escaping into another, shall, in consequence of any law or regulation therein, be discharged from such service or labor, but shall be delivered up, on claim of the party to whom such service or labor may be due."

This stipulation was so material to the compact, that without it that compact would not have been made. The greater number of the contracting parties held slaves, and they had previously evinced their estimate of the value of such a stipulation by making it a condition in the Ordinance for the government of the territory ceded by Virginia, which now composes the States north of the Ohio River.

*   *   *

The General Government, as the common agent, passed laws to carry into effect these stipulations of the States. For many years these laws were executed. But an increasing hostility on the part of the non-slaveholding States to the institution of slavery, has led to a disregard of their obligations, and the laws of the General Government have ceased to effect the objects of the Constitution. The States of Maine, New Hampshire, Vermont, Massachusetts, Connecticut, Rhode Island, New York, Pennsylvania, Illinois, Indiana, Michigan, Wisconsin and Iowa, have enacted laws which either nullify the Acts of Congress or render useless any attempt to execute them. In many of these States the fugitive is discharged from the service or labor claimed, and in none of them has the State Government complied with the stipulation made in the Constitution. . . . In the State of New York even the right of transit for a slave has been denied by her tribunals; and the States of Ohio and Iowa have refused to surrender to justice fugitives charged with murder, and with inciting servile insurrection in the State of Virginia. Thus the constituted compact has been deliberately broken and disregarded by the non-slaveholding States, and the consequence follows that South Carolina is released from her obligation.

*   *   *

. . . [In the Constitution, the] right of property in slaves was recognized by giving to free persons distinct political rights, by giving them the right to represent, and burthening them with direct taxes for three-fifths of their slaves; by authorizing the importation of slaves for twenty years; and by stipulating for the rendition of fugitives from labor.

We affirm that these ends for which this Government was instituted have been defeated, and the Government itself has been made destructive of them by the action of the non-slaveholding States. Those States have assumed the right of deciding upon the propriety of our domestic institutions; and have denied the rights of property established in fifteen of the States and recognized by the Constitution; they have denounced as sinful the institution of slavery; they have permitted the open establishment among them of societies, whose avowed object is to disturb the peace and to eloign the property of the citizens of other States. They have encouraged and assisted thousands of our slaves to leave their homes; and those who remain, have been incited by emissaries, books and pictures to servile insurrection.

For twenty-five years this agitation has been steadily increasing, until it has now secured to its aid the power of the common Government. Observing the forms of the Constitution, a sectional party has found within that Article establishing the Executive Department, the means of subverting the Constitution itself. A geographical line has been drawn across the Union, and all the States north of that line have united in the election of a man to the high office of President of the United States, whose opinions and purposes are hostile to slavery. He is to be entrusted with the administration of the common Government, because he has declared that that "Government cannot endure permanently half slave, half free," and that the public mind must rest in the belief that slavery is in the course of ultimate extinction.

This sectional combination for the submersion of the Constitution has been aided in some of the States by elevating to citizenship, persons who, by the supreme law of the land, are incapable of becoming citizens; and their votes have been used to inaugurate a new policy, hostile to the South, and destructive of its beliefs and safety.

On the 4th of March next, this party will take possession of the Government. It has announced that the South shall be excluded from the common territory, that the judicial tribunals shall be made sectional and that a war must be waged against slavery until it shall cease throughout the United States.

The guaranties of the Constitution will then no longer exist; the equal rights of the States will be lost. The slaveholding States will no longer have the power of self-government, or self-protection, and the Federal Government will have become their enemy.

*   *   *

We, therefore, the People of South Carolina, by our delegates Convention assembled, appealing to the Supreme Judge of the world for the rectitude of our intentions, have solemnly declared that the Union heretofore existing between this State and the other States of North America, is dissolved, and that the State of South Carolina has resumed her position among the nations of the world, as a separate and independent State; with full power to levy war, conclude peace, contract alliances, establish commerce, and to do all other acts and things which independent States may of right do.

ABRAHAM LINCOLN
First Inaugural Address
March 4, 1861

Upon taking office, Lincoln faced the greatest crisis in the nation's history. Seven states had seceded, and civil war seemed likely. Although personally opposed to slavery, Lincoln had made it clear throughout his campaign that he posed no threat to slavery where it already existed. While seeking peace, Lincoln was determined to preserve the Union and not to back down from his commitment to prevent the spread of slavery to the western territories.

Fellow citizens of the United States:

*   *   *

Apprehension seems to exist among the people of the Southern States, that by the accession of a Republican Administration, their property, and their peace, and personal security, are to be endangered. There has never been any reasonable cause for such apprehension. Indeed, the most ample evidence to the contrary has all the while existed, and been open to their inspection. It is found in nearly all [my] published speeches. . . . I do but quote from one of those speeches when I declare that "I have no purpose, directly or indirectly, to interfere with the institution of slavery in the States where it exists. I believe I have no lawful right to do so, and I have no inclination to do so." Those who nominated and elected me did so with full knowledge that I had made this, and many similar declarations, and had never recanted them. And more than this, they placed in the platform . . . [this] clear and emphatic resolution. . . .

"*Resolved*, That the maintenance inviolate of the rights of the States, and especially the right of each State to order and control its own domestic institutions according to its own judgment exclusively, is essential to that balance of power on which the perfection and endurance of our political fabric depend; and we denounce the lawless invasions by armed force of the soil of any State or Territory, no matter under what pretext, as among the gravest of crimes."

I now reiterate these sentiments: and in doing so, I only press upon the public attention the most conclusive evidence of which the case is susceptible, that the property, peace and security of no section are to be in anywise endangered by the now incoming Administration. I add too, that all the protection which, consistently with the Constitution and the laws, can be given, will be cheerfully given to all the States when lawfully demanded, for whatever cause—as cheerfully to one section, as to another.

*   *   *

I hold that in contemplation of universal law, and of the Constitution, the Union of these States is perpetual. Perpetuity is implied, if not expressed, in the fundamental law of all national governments. It is safe to assert that no government power, ever had a provision in its organic law for its own termination. Continue to execute all the express provisions of our national Constitution, and the Union will endure forever—it being impossible to destroy it, except by some action not provided for in the instrument itself.

*   *   *

Descending from these general principles, we find the proposition that, in legal contemplation, the Union is perpetual, confirmed by the history of the Union itself. The Union is much older than the Constitution. It was formed in fact, by the Articles of Association in 1774. It was matured and continued by the Declaration of Independence in 1776. It was further matured and the faith of all the then thirteen States expressly plighted and engaged that it should be perpetual, by the Articles of Confederation in 1778. And finally, in 1787, one of the declared objects for ordaining and establishing the Constitution, was "*to form a more perfect union.*"

But if destruction of the Union, by one, or by a part only, of the States, be lawfully possible, the Union is *less* perfect than before the Constitution, having lost the vital element of perpetuity.

It follows from these views that no State, upon its own mere motion, can lawfully get out of the Union,—that *resolves* and *ordinances* to that effect are legally void; and that acts of violence, within any State or States, against the authority of the United States, are insurrectionary or revolutionary. . . .

I therefore consider that, in view of the Constitution and the laws, the Union is unbroken; and, to the extent of my ability, I shall take care, as the Constitution itself expressly enjoins upon me, that the laws of the Union be faithfully executed in all the States. Doing this I deem to be only a simple duty on my part; and I shall perform it, so far as practicable, unless my rightful masters, the American people, shall withhold the requisite means, or, in some authoritative manner, direct the contrary. I trust this will not be regarded as a menace, but only as the declared purpose of the Union that it *will* constitutionally defend, and maintain itself.

In doing this there needs to be no bloodshed or violence; and there shall be none, unless it be forced upon the national authority. The power confided to me, will be used to hold, occupy, and possess the property, and places belonging to the government, and to collect the duties and imposts; but beyond what may be necessary for these objects, there will be no invasion—no using of force against, or among the people anywhere. Where hostility to the United States, in any interior locality, shall be so great and so universal, as to prevent competent resident citizens from holding the Federal offices, there will be no attempt to force obnoxious strangers among the people for that object. While the strict legal right may exist in the government to enforce the exercise of these offices, the attempt to do so would be so irritating, and so nearly impracticable with all, that I deem it better to forgo, for the time, the uses of such offices.

That there are persons in one section, or another who seek to destroy the Union at all events, and are glad of any pretext to do it . . . I need address no word to them. To those, however, who really love the Union, may I not speak?

Before entering upon so grave a matter as the destruction of our national fabric, with all its benefits, its memories, and its hopes, would it not be wise to ascertain precisely why we do it? Will you hazard so desperate a step, while there is any possibility that any portion of the ills you fly from, have no real existence? Will you, while the certain ills you fly to, are greater than all the real ones you fly from? Will you risk the commission of so fearful a mistake?

All profess to be content in the Union, if all constitutional rights can be maintained. Is it true, then, that any right, plainly written in the Constitution, has been denied? I think not. . . . Think, if you can, of a single instance in which a plainly written provision of the Constitution has ever been denied. . . . Shall fugitives from labor be surrendered by national or by State authority? The Constitution does not expressly say. *May* Congress prohibit slavery in the territories? The Constitution does not expressly say. *Must* congress protect slavery in the territories? The Constitution does not expressly say.

*   *   *

Plainly, the central idea of secession, is the essence of anarchy. A majority, held in restraint by constitutional checks, and limitations, and always changing easily, with deliberate changes of popular opinions and sentiments, is the only true sovereign of a free people. Whoever rejects it, does, of necessity, fly to anarchy or to despotism. Unanimity is impossible; the rule of a minority, as a permanent arrangement, is wholly inadmissible; so that, rejecting the majority principle, anarchy, or despotism . . . is all that is left.

I do not forget the position assumed by some, that constitutional questions are to be decided by the Supreme Court; nor do I deny that such decisions must be binding in any case, upon the parties to a suit, as to the object of that suit, while they are also entitled to very high respect and consideration, in all parallel cases, by all other departments of the government. And while it is obviously possible that such decision may be erroneous in any given case, still the evil effect following it, being limited to that particular case, with the chance that it may be over-ruled, and never become a precedent for other cases, can better be borne than could the evils of a different practice. At the same time the candid citizen must confess that if the policy of the government, upon vital questions, affecting the whole people, is to be irrevocably fixed by decisions of the Supreme Court, the instant they are made, in ordinary litigation between parties, in personal actions, the people will have ceased, to be their own rulers, having, to that extent, practically resigned their government, into the hands of that eminent tribunal. Nor is there, in this view, any assault upon the court, or the judges. It is a duty, from which they may not shrink, to decide cases properly brought before them; and it is no fault of theirs, if others seek to turn their decisions to political purposes.

One section of our country believes slavery is right, and ought to be extended, while the other believes it is wrong, and ought not to be extended. This is the only substantial dispute. The fugitive slave clause of the Constitution, and the law for the suppression of the foreign slave trade, are each as well enforced, perhaps, as any law can ever be in a community where the moral sense of the people imperfectly supports the law itself. The great body of the people abide by the dry legal obligation in both cases, and a few break over in each. This, I think, cannot be perfectly cured; and it would be worse in both cases after the separation of the sections, than before. The foreign slave trade, now imperfectly suppressed, would be ultimately revived without restriction, in one section; while fugitive slaves, now only partially surrendered, would not be surrendered at all, by the other.

Physically speaking, we cannot separate. We cannot remove our respective sections from each other, nor build an impassable wall between them. A husband and wife may be divorced, and go out of the presence, and beyond the reach of each other; but the different parts of our country cannot do this. They cannot but remain face to face; and intercourse, either amicable or hostile, must continue between them. Is it possible then to make that intercourse more advantageous, or more satisfactory, after separation than before? Can aliens make treaties easier than friends can make laws? Can treaties be more faithfully enforced between aliens, than laws can among friends? Suppose you go to war, you cannot fight always; and when, after much loss on both sides, and no gain on either, you cease fighting, the identical old questions, as to terms of intercourse, are again upon you.

*   *   *

While the people retain their virtue, and vigilance, no administration, by any extreme of wickedness or folly, can very seriously injure the government, in the short space of four years.

My countrymen, one and all, think calmly and well, upon this whole subject. Nothing valuable can be lost by taking time. If there be an object to hurry any of you, in hot haste, to a step which you would never take deliberately, that object will be frustrated by taking time; but no good object can be frustrated by it. Such of you as are now dissatisfied, still have the old Constitution unimpaired, and, on the sensitive point, the laws of your own framing under it; while the new administration will have no immediate power, if it would, to change either. If it were admitted that you who are dissatisfied, hold the right side in the dispute, there still is no single good reason for precipitate action. Intelligence, patriotism, Christianity, and a firm reliance on Him, who has never yet forsaken this favored land, are still competent to adjust, in the best way, all our present difficulty.

In your hands, my dissatisfied fellow countrymen, and not in mine, is the momentous issue of civil war. The government will not assail you. You can have no conflict, without being yourselves the aggressors. You have no oath registered in Heaven to destroy the government, while I shall have the most solemn one to "preserve, protect and defend" it.

I am loth to close. We are not enemies, but friends. We must not be enemies. Though passion may have strained, it must not break our bonds of affection. The mystic chords of memory, stretching from every battlefield, and patriot grave, to every living heart and hearthstone, all over this broad land, will yet swell the chorus of the Union, when again touched, as surely they will be, by the better angels of our nature.

The Civil War and Emancipation

During the Civil War, the president and Congress discovered new solutions to the problems created by the war. What could not be accomplished legally in peacetime became possible during the war. The president, Congress, and the Army were the chief actors in shaping constitutional developments.

At the beginning of the war, Lincoln unilaterally suspended habeas corpus while Congress was not in session. Acting in his capacity as a circuit judge, Chief Justice Taney, in *Ex parte Merryman* (1861), declared Lincoln's suspension of habeas corpus unconstitutional. Lincoln ignored Taney's order to release the Confederate activist Merryman. Congress subsequently ratified Lincoln's actions with the Habeas Corpus Act of 1863. After the *Merryman* case, all the federal courts showed enormous deference to the administration. In the *Prize Cases* (1863), the Supreme Court affirmed Lincoln's unilateral use of a blockade against southern ports. In *Ex parte Vallandingham* (1864), the Court refused to intervene on behalf of a civilian arrested, tried, and sentenced by a military tribunal.

The greatest legal change of the Civil War era was the conversion of billions of dollars' worth of slave property into millions of free citizens of the nation. In April 1862, Congress ended slavery in the District of Columbia through compensated emancipation. In June, Congress rejected the *Dred Scott* precedent by abolishing slavery in the territories. In July, Congress took the first step toward black citizenship by granting blacks the right to testify in all court cases in the nation's capital. No one challenged these laws in the courts. It is likely that the Supreme Court, with Taney still Chief Justice, would have sided with the slaveholders in such a case, but no one doubted that Lincoln and Congress would have ignored the Court on this issue. In 1862, Congress also passed the Second Confiscation Act, which declared forever free the slaves of certain rebellious masters and authorized the use of black troops. The Supreme Court would uphold this law in *Miller* v. *United States* (1870).

In many ways, the constitutional developments of the Civil War are extraordinarily ironic. Before the war, the South accused Lincoln of wanting to destroy slavery, while Lincoln claimed he had no plans and no power to take such an action. But during the war, both the president and Congress found powers to do what could not have been done in peacetime. Secession and war became self-fulfilling prophecies for the South. By leaving the Union, Southerners gave the Republicans a majority in Congress they would never have had otherwise. By fighting the war, the South gave

Lincoln powers he never dreamed of before 1861. The war began as a revolution by the South, and ended as a revolution in constitutional law, race relations, and national power.

ABRAHAM LINCOLN
The Emancipation Proclamation
January 1, 1863

Although few slaves actually gained their freedom under the law, the Second Confiscation Act and congressional abolition in federal jurisdictions set the stage for the Emancipation Proclamation, which Lincoln secretly drafted in July 1862. In August, Lincoln publicly denied any plans for emancipation, but on September 22, 1862, acting as commander-in-chief, Lincoln issued the Preliminary Emancipation Proclamation, declaring that it would go into effect in 100 days.

Now, therefore I, Abraham Lincoln, President of the United States, by virtue of the power in me vested as Commander-in-Chief, of the Army and Navy of the United States in time of actual armed rebellion against authority and government of the United States, and as a fit and necessary war measure for suppressing said rebellion, do, on this first day of January, in the year of our Lord one thousand eight hundred and sixty three, and in accordance with my purpose so to do publicly proclaimed for the full period of one hundred days, from the day first above mentioned, order and designate as the States and parts of States wherein the people thereof respectively, are this day in rebellion against the United States, the following, to wit:

Arkansas, Texas, Louisiana, (except [thirteen listed Parishes] . . . including the City of New-Orleans) Mississippi, Alabama, Florida, Georgia, South-Carolina, North-Carolina, and Virginia, (except the fortyeight counties designated as West Virginia, and also [seven listed counties] . . . [)]; and which excepted parts are, for the present, left precisely as if this proclamation were not issued.

And by virtue of the power, and for the purpose aforesaid, I do order and declare that all persons held as slaves within said designated States, and parts of States, are, and henceforward shall be free; and that the Executive government of the United States, including the military and naval authorities thereof, will recognize and maintain the freedom of said persons. And I hereby enjoin upon the people so declared to be free to abstain from all violence, unless in necessary self-defence; and I recommend to them that, in all cases when allowed, they labor faithfully for reasonable wages.

And I further declare and make known, that such persons of suitable condition, will be received into the armed service of the United States to garrison forts, positions, stations, and other places, and to man vessels of all sorts in said service.

And upon this act, sincerely believed to be an act of justice, warranted by the Constitution, upon military necessity, I invoke the considerate judgment of mankind, and the gracious favor of Almighty God.

Note: The Effect of the Emancipation Proclamation

The Emancipation Proclamation applied only to areas of the nation that were under Confederate control. Thus it emancipated no slaves when issued. However, each movement of Union troops farther south resulted in the emancipation of more slaves. From 1863 to 1865, the Union Army became the actual emancipator of millions of slaves. In 1864, Congress sent to the states the Thirteenth Amendment, declaring "neither slavery nor involuntary servitude . . . shall exist within the United States. . . ." When ratified in 1865, this amendment ended slavery everywhere in the nation. Meanwhile, between 1863 and 1865 many slaveowners in the border states allowed their male slaves to enlist in the Army. The owner usually claimed the enlistment bounty, while the slave gained his freedom and the opportunity to fight for the freedom of all American slaves.

ABRAHAM LINCOLN
Second Inaugural Address
March 4, 1865

Lincoln's Second Inaugural is a masterpiece of political writing. Lincoln set the agenda of reconstruction by attributing the underlying cause of the war to slavery and by stressing the shared heritage of Northerners and Southerners. Thus the inaugural set the stage for ending all vestiges of slavery and for bringing the nation back together with "malice toward none" and with "charity for all."

On the occasion corresponding to this four years ago all thoughts were anxiously directed to an impending civil war. All dreaded it, all sought to avert it. While the inaugural address was being delivered from this place, devoted altogether to saving the Union without war, insurgent agents were in the city seeking to destroy it without war—seeking to dissolve the Union and divide effects by negotiation. Both parties deprecated war, but one of them would make war rather than let the nation survive, and the other would accept war rather than let it perish, and the war came.

One-eighth of the whole population were colored slaves, not distributed generally over the Union, but localized in the southern part of it. These slaves constituted a peculiar and powerful interest. All knew that this interest was somehow the cause of the war. To strengthen, perpetuate, and extend this interest was the object for which the insurgents would rend the Union even by war, while the Government claimed no right to do more than to restrict the territorial enlargement of it. Neither party expected for the war the magnitude or the duration which it has already attained. Neither anticipated that the cause of the conflict might cease with or even before the conflict itself should cease. Each looked for an easier triumph, and a result less fundamental and astounding. Both read the same Bible and pray to the same God, and each invokes His aid against the other. It may seem strange that any men should dare to ask a just God's assistance in wringing their bread from the sweat of other men's faces, but let us judge not, that we be not judged. The prayers of both could not be answered. That of neither has been answered fully. The Almighty has His own purposes. "Woe unto the world because of offenses; for it must needs be that offenses come, but woe to that man by whom the offense cometh." If we shall suppose that American slavery is one of those offenses which, in the providence of God, must needs come, but which, having continued through His appointed time, He now wills to remove, and that He gives to both North and South this terrible war as the woe due to those by whom the offense came, shall we discern therein any departure from those divine attributes which the believers in a living God always ascribe to Him? Fondly do we hope, fervently do we pray, that this mighty scourge of war may speedily pass away. Yet, if God wills that it continue until all the wealth piled by the bondsman's two hundred and fifty years of unrequited toil shall be sunk, and until every drop of blood drawn with the lash shall be paid by another drawn with the sword, as was said three thousand years ago, so still it must be said "the judgments of the Lord are true and righteous altogether."

With malice toward none, with charity for all, with firmness in the right as God gives us to see the right, let us strive on to finish the work we are in, to bind up the nation's wounds, to care for him who shall have borne the battle and for his widow and his orphan, to do all which may achieve and cherish a just and lasting peace among ourselves and with all nations.

Reconstruction and Its Aftermath: Political Change, Black Freedom, and the Nadir of Black Rights

Peace brought as many complex constitutional and legal problems as had the war. The nation could not re-create itself into the antebellum federal system, with the states retaining great power. A new federalism had emerged that made the states unambiguously subordinate to the national government. State sovereignty was forever dead; the concept of states' rights remained, but it had been weakened and altered by the war. One price of peace was the repudiation of secession.

A second price was the recognition of the end of slavery. Emancipation had been accomplished by congressional action, presidential proclamation, and Union military success. The federal government demanded that the former Confederate states accept and endorse this change in their new state constitutions and with their ratification of the Thirteenth Amendment.

But what was to happen to the ex-slaves? Were they to be left to the mercies of their defeated masters? Were they to be enfranchised and made full citizens? Who would protect them from exploitation and violence? How would they feed themselves, gain an economic foothold, acquire an education? Such questions puzzled the victorious Republicans as they began to reconstruct the Union.

Complicating this task was the assassination of Lincoln and the ascension of Andrew Johnson, a native Southerner who hated slavery but also despised blacks. Johnson's views of black freedom were not in tune with those of most Republicans or most Northerners. Even by the standards of the 1860s, Johnson was a thoroughgoing racist. Poorly educated, unsophisticated, intemperate, and stubborn, Johnson's behavior would lead to the only presidential impeachment in the nation's history. More importantly, his policies undermined the "new birth of freedom" that Lincoln had spoken of shortly before his death.

Central to Reconstruction were the Thirteenth, Fourteenth, and Fifteenth Amendments. Debate still rages over the purpose or "intent" of these amendments. Historian Harold Hyman has persuasively argued that the Thirteenth Amendment was designed to do more than end slavery: it was a statement of "protection" guaranteed by the federal government "from involuntary servitude and violence" and a promise "of all the full and equal rights of freedom, some of which history had identified and a multitude of which remained for the inscrutable future to reveal."³ The enforcement provision of the amendment—the first in the Constitution—particularly troubled Southerners because it implied open-ended federal power to protect the freedmen and to regulate race relations. Congress quickly exercised power under the enforcement clause to protect the basic rights of the freedmen, through the Civil Rights Act of 1866, enacting it over President Johnson's veto.

The Thirteenth Amendment was the beginning of the process of constitutionalizing the revolution in federalism and race relations. The Fourteenth Amendment contained an enforcement provision as well, along with open-ended language guaranteeing the freedmen "privileges and immunities," "due process," and "equal protection of the law." We can never know exactly what the authors of this amendment had in mind. They probably did not completely know themselves. But, at a minimum, the framers of the two amendments believed they were expanding the Bill of Rights to the states and giving Congress broad plenary power to protect both civil rights and civil liberties throughout the nation. The Fifteenth Amendment, ratified in 1870, was designed to prohibit voting discrimination based on race.

Congress passed Civil Rights Acts in 1866 and 1875 and various other laws to protect black freedom. The Supreme Court, however, failed to appreciate the revolution in law that the Civil War and Reconstruction produced. Too often, the justices looked at congressional actions through the lens of antebellum legal theory, rather than through the expansive language of the new amendments. Uncomfortable with the revolution in federalism and race relations, the Court interpreted the new amendments in constricted and narrow ways.

By the end of the century, the Court had abandoned the freedmen to the tender mercies of southern white politicians. The results were political disfranchisement, legal isolation, economic peonage, and segregation everywhere. This was "the Nadir" of American black life, the "Betrayal of the Negro" by Congress and the courts, and the betrayal of the principles of the Reconstruction amendments.⁴

Political Change

With the Union preserved, the overwhelming political question facing the nation was how the Union should be reconstructed. Was Congress or the president to set policy? Should the southern states be readmitted quickly to encourage reconciliation, or should the former Confederate states be denied full political self-determination until they had fully accepted the consequences of the war, including black freedom, citizenship, and equality?

Starting in late 1863 (with the occupation of Louisiana), Lincoln sought to impose a reconstruction program through provisional governments under his control. Lincoln wanted a speedy reconstruction, but Republican congressional leaders opposed it and refused to seat senators and congressmen elected by the reconstructed states in 1864 and 1865.

The conflict between Congress and the president turned to open warfare under Andrew Johnson. Johnson consistently attempted to thwart Congress, often by failing to implement Reconstruction acts passed over his intemperate and unnecessarily antagonistic vetoes. He arbitrarily fired a large number of local federal officeholders in a clumsy attempt to control northern state politics. Johnson angered Congress by pardoning many former Confederates and pressing for a quick reconstruction of the South. Johnson's racism and hostility to black rights endangered the lives of blacks and white Unionists in the South. His policies had

> a staggering effect on the South. He converted a conquered people, bitter but ready to accept the consequences of defeat, into a hostile, aggressive, uncooperative unit. He restored them to political and economic power . . . [allowing them to dominate] the men and women they had recently held as slaves. He had set back the work of Reconstruction, as it turned out, two full years.[5]

Johnson undermined the Freedmen's Bureau, the 1866 Civil Rights Act, and other congressionally mandated policies and programs. He placated southern whites while ignoring the plight of southern blacks. In July 1866, Johnson overruled Philip Sheridan when the general removed from office local officials who were responsible for "the absolute massacre" in New Orleans of black Army veterans and Republican delegates to the Louisiana Constitutional Convention. Another general complained that Johnson's policy of overruling military commanders led to "barbarism" in Louisiana and throughout the South. To curb Johnson's obstruction of its will, Congress passed the Tenure of Office Act in 1867, barring Johnson from removing various federal officials until the Senate confirmed their replacements. This law was aimed at preventing the removal of Secretary of War Edwin Stanton, an ally of Congress and a supporter of black rights. In February 1868, Johnson nevertheless removed Stanton from office, which was the final event before his impeachment.

Articles of Impeachment of Andrew Johnson
March 2 and 3, 1868

ARTICLES EXHIBITED BY THE HOUSE OF REPRESENTATIVES OF THE UNITED STATES, IN THE NAME OF THEMSELVES AND ALL THE PEOPLE OF THE UNITED STATES, AGAINST ANDREW JOHNSON, PRESIDENT OF THE UNITED STATES, IN MAINTENANCE AND SUPPORT OF THEIR IMPEACHMENT AGAINST HIM FOR HIGH CRIMES AND MISDEMEANORS IN OFFICE.

Article I.   That said Andrew Johnson, President of the United States, on the 21st day of February, A.D. 1868 . . . unmindful of the high duties of his office, of his oath of office, and of the requirement of the Constitution that he should take care that the laws be faithfully executed, did unlawfully and in violation of the Constitution and laws of the United States issue an order in writing for the removal of Edwin M. Stanton from the office of Secretary for the Department of War, . . . and . . . on the 12th day of December, in the year last aforesaid—having reported to said Senate such suspension, with the evidence and reasons for his action in the case . . . and said Senate thereafterwards, on the 13th day of January, A.D. 1868, having duly considered the evidence and reasons reported by said Andrew Johnson for said suspension, and having refused to concur in said suspension, whereby and by force of the provisions of an act entitled "An act regulating the tenure of certain civil offices," passed March 2,

1867, said Edwin M. Stanton did forthwith resume the functions of his office, whereof the said Andrew Johnson . . . unlawfully issued with intent then and there to violate . . . [the Tenure of Office Act], and with the further intent, contrary to the provisions of said act, in violation thereof, and contrary to the provisions of the Constitution of the United States, and without the advice and consent of the Senate of the United States . . . to remove said Edwin M. Stanton from the office of the Secretary for the Department of War, the said Edwin M. Stanton being then and there Secretary for the Department of War, . . . whereby said Andrew Johnson, President of the United States, did then and there commit and was guilty of a high misdemeanor in office.

* * *

Art. X.   That said Andrew Johnson, President of the United States, unmindful of the high duties of his office and the dignity and proprieties thereof, and of the harmony and courtesies which ought to exist and be maintained between the executive and legislative branches of the Government of the United States, designing and intending to set aside the rightful authority and powers of Congress, did attempt to bring into disgrace, ridicule, hatred, contempt, and reproach the Congress of the United States and the several branches thereof, to impair and destroy the regard and respect of all the good people of the United States for the Congress and legislative power thereof (which all officers of the Government ought inviolably to preserve and maintain), and to excite the odium and resentment of all the good people of the United States against Congress and the laws by it duly and constitutionally enacted; and, in pursuance of his said design and intent, openly and publicly, and before divers assemblages of the citizens of the United States, convened in divers parts thereof to meet and receive said Andrew Johnson as the Chief Magistrate of the United States, did, on the 18th day of August, A.D. 1866, and on divers other days and times, as well before as afterwards, make and deliver with a loud voice certain intemperate, inflammatory, and scandalous harangues, and did therein utter loud threats and bitter menaces, as well against Congress as the laws of the United States, duly enacted thereby, amid the cries, jeers, and laughter of the multitudes then assembled and in hearing . . . [Here the charges included specific examples of his speeches, with long quotations from them] which said utterances, declarations, threats, and harangues, highly censurable in any, are peculiarly indecent and unbecoming in the Chief Magistrate of the United States, by means whereof said Andrew Johnson has brought the high office of the President of the United States into contempt, ridicule, and disgrace, to the great scandal of all good citizens; whereby said Andrew Johnson, President of the United States, did commit and was then and there guilty of a high misdemeanor in office.

Art. XI.   That said Andrew Johnson, President of the United States, unmindful of the high duties of his office and of his oath of office, and in disregard of the Constitution and laws of the United States, did heretofore, to wit, on the 18th day of August, A.D. 1866, at the city of Washington, in the District of Columbia, by public speech, declare and affirm in substance that the Thirty-ninth Congress of the United States was not a Congress of the United States authorized by the Constitution to exercise legislative power under the same, but, on the contrary, was a Congress of only part of the States; thereby denying and intending to deny that the legislation of said Congress was valid or obligatory upon him, the said Andrew Johnson, except in so far as he saw fit to approve the same, and also thereby denying and intending to deny the power of the said Thirty-ninth Congress to propose amendments to the Constitution of the United States; and in pursuance of said declaration the said Andrew Johnson, President of the United States, afterwards, to wit, on the 21st day of February, A.D. 1868, . . . did unlawfully, and in disregard of the requirement of the Constitution that he should take care that the laws be faithfully executed, attempt to prevent the execution of an act entitled "An act regulating the tenure of certain civil offices," passed March 2, 1867, by unlawfully devising and contriving, and attempting to devise and contrive, means by which he should prevent Edwin M. Stanton from forthwith resuming the functions of the office of Secretary for the Department of War, notwithstanding the refusal of the Senate to concur in the suspension theretofore made by said Andrew Johnson of said Edwin M. Stanton from said office of Secretary for the Department of War, and also by further unlawfully devising and contriving, and attempting to devise and contrive, means then and there to prevent the execution of an act entitled "An act making appropriations for the support of the Army for the fiscal year ending June 30, 1868 and for other purposes," approved March 2, 1867, and also to prevent the execution of an act entitled "An act to provide for the more efficient government of the rebel States," passed March 2, 1867, whereby the said Andrew Johnson, President of the United States, did then, to wit, on the 21st day of February, A.D. 1868, at the city of Washington, commit and was guilty of a high misdemeanor in office.

[On May 16, thirty-five senators voted for conviction, one short of the two-thirds majority needed for removal from office.]

Note: The Courts and the Politics of Reconstruction

For the most part, the courts rarely interfered with Reconstruction policy. In *Ex parte Milligan* (1866), the Supreme Court reversed Milligan's conviction because he was a civilian who had been tried by a military court in Indiana at a time when the civilian courts were open and functioning. Although a great victory for civil liberties, the case had little effect on Reconstruction policy. Somewhat more significant to Reconstruction policies were *Cummings* v. *Missouri* (1867) and *Ex parte Garland* (1867), striking down, as *ex post facto* laws, state and federal requirements of oaths that made voters, attorneys, and others swear that they had never aided the rebellion or even expressed sympathy for the Confederate cause.

The Supreme Court was exceedingly restrained on the key issue of congressional power over Reconstruction. The Court accepted the reality that Congress would decide the political issue of the status of the former Confederate states. In *Mississippi* v. *Johnson* (1867), *Georgia* v. *Stanton* (1868), and *Ex parte McCardle* (1869), the Court refused to interfere with the implementation of the Military Reconstruction Acts. In *Texas* v. *White* (1869), the Court accepted Congress's theory of Reconstruction— that "the rights of the State as a member" of the Union "were suspended" by secession and that only Congress could end that suspension.

Black Freedom

The Thirteenth Amendment, ratified in late 1865, proclaimed the end of slavery and empowered Congress to enforce the amendment "by appropriate legislation." The Fourteenth and Fifteenth Amendments, adopted in 1868 and 1870, contained similar enforcement clauses.

After the war, most southern whites acquiesced in the demise of chattel slavery but did not accept the freedmen as equals or as citizens. In 1865 and 1866, President Johnson allowed former Confederates to participate in the reorganization of state and local governments. These new governments quickly moved to force blacks into a state of subservience and subjugation with laws collectively known as the black codes. These laws required that blacks get licenses to own guns or other weapons, to "exercise the function of a minister of the Gospel," and to live in a city or town. Black children could be apprenticed against the wishes of their parents, while strict vagrancy laws allowed the virtual enslavement of any free black who was unwilling to work for his or her former master. The laws "created a quasi-slavery or serfdom which was offensive to liberal, humanitarian sentiment" and "represented an attempt to make the freedmen in effect slaves of the community by treating them as a distinct class and by severely restricting their access to the ordinary civil rights and liberties that white persons enjoyed."[6]

Congress countered the black codes with the Civil Rights Act of 1866. In *In re Turner* (1867), Chief Justice Salmon Chase held, while riding circuit, that a Maryland apprentice law leading to the virtual enslavement of the minor children of former slaves violated the 1866 act. Increased violence against blacks and white Unionists by the Ku Klux Klan led to the "Force Acts," adopted by Congress in 1870 and 1871. Congressional protection of blacks culminated with the Civil Rights Act of 1875.

Congressional support for black freedom had mixed results. President Johnson resisted Congress's attempts to protect the freedmen. Congress enacted both the Second Freedmen's Bureau Act and the Civil Rights Act of 1866 over Johnson's vetoes. Johnson refused to use his powers to protect blacks and, instead, removed numerous civilian and military authorities in the South who attempted to help blacks and treat them justly. More importantly, Johnson's policies encouraged white resistance to civil rights, which continued during the Grant administration. Ultimately, southern white resistance, a series of adverse Supreme Court decisions, and northern disinterest in the fate of southern blacks doomed the former slaves to poverty, political disfranchisement, segregation, and legally sanctioned second-class status.

Mississippi Black Codes
1865

By late 1865, President Johnson had established new governments in the South that were dominated by whites, including many former Confederates. Johnson required only that the governments ratify the Thirteenth Amendment, repudiate the Confederate debt, and repeal their ordinances of secession. These new governments sought to control the freedmen through black codes.

AN ACT to confer Civil Rights on Freedmen, and for other purposes.

Section 1.   Be it enacted by the Legislature of the State of Mississippi, That all freedmen, free negroes and mulattoes may sue and be sued, implead and be impleaded in all the courts of law and equity of this State, and may acquire personal property and choses in action, by descent or purchase, and may dispose of the same, in the same manner, and to the same extent that white persons may: Provided that the provisions of this section shall not be so construed as to allow any freedmen, free negro or mulatto, to rent or lease any lands or tenements, except in incorporated towns or cities in which places the corporate authorities shall control the same.

SEC. 2.   Be it further enacted, That all freedmen, free negroes, and mulattoes may intermarry with each other, in the same manner and under the same regulations that are provided by law for white persons: Provided, that the clerk of probate shall keep separate records of the same.

SEC. 3.   Be it further enacted, That all freedmen, free negroes and mulattoes, who do now and have heretofore lived and cohabitated together as husband and wife shall be taken and held in law as legally married, and the issue shall be taken and held as legitimate for all purposes. That it shall not be lawful for any freedmen [etc.] . . . to intermarry with any white person; nor for any white person to intermarry with any freedmen [etc.] . . . ; and any person who shall so intermarry shall be deemed guilty of felony, and on conviction thereof, shall be confined in the State Penitentiary for life; and those shall be deemed freedmen, free negroes and mulattoes who are of pure negro blood, and those descended from a negro to the third generation inclusive, though one ancestor of each generation may have been a white person.

*   *   *

SEC. 6.   Be it further enacted, That all contracts for labor made with freedmen, free negroes and mulattoes, for a longer period than one month shall be in writing and in duplicate, attested and read to said freedmen [etc.] . . . and if the laborer shall quit the service of the employer, before expiration of his term of service, without good cause, he shall forfeit his wages for that year, up to the time of quitting.

SEC. 7.   Be it further enacted, That every civil officer shall, and every person may arrest and carry back to his or her legal employer any freedman, free negro or mulatto, who shall have quit the service of his or her employer before the expiration of his or her term of service without good cause, and said officer and person shall be entitled to receive for arresting and carrying back every deserting employee aforesaid, the sum of five dollars, and ten cents per mile from the place of arrest to the place of delivery, and the same shall be paid by the employer, and held as a set-off for so much against the wages of said deserting employee: Provided that said arrested party after being so returned may appeal to a justice of the peace or member of the board of police of the county, who on notice to the alleged employer, shall try summarily whether said appellant is legally employed by the alleged employer and has good cause to quit said employer; either party shall have the right of appeal to the county court, pending which the alleged deserter shall be remanded to the alleged employer, or otherwise disposed of as shall be right and just, and the decision of the county court shall be final.

*   *   *

SEC. 9.   Be it further enacted, That if any person shall persuade or attempt to persuade, entice or cause any freedman [etc.] . . . to desert from the legal employment of any person, before the expiration of his or her term of service, or shall knowingly employ any such deserting freedman [etc.] . . . or shall knowingly give or sell to any such deserting freedman [etc.] . . . any food, payment or other thing, he or she shall be guilty of a misdemeanor, and upon conviction, shall be fined not less than twenty-five dollars and not more than two hundred dollars and the costs, and if said fine and costs shall not be immediately paid, the court shall sentence said convict to not exceeding two months imprisonment in the county jail, and he or she shall moreover be liable to the party injured in damages: Provided, if any person shall, or shall attempt to persuade, entice, or cause any freedman [etc.] . . . to desert from any legal employment of any person, with the view to employ said freedman [etc.] . . . without the limits of this State, such person, on conviction, shall be fined not less than fifty dollars and not more than five hundred dollars and costs, and if said fine and costs shall not be immediately paid, the court shall sentence said convict to not exceeding six months imprisonment in the county jail.

AN ACT to amend the Vagrant Laws of the State

*   *   *

Sec. 2.   Be it further enacted, That all freedmen, free negroes and mulattoes in this state, over the age of eighteen years, found on the second Monday in January, 1866, or thereafter, with no lawful employment or business, or found unlawfully assembling themselves together either in the day or night time, and all white persons so assembling with freedmen [etc.] . . . or usually associating with freedmen [etc.] . . . on terms of equality, or living in adultery or fornication with a freedwoman, free negro, or mulatto, shall be deemed vagrants, and on conviction thereof, shall be fined in the sum of not exceeding, in the case of a freedman, free negro or mulatto, fifty dollars and a white man twelve hundred dollars, and imprisoned at the discretion of the court, the free negro not exceeding ten days, and the white man not exceeding six months.

*   *   *

Sec. 7.   Be it further enacted, That if any freedman, free negro or mulatto shall fail, or refuse to pay any tax levied according to the provisions of the sixth section of this act, it shall be prima facie evidence of vagrancy, and it shall be the duty of the sheriff to arrest such freedman, free negro or mulatto or such person refusing or neglecting to pay such tax and proceed at once to hire, for the shortest time, such delinquent tax payer to any one who will pay the said tax, with accruing costs, giving preference to the employer, if there be one.

An Act to Protect All Persons in the United States in Their Civil Rights, and Furnish Means of Their Vindication
1866

Congress responded to the proliferation of southern black codes with the Civil Rights Act of 1866. This was the first congressional protection of individual liberty in American history. The bill became law over President Johnson's veto.

Be it enacted . . . That all persons born in the United States and not subject to any foreign power, excluding Indians not taxed, are hereby declared to be citizens of the United States; and such citizens, of every race and color, without regard to any previous condition of slavery or involuntary servitude . . . shall have the same right, in every state and Territory . . . to make and enforce contracts, to sue, be parties, and give evidence, to inherit, purchase, lease, sell, hold, and convey real and personal property, and to full and equal benefit of all laws and proceedings for the security of person and property, as is enjoyed by white citizens, and shall be subject to like punishment, pains, and penalties, and to none other. . . .

Sec. 2. . . . That any person who, under color of any law, statute, ordinance, regulation, or custom, shall subject, or cause to be subjected, any inhabitant of any State or Territory to the deprivation of any right secured or protected by this act, or to different punishment, pains, or penalties on account of such person having at any time been held in a condition of slavery or involuntary servitude, . . . or by reason of his color or race, than is prescribed for the punishment of white persons, shall be deemed guilty of a misdemeanor, and, on conviction, shall be punished by fine not exceeding one thousand dollars, or imprisonment not exceeding one year, or both. . . .

Sec[.] 3. . . . That the district courts of the United States, within their respective districts, shall have, exclusively of the courts of the several States, cognizance of all crimes and offenses committed against the provisions of this act, and also, concurrently with the circuit courts of the United States, of all causes, civil and criminal, affecting persons who are denied or cannot enforce in the courts of judicial tribunals of the State or locality where they may be any of the rights secured to them by the first section of this act. . . .

Sec. 4. . . . That the district attorneys, marshals, and deputy marshals of the United States, the commissioners appointed by the circuit and territorial courts of the United States . . . the officers and agents of the Freedmen's Bureau, and every other officer who may be specially empowered by the President of the United States . . . are hereby, specially authorized and required, at the expense of the United States, to institute proceedings against all and every person who shall violate the provisions of this act, and cause him or them to be arrested . . . for trial before such court of the United States or territorial court. . . . And with a view to affording reasonable protection to all persons in their constitutional rights of equality before the law, without distinction of race or color, or previous condition of slavery . . . and to the prompt discharge of the duties of this act, it shall be the duty of the circuit courts [and territorial courts] of the United States . . . from time to time, to increase the number of commissioners, so as to afford a speedy and convenient means for the arrest and examination of persons charged with a violation of this act. . . .

*   *   *

[The remaining sections of the law contained various enforcement provisions and penalties. These provisions included the use of federal troops and local militia for enforcement.]

Note: The Civil Rights Act and the Fourteenth Amendment

Some members of Congress doubted the constitutionality of the 1866 Civil Rights Act, but most were convinced that the enforcement provision of the Thirteenth Amendment gave Congress sufficient power to protect the freedmen against both private action and state action. Following the override of President Johnson's veto of the Civil Rights Act, Congress passed the Fourteenth Amendment and sent it to the states. In 1870, Congress "reenacted" the 1866 act, on the assumption that the newly adopted Fourteenth and Fifteenth Amendments gave additional constitutional authority to the law.

Note: Andrew Johnson's Veto of the 1866 Civil Rights Act

The Civil Rights Act of 1866 became law over Johnson's veto. In his veto message, Johnson complained that the bill gave citizenship to all persons born in the United States, including "the Chinese of the Pacific States, Indians subject to taxation, the people called gypsies, as well as the entire race designated as blacks, people of color, negroes, mulattos, and persons of African blood." He condemned the law for creating "a perfect equality of white and colored races . . . fixed by Federal law in every state of the Union," arguing that "in fact, the distinction of race and color is by the bill made to operate in favor of the colored and against the white race.".

Note: The Freedmen's Bureau

In 1865, Congress established the Bureau of Refugees, Freedmen, and Abandoned Lands as an arm of the Department of War, staffed by a combination of military and civilian agents and headed by a Civil War hero, General Oliver O. Howard. The bureau, which was the country's first federally funded public-welfare program, coordinated private relief efforts with government initiatives to provide food, shelter, education, and legal protection to the recently emancipated slaves. Its ties to private charity suggest the discomfort of most members of Congress with federal aid to individuals; its failure to redistribute land to former slaves underscores the conservative nature of Reconstruction. The Freedmen's Bureau was to be in existence for one year after the war ended, but in July 1866 Congress re-created the bureau, passing the law over Johnson's veto. The 1866 act created Freedmen's Bureau courts to hear cases where "the ordinary course of judicial proceedings" had been "interrupted" or until a state was "duly represented in Congress." These courts adjudicated a full range of cases, using the military to protect the privileges and immunities of black citizens, and provided some legal protection and due process to former slaves, who faced discrimination and legal harassment at the hands of their former masters. Ultimately, the bureau's greatest success was in establishing schools for the freedmen.

Note: The Civil Rights Act of 1875

Officially titled "An Act to Protect all Citizens in their Civil and Legal Rights," the Civil Rights Act of 1875 was the last gasp of Reconstruction legislation. The law's preamble asserted that it was "essential to a just government" to "recognize the equality of all men before the law" and that it was "the duty of government in all its dealing with the people to mete out equal and exact justice to all; of whatever nativity, race, color, or persuasion, religious or political. . . ." It prohibited racial discrimination in jury selection at the state and federal levels, and allowed both civil damages and criminal penalties for any individuals who discriminated in "public accommodations . . . inns, public conveyances on land or water, theaters, and other places of public assessment. . . ." The act had almost no effect on American blacks, and most of it was declared unconstitutional in the *Civil Rights Cases* (1883).

The End of Civil Rights

The revolution in civil rights law began in 1862 with the Confiscation Acts and the first steps at congressional emancipation. The legislative initiatives continued until the passage of the Civil Rights Act of 1875. However, by this time, the United States Supreme Court had already begun to undermine the statutes and the amendments of the Civil War era.

Initially, the federal courts supported civil rights. Two cases decided by Supreme Court Justices while on circuit court duty illustrate this. In *U.S.* v. *Rhodes* (1866), Justice Noah Swayne upheld the constitutionality of the 1866 Civil Rights Act under the enforcement clause of the Thirteenth Amendment. In *In re Turner* (1866), Chief Justice Salmon P. Chase used the new amendment and the 1866 act to prohibit virtual reenslavement of black children under apprentice laws. In 1870 and 1871, trials under the Enforcement Acts (or Ku Klux Klan Acts, as they were known) helped destroy the Klan.

However, after 1873, support for civil rights diminished. Reconciliation captured the imagination of the North, while Democrats, including former Confederates, began to take control of southern state governments. In *U.S.* v. *Cruikshank* (1874) and *U.S.* v. *Harris* (1883), the Court undermined the use of the Ku Klux Klan Acts, while in the *Civil Rights Cases* (1883) the Court found most of the 1875 Civil Rights Act to be unconstitutional. In the following decades, the Court and the national legislature did little to protect black rights and liberties. The beginning of the nadir for black civil rights was Justice Samuel F. Miller's majority opinion in the *Slaughterhouse Cases*.

The *Slaughterhouse Cases*
16 Wall. (83 U.S.) 36 (1873)

In 1869, Louisiana confined all slaughtering in New Orleans to the Crescent City Live-Stock Landing & Slaughterhouse Company. This monopoly required individ-

ual butchers to rent space from the Crescent City Company in order to carry out their business. The state and city claimed this was a legitimate health regulation under the state's police powers. The butchers argued that the monopoly violated the Thirteenth and Fourteenth Amendments to the Constitution. Slaughterhouse was the first case the Supreme Court heard under the Fourteenth Amendment. In rejecting the claims of the butchers, the Court severely limited the application of the Fourteenth Amendment and virtually destroyed the value of the privileges and immunities clause of that Amendment.

Mr. Justice Miller . . .

* * *

The most cursory glance at these articles [the Civil War Amendments] discloses a unity of purpose, when taken in connection with the history of the times, which cannot fail to have an important bearing on any question of doubt concerning their true meaning. Nor can such doubts, when any reasonably exist, be safely and rationally solved without a reference to that history; for in it is found the occasion and the necessity for recurring again to the great source of power in this country, the people of the States, for additional guarantees of human rights; additional powers to the Federal government; additional restraints upon those of the States. Fortunately that history is fresh within the memory of us all, and its leading features, as they bear upon the matter before us, free from doubt.

The institution of African slavery, as it existed in about half the states of the Union, and the contests pervading the public mind for many years, between those who desired its curtailment and ultimate extinction and those who desired additional safeguards for its security and perpetuation, culminated in the effort, on the part of most of the States in which slavery existed, to separate from the Federal government, and to resist its authority. This constituted the war of the rebellion, and whatever auxiliary causes may have contributed to bring about this war, undoubtedly the over-shadowing and efficient cause was African slavery.

In that struggle slavery, as a legalized social relation, perished. . . . Hence the thirteenth article of amendment. . . .

To withdraw the mind from the contemplation of this grand yet simple declaration of the personal freedom of all the human race within the jurisdiction of this government—a declaration designed to establish the freedom of four millions of slaves—and with a microscopic search endeavor to find in it a reference to servitudes, which may have been attached to property in certain localities, requires an effort, to say the least of it.

That a personal servitude was meant is proved by the use of the word "involuntary," which can only apply to human beings. The exception of servitude as a punishment for crime gives an idea of the class of servitude that is meant. The word servitude is of larger meaning than slavery, as the latter is popularly understood in this country, and the obvious purpose was to forbid all shades and conditions of African slavery. It was very well understood that in the form of apprenticeship for long terms, as it had been practiced in the West India Islands, on the abolition of slavery by the English government, or by reducing the slaves to the condition of serfs attached in the plantation, the purpose of the article might have been evaded, if only the word slavery had been used. The case of the apprentice slave, held under a law of Maryland, liberated by Chief Justice Chase [*In re Turner* (1866)], on a writ of habeas corpus under this article, illustrates this course of observation. And it is all that we deem necessary to say on the application of that article to the statute of Louisiana, now under consideration.

* * *

We repeat, then in the light of this recapitulation of events, almost too recent to be called history, but which are familiar to us all; and on the most casual examination of the language of these amendments, no one can fail to be impressed with the one pervading purpose found in them all, lying at the foundation of each, and without which none of them would have been even suggested; we mean the freedom of the slave race, the security and firm establishment of that freedom, and the protection of the newly-made freeman and citizen from the oppression of those who had formerly exercised unlimited dominion over him. It is true that only the fifteenth amendment, in terms, mentions the negro by speaking of his color and his slavery. But it is just as true that each of the other articles was addressed to the grievances of that race. . . .

* * *

The first section of the fourteenth article, to which our attention is more specially invited, opens with a definition of citizenship—not only citizenship of the United States, but citizenship of the States. . . .

* * *

It is quite clear, then, that there is a citizenship of the United States, and a citizenship of a State, which are distinct from each other, and which depend upon different characteristics or circumstances in the individual.

We think this distinction and its explicit recognition in this amendment of great weight in this argument, because the next paragraph of this same section, which is the one mainly relied on by the plaintiffs in error, speaks only of privileges and immunities of citizens of the United States, and does not speak of those of citizens of the several States. The argument, however, in favor of the plaintiffs rests wholly on the assumption that the citizenship is the same, and the privileges and immunities guaranteed by the clause are the same.

The language is "No state shall make or enforce any law which shall abridge the privileges or immunities of citizens of *the United States*." It is a little remarkable, if this clause was intended as a protection to the citizen of a State against the legislative power of his own State, that the word citizen of the State should be left out when it is so carefully used, and used in contradiction to citizens of the United States, in the very sentence which precedes it. It is too clear for argument that the change in phraseology was adopted . . . with a purpose.

Of the privileges and immunities of the citizen of the United States, and of the privileges and immunities of the citizen of the State, and what they respectively are, we will presently consider; but we wish to state here that it is only the former which are placed by this clause under the protection of the Federal Constitution, and that the latter, whatever they may be, are not intended to have any additional protection by this paragraph of the amendment.

* * *

. . . Was it the purpose of the fourteenth amendment, by the simple declaration that no State should make or enforce any law which shall abridge the privileges and immunities of citizens of the United States, to transfer the security and protection of all the civil rights which we have mentioned, from the States to the Federal government? And where it is declared that Congress shall have the power to enforce that article, was it intended to bring within the power of Congress the entire domain of civil rights heretofore belonging exclusively to the States?

All this and more must follow, if the proposition of the plaintiffs in error be sound. For not only are these rights subject to the control of Congress whenever in its discretion any of them are supposed to be abridged by State Legislation, but that body may pass laws in advance, limiting and restricting the exercise of legislative power by the States, in their most ordinary and usual functions, as in its judgment it may think proper on all such subjects. And still further, such a construction followed by the reversal of the judgments of the Supreme Court of Louisiana in these cases, would constitute this court a perpetual censor upon all legislation of the States, on the civil rights of their own citizens, with authority to nullify such as it did not approve as consistent with those rights, as they existed at the time of the adoption of this amendment. The argument we admit is not always the most conclusive which is drawn from the consequences urged against the adoption of a particular construction of an instrument. But when, as in the case before us, these consequences are so serious, so far reaching and pervading, so great a departure from the structure and spirit of our institutions; when the effect is to fetter and degrade the State governments by subjecting them to the control of Congress, in the exercise of powers heretofore universally conceded to them of the most ordinary and fundamental character; when in fact it radically changes the whole theory of the relations of the State and Federal governments to each other and of both these governments to the people; the argument has been a force that is irresistible, in the absence of language which expresses such a purpose too clearly to admit of doubt.

We are convinced that no such results were intended by the Congress which proposed these amendments, nor by the legislature of the States which ratified them.

*　　　*　　　*

But lest it should be said that no such privileges and immunities are to be found. . . .

*　　　*　　　*

. . . [The Court offered some examples of "privileges and immunities" protected by the Fourteenth Amendment. These included the right to travel and a right to claim protection of the government on the high seas.] The right to peaceably assemble and petition for redress of grievances, the privilege of the writ of habeas corpus, are rights of the citizen guaranteed by the Federal Constitution. The right to use the navigable waters of the United States, however they may penetrate the territory of the several States, all rights secured to our citizens by treaties with foreign nations, are dependent upon citizenship of the United States, and not citizenship of a State. One of these privileges is conferred by the very article under consideration. It is that a citizen of the United States can, of his own volition, become a citizen of any State of the Union by a bona fide residence therein, with the same rights as other citizens of that State. To these may be added the rights secured by the thirteenth and fifteenth articles of amendment, and by the other clause of the fourteenth, next to be considered.

*　　　　　*　　　　　*

The argument has not been much pressed in these cases that the defendant's charter deprives the plaintiffs of their property without due process of law, or that it denies them the equal protection of the law. [Here the court noted that such clauses existed in most state constitutions as well as in the Fifth Amendment to the United States Constitution.] . . .

We are not without judicial interpretation, therefore, both state and nation, of the meaning to this clause. And it is sufficient to say that under no construction of that provision that we have ever seen, or any that we deem admissible, can the restraint imposed by the state of Louisiana . . . be held to be a deprivation of property within the meaning of that provision.

*　　　　　*　　　　　*

"Nor shall any State deny to any person within its jurisdiction the equal protection of the laws."

In the light of the history of these amendments, and the pervading purpose of them, which we have already discussed, it is not difficult to give a meaning to this clause. The existence of laws in the States where the newly emancipated negroes resided, which discriminated with gross injustice and hardship against them as a class, was the evil to be remedied by this clause, and by it such laws are forbidden.

If, however, the States did not conform their laws to its requirements, then by the fifth section of the article of amendment Congress was authorized to enforce it by suitable legislation. We doubt very much whether any action of a State not directed by way of discrimination against the negroes as a class, or an account of their race, will ever be held to come within the purview of this provision. It is so clearly a provision for that race and that emergency, that a strong case would be necessary for its application to any other. . . .

*　　　　　*　　　　　*

. . . It was then discovered [when the Civil War occurred] that the true danger to the perpetuity of the Union was in the capacity of the State organization to combine and concentrate all the powers of the State, and of contiguous States, for a determined resistance to the General Government.

Unquestionably this has given great force to the argument, and added largely to the number of those who believe in the necessity of a strong National government.

But, however pervading this sentiment, and however it may have contributed to the adoption of the amendments we have been considering, we do not see in those amendments any purpose to destroy the main features of the general system. Under the pressure of all the excited feeling growing out of the war, our statesmen have still believed that the existence of the States with powers for domestic and local government, including the regulation of civil rights—the rights of person and of property—was essential to the perfect working of our complex form of government, though they have thought proper to impose additional limitations on the States, and to confer additional power on that of the Nation.

Note: The *Slaughterhouse* Legacy

Chief Justice Chase and Justices Swayne, Bradley, and Field dissented, arguing for a more expansive interpretation of the Fourteenth Amendment. These dissents stressed the nationalization of liberty under the amendment. The Bradley dissent in particular set the stage for the late-nineteenth-century developments in substantive due process, as is presented in Chapter 7 of this book.

The more pernicious result of *Slaughterhouse* is outlined in the following paragraph from a recent book on the constitutional history of this period.

> Herein lay a terrible irony for blacks. After having construed the "pervading purpose" of the Civil War amendments to be the freedom of black people, Miller relegated freedmen, for the effective protection of their new freedom, to precisely those governments—the southern states—least likely to respect either their rights or their freedom should the Republican regimes fall from power. The federal government could protect only the privileges and immunities of federal citizenship. As enumerated by Miller, these included the right of access to Washington, D.C., and the coastal seaports; the right to protection on the high seas and abroad; the right to use navigable waters of the United States; the right of assembly and petition; the privilege of habeas corpus. Of these, only the last two would be significant for most blacks.[7]

Note: *Civil Rights Cases*, 109 U.S. 3 (1883)

The *Civil Rights Cases* were five prosecutions and civil suits from California, Kansas, Missouri, New York, and Tennessee, for denying blacks access to public accommodations and facilities under the Civil Rights Act of 1875. The defendants had denied blacks access to hotels, theaters, and railroad cars. Speaking for the Court, Justice Joseph Bradley found the 1875 Civil Rights Act unconstitutional because he believed that the Fourteenth Amendment prohibited only state action and did not protect blacks against private discrimination. He admitted that the Thirteenth Amendment allowed for the elimination of "badges of slavery," but would not apply this to prohibitions of racial discrimination in "an inn, a public conveyance, or a theatre." He believed that antidiscrimination laws belonged to the jurisdiction of the states, not the national government. He concluded:

> When a man has emerged from slavery, and by the aid of beneficent legislation has shaken off the inseparable concomitants of that state, there must be some stage in the progress of his elevation when he takes the rank of a mere citizen, and ceases to be the special favorite of the laws, and when his rights as a citizen, or a man, are to be protected in the ordinary modes by which other men's rights are protected. There were thousands of free colored people in this country before the abolition of slavery, enjoying all the essential rights of life, liberty and property the same as white citizens; yet no one, at that time, thought that it was any invasion of his personal status as a freeman because he was not admitted to all the privileges enjoyed by white citizens, or because he was subjected to discriminations in the enjoyment of accommodations in inns, public conveyances and places of amusement. Mere discriminations on account of race or color were not regarded as badges of slavery. If, since that time, the enjoyment of equal rights in all these respects has become established by constitutional enactment, it is not by force of the Thirteenth Amendment (which merely abolishes slavery), but by force of the Fourteenth and Fifteenth Amendments.

Justice John Marshall Harlan, a former slaveowner from Kentucky, dissented, arguing that the Court's opinion rested "upon grounds entirely too narrow and artificial." He urged a broad reading of both the Thirteenth and Fourteenth Amendments. Of the former he noted:

The Thirteenth Amendment, it is conceded, did something more than to prohibit slavery as an *institution*, resting upon distinctions of race, and upheld by positive law. My brethren admit that it established and decreed universal *civil freedom* throughout the United States. But did the freedom thus established involve nothing more than exemption from actual slavery? Was nothing more intended than to forbid one man from owning another as property? Was it the purpose of the nation simply to destroy the institution, and then remit the race, theretofore held in bondage, to the several States for such protection, in their civil rights, necessarily growing out of freedom, as those States, in their discretion, might choose to provide? Were the States against whose protest the institution was destroyed, to be left free, so far as national interference was concerned, to make or allow discriminations against that race, as such, in the enjoyment of those fundamental rights which by universal concession, inhere in a state of freedom?

Harlan also argued that the discrimination in public carriers and public facilities amounted to state action because the roads and highways were "established by authority of these States." Public inns were historically obligated to serve "all travelers or Wayfarers who might choose to" enter them. Theaters were licensed by the state, and that was sufficient state action to justify federal protection under the Civil War Amendments. Most importantly, Harlan challenged the cynical conclusions of Bradley that the former slaves had been the "special favorite of the laws."

My brethren say, that when a man has emerged from slavery, and by the aid of beneficent legislation has shaken off the inseparable concomitants of that state, there must be some stage in the progress of his elevation when he takes the rank of a mere citizen, and ceases to be the special favorite of the laws, and when his rights as a citizen, or a man, are to be protected in the ordinary modes by which other men's rights are protected. It is, I submit, scarcely just to say that the colored race has been the special favorite of the laws. The statute of 1875, now adjudged to be unconstitutional, is for the benefit of citizens of every race and color. What the nation, through Congress, has sought to accomplish in reference to that race, is—what had already been done in every State of the Union for the white race—to secure and protect rights belonging to them as freemen and citizens; nothing more. It was not deemed enough "to help the feeble up, but to support him after." The one underlying purpose of congressional legislation has been to enable the black race to take the rank of mere citizens. The difficulty has been to compel a recognition of the legal right of the black race to take the rank of citizens, and to secure the enjoyment of privileges belonging, under the law, to them as a component part of the people for whose welfare and happiness government is ordained. At every step, in this direction, the nation has been confronted with class tyranny, which a contemporary English historian says is, of all tyrannies, the most intolerable, "for it is ubiquitous in its operation, and weighs, perhaps, most heavily on those whose obscurity or distance would withdraw them from the notice of a single despot." To-day, it is the colored race which is denied, by corporations and individuals wielding public authority, rights fundamental in their freedom and citizenship. At some future time, it may be that some other race will fall under the ban of race discrimination. If the constitutional amendments be enforced, according to the intent with which, as I conceive, they were adopted, there cannot be, in this republic, any class of human beings in practical subjection to another class, with power in the latter to dole out to the former just such privileges as they may choose to grant. The supreme law of the land has decreed that no authority shall be exercised in this country upon the basis of discrimination, in respect of civil rights, against freemen and citizens because of their race, color, or previous condition of servitude.

5

Nineteenth-Century Law and Society 1800–1900

Industrialization, urbanization, territorial growth, and immigration transformed nineteenth-century American society. When the Civil War began in 1861, agriculture propelled the country's economic growth; forty years later, manufacturing had taken its place. The benefits of economic growth showered unevenly across the social order; wealth became increasingly concentrated in the rising urban middle and upper classes, even as the absolute numbers of persons in the ranks of both groups continued to swell.

Economic growth and concomitant demographic changes had powerful social ramifications. The rising urban middle class, for example, fostered new expectations about the role of women, children, and family life in general. In the seventeenth and eighteenth centuries, most American families functioned as independent economic units. But as men became enmeshed in the nineteenth-century's money economy (whether through trade and commerce or market farming), the direct contributions of women and children to the family economy declined. The new order that began to emerge by the 1820s had women and men occupying separate spheres, with the former dominating the private realm of the home by serving as homemakers and guardians of their families' moral and cultural well-being.

The roles of women and children changed in other ways. Until the late eighteenth century, economic arrangements guided most marriages, but in the new century wedlock increasingly was based on the ideal of mutual emotional support. In this configuration, the children of middle and upper-class combinations were not economic assets but objects of emotional attachment. These changes in the underlying social basis of the family prompted new demands on the legal culture, and lawmakers and judges responded by revising the rules governing domestic relations, an area that government had previously regulated lightly. The law of marriage, birth control, abortion, divorce, and child custody all underwent significant changes in the nineteenth century.

The lines separating male and female spheres also became entangled during this century. Women social reformers, such as Elizabeth Cady Stanton, sought to broaden the legal status of women, but to do so, in most instances, meant removing them from the pedestal on which men had placed them and eliminating the laws that male legislators had crafted for the protection of women and the family. A small but vocal band of women also asserted their claims to a role in public life through activism on behalf of several social reform causes, including the abolition of slavery, penal reform, temperance, and, most significantly, women's suffrage.

Economic growth and social change converged through the law in other ways. Throughout the century, labor remained dear. Black slaves, as we have seen in Chapter 4, supplied much of the needs of southern planters before the Civil War. The small free black population in the South and North, while having little impact on the labor supply, did stir significant concern among the white population. The dominant ideology of free, white labor meant that many white workers not only fretted over competition with slave labor but viewed any black workers, under the prevailing climate of race relations, as social pariahs. The emancipation of approximately 4 million slaves after the Civil War further fueled racial discontent, especially in the South, where the bulk of the black population lived and where their service as la-borers was essential to the restoration of the devastated southern economy. The law of racial adjustment, for free blacks before the Civil War and for freed men and women after the war, heaped powerful new social demands on an already racist legal culture.

The experience of African-Americans was only the most prominent example of the tensions inherent in a legal culture that struggled to reconcile an ostensible commitment to an impartial rule of law with persistent racism and xenophobia. The growth of racial and ethnic diversity during the century only exacerbated this stress. A strong white nativist movement, for example, protested the massive influx of Irish and other European immigrants that beat on American shores, beginning in mid-century, and provided an enormous pool of labor. The nation's population soared because of this flood of immigrants. In the decade 1820 to 1829, only about 4 percent of the population increase came from the foreign born; between 1880 and 1889, the period of the highest percentage of foreign born entering the nation in its history, more than 40 percent of the population increase came from immigration. Most of these new immigrants swelled the population of American cities and stoked industrialization, but they also frightened the native-born Protestant population with their customs and religious beliefs.

Americanization, ethnic assimilation, and racism also became entwined with themes of law and order. Urban rioting, crime, and poverty were features of growing American cities, and public authorities, who were often native-born Protestants, linked these disorders to immigrants. Throughout the century, concerns about crime often merely disguised nativist wishes to control the "dangerous classes." Yet social control through the criminal justice system had another side: a genuinely free people required a stable social order in which their persons and property was secure.

Nativism and racism were invariably supportive of each other, and both lurked just below the surface of American society. The legal fate of the Chinese and Native Americans illustrates this point. The Chinese were the most exotic component of the nineteenth-century migration. They first arrived in America in the 1840s with the opening of the California gold fields, and they shortly became the objects of racial contempt and of public policies even more bizarre than those adopted to deal with free blacks. The Chinese labored with white settlers to open the American West, but they were as visibly different as blacks from the dominant Anglo-Saxon population, and their religious practices made then troublesome for a criminal justice system rooted in Christian oath taking.

Native Americans also drew the white population's contempt. As American settlers poured westward, they invariably competed with the Indians for lands. These successive collisions began in the Southeast early in the century, spread beyond the Mississippi in mid-century, and continued after the Civil War on the Great Plains. Ironically, while most of the white population viewed Native Americans with a degree of equanimity that they refused to extend to blacks and Chinese, no other racial group suffered greater cultural or physical destruction. At each turn in the history of white–Native American relations, the law figured prominently in defining the rights and duties of each group. The issue of Indian rights, however, was part of a greater debate about the relative power of the federal and state governments. If the tribes were treated as separate nations, then the states had limited authority to take tribal lands and impose state law. The white quest for Indian lands also raised questions about whether a policy of preserving tribal culture on reservations or granting Native Americans full citizenship made sense. Political expediency, philanthropy, and greed shaped white treatment, through the law, of Native Americans.

By 1900, the rural republic of a hundred years before had been swamped by a significantly more diverse and contentious social order. Whether involving matters of racial adjustment, domestic relations, women's rights, or crime and criminal justice, the relationship between law and society in the nineteenth century was typically one of demand and response. The documents that follow address the ways in which nineteenth-century Americans invoked legal authority to deal with the tensions created by a contradictory commitment to human equality, on the one hand, and sexism and racism, on the other.

Race

Nineteenth-century lawmakers invoked race to define personal status. Slavery, for example, attached exclusively to black people, and the southern system of Jim Crow segregation that rose to replace it was also directed toward nonwhites only. This shift from slavery to segregation underscores the dynamic and pliable character of the relationship between race and law, and this same quality figures in the treatment accorded Native Americans and Chinese. In each instance, the social and cultural assumptions of inferiority that whites attached to these groups found expression in the legal culture. Throughout the nineteenth century, a minority of white Americans embraced the arguments made by some anthropologists, physicians, and other scientists that nonwhites were actually a species of beings who had been placed on earth by God at a "separate creation." Most Americans rejected this extreme position, in large measure because it violated the biblical creation story set out in the book of Genesis. More common, at least in the South, was the view expressed by Senator James Henry Hammond of South Carolina in a famous 1858 speech on the floor of the Senate that blacks were simply a "race inferior" to whites who had a "low order of intellect" and "little skill," and were marked by "vigor, docility, [and] fidelity." Comparable statements about the Chinese and Native Americans were made by other nineteenth-century Americans. Not surprisingly, white Americans sought through the law to provide for the social control of each of these groups. But in each instance, the law also recognized important differences among these racial groups, and, as significant, there were important regional differences in ideas and practices. For example, after the Civil War, the Chinese, Native Americans, and Mexican Americans were a far greater source of concern than were blacks in the West; the opposite was true in the East and South.

Blacks

The Civil War had ironic consequences for the adjustment of race relations in the United States. The war simultaneously exacerbated racial disharmony by emancipating more than 4 million former slaves while it fostered political changes necessary to establish a seemingly color-blind legal order through the Thirteenth, Fourteenth, and Fifteenth Amendments to the federal Constitution. As we have seen in Chapter 4, these amendments and statutes passed by the Republican majority in Congress provided the legal scaffolding that made blacks citizens, promised them equal protection of the laws, and prohibited discrimination in federal elections. The amendments were only partially successful in creating substantive equality for black people. For example, in the late nineteenth century and twentieth century, southern state legislatures, with the acquiescence of the United States Supreme Court, enacted statutes that stripped blacks of their political rights and cast them into racial segregation. Conditions were better in the North, where blacks could testify against whites, freely migrate from state to state, enjoy public education, and vote. Yet even under the best circumstances, legal equality for nineteenth-century American blacks did not translate into equal social status with whites. In matters of public schooling, voting, and marrying, the legal order reflected an underlying social assumption that, for the most part, blacks were not to mix with whites.

Roberts v. The City of Boston
5 Cush. (59 Mass.) 198 (1849)

Roberts v. The City of Boston *(1849) was the first school desegregation case in the United States. Charles Sumner, a future United States senator, and Robert Morris, Jr., one of the first black attorneys in the nation, argued the case for Benjamin Roberts. He had sought to enroll his daughter, Sarah, in the school nearest to his house, rather than in a more distant school designated for black children. In order for Sarah to reach her assigned school, she had to pass five "whites only" schools. At the time, Boston was one of only a few places in Massachusetts that segregated black and white schoolchildren. Segregation in the schools was not required by any state statute or Boston ordinance. Rather, the Boston school committee used its powers to segregate the city's schools. Chief Justice Lemuel Shaw, one of the giant figures of nineteenth-century legal history, delivered the opinion of the court.*

[Sarah Roberts] The plaintiff, a colored child of five years of age, has commenced this action, by her father and next friend . . . upon the statute of 1845, c. 214, which provides, that any child unlawfully excluded from public school instruction, in this commonwealth, shall recover damages therefor, in an action against the city or town, by which such public school instruction is supported. The question therefore is, whether, upon the facts agreed, the plaintiff has been unlawfully excluded from such instruction.

By the agreed statement of facts, it appears that the defendants support a class of schools called primary schools, to the number of about one hundred and sixty, designed for the instruction of children of both sexes, who are between the ages of four and seven years. Two of these schools are appropriated by the primary school committee, having charge of that class of schools, to the exclusive instruction of colored children, and the residue to the exclusive instruction of white children.

The plaintiff, by her father, took proper measures to obtain admission into one of these schools appropriated to white children, but pursuant to the regulations of the committee . . . she was not admitted. Either of the schools appropriated to colored children was open to her; the nearest of which was about a fifth of a mile or seventy rods more distant from her father's house than the nearest primary school. It further appears, by the facts agreed, that the committee having charge of that class of schools, had, a short time previously to the plaintiff's application, adopted a resolution upon a report of a committee, that in the opinion of that board, the continuance of the separate schools for colored children and the regular attendance of all such children upon the schools, is not only legal and just, but is best adapted to promote the instruction of that class of the population.

*   *   *

The plaintiff had access to a school, set apart for colored children, as well conducted in all respects, and as well fitted, in point of capacity and qualification of the instructors, to advance the education of children under seven years old, as the other primary schools; the objection is, that the schools thus open to the plaintiff are exclusively appropriated to colored children, and are at a greater distance from her home. Under these circumstances, has the plaintiff been unlawfully excluded from public school instruction? Upon the best consideration we have been able to give the subject, the court are all of opinion that she has not.

It will be considered, that this is a question of power, or of the legal authority of the committee intrusted by the city with this department of public instruction; because, if they have the legal authority, the expediency of exercising it in any particular way is exclusively with them.

The great principle, advanced by the learned and eloquent advocate of the plaintiff, is, that by the constitution and laws of Massachusetts, all persons without distinction of age or sex, birth or color, origin or condition, are equal before the law. This, as a broad general principle, such as ought to appear in a declaration of rights, is perfectly sound; it is not only expressed in terms, but pervades and animates the whole spirit of our constitution of free government. But, when this great principle comes to be applied to the actual and various conditions of persons in society, it will not warrant the assertion, that men and women are legally clothed with the same civil and political powers, and that children and adults are legally to have the same functions and be subject to the same treatment; but only that the rights of all, as they are settled and regulated by law, are equally entitled to the paternal consideration and protection of the law, for their maintenance and security. What those rights are, to which individuals, in the infinite variety of circumstances by which they are surrounded in society, are entitled, must depend on laws adapted to their respective relations and conditions.

Conceding, therefore, in the fullest manner, that colored persons, the descendants of Africans, are entitled by law, in this commonwealth, to equal rights, constitutional and political, civil and social, the question then arises, whether the regulation in question, which provides separate schools for colored children, is a violation of any of these rights.

Legal rights must, after all, depend upon the provisions of law; certainly all those rights of individuals which can be asserted and maintained in any judicial tribunal. The proper province of a declaration of rights and constitution of government, after directing its form, regulating its organization and the distribution of its powers, is to declare great principles and fundamental truths, to influence and direct the judgment and conscience of legislators in making laws, rather than to limit and control them, by directing what precise laws they shall make. The provision, that it shall be the duty of legislatures and magistrates to cherish the interests of literature and the sciences, especially the university at Cambridge, public schools, and grammar schools, in the towns, is precisely of this character. Had the legislature failed to comply with this injunction, and neglected to provide public schools in the towns, or should they so far fail in their duty as to repeal all laws on the subject, and leave all education to depend on private means, strong and explicitly as the direction of the constitution is, it would afford no remedy or redress to the thousands of the rising generation, who now depend on these schools to afford them a most valuable education and an introduction to useful life.

                    *   *   *

The power of general superintendence vests a plenary authority in the committee to arrange, classify, and distribute pupils, in such a manner as they think best adapted to their general proficiency and welfare. If it is thought expedient to provide for very young children, it may be, that such schools may be kept exclusively by female teachers, quite adequate to their instruction, and yet whose services may be obtained at a cost much lower than that of more highly-qualified male instructors. So if they should judge it expedient to have a grade of schools for children from seven to ten, and another for those from ten to fourteen, it would seem to be within their authority to establish such schools. So to separate male and female pupils into different schools. It has been found necessary, that is to say, highly expedient, at times, to establish special schools for poor and neglected children, who have passed the age of seven, and have become too old to attend the primary school, and yet have not acquired the rudiments of learning, to enable them to enter the ordinary schools. If a class of youth, of one or both sexes, is found in that condition, and it is expedient to organize them into a separate school, to receive the special training, adapted to their condition, it seems to be within the power of the superintending committee, to provide for the organization of such special school.

                    *   *   *

In the absence of special legislation of this subject, the law has vested the power in the committee to regulate the system of distribution and classification; and when this power is reasonably exercised, without being abused or perverted by colorable pretences, the decision of the committee must be deemed conclusive. The committee, apparently upon great deliberation, have come to the conclusion, that the good of both classes of schools will be best promoted, by maintaining the separate primary schools for colored and for white children, and we can perceive no ground to doubt, that this is the honest result of their experience and judgment.

It is urged that this maintenance of separate schools tends to deepen and perpetuate the odious distinction of caste, founded in a deep-rooted prejudice in public opinion. This prejudice, if it exists, is not created by law, and probably cannot be changed by law. Whether this distinction and prejudice, existing in the opinion and feelings of the community, would not be as effectually fostered by compelling colored and white children to associate together in the same schools, may well be doubted; at all events, it is a fair and proper question for the committee to consider and decide upon, having in view the best interests of both classes of children placed under their superintendence, and we cannot say, that their decision upon it is not founded on just grounds of reason and experience, and in the results of a discriminating and honest judgment.

The increased distance, to which the plaintiff was obliged to go to school from her father's house, is not such, in our opinion, as to render the regulation in question unreasonable, still less illegal.

On the whole the court are of opinion, that upon the facts stated, the action cannot be maintained.

Note: Free Blacks and the Law

At the beginning of the Civil War, there were approximately 500,000 free blacks in the United States. More than half of them lived in the South, where they enjoyed a precarious existence at best. There was great variety in the laws limiting their actions, but several broad trends were evident. They could not travel without passes, move to other slave states, practice certain professions, gather in groups, own weapons, and learn to read or write. The highpoint of southern antebellum hostility to free blacks appeared in *Mitchell* v. *Wells*, 37 Miss. 235 (1859). Nancy Wells was the daughter of a Mississippi slaveowner, Edward Wells, and his slave mistress. Before his death, Edward Wells took his daughter to Ohio and emancipated her there. In his will, Wells bequeathed $3,000, a bed, and some property to his daughter. The executor of the will, William Mitchell, refused to give Nancy her legacy, even after a lower court ordered him to do so. Judge William Harris of the Mississippi High Court of Errors and Appeals reversed that decision and held that Nancy Wells, whatever her status in Ohio, would always be a slave in Mississippi.

The issue of the rights of free blacks also turned on the important question of the legal definition of race. The 1802 and 1851 constitutions of Ohio, for example, enfranchised only white males. But in *Anderson* v. *Millikin et al.*, 9 Ohio St. 586 (1859), the Ohio Supreme Court declared that the constitutional prohibition on black suffrage was limited to persons who were more than half-black. The decision declared mulattos white, and it made Ohio one of two states (the other was Louisiana) to reject what might be called "the American rule of race"—that any visible black ancestry made a person black, rather than white.

The *Roberts* and *Anderson* cases illustrate the complexity of northern race relations. While the legislature in Massachusetts took a more liberal view of race relations
than did the state's highest court, in Ohio the reverse happened. Moreover, while
Massachusetts, Ohio, and some other northern states liberalized their laws on race in
the antebellum period, Indiana and Illinois moved in the opposite direction. For example, in *Nelson (a mulatto) v. The People*, 33 Ill. 390 (1864), the Illinois Supreme Court
in 1864 was openly hostile to the rights of free blacks. The judges upheld the constitutionality of a law that prohibited free blacks from immigrating into the state. The same
year, however, the Iowa legislature repealed a statute that had prohibited the immigration of blacks into the state (see 10 Iowa Laws 6 [1864]).

Plessy v. *Ferguson*
163 U.S. 537 (1896)

*Plessy, a man of mixed racial ancestry, was prosecuted for sitting in a railroad
car in the "whites only" section. He sought relief from the United States Supreme
Court, asking for a writ of prohibition against Ferguson, the judge of the Orleans
Parish criminal court, to end the prosecution. This litigation was organized by
citizens in Louisiana, as a test case, to help stem the growing tide of southern
segregation.*

Mr. Justice Brown . . .
   This case turns upon the constitutionality of an act of the General Assembly of
the State of Louisiana, passed in 1890, providing for separate railway carriages for
the white and colored races.
   The first section of the statute enacts "that all railway companies carrying
passengers in their coaches in this State, shall provide equal but separate accommodations for the white, and colored races, by providing two or more passenger
coaches for each passenger train, or by dividing the passenger coaches by a partition
so as to secure separate accommodations." . . .

*   *   *

   1.   That it does not conflict with the Thirteenth Amendment, which abolished
slavery and involuntary servitude, except as a punishment for crime, is too clear for
argument. Slavery implies involuntary servitude—a state of bondage; the ownership
of mankind as a chattel, or at least the control of the labor and services of one man
for the benefit of another, and the absence of a legal right to the disposal of his own
person, property and services. . . .

*   *   *

[Here the Court cited the *Slaughterhouse Cases* and the *Civil Rights Cases*.]
   A statute which implies merely a legal distinction between the white and colored
races—a distinction which is founded in the color of the two races, and which must
always exist so long as white men are distinguished from the other race by color—
has no tendency to destroy the legal equality of the two races, or reestablish a state
of involuntary servitude. Indeed, we do not understand that the Thirteenth Amendment is strenuously relied upon by the plaintiff in error in this connection.

*   *   *

The object of the [Fourteenth] amendment was undoubtedly to enforce the absolute equality of the two races before the law, but in the nature of things it could not have been intended to abolish distinctions based upon color, or to enforce social, as distinguished from political equality, or a commingling of the two races upon terms unsatisfactory to either. Laws permitting, and even requiring, their separation in places where they are liable to be brought into contact do not necessarily imply the inferiority of either race to the other, and have been generally, if not universally, recognized as within the competency of the state legislatures in the exercise of their police power. The most common instance of this is connected with the establishment of separate schools for white and colored children, which has been held to be a valid exercise of the legislative power even by courts of States where the political rights of the colored race have been longest and most earnestly enforced.

One of the earliest of these cases is that of *Roberts* v. *City of Boston* (1849), in which the Supreme Judicial Court of Massachusetts held that the general school committee of Boston had power to make provision for the instruction of colored children in separate schools established exclusively for them, and to prohibit their attendance upon the other schools. . . .

*   *   *

So far, then as a conflict with the Fourteenth Amendment is concerned, the case reduces itself to the question whether the statute of Louisiana is a reasonable regulation, and with respect to this there must necessarily be a large discretion on the part of the legislature. In determining the question of reasonableness it is at liberty to act with reference to the established usages, customs and traditions of the people, and with a view to the promotion of their comfort, and the preservation of the public peace and good order. Gauged by this standard, we cannot say that a law which authorizes or even requires the separation of the two races in public conveyances is unreasonable, or more obnoxious to the Fourteenth Amendment than the acts of Congress requiring separate schools for colored children in the District of Columbia, the constitutionality of which does not seem to have been questioned, or the corresponding acts of state legislatures.

We consider the underlying fallacy of the plaintiff's argument to consist in the assumption that the enforced separation of the two races stamps the colored race with a badge of inferiority. If this be so, it is not by reason of anything found in the act, but solely because the colored race chooses to put that construction upon it. The argument necessarily assumes that if, as has been more than once the case, and is not unlikely to be so again, the colored race should become the dominant power in the state legislature, and should enact a law in precisely similar terms, it would thereby relegate the white race to an inferior position. We imagine that the white race, at least, would not acquiesce in this assumption. The argument also assumes that social prejudices may be overcome by legislation, and that equal rights cannot be secured to the negro except by an enforced commingling of the two races. We cannot accept this proposition. If the two races are to meet upon terms of social equality, it must be the result of natural affinities, a mutual appreciation of each other's merits and a voluntary consent of individuals. . . . Legislation is powerless to eradicate racial instincts or to abolish distinctions based upon physical differences, and the attempt to do so can only result in accentuating the difficulties of the present situation. If the civil and political rights of both races be equal one cannot be inferior to the other civilly or politically. If one race be inferior to the other socially, the Constitution of the United States cannot put them upon the same plane.

*   *   *

Mr. Justice Harlan dissenting.

*   *   *

In respect of civil rights, common to all citizens, the Constitution of the United States does not, I think, permit any public authority to know the race of those entitled to be protected in the enjoyment of such rights. Every true man has pride of race, and under appropriate circumstances when the rights of others, his equals before the law, are not to be affected, it is his privilege to express such pride and to take such action based upon it as to him seems proper. But I deny that any legislative body or judicial tribunal may have regard to the race of citizens when the civil rights of those citizens are involved. Indeed, such legislation, as that here in question, is inconsistent not only with that equality of rights which pertains to citizenship, National and State, but with the personal liberty enjoyed by everyone within the United States.

The Thirteenth Amendment does not permit the withholding or the deprivation of any right necessarily inhering in freedom. It not only struck down the institution of slavery as previously existing in the United States, but it prevents the imposition of any burdens or disabilities that constitute badges of slavery or servitude. It decreed universal civil freedom in this country. This court has so adjudged. But that amendment having been found inadequate to the protection of the rights of those who had been in slavery, it was followed by the Fourteenth Amendment, which added greatly to the dignity and glory of American citizenship, and to the security of personal liberty, by declaring that "all persons born or naturalized in the United States, and subject to the jurisdiction thereof, are citizens of the United States and of the State wherein they reside," and that "no State shall make or enforce any law which shall abridge the privileges or immunities of citizens of the United States; nor shall any State deprive any person of life, liberty or property without due process of law, nor deny to any person within its jurisdiction the equal protection of the laws." These two amendments, if enforced according to their true intent and meaning, will protect all the civil rights that pertain to freedom and citizenship. . . .

*   *   *

It was said in argument that the statute of Louisiana does not discriminate against either race, but prescribes a rule applicable alike to white and colored citizens. But this argument does not meet the difficulty. Every one knows that the statute in question had its origin in the purpose, not so much to exclude white persons from railroad cars occupied by blacks, as to exclude colored people from coaches occupied by or assigned to white persons. Railroad corporations of Louisiana did not make discrimination among whites in the matter of accommodation for travellers. The thing to accomplish was, under the guise of giving equal accommodation for whites and blacks, to compel the latter to keep to themselves while travelling in railroad passenger coaches. No one would be so wanting in candor as to assert the contrary. The fundamental objection, therefore, to the statute is that it interferes with the personal freedom of citizens. . . .

*   *   *

The white race deems itself to be the dominant race in this country. And so it is, in prestige, in achievements, in education, in wealth and in power. So, I doubt not, it will continue to be for all time, if it remains true to its great heritage and holds fast to the principles of constitutional liberty. But in view of the Constitution, in the eye of the law, there is in this country no superior, dominant, ruling class of citizens. There is no caste here. Our Constitution is color-blind, and neither knows nor tolerates classes among citizens. In respect of civil rights, all citizens are equal before the law. The humblest is the peer of the most powerful. The law regards man as man, and takes no account of his surroundings or of his color when his civil rights as guaranteed by the supreme law of the land are involved. It is, therefore, to be regretted that this high tribunal, the final expositor of the fundamental law of the land, has reached the conclusion that it is competent for a State to regulate the enjoyment by citizens of their civil rights solely upon the basis of race.

In my opinion, the judgment this day rendered will, in time, prove to be quite as pernicious as the decision made by this tribunal in the *Dred Scott* case (1857). It was adjudged in that case that the descendants of Africans who were imported into this country and sold as slaves were not included nor intended to be included under the word "citizens" in the Constitution, and could not claim any of the rights and privileges which that instrument provided for and secured to citizens of the United States; that at the time of the adoption of the Constitution they were "considered as a subordinate and inferior class of beings, who . . . had no rights or privileges but such as those who held the power and the government might choose to grant them." The recent amendments of the Constitution, it was supposed, had eradicated these principles from our institutions. But it seems that we have yet, in some of the States, a dominant race—a superior class of citizens, which assumes to regulate the enjoyment of civil rights, common to all citizens, upon the basis of race. The present decision, it may well be apprehended, will not only stimulate aggressions, more or less brutal and irritating, upon the admitted rights of colored citizens, but will encourage the belief that it is possible, by means of state enactments, to defeat the beneficent purposes which the people of the United States had in view when they adopted the recent amendments of the Constitution, by one of which the blacks of this country were made citizens of the United States and of the States in which they respectively reside, and whose privileges and immunities, as citizens, the States are forbidden to abridge. Sixty millions of whites are in no danger from the presence here of eight millions of blacks. The destinies of the two races, in this country, are indissolubly linked together, and the interests of both require that the common government of all shall not permit the seeds of race hate to be planted under the sanction of law. What can more certainly arouse race hate, what more certainly create and perpetuate a feeling of distrust between these races, than state enactments, which, in fact, proceed on the ground that colored citizens are so inferior and degraded that they cannot be allowed to sit in public coaches occupied by white citizens? That, as all will admit, is the real meaning of such legislation as was enacted in Louisiana. . . .

State enactments, regulating the enjoyment of civil rights, upon the basis of race, and cunningly devised to defeat legitimate results of the war, under the pretence of recognizing equality of rights, can have no other result than to render permanent peace impossible, and to keep alive a conflict of races, the continuance of which must do harm to all concerned. This question is not met by the suggestion that social equality cannot exist between the white and black races in this country. That argument, if it can be properly regarded as one, is scarcely worthy of consideration; for social equality no more exists between two races when travelling in a passenger coach or a public highway than when members of the same races sit by each other in a street car or in the jury box, or stand or sit with each other in a political assembly, or when they use in common the streets of a city or town, or when they are in the same room for the purpose of having their names placed on the registry of voters, or when they approach the ballot-box in order to exercise the high privilege of voting.

There is a race so different from our own that we do not permit those belonging to it to become citizens of the United States. Persons belonging to it are, with few exceptions, absolutely excluded from our country. I allude to the Chinese race. But by the statute in question, a Chinaman can ride in the same passenger coach with white citizens of the United States, while citizens of the black race in Louisiana, any of whom, perhaps, risked their lives for the preservation of the Union, who are entitled, by law, to participate in the political control of the State and nation, who are not excluded, by law or by reason of their race, from public stations of any kind, and who have all the legal rights that belong to white citizens, are yet declared to be criminals, liable to imprisonment, if they ride in a public coach occupied by citizens of the white race. It is scarcely just to say that a colored citizen should not object of occupying a public coach assigned to his own race. He does not object, nor, perhaps, would he object to separate coaches for his race, if his rights under the law were recognized. But he objects, and ought never to cease objecting to the proposition, that citizens of the white and black races can be adjudged criminals because they sit, or claim the right to sit, in the same public coach on a public highway.

The arbitrary separation of citizens, on the basis of race, while they are on a public highway, is a badge of servitude wholly inconsistent with the civil freedom and the quality before the law established by the Constitution. It cannot be justified upon any legal grounds.

If evils will result from the commingling of the two races upon public highways established for the benefit of all, they will be infinitely less than those that will surely come from state legislation regulating the enjoyment of civil rights upon the basis of race. We boast of the freedom enjoyed by our people above all other peoples. But it is difficult to reconcile that boast with a state of the law which, practically, puts the brand of servitude and degradation upon a large class of our fellow-citizens, our equals before the law. The thin disguise of "equal" accommodations for passengers in railroad coaches will not mislead any one, nor atone for the wrong this day done.

Note: Separate But Equal in the North

In *Board of Education of Ottawa* v. *Tinnon* (1881), the Kansas Supreme Court ordered Ottawa to integrate its schools. The court held that Kansas law did not allow Ottawa to impose segregation. Because the case turned on state law, the court did not decide the constitutionality of segregation. *Tinnon* illustrates the divergence between the North and the South on race at this time. Ironically, the case that ended school segregation, *Brown* v. *Board of Education of Topeka* (1954), would come out of Kansas.

In *Plessy*, Justice Brown cited the nation's first school desegregation case, *Roberts* v. *City of Boston*, 5 Cush. (59 Mass.) 198 (1849), to support segregation in Louisiana. In *Roberts*, Chief Justice Lemuel Shaw upheld Boston's segregated school system with a theory that resembled "separate but equal." The validity of the *Roberts* precedent in *Plessy* is undermined by three points. First, *Roberts* took place before the Civil War and Reconstruction worked a revolution in race relations. Did it make sense to use an antebellum case to justify segregation almost fifty years, a war, and three constitutional amendments later? Second, *Roberts* was decided under the Massachusetts Constitution, which did not have an equal protection clause similar to that in the Fourteenth Amendment. Finally, in 1855 the Massachusetts legislature banned all segregation in the state's public schools.

Segregation on the Eve of a New Century
1898

In 1898, an editor of the Charleston, South Carolina, News and Courier *attacked the growing segregation in his state with an argument of* reductio ad absurdum, *but, as C. Vann Woodward has observed, "apart from the Jim Crow counties and Jim Crow witness stands, all the improbable applications of the principle suggested by the editor in derision had been put into practice—down to and including the Jim Crow Bible."'*

If there must be Jim Crow cars on the railroads, there should be Jim Crow cars on the street railways. Also on all passenger boats. . . . If there are to be Jim Crow cars, moreover, there should be Jim Crow waiting saloons at all stations, and Jim Crow eating houses. . . . There should be Jim Crow sections of the jury box, and a separate Jim Crow dock and witness stand in every court—and a Jim Crow Bible for colored witnesses to kiss. It would be advisable to also have a Jim Crow section in county auditors' and treasurers' offices for the accommodation of colored taxpayers. . . . Perhaps, the best plan would be, after all, to take the short cut to the general end . . . by establishing two or three Jim Crow counties at once. . . .

Native Americans

As white settlers flooded into the interior of the new American nation, they found a land already occupied by Native Americans. By 1800, white settlement, disease, and warfare had decimated Native Americans along the Atlantic coast, leaving only a few tribal remnants scattered from Maine to Georgia. In the trans-Appalachian interior, powerful tribes still dominated, although by 1820 they too would succumb to the tide of white migration.

During these years, the federal government established formative policies that framed the course of white–Native American relations for the rest of the century. Lawmakers attempted to balance competing goals. They at once pursued a paternalistic policy intended to protect Native Americans from unscrupulous traders and settlers while Christianizing them in preparation for admission into white society. The same federal government also championed a policy of territorial expansion that with each successive wave of white settlement pushed Native Americans ever farther west.

The acquisition of Native American lands emerged as the dominant objective of federal Indian policy, but the means to that end varied during the century. Initially, the federal government had set on a course of conquest, but during the 1790s that program changed to one that recognized the inherent rights of Native Americans to their lands. Land transfers were accomplished through treaty agreements, a policy that rested on the assumption that the several tribes composed a distinct nation capable of entering into treaty negotiations. The nature and scope of Native American sovereignty, therefore, emerged as the most important issue in the legal history of nineteenth-century Native American relations with the federal government.

The Framers of the federal Constitution left the status of Native Americans indefinite, although, by implication, they were outside the constitutional system. They were denied citizenship, exempted from taxation, and not counted in the apportionment of representation and direct taxes. Congress had authority to regulate commerce with the Indian tribes, and a succession of presidents acted under the treaty-making and war powers to negotiate with the tribes. Throughout the nineteenth century, the federal government pursued a policy that inexorably eroded the independence of the tribes, reaching a point late in the century when, under the Dawes Act of 1887, it called for the wholesale assimilation of the tribes.

Cherokee Nation v. Georgia
5 Pet. (30 U.S.) 1 (1831)

The disposition of Native American lands was a point of controversy between federal and state governments, with each claiming that it had exclusive authority to deal with the tribes. During the 1820s, Georgia became dissatisfied with the slowness of the United States government in removing the Creek and Cherokee populations. Georgia lawmakers aggressively pushed for the removal of the tribes, so much so that they dispatched surveyors to prepare the land for sale. The Cherokees reacted by adopting a written constitution and proclaiming themselves an independent nation. When Andrew Jackson became president in 1829, he refused to take any action in defense of Indian treaty rights, as previous chief executives, especially John Quincy Adams, had done. Friends of the Cherokees, however, sought an injunction from the Supreme Court to restrain Georgia from enforcing its laws over the Cherokees and from seizing their lands. Against this backdrop of events, Chief Justice John Marshall wrote the opinion of the Court.

Mr. Chief Justice Marshall delivered the opinion of the Court.

This bill is brought by the Cherokee nation, praying an injunction to restrain the state of Georgia from the execution of certain laws of that state, which, as is alleged, go directly to annihilate the Cherokees as a political society, and to seize, for the use of Georgia, the lands of the nation which have been assured to them by the United States in solemn treaties repeatedly made and still in force.

If courts were permitted to indulge their sympathies, a case better calculated to excite them can scarcely be imagined. A people once numerous, powerful, and truly independent, found by our ancestors in the quiet and uncontrolled possession of an ample domain, gradually sinking beneath our superior policy, our arts and our arms, have yielded their lands by successive treaties, each of which contains a solemn guarantee of the residue, until they retain no more of their formerly extensive territory than is deemed necessary to their comfortable subsistence. To preserve this remnant, the present application is made.

Before we can look into the merits of the case, a preliminary inquiry presents itself. Has this court jurisdiction of the cause?

The third article of the constitution describes the extent of the judicial power. The second section closes an enumeration of the cases to which it is extended, with "controversies" "between a state or the citizens thereof, and foreign states, citizens, or subjects." A subsequent clause of the same section gives the supreme court original jurisdiction in all cases in which a state shall be a party. The party defendant may then unquestionably be sued in this court. May the plaintiff sue in it? Is the Cherokee nation a foreign state in the sense in which that term is used in the constitution?

The counsel for the plaintiffs have maintained the affirmative of this proposition with great earnestness and ability. So much of the argument as was intended to prove the character of the Cherokees as a state, as a distinct political society, separated from others, capable of managing its own affairs and governing itself, has, in the opinion of a majority of the judges, been completely successful. They have been uniformly treated as a state from the settlement of our country. The numerous treaties made with them by the United States recognize them as a people capable of maintaining the relations of peace and war, of being responsible in their political character for any violation of their engagements, or for any aggression committed on the citizens of the United States by any individual of their community. Laws have been enacted in the spirit of these treaties. The acts of our government plainly recognize the Cherokee nation as a state, and the courts are bound by those acts.

A question of much more difficulty remains. Do the Cherokees constitute a foreign state in the sense of the constitution?

The counsel have shown conclusively that they are not a state of the union, and have insisted that individually they are aliens, not owing allegiance to the United States. An aggregate of aliens composing a state must, they say, be a foreign state. Each individual being foreign, the whole must be foreign.

This argument is imposing, but we must examine it more closely before we yield to it. The condition of the Indians in relation to the United States is perhaps unlike that of any other two people in existence. In the general, nations not owing a common allegiance are foreign to each other. The term *foreign nation* is, with strict propriety, applicable by either to the other. But the relation of the Indians to the United States is marked by peculiar and cardinal distinctions which exist no where else.

The Indian territory is admitted to compose a part of the United States. In all our maps, geographical treatises, histories, and laws, it is so considered. In all our intercourse with foreign nations, in our commercial regulations, in any attempt at intercourse between Indians and foreign nations, they are considered as within the jurisdictional limits of the United States, subject to many of those restraints which are imposed upon our own citizens. They acknowledge themselves in their treaties to be under the protection of the United States; they admit that the United States shall have the sole and exclusive right of regulating the trade with them, and managing all their affairs as they think proper; and the Cherokees in particular were allowed by the treaty of Hopewell, which preceded the constitution, "to send a deputy of their choice, whenever they think fit, to congress." Treaties were made with some tribes by the state of New York, under a then unsettled construction of the confederation, by which they ceded all their lands to that state, taking back a limited grant to themselves, in which they admit their dependence.

Though the Indians are acknowledged to have an unquestionable, and, here-tofore, unquestioned right to the lands they occupy, until that right shall be extin-guished by a voluntary cession to our government; yet it may well be doubted whether those tribes which reside within the acknowledged boundaries of the United States can, with strict accuracy, be denominated foreign nations. They may, more correctly, perhaps, be denominated domestic dependent nations. They occupy a territory to which we assert a title independent of their will, which must take effect in point of possession when their right of possession ceases. Meanwhile they are in a state of pupilage. Their relation to the United States resembles that of a ward to his guardian.

They look to our government for protection; rely upon its kindness and its power; appeal to it for relief to their wants; and address the president as their great father. They and their country are considered by foreign nations, as well as by ourselves, as being so completely under the sovereignty and dominion of the United States, that any attempt to acquire their lands, or to form a political connexion with them, would be considered by all as an invasion of our territory, and an act of hostility.

These considerations go far to support the opinion, that the framers of our constitution had not the Indian tribes in view, when they opened the courts of the union to controversies between a state or the citizens thereof, and foreign states.

In considering this subject, the habits and usages of the Indians, in their inter-course with their white neighbours, ought not to be entirely disregarded. At the time the constitution was framed, the idea of appealing to an American court of justice for an assertion of right or a redress of wrong, had perhaps never entered the mind of an Indian or of his tribe. Their appeal was to the tomahawk, or to the government. This was well understood by the statesmen who framed the constitution of the United States, and might furnish some reason for omitting to enumerate them among the parties who might sue in the courts of the union. Be this as it may, the peculiar relations between the United States and the Indians occupying our territory are such, that we should feel much difficulty in considering them as designated by the term *foreign state*, were there no other part of the constitution which might shed light on the meaning of these words. But we think that in construing them, consider-able aid is furnished by that clause in the eighth section of the third article; which empowers congress to "regulate commerce with foreign nations, and among the several states, and with the Indian tribes."

In this clause they are as clearly contradistinguished by a name appropriate to themselves, from foreign nations, as from the several states composing the union. They are designated by a distinct appellation; and as this appellation can be applied to neither of the others, neither can the appellation distinguishing either of the others be in fair construction applied to them. The objects, to which the power of regulating commerce might be directed, are divided into three distinct classes—foreign nations, the several states, and Indian tribes. When forming this article, the convention considered them as entirely distinct. We cannot assume that the distinction was lost in framing a subsequent article, unless there be something in its language to authorize the assumption.

The counsel for the plaintiffs contend that the words "Indian tribes" were introduced into the article, empowering congress to regulate commerce, for the purpose of removing those doubts in which the management of Indian affairs was involved by the language of the ninth article of the confederation. Intending to give the whole power of managing those affairs to the government about to be instituted, the convention conferred it explicitly; and omitted those qualifications which embarrassed the exercise of it as granted in the confederation. This may be admitted without weakening the construction which has been intimated. Had the Indian tribes been foreign nations, in the view of the convention; this exclusive power of regulating intercourse with them might have been, and most probably would have been, specifically given, in language indicating that idea, not in language contradistinguishing them from foreign nations. Congress might have been empowered "to regulate commerce with foreign nations, including the Indian tribes, and among the several states." This language would have suggested itself to statesmen who considered the Indian tribes as foreign nations, and were yet desirous of mentioning them particularly.

*   *   *

The court has bestowed its best attention on this question, and, after mature deliberation, the majority is of opinion that an Indian tribe or nation within the United States is not a foreign state in the sense of the constitution and cannot maintain an action in the courts of the United States.

*   *   *

If it be true that the Cherokee nation have rights, this is not the tribunal in which those rights are to be asserted. If it be true that wrongs have been inflicted, and that still greater are to be apprehended, this is not the tribunal which can redress the past or prevent the future.

The motion for an injunction is denied.

Note: The Federal Government and Native Americans

The year following *Cherokee Nation*, the Court decided *Worcester* v. *Georgia*, 6 Pet. 515 (1832). Samuel Worcester had been convicted in a state court of living on Indian lands without a state license. In this instance, Chief Justice Marshall, speaking for the Court, recognized the Cherokees as a distinct political community having territorial boundaries within which Georgia had no right of action. Georgia declined to appear in the Supreme Court to argue its position, and state officials refused to release Worcester from custody. President Andrew Jackson also dismissed the Chief Justice's opinion, supposedly proclaiming that "John Marshall had made his decision, now let him enforce it." Jackson decided that the best course of action was to apply further pressure on the Cherokees to give up their lands, and his administration oversaw the wholesale removal of the native tribes of the Southeast to lands beyond the Mississippi River. The federal Constitution failed to provide meaningful protection to the nation's largest free minority, the American Indians. The *Cherokee Nation* and *Worcester* cases also coincided with the Nullification Crisis. The defiance of Georgia officials seems to have further emboldened radical states'-rights elements in South Carolina. President Jackson acted with far greater energy in stemming that threat to federal authority than he did in dealing with recalcitrant Georgia officials.

The concept of tribal sovereignty came under attack after the Civil War. The federal government, for example, permitted gold prospectors to stream into the Black Hills, an area considered sacred by the Sioux. Despite a stunning victory in 1876 over General George Armstrong Custer at Little Big Horn, the native tribes proved no match for the U.S. Army. Furthermore, the slaughter of the buffalo by white hunters (some 13 million animals by 1883) decimated the natural supply of food and clothing of the tribes, to which the federal government turned a blind eye.

The concept of tribal sovereignty also came under congressional attack in the post–Civil War era. The Dawes Severalty Act of 1887 was the most important piece of congressional legislation involving Indians in the nineteenth century. The purpose of the act was simple: to end the traditional policy of treating individual Indians as members of their tribes. The Dawes Act sought to lure Indians away from their tribal commitments by offering them a homestead grant that promised both to destroy their culture and to turn them into white farmers. The great bulk of Native Americans opposed the Dawes Act, and Indian agents representing them in Washington made these sentiments known to Congress. The idea of making Indians American citizens, however, had great allure for lawmakers, since it held forth the promise of permanently settling the Indian question. More important, however, the Dawes Act, even with its allotment of 160 acres per Indian, created millions of "surplus" acres that could be sold to white settlers. By the end of the century, Native Americans had lost 60 percent of their lands, the sale of which went into a trust fund for use in further "civilizing" the tribes.

Chinese

Although only 264,000 Chinese came to the United States between 1860 and 1900, they constituted a significant minority on the West Coast. The Chinese initially labored in the gold fields, where they were particularly adept at finding what other miners overlooked. White American miners resented the Chinese presence, and they gradually applied physical violence and political pressure to force them out. The California General Assembly, for example, made an abortive attempt to declare illegal all mining by foreign persons, settling instead for a stiff tax on foreign miners (that the California Supreme Court ultimately declared unconstitutional). Under continuing pressure from the American population, the Chinese gravitated into San Francisco, Sacramento, and other urban areas. They did, however, continue throughout the

West to perform some of the dirtiest and hardest work, ranging from railroad and levee construction to factory labor. They also engaged in a variety of trades, most notably the laundry business. American settlers in the West viewed the Chinese with double suspicion. They were considered as heathens, exotic, backward, and immoral; they were also deeply resented by a white work force fearful of its jobs and wages.

Yick Wo v. *Hopkins*
118 U.S. 356 (1886)

The hatred of white Americans for the Chinese surfaced in several ways, some of which appeared in what today would seem bizarre statutes and ordinances. Just as Southerners were erecting Jim Crow laws to segregate blacks and other non-whites, Westerners sought to control the Chinese. A California statute of 1872, for example, authorized school districts to establish separate schools for the Chinese and Japanese. But it was their pocketbooks that Westerners were most interested in protecting, as the following case involving a San Francisco ordinance of 1880 makes clear. The ordinance made it unlawful to carry on a laundry in the city without the consent of the board of supervisors, unless the laundry was located in a building constructed of either brick or stone. Almost every San Francisco laundry was in a wooden building. The board turned down all applications of Chinese and granted all those of Caucasians. Its actions raised important questions about the meaning of the equal protection clause of the Fourteenth Amendment.

Mr. Justice Matthews delivered the opinion of the court.

In the case of the petitioner, brought here by writ of error to the Supreme Court of California, our jurisdiction is limited to the question, whether the plaintiff in error has been denied a right in violation of the Constitution, laws, or treaties of the United States.

We are consequently constrained at the outset to differ from the Supreme Court of California upon the real meaning of the ordinances in question. That court considered these ordinances as vesting in the board of supervisors a not unusual discretion in granting or withholding their assent to the use of wooden buildings as laundries, to be exercised in reference to the circumstances of each case, with a view to the protection of the public against the dangers of fire. We are not able to concur in that interpretation of the power conferred upon the supervisors. There is nothing in the ordinances which points to such a regulation of the business of keeping and conducting laundries. They seem intended to confer, and actually do confer, not a discretion to be exercised upon a consideration of the circumstances of each case, but a naked and arbitrary power to give or withhold consent, not only as to places, but as to persons.

* * *

The ordinance drawn in question . . . does not prescribe a rule and conditions for the regulation of the use of property for laundry purposes, to which all similarly situated may conform. It allows without restriction the use for such purposes of buildings of brick or stone; but, as to wooden buildings, constituting nearly all those in previous use, it divides the owners or occupiers into two classes, not having respect to their personal character and qualifications for the business, nor the situation and nature and adaptation of the buildings themselves, but merely by an arbitrary line, on one side of which are those who are permitted to pursue their industry by the mere will and consent of the supervisors, and on the other those from whom that consent is withheld at their mere will and pleasure. And both classes are alike only in this, that they are tenants at will, under the supervisors, of their means of living. The ordinance, therefore, also differs from the not unusual case, where discretion is lodged by law in public officers or bodies to grant or withhold licenses to keep taverns, or places for the sale of spirituous liquors, and the like, when one of the conditions is that the applicant shall be a fit person for the exercise of the privilege, because in such cases the fact of fitness is submitted to the judgment of the officer, and calls for the exercise of a discretion of a judicial nature.

*   *   *

The rights of the petitioners, as affected by the proceedings of which they complain, are not less, because they are aliens and subjects of the Emperor of China.

*   *   *

The Fourteenth Amendment to the Constitution is not confined to the protection of citizens. It says: "Nor shall any State deprive any person of life, liberty, or property without due process of law; nor deny to any person within its jurisdiction the equal protection of the laws." These provisions are universal in their application, to all persons within the territorial jurisdiction, without regard to any differences of race, of color, or of nationality; and the equal protection of the laws is a pledge of the protection of equal laws. . . . The questions we have to consider and decide in these cases, therefore, are to be treated as involving the rights of every citizen of the United States equally with those of the strangers and aliens who now invoke the jurisdiction of the court.

*   *   *

When we consider the nature and the theory of our institutions of government, the principles upon which they are supposed to rest, and review the history of their development, we are constrained to conclude that they do not mean to leave room for the play and action of purely personal and arbitrary power. Sovereignty itself is, of course, not subject to law, for it is the author and source of law; but in our system, while sovereign powers are delegated to the agencies of government, sovereignty itself remains with the people, by whom and for whom all government exists and acts. And the law is the definition and limitation of power. It is, indeed, quite true, that there must always be lodged somewhere, and in some person or body, the authority of final decision; and in many cases of mere administration the responsibility is purely political, no appeal lying except to the ultimate tribunal of the public judgment, exercised either in the pressure of opinion or by means of the suffrage. But the fundamental rights to life, liberty, and the pursuit of happiness, considered as individual possessions, are secured by those maxims of constitutional law which are the monuments showing the victorious progress of the race in securing to men the blessings of civilization under the reign of just and equal laws, so that, in the famous language of the Massachusetts Bill of Rights, the government of the commonwealth "may be a government of laws and not of men." For, the very idea that one man may be compelled to hold his life, or the means of living, or any material right essential to the enjoyment of life, at the mere will of another, seems to be intolerable in any country where freedom prevails, as being the essence of slavery itself.

There are many illustrations that might be given of this truth, which would make manifest that it was self-evident in the light of our system of jurisprudence. The case of the political franchise of voting is one. Though not regarded strictly as a natural right, but as a privilege merely conceded by society according to its will, under certain conditions, nevertheless it is regarded as a fundamental political right, because preservative of all rights.

*   *   *

[T]he cases present the ordinances in actual operation, and the facts shown establish an administration directed so exclusively against a particular class of persons as to warrant and require the conclusion, that, whatever may have been the intent of the ordinances as adopted, they are applied by the public authorities charged with their administration, and thus representing the State itself, with a mind so unequal and oppressive as to amount to a practical denial by the State of that equal protection of the laws which is secured to the petitioners, as to all other persons, by the broad and benign provisions of the Fourteenth Amendment to the Constitution of the United States. Though the law itself be fair on its face and impartial in appearance, yet, if it is applied and administered by public authority with an evil eye and an unequal hand, so as practically to make unjust and illegal discriminations between persons in similar circumstances, material to their rights, the denial of equal justice is still within the prohibition of the Constitution.

*   *   *

The present case, as shown by the facts disclosed in the record, are within this class. It appears that both petitioners have complied with every requisite, deemed by the law or by the public officers charged with its administration, necessary for the protection of neighboring property from fire, or as a precaution against injury to the public health. No reason whatever, except the will of the supervisors, is assigned why they should not be permitted to carry on, in the accustomed manner, their harmless and useful occupation, on which they depend for a livelihood. And while this consent of the supervisors was withheld from them and from two hundred others who have also petitioned, all of whom happen to be Chinese subjects, eighty others, not Chinese subjects, are permitted to carry on the same business under similar conditions. The fact of this discrimination is admitted. No reason for it is shown, and the conclusion cannot be resisted, that no reason for it exists except hostility to the race and nationality to which the petitioners belong, and which in the eye of the law is not justified. The discrimination is, therefore, illegal, and the public administration which enforces it is a denial of the equal protection of the laws and a violation of the Fourteenth Amendment of the Constitution. The imprisonment of the petitioners is, therefore, illegal, and they must be discharged.

Note: The Chinese and Jim Crow

On first impression, the Court's treatment of the Chinese under the Fourteenth Amendment seems to contrast sharply with its approval of southern Jim Crow legislation. Yet there was an important difference, one that helps to place not just the Court but the role of race in late-nineteenth-century legal culture in clearer perspective. What the justices worried about in *Yick Wo* was the threat posed by the city ordinance to property rights. The justices were certainly willing to recognize broad authority for local and state governments to regulate human activity in the name of health, safety, morals, and welfare. But in this instance, such regulation seemed capricious, arbitrary, and a species of class legislation. That is, the law, while not blatantly discriminatory on racial grounds, did threaten private property rights, which the justices held particularly dear. Most Jim Crow legislation did not labor under that particular handicap.

Gender and Domestic Relations

The American Revolution unleashed forces that had long-term effects on the status of women and the family. Republican ideology fostered a family order in which authority was accountable, property rights were equated with independence, and human relations were set in contractual terms. The family in the nineteenth century became a private, inward-looking institution, one sharply in contrast with the community-oriented little commonwealths of the colonial era. Market capitalism also molded the status of women, the family, and the role of children. The gradual separation of the workplace from the home granted wives new autonomy over the domestic sphere, opened men even more directly to the competitive forces of a market economy, and gave rise to the "economically worthless child." Thus new economic and social demands precipitated changes in the law affecting women and domestic relations (marriage, divorce, child custody, and birth control).

The Rights of Women

Gender, like race, was a defining category of nineteenth-century American law, and it is conspicuous in matters as diverse as protective legislation, domestic relations, suffrage, property rights, birth control, and abortion. Being female, and being female and married, in particular, made a difference in the eyes of the law. Male lawmakers clung to paternalistic ideas that at once placed women on a pedestal and condemned them to second-class status. As the century progressed, however, a small group of feminist reformers sought to chart an independent course for women. They did so at a time when the growing pressures of a burgeoning market economy placed new pressures not only on women, but on men and the family unit as a whole.

"The Seneca Falls Declaration of Sentiments" 1848

In 1848, Elizabeth Cady Stanton and Lucretia Mott organized the Seneca Falls Convention, one of the most significant protest meetings of the antebellum era. They and other women had participated actively in a host of other social reforms, especially the antislavery movement. Males, however, dominated the leadership of these groups, often relegating women to second-class roles. At the World Anti-

Slavery Conference in 1840, for example, male delegates refused to allow women to participate; they ordered both Stanton and Mott to sit behind curtains where they could not be seen. Modeling the language of their "Declaration of Senti-ments" on that of the Declaration of Independence, the women at Seneca Falls charged that men had usurped women's freedom and dignity. The resolutions they appended to the Declaration underscored their concern with gender bias in the law and the legal system.

When, in the course of human events, it becomes necessary for one portion of the family of man to assume among the people of the earth a position different from that which they have hitherto occupied, but one to which the laws of nature and of nature's God entitle them, a decent respect to the opinions of mankind requires that they should declare the causes that impel them to such a course.

We hold these truths to be self-evident: that all men and women are created equal; that they are endowed by their Creator with certain inalienable rights; that among these are life, liberty, and the pursuit of happiness; that to secure these rights governments are instituted, deriving their just powers from the consent of the governed. Whenever any form of government becomes destructive of these ends, it is the right of those who suffer from it to refuse allegiance to it, and to insist upon the institution of a new government, laying its foundation on such principles, and organizing its powers in such form, as to them shall seem most likely to effect their safety and happiness. Prudence, indeed, will dictate that governments long estab-lished should not be changed for light and transient causes; and accordingly all experience hath shown that mankind are more disposed to suffer, while evils are sufferable, than to right themselves by abolishing the forms to which they were accustomed. But when a long train of abuses and usurpations, pursuing invariably the same object evinces a design to reduce them under absolute despotism, it is their duty to throw off such government, and to provide new guards for their future security. Such has been the patient sufferance of the women under this government, and such is now the necessity which constrains them to demand the equal station to which they are entitled.

The history of mankind is a history of repeated injuries and usurpations on the part of man toward woman, having in direct object the establishment of an absolute tyranny over her. To prove this, let facts be submitted to a candid world.

He has never permitted her to exercise her inalienable right to the elective franchise.

He has compelled her to submit to laws, in the formation of which she had no voice.

He has withheld from her rights which are given to the most ignorant and degraded men—both natives and foreigners.

Having deprived her of this first right of a citizen, the elective franchise, thereby leaving her without representation in the halls of legislation, he has oppressed her on all sides.

He has made her, if married, in the eye of the law, civilly dead.

He has taken from her all right in property, even to the wages she earns.

He has made her, morally, an irresponsible being, as she can commit many crimes with impunity, provided they be done in the presence of her husband. In the covenant of marriage, she is compelled to promise obedience to her husband, he becoming, to all intents and purposes, her master—the law giving him power to deprive her of her liberty, and to administer chastisement.

He has so framed the laws of divorce, as to what shall be the proper causes, and in case of separation, to whom the guardianship of the children shall be given, as to be wholly regardless of the happiness of women—the law, in all cases, going upon a false supposition of the supremacy of man, and giving all power into his hands.

After depriving her of all rights as a married woman, if single, and the owner of property, he has taxed her to support a government which recognizes her only when her property can be made profitable to it.

He has monopolized nearly all the profitable employments, and from those she is permitted to follow, she receives but a scanty remuneration. He closes against her all the avenues to wealth and distinction which he considers most honorable to himself. As a teacher of theology, medicine, or law, she is not known.

He has denied her the facilities for obtaining a thorough education, all colleges being closed against her.

He allows her in Church, as well as State, but a subordinate position, claiming Apostolic authority for her exclusion from the ministry, and, with some exceptions, from any public participation in the affairs of the Church.

He has created a false public sentiment by giving to the world a different code of morals for men and women, by which moral delinquencies which exclude women from society, are not only tolerated, but deemed of little account in man.

He has usurped the prerogative of Jehovah himself, claiming it as his right to assign for her a sphere of action, when that belongs to her conscience and to her God.

He has endeavored, in every way that he could, to destroy her confidence in her own powers, to lessen her self-respect, and to make her willing to lead a dependent and abject life.

Now, in view of this entire disfranchisement of one-half the people of this country, their social and religious degradation—in view of the unjust laws above mentioned, and because women do feel themselves aggrieved, oppressed, and fraudulently deprived of their most sacred rights, we insist that they have immediate admission to all the rights and privileges which belong to them as citizens of the United States.

In entering upon the great work before us, we anticipate no small amount of misconception, misrepresentation, and ridicule; but we shall use every instrumentality within our power to effect our object. We shall employ agents, circulate tracts, petition the State and National legislatures, and endeavor to enlist the pulpit and the press in our behalf. We hope this Convention will be followed by a series of Conventions embracing every part of the country.

The New York Married Women's Property Acts
1848

Unmarried women enjoyed the same legal position as men, save for the fact that they could not vote. Such was not the case for wives, whose condition some antebellum legal commentators equated with that of slaves. Such dependence, while suited to low-level economic activity, became increasingly costly as the mid-century American economy reached the stage of take-off into sustained growth. Economic growth carried with it certain costs of credit associated with risk taking and with pauperization of the family should a husband slide into insolvency. State legislatures adopted married women's property acts as a means of dealing with the twin problems of providing greater stability to the economy and ensuring the equitable treatment of women (and minor children under their care) from spendthrift husbands. The first statutes appeared in Arkansas and Florida territories in the mid-1830s, but the first major state act was that of Mississippi, which came hard on the heels of the devastating Panic of 1837. The New York State act, passed in 1848 (the same year as the Seneca Falls Convention), emerged as the national model. During the next half-century, New York legislators refashioned and expanded this initial legislation, attempting to keep pace with changing economic demands and with growing pressure from increasingly well-organized women's groups.

Chap. 200

AN ACT *for the more effectual protection of the property of* married women. Passed April 7, 1848.

The People of the State of New York, represented in Senate and Assembly, do enact as follows:

    1.   The real and personal property of any female who may hereafter marry, and which she shall own at the time of marriage, and the rents, issues and profits thereof shall not be subject to the disposal of her husband, nor be liable for his debts, and shall continue her sole and separate property, as if she were a single female.

    2.   The real and personal property, and the rents, issues and profits thereof of any female now married shall not be subject to the disposal of her husband; but shall be her sole and separate property as if she were a single female except so far as the same may be liable for the debts of her husband heretofore contracted.

    3.   It shall be lawful for any married female to receive, by gift, grant, devise or bequest, from any person other than her husband and hold to her sole and separate use, as if she were a single female, real and personal property, and the rents, issues, and profits thereof, and the same shall not be subject to the disposal of her husband, nor be liable for his debts.

    4.   All contracts made between persons in contemplation of marriage shall remain in full force after such marriage takes place.

Chap. 375

AN ACT *to amend an act entitled "An Act for the more effectual protection of the property of married women," passed April 7, 1848.* Passed April 11, 1849.

The people of the State of New York, represented in Senate and Assembly, do enact as follows:

1.   The third section of the act entitled "An act for the more effectual protection of the property of married women," is hereby amended so as to read as follows:

2.   Any married female may take by inheritance or by gift, grant, devise or bequest, from any person other than her husband and hold to her sole and separate use and convey and devise real and personal property, and any interest of estate therein, and the rents, issues and profits thereof in the same manner and with like effect as if she were unmarried, and the same shall not be subject to the disposal of her husband nor be liable for his debts.

3.   Any person who may hold or who may hereafter hold as trustee for any married woman, any real or personal estate or other property under any deed of conveyance or otherwise, on the written request of such married woman accompanied by a certificate of a justice of the supreme court that he has examined the condition and situation of the property, and made due enquiry into the capacity of such married woman to manage and control the same, may convey such married woman by deed or otherwise, all or any portion of such property, or the rents issues or profits thereof, for her sole and separate use and benefit.

4.   All contracts made between persons in contemplation of marriage shall remain in full force after such marriage takes place.

Note: Married Women and the Law

Under the doctrine of coverture, which had historical roots tracing back to the Middle Ages, the property of the wife came under the control of her husband. This practice left many wives economically dependent on their husbands. There were exceptions, however. For example, the practice of dower gave to widows a one-third life estate in the property of their husbands. Married women also could receive protection through separate equitable estates. This trust arrangement could be fashioned before marriage (in which case it became a prenuptial agreement) or later. The document, which was created in equity rather than law, designated a trustee who was charged with holding the property for the separate use of a particular married woman. The device protected the property of women from being ravaged by their husbands' creditors. Nevertheless, the impetus behind these measures was not to place women on an equal footing with men, but to secure them against financial ruin. Most married women did not have prenuptial agreements or separate equitable estates. The first wave of married women's property acts freed wives' estates from the debts of their husbands, leaving the traditional marital estate and coverture rules intact. Subsequent legislation extended the sweep of these laws by taking into account the changing workplace where women entered in small but growing numbers in the late nineteenth century. Married women's property acts were modest incursions on traditional patriarchy that provided for equity in wives' treatment rather than equality with husbands.

Minor v. *Happersett*
21 Wall. (88 U.S.) 162 (1875)

The United States Supreme Court refused to recognize women as the constitutional equals of men. In this case, Virginia Minor, a Missouri woman, claimed a

Fourteenth Amendment right to vote as one of her "privileges or immunities," despite Missouri's men-only suffrage laws.

The CHIEF JUSTICE, Morrison R. Waite, delivered the opinion of the court.

The question is presented in this case, whether, since the adoption of the fourteenth amendment, a woman, who is a citizen of the United States and of the State of Missouri, is a voter in that State, notwithstanding the provision of the constitution and laws of the State, which confine the right of suffrage to men alone.

*   *   *

There is no doubt that women may be citizens. They are persons, and by the fourteenth amendment "all persons born or naturalized in the United States and subject to the jurisdiction thereof" are expressly declared to be "citizens of the United States and of the State wherein they reside." But, in our opinion, it did not need this amendment to give them that position. Before its adoption the Constitution of the United States did not in terms prescribe who should be citizens of the United States or of the several States, yet there were necessarily such citizens without such provision. There cannot be a nation without a people. The very idea of a political community, such as a nation is, implies an association of persons for the promotion of their general welfare. Each one of the persons associated becomes a member of the nation formed by the association. He owes it allegiance and is entitled to its protection. Allegiance and protection are, in this connection, reciprocal obligations. The one is a compensation for the other; allegiance for protection and protection for allegiance.

*   *   *

Sex has never been made one of the elements of citizenship in the United States. In this respect men have never had an advantage over women. The same laws precisely apply to both. The fourteenth amendment did not affect the citizenship of women any more than it did of men. In this particular, therefore, the rights of Mrs. Minor do not depend upon the amendment. She has always been a citizen from her birth, and entitled to all the privileges and immunities of citizenship. The amendment prohibited the State, of which she is a citizen, from abridging any of her privileges and immunities as a citizen of the United States; but it did not confer citizenship on her. That she had before its adoption.

If the right of suffrage is one of the necessary privileges of a citizen of the United States, then the constitution and laws of Missouri confining it to men are in violation of the Constitution of the United States, as amended, and consequently void. The direct question is, therefore, presented whether all citizens are necessarily voters.

The Constitution does not define the privileges and immunities of citizens. For that definition we must look elsewhere. In this case we need not determine what they are, but only whether suffrage is necessarily one of them.

*   *   *

The amendment did not add to the privileges and immunities of a citizen. It simply furnished an additional guaranty for the protection of such as he already had. No new voters were necessarily made by it. Indirectly it may have had that effect, because it may have increased the number of citizens entitled to suffrage under the constitution and laws of the States, but it operates for this purpose, if at all, through the States and the State laws, and not directly upon the citizen.

It is clear, therefore, we think, that the Constitution has not added the right of suffrage to the privileges and immunities of citizenship as they existed at the time it was adopted. This makes it proper to inquire whether suffrage was coextensive with the citizenship of the States at the time of its adoption. If it was, then it may with force be argued that suffrage was one of the rights which belonged to citizenship, and in the enjoyment of which every citizen must be protected. But if it was not, the contrary may with propriety be assumed.

                    *   *   *

In respect to suffrage in the several States it cannot for a moment be doubted that if it had been intended to make all citizens of the United States voters, the framers of the Constitution would not have left it to implication. So important a change in the condition of citizenship as it actually existed, if intended, would have been expressly declared.

                    *   *   *

After the adoption of the fourteenth amendment, it was deemed necessary to adopt a fifteenth, as follows: "The right of citizens of the United States to vote shall not be denied or abridged by the United States, or by any State, on account of race, color, or previous condition of servitude." The fourteenth amendment had already provided that no State should make or enforce any law which should abridge the privileges or immunities of citizens of the United States. If suffrage was one of these privileges or immunities, why amend the Constitution to prevent its being denied on account of race, &c? Nothing is more evident than that the greater must include the less, and if all were already protected why go through with the form of amending the Constitution to protect a part?

                    *   *   *

It is true that the United States guarantees to every State a republican form of government. . . . The guaranty is of a republican form of government. No particular government is designated as republican, neither is the exact form to be guaranteed, in any manner especially designated.

                    *   *   *

All the citizens of the States were not invested with the right of suffrage. In all, save perhaps New Jersey, this right was only bestowed upon men and not upon all of them. Under these circumstances it is certainly now too late to contend that a government is not republican, within the meaning of this guaranty in the Constitution, because women are not made voters.

The same may be said of the other provisions just quoted. Women were excluded from suffrage in nearly all the States by the express provision of their constitutions and laws. If that had been equivalent to a bill of attainder, certainly its abrogation would not have been left to implication. Nothing less than express language would have been employed to effect so radical a change. So also of the amendment which declares that no person shall be deprived of life, liberty, or property without due process of law, adopted as it was as early as 1791. If suffrage was intended to be included within its obligations, language better adapted to express that intent would most certainly have been employed. The right of suffrage, when granted, will be protected. He who has it can only be deprived of it by due process of law, but in order to claim protection he must first show that he has the right.

*   *   *

Certainly, if the courts can consider any question settled, this is one. For nearly ninety years the people have acted upon the idea that the Constitution, when it conferred citizenship, did not necessarily confer the right of suffrage. If uniform practice long continued can settle the construction of so important an instrument as the Constitution of the United States confessedly is, most certainly it has been done here. Our province is to decide what the law is, not to declare what it should be.

We have given this case the careful consideration its importance demands. If the law is wrong, it ought to be changed; but the power for that is not with us. The arguments addressed to us bearing upon such a view of the subject may perhaps be sufficient to induce those having the power, to make the alteration, but they ought not to be permitted to influence our judgment in determining the present rights of the parties now litigating before us. No argument as to woman's need of suffrage can be considered. We can only act upon her rights as they exist. It is not for us to look at the hardship of withholding. Our duty is at an end if we find it is within the power of a State to withhold.

Being unanimously of the opinion that the Constitution of the United States does not confer the right of suffrage upon any one, and that the constitutions and laws of the several States which commit that important trust to men alone are not necessarily void, we

AFFIRM THE JUDGMENT.

Domestic Relations: Marriage and Divorce

In 1800, the law of domestic relations was scattered through such diverse categories as contracts, property, and tort. By 1900, a more or less unified body of law had emerged. Economic change, the rise of companionate marriage, and the increasing assertiveness of women about their rights generated demands for legal reforms in marriage, divorce, child custody, birth control, and abortion. In most instances, greater certainty in the law was accompanied by growing state intervention in matters that had historically been left to private decision making and by increasing judicial oversight.

JOEL P. BISHOP

"The Nature of Marriage and How Defined"
1881

Joel Bishop, a Whiggish Massachusetts lawyer, dominated the law of domestic relations during the nineteenth century. He led the way in clarifying and adjusting the law of husband and wife, and his Commentaries, *which first appeared in 1852 and went through successive revisions and new editions into the twentieth century, was the standard treatise on the subject of domestic relations.*

1.   Harmony and Diversities of Opinion – The universal sentiment of mankind accepts the fundamental doctrine of the law of marriage, that the sexes should not associate promiscuously as prompted by mere animal instinct, but "pair off," to use an expression applied to the birds of the air. Even where polygamy is tolerated, fidelity to and among the family of wives is enjoined, the same as is the more restricted fidelity in monogamy. In Christian countries, marriage comprehends the union of one man with one woman only, and all outside commerce of the sexes is forbidden, though, like other admitted evils, it is less severely dealt with in some countries than in others. . . .

2.   Assumed by Contract – [M]arriage is entered into by contract. The meaning of which is, that those and those only who mutually agree to marry, being legally capable of intermarrying, are by the laws made husband and wife. This contract of marriage differs from the marriage itself, as the agreement to build a house differs from the completed structure, or as the egg and the incubation differ from the bird produced. It has the properties of any other ordinary contract: as, for example, the parties must be capable of contracting, and those already married cannot agree to marry others, though one who has concealed his incapacity may be sued by the other . . . ; it must be founded on a consideration, which, in the facts of most cases and in a certain sense of necessity, consists of mutual promises, the consideration must not involve what is immoral or against public policy; fraud or mistake, such as a concealed or undisclosed lack of chastity, will justify the breaking of the promise; the contract between an infant and an adult is binding on the adult but voidable by the infant; the "act of God," occurring after the contract is made, whereby one becomes physically incapable of performing the functions of marriage, will justify its breach by either of the parties; an action of damages for a breach may be maintained; and this contract, like any other, ends when performance is fully done and accepted. Actual marriage, in any form which makes the parties in law husband and wife, is performance. Nothing short is. At marriage, therefore, the contract ceases. Hence,—

3.   Marriage Defined. – Marriage . . . is the civil status of one man and one woman united in law for life, for the discharge, to each other and the community, of the duties legally incumbent on those whose association is founded on the distinction of sex. . . .

Source of Marriage—Further of the Definition. – The source of marriage is the law of nature, whence it has flowed into the municipal laws of every civilized country, and into the general law of nations. And since it can exist only in pairs, and since none are compelled, but all who are capable are permitted, to assume it,— marriage may be said to proceed, as just explained, from a civil contract between one man and one woman, of the needful physical and civil capacity. While the contract remains a mere agreement to marry, it is not essentially different from other executory civil contracts; it does not superinduce the status; and, on its violation, an action may be maintained by the injured party to recover his damages of the other. But when it is executed in what the law accepts as a valid marriage, its nature as a contract is merged in the higher nature of the status. And though the new relation— that is, the status—retains some similitudes reminding us of its origin, the contract does in truth no longer exist, but the parties are governed by the law of husband and wife. In other words, the parties, when they agreed to marry, undertook only to assume the marital status; and, on its assumption, the agreement, being fully performed according to its terms, bound them no longer.

*   *   *

4. Further of the Definition of Marriage. – We know that the foregoing definition of marriage is correct, because it accurately describes what the courts constantly decide. That marriage executed is not a contract we know, because the parties cannot mutually dissolve it, because the act of God incapacitating one to discharge its duties will not release the bond, because there is no accepted performance which will end it, because a minor of marriageable age can no more recede from it than an adult, because it is not dissolved by a failure of the original consideration, because no suit for damages will lie for the non-fulfillment of its duties, because its duties are not derived from its terms but from the law, because legislation may annul it at pleasure, and because none of its other elements are those of contract, but all are of status. Still,—

5. Continued. – Plain as this view is, and incredible as it may seem that anything contrary to it should be seriously entertained, marriage was generally in our books, prior to the present one, defined as a contract. But this definition, thus broadly stated, was so obviously inaccurate that it was commonly more or less qualified; and, by some, so much was excepted out of it as to leave little or nothing of the original. So that, if marriage was pronounced a contract, it was said also to be more than a contract, and to differ from all other contracts. A frequent question was, whether it is a civil contract, or a religious vow. The Roman Catholic Church holds it to be a sacrament; and, though Protestants do not generally so esteem it, they account it as of Divine origin, and invest it with the sanctions of religion. Therefore it has been said, that, "according to juster notions of the nature of the marriage contract, it is not merely either a civil or religious contract; and at the present time it is not to be considered as originally and simply one or the other." Yet all the decisions attest, that, however deeply the religious nature of marriage may engage the affections of the community, the law leaves this nature to the sole care of religion, and contemplates it only as a civil institution. . . .

Wightman v. Coates
15 Mass. 1 (1833)

Through the first half of the nineteenth century, breach-of-promise suits were an important means by which private parties policed courtship. Marriage among the English upper class was a property transaction in which love played a minor role. Under such circumstances, courtship was like a stage in bargaining about the economic terms of wedlock, and men who jilted would-be brides were guilty of breaching a promise with often significant economic implications. As the explicit economic basis of marriage declined and the concept of companionate marriage increased in significance during the century, the underlying basis of the breach-of-promise suit changed. It increasingly rested on the assumption that women had to marry to become mothers in order to fulfill their social responsibilities.

ASSUMPSIT on a promise to marry the plaintiff, and a breach thereof by refusal, and having married another woman.

At the trial on the general issue, at the last November term before *Parker C. J.* the evidence of a promise resulted from sundry letters written to the plaintiff by the defendant, and from his attentions to her for a considerable length of time.

It was objected by the defendant, that there being no direct evidence of an express promise, the action could not be maintained.

This objection was overruled by the judge; and the jury were instructed that if, from the letters of the defendant read in evidence, and the course of his conduct towards the plaintiff, they were satisfied that there was a mutual understanding and engagement between the parties to marry each other, they might find for the plaintiff, which they did.

If the said direction was right, judgment was to be rendered on the verdict: otherwise a new trial was to be granted.

PARKER C. J. delivered the opinion of the court. Respectable counsel having expressed doubts upon the point reserved in this case, and having also suggested an opinion that the action was of a nature to be discountenanced rather than favored; we have given more consideration to the case, than our impression of the merits of the objections would have required.

We can conceive of no more suitable ground of application to the tribunals of justice for compensation, than that of a violated promise to enter into a contract, on the faithful performance of which the interest of all civilized countries so essentially depends. When two parties, of suitable age to contract, agree to pledge their faith to each other, and thus withdraw themselves from that intercourse with society, which might probably lead to a similar connexion with another; the affections being so far interested as to render a subsequent engagement not probable or desirable; and one of the parties wantonly and capriciously refuses to execute the contract, which is thus commenced; the injury may be serious, and circumstances may often justify a claim of pecuniary indemnification.

When the female is the injured party, there is generally more reason for a resort to the laws, then when the man is the sufferer. Both have a right of action, but the jury will discriminate and apportion the damages according to the injury sustained. A deserted female, whose prospects in life may be materially affected by the treachery of the man, to whom she has plighted her vows, will always receive from a jury the attention which her situation requires. And it is not disreputable for one, who may have to mourn for years over lost prospects and broken vows, to seek such compensation as the laws can give her. It is also for the public interest, that conduct tending to consign a virtuous woman to celibacy, should meet with that punishment, which may prevent it from becoming common. That delicacy of the sex, which happily in this country gives the man so much advantage over the woman, in the intercourse which leads to matrimonial engagements, requires for its protection and continuance the aid of the laws. When it shall be abused by the injustice of those who would take advantage of it, moral justice as well as public policy dictate the propriety of a legal indemnity.

This is not a new doctrine. As early as the time of Lord *Holt*, it was enforced, as the common law, by that wise and learned judge and his brethren, that a breach of promise of marriage was a meritorious cause of action, and although the value of a marriage in money might have had some influence in that decision, there is no doubt that the loss sustained in other respects,—the wounded spirit, the unmerited disgrace, and the probable solitude,—which would be the consequences of desertion after a long courtship, were considered to be as legitimate claims for pecuniary compensation, as the loss of reputation by slander, or the wounded pride in slight assaults and batteries.

Nor is this English law become obsolete. It is the common law of our country, always recognized when occasions have offered; and the occasions have not been infrequent since the adoption of our constitution. . . . Several actions of this nature have been before this court, since I have been upon the bench, and I remember several when I was in practice at the bar, in which I was counsel. Indeed there is no country, in which the relative situation of the sexes, and their joint influence on society, would render such a principle of jurisprudence more useful or necessary.

As to the technical ground, upon which the objection to the verdict now rests, we entertain no doubts. The exception taken is, that there was no direct evidence of an express promise of marriage made by the defendant. The objection implies that there was indirect evidence, from which such a promise may have been inferred; and the jury were instructed that if, from the letters written by the defendant, as well as his conduct, they believed that a mutual engagement subsisted between the parties, they ought to find for the plaintiff. They made the inference, and without doubt it was justly drawn.

Is it then necessary that an express promise in direct terms should be proved? A necessity for this would imply a state of public manners by no means desirable. That young persons of different sexes, instead of having their mutual engagements inferred from a course of devoted attention, and apparently exclusive attachment, which is now the common evidence, should be obliged, before they considered themselves bound, to call witnesses, or execute instruments under hand and seal, would be destructive of that chaste and modest intercourse, which is the pride of our country; and a boldness of manners would probably succeed, by no means friendly to the character of the sex, or the interests of society.

A mutual engagement must be proved, to support this action: but it may be proved by those circumstances, which usually accompany such a connexion. No case has been cited, in support of the defendant's objection. On the contrary, it is very clear from all the *English* cases, that a promise may be inferred, and that direct proof is not necessary. In the case before referred to of *Hutton* vs. *Mansell*, Lord *Holt* says expressly, that where one has promised, and the behavior of the other is such as to countenance the belief that an engagement has taken place, this is evidence enough of a promise on the part of the person so conducting; and the same principle will apply to both the parties.

In the present case, however, the evidence on which the jury relied, was of a decisive nature; for the letters of the defendant, which were submitted to them, were couched in terms which admit only of the alternative, that he was bound in honor and conscience to marry the plaintiff, or that he was prosecuting a deeply laid scheme of fraud and deception, with a view to seduction. The jury believed the former; and in so doing, have vindicated his character from the greater stain: and he ought to be content with the damages, which they thought it reasonable to assess for the lighter injury. *Judgment on the verdict.*

Reynolds v. United States
98 U.S. 145 (1878)

Marriage also carried with it powerful cultural values. The following case involved polygamy, a practice adopted on religious grounds by the Church of Jesus Christ of Latter-day Saints in Utah Territory. Much of the Court's decision in Reynolds *dealt with the power of the federal government to interfere with freedom of religion, but it also touched on important questions about whether the state had a responsibility to define the marriage agreement.*

[Chief Justice Waite] On the trial, the plaintiff in error, the accused, proved that at the time of his alleged second marriage he was, and for many years before had been, a member of the Church of Jesus Christ of Latter-Day Saints, commonly called the Mormon Church, and a believer in its doctrines; that it was an accepted doctrine of that church "that it was the duty of male members of said church, circumstances permitting, to practice polygamy; . . . that this duty was enjoined by different books which the members of said church believed to be of divine origin, and among others the Holy Bible, and also that the members of the church believed that the practice of polygamy was directly enjoined upon the male members thereof by the Almighty God, in a revelation to Joseph Smith, the founder and prophet of said church; that the failing or refusing to practice polygamy by such male members of said church, when circumstances would admit, would be punished, and that the penalty for such failure and refusal would be damnation in the life to come." He also proved "that he had received permission from the recognized authorities in said church to enter into polygamous marriage; . . ." that Daniel H. Wells, one having authority in said church to perform the marriage ceremony, married the said defendant on or about the time the crime is alleged to have been committed, to some woman by the name of Schofield, and that such marriage ceremony was performed under and pursuant to the doctrines of said church.

Upon this proof he asked the court to instruct the jury that if they found from the evidence that he "was married as charged—if he was married—in pursuance of and in conformity with what he believed at the time to be a religious duty, that the verdict must be 'not guilty.'" This request was refused, and the court did charge "that there must have been a criminal intent, but that if the defendant, under the influence of a religious belief that it was right,—under an inspiration, if you please, that it was right,—deliberately married a second time, having a first wife living, the want of consciousness of evil intent—the want of understanding on his part that he was committing a crime—did not excuse him; but the law inexorably in such case implies the criminal intent."

Upon this charge and refusal to charge the question is raised, whether religious belief can be accepted as a justification of an overt act made criminal by the law of the land. The inquiry is not as to the power of Congress to prescribe criminal laws for the Territories, but as to the guilt of one who knowingly violates a law which has been properly enacted, if he entertains a religious belief that the law is wrong.

Congress cannot pass a law for the government of the Territories which shall prohibit the free exercise of religion. The first amendment to the Constitution expressly forbids such legislation. Religious freedom is guaranteed everywhere throughout the United States, so far as congressional interference is concerned. The question to be determined is, whether the law now under consideration comes within this prohibition.

[Here Chief Justice Waite explored the history of religious freedom in America, finding that Congress had authority to control those religious actions that violated the social order.]

Polygamy has always been odious among the northern and western nations of Europe, and, until the establishment of the Mormon Church, was almost exclusively a feature of the life of Asiatic and of African people. At common law, the second marriage was always void and from the earliest history of England polygamy has been treated as an offence against society. After the establishment of the ecclesiastical courts, and until the time of James I, it was punished through the instrumentality of those tribunals, not merely because ecclesiastical rights had been violated, but because upon the separation of the ecclesiastical courts from the civil the ecclesiastical were supposed to be the most appropriate for the trial of matrimonial causes and offences against the rights of marriage, just as they were for testamentary causes and the settlement of the estates of deceased persons.

By the statute of 1 James I, the offence, if committed in England or Wales, was made punishable in the civil courts, and the penalty was death. As this statute was limited in its operation to England and Wales, it was at a very early period re-enacted, generally with some modifications, in all the colonies. In connection with the case we are now considering, it is a significant fact that on the 8th of December, 1788, after the passage of the act establishing religious freedom, and after the convention of Virginia had recommended as an amendment to the Constitution of the United States the declaration in a bill of rights that "all men have an equal, natural, and unalienable right to the free exercise of religion, according to the dictates of conscience," the legislature of that State substantially enacted the statute of James I., death penalty included, because, as recited in the preamble, "it hath been doubted whether bigamy or polygamy be punishable by the laws of this Commonwealth." From that day to this we think it may safely be said there never has been a time in any State of the Union when polygamy has not been an offence against society, cognizable by the civil courts and punishable with more or less severity. In the face of all this evidence, it is impossible to believe that the constitutional guaranty of religious freedom was intended to prohibit legislation in respect to this most important feature of social life. Marriage, while from its very nature a sacred obligation, is nevertheless, in most civilized nations, a civil contract, and usually regulated by law. Upon it society may be said to be built, and out of its fruits spring social relations and social obligations and duties, with which government is necessarily required to deal. In fact, according as monogamous or polygamous marriages are allowed, do we find the principles on which the government of the people, to a greater or less extent, rests. Professor Lieber says, polygamy leads to the patriarchal principle, and which, when applied to large communities, fetters the people in stationary despotism, while that principle cannot long exist in connection with monogamy. . . .

*   *   *

In our opinion, the statute immediately under consideration is within the legislative power of Congress. It is constitutional and valid as prescribing a rule of action for all those residing in the Territories, and in places over which the United States have exclusive control. This being so, the only question which remains is, whether those who make polygamy a part of their religion are an exception from the operation of the statute. If they are, then those who do not make polygamy a part of their religious belief may be found guilty and punished, while those who do, must be acquitted and go free. This would be introducing a new element into criminal law. Laws are made for the government of actions, and while they cannot interfere with mere religious belief and opinions, they may with practices. Suppose one believed that human sacrifices were a necessary part of religious worship, would it be seriously contended that the civil government under which he lived could not interfere to prevent a sacrifice? Or if a wife religiously believed it was her duty to burn herself upon the funeral pile of her dead husband, would it be beyond the power of the civil government to prevent her carrying her belief into practice?

So here, as a law of the organization of society under the exclusive dominion of the United States, it is provided that plural marriages shall not be allowed. Can a man excuse his practices to the contrary because of his religious belief? and there are pure-minded women and there are innocent children,—innocent in a sense even beyond the degree of the innocence of childhood itself. These are to be the sufferers; and as jurors fail to do their duty, and as these cases come up in the Territory of Utah, just so do these victims multiply and spread themselves over the land.

While every appeal by the court to the passions or the prejudices of a jury should be promptly rebuked, and while it is the imperative duty of a reviewing court to take care that wrong is not done in this way, we see no just cause for complaint in this case. Congress, in 1862, saw fit to make bigamy a crime in the Territories. This was done because of the evil consequences that were supposed to flow from plural marriages. All the court did was to call the attention of the jury to the peculiar character of the crime for which the accused was on trial, and to remind them of the duty they had to perform. There was no appeal to the passions, no instigation of prejudice. Upon the showing made by the accused himself, he was guilty of a violation of the law under which he had been indicted: and the effort of the court seems to have been not to withdraw the minds of the jury from the issue to be tried, but to bring them to it; not to make them partial, but to keep them impartial.

Upon a careful consideration of the whole case, we are satisfied that no error was committed by the court below.

Judgment affirmed.

Note: Divorce

Divorce had been extremely rare in colonial America. When couples divorced from "bed and board," they simply separated without legally dissolving their relationship. Although the incidence of divorce increased in the nineteenth century, the practice grew more rapidly during the last forty years of the century as industrialization took hold. Most divorces were granted to women, and most of these were based on either a husband's alleged adultery or his cruelty. By the end of the nineteenth century, a liberal view of divorce began to emerge, one that recognized the sweeping economic changes of the era and had vast implications for the marriage contract. Judicial divorce became more popular as a means of allocating property when things went sour.

Waldron v. *Waldron*
85 Cal. 251 (1890)

The rise of companionate marriage invited matrimonial dissolutions because the expectations of love and affection that it raised were often unattainable. Legislators set the terms for divorce; judges applied them. Adultery figured prominently in every state, but by the end of the century, cruelty was also widely accepted as grounds for divorce. What this vague term meant was another matter. The court in 1863 had rejected the idea that physical harm alone constituted cruelty. In Powelson v. Powelson, *22 Cal. 360, the judges concluded that any "conduct sufficiently aggravated to produce ill-health or bodily pain . . . though operating primarily upon the mind only, should be regarded as legal cruelty." The court's finding in* Waldron, *although it worked against the wife, did provide that if the indignities were sufficient they could destroy a marriage, even if there had been no physical harm. In 1892, the California General Assembly ratified this view in legislation that made it possible to prove mental suffering even if there was no evidence of deterioration in a spouse's physical health.*

VANCLIEF, C.—This is an action for divorce on the ground of extreme cruelty, by the use of vile and offensive language, without any physical force or violence applied to the person of the plaintiff.

The answer of the defendant denies the cruelty and the use of the language alleged. The court found for the plaintiff, and decreed a divorce and permanent alimony of one hundred dollars per month while she shall remain unmarried, and one thousand dollars for her attorneys fees; and defendant appeals from the judgment, and from an order denying his motion for a new trial.

The material substance of the findings as to extreme cruelty is as follows:—

That, upon occasions when the defendant was intoxicated, he wrongfully and unjustly, and without sufficient provocation to justify him in so doing, called the plaintiff vile names, once called her a "whore," and on several different occasions called her a "damned bitch," and a "damned witch from hell," in the presence and hearing of other people, and thereby inflicting upon her grievous mental suffering, but without injury to her health; that when he called her such vile names she was not without fault, and that she was not uniformly kind to him; that there is reasonable apprehension to believe that such cruel treatment will be continued if a divorce is not granted.

*   *   *

Although the character of the ill treatment, whether it operates directly upon the body or primarily upon the mind alone, and all the attending circumstances, are to be considered for the purpose of estimating the degree of the cruelty, yet the final test of its sufficiency, as a cause of divorce, must be its actual or reasonably apprehended injurious effect upon the body or health of the complaining party. . . . This is the only practically safe rule. The grave remedy of divorce is disproportioned to the petty marital wrongs and annoyances whose injurious effect upon the body or health cannot be shown and sensibly appreciated, and it is not to be administered on the ground of cruelty, except in conservation of life or health. Many of such wrongs and annoyances, productive of more or less unhappiness, must be borne, if they cannot be justly remedied or avoided by the parties themselves.

*   *   *

Yet the practical view of the law is, that a degree of cruelty which cannot be perceived to injure the body or the health of the body, "can be practically endured," and *must* be endured, if there is no other remedy than by divorce; because no "scale" by which to gauge the purely mental susceptibilities and sufferings has yet been invented or discovered, except such as indicate the degrees thereof by their *perceptible* effects upon the physical organization of the body.

From the foregoing considerations, it follows that the findings of fact are not sufficient to sustain the judgment. "Extreme cruelty" is not expressly found in any sense; nor does it, in the legal sense above described, follow, as a necessary inference, from the facts found. The finding of "grievous mental suffering" is, and purports to be, only an inference or conclusion from the opprobrious language found to have been used by the defendant.

*   *   *

Plaintiff admitted that the defendant was an honest man in all his business transactions, and that he liberally supplied her and her children and niece. She complained of no unkindness when he was sober, and feared no physical violence from him when he was drunk. In their quarrels she appears to have been more than his match, though she could not descend to answer his profanity and obscenity in kind. While drunkenness was no excuse for calling her vile names under any circumstances, yet the injurious effect thereof upon her mind should not have been, and probably was not, so bad as if he had deliberately called her by those names when he was sober. No mental suffering produced by his drunkenness, merely, can be considered, because not complained of. The mental suffering, caused by his words alone, can be considered in this case.

The finding that defendant called the plaintiff a whore and a bitch, *in the presence and hearing of other people*, should be qualified by the admitted facts that none but the niece and her caller and the colored servant heard him call out her name, and that he was not aware that even they heard what he said, or that the caller upon the niece was in the house at the time. This seems material, as tending both to modify the otherwise apparent motive of the defendant, and to mitigate the alleged painful effect upon the mind of the plaintiff, as without this qualification it would appear that the defendant intended to defame the plaintiff in public estimation, which would indicate a worse motive on his part, and produce a more painful effect upon her mind than would the mere intention privately to annoy her, or to revenge himself for the fancied wrongs of having been barred out of her room and threatened with the police.

While the defamatory, obscene, and profane language of the defendant was wholly unjustified, inexcusable, and unmanly, it may be said that the conduct of the plaintiff was at least unkind and censorious, and tended to provoke anger and harsh language on the part of the defendant. It probably resulted from her ill temper, bad judgment, and a mistaken view of the duty of a wife under the circumstances. She probably deemed it her duty, by means of censure, reproach, and scolding, to make her husband "do what was right," and it seems that she faithfully, in season and out of season, applied such means. In this I think she was mistaken. Intemperate husbands are seldom, if ever, reformed by such treatment, whereas uniform kindness may often prove effectual, and never harmful; but should kindness fail, and the intemperance of the husband become habitual, the wife will be entitled to a divorce on that ground alone.

I think the judgment should be reversed, and the court below directed to render judgment for the defendant on the findings, without costs, and that the appellant pay his own costs of the appeal.

Birth Control and Abortion

A dramatic decline in female fertility (and, hence, family size) was an important demographic feature of nineteenth-century America. By the beginning of the twentieth century, the United States had one of the lowest fertility rates in the world. Historians have debated why this decline took place and on whose initiative (husband, wife, or both). The companionate form of marriage and the greater emotional attention given to children may explain some of the decline in births. Women also seem to have viewed the practice of birth control as one way of increasing their autonomy. Yet male lawmakers grew increasingly wary of these practices and intervened, with greater and greater frequency, in an area that had been deemed exclusively private, going so far as to criminalize the dissemination of birth-control information and the practice of abortion.

State v. Slagle
82 N.C. 653 (1880)

Abortion carried a far heavier moral and legal burden than did birth control. Infanticide had been a feature of colonial America, but as the fertility rate dropped and birth-control practices became better and more widespread its significance also declined. Abortion, however, at the beginning of the nineteenth century, carried no legal penalties so long as it was performed before "quickening," the period at about four or five months when the fetus begins to move in the womb. The leading American case was Commonwealth v. Bangs, 9 Mass. 369 (1812), *which gave the quickening doctrine, with its long roots in English common law, a firm hold in nineteenth-century American common law. By the end of the century, however, American judges began to deemphasize the quickening doctrine.*

ASHE, J. The indictment contained four counts; the first two charged the defendant with having *wilfully* and *feloniously* administered a poisonous drug to one Eva Bryson, with intent to kill and murder her, varying only in the description of the drug used. The last two counts charged him with having unlawfully and wickedly administered a noxious potion to the said Eva, then being quick with child, with the intent to cause and procure the miscarriage of the said Eva, and the premature birth of the said child; these two counts only differing as to the nature of the drugs employed to effect the purpose. The defendant . . . argued [t]hat the facts set forth and charged against him in said bill of indictment do not constitute an offence or crime against the laws of North Carolina. . . .

            *   *   *

The defendant is . . . charged in the indictment with a crime under the laws of the state. And when one in this state is indicted and tried as for a felony, yet the facts averred in the indictment do not support the charge of felony, but a misdemeanor, the court may give judgment for such misdemeanor.

            *   *   *

We have no statute making it indictable to administer "drugs" to produce abortion, and there is very little to be found on the subject in either the English or American writers on criminal law, but it is held by the highest authority that it is a misdemeanor at common law. . . . And Wharton in his work on Criminal Law, 1220 says: "There is no doubt at common law the destruction of an infant unborn is a high misdemeanor and at an early period, it seems to have been murder." It has been said it is not an indictable offence to administer a drug to a woman and thereby to procure an abortion, unless the mother is quick with child, though such a distinction, it is submitted, is neither in accordance with the results of medical experience or with the principles of the common law.

            *   *   *

PER CURIAM.   No error.

Note: Abortion and the Quickening Doctrine

The decision in *Slagle* marked a growing retreat by both courts and legislatures from the quickening doctrine. To some extent, this change in direction revealed the influence of an increasingly vocal and well-organized antiabortion campaign by the medical profession. The American Medical Association made an end to abortion one of its chief goals: its leaders considered abortion-law reform a means by which the profession could enhance its moral influence, extend the influence of scientific medical practices against midwives, and monopolize the health-care business generally. Legislatures cooperated by adopting more comprehensive acts that imposed stiffer penalties, on both the woman and the abortionist. Abortion was a risky procedure, and the states had a plausible role in saving women from death and sterility as a result of hemorrhage and infection. The Massachusetts Supreme Judicial Court in 1882 reversed its earlier holding in *Bangs* by disposing of the quickening doctrine altogether in considering whether an abortion was illegal (see *Commonwealth* v. *Taylor*, 132 Mass. 261 [1882]). But quickening did continue to play some part in determining the extent of criminal penalty. The aborting of a prequickened fetus was generally treated as a misdemeanor; that of a fully animated fetus was considered a felony.

Despite the criminalization of abortion in most states, the practice continued to flourish. Only a small percentage of those persons who performed abortions were ever convicted. Like birth-control information and devices, the public demand for abortion produced its own black market, one in which women of standing and wealth had far greater access to competent treatment than did lower-class and poor women. New abortion statutes limited the discretionary rights of all women.

People v. *Sanger*
222 N.Y. 192 (1918)

Like abortion, birth control came under increased scrutiny by state government. By the end of the nineteenth century, moral reformers had made limitation of such knowledge one of their chief objectives. Margaret Sanger was a prominent advocate of birth control, and she and her sister sought to test the constitutionality of a New York State law against distributing birth-control information by purposely being convicted under it.

CRANE, J. Section 1142 of the Penal Law, among other things, makes it a misdemeanor for a person to sell, or give away, or to advertise or offer for sale, any instrument or article, drug or medicine, for the prevention of conception; or to give information orally stating when, where or how such an instrument, article or medicine can be purchased or obtained.

The appellant was convicted . . . for a violation of this section, and sentenced to thirty days in the workhouse. She claims that the law is unconstitutional.

Some of the reasons assigned below for the illegality of this act have now been abandoned and it is conceded to be within the police power of the legislature, for the benefit of the morals and health of the community, to make such a law as this applicable to unmarried persons. But it is argued that if this law be broad enough to prevent a duly licensed physician from giving advice and help to his married patients in a proper case, it is an unreasonable police regulation, and, therefore, unconstitutional. There are two answers to this suggestion.

In the first place, the defendant is not a physician, and the general rule applies in a criminal as well as a civil case that no one can plead the unconstitutionality of a law except the person affected thereby. . . .

Secondly, by section 1145 of the Penal Law, physicians are excepted from the provisions of this act under circumstances therein mentioned. This section reads: "An article or instrument, used or applied by physicians lawfully practicing, or by their direction or prescription, for the cure or prevention of disease, is not an article of indecent or immoral nature or use, within this article. The supplying of such articles to such physicians or by their direction or prescription, is not an offense under this article."

This exception in behalf of physicians does not permit advertisements regarding such matters, nor promiscuous advice to patients irrespective of their condition, but it is broad enough to protect the physician who in good faith gives such help or advice to a married person to cure or prevent disease. "Disease," by Webster's International Dictionary, is defined to be, "an alteration in the state of the body, or of some of its organs, interrupting or disturbing the performance of the vital functions, and causing or threatening pain and sickness; illness; sickness; disorder."

The protection thus afforded the physician would also extend to the druggist, or vendor, acting upon the physician's prescription or order.

Much of the argument presented to us by the appellant touching social conditions and sociological questions are matters for the legislature and not for the courts.

Judgment affirmed.

Crime and Criminal Justice

Criminal law involves the power of the state to deprive individuals of their liberty (through imprisonment, even death) and property (through fines and confiscations). In the American federal system, the states almost entirely created and enforced this body of law. Nineteenth-century state lawmakers did so based on the police powers—powers to provide for the morals, health, welfare, and safety of the public. Both the criminal law and the criminal justice system underwent significant change during the century, although historians disagree sharply about the causes and consequences of those changes. For example, the rate of serious crime dropped during the nineteenth century, a decline that continued well into the twentieth century. But why this decrease (the amount of crime increased, but so did the population) occurred remains uncertain. The debate over the crime rate revolves around two of the most important developments of the century—industrialization and urbanization. Some scholars argue that a greater concentration of people in urban areas and the rise of an industrial market economy should have produced social dislocations sufficient to encourage crime. Others contend that capitalism and the emerging American city actually encouraged a system of discipline and order that inhibited crime. Still others insist that neither of these broad developments had much to do directly with the decline in the rate of serious crime: rather, they argue that the emergence of professional police forces, beginning in mid-century, effectively deterred crime.

Students of the era have also argued that crime was endemic in rural, frontier areas where the arm of the law failed to reach. Such a view holds that what law did exist flowed out of the barrel of a gun and that vigilantism was an everyday occurrence. Other scholars have concluded that there was far more stability and order than previously believed. John P. Reid, for example, has argued persuasively that travelers on the Overland Trail during mid-century displayed an extraordinary commitment to law and order, a commitment that they learned in the more civilized East and carried with them into the West.[2]

There is also disagreement about the nature of nineteenth-century crime. William E. Nelson, for instance, has noted that by the beginning of the century crimes against property rather than moral crimes (adultery, fornication, and such) received greatest attention from the criminal justice system.[3] Yet by the end of the century, as some of the previous material in this chapter makes clear, social reformers turned increasingly to criminal law to control abortion, birth control, and supposedly obscene materials, such as birth-control literature.

Nineteenth-century Americans also wrestled with the problem of punishing criminal offenders, and social reformers gave great attention to prison reform and the abolition of the death penalty. Perhaps the most dramatic response during the first half of the century was the discovery of the asylum. Penitentiaries, madhouses, and poorhouses were institutional responses to the problems of deviancy and dependency. Advocates of the penitentiary insisted that the causes of crime had environmental roots and that, by taking offenders out of degraded surroundings and placing them in an atmosphere of discipline and order, change was possible. The quest to rehabilitate the individual, however, always clashed with persistent societal demands that retribution be meted out to wrongdoers.

By the end of the century, the rehabilitative ideal that undergirded the asylum movement came under increasing attack from proponents of biological inheritance and eugenics. There were, in short, born criminals. A bad environment, like crowded urban slums, only exacerbated the problems created by a faulty inheritance.

Conflicts over the proper method of punishment and the relationship of environment and inheritance to crime also surfaced in the growing debate over what constituted a proper legal excuse for crime. Pleas of insanity and self-defense, for example, became increasingly important in nineteenth-century homicide law.

Crime and Punishment

Nineteenth-century students of American crime expounded conflicting views about its causes. Some spokesmen stressed environment; others, especially as the eugenics movement gathered momentum at century's end, emphasized biological inheritance; and still others claimed that both elements explained criminal behavior. Crime, of course, is a wholly subjective designation; it is what those who control the power of the state say it is. For most of the century, however, lawmakers drew from an Enlightenment inheritance that stressed reason and environment over innate sinfulness. By the end of the century, however, a scientific explanation that derived from eugenics gained increasing currency.

CESARE BECCARIA
On Crimes and Punishments
1764

Cesare Bonesana, Marquis of Beccaria, was an Italian nobleman who founded the classical or rational school of criminology. In 1764 Beccaria published his now-famous essay On Crimes and Punishments, *and it received wide attention in pre- and post-Revolutionary America. The first English translation in America appeared in Charleston, South Carolina, in 1777, and Thomas Jefferson's* Commonplace Book *contained twenty-six extracts from the essay. Jefferson in 1776 also drew heavily on it to formulate his proposed reforms to Virginia's penal laws.*

It is better to prevent crimes than to punish them. This is the ultimate end of every good legislation, which, to use the general terms for assessing the good and evils of life, is the art of leading men to the greatest possible happiness or to the least possible unhappiness.

*   *   *

Do you want to prevent crimes? See to it that the laws are clear and simple and that the entire force of a nation is united in their defense, and that no part of it is employed to destroy them. See to it that the laws favor not so much classes of men as men themselves. See to it that men fear the laws and fear nothing else. For fear of the laws is salutary, but fatal and fertile for crimes is one man's fear of another. Enslaved men are more voluptuous, more depraved, more cruel than free men. These study the sciences, give thought to the interests of their country, contemplate grand objects and imitate them, while enslaved men, content with the present moment, seek in the excitement of debauchery a distraction from the emptiness of the condition in which they find themselves. Accustomed to an uncertainty of outcome in all things, the outcome of their crimes remains for them problematical, to the advantage of the passions that determine them. If uncertainty regarding the laws befalls a nation which is indolent because of climate, its indolence and stupidity are confirmed and increased; if it befalls a voluptuous but energetic nation, the result is a wasteful diffusion of energy into an infinite number of little cabals and intrigues that sow distrust in every heart, make treachery and dissimulation the foundation of prudence; if it befalls a brave and powerful nation, the uncertainty is removed finally, but only after having caused many oscillations from liberty to slavery and from slavery back to liberty.

Do you want to prevent crimes? See to it that enlightenment accompanies liberty. Knowledge breeds evils in inverse ratio to its diffusion, and benefits in direct ratio. A daring impostor, who is never a common man, is received with adoration by an ignorant people, and with hisses by an enlightened one. Knowledge, by facilitating comparisons and by multiplying points of view, brings on a mutual modification of conflicting feelings, especially when it appears that others hold the same views and face the same difficulties. In the face of enlightenment widely diffused throughout the nation, the calumnies of ignorance are silenced and authority trembles if it be not armed with reason. The vigorous force of the laws, meanwhile, remains immovable, for no enlightened person can fail to approve of the clear and useful public compacts of mutual security when he compares the inconsiderable portion of useless liberty he himself has sacrificed with the sum total of liberties sacrificed by other men, which, except for the laws, might have been turned against him. Any person of sensibility, glancing over a code of well-made laws and observing that he has lost only a baneful liberty to injure others, will feel constrained to bless the throne and its occupant.

CHARLES LORING BRACE
"The Causes of Crime"
1880

By the end of the nineteenth century, Beccaria's rational view came under attack from authorities who tied crime to biological inheritance. Cesare Lomborso, an Italian physician and the father of modern criminology, for example, pioneered the science of anthropometry, which purported to describe a set of physical characteristics, such as a low-sloping forehead and heavily massed ears, that all criminals supposedly shared. Lomborso outlined his theory in Criminal Man *(1876), and its claims that criminals were born, not made, received considerable attention in the United States. Charles Loring Brace, a leader of the New York Children's Aid Society, added yet another dimension to these arguments by borrowing ideas from both the environmental and inheritance schools. He described the existence of a "dangerous class," composed of the masses of poor, foreign-born immigrants who were filling up American cities. Brace's anti-Irish bias paralleled racial stereotypes formed of blacks, Chinese, and Native Americans. Yet Brace also believed that the city, more so than small villages and towns, was best suited to deal with the causes of crime.*

There is no question that the breaking of the ties with one's country has a bad moral effect, especially on a laboring class. The Emigrant is released from the social inspection and judgment to which he has been subjected at home, and the tie of church and priesthood is weakened. If a Roman Catholic, he is often a worse Catholic, without being a better Protestant. If a Protestant, he often becomes indifferent. Moral ties are loosened with the religious. The intervening process which occurs here, between his abandoning the old state of things and fitting himself to the new, is not favorable to morals or character.

The consequence is, that an immense proportion of our ignorant and criminal class are foreign-born; and of the dangerous classes here, a very large part, though native-born, are of foreign parentage.

*   *   *

It is another marked instance of the demoralizing influence of emigration, that so large a proportion of the female criminal class should be Irish-born, though the Irish female laboring class are well known to be at home one of the most virtuous in the world.

A hopeful fact, however, begins to appear in regard to this matter; the worst effects of emigration in this country seem over. The machinery for protecting and forwarding the newly-arrived immigrants, so that they may escape the dangers and temptations of the city, has been much improved. Very few, comparatively, now remain in our sea-ports to swell the current of poverty and crime. The majority find their way at once to the country districts. The quality, too, of the immigration has improved. More well-to-do farmers and peasantry, with small savings, arrive than formerly, and the preponderance, as to nationality, is inclining to Germany. It comparatively seldom happens now that paupers or persons absolutely without means, land in New York.

As one of the great causes of crime, Emigration will undoubtedly have a much feebler influence in the future in New York [City] than it has had in the past.

*   *   *

A most powerful and continual source of crime with the young is Inheritance—the transmitted tendencies and qualities of their parents, or of several generations of ancestors.

It is well-known to those familiar with the criminal classes, that certain appetites or habits, if indulged abnormally and excessively through two or more generations, come to have an almost irresistible force, and, no doubt, modify the brain so as to constitute almost an instance condition. This is especially true of the appetite for liquor and of the sexual passion, and sometimes of the peculiar weakness, dependence, and laziness which make confirmed paupers.

The writer knows of an instance in an almshouse in Western New York, where four generations of females were paupers and prostitutes. Almost every reader who is familiar with village life will recall poor families which have had dissolute or criminal members beyond the memory of the oldest inhabitant, and who still continue to breed such characters. I have known a child of nine or ten years, given up, apparently beyond control, to licentious habits and desires, and who in all different circumstances seemed to show the same tendencies; her mother had been of similar character, and quite likely her grandmother. The "gemmules," or latent tendencies, or forces, or cells of her immediate ancestors were in her system, and working in her blood, producing irresistible effects on her brain, nerves, and mental emotions, and finally, not being met early enough by other moral, mental, and physical influences, they have modified her organization, until her will is scarcely able to control them and she gives herself up to them. All those who instruct or govern "Houses of Refuge," or "Reform Schools," or Asylums for criminal children and youths, will recall many such instances.

They are much better known in the Old World than this; they are far more common here in the country than in the city.

My own experience during twenty years has been in this regard singularly hopeful. I have watched great numbers of degraded families in New York, and exceedingly few of them have transmitted new generations of paupers, criminals, or vagrants.

The causes of this encouraging state of things are not obscure. The action of the great law of "Natural Selection," in regard to the human race, is always towards temperance and virtue. That is, vice and extreme indulgence weaken the physical powers and undermine the constitution; they impair the faculties by which man struggles with adverse conditions and gets beyond the reach of poverty and want. The vicious and sensual and drunken die earlier, or they have fewer children, or their children are carried off by diseases more frequently, or they themselves are unable to resist or prevent poverty and suffering. As a consequence, in the lowest class, the more self-controlled and virtuous tend constantly to survive, and to prevail in "the struggle for existence," over the vicious and ungoverned, and to transmit their progeny. The natural drift among the poor is towards virtue. Probably no vicious organization with very extreme and abnormal tendencies is transmitted beyond the fourth generation; it ends in insanity or cretinism or the wildest crime.

The result is then, with the worst-endowed families, that the "gemmules," or latent forces of hundreds of virtuous, or at least, not vicious, generations, lie hid in their constitutions. The immediate influences of parents or grandparents are, of course, the strongest in heritance; but these may be overcome, and the latent tendencies to good, coming down from remote ancestors, be aroused and developed.

Thus is explained the extraordinary improvement of the children of crime and poverty in our Industrial Schools; and the reforms and happy changes seen in the boys and girls of our dangerous classes when placed in kind Western homes. The change of circumstances, the improved food, the daily moral and mental influences, the effect of regular labor and discipline, and, above all, the power of Religion, awaken these hidden tendencies to good, both those coming from many generations of comparative virtue and those inherent in the soul, while they control and weaken and cause to be forgotten those diseased appetites or extreme passions which these unfortunate creatures inherit directly, and substitute a higher moral sense for the low moral instincts which they obtained from their parents. So it happens, also, that American life, as compared with European, and city life, as compared with country, produces similar results. In the United States, a boundless hope pervades all classes; it reaches down to the outcast and vagrant. There is no fixity, as is so often the fact in Europe, from the sense of despair. Every individual, at least till he is old, hopes and expects to rise out of his condition.

The daughter of the rag-picker or vagrant sees the children she knows, continually dressing better or associating with more decent people; she beholds them attending the public schools and improving in education and manners; she comes in contact with the greatest force the poor know—public opinion, which requires a certain decency and respectability among themselves. She becomes ashamed of her squalid, ragged, or drunken mother. She enters an Industrial School, or creeps into a Ward School, or "goes out" as a servant. In every place, she feels the profound forces of American life; the desire of equality, ambition to rise, the sense of self-respect and the passion for education.

These new desires overcome the low appetites in her blood, and she continually rises and improves. If Religion in any form reach her, she attains a still greater height over the sensual and filthy ways of her parents. She is in no danger of sexual degradation, or of any extreme vice. The poison in her blood has found an antidote. When she marries, it will inevitably be with a class above her own. This process goes on continually throughout the country, and breaks up criminal inheritance.

Moreover, the incessant change of our people, especially in cities, the separation of children from parents, of brothers from sisters, and of all from their former localities, destroy that continuity of influence which bad parents and grandparents exert, and do away with those neighborhoods of crime and pauperism where vice concentrates and transmits itself with ever-increasing power. The fact that tenants must forever be "moving" in New York, is a preventive of some of the worst evils among the lower poor. The mill of American life, which grinds up so many delicate and fragile things, has its uses, when it is turned on the vicious fragments of the lower strata of society.

Villages, which are more stable and conservative, and tend to keep families together more and in the same neighborhoods, show more instances of inherited and concentrated wickedness and idleness. In New York the families are constantly broken up; some members improve, some die out, but they do not transmit a progeny of crime. There is little inherited criminality and pauperism.

Note: The Police and the Prison

Although Brace did not touch on the matter in the selection above, he also believed that in every major urban area an organized and professional police force contributed significantly to law and order. During the nineteenth century, the police had undergone a metamorphosis. The informal and typically nonuniformed police of the pre-

Civil War years gave way after the war to an increasingly professional police order, one that took on a paramilitary style of organization including uniforms and, unlike the Metropolitan Police of London (the prototypal modern police force formed in the 1850s), arms. Until about the mid-1880s, the police were as much social welfare agents, providing temporary housing for the homeless and collecting lost children, as they were crime preventors and detectors. Thereafter, however, their role narrowed, and they became much more agents of the criminal justice system who detected and prevented crimes by the "dangerous classes" that Brace describes.

The prison also emerged during the nineteenth century as an essential element in the criminal justice systems of most states. Two major prison systems vied for acceptance—the separate and the congregate. The former was associated with the Eastern State Penitentiary in Philadelphia; the latter was represented by the Auburn State Penitentiary in Auburn, New York. These two institutions also underscored the age-old tensions that have beset prison as a form of punishment: the need to keep costs within reason (the congregate system) while designing individualized approaches (the separate system) to the treatment of criminals. Both systems, however, imbibed the rehabilitative ideal—the notion that the purpose of punishment was to return the individual to society.

The Excuse of Crime

Nineteenth-century lawmakers responded to the threat of criminal disorder by passing more laws. Rhode Island, for example, listed only 50 criminal acts in 1822; by 1872, that number had jumped to 128. The substantive criminal law also gradually shifted in its underlying assumptions. Colonial Americans had generally equated crime with sin, but nineteenth-century lawmakers, influenced by a rising tide of scientific learning, rooted it in hereditary, environmental, and emotional conditions. More so than in the colonial era, therefore, the question of excusing criminal behavior became more complex, as the debate over insanity and self-defense reveals.

The insanity defense was a product of scientific naturalism, a body of thought that held that physical and emotional causes, rather than moral wickedness, explained human behavior. The infant discipline of psychiatry was one offshoot of scientific naturalism, but so was the eugenics movement, with its stress on inherited criminal behavior. Isaac Ray, the most famous American student of medical jurisprudence in the nineteenth century, disagreed with the latter approach. Instead, he stressed that a physical disease of the brain forced persons to act contrary to their own moral standards. Ray insisted that the traditional common-law test, which the English court had outlined in *Regina* v. *McNaghten* (1843), was needlessly narrow in considering the question of whether the defendant knew right from wrong and that it flew in the face of advancing scientific knowledge. He subscribed to the "irresistible impulse" test, but only a handful of jurisdictions agreed with him.

State v. *Felter*
25 Iowa 67 (1868)

The following is the leading case on "irresistible impulse." Its author, John Forrest Dillon, after serving as Chief Justice of the Iowa Supreme Court, became a prominent Wall Street lawyer, an authority on municipal bonds, and the president of the American Bar Association in 1892.

[Dillon, C. J.] Finally, it is insisted that the court erred in its instructions to the jury, and in its refusal to give certain instructions prayed by the defendant relative to the defense of insanity. Before noticing the assignment of error, it is proper, briefly, to refer to the circumstances of the homicide. That the defendant took the life of his wife was not disputed; and the only defense made or relied on was that species of mental unsoundness which has received the name of homicidal mania.

The testimony tends to show that the defendant was about forty years of age, and resided with his wife and a child (who was a witness on the trial), in Tama county, on a farm, about one mile distant from neighbors. He had resided in that county for over ten years, and had served in the army during the war. He had, during the forenoon of the day on which the homicide was committed, been at work in the usual manner. Shortly after dinner the neighbors, from seeing the fire, or some other reason, visited the premises of the defendant, and found the house in ashes, and the defendant's wife within a few feet of it, dead, without clothing upon her person, one of her feet burned off, her features so destroyed by fire that they could not be recognized, and her skull badly fractured, evidently in consequence of heavy blows with a club or other deadly instrument. The defendant himself was found (although he had been seen walking around by persons when approaching the premises) lying near some stacks a few rods from the dwelling-house, with his throat cut from ear to ear, and very weak from the loss of blood. His hair and whiskers were singed, and there was a blister on his nose, but no evidence of fire on any other part of his person, and his clothes were not burned.

There was but one eyewitness to the terrible occurrence—a very young daughter of the defendant, whose age is not stated in the record; and she saw only the first portion of it. The testimony in the case is very imperfectly reported, having been taken down by an unskilled person. The daughter testified, in substance, thus:

"My mother is dead—my father killed her; he struck her—I don't know with what; he was mad at her before I left; it was because she poured the buttermilk out; I left because he was going to kill me; I knew this by the way he acted; mother told me to go to Mr. P.'s (a neighbor's); it was in front of the house that father struck her, about a rod from the house; he shot the gun off by her head; my father was cross to her and did everything mean he could."

*   *   *

There was other evidence, showing that they did not at times live happily together, and that the defendant was fault-finding and cross toward her. The physician who examined the deceased, gave it as his opinion, that the blow upon her skull would produce instant death. When Doctor Daniels afterward dressed the defendant's wound in his throat, he had a conversation with him in respect to the homicide. The defendant said, "that the reason he shot at her was, that he wanted to scare her." He said he wanted to destroy everything, so that she would not get anything, and this was the reason why he burned the house.

*   *   *

A great number of witnesses who had known the defendant for many years, testified that they never saw anything strange in his conduct, or anything that lead them to suspect that he was of unsound mind.

The defendant stated that he cut his throat with a razor, and told where it could be found.

*   *   *

It was admitted by the State that the defendant intended to take his own life when he cut his own throat. There were no witnesses upon the stand who knew of or testified respecting the alleged insanity of the defendant when at home, or the alleged insanity of his father.

The medical witnesses examined on the trial, as not unfrequently happens, differed in opinion as to the defendant's sanity. Most of these witnesses, however, had given to the subject of insanity no special attention.

The court charged the jury that "if the defendant, at the time of the commission of the act (if he did commit it), was laboring under such a degree of insanity as irresistibly and uncontrollably forced him to commit the act, and if he did not at the time of the act, have reason sufficient to discriminate between right and wrong in reference to the act about to be committed by him, it is your duty to acquit wholly; in other words, if you believe from the evidence that the defendant's mind, at the time of committing the act (if he did commit it), was so insane that he did not know the nature of the crime, and did not know that *he was doing wrong in doing the act*, it is your duty to acquit him altogether."

The defendant's counsel complain of this instruction, and in their written argument make to it this objection: "The court did not state the law; only a part of it. It told the jury if the defendant had sufficient mind to discriminate between right and wrong he was responsible. This is not sufficient. He must have mind enough to know that he will be held responsible for his act."

*   *   *

With reference to the right and wrong test referred to in the instructions given, it will be seen that the court does not adopt this criterion as a general one, that is the court does not say if the defendant has capacity to distinguish between right and wrong generally, he is criminally responsible.

But it held that if at the time and with respect to the *act* about to be committed, the defendant had not reason enough to discriminate between right and wrong with reference to that act, had not reason enough to know the nature of the crime, and did not *know that he was doing wrong in committing it*, he is not criminally punishable. The court in substance held that if the defendant's reason was so far gone or overwhelmed that his perception of right or wrong with respect to the comtemplated act was destroyed, if he did not rationally comprehend the character of the act he was about to commit, he should be acquitted.

*   *   *

On the other hand, the right and wrong test, even when guarded as carefully as in the court's instruction, has been very vehemently opposed as incorrect and delusive, especially as a criterion of responsibility in cases of moral insanity.

In my opinion, the right and wrong test is not to be applied too strictly, and belongs more properly to intellectual than to moral insanity. Intelligent medical observers who have made insanity a special study, insist that it not unfrequently happens that persons undoubtedly insane, and who are confined on that account in asylums, are able to distinguish right from wrong, and to know the moral qualities of acts.

Perhaps the profession of law has not fully kept pace with that of medicine on the subject of insanity. And yet medical theorists have propounded doctrines respecting insanity as an excuse for criminal acts, which a due regard for the safety of the community and an enlightened public policy must prevent jurists from adopting as part of the law of the land.

If, as the court charged, the defendant committed the act from an irresistible and uncontrollable insane impulse, not knowing it was wrong, it is clear that he is not criminally responsible.

But suppose he knew it was wrong, but yet was driven to it by an uncontrollable and irresistible impulse, arising, not from natural passion, but from an insane condition of the mind, would he then be criminally responsible?

Most of the cases before cited have recognized the doctrine, that there is a responsibility for the criminal act if the accused knew at the time it was wrong; or, as it would be better expressed, if he rationally comprehended the character and consequences of the act.

But, if, from the observation and concurrent testimony of medical men who make the study of insanity a specialty, it shall be definitely established to be true, that there is an unsound condition of the mind,—that is a diseased condition of the mind, in which, though a person abstractly knows that a given act is wrong, he is yet by an *insane impulse*, that is, an impulse proceeding from a diseased intellect, irresistibly driven to commit it,—the law must modify its ancient doctrines and recognize the truth, and give to this condition, when it is satisfactorily shown to exist, its exculpatory effect.

It is not too much to say, that both medicine and law now recognize the existence of such a mental disease as homicidal insanity; the remaining question in jurisprudence being what must be shown to make it available as a defense to a charge of murder.

*   *   *

If this want of power of control arose from the *insane* condition of the mind of the accused, he should not be held responsible. But if want of power to control his actions arose from violent and ungovernable passions, in a mind not diseased or unsound, he would and ought to be criminally punishable for his acts.

Without further discussion, we conclude by stating what, under the facts of this case, would be safe and proper directions to be given to the jury respecting the point under consideration. The jury, in substance, should be told that if the defendant's act in taking the life of his wife (if he did take it), was caused by mental disease or unsoundness, which dethroned his reason and judgment with respect to that act, which destroyed his power rationally to comprehend the nature and consequences of that act, and which, overpowering his will, irresistibly forced him to its commission, then he is not amenable to legal punishment. But if the jury believe from all the evidence and circumstances, that the defendant was in the possession of a rational intellect or sound mind, and allowed his passions to escape control, then, though *passion* may for the time being have driven *reason* from her seat and usurped it, and have urged the defendant with a force at the moment irresistible to desperate acts, he cannot claim for such acts the protection of insanity.

Whether *passion* or *insanity* was the ruling force and controlling agency which led to the homicide,—in other words, whether the defendant's act was the insane act of an unsound mind, or the outburst of violent, reckless and uncontrolled passion in a mind not diseased,—is the practical question which the jury should be told to determine according to their best judgment upon the evidence before them. If they believe that the homicide was the direct result or offspring of *insanity*, they should acquit; if of *passion*, unless it be an insane passion, they should convict. This is a much more practical inquiry than to direct their attention solely to the defendant's capacity at the time to distinguish right from wrong—an inquiry which must often be speculative and difficult of determination from the data possible to be laid before the jury, and which as a test or criterion of responsibility rather belongs, when applicable, to what is known as *intellectual*, as distinguished from *moral* insanity.

Note: Insanity Tests

The "irresistible impulse," or "wild beast," test meant that a person could know that he or she was doing wrong, yet still be excused from doing it because the individual was driven to do so by an insane condition of the mind. Ray approved of the test because it broadened the scope of the insanity defense in keeping with the best psychiatric learning of the day.

McNaghten was the majority test; *Felter* sketched the minority position. Chief Justice Charles Doe of the New Hampshire Supreme Court urged yet a third and even broader guideline. In *State* v. *Pike*, 49 N.H. 399 (1869), Doe held that neither delusion nor knowledge of right and wrong, as a matter of law, should be the test of mental disease. Instead, he preferred to leave the matter entirely as a fact in question to the jury to decide. This rule stood by itself in New Hampshire and was adopted nowhere else.

Felter was retried and his counsel failed to prove hereditary insanity, resulting in a conviction of manslaughter.

Bill Bell v. *The State*
17 Tex. Crim. 538 (1885)

Violence riddled nineteenth-century America, and nowhere was it more apparent than in the South, where the code duello persisted long after lawmakers banned it. Statistical compilations on homicide go back more than a century, and they leave little doubt that an extraordinary level of personal violence plagued the South. The reasons for this record are hotly debated among scholars, but cultural influences that stressed a strong code of honor were certainly critical. Not surprisingly, the excuse of self-defense had a particularly luxuriant growth in that region, nowhere more so than in the most violent state—Texas.

In the following case, the defendant, who drove a horse-drawn hack in Waco,

*Texas, stabbed to death a customer who became belligerent and refused to pay the
proper fare. He was found guilty of second-degree murder and sentenced to seven
years in the penitentiary.*

WILSON, JUDGE. It cannot be questioned but that the evidence is sufficient to sustain
the conviction. It is not so clear and conclusive of the defendant's guilt, however, as
to exclude a lower grade of homicide than murder in the second degree, or justifiable homicide in self-defense. As we view the evidence, it demanded of the trial
court to instruct the jury, lst. Upon the law of murder in the second degree; 2nd.
Upon the law of manslaughter; and, 3d. Upon the law of self-defense. In the main
charge the court sufficiently, and with substantial correctness, explained to the jury
the law of murder in the second degree and of manslaughter.

It omitted entirely to submit the issue of self-defense. To supply this omission,
defendant's counsel requested a special instruction in the following language, viz.:
"If the jury believe, from all the facts and circumstances in evidence, that, at the
time of the difficulty between the deceased Moreland and the defendant Bell, and at
the time Bell inflicted the injury which proved fatal (if the jury find that Bell did
inflict the injury), that Bell did not intend to kill Moreland, and only intended by his
acts to defend himself from an unlawful and violent attack made upon him by
Moreland, and used no means in such resistance disproportioned to such attack,
considering the relative disproportion in size of the combatants (if there was such
disproportion), and Bell had reason to believe and did believe that such attack was
likely to endanger his own life, or result in serious bodily injury to himself, then the
homicide would be justifiable, and the jury will acquit." This special charge was
given, and it consitutes the only charge given to the jury upon the issue of self-
defense,—nor did the defendant request any additional charge upon the subject.

At the time of the trial no exceptions were taken by the defendant to the charge
of the court or any portion of it, but in his motion for a new trial several objections
to it are urged, which are insisted upon in this court, and among them, that "the
court erred in failing to define justifiable homicide, and in failing to submit to the
jury proper issues arising upon the evidence as to the law of self-defense and
justifiable homicide." This objection is, we think, well taken. As far as it goes the
special charge we have quoted is correct and applicable to the evidence. It does not,
however, go far enough. It does not give *all* the law of self-defense demanded by the
evidence. It should have stated that the defendant, if unlawfully attacked by the
deceased, was not bound to retreat in order to avoid the necessity of killing
him. . . . This is a very material part of the law of self-defense, and is a statutory
innovation upon the common law, and upon the common view of what constitutes
self-defense. The common law required the assailed party to "retreat to the wall,"
and this requirement, while it no longer exists as the law of this State, is still
believed by many who are unlearned in the law to be in force. In all cases, therefore,
where the issue of self-defense arises from the evidence, the jury should be instructed that the assailed party is not bound to retreat in order to make perfect his
right of self-defense. And when the evidence presents the issue of self-defense, the
law, and *all* the law, applicable to that issue, as made by the evidence, should be
given in charge to the jury, whether requested or not. . . .

When the court omits to do this it is error, and, if excepted to at the time of the trial, the conviction would necessarily be set aside. But if the error be not excepted to, but be called to the attention of the trial court for the first time in a motion for new trial, it will not be cause for reversal unless it should appear to this court that the defendant's rights have probably been injured thereby. . . .

In the case before us, the inquiry therefore arises, did the error of the court, in failing to instruct the jury that the defendant was not bound to retreat, probably weaken his plea of self-defense, and prejudice his legal rights in respect thereto? In view of the evidence in the case, we must say that in our opinion it was calculated to have that effect. It was within the power of the defendant to have retreated, and by this means to have avoided the necessity of killing the deceased. It may have been the opinion of the jury that he should have retreated, and that, as he did not in this way avoid his assailant, he was not justified in slaying him. They should have been told by the court that the law of this State does not require retreat under any circumstances. By giving the special charge requested, the trial judge conceded, and we think correctly, that the issue of self-defense was presented by the evidence, and this special charge called his attention to that issue, and, being imperfect, it was the duty of the court to supply its defects by additional instructions. Because the charge as requested was not as full as the law required, should not, we think, be regarded as a waiver by the defendant of his right to a full and correct charge, and should not be held to relieve the court of the duty of giving such charge. Considering the evidence of this case, we think the failure of the court to give in charge article 573 of the Penal Code was material error calculated to injure the rights of the defendant, and is therefore reversible error although not excepted to at the time of the trial.

*   *   *

But we are not prepared to say that the special charge was even abstractly correct, especially in view of the evidence in the case. It was not shown clearly that the wounds inflicted upon deceased were inflicted with a knife, and, if with a knife, that it was such a one as was calculated ordinarily to produce death or serious bodily injury, when used in the manner and under the circumstances here shown. There were but two wounds upon deceased, one in the arm, which was slight, and the other in the temple above the eye, which proved fatal. These wounds were made with some sharp pointed instrument and were small. It is quite reasonable to infer that the wounds were made with a knife, but still the testimony does not place this conclusion beyond doubt. If made with a knife, evidently it was a small one, as demonstrated by the small size of the wounds. The fatal wound was fatal because perhaps of its locality. The instrument used penetrated at the suture or lap in the skull bone, fracturing the bone to some extent, and wounding the brain, producing meningitis which caused death. Had the blow fallen on almost any other portion of the body it might not have been serious, much less mortal. Therefore, the fact that the wound produced death does not of itself warrant the deduction that the instrument used was of a character calculated ordinarily, when so used, to produce death or serious bodily injury.

It is not every *knife* that is a deadly or even a dangerous weapon, and yet with any kind of a knife it is possible, no doubt, to produce death or serious bodily injury.

A small sewing needle is not an instrument that could be considered deadly or dangerous, and yet one skilled in human anatomy might, under favorable circumstances, use it with fatal effect, or it might be so used accidentally, or without any intention to kill or seriously injure. Considering the absence of any evidence, except the fatal result of the wound, to show the deadly or dangerous character of the weapon used, we are of the opinion that the special charge is not even abstractly correct when viewed with reference to the facts of this case, and that under the circumstances it was erroneous, and prejudicial to the defendant's rights. It was furthermore not in harmony with the main charge, which submitted to the jury, as a question to be determined from the evidence, whether or not, in inflicting the blows, it was the intention of the defendant to kill or inflict serious bodily injury. The special charge, in a great measure, supplied this question of fact with a presumption of the law, and that, too, without explaining that this presumption of the law was not a conclusive one, but that it might be removed by other evidence showing an absence of such criminal intent. The *intent* with which the wounds were inflicted was a most vital issue to the defendant. Upon this pivot hung his fate. In the main charge this issue was properly submitted to the jury to be determined by them from the evidence, without the aid of any presumption of law, except that the defendant should be presumed innocent until his guilt was established by competent evidence. Here, we think, upon this issue, the charge should have rested.

*   *   *

We are of the opinion that the facts of this case are of a character which demanded of the trial court a full and correct charge upon justifiable homicide in self-defense, and also a full and correct charge upon the issue of the defendant's intent in inflicting the wounds, leaving the jury to determine that intent from the evidence in the case, without incumbering such determination with any arbitrary presumption of the law, adverse to the presumption of innocence. Believing that he has not had the benefit of such a charge, and that thereby his rights have probably been prejudiced, the judgment is reversed and the cause is remanded.

Reversed and remanded.

Note: The South and Self-Defense

The penal codes of several southern states tolerated the taking of lives in personal disputes. Texas, however, was exceptional. All other southern states (and northern ones as well) adopted the rule of "duty to retreat." Simply put, it meant that in a life-threatening situation an assailed person was required to "retreat to the wall." Only after having done so could that person claim that he had acted in self-defense. The so-called Texas rule put forth in *Bell* was strikingly different. It permitted a person under attack to "stand his ground" and kill his assailant; he had no duty to retreat.

Differences in the rules of self-defense did not predict the incidence of personal assault and homicide. For example, the Alabama Supreme Court strongly endorsed the "duty to retreat" rule, but bloodletting in that state was above the national average and close to that of Texas. Different legal rules for self-defense, along with the insanity defense, seem to have reflected cultural and moral assumptions. The "stand-one's-ground" rule merely supported the ethical etiquette of duelists.

Late-Nineteenth-Century Crime and Morality

Colonial lawmakers had lavished great attention on regulating moral behavior by proscribing sexual practices, such as adultery and fornication. During the nineteenth century, these concerns ebbed as lawmakers shifted their attention to crimes against property. By the end of the century, however, another wave of moral purity swept the nation. For instance, several states passed legislation that regulated the production, sale, and consumption of alcoholic beverages. This new moral reform movement, as we have seen, also sought to criminalize abortion and the dissemination of birth-control information in the belief that both of these practices were already fomenting moral debauchery.

The increasingly independent and national character of late-nineteenth-century American society continually frustrated proponents of moral purity. They achieved some success at the state level, but they realized that only federal laws could stem what they believed to be a rush of immorality. The most important federal statute was the Comstock Act (1873), named after Anthony Comstock, a failed New York businessman and prominent moral reformer.

The Comstock Act was passed at the urging of Comstock, Vice President Henry Wilson, and Supreme Court Justice William Strong. Comstock personified the excesses of the moral purity movement that formed such a central part of the Victorian era. For example, he hounded Madame Restell, a wealthy operator of a New York City bordello and abortion clinic, until she committed suicide. For his efforts, Comstock was made special agent to enforce the act named for him.

Several states passed their own versions of the national legislation. In 1879, the Connecticut legislature adopted the harshest of these "Little" Comstock Acts. There, the great circus promoter Phineas T. Barnum successfully urged legislators to make the *use* of contraceptive materials a crime.

Ex parte Jackson
96 U.S. 727 (1877)

The Comstock Act derived its authority from the power vested in Congress to establish "post-offices and post-roads." But the act was also an opening chapter in Congress's development of a federal police power. The act chipped away at the once exclusive authority of the states to provide for the health, safety, morals, and welfare of their residents. In this case, Jackson sought a writ of habeas corpus on the grounds that he was being restrained by the United States marshal for the Southern District of New York after having been convicted of violating that provision of the Comstock Act that made it illegal to mail a circular concerning a lottery that offered prizes.

MR. JUSTICE FIELD, after stating the case, delivered the opinion of the court.

The power vested in Congress "to establish post-offices and post-roads" has been practically construed, since the foundation of the government, to authorize, not merely the designation of the routes over which the mail shall be carried, and the offices where letters and other documents shall be received to be distributed or forwarded, but the carriage of the mail, and all measures necessary to secure its safe and speedy transit, and the prompt delivery of its contents. The validity of legislation prescribing what should be carried, and its weight and form, and the charges to which it should be subjected, has never been questioned. What should be mailable has varied at different times, changing with the facility of transportation over the post-roads. At one time, only letters, newspapers, magazines, pamphlets, and other printed matter, not exceeding eight ounces in weight, were carried; afterwards books were added to the list; and now small packages of merchandise, not exceeding a prescribed weight, as well as books and printed matter of all kinds, are transported in the mail. The power possessed by Congress embraces the regulation of the entire postal system of the country. The right to designate what shall be carried necessarily involves the right to determine what shall be excluded. The difficulty attending the subject arises, not from the want of power in Congress to prescribe regulations as to what shall constitute mail matter, but from the necessity of enforcing them consistently with rights reserved to the people, of far greater importance than the transportation of the mail. In their enforcement, a distinction is to be made between different kinds of mail matter,—between what is intended to be kept free from inspection, such as letters, and sealed packages subject to letter postage; and what is open to inspection, such as newspapers, magazines, pamphlets, and other printed matter, purposely left in a condition to be examined. Letters and sealed packages of this kind in the mail are as fully guarded from examination and inspection, except as to their outward form and weight, as if they were retained by the parties forwarding them in their own domiciles. The constitutional guaranty of the right of the people to be secure in their papers against unreasonable searches and seizures extends to their papers, thus closed against inspection, wherever they may be. Whilst in the mail, they can only be opened and examined under like warrant, issued upon similar oath or affirmation, particularly describing the thing to be seized, as is required when papers are subjected to search in one's own household. No law of Congress can place in the hands of officials connected with the postal service any authority to invade the secrecy of letters and such sealed packages in the mail; and all regulations adopted as to mail matter of this kind must be in subordination to the great principle embodied in the fourth amendment of the Constitution.

Nor can any regulations be enforced against the transportation of printed matter in the mail, which is open to examination, so as to interfere in any manner with the freedom of the press. Liberty of circulating is as essential to that freedom as liberty of publishing; indeed, without the circulation, the publication would be of little value. If, therefore, printed matter be excluded from the mails, its transportation in any other way cannot be forbidden by Congress.

*   *   *

In excluding various articles from the mail, the object of Congress has not been to interfere with the freedom of the press, or with any other rights of the people; but to refuse its facilities for the distribution of matter deemed injurious to the public morals. Thus, by the act of March 3, 1873, Congress declared "that no obscene, lewd, or lascivious book, pamphlet, picture, paper, print, or other publication of an indecent character, or any article or thing designed or intended for the prevention of conception or procuring of abortion, nor any article or thing intended or adapted for any indecent or immoral use or nature, nor any written or printed card, circular, book, pamphlet, advertisement, or notice of any kind, giving information, directly or indirectly, where, or how, or of whom, or by what means, either of the things before mentioned may be obtained or made, nor any letter upon the envelope of which, or postal-card upon which indecent or scurrilous epithets may be written or printed, shall be carried in the mail; and any person who shall knowingly deposit, or cause to be deposited, for mailing or delivery, any of the hereinbefore mentioned articles or things, . . . shall be deemed guilty of a misdemeanor, and, on conviction thereof, shall, for every offence, be fined not less than $100, nor more than $5,000, or imprinment at hard labor not less than one year nor more than ten years, or both, in the discretion of the judge."

All that Congress meant by this act was, that the mail should not be used to transport such corrupting publications and articles, and that any one who attempted to use it for that purpose should be punished. The same inhibition has been extended to circulars concerning lotteries,—institutions which are supposed to have a demoralizing influence upon the people. There is no question before us as to the evidence upon which the conviction of the petitioner was had; nor does it appear whether the envelope in which the prohibited circular was deposited in the mail was sealed or left open for examination. The only question for our determination relates to the constitutionality of the act; and of that we have no doubt.

The commitment of the petitioner to the county jail, until his fine was paid, was within the discretion of the court under the statute.

[Motion] Denied.

Note

Justice Stephen J. Field's opinion in *Jackson* underscored the great tensions in late-nineteenth-century jurisprudence. On the one hand, Field and other critics of legislative action, such as Thomas M. Cooley and Christopher Tiedeman, complained that government should leave individuals alone to make their own economic choices. On the other hand, Field's opinion makes clear that he, and his brethren, believed that government had a duty to promote moral behavior, even at the expense of individual rights.

People v. *Plath*
100 N.Y. 590 (1885)

Nowhere in the late nineteenth century were the ambiguities of criminal law greater and the tensions over sex roles and morality clearer than with regard to prostitution, a practice that was thoroughly illegal in every state.

RUGER, CH. J. The defendant was indicted and upon trial convicted of the crime of abduction, in that he "with force and arms feloniously did take one Katie Kavanaugh for the purpose of prostitution, she the said Katie Kavanaugh being then and there a female under the age of sixteen years." It was essential to the support of this conviction that the people show, not only a taking by the defendant within the meaning of the statute, but also that such taking was for the purpose of prostitution. Penal Code, 282; as amended by 2 chap. 46, Laws of 1884. If the evidence establishes only a taking and fails to show that it was *for the prohibited purpose* it is insufficient to sustain the conviction, and so proof of the fact that the person of the female was used for purposes of prostitution without proof of the abduction would not bring the accused within the condemnation of the statute. It is elementary, when a specific intent is required to make an act an offense, that the doing of the act does not raise a presumption that it was done with the specific intent. . . . Neither can a conviction under this act be sustained upon the unsupported evidence of the female abducted.

* * *

An examination of the proof in this case fails to disclose any evidence corroborating the testimony of the female alleged to have been abducted, as to the participation of the defendant in the abduction, assuming that her evidence established a taking within the meaning of the statute. We have, however, grave doubts as to the sufficiency of such evidence to establish such taking. . . . But passing over that question, we will examine the evidence which it is claimed corroborated the testimony of the abducted female.

Her evidence was to the effect that in July, 1884, the defendant kept a dance hall or concert saloon and drinking place in Chatham street, New York, and had no previous acquaintance with, or knowledge of the witness, her friends or family; that she was a young girl about fifteen years of age, of somewhat dissolute character, residing with her parents at Newark; that some time in the latter part of July, in company with a young companion, the former inmate of a house of prostitution, of her own free will, she visited New York without the consent of her parents, and in strolling about the streets came to the defendant's saloon and entered. After sitting in the bar room for awhile she saw the defendant go behind the bar, and asked him "how much it was to see the entertainment;" he replied "nothing, my little dear, come in." He then treated the girls to soda water and asked them if they came to stay, to which Kavanaugh replied that she did. He then invited the girls to go upstairs and while there offered Kavanaugh a dress which she declined. He also took indecent liberties with the persons of both girls and after remaining there about twenty minutes left them. Both girls voluntarily remained in the place several days, and the Kavanaugh girl for about one month, during which time she had intercourse with a large number of men. No evidence was furnished by the prosecution showing that the defendant knew the true name of the girl *or the place of residence of herself or family, or that he had had any previous acquaintance with her or knowledge of her family*, or their circumstances or condition. No direct proof was given to establish the existence of any fact testified to by Kavanaugh, but she was attempted to be supported by circumstances alone. Two witnesses testified that they visited defendant's saloon the latter part of August and found quite a number of women and men assembled there engaged in dancing, drinking, and sitting around together among whom was Kavanaugh. They asked defendant if he had there a girl by the name of Kavanaugh who came from Newark. Defendant denied any knowledge of such a girl, and offered to allow them to search the premises for her. While they were talking Kavanaugh disappeared. It nowhere appeared that defendant was acquainted with the true name of Kavanaugh, or that she came from Newark. The witnesses also inspected the upper rooms of the saloon and there found a number of small apartments filled with beds and bunks; they saw women intoxicated and some quarreling and fighting going on. Afterward in September, one of the witnesses saw a man and woman in bed together there, and the man stated that he was not the husband of the woman. A physical examination of the girl revealed appearances indicating that attempts at sexual intercourse with her had been made, but that in fact it never had been accomplished. Beyond this no evidence was given looking toward corroboration of the testimony of the alleged abducted female.

We are utterly unable to see how this evidence tends to prove any of the facts going to show the agency of the defendant, in inducing Kavanaugh either to come to or remain in his place, unless a presumption of criminal persuasion is always to be imputed to a person with whom a dissolute female is domiciled. That he kept a disorderly house and was engaged in a vile and reprehensible occupation is quite sufficiently demonstrated, and that the object of Kavanaugh's residence in his house was presumably for the purpose of prostitution; but there is nothing in the corroborative proof inconsistent with the theory that her stay there was the result of her own will, uninfluenced by any persuasion, allurement or device of the defendant. The evidence does not tend to show that the influences inducting Kavanaugh to come or remain at the defendant's house were any different from those operating upon the other inmates of the place or upon females generally, who had not become inmates.

It is a lamentable fact that a life of prostitution presents attractions to some young and inexperienced females and that many are induced to enter upon it by the expectation of pleasures to be derived, wants to be supplied, or disagreeable social conditions to be escaped, and that from some or all of these causes combined, the haunts of vice and immorality are too largely supplied; but the statute in question was not intended to provide a remedy for this evil, or prescribe a punishment for those who keep such places. There is nothing in the section of the act under which defendant was convicted making the employment of a female under sixteen years of age for purposes of prostitution or sexual intercourse a criminal offense, *except where it is accompanied with a taking of her person by some active agency for such purpose*. The word "takes" seems to be used to distinguish the act prohibited, from those where the female is merely received, or permitted and allowed to follow a life of prostitution without persuasive inducement by the person accused.

The statutory age under which the consent of the female does not deprive the act of sexual intercourse of its criminal effect is fixed at ten years, but over that age the act in question does not make such intercourse a crime if effected without persuasion or device, by the free will and consent of the female. The same evidence which has been produced against the defendant in this case could doubtless be given as to every keeper of a brothel or disorderly house in New York, and it would tend to impair confidence in the administration of the law and confound the distinction in crimes made by statute to permit this conviction to be upheld upon the proof shown by the record. Every criminal, however vile, has a right to require that the elements of his offense shall be clearly defined by law and established by legal proof before he can be convicted thereof, and until then he may safely assert his immunity from punishment for any offense which is not thus defined and proved. The defendant in this case is entitled to the same presumption of innocence which prevails in other cases, and we are constrained to say that evidence has not been given here rebutting such presumption.

We think the evidence was insufficient in the absence of the proper confirmatory proof to warrant his conviction, and that the judgment of the General Term and Sessions should be reversed and a new trial granted.

All concur.

Judgment reversed.

Note: Prostitution in Nineteenth-Century America

In many ways, what public authorities sought to deal with in the nineteenth century was not so much sin as sin in public. Prostitution was thoroughly illegal, but it flourished everywhere; it continued to exist by tacit agreement between brothel owners and public authorities. That understanding required, however, that prostitution remain within specific geographical limits and that owners not force or entice young girls into the world's oldest profession. In the American West, where until the early twentieth century men greatly outnumbered women, prostitution was an important and apparently profitable business. However, in major urban areas, prostitution was closely linked with vice and other criminal activities associated with the dangerous classes. In some cities, such as Detroit, brothel riots occurred, in which local citizens, angry that authorities continued to countenance the practice, took matters into their own hands. But in most instances, an accommodation was reached. As long as prostitution remained underground and off the streets, the authorities winked at it.

A few nineteenth-century cities, most notably St. Louis and New Orleans, attempted to regulate the practice by passing ordinances defining so-called red-light districts. The punishments meted out were invariably greater for those who ran houses of prostitution or procured girls and women into the service than it was for the prostitute.

Brothels became the object of special attack during the late nineteenth century as the moral purity movement swung into action. These establishments served as more than sexual pleasure domes; they were also centers of information about birth control and abortion.

The New York statute at issue in *Plath* was typical of measures passed in most states that made the "taking" of a female under a certain age (usually sixteen) for the purposes of prostitution a crime. Legislators sought not so much to eliminate prostitution as to shield children from its scourge. The concern of men like Comstock for moral purity fitted nicely with a growing drive to provide juvenile justice.

6

Bench, Bar, and Legal Reform
in the Nineteenth Century

No living legal system can remain static; change here, as elsewhere, is inevitable. American law from the Jacksonian era through World War I was no exception. John Adams, Thomas Jefferson, and other legal reformers of the late eighteenth century modified the inherited British legal order to eliminate all traces of monarchy, aristocracy, and any legal institutions, such as an established church and a standing army, that seemed incompatible with the republican societies they were creating. But beyond such innovations, American lawyers trod carefully. Cautious and piecemeal reform, not revolution, was the norm. American lawyers of the Revolutionary generation saw to it that the basis of legal systems in the new republic was to be the common law. They cherished this body of law as venerable and familiar, especially because it seemed an anchor of stability in a time of rapid social change.

Legal reform evoked ambivalent reactions from American lawyers. As heirs to the republican Revolution, they championed renovation of law and social institutions (e.g., abolition of imprisonment for debt and reduction of the catalogue of capital offenses). But, conversely, they did not want to move too fast. This ambivalence gave the internal impetus for law reform its cautious, sometimes reluctant, character.

The antebellum era was a time of unequaled reform. America's future, like the North American continent itself, seemed boundless, an infinite field on which to realize the dreams of republicanism, democracy, and reformed religion. Dazzled by this prospect and little restrained by the past, Americans seemed to proliferate endless ideas for reforming their society. Nothing in American society seemed to be immune from demands that it be new-modeled. Religion, government, education, care for society's outcasts, family life, personal health and hygiene, recreation, business practice were all vulnerable to criticism. In such a climate, law itself could not be exempt from the universal demand for reform. Law was also an instrument to realize many nonlegal reforms, such as the fight against Demon Rum.

But not everyone embraced change, especially when it seemed to affect their personal interests or beliefs, and so some Americans looked askance at demands for reform. As we might expect, lawyers were foremost among those skeptical of change, particularly when reform would have an impact on the law itself. Yet their resistance to innovation in the law imposed from the outside conflicted with their need to promote renovation from within.

Many aspects of the law's development in the nineteenth century were affected by the crosscurrents of reform. The documents in this chapter first sketch the lawyer's place in American society, seen through the eyes of both lay people and lawyers themselves, since the image of lawyers had as great an impact on legal change as the role they actually played in society. Next we will review attacks on the common law itself, and lawyers' defensive reactions to that assault. Then we will review the mode of selecting judges, which provided a ready target for reformers' attentions.

Lawyers are not born; they are made, and the process of making them is accomplished by legal education. The methods of schooling future lawyers came under critical scrutiny. While lawyers monopolized all avenues of professional socialization, they had no ready-made formula for instructing those who would follow them. The evolution of legal education reflected ideological developments in the way that lawyers thought about the law. But those ideological currents in their turn reflected the way that lawyers perceived the law's relationship to the larger society. We conclude this chapter with turn-of-the-century lawyers' visions of the role of law in American life.

The Lawyer in American Society

The lawyer has been a by-word of notoriety in English and American society for at least four centuries. The attitudes of early Americans toward attorneys were ambivalent at best. Some seventeenth-century colonies prohibited lawyering altogether. It was to be expected in homogeneous colonies, like Connecticut, that were established as religious utopias, but it appeared in purely commercial colonies too. John Locke declared in the 1669 Fundamental Constitutions of Carolina that it is "a base and vile thing to plead for money or reward."[1] Quaker settlements discouraged litigation in favor of what is today called alternative dispute resolution. An early-eighteenth-century observer wrote back home about Pennsylvania: "They have no lawyers. Everyone is to tell his own case, or some friend for him. . . . 'Tis a happy country."[2]

But Americans in the eighteenth century discovered that lawyers were a necessary evil, as their societies and economies grew more complex, as homogeneous and close-knit towns gave way to heterogeneous, scattered communities, and as religious constraints on behavior weakened. Antilawyer animosity persisted, however. In 1765, Cadwallader Colden, the lieutenant governor of New York, complained to the Board of Trade that law practice in his colony was "carried on by the same wicked artifices that the Domination of Priests formerly was in the times of ignorance."[3] Yet the bar and the common law it administered survived the Revolution, emerging more powerful than ever. Despite the adverse public-relations climate in which lawyers seem doomed to labor inescapably, the legal profession has triumphantly weathered all attacks on it, emerging from each successive assault more firmly ensconced in the seats of power.

Lemuel Shaw on Lawyering
1827

Chief Justice Lemuel Shaw of the Massachusetts Supreme Judicial Court believed that law is a science and that its practitioners have an exalted mission as guard-

ians of the American republican tradition. In this address to Boston lawyers in
1827, Shaw provided a rationale for professional resistance to the spread of
popular democracy in the age of Jackson.

Let us then, gentlemen, proceed to consider the condition, the importance and
utility of the profession of the law, in the actual situation and prospects of the United
States.

*   *   *

In a free, representative government, founded upon enlarged and liberal views,
designed to secure the rights, to promote the industry and to advance the happiness
of a great community, and adapted to a high state of civilization and improvement, it
is of the highest importance that there should be a body of men, trained, by a well
adapted course of education and study, to a thorough and profound knowledge of the
law, and practically skilled in its application, whose privilege and duty it is, in
common with their fellow citizens, to exert a fair share of influence in the enactment
of laws, and whose peculiar duty and exclusive occupation it is, to assist in the
application of them to practice in the administration of justice, in its various
departments.

*   *   *

. . . As those who govern, claim not to exercise an inherent power, but simply
to execute a delegated authority, created, regulated, and limited by law, there is no
inconsistency in considering such authority as equally supreme, over those who
exercise it, and those upon whom it operates. Whilst [free government] thus professes to derive its whole authority from the natural right and power of the people to
provide for their own safety and happiness, and thus absolutely exclude the assumption of all arbitrary and extrinsic power, it guards with equal vigilance against the
violence and encroachments of a wild and licentious democracy, by a well balanced
constitution; such a constitution as at once restrains the violent and irregular action
of mere popular will, and calls to the aid, and secures in the service of the government, the enlightened wisdom, the pure morals, the cultivated reason, and matured
experience of its ablest and best members.

*   *   *

Our government, throughout its entire fabric, professes to be a free, representative government. It is peculiarly, exclusively, and emphatically a government of
laws. The constitutions of the United States, and of the several states, with all their
provisions and limitations, are regarded, and very properly regarded, as part of the
laws. . . . To these fundamental laws, every individual citizen has a right to appeal,
and does constantly appeal, in the discussion and establishment of his rights, civil as
well as political. In an equal degree, they regulate and control the highest functions
of government, determine the just sources and limits, and regulate the distribution
of all powers, executive, legislative, and judicial. These principles may, at any
time, be drawn in question before the tribunals of justice, and are subject to the
same rules of judicial interpretation, with all other legal provisions. It is difficult to
conceive of the vast extent, to which this consideration enlarges the field of American jurisprudence, and increases the functions, and elevates the duties and character
of the American lawyer.

"If," says Sir William Jones, "law be a science, and really deserve so sublime a name, it must be founded on principle, and claim an exalted rank in the empire of reason." If such be the just character of the law, when regarded as a system of civil and criminal jurisprudence, how much more eminently does it maintain that character, when, in addition to these subjects, it embraces within its range, the whole science of political philosophy. Hence we daily witness, under the head of "constitutional law," a title hardly known in any other system of jurisprudence the profoundest discussions at the bar, and the ablest decisions from the bench, almost without the aid of precedent, because they involve questions, which have never before been raised, in which the principles of social duty, of natural and conventional obligation, are considered, distinguished, and applied, with that sagacity, reach of thought, and scientific skill, which can be derived only from a thorough and intimate acquaintance with the philosophy of the mind.

*   *   *

. . . I am aware that there are some persons who maintain, that the law is a system of artifical and technical rules, having little regard to principle, and that he is the best lawyer, who has the most tenacious memory, and who is most skilful and adroit in using the weapons furnished by these rules. Others again maintain, that natural justice is sufficient to settle all controverted questions, and that every case may be well settled upon its own particular equities. Both of these views are unquestionably partial and erroneous. Whilst the law is a science founded upon reason and principle, and no law can stand the test of strict inquiry which palpably violates the dictates of natural justice, yet it is also a system of precise and practical rules, adapted to regulate the rights and duties of persons in an infinite variety of cases, in which natural law is silent or indifferent, and yet where it is of the utmost importance that there should be a fixed rule.

Alexis de Tocqueville on Lawyers and Judges
1835

In 1835, the French visitor Alexis de Tocqueville offered striking observations on the actual workings of popular sovereignty, judicial power, and lawyers in the bumptious American democracy that so fascinated him. Tocqueville was astonishingly perceptive in his own time; do his remarks remain as relevant and valid for today's society?

Whenever a law that the judge holds to be unconstitutional is invoked in a tribunal of the United States, he may refuse to admit it as a rule; this power is the only one peculiar to the American magistrate, but it gives rise to immense political influence. In truth, few laws can escape the searching analysis of the judicial power for any length of time, for there are few that are not prejudicial to some private interest or other, and none that may not be brought before a court of justice by the choice of parties or by the necessity of the case. But as soon as a judge has refused to apply any given law in a case, that law immediately loses a portion of its moral force.

*   *   *

Within these limits the power vested in the American courts of justice of pronouncing a statute to be unconstitutional forms one of the most powerful barriers that have ever been devised against the tyranny of political assemblies.

*   *   *

When we have examined in detail the organization of the [United States] Supreme Court and the entire prerogatives which it exercises, we shall readily admit that a more imposing judicial power was never constituted by any people. The Supreme Court is placed higher than any other known tribunal, both by the nature of its rights and the class of justiciable parties which it controls.

*   *   *

The peace, the prosperity, and the very existence of the Union are vested in the hands of the seven Federal judges [of the United States Supreme Court]. Without them the Constitution would be a dead letter: the executive appeals to them for assistance against the encroachments of the legislative power; the legislature demands their protection against the assaults of the executive; they defend the Union from the disobedience of the states, the states from the exaggerated claims of the Union, the public interest against private interests, and the conservative spirit of stability against the fickleness of the democracy. Their power is enormous, but it is the power of public opinion. They are all-powerful as long as the people respect the law; but they would be impotent against popular neglect or contempt of the law. The force of public opinion is the most intractable of agents, because its exact limits cannot be defined; and it is not less dangerous to exceed than to remain below the boundary prescribed.

*   *   *

Democratic laws generally tend to promote the welfare of the greatest possible number; for they emanate from the majority of the citizens, who are subject to error, but who cannot have an interest opposed to their own advantage. The laws of an aristocracy tend, on the contrary, to concentrate wealth and power in the hands of the minority; because an aristocracy, by its very nature, constitutes a minority. It may therefore be asserted, as a general proposition, that the purpose of a democracy in its legislation is more useful to humanity than that of an aristocracy. This, however, is the sum total of its advantages.

*   *   *

No political form has hitherto been discovered that is equally favorable to the prosperity and the development of all the classes into which society is divided. These classes continue to form, as it were, so many distinct communities in the same nation; and experience has shown that it is no less dangerous to place the fate of these classes exclusively in the hands of any one of them than it is to make one people the arbiter of the destiny of another. When the rich alone govern, the interest of the poor is always endangered; and when the poor make the laws, that of the rich incurs very serious risks. The advantage of democracy does not consist, therefore, as has sometimes been asserted, in favoring the prosperity of all, but simply in contributing to the well-being of the greatest number.

The men who are entrusted with the direction of public affairs in the United States are frequently inferior, in both capacity and morality, to those whom an aristocracy would raise to power. But their interest is identified and mingled with that of the majority of their fellow citizens. They may frequently be faithless and frequently mistaken, but they will never systematically adopt a line of conduct hostile to the majority; and they cannot give a dangerous or exclusive tendency to the government.

*   *   *

It is not always feasible to consult the whole people, either directly or indirectly, in the formation of law; but it cannot be denied that, when this is possible, the authority of law is much augmented. This popular origin which impairs the excellence and the wisdom of legislation, contributes much to increase its power. There is an amazing strength in the expression of the will of a whole people; and when it declares itself, even the imagination of those who would wish to contest it is overawed. The truth of this fact is well known by parties, and they consequently strive to make out a majority whenever they can. If they have not the greater number of voters on their side, they assert that the true majority abstained from voting; and if they are foiled even there, they have recourse to those persons who had no right to vote.

In the United States, except slaves, servants, and paupers supported by the townships, there is no class of persons who do not exercise the elective franchise and who do not indirectly contribute to make the laws. Those who wish to attack the laws must consequently either change the opinion of the nation or trample upon its decision.

A second reason, which is still more direct and weighty, may be adduced: in the United States everyone is personally interested in enforcing the obedience of the whole community to the law; for as the minority may shortly rally the majority to its principles, it is interested in professing that respect for the decrees of the legislator which it may soon have occasion to claim for its own. However irksome an enactment may be, the citizen of the United States complies with it, not only because it is the work of the majority, but because it is his own, and he regards it as a contract to which he is himself a party.

In the United States, then, that numerous and turbulent multitude does not exist who, regarding the law as their natural enemy, look upon it with fear and distrust. It is impossible, on the contrary, not to perceive that all classes display the utmost reliance upon the legislation of their country and are attached to it by a kind of parental affection.

*   *   *

In visiting the Americans and studying their laws, we perceive that the authority they have entrusted to members of the legal profession, and the influence that these individuals exercise in the government, are the most powerful existing security against the excesses of democracy. This effect seems to me to result from a general cause, which it is useful to investigate, as it may be reproduced elsewhere. . . .

Men who have made a special study of the laws derive from [that] occupation certain habits of order, a taste for formalities, and a kind of instinctive regard for the regular connection of ideas, which naturally render them very hostile to the revolutionary spirit and the unreflecting passions of the multitude.

The special information that lawyers derive from their studies ensures them a separate rank in society, and they constitute a sort of privileged body in the scale of intellect. This notion of their superiority perpetually recurs to them in the practice of their profession: they are the masters of a science which is necessary, but not very generally known; they serve as arbiters between the citizens; and the habit of directing to their purpose the blind passions of parties in litigation inspires them with a certain contempt for the judgment of the multitude. Add to this that they naturally constitute a body; not by any previous understanding, or by an agreement that directs them to a common end; but the analogy of their studies and the uniformity of their methods connect their minds as a common interest might unite their endeavors.

Some of the tastes and the habits of the aristocracy may consequently be discovered in the characters of lawyers. They participate in the same instinctive love of order and formalities; and they entertain the same repugnance to the actions of the multitude, and the same secret contempt of the government of the people. I do not mean to say that the natural propensities of lawyers are sufficiently strong to sway them irresistibly; for they, like most other men, are governed by their private interests, and especially by the interests of the moment.

*   *   *

I do not, then, assert that all the members of the legal profession are at all times the friends of order and the opponents of innovation, but merely that most of them are usually so. In a community to which lawyers are allowed to occupy without opposition that high station which naturally belongs to them, their general spirit will be eminently conservative and anti-democratic. When an aristocracy excludes the leaders of that profession from its ranks, it excites enemies who are the more formidable as they are independent of the nobility by their labors and feel themselves to be their equals in intelligence though inferior in opulence and power.

*   *   *

Lawyers are attached to public order beyond every other consideration, and the best security of public order is authority. It must not be forgotten, also, that if they prize freedom much, they generally value legality still more; they are less afraid of tyranny than of arbitrary power; and, provided the legislature undertakes of itself to deprive men of their independence, they are not dissatisfied.

*   *   *

The government of democracy is favorable to the political power of lawyers; for when the wealthy, the noble, and the prince are excluded from the government, the lawyers take possession of it, in their own right, as it were, since they are the only men of information and sagacity, beyond the sphere of the people, who can be the object of the popular choice. If, then, they are led by their tastes towards the aristocracy and the prince, they are brought in contact with the people by their interests. They like the government of democracy without participating in its propensities and without imitating its weaknesses; whence they derive a two-fold authority from it and over it. The people in democratic states do not mistrust the members of the legal profession, because it is known that they are interested to serve the popular cause; and the people listen to them without irritation, because they do not attribute to them any sinister designs. The lawyers do not, indeed, wish to overthrow the institutions of democracy, but they constantly endeavor to turn it away from its real direction by means that are foreign to its nature. Lawyers belong to the people by birth and interest, and to the aristocracy by habit and taste; they may be looked upon as the connecting link between the two great classes of society.

The profession of the law is the only aristocratic element that can be amalgamated without violence with the natural elements of democracy and be advantageously and permanently combined with them. I am not ignorant of the defects inherent in the character of this body of men; but without this admixture of lawyer-like sobriety with the democratic principle, I question whether democratic institutions could long be maintained; and I cannot believe that a republic could hope to exist at the present time if the influence of lawyers in public business did not increase in proportion to the power of the people.

        *   *   *

In America there are no nobles or literary men, and the people are apt to mistrust the wealthy; lawyers consequently form the highest political class and the most cultivated portion of society. They have therefore nothing to gain by innovation, which adds a conservative interest to their natural taste for public order. If I were asked where I place the American aristocracy, I should reply without hesitation that it is not among the rich, who are united by no common tie, but that it occupies the judicial bench and the bar.

The more we reflect upon all that occurs in the United States, the more we shall be persuaded that the lawyers, as a body, form the most powerful, if not the only, counterpoise to the democratic element. In that country we easily perceive how the legal profession is qualified by its attributes, and even by its faults, to neutralize the vices inherent in popular government. When the American people are intoxicated by passion or carried away by the impetuosity of their ideas, they are checked and stopped by the almost invisible influence of their legal counselors. These secretly oppose their aristocratic propensities to the nation's democratic instincts, their superstitious attachment to what is old to its love of novelty, their narrow views to its immense designs, and their habitual procrastination to its ardent impatience.

The courts of justice are the visible organs by which the legal profession is enabled to control the democracy. The judge is a lawyer who, independently of the taste for regularity and order that he has contracted in the study of law, derives an additional love of stability from the inalienability of his own functions. His legal attainments have already raised him to a distinguished rank among his fellows; his political power completes the distinction of his station and gives him the instincts of the privileged classes.

        *   *   *

It must not be supposed, moreover, that the legal spirit is confined in the United States to the courts of justice; it extends far beyond them. As the lawyers form the only enlightened class whom the people do not mistrust, they are naturally called upon to occupy most of the public stations. They fill the legislative assemblies and are at the head of the administration; they consequently exercise a powerful influence upon the formation of the law and upon its execution. The lawyers are obliged, however, to yield to the current public opinion, which is too strong for them to resist; but it is easy to find indications of what they would do if they were free to act. The Americans, who have made so many innovations in their political laws, have introduced very sparing alterations in their civil laws, and that with great difficulty, although many of these laws are repugnant to their social condition. The reason for this is that in matters of civil law the majority are obliged to defer to the authority of the legal profession, and the American lawyers are disinclined to innovate when they are left to their own choice.

*   *   *

The influence of legal habits extends beyond the precise limits I have pointed out. Scarcely any political question arises in the United States that is not resolved, sooner or later, into a judicial question. Hence all parties are obliged to borrow, in their daily controversies, the ideas, and even the language, peculiar to judicial proceedings. As most public men are or have been legal practitioners, they introduce the customs and technicalities of their profession into the management of public affairs. The jury extends this habit to all classes. The language of the law thus becomes, in some measure, a vulgar tongue; the spirit of the law, which is produced in the schools and courts of justice, gradually penetrates beyond their walls into the bosom of society, where it descends to the lowest classes, so that at last the whole people contract the habits and the tastes of the judicial magistrate. The lawyers of the United States form a party which is but little feared and scarcely perceived, which has no badge peculiar to itself, which adapts itself with great flexibility to the exigencies of the time and accommodates itself without resistance to all the movements of the social body. But this party extends over the whole community and penetrates into all the classes which compose it; it acts upon the country imperceptibly, but finally fashions it to suit its own purposes.

P. W. GRAYSON [pseud.]
"Vice Unmasked, an Essay: Being a Consideration of the Influence of Law upon the Moral Essence of Man . . ."
1830

The anonymous author of this diatribe reflected the tradition of popular hostility to lawyers. His condemnation was entirely negative, unlike both earlier and later examples of the genre, which offered constructive solutions to the problems presented by the stereotype of lawyers. Other critics would soon supply this defect, however, by proposing codification and an elective judiciary.

I have already sufficiently considered the demoralizing influence of law, as far as respects its own unaided operation, on the temper and principles of men. But I have yet to unfold another influence, of an entirely congenial stamp with the former, that operates, as I think, with wonderful force to inflame its mischievous power. It is that of a certain class of men, in short, we know by the name of lawyers, whom we find swarming in every hole and corner of society. I fear I shall present in them a picture of the seeds of depravity, at which philanthropy may fold her arms, in utter despair, and weep as though the cause of mankind were indeed irredeemably lost forever!

*   *   *

Their business is with statutes, dictates, decisions, and authority. They go on, emptying volume after volume, of all their heterogeneous contents, till they become so laden with other men's thoughts, as scarce to have any of their own. Seldom do their sad eyes look beyond the musty walls of authority, in which their souls are all perpetually immured. And now, as soon as their minds have come to be duly instructed, first, in the antique sophistries, substantial fictions, wise absurdities, and profound dogmas of buried sages, and then fairly liberalized by all the light of modern innovation, and of precious salutary change, do we see them step forward into the world, blown with the most triumphant pretensions, to deal out blessings to mankind. Now, indeed, they are ready to execute any prescription of either justice or injustice—to lend themselves to any side—to advocate any doctrine, for they are well provided with the means in venerable print. Eager for employment, they pry into the business of men, with snakish smoothness slip into the secrets of their affairs, discern the ingredients of litigation, and blow them up into strife. This is, indeed, but laboring in their vocation. For an honest lawyer, if, in strictness, there be such a phenomenon on earth, is an appearance entirely out of the common course of nature—a violent exception, and must therefore be esteemed a sort of prodigy.

Abject slaves of authority themselves, these counterfeits of men are now to be the proud dictators of human destiny, and withal the glittering favorites of fortune!

*   *   *

Again we hear it urged in their favor, that from dire necessity they must be true to their clients, at whatever cost of principle to themselves—that this fidelity to their client, who consigns his dearest interests, it may be even liberty or life, to their official custody, sufficiently cancels all the claims of morality, and amply atones for every obliquity they may find it convenient to practice, in the faithful discharge of grave professional duty. By the force of this venerable custom of thought, we find it has really become a matter of conscience, of high professional honor, for these men of the law to go all lengths that are possible—snatch all advantages, too, in their crafty endeavors to gain even the most unrighteous ends of their clients. Nothing, indeed, is more common, at this time of day, than to hear them gravely extolled as patterns of excellence, for no other merit, than, merely, the cunning trick and devotion they show in the unconscientious cause of their client.

*   *   *

Can there be a more pitiable sight than that we are here constrained to behold? Quite certain it is, that the law, if it do not absorb all the talents and genius of the country, attracts, at least, the choice of it all, and leaves but little more than the refuse for other callings. What then is this sight?—genius putting itself to sale —the brightest intelligence of the land offering itself a loose prostitute to the capricious use of all men alike, for gold!

RUFUS CHOATE

"The Position and Functions of the American Bar, as an Element of Conservatism in the State . . ."
1845

Rufus Choate was a prominent and conservative Massachusetts Whig attorney. His 1845 address, delivered to the students of Harvard Law School, summed up most of the ideological strands of Whiggish conservatism in antebellum America.

Had Choate's vision been fully realized, law in the United States would have developed into a barrier to all but the most incremental change. However, pressures from all points on the ideological compass rendered such a development impossible from the outset.

Instead of diffusing myself in a display of all the modes by which the profession of the law may claim to serve the State, I shall consider but a single one, and that is its agency as an element of conservation. The position and functions of the American Bar, then, as an element of conservation in the State,—this precisely and singly is the topic to which I invite your attention.

*   *   *

In our jurisprudence of liberty, which guards our person from violence and our goods from plunder, and which forbids the whole power of the State itself to take the ewe lamb, or to trample on a blade of grass of the humblest citizen without adequate remuneration; which makes every dwelling large enough to shelter a human life its owner's castle which winds and rain may enter but which the government cannot,—in our written constitutions, whereby the people, exercising an act of sublime self-restraint, have intended to put it out of their own power for ever, to be passionate, tumultuous, unwise, unjust; whereby they have intended, by means of a system of representation; by means of the distribution of government into departments, independent, coordinate for checks and balances; by a double chamber of legislation; by the establishment of a fundamental and paramount organic law; by the organization of a judiciary whose function, whose loftiest function it is to test the legislation of the day by this standard for all time,—constitutions, whereby by all these means they have intended to secure a government of laws, not of men; of reason, not of will; of justice, not of fraud,—in that grand dogma of equality, equality of right, of burthens, of duty, of privileges, and of chances, which is the very mystery of our social being,—to the Jews, a stumbling block; to the Greeks, foolishness,—our strength, our glory,—in that liberty which we value solely because it is a principle of individual energy and a guaranty of national renown; not at all because it attacts a procession and lights a bonfire, but because, when blended with order, attended by law, tempered by virtue, graced by culture, it is a great practical good; because in her right hand are riches, and honor, and peace; because she has come down from her golden and purple cloud to walk in brightness by the weary ploughman's side, and whisper in his ear as he casts the seed with tears, that the harvest which frost and mildew and canker-worm shall spare, the government shall spare also; in our distribution into separate and kindred States, not wholly independent, not quite identical, in "the wide arch of the ranged empire": above,—these are they in which the fruits of our age and our agency of reform are embodied; and these are they by which, if we are wise,—if we understand the things that belong to our peace,—they may be perpetuated. It is for this that I say the fields of reform, the aims of reform, the uses of reform here, therefore, are wholly unlike the fields, uses, and aims of reform elsewhere. Foreign examples, foreign counsel,—well or ill meant,—the advice of the first foreign understandings, the example of the wisest foreign nations, are worse than useless for us. Even the teachings of history are to be cautiously consulted, or the guide of human life will lead us astray.

We need reform enough, Heaven knows; but it is the reformation of our individual selves, the bettering of our personal natures; it is a more intellectual industry; it is a more diffused, profound, and graceful, popular and higher culture; it is a wider development of the love and discernment of the beautiful in form, in color, in speech, and in the soul of man,—this is what we need,—personal, moral, mental reform,—not civil—not political! No, no! Government, substantially as it is; jurisprudence, substantially as it is; the general arrangements of liberty, substantially as they are; the Constitution and the Union, exactly as they are,—this is to be wise, according to the wisdom of America.

*   *   *

It is one of the distempers to which an unreasoning liberty may grow, no doubt, to regard law as no more nor less than just the will—the actual and present will—of the actual majority of the nation. The majority govern. What the majority pleases, it may ordain. What it ordains is law. So much for the source of law, and so much for the nature of law. But, then, as law is nothing but the will of a major number, as that will differs from the will of yesterday, and will differ from that of to-morrow, and as all law is a restraint on natural right and personal independence, how can it gain a moment's hold on the reverential sentiments of the heart, and the profounder convictions of the judgment? How can it impress a filial awe; how can it conciliate a filial love; how can it sustain a sentiment of veneration, how can it command a rational and animated defence? Such sentiments are not the stuff from which the immortality of a nation is to be woven! Oppose now to this the loftier philosophy which we have learned. In the language of our system, the law is not the transient and arbitrary creation of the major will, nor of any will. It is not the offspring of will at all. It is the absolute justice of the State, enlightened by the perfect reason of the State. That is law. Enlightened justice assisting the social nature to perfect itself by the social life. It is ordained, doubtless, that is, it is chosen, and is ascertained by the wisdom of man. But, then, it is the master-work of man.

*   *   *

It is certain that in the American theory, the free theory of government, it is the right of the people, at any moment of its representation in the legislature, to make all the law, and, by its representatives in conventions, to make the Constitution anew. It is their right to do so peaceably and according to existing forms, and to do it by revolution against all forms. This is the theory. But I do not know that any wise man would desire to have this theory every day, or ever, acted upon up to its whole extent, or to have it eternally pressed, promulgated, panegyrized as the grand peculiarity and chief privilege of our condition. Acting upon this theory, we have made our constitutions, founded our policy, written the great body of our law, set our whole government going. It worked well. It works to a charm. . . . True wisdom would seem to advise the culture of dispositions of rest, contentment, conservation. True wisdom would advise to lock up the extreme medicine till the attack of the alarming malady. True wisdom would advise to place the power of revolution, overturning all to begin anew, rather in the background, to throw over it a politic, well-wrought veil, to reserve it for crises, exigencies, the rare and distant days of great historical epochs. These great, transcendental rights should be preserved, must be, will be. But perhaps you would place them away, reverentially, in the profoundest recesses of the chambers of the dead, down in deep vaults of black marble, lighted by a single silver lamp,—as in that vision of the Gothic king,—to which wise and brave men may go down, in the hour of extremity, to evoke the tremendous divinities of change from their sleep of ages.

*   *   *

Is there not somewhat in sharing in that administration, observing and enjoying it, which tends to substitute in the professional and in the popular mind, in place of the wild consciousness of possessing summary power, ultimate power, the wild desire to exert it, and to grasp and subject all things to its rule,—to substitute for this the more conservative sentiments of reverence for a law independent of, and distinct from, and antagonistical to, the humor of the hour? Is there not something in the study and administrative enjoyment of an elaborate, rational, and ancient juris-prudence, which tends to raise the law itself, in the professional and in the general idea, almost up to the nature of an independent, superior reason, in one sense out of the people, in one sense above them,—out of and above, and independent of, and collateral to, the people of any given day? In all its vast volumes of provisions, very little of it is seen to be produced by the actual will of the existing generation. The first thing we know about it is, that we are actually being governed by it. The next thing we know is, we are rightfully and beneficially governed by it. We did not help make it. No man now living helped to make much of it. The judge does not make it. Like the structure of the State itself, we found it around us at the earliest dawn of reason, it guarded the helplessness of our infancy, it restrained the passions of our youth, it protects the acquisitions of our manhood, it shields the sanctity of the grave, it executes the will of the departed. Invisible, omnipresent, a real yet impal-pable existence, it seems more a spirit, an abstraction,—the widespread yet au-thoritative voice of all the past and all the good,—than like the transient contrivance of altogether such as ourselves. We come to think of it, not so much as a set of provisions and rules which we can unmake, amend, and annul, as of a guide whom it is wiser to follow, an authority whom it is better to obey, a wisdom which it is not unbecoming to revere, a power,—a superior—whose service is perfect freedom. Thus at last the spirit of the law descends into the great heart of the people for healing and for conservation.

Codification

Lay people's distrust of lawyers reflected their doubts about the legal system that American lawyers administered—the common law. Some Americans projected law-reform schemes that included a complete or partial codification of the common law— that is, a comprehensive legislative enactment of the rules and principles that inhered in the common law. The ensuing struggle over codification distracted the attention of lawyers for most of the nineteenth century.

In one sense, there was nothing controversial or innovative about codification. Legislatures had been reorganizing their laws since the seventeenth century: omit-ting obsolete, contradictory, or superfluous statutes, updating old enactments, and compiling and reducing the work-product of annual or semiannual legislative sessions into coherent, comprehensive bodies of law reenacted as statutes. For example, South Carolina's slave law of 1740 was one such measure.

But this was not the kind of codification that more radical law reformers of the nineteenth century had in mind. They sought to reduce all law to a legislatively enacted body of general principles. Such a code would guide the deliberations of juries and limit judges' discretion. Under such a system, courts would simply apply the principles given them by the legislatures, rather than making up law as they went along, as in the common-law system.

ROBERT RANTOUL
"Oration at Scituate"
1836

Robert Rantoul was that rarest of creatures in the Jacksonian era—a liberal antislavery Democrat. He supported numerous reform causes, serving as counsel for the bootmakers in the case of Commonwealth v. Hunt *(1842) and for some of the Dorrites indicted in the aftermath of the Dorr Rebellion. Thus his critical attitude toward the common law, although unusual in a lawyer of his time, was compatible with his reformist bent. His Fourth of July oration went beyond the merely negative posture of condemning the common law, to a positive recommendation for reform—codification.*

The Common Law sprang from the dark ages; the fountain of justice is the throne of the Deity. The Common Law is but the glimmering taper by which men groped their way through the palpable midnight in which learning, wit, and reason were almost extinguished; justice shines with the splendor of that fulness of light which beams from the Ineffable Presence. The Common Law had its beginning in time, and in the time of ignorance; justice is eternal, even with the eternity of the allwise and just Lawgiver and Judge. The Common Law had its origin in folly, barbarism, and feudality; justice is the irradiance of divine wisdom, divine truth, and the government of infinite benevolence. While the Common Law sheds no light, but rather darkness visible, that serves but to discover sights of woe,—justice rises, like the Sun of Righteousness, with healing on his wings, scatters the doubts that torture without end, dispels the mists of scholastic subtilty, and illuminates with the light that lighteth every man that cometh into the world. Older, nobler, clearer, and more glorious, then, is everlasting justice, than ambiguous, base-born, purblind, perishable Common Law. That which is older than the creation may indeed be extolled for its venerable age; but among created things, the argument from antiquity is a false criterion of worth. Sin and death are older than the Common Law; are they, therefore, to be preferred to it? The mortal transgression of Cain was anterior to the Common Law: does it therefore furnish a better precedent?

Judge-made law is ex post facto law, and therefore unjust. An act is not forbidden by the statute law, but it becomes void by judicial construction. The legislature could not effect this, for the Constitution forbids it. The judiciary shall not usurp legislative power, says the Bill of Rights: yet it not only usurps, but runs riot beyond the confines of legislative power.

Judge-made law is special legislation. The judge is human, and feels the bias which the coloring of the particular case gives. If he wishes to decide the next case differently, he has only to distinguish, and thereby make a new law. The legislature must act on general views, and prescribe at once for a whole class of cases.

No man can tell what the Common Law is; therefore it is not law: for a law is a rule of action; but a rule which is unknown can govern no man's conduct. Notwithstanding this, it has been called the perfection of human reason.

The Common Law is the perfection of human reason,—just as alcohol is the perfection of sugar. The subtle spirit of the Common Law is reason double distilled, till what was wholesome and nutritive becomes rank poison. Reason is sweet and pleasant to the unsophisticated intellect; but this sublimated perversion of reason bewilders, and perplexes, and plunges its victims into mazes of error.

The judge makes law, by extorting from precedents something which they do not contain. He extends his precedents, which were themselves the extension of others, till, by this accommodating principle, a whole system of law is built up without the authority or interference of the legislator.

The judge labors to reconcile conflicting analogies, and to derive from them a rule to decide future cases. No one knows what the law is, before he lays it down; for it does not exist even in the breast of the judge. All the cases carried up to the tribunal of the last resort, are capable of being argued, or they would not be carried there. Those which are not carried up are not law, for the Supreme Court might decide them differently. Those which are carried up, argued, and decided, might have been decided differently, as will appear from the arguments. It is, therefore, often optional with the judge to incline the balance as he pleases. In forty per cent of the cases carried up to a higher court, for a considerable term of years, terminating not long ago, the judgment was reversed. Almost any case, where there is any difference of opinion, may be decided either way, and plausible analogies found in the great storehouse of precedent to justify the decision. The law, then, is the final will or whim of the judge, after counsel for both parties have done their utmost to sway it to the one side or the other.

No man knows what the law is after the judge has decided it. Because, as the judge is careful not to decide any point which is not brought before him, he restricts his decision within the narrowest possible limits; and though the very next case that may arise may seem, to a superficial observer, and even upon a close inspection by an ordinary mind, to be precisely similar to the last, yet the ingenuity of a thorough-bred lawyer may detect some unsuspected shade of difference upon which an opposite decision may be founded. Great part of the skill of a judge consists in avoiding the direct consequences of a rule, by ingenious expedients and distinctions, whenever the rule would operate absurdly; and as an ancient maxim may be evaded, but must be annulled, the whole system has been gradually rendered a labyrinth of apparent contradictions, reconciled by legal adroitness.

Statutes, enacted by the legislature, speak the public voice. Legislators, with us, are not only chosen because they possess the public confidence, but after their election, they are strongly influenced by public feeling. They must sympathize with the public, and express its will: should they fail to do so, the next year witnesses their removal from office, and others are selected to the organs of the popular sentiment. The older portions of the Common Law are the work of judges, who held their places during the good pleasure of the king, and of course decided the law so as to suit the pleasure of the king. In feudal times it was made up of feudal principles, warped, to be sure, according to the king's necessities. Judges now are appointed by the executive, and hold their offices during good behavior,—that is, for life, and consequently out of the reach of popular influence. They are sworn to administer Common Law as it came down from the dark ages, excepting what has been repealed by the Constitution and the statutes, which exception they are always careful to reduce to the narrowest possible limits. With them, wrong is right, if wrong has existed from time immemorial: precedents are every thing: the spirit of the age is nothing. And suppose the judge prefers the Common Law to the Constitutions of the State and of the Union; or decides in defiance of the statute; what is the remedy? An astute argument is always at hand to reconcile the open violation of that instrument with the express letter of the Constitution, as in the case of the United States Bank—or to prove an obnoxious statute unconstitutional, as would have happened in the case of Warren Bridge, but for the firmness of Judge Morton. Impeachment is a bugbear, which has lost its terrors. We must have democratic governors, who will appoint democratic judges, and the whole body of the law must be codified.

JOSEPH STORY
"Report of the Commissioners [on codification] to the Governor of the Commonwealth of Massachusetts"
1837

Justice Joseph Story's report on behalf of the Massachusetts codification commission he chaired represented a moderate and cautious approach to codification. Story had little admiration for legislative intrusions on the common law, but he recognized that some degree of codification was inevitable and desirable, provided it was held on a tight leash. He had long believed that some areas of the law, particularly procedure and commercial law, lent themselves to codification, and that is just what he proposed here. But he insisted that codification not displace the common law or be used as a vehicle for more radical law-reform projects.

I.   The Commissioners are, in the first place, of opinion, that it is not expedient to attempt the reduction to a Code of the entire body of the common law of Massachusetts, either in its general principles, or in the deductions from or the applications of those principles, so far as they have been ascertained by judicial decisions, or are incontrovertibly established.

II.   The Commissioners are, in the next place, of opinion that it is expedient to reduce to a Code those principles and details of the common law of Massachusetts, in civil cases, which are of daily use and familiar application to the common business life and the present state of property and personal rights [and] contracts, and which are now so far ascertained and established as to admit of a scientific form and arrangement, and are capable of being announced in distinct and determinate propositions. What portions of the common law properly fall under the predicament will be in some measure considered hereafter.

III.   The Commissioners are, in the next place, of opinion, that it is expedient to reduce to a Code the common law, as to the definition, trial and punishment of crimes, and the incidents thereto.

IV.   The Commissioners are, in the next place, of opinion, that the law of evidence, as applicable both to civil and criminal proceedings, should be reduced to a Code.

*   *   *

[Story then provided a] consideration of the benefits, which may be derived from a codification of the common law. It has been already admitted, that every such codification must, from the nature of things, be imperfect; for it never can embrace all the past, present, and future changes in society, which may require new rules to govern them. But this is an objection, in its general form, founded upon the absolute infirmity of human nature for every purpose of perfect action, and is not limited to codification. It by no means follows, that because legislation cannot do every thing, or foresee every thing, therefore no legislation should exist, either to remedy evils, to ascertain rights, or to secure property. The benefits proposed by a Code may be summed up in the following propositions.

I.   In the first place, certainty, clearness, and facility of reference are of great importance in all matters of law, which concern the public generally. It is desirable, in every community, that the laws, which govern the rights, duties, relations, and business of the people, should, as far as practicable, be accessible to them for daily use or consultation.

*   *   *

Now, certainly, if a rule or doctrine of the common law exists in a determinate form or with a determinate certainty, it is capable of being so expressed in the text of a Code. If so capable, then it is not easy to perceive why it should not be so expressed that it may furnish a guide for inquirers, to clear away a private doubt, or to satisfy a hesitating judgment.

But this is not all. At present the known rules and doctrines of the common law are spread over many ponderous volumes. They are nowhere collected together in a concise and systematic form, having a positive legislative sanction. They are to be gathered from treatises upon distinct and independent subjects, of very different merit and accuracy; from digests and abridgments; from books of practice and from professional practice; and above all, from books of reports of adjudged cases, many hundreds of which now exist, and which require to be painfully and laboriously consulted in order to ascertain them. These rules and doctrines may be well known and well understood by eminent lawyers and judges, by profound students, who possess an ample library of law books, and by others, who devote their whole leisure to the purpose. And yet men less eminent, less studious, or with less means to provide a library, or to consult it, may be unable to arrive at the same certainty, any may even be misled by their partial examinations, into serious errors and mistakes. A leading rule may have some exceptions, which have escaped the researches of the party and yet be as well established as the rule itself. Many lawsuits are now founded upon errors and mistakes of this sort, which the mere imperfection of the means within the reach of the interested party, or of his counsel, has unavoidably produced. A single line of a Code, properly and accurately prepared upon such a subject, might at once have dissipated every doubt and uncertainty, as to the nature, extent and operation of the existing rule.

*   *   *

One great advantage, therefore, of a Code, an advantage which in a practical view can scarcely be over estimated, is, that it supersedes the necessity, in ordinary cases at least, of very elaborate researches into other books; and, indeed, it often supersedes, in all cases but those of rare and extraordinary occurrence, the necessity of consulting an immense mass of learned collections and digests of antecedent decisions.

*   *   *

III.   In the next place, it may be stated, in connection with the preceding head, and as illustrative of it, that there are in the common law many points, which, though on the whole now established by a considerable weight of judicial authority, are not absolutely beyond the reach of forensic controversy, if learned counsel should choose to stir them. There are, for example, many questions, which have given rise to litigation in different ages, and upon which there may be found in the reports, not only occasional diversities of judicial opinion, but many nice distinctions and differences, and many incidental dicta, which serve greatly to perplex the inquiries of the ablest lawyers. Where authorities are to be found on each side of a point; where the circumstances of cases, very nearly resembling each other in most respects, are yet distinguishable from each other by nice shades of difference, or have been so distinguished, thus furnishing grounds for reasoning and controversy as to the precise extent of a principle, no judges would feel at liberty to stop the argument, although in their judgment, the weight of authority should be clearly against the suggested distinction or difference. Much of the time of courts of justice is consumed in arguments of this sort, where there are numerous cases, with some slight differences of circumstances, bearing on the same general rule, all of which may be required to be examined and distinguished. It was said by an eminent Judge (Lord Eldon), upon an occasion, where some question of artificial or technical law was under discussion before him, that there were upwards of three hundred cases bearing on that question, which had already been decided. To master them, with all their minute distinctions of circumstances, would of itself be a vast labor. And yet it is not perhaps too much to say, that four or five lines of text in a Code, stating the true general rule, deducible from the best of them, would at once have put aside the necessity of any further consideration of most of these cases.

There are, besides, numerous points, upon which there are now to be found conflicting decisions, or dicta of courts of justice, which shake the authority of certain doctrines. In cases of this sort, it seems desirable to establish which of these decisions constitutes the true rule, or at least to give a positive affirmance of the true rule, when it can be fairly ascertained what that is. And perhaps also in some instances of daily practical importance, where there is a real doubt what the true rule of the common law is, it may not be without use to fix it in a like positive form.

The Commissioners do not indulge the rash expectation, that any Code of the known existing common law will dry up all the common sources of litigation. New cases must arise, which no Code can provide for, or even ascertain. These must necessarily be left to be disposed of by courts of justice, as they shall occur in future. But the Commissioners are of opinion, that a Code which shall contain the clearly established principles of the common law, will be attended with great benefits to the public, for the reasons already stated. It will show what the existing law is, as far as it goes, in a clear and intelligible manner. It will have a tendency to suppress useless and expensive litigation. It will greatly abridge the labors of judges, as well as of the profession, by furnishing a starting point for future discussions, instead of imposing the necessity of constant researches through all the past annals of the law.

DAVID DUDLEY FIELD

"What Shall Be Done with the Practice of the Courts?"

1847

David Dudley Field was a member of a prominent New York family; one of his brothers was Stephen J. Field, Associate Justice of the United States Supreme Court, and another, Cyrus, was an entrepreneur who laid the first trans-Atlantic cable. David Field enjoyed a lucrative practice in New York City and before the United States Supreme Court. Despite his professional eminence, however, he labored throughout his long career for the codification of all branches of the law. He was most successful in the field of civil procedure, being almost singlehandedly responsible for the abolition of common-law pleading and the substitution of what came to be called code pleading. His 1847 essay, excerpted below, stated the case for reform in the area of civil procedure in the state courts.

The Constitution of this State [New York, 1846], which goes into effect to-day, will render great changes necessary in our system of legal procedure. It remodels our Courts; unites the administration of law and equity in the same tribunal; directs testimony to be taken in like manner in both classes of cases; abolishes the offices of Master and Examiner in Chancery, hitherto important parts of our equity system; and, finally, directs that the next Legislature shall provide for the appointment of three commissioners, "whose duty it shall be to revise, reform, simplify, and abridge the rules of practice, pleadings, forms, and proceedings of the courts of record," and report thereon to the Legislature for its action.

Important modifications of the equity practice are thus made indispensable, in order to adapt it to the new mode of taking testimony. But I think that the Convention intended, and that the people expect, much greater changes than these. We know that radical reform in legal proceedings has long been demanded by no inconsiderable number of the people; that a more determined agitation of the subject has been postponed by its friends, till such time as there should be a reorganization of the judicial establishment, upon the idea that a new system of procedure and a new system of Courts ought to come in together; that it was a prominent topic in the Convention itself, where its friends were in an undoubted majority; and that the manifestations of public sentiment out of doors were no less clear than were the sentiments of that body. Indeed, if now, after all that has been done within the last five years, there should be made only such changes as the Constitution absolutely commands, there will be great and general disappointment.

*   *   *

Every consideration, as it seems to me, makes it expedient for us all now to enter heartily upon the work of amendment. Those of us who have long been laboring for a radical reformation of the law, and those who have felt less inclination for it, should find this an occasion to act together in the common pursuit of thorough and wise reforms. We feel the inconvenience of the present state of things. We know that the technicality and the drudgery of legal proceedings are discreditable to our profession. Justice is entangled in the net of forms.

*   *   *

Believing, therefore, that great changes are inevitable in any event, and that this is a period favorable to the adoption of all the reforms which are really required, I wish it were possible to engage every member of the legal profession in the promotion of a wise, safe, and radical reform. Radical reform will come sooner or later, with us or without us. Shall we cooperate to make it at the same time wise and safe?

Such a reform, I am persuaded, should have in view nothing less than a uniform course of proceeding, in all cases, legal and equitable.

*   *   *

What I propose, then, in respect to cases of legal cognizance, is this: that the present forms of action be abolished, and in their stead a complaint and answer required, each setting forth the real claim and defense of the parties. Such pleadings would be precisely similar to those proposed for equity cases, and we should thus have a uniform course of pleading for all cases, legal and equitable. The distinction between the two classes of cases is now merely a distinction in the forms of proceeding. The Court of Chancery has existed only in consequence of the narrow and fixed forms of the common law. If those forms had been abolished, and a natural procedure adopted, the course of the two Courts would long ago have been assimilated.

Let the plaintiff set forth his cause of action in his complaint briefly, in ordinary language, and without repetition; and let the defendant make his answer in the same way. Let each party verify his allegation by making oath that he believes it to be true. The complaint will then acquaint the defendant with the real charge, while the answer will inform the plaintiff of the real defense. The disputed facts will be sifted from the undisputed, and the parties will go to trial knowing what they have to answer. The plaintiff will state his case as he believes it, and as he expects to prove it. The defendant, on his part, will set forth what he believes and expects to establish, and he need set forth no more. He will not be likely to aver what he does not believe. His answer will disclose the whole of his defense, because he will not be allowed to prove anything which the answer does not contain. He will not be perplexed with questions of double pleading, nor shackled by ancient technical rules.

*   *   *

The legitimate end of every administration of law is to do justice, with the least possible delay and expense. Every system of pleading is useful only as it tends to this end. This it can do but one of two ways: either by enabling the parties the better to prepare for trial, or by assisting the jury and the Court in judging the causes.

*   *   *

If we adopt the plan of pleading which I propose, we shall save both time and expense. We shall avoid the risk of losing causes from mistaking the rules of pleading; and we take one step, and that a great one, toward introducing simplicity and directness into the machinery of the law.

*   *   *

And is, indeed, the learning of the profession bound up with the system of common-law pleading? Is the noble science of jurisprudence—the fruit of the experience of ages, at once the monument and the record of civilization— inseparable from such paltry learning as that, "after the declaration, the parties must at each stage demur, or plead by way of traverse, or by way of confession and avoidance," or that "upon a traverse issue must be tendered," or anything of that sort? Lawyers have enough to learn if their studies are confined to useful knowledge. To assert that the great body of the law, civil and criminal—the law which defines rights and punishes crimes; the law which regulates the proprietorship, the enjoyment, and the transmission of property in all its forms; which explains the nature and the obligations of contracts through all their changes; the law that prevails equally on the sea and the land; the law that is enforced in courts of chancery and courts of admiralty, as well as in the courts of common law—to assert that this vast body of law requires the aid of that small portion which regulates the written statement of the parties in the courts of common law, is to assert a monstrous paradox, fitter for ridicule than for argument.

Note: The Fate of the Field Codes

Procedural reform was long overdue in most American jurisdictions by mid-century, so Field's project for the simplification of civil procedure was an idea whose time had come. The New York legislature, in compliance with the mandate of the 1846 Constitution, created a three-man commission, eventually chaired by Field, to reform procedure in the New York courts. The result was "An Act to simplify and abridge the Practice, Pleadings, and Proceedings of the Courts" (1848)—the Field procedural code. This statute realized the objectives and ideals that Field had called for in his essay of 1847. In the eyes of horrified conservatives, its Section 62 was revolutionary.

> The distinction between actions at law and suits in equity, and for the forms of all such actions and suits heretofore existing, are abolished; and, there shall be in this state, hereafter, but one form of action, for the enforcement or protection of private rights and the redress or prevention of private wrongs, which shall be denominated a civil action.[4]

Although the procedural codes were to rout common-law pleading in nearly every American jurisdiction by the turn of the century, the Field code had a curiously uneven reception in its home state. Some appellate judges resisted it; Lawrence M. Friedman quotes one of them, Samuel Selden, "who remained convinced that law and equity were categories of the real world. He simply could not grasp the idea of merging the two: 'It is possible to abolish one or the other . . . but it certainly is not possible to abolish the distinction between them.'"[5] The New York legislature tinkered with the code incessantly, adding section upon section as the century progressed and producing an 1876 descendant that a nineteenth-century historical scholar condemned as "reactionary in spirit[,] . . . a figure of Falstaffian proportions among the other codes."[6]

A southern legal scholar condemned North Carolina's adoption of the Field procedural code in racy metaphors seldom found in legal writing:

> [T]his new-fangled commercial machine . . . was as well adapted to [North Carolina's] condition as were the light driving buggies of the Riverside Park to the rough roads of the Black mountains, or the garb of the Broadway dandy to the turpentine stiller on the Big Tar river. . . . North Carolina had about as much use for the system as she had for a clearing-house, a Central Park or a Stock Exchange. The clamors of the bar soon brought about an amendment . . . and left [the code] . . . a great heavy cumbrous piece of machinery without driving-wheels, steam-chest or boiler, propelled alone by the typical slow ox-team.[7]

The Field procedural code was at first much more warmly received in the western states than in the East or South, being adopted in the trans-Mississippi region more readily, and with fewer barnacled amendments, than it had been in the eastern states. For whatever reason, the western states were more hospitable to the codification of procedure. This reform slowly returned to its eastern home, sometimes in imitation of the procedural streamlining accomplished in the West, sometimes via imitation of the English Judicature Act of 1873,[8] which was influenced by the original New York code.

Field had called for more than procedural reform, though; he projected civil, criminal, and political (i.e., constitutional) codes. Toward the end of his career, he even projected an international code. New York adopted his penal code in 1881, and a handful of western states—Dakota Territory, Idaho, Montana, and, above all, California—adopted the civil code or something derived from it. But substantive codification, whether civil or criminal, was definitely not a reality in the late nineteenth century. Legal conservatives successfully fought it on ideological and practical grounds.

Even where adopted, California being the classic illustrative case, judges viewed a civil code askance and adopted rules of interpretation that smuggled much of the common law back in. In an 1888 decision, the California Supreme Court declared that

> the common law underlies all our legislation, and furnishes the rule of decision except in so far as the statutes have changed the common law. When the common law is departed from by a provision of the code, effect is to be given to the provision to the extent—and only to the extent—of the departure.[9]

Codification could not succeed over the opposition of the bar; Field essentially took on the entire New York bar in fighting for the civil code, and he lost. But some form or other of rationalization of the common law triumphed when the organized bar, particularly its practicing and academic elites, supported such movements. Two twentieth-century examples are outstanding: the Restatements of the Laws produced by the American Law Institute, and the various uniform laws that are the products of the Conference of Commissioners on Uniform State Laws. The most notable and influential of the latter is the Uniform Commercial Code, which is the law today in all American jurisdictions except Louisiana.

The Judge in American Society

The exuberant democracy of the Jacksonian era produced demands that the law and the lawmaking processes themselves be democratized. As the conservatism of Choate and Shaw was the natural extension of lawyers' cautious impulses in the era of the American Revolution, the effort to make all sources of law responsive to democratic control naturally grew out of the contemporaneous impulse to popular sovereignty. Throughout the nineteenth century, the states inexorably moved toward popular election of their judges, to replace the original methods of legislative selection or nomination by the governor and confirmation by the senate.

The movement toward an elective bench was largely successful by the end of the century at the state level, but the federal courts resisted the trend and remain appointive. The movement for an elective bench receded in the twentieth century after it proved not to be a democratic panacea.

The Elective Judiciary

CHARLES REEMELIN
Statements Regarding an Elective Judiciary
July 5, 1850

The idea of electing judges rather than appointing them was promoted (and resisted) in stark ideological terms in the nineteenth century. Proponents of the elective bench claimed that electorally responsive judges would return power to the sovereign people and prevent a nonresponsible judicial elite from interposing a conservative shield that protected private property and corporations from regulation by the people's representatives. Conservatives countered that appointive judges were all that stood between demagogue-dominated popular majorities and the vested rights of property and contract. The excerpt below gives a radical argument in favor of an elective bench made at the 1851 Ohio constitutional convention.

Mr. Chairman, my opponents upon this question are most valiant men in fighting men of straw, set up by themselves. Who, on this side has asked for a political court? Who, on this side, has asked for a partisan judge? Who has asked any judge to violate his oath? Who has asked him to become corrupt? Who has even admitted, on our side of the question, that to elect judges by the people, at short periods, would bring about any such results? All such remarks are the mere fanciful imaginings raised up for the purpose of making fine speeches on the independence of the judiciary—upon its impartiality—and upon the safeguards of the constitution, and claptrap terms of that kind. Let me recapitulate, very briefly, what I did say, the points I made, and the arguments I used to sustain them.

*   *   *

. . . I said that the election of judges by the people was asked for by the people, for the purpose of bringing within their control more fully that department of our government, which alone, of all other departments of American governments, had not felt the chastening and reforming hand of American public opinion. . . .

I said that the longer the term of office for the judge, the more effectually would the people be balked in their endeavors thus to bring the judiciary within the control of public opinion. I said that it was a question of mathematics, that those who desired the people to rule who were democratic, using this term as I distinctly stated, in its legitimate sense, and not as a partisan term, should go for as short terms as could be obtained under the circumstances. I also said that the great difference between a democrat and an aristocrat, and I certainly used these terms with a general meaning, rather than with any special one to persons then about me, existed upon the point whether a man had confidence in the people. A democrat desired the people to rule, not only because he believed the people wanted the right, but that also as a general question, the people would do what was right. An aristocrat, on the other side, would naturally seek for a good government, not with the people, for he had no confidence in them, but he would seek it in age, experience, in the rectitude of a few men, in their independence of character, in their superior legal attainments, and in some conservative provisions to be put into the government machinery here and there, for the purpose of balancing what they call the whims and prejudices and the passions of the people.

Sir, the main point between us, disguise it as they may, is that we on our side desire the people to govern, while on the other side, the idea of the people ruling is associated with hob-goblins of every description that frightens them out of their senses; and we have therefore presented to us, the raw-head and bloody-bones of mobs and popular outbreaks; of a little stormy meeting in this village, and in that town; of a little difficulty here, and a little difficulty there; and as if these constituted the people at the ballot-boxes, and as if the errors of a part were to be charged upon the whole. It is want of confidence in the people, I repeat it again, that will make them vote for long terms for judges in office, and it was that difficulty that prevented them coming out early in favor of electing judges by the people. Why, sir, they call it the "downward tendency." Downward! where, and to whom? Downward to the people? Why, sir, I call that going upward; and this little word, insignificant as it may appear in the speeches of the gentleman, shows conclusively how adverse his mind and the minds of his friends are, to granting to the people more power, and more frequent chances to act upon their government.

*   *   *

I look to the people, and to their action on the government only for the preservation of my rights and those of my family. I have but little confidence in that ever vaunted "legal talent," "experienced age," "independent courts," etc., unless backed and kept alive by republican habits, and a perfect equality among all classes of people. It was, therefore, not the outside machinery of government which brought me here, but it is an ever-abiding trust in the rectitude and foresighted correctness of our people.

Note: The Elective Judiciary and Judicial Review

Since all states provided for election of some or all of their judges by the end of the nineteenth century, it has seemed to some historians that the radical argument triumphed, perhaps because of the political power of Jacksonian democracy. Yet an anomaly cautions us that this explanation is too simple. For while the popular election of judges was triumphing, the judiciary was expanding the scope of judicial review. Indeed, at the moment of complete triumph of the elective branch at the state level in the nineteenth century, state judges also reached the apogee of substantive due process judicial review.

Rather than popular election of judges vindicating radical views, a more careful analysis of state constitutional conventions held between 1846 and 1860 reveals that it was moderates in a bipartisan coalition dominated by lawyers and judges, not Democratic radicals, who supported popular election. They did so to enhance judicial power, improve judicial administration by clearing backlogs of cases, remove the judicial appointment process from the influence of partisan patronage, and enhance the ability of judges to curb legislative excesses of the era, such as ill-considered legislative support for railroad financing.

WILLIAM HOWARD TAFT
Veto of the Arizona Enabling Act
1911

President William Howard Taft vetoed the Arizona statehood bill of 1911 because the nascent state's constitution contained a provision permitting the recall of judges. The president's heartfelt arguments reflect the anxiety that beset conservatives when they perceived the state and federal judiciary to be under assault from proponents of democracy. Recurring to eighteenth-century principles concerning the separation of powers and the independence of the judiciary, Taft and other conservatives resurrected the arguments of Alexander Hamilton that justified judicial review, to stave off the encroachments of popular influence on the judiciary.

VETO MESSAGE

Returning without approval a joint resolution for the
admission of the Territories of New Mexico and Arizona
into the Union as States

The White House, August 22, 1911

This provision of the Arizona constitution, in its application to county and State judges, seems to me so pernicious in its effect, so destructive of independence in the judiciary, so likely to subject the rights of the individual to the possible tyranny of a popular majority, and, therefore, to be so injurious to the cause of free government, that I must disapprove a constitution containing it.

*   *   *

A government is for the benefit of all the people. We believe that this benefit is best accomplished by popular government, because in the long run each class of individuals is apt to secure better provision for themselves through their own voice in government than through the altruistic interest of others, however intelligent or philanthropic. The wisdom of ages has taught that no government can exist except in accordance with laws and unless the people under it either obey the laws voluntarily or are made to obey them. In a popular government the laws are made by the people—not by all the people—but by those supposed and declared competent for the purpose, as males over 21 years of age, and not by all of these—but by a majority of them only. Now, as the government is for all the people, and is not solely for a majority of them, the majority in exercising control either directly or through its agents is bound to exercise the power for the benefit of the minority as well as the majority. But all have recognized that the majority of a people, unrestrained by law, when aroused and without the sobering effect of deliberation and discussion, may do injustice to the minority or to the individual when the selfish interest of the majority prompts. Hence arises the necessity for a constitution by which the will of the majority shall be permitted to guide the course of the government only under controlling checks that experience has shown to be necessary to secure for the minority its share of the benefit to the whole people that a popular government is established to bestow. A popular government is not a government of a majority, by a majority, for a majority of the people. It is a government of the whole people, by a majority of the whole people under such rules and checks as will secure a wise, just, and beneficent government for all the people. It is said you can always trust the people to do justice. If that means all the people and they all agree, you can. But ordinarily they do not all agree, and the maxim is interpreted to mean that you can always trust a majority of the people. This is not invariably true; and every limitation imposed by the people upon the power of the majority in their constitutions is an admission that it is not always true. No honest, clear-headed man, however great a lover of popular government, can deny that the unbridled expression of the majority of a community converted hastily into law or action would sometimes make a government tyrannical and cruel. Constitutions are checks upon the hasty action of the majority. They are the self-imposed restraints of a whole people upon a majority of them to secure sober action and a respect for the rights of the minority, and of the individual in his relation to other individuals, and in his relation to the whole people in their character as a state or government.

The Constitution distributes the functions of government into three branches—the legislative, to make the laws; the executive, to execute them; and the judicial, to decide in cases arising before it the rights of the individual as between him and others and as between him and the Government. This division of government into three separate branches has always been regarded as a great security for the maintenance of free institutions, and the security is only firm and assured when the judicial branch is independent and impartial. The executive and legislative branches are representative of the majority of the people which elected them in guiding the course of the Government within the limits of the Constitution. They must act for the whole people, of course; but they may properly follow, and usually ought to follow, the views of the majority which elected them in respect to the governmental policy best adapted to secure the welfare of the whole people. But the judicial branch of the Government is not representative of a majority of the people in any such sense, even if the mode of selecting the judges is by popular election. In a proper sense, judges are servants of the people; that is, they are doing work which must be done for the Government and in the interest of all the people, but it is not work in the doing of which they are to follow the will of the majority except as that is embodied in statutes, lawfully enacted according to constitutional limitations.

They are not popular representatives. On the contrary, to fill their office properly, they must be independent. They must decide every question which comes before them according to law and justice.

*   *   *

This power conferred on the judiciary in our form of government is unique in the history of governments, and its operation has attracted and deserved the admiration and commendation of the world. It gives to our judiciary a position higher, stronger, and more responsible than that of the judiciary of any other country, and more effectively secures adherence to the fundamental will of the people.

What I have said has been to little purpose if it has not shown that judges to fulfill their functions properly in our popular Government must be more independent than in any other form of government, and that need of independence is greater where the individual is one litigant and the State, guided by the successful and governing majority, is the other. In order to maintain the rights of the minority and the individual and to preserve our constitutional balance we must have judges with courage to decide against the majority when justice and law require.

By the recall in the Arizona constitution it is proposed to give to the majority power to remove arbitrarily, and without delay, any judge who may have the courage to render an unpopular decision.

*   *   *

Could there be a system more ingeniously devised to subject judges to momentary gusts of popular passion than this? We can not be blind to the fact that often an intelligent and respectable electorate may be so roused upon an issue that it will visit with condemnation the decision of a just judge, though exactly in accord with the law governing the case, merely because it affects unfavorably their contest. Controversies over elections, labor troubles, racial or religious issues, issues as to the construction or constitutionality of liquor laws, criminal trials of popular or unpopular defendants, the removal of county seats, suits by individuals to maintain their constitutional rights in obstruction of some popular improvement—these and many other cases could be cited in which a majority of a district electorate would be tempted by hasty anger to recall a conscientious judge if the opportunity were open all the time. No period of delay is interposed for the abatement of popular feeling. The recall is devised to encourage quick action, and to lead the people to strike while the iron is hot. The judge is treated as the instrument and servant of a majority of the people and subject to their momentary will.

*   *   *

Think of the enormous power for evil given to the sensational, muckraking portion of the press in rousing prejudice against a just judge by false charges and insinuations, the effect of which in the short period of an election by recall it would be impossible for him to meet and offset! Supporters of such a system seem to think that it will work only in the interest of the poor, the humble, the weak and the oppressed; that it will strike down only the judge who is supposed to favor corporations and be affected by the corrupting influence of the rich. Nothing could be further from the ultimate result. The motive it would offer to unscrupulous combinations to seek to control politics in order to control judges is clear.

Again judicial recall is advocated on the ground that it will bring the judges more into sympathy with the popular will and the progress of ideas among the people. It is said that now judges are out of touch with the movement toward a wider democracy and a greater control of governmental agencies in the interest and for the benefit of the people. The righteous and just course for a judge to pursue is ordinarily fixed by statute or clear principles of law, and the cases in which his judgment may be affected by his political, economic, or social views are infrequent. But even in such cases, judges are not removed from the people's influence. Surround the judiciary with all the safeguards possible, create judges by appointment, make their tenure for life, forbid diminution of salary during their term, and still it is impossible to prevent the influence of popular opinion from coloring judgments in the long run. Judges are men, intelligent, sympathetic men, patriotic men, and in those fields of the law in which the personal equation unavoidably plays a part, there will be found a response to sober popular opinion as it changes to meet the exigency of social, political, and economic changes. Indeed this should be so. Individual instances of a hidebound and retrograde conservatism on the part of courts in decisions which turn on the individual economic or sociological views of the judges may be pointed out; but they are not many, and do not call for radical action.

Note: The Role of Juries

While the democratic-minded were demanding that judges be held politically accountable, the judges themselves were attempting to restrict the role of juries, principally in two ways. First, judges insisted that jurors, who were all laymen with no legal training, were competent to decide only questions of fact, not of law. (In the eighteenth century, juries often decided questions both of fact and of law.) Second, judges tried to eliminate the jurors' ability to ignore law they deemed unjust or unconstitutional and to ignore the instructions of the judges. In short, judges tried to reduce or abolish the discretion of jurors to decide cases on the basis of community standards of justice. Before the Civil War, the petit jury underwent a remarkable transformation. The legal historian William E. Nelson has summed up that change:

> The role of the jury as a finder both of law and fact had been totally transformed. The jury had ceased to be an adjunct of local communities which articulated into positive law the ethical standards of those communities and which in doing so completely dominated the legal system's decision-making processes. It had become instead the adjunct of the court and had been left only . . . fact-finding tasks. . . .[10]

Although Nelson was writing of Massachusetts in the first decade of the nineteenth century, his remarks are applicable to all American jurisdictions.

Judges narrowed the jury's role by a number of procedural devices. First among these was the practice of encouraging opposing counsel to submit their cases on an agreed statement of facts. Under a procedure known as "case reserved," judges could arrange to decide questions of law if there was no factual dispute between the parties. The agreed statement of facts thus removed this fact-finding function from juries. More significant was the increased use of postverdict motions, especially the motion to award a new trial on the ground that the verdict was contrary to the weight of the evidence. In the eighteenth century, such a motion was rare because it effectively substituted the opinion of the judge for that of the jury, at least once, on questions of fact.

Finally, the fact–law distinction expanded in importance. Speaking of eighteenth-century practice, the Connecticut jurist Zephaniah Swift stated that "the jury [are] the proper judges not only of the facts but of the laws."[11] That changed in the early nineteenth century, as judges became troubled over jury discretion. Judges first sharpened the distinction between questions of fact and questions of law. Then they assigned those responsibilities functionally—facts to juries, law to judges—beginning the process of withdrawing from juries any authority over issues of law, including the constitutionality of a statute. Such a distribution of functions enhanced the role of judges. This heightened role, in turn, made some Americans ever more suspicious of the judges' power in a democracy.

Although juries inexorably lost the broad powers they had enjoyed in the eighteenth century, the narrowing of their role did not go unchallenged. The most vigorous defense of the jury to appear in the nineteenth century came from the pen of a man whom modern anarchists hail as their intellectual ancestor, the Massachusetts abolitionist Lysander Spooner. Not so much an anarchist as an antistatist, Spooner came to his views through pondering the use of state power to sustain slavery. Thenceforth suspicious of every exercise of the coercive power of the state, Spooner attempted to restore the jury to some mythical position as a check on the state. In an 1852 essay on the topic, he outlined the idealized functioning of the jury:

> For more than six hundred years—that is, since Magna Carta, in 1215—there has been no clearer principle of English or American constitutional law, than that, in criminal cases, it is not only the right and duty of juries to judge what are the facts, what is the law, and what was the moral intent of the accused; but it is also their right, and their primary and paramount duty, to judge of the justice of the law, and to hold all laws invalid, that are, in their opinion, unjust or oppressive, and all persons guiltless in violating, or resisting the execution of such laws.
>
>   *   *   *
>
> Any people, that judge of, and determine authoritatively for the government, what are their own liberties against the government, of course retain all the liberties they wish to enjoy. And this is freedom. At least, it is freedom to them; because, although it may be theoretically imperfect, nevertheless, corresponds to their highest notions of freedom.[12]

Legal Education

Formal legal education in America started late and grew slowly, when compared with higher education in general or the growth of the bar. Before the appearance of the university-affiliated law schools in the nineteenth century, legal education evolved gradually out of apprenticeship into something more formal and academic.

Apprenticeship or clerking has always been a form of legal education and, in attenuated forms, remains so today. (Current forms of apprenticeship include summer employment in law firms or legal agencies, such as district attorneys' offices, after the first or second year of law school; judicial clerkships after graduation; and, here and there in the few remaining jurisdictions, such as Virginia, that still permit it, reading for the bar without attending law school.) Before and throughout the nineteenth century, an aspiring legal tyro would agree with an established lawyer to serve a period of time or at will, providing menial services like drafting or being a general gofer, in return for some more or less (usually less) rudimentary tutoring in the elements of law practice, supplemented by some reading in a handful of legal classics: Blackstone, Coke on Littleton, the statutes of the jurisdiction. Sometimes these arrangements included room and board with the lawyer. Such training was necessarily hit-or-miss: a lucky apprentice would get a conscientious mentor or, in the early nineteenth century, an established lawyer who had a taste for teaching, such as Lemuel Shaw and Theophilus Parsons in Massachusetts.

After independence, some colleges began experimenting with legal education, usually like that offered by holders of the Vinerian Chair at Oxford, such as Sir William Blackstone—that is, lectures to undergraduates, not the postgraduate professional education we identify with legal training today. The first university-affiliated chair for teaching law was established in "Law and Police" at the College of William and Mary in 1779. Its original occupant was George Wythe, a chancellor of Virginia's equity court, who resigned from the position eleven years later and opened his own proprietary school. Wythe was the law teacher of both Thomas Jefferson and John Marshall. Other eminent pioneer law teachers included St. George Tucker, Wythe's successor at William and Mary and editor of a widely used American edition of Blackstone that was adorned with important essays on American law; James Wilson, who delivered occasional lectures at the University of Pennsylvania while serving as an Associate Justice of the United States Supreme Court; and James Kent, who, although unsuccessful and unhappy during his two stints as a law teacher at Columbia College (1793–1798, 1824–1826), published his lectures there in the influential *Commentaries on American Law* (1826).

Advertisement for the Litchfield Law School
1828

Formal systems of legal education evolved out of the apprenticeship system. Teaching lawyers like Judge Tapping Reeve in Connecticut created proprietary schools where instruction was systematized in a prescribed curriculum. As the most successful and renowned of the proprietary American law schools, Litchfield was fully justified in its boast that many of its graduates "have since been eminently conspicuous, both as Jurists, and as Statesmen." Among the latter was John C. Calhoun. The little village law school of Judges Reeve and Gould proved to be the nursery of statesmen in the Jacksonian years.

This Law School was established in 1782 by the Hon. Tapping Reeve, late Chief Justice of this State, and continued under his sole direction until the year 1798, when the Hon. J. Gould was associated with him. These gentlemen continued their joint labours until 1820, since which period Judge Gould has lectured alone.

*   *   *

According to the plan pursued by Judge Gould, the Law is divided into forty-eight Titles, which embrace all its important branches, and of which he treats in systematic detail. . . . The Lectures, which are delivered every day, and which usually occupy an hour and a half, embrace every principle and rule falling under the several divisions of the different Titles. These principles and rules are supported by numerous authorities, and generally accompanied with familiar illustrations. . . . These lectures, thus classified, are taken down in full by the students, and after being compared with each other, are generally transcribed in a more neat and legible hand. The remainder of the day is occupied in examining the authorities cited in support of the several rules, and in reading the most approved authors upon those branches of the Law, which are at the time the subject of the lectures. These notes, thus written out, are, when complete, comprised in five large volumes, which constitute books of reference, the great advantages of which must be apparent to every one of the slightest acquaintance with the comprehensive and abstruse science of the Law. The examinations, which are held every Saturday, upon the lectures of the preceding week, consist of a thorough investigation of the principles of each rule, and not merely of such questions as can be answered from memory without any exercise of the judgment.

*   *   *

There is also connected with this insitution, a Moot Court for the argument of law questions, at which Judge Gould presides. The questions that are discussed, are prepared by him in the forms in which they generally arise. These courts are held once at least in each week, two students acting as Counsellors, one on each side, and the arguments that are advanced, together with the opinion of the Judge, are carefully recorded in a book kept for that purpose. For the preparation of these questions, access may at all times be had to an extensive library. Besides these courts, there are societies established for improvement in forensic exercises, which are entirely under the control of the students.

The whole course is completed in fourteen months, including two vacations of four weeks each, one in the spring, the other in the autumn. No student can enter for a shorter period than three months. The terms of instruction are $100 for the first year, and $60 for the second, payable either in advance or at the end of the year.

DAVID HOFFMAN
"A Lecture, Introductory to a Course of Lectures, Now Delivering in the University of Maryland . . ."
1823

David M. Hoffman was one of America's earliest full-time professional legal educators, abandoning his Baltimore practice on his appointment as professor of law at the University of Maryland. There, in 1823, he not only published lectures (to which the following is an introduction) that systematized public and private law, but also developed the outlines of the content of professional legal education. Joseph Story admired these efforts, extolling them as pathbreaking. Story's warm and generous reception reflected Hoffman's insistence that the law was a science, a concept that Story heartily endorsed.

To taste the pleasures which spring from legal research, we must have entered into the principles, discovered the harmonies, and arranged with method and curiosity the innumerable topicks of the science; as in the caverns of the earth the accomplished and inquisitive mineralogist and geologist reap a satisfaction, and an interest unknown to the uninformed spectators.

With these views of the science, to which you are pledged to devote yourselves, the number and variety of its subjects, instead of alarming your patience, should animate your enterprise.

A profession so liberal and extended, so sublime and important, should be cultivated by those only who are actuated by principles of the purest, and most refined honour. Regarding law as a science equally venerable from its objects, and noble from the ingenuity and mental expansion employed and excited in its acquisition and practice, it should be the ardent desire of its votaries to see its shrine unprofaned by knavery and ignorance, and its retainers not more eminent, from the importance of their functions, than from the honesty and skill with which they discharge them.

*   *   *

If the intrinsick excellence of the profession, and its natural tendency to beget elevated and honest dispositions, be not sufficient to check the wayward proclivity of some men's minds towards vice and dishonour, it is fortunate that our profession has a powerful control over its members, in the authority possessed by courts of justice (whose officers lawyers are, and under whose commission alone, are they competent to act) to suspend them, or wholly to deprive them of the privilege of practice; and, if this be once done, by any court of judicature, all others, by courtesy, would, at once, adjudge them unworthy members, and close every hope of amending this condition, by a change of residence.

You have then, every motive for exerting the utmost assiduity in your studies, and the most sacred honour in the practice of your profession. Respect and influence in society, professional reputation, the highest stations of honour and profit, in a great and enlightened republick, and all the goods of intellectual and worldly wealth are proffered to you. The character of a lawyer who does justice to his profession, and to the important station he holds in life, is, indeed, truly excellent and dignified. He is one, whom early education has imbued with the principles of probity, and habituated to labour and research, in that which enlarges, and refines the mind. He desires to impart lustre to the utility of his learning, by fostering every honourable and amiable affection. The fountains of liberal science and polite letters he has tasted of, before he enters on the pursuit of his more technical studies, and has thus protected himself from pedantry and narrow views. Versed in the sciences most necessary to the purposes of society, he naturally obtains over it a large and legitimate control, which he exercises only that he may become in it a more useful member. He is the asserter of right, the accuser of wrong, the protector of innocence, and the terror of crime. He labours not for those alone who can afford the honorarium, but the widow, the fatherless, and the oppressed are ever in his mind. No prospect of gain will ever induce him to advise the pursuit of law against right, or sober judgment; nor will any man's greatness be a shield against the justice due to his client. If he assist in the enaction of laws, which he may afterwards be called on to vindicate, it is done with an eye solely to his country's good, and whilst he respects its legislature and judiciary, he learns to reverence the constitution more than either. History is his field as he learns in it the rudiments and revolutions of his science. Rehetorick and logic are the weapons by which he imparts to his oratory warmth and grace, force and clearness.

* * *

Hence . . . the importance, nay, necessity, as adjudicated cases multiply, of arranging them in classes, and extracting their spirit in treatises. This method subserves a double purpose; it gives the student a comprehensive view of the subject, and collects under his eye the cases from which it has been extracted, to which he may, and often should refer for confirmation or correction. It is true, that while a student has the power to inquire at the fountains themselves; while the amount of collected knowledge is not yet so great but that within the usual legal novitiate, he may himself survey the whole ground, it is all important, for correct and certain knowledge, that he mark, learn, and digest for himself. Such, however, is the vast extent of most of the branches of legal science, that such a mode of study would be nearly impossible. But should he pursue this course to the greatest extent, the methodized treatises, especially of our own time, are of infinite use; they give the natural order of inquiry, they show what is to be sought, and where it is to be found—with such aids, if we inquire for ourselves, it is of little importance that our conclusion shall be exactly the same.

* * *

Even municipal law (in its most restricted signification) is not a system of merely positive and arbitrary rules. It has its deep foundations in the universal laws of our moral nature, and, all its positive enactments, proceeding on these, must receive their just interpretation with a reference to them. Would it be possible (for instance) to interpret justly a law, or explain a contract, without knowledge of the general principles on which they are promulgated or entered into? Whence proceeds the rule that laws should not be retrospective, but from the principle of natural law, or ethicks, that associations are bound only by rules to which they may be supposed to have consented? What are the rules of evidence, but metaphysical and ethical modes of investigating truth on the one hand, and limiting our deductions by a regard to human rights and feelings, and to our moral constitution, on the other? How else is the great point of expatriation (on which there have been so many positive enactments) to be settled but by reference to the universal principles on which political association at first arose? In these and infinite other cases, nay, in all modifications of positive institutions, there can be no just design on the part of legislators, nor correct interpretation on those who administer their provisions, without knowledge of the true principles of moral and political philosophy. Nay, the very obedience of the governed proceeds, doubtless, from an apprehension, however imperfect, of the great and obvious principles of moral justice.

Note: The Evolution of Legal Education

Through the nineteenth century, apprenticeship slowly gave way to more structured modes of legal instruction, increasingly associated with colleges and universities. Although early proprietary law schools, like Litchfield, were successful for a time, the conservative bar's demand for classically educated lawyers gradually forced law schools that were not affiliated with universities to the margins of legal education. The university law schools assumed the role of inculcating an ideology in their students, one that stressed professionalism, the supposedly apolitical character of law, and respect for extant institutions, thus reinforcing the inherently conservative inclinations of the bar noted earlier by Tocqueville.

But the university law schools grew somnolent and complacent as the century wore on, until they were shaken to their intellectual foundations by the revolution in legal education begun by Christopher C. Langdell at Harvard Law School after he became dean in 1870. The triumph of what in its time was called "the Harvard method" was complete within a generation, driving other forms of legal education to the periphery.

Langdell transformed Harvard Law School in numerous ways. He required either a baccalaureate degree or passage of a stiff entrance examination as a condition of matriculation; extended the course of study from two to three years; devised both the Socratic method of classroom teaching and its indispensable ancillary, the casebook; required final examinations in courses; instituted the Law Review; hired full-time law teachers in place of the practitioner part-timers who had been the rule; persistently raised both the number and the quality of the students admitted and, not coincidentally, the tuition that they paid; increased the size of the faculty; expanded the law library; built Austin Hall to replace the noisy, unsafe, wooden Dane Hall; and, most important, indelibly impressed the ideology of law-as-science on the teaching of law at Harvard.

Langdell believed that law is a science and that all the available materials of this science are contained in printed books:

> If law be not a science, a university will best consult its own dignity in declining to teach it. If it be not a science, it is a species of handicraft, and may best be learned by serving an apprenticeship to one who practices it. If it be a science, it will scarcely be disputed that it is one of the greatest and most difficult of sciences, and that it needs all the light that the most enlightened seat of learning can throw upon it. Again, law can be learned and taught in a university by means of printed books. If, therefore, there are other and better means of teaching and learning law than printed books, or if printed books can only be used to the best advantage in connection with other means,—for instance, the work of a lawyer's office, or attendance upon the proceedings of courts of justice,—it must be confessed that such means cannot be provided by a university. But if printed books are the ultimate sources of all legal knowledge; if every student who would obtain any mastery of law as a science must resort to these ultimate sources; and if the only assistance which it is possible for the learner to receive is such as can be afforded by teachers who have travelled the same road before him,—then a university, and a university alone, can furnish every possible facility for teaching and learning law. . . . We have also constantly inculcated the idea that the library is the proper workshop of professors and students alike; that it is to us all that the laboratories of the university are to the chemists and physicists, all that the museum of natural history is to the zoologists, all that the botanical garden is to the botanists.[13]

Formalism in Legal Education

CHRISTOPHER C. LANGDELL
A Selection of Cases on the Law of Contracts
1871

The concept of law as a science contained within itself the potential for directing legal thought toward arid sterility. If the scientific comparison was taken too literally, it would lead to the intellectual dead end of formalism. Langdell anticipated just such a route in the Preface to his pathbreaking Contracts *casebook.*

Oliver Wendell Holmes, Jr., in turn, warned of the dangers such a direction posed, in his review of the second edition (1880) of that casebook.

Preface

I entered upon the duties of my present position, a year and a half ago, with a settled conviction that law could only be taught or learned effectively by means of cases in some form. I had entertained such an opinion ever since I knew anything of the nature of law or legal study; but it was chiefly through my experience as a learner that it was formed, as well as subsequently strengthened and confirmed. Of teaching indeed, as a business, I was entirely without experience; nor had I given much consideration to that subject, except so far as proper methods of teaching are involved in proper methods of study.

Now, however, I was called upon to consider directly the subject of teaching, not theoretically but practically, in connection with a large school with its more or less complicated organization, its daily routine, and daily duties. I was expected to take a large class of pupils, meet them regularly from day to day, and give them systematic instruction in such branches of law as had been assigned to me. To accomplish this successfully, it was necessary, first, that the efforts of the pupils should go hand in hand with mine, that is, that they should study with direct reference to my instruction; secondly, that the study thus required of them should be of the kind from which they might reap the greatest and most lasting benefit; thirdly, that the instruction should be of such a character that the pupils might at least derive a greater advantage from attending it than from devoting the same time to private study. How could this threefold object be accomplished? Only one mode occurred to me which seemed to hold out any reasonable prospect of success; and that was, to make a series of cases, carefully selected from the books of reports, the subject alike of study and instruction. But here I was met by what seemed at first to be an insuperable practical difficulty, namely, the want of books; for though it might be practicable, in case of private pupils having free access to a complete library, to refer them directly to the books of reports, such a course was quite out of the question with a large class, all of whom would want the same books at the same time. Nor would such a course be without great drawbacks and inconveniences, even in the case of a single pupil. As he would always have to go where the books were, and could only have access to them there during certain prescribed hours, it would be impossible for him to economize his time or work to the best advantage; and he would be liable to be constantly haunted by the apprehension that he was spending time, labor, and money in studying cases which would be inaccessible to him in after life.

It was with a view to removing these obstacles, that I was first led to inquire into the feasibility of preparing and publishing such a selection of cases as would be adapted to my purpose as a teacher. The most important element in that inquiry was the great and rapidly increasing number of reported cases in every department of law. In view of this fact, was there any satisfactory principle upon which such a selection could be made? It seemed to me that there was. Law, considered as a science, consists of certain principles or doctrines. To have such a mastery of these as to be able to apply them with constant facility and certainly to the ever-tangled skein of human affairs, is what constitutes a true lawyer; and hence to acquire that mastery should be the business of every earnest student of law. Each of these doctrines has arrived at its present state by slow degrees; in other words, it is a growth, extending in many cases through centuries. This growth is to be traced in the main through a series of cases; and much the shortest and best, if not the only way of mastering the doctrine effectually is by studying the cases in which it is embodied. But the cases which are useful and necessary for this purpose at the present day bear an exceedingly small proportion to all that have been reported. The vast majority are useless and worse than useless for any purpose of systematic study. Moreover, the number of fundamental legal doctrines is much less than is commonly supposed; the many different guises in which the same doctrine is constantly making its appearance, and the great extent to which legal treatises are a repetition of each other, being the cause of much misapprehension. If these doctrines could be so classified and arranged that each should be found in its proper place, and nowhere else, they would cease to be formidable from their number. It seemed to me, therefore, to be possible to take such a branch of the law as Contracts, for example, and, without exceeding comparatively moderate limits, to select, classify, and arrange all the cases which had contributed in any important degree to the growth, development, or establishment of any of its essential doctrines; and that such a work could not fail to be of material service to all who desire to study that branch of law systematically and in its original sources.

Note: Critics of Langdellian Assumptions

Not every legal educator enthusiastically endorsed Langdell's theories. One of the earliest critics was Oliver Wendell Holmes, Jr., who wrote scathingly of Langdell that his

> ideal in the law, the end of all his striving, is the elegantia juris, or logical integrity of the system as a system. He is, perhaps, the greatest living legal theologian. But as a theologian he is less concerned with his postulates than to show that the conclusions from them hang together.

*   *   *

> If Mr. Langdell could be suspected of ever having troubled himself about Hegel, we might call him a Hegelian in disguise, so entirely is he interested in the formal connection of things, or logic, as distinguished from the feelings which make the content of logic, and which have actually shaped the substance of law. The life of the law has not been logic; it has been experience. The seed of every new growth within its sphere has been a felt necessity.[14]

Legal Theory in the Late Nineteenth Century

In the late nineteenth century, some American lawyers rethought the premises of the American legal order. Prominent lawyers and judges gave voice to the fears gripping the emergent professional elite. Bar leaders were deeply shaken by labor unrest and socialist ideology; they responded in frightened reaction, going further than Rufus

Choate had done a half-century earlier in identifying law as a bulwark against change. Treatise writers like Thomas M. Cooley and Christopher Tiedemann reassured the bar that lawyers would continue to fend off the evils of unions, socialism, and democracy. Joseph Choate used such ideas in his arguments in the *Income Tax Cases* of 1895, condemning innovations like the federal income tax as the opening salvo of a cataclysmic class warfare.

The formalism of such views invited rebuttal, and it was not long in coming, partly from Oliver Wendell Holmes, Jr., on the Massachusetts Supreme Judicial Court and the United States Supreme Court. Roscoe Pound of the Harvard Law School condemned a mode of thinking that he called "Mechanical Jurisprudence" and suggested a more realistic approach to law that took account of empirical evidence.

This clash of ideas set the stage for the struggles over the direction of public law in the first third of the twentieth century. Holmes and Pound were precursors of the post–World War I movement known as Legal Realism, which dethroned turn-of-the-century formalism, at least for a time.

THOMAS M. COOLEY
A Treatise on the Constitutional Limitations which Rest upon the Legislative Power of the States of the American Union
1868

Thomas M. Cooley towered over the legal landscape of the late nineteenth century. In influence, he had few peers, even in an age when lawyers and judges were achieving unprecedented extensions of their power to make public policy. Cooley was successively professor of law at the University of Michigan, justice of the Michigan Supreme Court, and first chairman of the Interstate Commerce Commission. But his authority cannot be measured only by the positions he held. His Treatise on the Constitutional Limitations *was canonical for constitutional interpretation well into the twentieth century. As the title of his treatise indicates, Cooley's emphasis was not on empowerment, but on its opposite—the inhibition of power. To him, the genius of the American republican experiment was that it restricted power. That axiomatic premise went far to baffle the emergence of the regulatory state.*

Of the Protection to Property by "The Law of the Land"

The protection of the subject in the free enjoyment of his life, his liberty, and his property, except as they might be declared, by the judgment of his peers or the law of the land, to be forfeited, was guaranteed by the thirty-ninth chapter of Magna Charta, "which alone," says Blackstone, "would have merited the title that it bears, of the great charter." The people of the American States, holding the sovereignty in their own hands, have no occasion to exact pledges for a due observance of individual rights from anyone; but the aggressive tendency of power is such, that in framing the instruments under which their governments are to be administered by their agents, they have deemed it important to repeat the guaranty, and thereby adopted it as a principle of constitutional protection.

*   *   *

What then is meant by "due process of law," and "the law of the land," in the constitutional provisions which we have referred to, as they are applied to the protection of rights in property, and in what cases can legislative action be annulled as not being "the law of the land," or judicial or ministerial action set aside as not being "due process of law" in the constitutional sense?

*   *   *

When the government, through its established agencies, interferes with the title to one's property, or with his independent enjoyment of it, and its act is called in question as not in accordance with the law of the land, we are to test its validity by those principles of civil liberty and constitutional defence which have become established in our system of law, and not by any rules that pertain to forms of procedure merely. In judicial proceedings the law of the land requires a hearing before condemnation, and judgment before dispossession; but when property is appropriated by the government to public uses, or the legislature attempts to control it through remedial statutes, different considerations prevail from those which relate to controversies between man and man, different proceedings are required, and we have only to see whether the interference can be justified by the established rules applicable to the case. Due process of law in each particular case means, such an exertion of the powers of government as the settled maxims of law sanction, and under such safeguards for the protection of individual rights as those maxims prescribe for the class of cases to which the one in question belongs.

*   *   *

There is no rule or principle known to our system under which private property can be taken from one man and transferred to another for the private use and benefit of such other person, whether by general laws or by special enactment. The purpose must be public, and must have reference to the needs of the government. No reason of general public policy will be sufficient to protect such transfers where they operate upon existing vested rights.

*   *   *

The doubt might also arise whether a regulation made for any one class of citizens, entirely arbitrary in its character, and restricting their rights, privileges, or legal capacities in a manner before unknown to the law, could be sustained, notwithstanding its generality. Distinctions in these respects should be based upon some reason which renders them important,—like the want of capacity in infants, and insane persons; but if the legislature should undertake to provide that persons following some specified lawful trade or employment should not have capacity to make contracts, or to receive conveyances, or to build such houses as others were allowed to erect, or in any other way to make such use of their property as was permissible to others, it can scarcely be doubted that the act would transcend the due bounds of legislative powers, even if it did not come in conflict with express constitutional provisions. The man or the class forbidden the acquisition or enjoyment of property in the manner permitted to the community at large would be deprived of liberty in particulars of primary importance to his or their "pursuit of happiness."

Equality of rights, privileges, and capacities unquestionably should be the aim of the law; and if special privileges are granted, or special burdens or restrictions imposed in any case, it must be presumed that the legislature designed to depart as little as possible from this fundamental maxim of government. The State, it is to be presumed, has no favors to bestow, and designs to inflict no arbitrary deprivation of rights. Special privileges are obnoxious and discriminations against persons or classes are still more so.

*　　　*　　　*

[T]here are other cases where it becomes necessary for the public authorities to interfere with the control by individuals of their property, and even to destroy it, where the owners themselves have fully observed all their duties to their fellows and to the State, but where, nevertheless, some controlling public necessity demands the interference or destruction. A strong instance of this description is where it becomes necessary to take, use, or destroy the private property of individuals to prevent the spreading of a fire, the ravages of a pestilence, the advance of a hostile army, or any other great public calamity. Here the individual is in no degree in fault, but his interest must yield to that "necessity" which "knows no law." The establishment of limits within the denser portions of cities and villages, within which buildings constructed of inflammable materials shall not be erected or repaired, may also, in some cases, be equivalent to a destruction of private property; but regulations for this purpose have been sustained notwithstanding this result. Wharf lines may also be established for the general good, even though they prevent the owners of water-fronts from building out on that which constitutes private property. And, whenever the legislature deem it necessary to the protection of a harbor to forbid the removal of stones, gravel, or sand from the beach, they may establish regulations to that effect under penalties, and make them applicable to the owners of the soil equally with other persons. Such regulations are only "a just restraint of an injurious use of property, which the legislature have authority" to impose.

*　　　*　　　*

The preservation of the public morals is peculiarly subject to legislative supervision, which may forbid the keeping, exhibition, or sale of indecent books or pictures, and cause their destruction if seized; or prohibit or regulate the places of amusement that may be resorted to for the purpose of gaming; or forbid altogether the keeping of implements of gaming for unlawful games; or prevent the keeping and exhibition of stallions in public places. And the power to provide for the compulsory observance of the first day of the week is also to be referred to the same authority.

Note: The "Conservative Crisis" of the Law in the 1890s

To concerned observers of American society from the 1870s to the 1890s, symptoms of social crisis abounded. Labor violence was the most conspicuous. Although today we see workers and their unions as the victims of management repression, contemporaries saw it largely the other way around: workers threatened to thwart the benefits that industrialization was supposed to bring; they sought to redistribute wealth from the rich to the working classes by violence; unions demanded a share in management's prerogatives; and the march of democracy provided a political means to accomplish these ends short of violence. But there was violence aplenty too: the Molly Maguires in the mines of eastern Pennsylvania, the General Strike of 1877, the Haymarket bombing of 1886, the Homestead Massacre and the Coeur d'Alene strike of 1892, the Pullman strike of 1894. The rise of European radical movements, such as the Marxian Socialists, the Bakuninite Anarchists, and politically oriented socialists, seemed to precede a wave of assassinations, which in turn seemed to have their American echoes: the attempted assassination of industrialist Henry Frick in connection with the Homestead Massacre, the assassination of President William McKinley by an anarchist in 1901. The experience of actual communism in the Paris Commune of 1871 terrified Americans who followed the news from Europe, providing as Napoleon had done earlier a superficial but convenient proof of the validity of conservative political theories.

Immigration poured masses of aliens into the country in response to the demand for unskilled labor. These "new" immigrants were largely non-Protestant: Roman Catholic, Jewish, Orthodox. Their eastern and southern European languages added a Babel to a nation only beginning to assimilate earlier waves of German and Irish immigrants. Strange in clothing and manners, they challenged what contemporaries considered to be the ethnic and religious homogeneity of an older, rural America. At a minimum, they had to be "Americanized": stripped of their languages, religions, and customs, and bent to the yoke of industrial discipline.

Urbanization seemed to validate Thomas Jefferson's vision of cities as "great sores" on the body politic, pustulating civic ulcers oozing political corruption, alien manners, and decaying public health. Mugwump political reform efforts, enfeebled by their middle-class origins and orientation, appeared inadequate to cope with the rise of the cities.

Such an unraveling of the social fabric would unavoidably have an impact on the rule of law. Lawyers and judges mobilized all their considerable resources to shore up law's hegemonic dominance and repulse the labor-socialist-immigrant hordes.

CHRISTOPHER G. TIEDEMANN
A Treatise on the Limitations of Police Power in the United States
1886

Christopher Tiedemann, a twenty-nine-year-old law professor at the time his influential treatise was first published, provided the most candid expression of the fears felt by the legal elite. Politics and ideology were not far below the surface of legal doctrine in works like Tiedemann's. When lawyers considered democracy to be the foe of the rule of law, formalist doctrine provided the rationale for judicial and legal reaction.

Socialism, Communism, and Anarchism are rampant throughout the civilized world. The State is called on to protect the weak against the shrewdness of the stronger, to determine what wages a workman shall receive for his labor, and how many hours daily he shall labor. Many trades and occupations are being prohibited because some are damaged incidentally by their prosecution, and many ordinary pursuits are made government monopolies. The demands of the Socialists and Communists vary in degree and in detail, and the most extreme of them insist upon the assumption by government of the paternal character altogether, abolishing all private property in land, and making the State the sole possessor of the working capital of the nation.

Contemplating these extraordinary demands of the great army of discontents, and their apparent power, with the growth and development of universal suffrage, to enforce their views of civil polity upon the civilized world, the conservative class stand in constant fear of the advent of an absolutism more tyrannical and more unreasoning than any before experienced by man, the absolutism of a democratic majority.

The principal object of the present work is to demonstrate, by a detailed discussion of the constitutional limitations upon the police power in the United States, that under the written constitutions, Federal and State, democratic absolutism is impossible in this country, as long as the popular reverence for the constitutions, in their restrictions upon governmental activity, is nourished and sustained by a prompt avoidance by the courts of any violations of their provisions, in word or in spirit. The substantial rights of the minority are shown to be free from all lawful control or interference by the majority, except so far as such control or interference may be necessary to prevent injury to others in the enjoyment of their rights.

Populist Platform Adopted at St. Louis
1892

The "conservative-crisis" mentality was not a fantasy having no grounding in reality. While we may think, with the benefit of a century's hindsight, that the legal-judicial conservatives of the Victorian era overreacted, there was some basis in the world around them for their anxieties. The Populist party of the 1890s provided a political expression of workers' and farmers' discontents. Its 1892 St. Louis Platform contained most of the prevalent proposals and nostrums for political and economic reform, including electoral reforms like the Australian (secret) ballot, restrictions on open immigration, an eight-hour working day, an income tax, the initiative and referendum, and opposition to subsidies to corporations. Conservatives saw portents of class warfare and expropriation of property in the Populists' attacks on railroads and telegraph companies.

Preamble

The conditions which surround us best justify our co-operation; we meet in the midst of a nation brought to the verge of moral, political, and material ruin. Corruption dominates the ballot-box, the Legislatures, the Congress, and touches even the ermine of the bench. The people are demoralized; most of the States have been compelled to isolate the voters at the polling places to prevent universal intimidation and bribery. The newspapers are largely subsidized or muzzled, public opinion silenced, business prostrated, homes covered with mortgages, labor impoverished, and the land concentrating in the hands of the capitalists. The urban workmen are denied the right to organize for self-protection, imported pauperized labor beats down their wages, a hireling standing army, unrecognized by our laws, is established to shoot them down, and they are rapidly degenerating into European conditions. The fruits of the toil of millions are boldly stolen to build up colossal fortunes for a few, unprecedented in the history of mankind; and the possessors of these, in turn, despise the Republic and endanger liberty. From the same prolific womb of governmental injustice we breed the two great classes—tramps and millionaires.

The national power to create money is appropriated to enrich bond-holders; a vast public debt payable in legal-tender currency has been funded into gold-bearing bonds, thereby adding millions to the burdens of the people.

Silver, which has been accepted as coin since the dawn of history, has been demonetized to add to the purchasing power of gold by decreasing the value of all forms of property as well as human labor, and the supply of currency is purposely abridged to fatten usurers, bankrupt enterprise, and enslave industry. A vast conspiracy against mankind has been organized on two continents, and it is rapidly taking possession of the world. If not met and overthrown at once it forebodes terrible social convulsions, the destruction of civilization, or the establishment of an absolute despotism.

We have witnessed for more than a quarter of a century the struggles of the two great political parties for power and plunder, while grievous wrongs have been inflicted upon the suffering people. We charge that the controlling influences dominating both these parties have permitted the existing dreadful conditions to develop without serious effort to prevent or restrain them. Neither do they now promise us any substantial reform. They have agreed together to ignore, in the coming campaign, every issue but one. They propose to drown the outcries of a plundered people with the uproar of a sham battle over the tariff, so that capitalists, corporations, national banks, rings, trusts, watered stock, the demonetization of silver and the oppressions of the usurer may all be lost sight of. They propose to sacrifice our homes, lives, and children on the altar of mammon; to destroy the multitude in order to secure corruption funds from the millionaires.

*   *   *

Our country finds itself confronted by conditions for which there is no precedent in the history of the world; our annual agricultural productions amount to billions of dollars in value, which must, within a few weeks or months, be exchanged for billions of dollars' worth of commodities consumed in their production; the existing currency supply is wholly inadequate to make this exchange; the results are falling prices, the formation of combines and rings, the impoverishment of the producing class. We pledge ourselves that if given power we will labor to correct these evils by wise and reasonable legislation, in accordance with the terms of our platform.

We believe that the power of government—in other words, of the people—should be expanded (as in the case of the postal service) as rapidly and as far as the good sense of an intelligent people and the teachings of experience shall justify, to the end that oppression, injustice, and poverty shall eventually cease in the land.

JOSEPH H. CHOATE
Arguments for Appellant in the *Income Tax Cases (Pollock* v. *Farmers' Loan and Trust Co.)*
157 U.S. 429 (1895)

Joseph Choate was one of the most eminent practitioners at the bar of the United States Supreme Court in his day, so the arguments quoted below cannot be dismissed as the rantings of a provincial crank; on the contrary, they represent the considered judgment of America's legal elite. Choate's arguments illustrate the process whereby fear and insecurity produce ideology and dogma; then ideology and dogma become embodied in legal argument; and finally, in the Field excerpt that follows this one, legal argument is endorsed by judges predisposed by their own ideology to absorb it into the structure of constitutional doctrine. Thus it was that in the name of one of America's oldest and loftiest legal ideals— the rule of law—a class bias was transformed into law. The holding of the Income Tax Cases *was consigned to the dump of discarded laws by constitutional amendment (the Sixteenth) within less than twenty years.*

I look upon this case with very different eyes from those of either the Attorney General or his associate who has just closed. I believe there are private rights of property here to be protected; that we have a right to come to this court and ask for their protection, and that this court has a right, without asking leave of the Attorney General or of any counsel, to hear our plea. The act of Congress which we are impugning before you is communistic in its purposes and tendencies, and is defended here upon principles as communistic, socialistic—what shall I call them— populistic as ever have been addressed to any political assembly in the world.

I do not believe that any member of this court ever has sat or ever will sit to hear and decide a case the consequences of which will be so far-reaching as this—not even the venerable member [Justice Field] who survives from the early days of the civil war, and has sat upon every question of reconstruction, of national destiny, of state destiny that has come up during the last thirty years. No member of this court will live long enough to hear a case which will involve a question of more importance than this, the preservation of the fundamental rights of private property and equality before the law, and the ability of the people of these United States to rely upon the guaranties of the Constitution. If it be true, as my friend said in closing, that the passions of the people are aroused on this subject, if it be true that a mighty army of sixty million citizens is likely to be incensed by this decision, it is the more vital to the future welfare of this country that this court again resolutely and courageously declare, as Marshall did, that it has the power to set aside an act of Congress violative of the Constitution, and that it will not hesitate in executing that power, no matter what the threatened consequences of popular or populistic wrath may be.

The *Income Tax Cases*
(*Pollock* v. *Farmers' Loan and Trust Co.*)

Perhaps it is unfair to quote the words of a great jurist written when he had slipped into dotage. Nevertheless, Justice Stephen J. Field's passionate jeremiad demonstrates the stampede mentality of legal and judicial conservatives at the turn of the century as they came to believe their own rhetoric and heed one another's overwrought warnings about the expansion of popular political power.

Field, J. Concurring:

Here I close my opinion. I could not say less in view of questions of such gravity that go down to the very foundation of the government. If the provisions of the Constitution can be set aside by an act of Congress, where is the course of usurpation to end? The present assault upon capital is but the beginning. It will be but the stepping-stone to others, larger and more sweeping, till our political contests will become a war of the poor against the rich; a war constantly growing in intensity and bitterness.

OLIVER WENDELL HOLMES, JR.
The Common Law
1881

Oliver Wendell Holmes, Jr., took up the first phase of his life's work at a most auspicious time. After his dogged labor in preparing the twelfth edition of James Kent's Commentaries on American Law *(1873), Holmes was determined to reconsider the fundamental nature of legal concepts and obligations. Influenced by the empiricism of William James and Charles Peirce, Holmes was ready to question the philosophical bases of Anglo-American common-law rules.*

The following excerpts, taken from his chapters on tort law, illustrate some of the dominant themes of Holmes's work. He was determined to rid law of moral concepts, grounding it instead on views of public policy. So conceived, law would take into account only an individual's self-interest, while ignoring his subjective state of mind. Law had to evolve external and objective criteria to measure liability in crimes, torts, and contracts. It also had to acknowledge the primacy of the majority's view of what is desirable as a matter of policy.

The object of this book is to present a general view of the Common Law. To accomplish the task, other tools are needed besides logic. It is something to show that the consistency of a system requires a particular result, but it is not all. The life of the law has not been logic; it has been experience. The felt necessities of the time, the prevalent moral and political theories, intuitions of public policy, avowed or unconscious, even the prejudices which judges share with their fellow-men, have had a good deal more to do than the syllogism in determining the rules by which men should be governed. The law embodies the story of a nation's development through many centuries, and it cannot be dealt with as if it contained only the axioms and corollaries of a book of mathematics. In order to know what it is, we must know what it has been, and what it tends to become. We must alternately consult history and existing theories of legislation. But the most difficult labor will be to understand the combination of the two into new products at every stage. The substance of the law at any given time pretty nearly corresponds, so far as it goes, with what is then understood to be convenient; but its form and machinery, and the degree to which it is able to work out desired results, depend very much upon its past.

*   *   *

In substance the growth of the law is legislative. And this in a deeper sense than what the courts declare to have always been the law is in fact new. It is legislative in its grounds. The very considerations which judges most rarely mention, and always with an apology, are the secret root from which the law draws all the juices of life. I mean, of course, consideration of what is expedient for the community concerned. Every important principle which is developed by litigation is in fact and at bottom the result of more or less definitely understood views of public policy; most generally, to be sure, under our practice and traditions, the unconscious result of instinctive preferences and inarticulate convictions, but none the less traceable to views of public policy in the last analysis. And as the law is administered by able and experienced men, who know too much to sacrifice good sense to syllogism, it will be found that, when ancient rules maintain themselves in the way that has been and will be shown in this book, new reasons more fitted to the time have been found for them, and that they gradually receive a new content, and at last a new form, from the grounds to which they have been transplanted.

But hitherto this process has been largely unconscious. It is important, on that account, to bring to mind what the actual course of events has been. If it were only to insist on a more conscious recognition of the legislative function of the courts, as just explained, it would be useful, as we shall see more clearly further on.

What has been said will explain the failure of all theories which consider the law only from its formal side, whether they attempt to deduce the corpus from a priori postulates, or fall into the humbler error of supposing the science of the law to reside in the elegantia juris, or logical cohesion of part with part. The truth is, that the law is always approaching, and never reaching, consistency. It is forever adopting new principles from life at one end, and it always retains old ones from history at the other, which have not yet been absorbed or sloughed off. It will become entirely consistent only when it ceases to grow.

Since the ancient forms of action have disappeared, a broader treatment of the subject ought to be possible. Ignorance is the best of law reformers. People are glad to discuss a question on general principles, when they have forgotten the special knowledge necessary for technical reasoning. But the present willingness to generalize is founded on more than merely negative grounds. The philosophical habit of the day, the frequency of legislation, and the ease with which the law may be changed to meet the opinions and wishes of the public, all make it natural and unavoidable that judges as well as others should openly discuss the legislative principles upon which their decisions must always rest in the end, and should base their judgments upon broad considerations of policy to which the traditions of the bench would hardly have tolerated a reference fifty years ago.

*   *   *

The business of the law of torts is to fix the dividing lines between those cases in which a man is liable for harm which he has done, and those in which he is not. But it cannot enable him to predict with certainty whether a given act under given circumstances will make him liable, because an act will rarely have that effect unless followed by damage, and for the most part, if not always, the consequences of an act are not known, but only guessed at as more or less probable. All the rules that the law can lay down beforehand are rules for determining the conduct which will be followed by liability if it is followed by harm,—that is, the conduct which a man pursues at his peril. The only guide for the future to be drawn from a decision against a defendant in an action of tort is that similar acts, under circumstances which cannot be distinguished except by the result from those of the defendant, are done at the peril of the actor; that if he escapes liability, it is simply because by good fortune no harm comes of his conduct in the particular event.

If, therefore, there is any common ground for all liability in tort, we shall best find it by eliminating the event as it actually turns out, and by considering only the principles on which the peril of his conduct is thrown upon the actor. We are to ask what are the elements, on the defendant's side, which must all be present before liability is possible, and the presence of which will commonly make him liable if damage follows.

The law of torts abounds in moral phraseology. It has much to say of wrongs, of malice, fraud, intent, and negligence. Hence it may naturally be supposed that the risk of a man's conduct is thrown upon him as the result of some moral short-coming. But while this notion has been entertained, the extreme opposite will be found to have been a far more popular opinion;—I mean the notion that a man is answerable for all the consequences of his acts, or, in other words, that he acts at his peril always, and wholly irrespective of the state of his consciousness upon the matter.

*   *   *

The general principle of our law is that loss from accident must lie where it falls, and this principle is not affected by the fact that a human being is the instrument of misfortune. But relatively to a given human being anything is accident which he could not fairly have been expected to contemplate as possible, and therefore to avoid. In the language of the late Chief Justice Nelson of New York: "No case or principle can be found, or if found can be maintained, subjecting an individual to liability for an act done without fault on his part. . . . All the cases concede that an injury arising from inevitable accident, or, which in law or reason is the same thing, from an act that ordinary human care and foresight are unable to guard against, is but the misfortune of the sufferer, and lays no foundation for legal responsibility." If this were not so, any act would be sufficient, however remote, which set in motion or opened the door for a series of physical sequences ending in damage; such as riding the horse, in the case of the runaway, or even coming to a place where one is seized with a fit and strikes the plaintiff in an unconscious spasm. Nay, why need the defendant have acted at all, and why is it not enough that his existence has been at the expense of the plaintiff? The requirement of an act is the requirement that the defendant should have made a choice. But the only possible purpose of introducing this moral element is to make the power of avoiding the evil complained of a condition of liability. There is no such power where the evil cannot be foreseen. Here we reach the argument from policy. . . .

A man need not, it is true, do this or that act,—the term act implies a choice,—but he must act somehow. Furthermore, the public generally profits by individual activity. As action cannot be avoided, and tends to the public good, there is obviously no policy in throwing the hazard of what is at once desirable and inevitable upon the actor.

The state might conceivably make itself a mutual insurance company against accidents, and distribute the burden of its citizens' mishaps among all its members. There might be a pension for paralytics, and state aid for those who suffered in person or estate from tempest or wild beasts. As between individuals it might adopt the mutual insurance principle pro tanto, and divide damages when both were in fault, as in the rusticum judicium of the admiralty, or it might throw all loss upon the actor irrespective of fault. The state does none of these things, however, and the prevailing view is that its cumbrous and expensive machinery ought not to be set in motion unless some clear benefit is to be derived from disturbing the status quo. State interference is an evil, where it cannot be shown to be a good. Universal insurance, if desired, can be better and more cheaply accomplished by private enterprise. The undertaking to redistribute losses simply on the ground that they resulted from the defendant's act would not only be open to these objections, but, as it is hoped the preceding discussion has shown, to the still graver one of offending the sense of justice. Unless my act is of a nature to threaten others, unless under the circumstances a prudent man would have foreseen the possibility of harm, it is no more justifiable to make me indemnify my neighbor against the consequences, than to make me do the same thing if I had fallen upon him in a fit, or to compel me to insure him against lightning.

OLIVER WENDELL HOLMES, JR.
"The Path of the Law"
1897

This, Holmes's best-known extrajudicial essay, carried forward themes first developed in The Common Law: *the dissociation of law and morality, the search for external criteria for legal liability, and the emphasis on policy as opposed to logic. But new emphases appeared as well, particularly a forcefully stated positivism, where Holmes defined law as a prediction of what the courts would do. Holmes's effort to strip law of moralistic concepts was now clothed in a striking metaphor: the "bad man theory" of law. The influence of Charles Darwin on Holmes's thought was evident here too. All the metaphors were biological: the law grows; it is not a machine or an equation.*

I wish, if I can, to lay down some first principles for the study of this body of dogma or systematized prediction which we call law, for men who want to use it as the instrument of their business to enable them to prophesy in their turn, and, as bearing upon the study, I wish to point out an ideal which as yet our law has not attained.

The first thing for a business-like understanding of the matter is to understand its limits, and therefore I think it desirable at once to point out and dispel a confusion between morality and law, which sometimes rises to the height of conscious theory, and more often and indeed constantly is making trouble in detail without reaching the point of consciousness. You can see very plainly that a bad man has as much reason as a good one for wishing to avoid an encounter with the public force, and therefore you can see the practical importance of the distinction between morality and law. A man who cares nothing for an ethical rule which is believed and practised by his neighbors is likely nevertheless to care a good deal to avoid being made to pay money, and will want to keep out of jail if he can.

*   *   *

If you want to know the law and nothing else, you must look at it as a bad man, who cares only for the material consequences which such knowledge enables him to predict, not a good one, who finds his reasons for conduct, whether inside the law or outside of it, in the vaguer sanctions of conscience.

The confusion with which I am dealing besets confessedly legal conceptions. Take the fundamental question, What constitutes the law? You will find some text writers telling you that it is something different from what is decided by the courts of Massachusetts or England, that it is a system of reason, that it is a deduction from principles of ethics or admitted axioms or what not, which may or may not coincide with the decisions. But if we take the view of our friend the bad man we shall find that he does not care two straws for the axioms or deductions, but that he does want to know what the Massachusetts or English courts are likely to do in fact. . . . The prophecies of what the courts will do in fact, and nothing more pretentious, are what I mean by the law.

Nowhere is the confusion between legal and moral ideas more manifest than in the law of contract. Among other things, here again the so-called primary rights and duties are invested with a mystic significance beyond what can be assigned and explained. The duty to keep a contract at common law means a prediction that you must pay damages if you do not keep it,—and nothing else. If you commit a tort, you are liable to pay a compensatory sum. If you commit a contract, you are liable to pay a compensatory sum unless the promised event comes to pass, and that is all the difference. But such a mode of looking at the matter stinks in the nostrils of those who think it advantageous to get as much ethics into the law as they can.

*   *   *

The danger of which I speak is not the admission that the principles governing other phenomenon also govern the law, but the notion that a given system, ours, for instance, can be worked out like mathematics from some general axioms of conduct. This is the natural error of the schools, but it is not confined to them. I once heard a very eminent judge say that he never let a decision go until he was absolutely sure that it was right. So judicial dissent often is blamed, as if it meant simply that one side or the other were not doing their sums right, and, if they would take more trouble, agreement inevitably would come.

This mode of thinking is entirely natural. The training of lawyers is a training in logic. The processes of analogy, discrimination and deduction are those in which they are most at home. The language of judicial decision is mainly the language of logic. And the logical method and form flatter that longing for certainty and for repose which is in every human mind. But certainty generally is illusion, and repose is not the destiny of man. Behind the logical form lies a judgment as to the relative worth and importance of competing legislative grounds, often an inarticulate and unconscious judgment, it is true, and yet the very root and nerve of the whole proceeding. You can give any conclusion a logical form. You always can imply a condition in a contract. But why do you imply? It is because of some belief as to the practice of the community or of a class, or because of some opinion as to policy, or, in short, because of some attitude of yours upon a matter not capable of founding exact logical conclusions. Such matters really are battle grounds where the means do not exist for determinations that shall be good for all time, and where the decision can do no more than embody the preference of a given body in a given time and place. We do not realize how large a part of our law is open to reconsideration upon a slight change in the habit of the public mind.

                             *   *   *

I think that the judges themselves have failed adequately to recognize their duty of weighing considerations of social advantage. The duty is inevitable, and the result of the often proclaimed judicial aversion to deal with such considerations is simply to leave the very ground and foundation of judgments inarticulate, and often unconscious, as I have said. When socialism first began to be talked about, the comfortable classes of the community were a good deal frightened. I suspect that this fear has influenced judicial action both here and in England, yet it is certain that it is not a conscious factor in the decisions to which I refer. I think that something similar has led people who no longer hope to control the legislatures to look to the courts as expounders of the Constitutions, and that in some courts now principles have been discovered outside the bodies of those instruments, which may be generalized into acceptance of the economic doctrines which prevailed about fifty years ago, and a wholesale prohibition of what a tribunal of lawyers does not think about right. I cannot but believe that if the training of lawyers led them habitually to consider more definitely and explicitly the social advantage on which the rule they lay down must be justified, they sometimes would hesitate where now they are confident, and see that really they were taking sides upon debatable and often burning questions.

7

Industrialization and the Regulatory State 1860–1920

The role of the state and federal governments changed profoundly in late-nineteenth-century America. Before the Civil War, the responsibilities of government had been distributive and promotional: states and nation conferred mostly benefits, such as charters, monopolies, patents, and land grants. The hand of government doled out opportunities to individuals; it did not restrain or discipline them by regulatory inhibitions. The Civil War changed that by demonstrating the necessity and advantages of governmental regulation.

This change did not sit well with people who had known only government's largesse and who now felt the hand of the constable on their shoulder. Antebellum lawyers assumed that private law was not redistributive; that is, in theory, law did not direct the force of the state to take property or money from one class of people and give it to another. In the classic *Calder* v. *Bull* (1798) formulation, a legislature could not take the property of A and give it to B. Morton Horwitz and others have contended, however, that private law was in fact highly redistributive, privileging certain forms of property by disadvantaging others—for example, through the railroads' exercise of eminent domain. Public law could be redistributive and regulatory, hence the protections for property and contract written into the federal and state constitutions.

The dichotomy between private law and public law began to dissolve after 1865. The wartime experience of mobilizing masses of men and materiel, of moving them by rail, barge, and ship, of outfitting soldiers and mass-producing weapons and ordnance, of coordinating communications and command, and of protecting the public health of soldiers and civilians alike convinced many Americans of the need and the usefulness of governmental regulatory control. Lessons learned during the war were applied to peacetime problems. Symbolic of such regulatory changes were the adoption of standard time and time zones (1883) and a uniform railroad track gauge (1886), necessities learned by military commanders and civilian dispatchers during the war. (The initiative for these particular innovations came from the private sector, not government.)

But while regulatory control may have appeared to some to be necessary or even valuable, it was not welcome to an individual whose dreams or greed it thwarted. Thus much of the conservative opposition to regulation was justified on pleas of

353

retaining an older system of governance, according to which government's role was limited to distributing benefits and maintaining the peace.

Resentment at the emergence of the regulatory state was fueled by an unwelcome change in Americans' vision of themselves and their future. For the first time in their existence as a people, Americans came to see that their continent—and, by extension, their destiny—had limits. The United States and its riches were not infinite, after all. This disagreeable realization was the starting point for historian Frederick Jackson Turner's frontier hypothesis (first presented in 1893 at the Columbian Exposition in Chicago), which warned that the frontier, supposedly a safety valve for American society and the nursery of democracy, had now disappeared. Many Americans now lived in crowded cities and therefore had to accept regulation in such matters as sanitation, education, and land use. Would capitalism as it had flourished until then be able to survive in a regulated state?

Another source of the constitutional paradigm that emerged in the 1890s was a reaffirmation of traditional American concepts of liberty. The constitutional historian Michael Les Benedict has written that

> there were two related but distinct justifications for the laissez-faire principle in the later nineteenth century. The first was based directly upon classical economists' conception of the "laws" of economics. It suggested that almost any government effort to overcome or channel those laws was doomed to failure. The second was based on a concept of human liberty implicit in the principles of classical economics. It militated only against certain kinds of government interferences in the economy, not against all interference. That concept was that the power of government could not legitimately be exercised to benefit one person or group at the expense of others. It was this conviction—the notion that all government economic activity violated "immutable" economic laws—that lay at the heart of laissez-faire constitutionalism. . . .Laissez-faire constitutionalism received wide support in late nineteenth-century America not because it was based on widely adhered-to economic principles, and certainly not because it protected entrenched economic privilege, but rather because it was congruent with a well-established and accepted principle of American liberty.[1]

But if unwelcome to some, the regulatory state was inevitable, and resistance became marginalized as the sort of fatuous romanticism that appeals to people who get indignant or nostalgic about lost causes. For the most part, late-nineteenth-century businessmen were not fools. They not only bowed to the inevitable, but seized it opportunistically in order to turn it to their own ends. Thus the large-scale integrated industries of the period pioneered in the development of bureaucracies that improved the flow of information and control throughout their systems. The administrative regulatory state would not have been possible without the development of a corps of administrators—in other words, a bureaucracy. No such class existed in the United States before the Civil War. It proliferated after the war, in both the public and the private sectors, in time to serve the needs of industrializing America.

It was the states rather than the federal government that first experimented with regulatory bodies like commissions and boards. Before the Civil War, Ohio, New York, and a few other states created canal commissions to oversee the construction, maintenance, and operation of canal networks. From this came the experiment, unsuccessful before the Civil War, of railroad regulatory bodies, chiefly in New England.

The judiciary provided a temporary surrogate for an administrative regulatory structure, with the Massachusetts Supreme Judicial Court under Chief Justice Lemuel Shaw creating a body of common law that provided some measure of legal control of railroads.

The Civil War proved that some forms of administrative regulation were useful and, in any event, necessary. The United States Sanitary Commission, an unofficial corps that functioned as a public-health auxiliary to the Union Army, demonstrated the value of public-health controls, first in military encampments and then in cities. The success of the Union occupying army in controlling yellow fever in New Orleans provided a dramatic example of the benefits of administrative control.

This experience in New Orleans anticipated Massachusetts' and New York's experiments with statewide boards of health, both established shortly after the war. Antebellum pioneering efforts by Dorothea Dix on behalf of the insane and Horace Mann for public education provided the inspiration for postwar welfare services for those members of society not able to care for themselves. In a related vein, the Freedmen's Bureau worked throughout the Reconstruction South to regulate labor contracts of the freed slaves, provide minimal and temporary assistance to both races dislocated by the war, and supplement the peacekeeping operations of the army.

The emergence of professional self-consciousness after the war resulted not only in the formation of professional societies, such as the American Bar Association and its state counterparts, but also in the establishment of licensing standards and procedures for numerous occupations and professions. At the same time, some states began to supervise animals and inanimate objects to protect public health. Ohio created a body of inspectors of illuminating oils in 1867 to eradicate the practice of adulterating kerosene with naphtha, a dangerous and flammable combination. In the same period, Kansas and the U.S. Army cooperated to control the movement of cattle with Texas spotted fever across state lines.

When Americans began to experiment with regulatory administration in a serious way after the war, many assumed that coercive control was both unnecessary and undesirable. Instead, they placed their faith in two techniques: the gathering and dissemination of facts, and what in our day is called jawboning—persuading the reluctant subjects of regulation. To go beyond this and force compliance with regulatory edicts, some thought, would be incompatible with the freedoms that Americans had hitherto enjoyed. This spirit was exemplified in Charles Francis Adams, Jr., the first chairman of the Massachusetts Railroad Commission. Historian Thomas McCraw wrote of his outlook that

> above all, the Massachusetts agency must shun coercion. Legal process could not be employed merely as a matter of course. Accordingly, the board almost never instituted lawsuits on its own motion. It issued no orders that the corporations were legally bound to obey, except for orders to produce information. . . . This was to set an early precedent of voluntary, cooperative, state-sponsored negotiation. Such a design for business–government relations was particularly compelling in the early decades of industrialization, when no powerful public bureaucracies yet existed to help manage the economy and offset the political strength of corporations.[2]

Historians refer to regulatory agencies organized on such premises as "weak" commissions.

The "strong" commissions, by contrast, appeared in the Granger states of the Middle West and South, where angry farmers demanded stringent regulatory controls on rail carriers, public utilities, and grain elevators. These strong commissions directly set rates and mandated equal access to transportation facilities. Two landmark United States Supreme Court decisions, the *Slaughterhouse Cases* of 1873 and *Munn* v. *Illinois* in 1877, ratified the exercise of these new regulatory powers.

Because of lingering antebellum assumptions about the nature of the federal Union, the national government was something of a johnny-come-lately in the new regulatory state. Opponents of federal regulatory authority assumed hopefully that the Civil War–era experiments in regulation would prove to be a wartime aberration, and for a time federal regulation seemed to be just that. But pressures mounted for national regulation, and Congress responded with the Interstate Commerce Act of 1887, creating the first national regulatory agency, the Interstate Commerce Commission, and then with the Sherman Anti-Trust Act of 1890, which entrusted regulatory responsibility not to an administrative agency but to the federal courts. A federal income tax and abortive child-labor legislation followed, but the real geyser of federal regulation did not spout until World War I.

The reaction of state and federal judges to the regulatory state was mixed. State courts picked up the thread of antebellum higher-law jurisprudence and spun the doctrine of substantive due process out of it. The supreme courts of the leading industrial and commercial states, particularly New York and Illinois, concocted novel doctrines of property and contractual relationships that attempted to stymie state regulatory efforts. The state judges were shortly abetted by their federal brethren, who expounded doctrines of liberty of contract and substantive due process to inhibit state and federal efforts to regulate economic relationships.

Thus the turn of the century proved to be a confusing era to contemporaries and to those who gaze back on it from later times. The nation and the states coped clumsily with unprecedented social and economic change. Their early toddling steps toward administrative regulation met first with tolerance, and then with erratic hostility from judges in the grip of apocalyptic visions of social conflict. Out of this confused response there emerged the beginnings of the regulatory state we know today.

State Regulation and the Public Interest

After the Civil War, the states began to exercise their regulatory power through legislation, constitutional revision, administrative action, and judicial decision. These changes were based on the state's "police power," which Chief Justice Lemuel Shaw of the Massachusetts Supreme Judicial Court had defined in sweeping terms in *Commonwealth* v. *Alger* in 1851:

> We think it is a settled principle, growing out of the nature of well ordered civil society, that every holder of property, however absolute and unqualified may be his title, holds it under the implied liability that his use of it may be so regulated, that it shall not be injurious to the equal enjoyment of others having an equal right to the enjoyment of their property, nor injurous to the rights of the community. All property in the commonwealth, as well that in the interior as that bordering on tide water, is derived directly or indirectly from the government, and held subject to those general regulations, which

are necessary to the common good and general welfare. Rights of property, like all other social and conventional rights, are subject to such reasonable limitations in their enjoyment, as shall prevent them from being injurious, and to such reasonable restraints and regulations established by law, as the legislature, under the governing and controlling power vested in them by the constitution, may think necessary and expedient.[3]

The growing power of labor unions seemed to require state regulatory intervention through the exercise of the police power after the Civil War. Judges reacted with hostility to labor organization before mid-century, while displaying an occasional concern for the well-being of individual industrial workers. Thus it would be a reductionist error to assume that because bar and bench were hostile to unions, they were equally hostile to workingmen and -women. Reality was more complex than that. Side by side with their antiunion biases, lawyers and judges displayed a paternalistic attitude toward workers, warily tolerating protective measures enacted by legislatures that were designed to meliorate the harshest of common-law doctrines, such as the fellow servant rule. Bench and bar did not exactly welcome legislative intervention on the side of labor when it occurred, but they displayed a surprising tolerance, even a mild sympathy, for legislative efforts to ease the lot of workers.

Paternalism: Child Labor and Maximum Hours

Legislatures displayed some solicitude for workers who were not fully capable of looking after their own interests. Children and women were the most obvious beneficiaries. But some legislation also regulated the length of time that adult males could work, indicating that legislative paternalism was not limited to women and children.

New Jersey Child Labor Act
1851

1. Be it enacted by the Senate and General Assembly of the State of New Jersey, That labor performed during a period of ten hours, on any day, in all cotton, woollen, milk, paper, glass and flax factories, and in manufactories of iron and brass, shall be considered a legal day's labor.
2. And be it enacted, That hereafter no minor engaged in any factory, shall be holden or required to work more than ten hours on any day, or sixty hours in any week; and that hereafter no minor shall be admitted as a worker under the age of ten years in any factory within this state; that if any owner of, or employer in any factory shall knowingly employ any such minor, or shall require any minor over the age of ten years to work more than ten hours on any day, or sixty hours in any week, he shall be adjudged to pay a penalty of fifty dollars. . . .

Utah Smelter Acts
1896

Be it enacted by the Legislature of the State of Utah:
Section 1.   That it shall be unlawful for any person, firm or corporation to employ

any child under fourteen years of age, or any female, to work in any mine or smelter in the State of Utah.

Section 2.   Any person, firm or corporation who shall violate any of the provisions of this act shall be deemed guilty of a misdemeanor.

Be it enacted by the Legislature of the State of Utah:

Section 1.   The period of employment of working men in all underground mines or workings shall be eight (8) hours per day, except in cases of emergency where life or property is in imminent danger.

Section 2.   The period of employment of workingmen in smelters and all other institutions for the reduction or refining of ores or metals shall be eight (8) hours per day, except in cases of emergency where life or property is in imminent danger.

Section 3.   Any person, body corporate, agent, manager or employer, who shall violate any of the provisions of sections 1 and 2 of this act shall be deemed guilty of a misdemeanor.

The Repressive Approach

Illinois Criminal Syndicalism Act
1887

Mild and benevolent legislative responses to labor organization appeared to-
gether with harsh and repressive ones. Legislators, almost as much as judges,
became caught up in the climate of fear that attended industrialization and union
organization in the late nineteenth century. Although legislators generally moved
ahead of judges in providing relief to individual workers (as in legislative modi-
fication or repeal of the fellow servant rule), they too were stampeded by fear of
labor violence, even when that violence was initiated by management and di-
rected at workers. Under these conditions, it took only one dramatic incident to
do what lightning did in cattle stampedes: touch off a panicked reaction, with
lawmakers running helter-skelter to enact legislation that would drive away the
bugaboos of the union organizer and the foreign anarchist. That incident was
Chicago's Haymarket Riot of 1886.

The riot began when police broke up a street tumult and in doing so killed or
wounded a half-dozen striking workers. The next day at a street rally called to
protest the slaying, someone (who has never been identified) threw a bomb into
the police line. The police opened fire, and in the aftermath, seven policemen
were killed. Chicago authorities rounded up organizers of the rally as principals
to the homicide. No one was ever charged with participating in the bombing or
even advocating it. Nevertheless, seven anarchists were sentenced to be hanged.
The punishments of two were commuted, one committed suicide, and four went to
the gallows.

The long-run consequences of the Haymarket bombing and its retaliatory
aftermath remain incalculable. First, the statute excerpted below was the fore-
runner of similar laws that were used to suppress labor organization and political
radicalism through World War I. Another consequence was the delay, by at least a

generation, in adoption of the eight-hour workday. Most pervasive was the con-firmation in the minds of America's middle class of the stereotype of the alien bomb-throwing anarchist. Organized labor suffered severely from the associa-tion.

If any person shall, by speaking to any public or private assemblage of people, or in any public place, or shall by writing, printing or publishing, or by causing to be written, printed, published or circulated, any written or printed matter, advise, encourage, aid, abet, or incite a local revolution, or the overthrowing or destruction of the existing order of society by force or violence, or the resistance to and destruction of the lawful power and authority of the legal authorities of this State or of any of the towns, cities or counties of this State, or resistance to the same, by force and violence, or by any of the means aforesaid shall advise, abet, encourage or incite the disturbance of the public peace, and by such disturbance [an] attempt at revolution or destruction of public order or resistance to such authorities shall thereafter ensue, and human life is taken or any person is injured, or property is destroyed by any person or by any of the means employed to carry into effect the purpose so advised, encouraged, aided, abetted or incited as aforesaid: every person so aiding, advising, encouraging, abetting or inciting the same shall be deemed as having conspired with the person or persons who actually commit the crime, and shall be deemed a principal in the perpetration of the same and be punished accord-ingly, and it shall not be necessary for the prosecution to show that the speaking was heard or the written or printed matter aforesaid was read or communicated to the person or persons actually committing the crime, if such speaking, writing, printing or publishing is shown to have been done in a public manner within this State.

New York Worker's Compensation Act
1910

As social tensions eased at the turn of the century, state legislatures returned to policy questions involving the problems of labor. In the interlude of relative calm that preceded World War I, they were able to distance themselves sufficiently from the hysteria that spawned the criminal syndicalism statutes to provide rational solutions to labor issues. Foremost among these were the intertwined subjects of allocating the burdens of industrial accidents and modifying the fellow servant rule. The solution adopted in all industrial states by World War I was workers' compensation (known at the time of its origin as workmen's compensation). The basic policy of workers' comp was a guaranteed recovery for death or disability and statutory abolition of the fellow servant rule, offset by a cap on liability (and a low one at that) plus abrogation of tort remedies for the injured worker. This statutory remedy replaced suits at common law by workers against their employ-ers. Adoption of the New York statute excerpted below was a milestone in the progress of workers' compensation.

AN ACT to amend the labor law, in relation to workmen's compensation in certain dangerous employments.

Application of article. This article shall apply only to workmen engaged in manual or mechanical labor in the following employments, each of which is hereby determined to be especially dangerous, in which from the nature, conditions or means of prosecution of the work therein, extraordinary risks to the life and limb of workmen engaged therein are inherent, necessary or substantially unavoidable, and as to each of which employments it is deemed necessary to establish a new system of compensation for accidents to workmen.

[The statute then itemized eight categories of dangerous labor, including demolition, blasting, tunneling, electrical construction, and railroad operation.]

*   *   *

Sec. 217.   Basis of liability. If, in the course of any of the employments above described, personal injury by accident arising out of and in the course of the employment after this article takes effect is caused to any workman employed therein, in whole or in part, or the damage or injury caused thereby is in whole or in part contributed to by

a.   A necessary risk or danger of the employment or one inherent in the nature thereof; or

b.   Failure of the employer of such workman or any of his or its officers, agents or employees to exercise due care, or to comply with any law affecting such employment; then such employer shall . . . be liable to pay compensation at the rates set out in section two hundred and nineteen-a of this title; provided that the employer shall not be liable in respect of any injury which does not disable the workman for a period of at least two weeks from earning full wages at the work at which he was employed, and provided that the employer shall not be liable in respect of any injury to the workman which is caused in whole or in part by the serious and willful misconduct of the workman.

*   *   *

Sec. 219-a.   Scale of compensation. The amount of compensation shall be in case death results from injury:

a.   If the workman leaves a widow or next of kin at the time of his death wholly dependent on his earnings, a sum equal to twelve hundred times the daily earnings of such workman at the rate at which he was being paid by such employer at the time of the injury subject as hereinafter provided, and in no event more than three thousand dollars. Any weekly payments made under this article shall be deducted in ascertaining such amount.

*   *   *

2.   Where total or partial incapacity for work at any gainful employment results to the workman from the injury, a weekly payment commencing at the end of the second week after the injury and continuing during such incapacity . . . equal to fifty per centum of his average weekly earnings when at work on full time during the preceding year during which he shall have been in the employment of the same employer[.]

*   *   *

In no event shall any compensation paid under this article exceed the damage suffered, nor shall any weekly payment payable under this article in any event exceed ten dollars a week or extend over more than eight years from the date of the accident.

Eminent Domain

Colorado Constitution
1876

Colorado, the Centennial State, was admitted to the Union in 1876. Its constitu-
tion reflected many of the trends in state constitution-making that had been
unleashed or accelerated by the Civil War. One of the more suggestive of these
trends was the expansion of the power of eminent domain.

Before the war, eminent domain had been "lent" by the state to private
corporations, such as railroads, which were permitted to condemn private prop-
erty as long as the taking conformed to the two traditional requirements of the
state and federal constitutions' takings clauses: the taking had to be for a public
purpose, and the taker had to provide the involuntary donor with just compensa-
tion. In the leading case of Inhabitants of Worcester v. *Western Railroad Co.*
(1842),4 Chief Justice Shaw of the Massachusetts Supreme Judicial Court ration-
alized this practice by holding that although run by a private corporation, a
railroad "is regarded as a public work . . . for the public use . . . [held by the
corporation] in trust for the public." In the pell-mell industrialization of the
post–Civil War era, eminent domain beckoned invitingly, particularly in the new
western states short of capital and avid for development, as a substitute for or
shortcut to capital formation. The difficulty lay in permitting it to be lent to
private concerns for private use; Shaw's rationalization could not be stretched far
enough to cover mines. The solution involved cutting the Gordian knot by autho-
rizing just such a private benefit through constitutional change. The delegates to
Colorado's constitutional convention also added an eminent domain provision
that ensured the state's control over corporations.

Art. II – Bill of Rights

Section 14.   That private property shall not be taken for private use unless by consent of the owner, except for private ways of necessity, and except for reservoirs, drains, flumes or ditches on or across the lands of others, for agricultural, mining, milling, domestic or sanitary purposes.

Section 15.   That private property shall not be taken or damaged, for public or private use without just compensation. Such compensation shall be ascertained by a Board of Commissioners, of not less than three freeholders, or by a jury, when required by the owner of the property, in such manner as may be prescribed by law, and until the same shall be paid to the owner, or into Court for the owner, the property shall not be needlessly disturbed, or the proprietary rights of the owner therein divested; and whenever an attempt is made to take private property for a use alleged to be public, the question whether the contemplated use be really public, shall be a judicial question, and determined as such without regard to any legislative assertion that the use is public.

*   *   *

Art. XV – Corporations

Section 8.   The right of eminent domain shall never be abridged nor so construed as to prevent the General Assembly from taking the property and franchises of incorporated companies, and subjecting them to public use, the same as the property of individuals; and the police power of the State shall never be abridged or so construed as to permit corporations to conduct their business in such manner as to infringe the equal rights of individuals or the general well being of the State.

*   *   *

Article XVI – Mining and Irrigation

Section 7.   All persons and corporations shall have the right of way across public, private and corporate lands for the construction of ditches, canals and flumes for the purpose of conveying water for domestic purposes, for the irrigation of agricultural land, and for mining and manufacturing purposes, and for drainage, upon payment of just compensation.

Federal Regulation and the Public Interest

The emergence of the regulatory state at the federal level came as more of a shock to conservative lawyers because the constitutional tradition of state police power had been well established before the Civil War. No comparable tradition supported an analogous federal police power, however, lending some credence to constitutional objections that the innovation was unprecedented.

A large component of conservative difficulty with federal regulation derived from assumptions about separation of powers. The symmetry of three branches of government—legislative, executive, judicial—seemed compelling. To the traditional mind, there seemed no room for a fourth branch of government. Worse, this new branch, the administrative, blurred the separation of powers by combining executive, legislative, and judicial functions in the same body. This blurring stirred up old fears of autocratic, tyrannical government, in which one branch gathered all powers into its own hands. Since the administrative agencies appeared predominantly executive in their origin and character, they portended one of the oldest threats to republican government—executive tyranny. This in turn might imperil judicial review and legislative autonomy.

The burden of demonstrating the constitutionality of the administrative state at the federal level lay with proponents of the innovation. This burden accounts for what otherwise appears to be willful obstructionism on the part of the United States Supreme Court, which greeted the fledgling administrative agencies in the 1890s and

1920s with cold suspicion, if not outright hostility. It was not so much that the judges thought any administrative innovation at all was unconstitutional, but that a new fourth element was being engrafted on a constitutional order that in its intrinsic character seemed to accommodate only three.

The emergence of the federal administrative structure followed state experience. Federal agencies at first had a predominantly fact-gathering mission; few in Congress believed that federal agencies should have law-enforcing or rate-setting authority. With Congress indecisive, federal judges, conservative by nature, did not rush to embrace innovation. A pattern of legislative–judicial dialogue emerged between 1890 and World War I. Congress would essay some legislative initiative, like the Interstate Commerce Act, with only vague and inconsistent suggestions about its intent in creating the new agency. Federal courts, faced with challenges to the constitutionality of the new body, would react cautiously, refusing to ascribe powers to it that congressional intent did not unambiguously support. Congress would return to the matter a few years later, restating (or articulating for the first time) its intent in setting up the new agency. If that congressional statement was sufficiently free from ambiguity, the courts would usually accept the new role being carved out for the agency.

There was also a concern for federalism running throughout federal judges' reception of the new administrative state. Some judges, especially those of antebellum Democratic antecedents, envisioned a constitutional order in which primary or exclusive responsibility for regulating matters that affected most Americans would continue to reside with the states, not with the federal government. Thus any apparent transfer of responsibility from states to nation would be greeted suspiciously, as an innovation at best, a violation of the Constitution at worst. This was only partially offset by a slowly expanding vision of congressional power under the commerce clause or other sources of federal authority. Traditional concepts of federalism died hard, despite the upheaval of the Civil War, and the old order of federalism yielded slowly and reluctantly to a new configuration of federal relations.

The Interstate Commerce Commission

Interstate Commerce Act
1887

In one way or another after the Civil War, the states tried to regulate railroads and the rates they charged. But whether this regulation took the form of the strong commissions favored in the midwestern states or the weak commissions of the eastern states, regulation at the state level proved to be inadequate to deal with emergent problems, chief of which was the inability of a single state to control an interstate enterprise. Recognizing this, Justice Samuel Miller of the United States Supreme Court asserted in 1886 that an Illinois statutory ban on long-haul–short-haul discrimination was a "species of regulation . . . which must be, if established at all, of a general and national character, and cannot be safely and wisely remitted to local rules and local regulations. . . ."[5] Miller's thinly veiled hint bore fruit within a year when Congress enacted the Interstate Commerce Act of 1887.

From a railroad's point of view, the principal problem facing it was excessive and unregulated competition in a capital-intensive industry. Railroads tried to cope with that problem by organizing pooling arrangements among themselves to distribute traffic and profits in competitive routes; in a word, they created cartels. But purely private cartels were not a satisfactory long-term solution because individual participants could opt out and because the legitimacy of the cartel might be challenged by disaffected customers. What railroads needed was government sanction of cartels.

From the viewpoint of the railroads' consumers, principally farmers, the situation looked altogether different. Railroad rates seemed inordinately high. In most areas, railroads were what economists call natural monopolies. They abused their power by offering rebates to favored customers, which were usually large corporations. They discriminated between long and short hauls in their rate structure, charging as much or more for short hauls as they did for a haul ten times the length, a practice that discriminated against certain localities.

Faced with conflicting pressures, Congress responded by evading a decisive preference for either. Instead, in 1887 it created an administrative body, the Interstate Commerce Commission, which was the first national regulatory agency, giving it power to hold hearings and issue cease-and-desist orders.

The provisions of this act shall apply to any common carrier or carriers engaged in the transportation of passengers or property wholly by railroad, or partly by railroad and partly by water when both are used, under a common control, management, or arrangement, for a continuous carriage or shipment, from one State or Territory of the United States, or the District of Columbia, to any other State or Territory of the United States, or the District of Columbia. . . .

All charges made for any service rendered or to be rendered in the transportation of passengers or property as aforesaid, or in connection therewith, or for the receiving, delivering, storage, or handling of such property, shall be reasonable and just; and every unjust and unreasonable charge for such service is prohibited and declared to be unlawful.

Sec. 2.   That if any common carrier subject to the provisions of this act shall, directly or indirectly, by any special rate, rebate, drawback, or other device, charge, demand, collect, or receive from any person or persons a greater or less compensation for any service rendered, or to be rendered, in the transportation of passengers or property, subject to the provisions of this act, than it charges, demands, collects, or receives from any other person or persons for doing for him or them a like and contemporaneous service in the transportation of a like kind of traffic under substantially similar circumstances and conditions, such common carrier shall be deemed guilty of unjust discrimination, which is hereby prohibited and declared to be unlawful.

Sec. 3.   That it shall be unlawful for any common carrier subject to the provisions of this act to make or give any undue or unreasonable preference or advantage to any particular person, company, firm, corporation, or locality, or any particular description of traffic, in any respect whatsoever, or to subject any particular person, company, firm, corporation, or locality, or any particular description of traffic, to any undue or unreasonable prejudice or disadvantage in any respect whatsoever.

Sec. 4.   That it shall be unlawful for any common carrier subject to the provisions of this act to charge or receive any greater compensation in the aggregate for the transportation of passengers or of like kind of property, under substantially similar circumstances and conditions, for a shorter than for a longer distance over the same line, in the same direction, the shorter being included within the longer distance. . . .

Sec. 5.   That it shall be unlawful for any common carrier subject to the provisions of this act to enter into any contract, agreement, or combination with any other common carriers for the pooling of freights of different and competing railroads, or to divide between them the aggregate or net proceeds of the earnings of such railroads, or any portion thereof; and in any case of an agreement for the pooling of freights as aforesaid, each day of its continuance shall be deemed a separate offense.

Note: Judicial Reaction to the Interstate Commerce Commission

The ICC, created by the 1887 statute, had judicial, executive, and legislative functions, which made it a suspect hybrid in conservative eyes. The United States Supreme Court at first demonstrated little sympathy for the act. It denied the ICC power to set rates and permitted federal courts to make fact-findings anew despite the statute's seeming assumption of finality for agency fact-finding.[6] These decisions left the agency virtually powerless, comparable to the weak rather than the strong state regulatory agencies.

Congress returned to the problem in the next decade, first by prohibiting rebates in the Elkins Act of 1903—a measure supported by the railroads, which wanted to eliminate any practice that diminished their earnings. The Hepburn Act of 1906 addressed the more difficult matter of giving the ICC greater power and according greater finality to its decisions. Congress once again temporized, shunting the question of the extent of judicial review over ICC rate setting to the courts. But the problem of whether the ICC should legitimate railroad cartels remained unsettled until American involvement in World War I.

The "Capture" of Regulatory Agencies

RICHARD S. OLNEY TO CHARLES C. PERKINS
Letter of
December 2, 1892

It is a commonplace among political scientists and students of public administration that administrative agencies in the twentieth century have experienced "capture." Over the years, they have come to adopt the outlook of the industries they are supposed to be regulating and have thus become lapdogs rather than watchdogs. According to the capture hypothesis, the agency protects the industry against competition and the public, rather than protecting the public from the industry.

Astute lawyers glimpsed this possibility from the start. Richard Olney, a prominent railroad lawyer, wrote to Charles Perkins, a railroad president, in the letter excerpted below, soothing Perkins's anxieties about the threat posed by the infant ICC. With astonishing prescience, Olney predicted the phenomenon of capture.

My impression would be that, in looking at the matter from a railroad point of view exclusively, it would not be a wise thing to undertake to abolish the [Interstate Commerce] Commission. The attempt would not be likely to succeed—if it did not succeed and were made on the ground of the inefficiency and uselessness of the Commission, the result would very probably be giving it the powers it now lacks. The Commission, as its functions have now been limited by the Courts, is, or can be made of great use to the railroads. It satisfies the popular clamor for a government supervision of railroads, at the same time that the supervision is almost entirely nominal. Further, the older such a commission gets to be, the more inclined it will be found to be to take the business and railroad view of things. It thus becomes a sort of barrier between the railroad corporations and the people and a sort of protection against hasty and crude legislation hostile to railroad interests. The Commission costs something, of course. But so long as its powers are advisory merely, for the reasons just stated, it strikes me it is well worth the money. The part of wisdom is not to destroy the Commission, but to utilize it. . . .

Trustbusting: The Statutory Basis

Sherman Anti-Trust Act
1890

Congress had two alternatives before it when it contemplated some kind of legislative action against trusts. On the one hand, it might follow the trail blazed by Charles Francis Adams, Jr., and the weak state regulatory commissions, entrusting some vaguely defined regulatory responsibility to commissions staffed by experts who might have powers of investigation and publicity. On the other, Congress could formulate as definite a statement of legislative policy as conflicting political pressures permitted, and then leave further articulation and enforcement of policy to courts. It chose the latter approach in the Sherman Anti-Trust Act.

Sec. 1. Every contract, combination in the form of trust or otherwise, or conspiracy, in restraint of trade or commerce among the several States, or with foreign nations, is hereby declared to be illegal. Every person who shall make any such contract or engage in any such combination or conspiracy, shall be deemed guilty of a misdemeanor, and, on conviction thereof, shall be punished by fine not exceeding five thousand dollars, or by imprisonment not exceeding one year, or by both said punishments, in the discretion of the court.

Sec. 2. Every person who shall monopolize, or attempt to monopolize, or combine or conspire with any other person or persons, to monopolize any part of the trade or commerce among the several States, or with foreign nations, shall be deemed guilty of a misdemeanor, and, on conviction thereof, shall be punished by fine not exceeding five thousand dollars, or by imprisonment not exceeding one year, or by both said punishments, in the discretion of the court.

Note: The Federal Police Power

Although the idea struck some as heretical, by the turn of the century it was becoming apparent that there was such a thing as a *federal* police power. Such a power had been an acknowledged part of the American constitutional order at the state level long before its formal recognition in the 1851 Massachusetts case of *Commonwealth v. Alger*. Conservative antebellum Democrats and laissez-faire jurists of the late nineteenth century were reluctant to recognize an analogous power in the national government. But the momentum of federal regulatory authority was becoming irresistible. Congress provided for the rudiments of a professional bureaucracy to administer federal departments and agencies by the Pendleton Civil Service Act of 1883. Imitating the Massachusetts weak-commission model, it created the information-gathering Bureau of Corporations within the Department of Commerce and Labor in 1903.

A miscellany of seemingly minor and innocuous police measures provided much grist for the mill of the United States Supreme Court: an 1895 statute prohibiting interstate shipment of lottery materials; the Erdman Act of 1898, barring yellow-dog contracts on railway labor; a prohibitive tax on artificially colored oleomargarine in 1902; the Meat Inspection Act of 1906 (inspired by publication of Upton Sinclair's *The Jungle*) and the Pure Food and Drug Act of the same year; the first and second Federal Employer's Liability Acts (1906 and 1908); the Mann or White Slave Trade Act of 1910; creation of the Federal Reserve Board in 1913; creation of the Federal Trade Commission in 1914; the Keating-Owen Child Labor Act of 1916; creation of the Federal Farm Loan Board, the United States Shipping Board, and the Railway Labor Board before American entry into World War I; and wartime centralization of control of the economy through the Lever Act of 1917, the War Industries Board, and the nationalization of the railroads, an experiment not totally abandoned in the Esch-Cummings or Transportation Act of 1920.

In addition, Congress had begun setting aside federal lands for national parks in 1872, with the creation of Yellowstone, and for national monuments in the Antiquities Act of 1906, later providing for the administration of these by creation of the National Park Service in 1916. In a comparable move, the Forest Reserve Act of 1891 authorized the president to set aside forest lands in the public domain. Theodore Roosevelt's conspicuous interest in conservation, signaled by the 1908 White House Conservation Conference, led to the adoption of U.S. Forester Gifford Pinchot's approach to the problem of natural resources and scenic lands. Pinchot popularized the concept of "multiple use," a policy that encouraged exploitation of national lands and was opposed to the lock-up or set-aside policies advocated by John Muir. The Newlands or National Reclamation Act of 1902 began the federal government's program of large-scale irrigation in arid lands.

Judicial Reaction to the Regulatory State

So pervasive an innovation in the structure and functioning of American government as the administrative state was bound to raise constitutional questions that had to be resolved in the courts. Two themes dominate judicial reaction to regulation after the

Civil War. The first was the appearance of the doctrine of substantive due process, as articulated by Thomas M. Cooley in his treatise *Constitutional Limitations* (see Chapter 6). Substantive due process provided a modernized replacement for the old concept of higher law articulated in Justice Samuel Chase's opinion in *Calder* v. *Bull* (1798). The acceptance of the doctrine was followed by the emergence of a corollary, the doctrine of liberty of contract, which in time came to overshadow its parent and was to bedevil labor reform well into the twentieth century. Substantive due process and liberty of contract provided paradigms of constitutional adjudication that dominated American law until the constitutional revolution of 1937.

The second theme developed out of the first. Substantive due process came into conflict with doctrines of police power at both the state and the federal levels. The two were incompatible, although they could coexist in uneasy tension for long periods of time. Out of this coexistence flowed two inconsistent streams of precedent, the one upholding governmental regulatory power and the other subordinating it to doctrines of individual liberty. Sooner or later, the conflict between these two lines of precedent would have to be resolved, lest legal doctrine appear fundamentally incoherent. But until that resolution came—in 1937—the United States Supreme Court oscillated unpredictably between upholding and invalidating state and federal regulatory legislation.

The Origins of Substantive Due Process

Wynehamer v. *The People*
13 N.Y. 378 (1856)

The natural-law tradition that traced back to Calder v. Bull *was losing its efficacy in the state courts by the mid-nineteenth century for a number of reasons. Among them were the widespread popular suspicion of lawyers, judges, and the common law that erupted recurrently after independence; the triumph of Jacksonian Democratic assumptions about democracy and privileged elites; and the disuse into which the doctrine had fallen in the federal courts. But the idea of transcendent constitutional restraints on legislative power by no means disappeared. On the contrary, as legislatures became more active in policy-making, conservative jurists saw a greater need than ever for a source of restraints on that popular branch of government. Shortly before the Civil War, the New York Court of Appeals hit on a workable formula to do just that, anchoring the nebulous metaphysics of* Calder *onto a specific clause of the state constitution.* Wynehamer *involved the constitutionality of a prohibition statute that banned the sale of intoxicating beverages. The law applied to existing stocks of alcohol, and a convicted barkeep challenged it as confiscatory.*

When the simple question is, whether [the legislature] can confiscate and destroy property lawfully acquired by the citizen in intoxicating liquors, then we are to remember that all property is equally sacred in the view of the constitution, and therefore that speculations as to its chemical or scientific qualities, or the mischief engendered by its abuse, have very little to do with the inquiry. Property, if protected by the constitution from such legislation as that we are now considering, is protected because it is property innocently acquired under existing laws, and not upon any theory which even so much as opens the question of its utility. If intoxicating liquors are property, the constitution does not permit a legislative estimate to be made of its usefulness, with a view to its destruction. In a word, that which belongs to the citizen in the sense of property, and as such has to him commercial value, cannot be pronounced worthless or pernicious, and so destroyed or deprived of its essential attributes.

* * *

In a government like ours, theories of public good or public necessity may be so plausible, or even so truthful, as to command popular majorities. But whether truthful or plausible merely, and by whatever numbers they are assented to, there are some absolute private rights beyond their reach, and among these the constitution places the right of property. It must follow that any scheme of legislation which, aiming at the destruction of this use, makes the keeping or sale of them as a beverage, in any quantity and by any person, a criminal offence—which declares them a public nuisance—which subjects them to seizure and physical destruction, and denies a legal remedy if they are taken by lawless force or robbery, must be deemed, in every beneficial sense, to deprive the owner of the enjoyment of his property.

* * *

It has been urged upon us, that the power of the legislature is restricted, not only by the express provisions of the written constitution, but by limitations implied from the nature and form of our government; that, aside from all special restriction, the right to enact such laws is not among the delegated powers of the legislature, and that the act in question is void, as against the fundamental principles of liberty, and against common reason and natural rights. High authority, certainly, has been cited to show that laws which, although not specially prohibited by written constitutions are repugnant to reason, and subvert clearly vested rights, are invalid, and must so be declared by the judiciary.

I am reluctant to enter upon this field of inquiry, satisfied as I am that no rule can be laid down in terms which may not contain the germ of great mischief to society, by giving to private opinion and speculation a license to oppose themselves to the just and legitimate powers of government.

* * *

I am brought, therefore to a more particular consideration of the limitations of power contained in the fundamental law: "No member of this state shall be disfranchised or deprived of any of the rights or privileges secured to any citizen thereof, unless by the law of the land of the judgment of his peers. No person shall be deprived of life, liberty or property, without due process of law; nor shall private property be taken for public use without just compensation." These provisions have been incorporated, in substance, into all our state constitutions.

No doubt, it seems to me, can be admitted of the meaning of these provisions. To say, as has been suggested, that "the law of the land," or "due process of law," may mean the very act of legislation which deprives the citizen of his rights, privileges or property, leads to a simple absurdity. The constitution would then mean, that no person shall be deprived of his property or rights, unless the legislature shall pass a law to effectuate the wrong, and this would be throwing the restraint entirely away. The true interpretation of these constitutional phrases is, that where rights are acquired by the citizen under the existing law, there is no power in any branch of the government to take them away; but where they are held contrary to the existing law, or are forfeited by its violation, then they may be taken from him—not by an act of the legislature, but in the due administration of the law itself, before the judicial tribunals of the state.

The Bradley Dissent in *Slaughterhouse*

The *Slaughterhouse Cases*
16 Wall. (83 U.S.) 36 (1873)

The origins of substantive due process in the United States Supreme Court may be traced to dissenting opinions in the Slaughterhouse Cases *of 1873. Justices Stephen J. Field and Joseph P. Bradley correctly perceived that the new Civil War Amendments had fundamentally altered both the nature of the federal system and the structure of protections for the rights of individuals. They differed in their emphases, with Field finding protection for the right to pursue a calling in the new privileges-and-immunities clause of the Fourteenth Amendment exclusively. Bradley adverted to the due process clause as well, and articulated the doctrine of substantive due process. His vision would triumph within two decades.*

Mr. Justice BRADLEY, . . . dissenting:
In my judgment, the right of any citizen to follow whatever lawful employment he chooses to adopt (submitting himself to all lawful regulations) is one of his most valuable rights, and one which the legislature of a State cannot invade, whether restrained by its own constitution or not.

The right of a State to regulate the conduct of its citizens is undoubtedly a very broad and extensive one, and not to be lightly restricted. But there are certain fundamental rights which this right of regulation cannot infringe. It may prescribe the manner of their exercise but it cannot subvert the rights themselves. I speak now of the rights of citizens of any free government.

The people of this country brought with them to its shores the rights of Englishmen; the rights, which had been wrested from English sovereigns at various periods of the nation's history. One of these fundamental rights was expressed in these words, found in Magna Charta: "No freeman shall be taken or imprisoned, or be disseized of his freehold or liberties or free customs, or be outlawed or exiled, or any otherwise destroyed; nor will we pass upon him or condemn him but by lawful judgment of his peers or by the law of the land." English constitutional writers expound this article as rendering life, liberty, and property inviolable, except by due process of law. This is the very right which the plaintiffs in error claim in this case. Another of these rights was that of habeas corpus, or the right of having any invasion of personal liberty judicially examined into, at once, by a competent judicial magistrate. Blackstone classifies these fundamental rights under three heads, as the absolute rights of individuals, to wit: the right of personal security, the right of personal liberty, and the right of private property. And of the last he says: "The third absolute right, inherent in every Englishman, is that of property, which consists in the free use, enjoyment, and disposal of all his acquisitions, without any control or diminution save only by the laws of the land."

Rights to life, liberty, and the pursuit of happiness are equivalent to the rights of life, liberty and property. These are the fundamental rights which can only be taken away by due process of law, and which can only be interfered with, or the enjoyment of which can only be modified, by lawful regulations necessary or proper for the mutual good of all; and the rights, I contend, belong to the citizens of every free government.

For the preservation, exercise, and enjoyment of these rights the individual citizen, as a necessity, must be left free to adopt such calling, profession, or trade as may seem to him most conducive to that end. Without this right he cannot be a freeman. This right to choose one's calling when chosen, is a man's property and right. Liberty and property are not protected where these rights are arbitrarily assailed.

II.   The next question to be determined in this case is: Is a monopoly or exclusive right, given to one person, or corporation, to the exclusion of all others, to keep slaughterhouses in a district of nearly twelve hundred square miles, for the supply of meat for a great city, a reasonable regulation of that employment which the legislature has a right to impose?

The keeping of a slaughter-house is part of, and incidental to, the trade of a butcher—one of the ordinary occupations of human life. To compel a butcher, or rather all the butchers of a large city and an extensive district, to slaughter their cattle in another person's slaughter-house and pay him a toll therefor, is such a restriction upon the trade as materially to interfere with its prosecution. It is onerous, unreasonable, arbitrary, and unjust. It has none of the qualities of a police regulation. If it were really a police regulation, it would undoubtedly be within the power of the legislature. That portion of the act which requires all slaughter-houses to be located below the city, and to be subject to inspection, &c., is clearly a police regulation. That portion which allows no one but the favored company to build, own, or have slaughter-houses is not a police regulation, and has not the faintest semblance of one. It is one of those arbitrary and unjust laws made in the interest of a few scheming individuals, by which some of the Southern States have, within the past few years, been so deplorably oppressed and impoverished. It seems to me strange that it can be viewed in any other light.

The amendment also prohibits any State from depriving any person (citizen or otherwise) of life, liberty, or property, without due process of law.

In my view, a law which prohibits a large class of citizens from adopting a lawful employment, or from following a lawful employment previously adopted, does deprive them of liberty as well as property, without due process of law. Their right of choice is a portion of their liberty; their occupation is their property. Such a law also deprives those citizens of the equal protection of the laws, contrary to the last clause of the section.

It is futile to argue that none but persons of the African race are intended to be benefited by this amendment. They may have been the primary cause of the amendment, but its language is general, embracing all citizens, and I think it was purposely so expressed.

The mischief to be remedied was not merely slavery and its incidents and consequences; but that spirit of insubordination and disloyalty to the National government which had troubled the country for so many years in some of the States, and that intolerance of free speech and free discussion which often rendered life and property insecure, and led to much unequal legislation. The amendment was an attempt to give voice to the strong National yearning for that time and that condition of things, in which American citizenship should be a sure guaranty of safety, and in which every citizen of the United States might stand erect on every portion of its soil, in the full enjoyment of every right and privilege belonging to a freeman, without fear of violence or molestation.

Reaffirmation of the Police Power

Munn v. Illinois
94 U.S. 113 (1877)

The opinion in this case, confirming the police power, established the opposite pole of the emerging constitutional dualism between substantive due process (heralded by Bradley's Slaughterhouse *dissent) and state and federal regulatory power.* Munn *upheld the constitutionality of the Illinois Granger Laws and the strong regulatory commission they created. But the scope of* Munn *would soon be curtailed. Even Chief Justice Morrison R. Waite, writing for the majority here, conceded that a regulatory statute might impinge on due process constraints, thus according implicit recognition to substantive due process.*

The question to be determined in this case is whether the general assembly of Illinois can, under the limitations upon the legislative power of the States imposed by the Constitution of the United States, fix by law the maximum of charges for the storage of grain in warehouses at Chicago and other places in the State having not less than one hundred thousand inhabitants. It is claimed that such a law is repugnant . . . to that part of amendment 14 which ordains that no State shall "deprive any person of life, liberty, or property, without due process of law, nor deny to any person within its jurisdiction the equal protection of the laws."

       *   *   *

While this provision of the amendment is new in the Constitution of the United States, as a limitation upon the powers of the States, it is old as a principle of civilized government. It is found in Magna Charta, and, in substance if not in form, in nearly or quite all the constitutions that have been from time to time adopted by the several States of the Union. By the Fifth Amendment it was introduced into the Constitution of the United States as a limitation upon the powers of the national government, and by the Fourteenth, as a guaranty against any encroachment upon the acknowledged right of citizenship by the legislatures of the states.

*   *   *

When one becomes a member of society, he necessarily parts with some rights or privileges which, as an individual not affected by his relations to others, he might retain. "A body politic," as aptly defined in the preamble of the Constitution of Massachusetts, "is a social compact by which the whole people convenants with each citizen, and each citizen with the whole people, that all shall be governed by certain laws for the common good." This does not confer power upon the whole people to control rights which are purely and exclusively private . . . but it does authorize the establishment of laws requiring each citizen to so conduct himself, and so use his own property, as not unnecessarily to injure another. This is the very essence of government. . . . From this source came the police powers of government . . . inherent in every sovereignty, . . . that is to say, . . . the power to govern men and things. Under these powers the government regulates the conduct of its citizens one towards another, and the manner in which each shall use his own property, when such regulation becomes necessary for the public good. In their exercise it has been customary in England from time immemorial, and in this country from its first colonization, to regulate ferries, common carriers, bakers, millers, wharfingers, innkeepers, &c., and in so doing to fix a maximum of charge to be made for services rendered, accommodations furnished, and articles sold.

*   *   *

From this it is apparent that, down to the time of the adoption of the Fourteenth Amendment, it was not supposed that statutes regulating the use, or even the price of the use, of private property necessarily deprived an owner of his property without due process of law. Under some circumstances they may, but not under all. The amendment does not change the law in this particular: it simply prevents the States from doing that which will operate as such a deprivation.

This brings us to inquire as to the principles upon which this power of regulation rests, in order that we may determine what is within and what [is] without its operative effect. Looking, then, to the common law, from whence came the right which the Constitution protects, we find that when private property is "affected with a public interest, it ceases to be *juris privati* only." This was said by Lord Chief Justice Hale more than two hundred years ago, in his treatise *De Portibus Maris*, . . . and has been accepted without objection as an essential element in the law of property ever since. Property does become clothed with a public interest when used in a manner to make it of public consequence, and affect the community at large. When, therefore, one devotes his property to a use in which the public has an interest, he in effect, grants to the public an interest in that use, and must submit to be controlled by the public for the common good, to the extent of the interest he has thus created. He may withdraw his grant by discontinuing the use; but, so long as he maintains the use, he must submit to the control.

*   *   *

This indicates very clearly that during the twenty years in which this peculiar business had been assuming its present "immense proportions," something had occurred which led the whole body of people to suppose that remedies such as are usually employed to prevent abuses by virtual monopolies might not be inappropriate here. For our purposes we must assume that, if a state of facts could exist that would justify such legislation, it actually did exist when the statute now under consideration was passed. For us the question is one of power, not of expediency. If no state of circumstances could exist to justify such a statute, then we may declare this one void, because in excess of the legislative power of the State. But if it could we must presume it did. Of the propriety of legislative interference within the scope of legislative power, the legislature is the exclusive judge.

Neither is it a matter of any moment that no precedent can be found for a statute precisely like this. It is conceded that the business is one of recent origin, that its growth has been rapid, and that it is already of great importance. And it must also be conceded that it is a business in which the whole public has a direct and positive interest. It presents, therefore, a case for the application of a long-known and well-established principle in social science, and this statute simply extends the law so as to meet this new development of commercial progress. There is no attempt to compel these owners to grant the public an interest in their property, but to declare their obligations if they use it in this particular manner.

*   *   *

It is insisted, however, that the owner of property is entitled to a reasonable compensation for its use, even though it be obtained with a public interest, and that what is reasonable is a judicial and not a legislative question.

As has already been shown, the practice has been otherwise. In countries where the common law prevails, it has been customary from time immemorial for the legislature to declare what shall be a reasonable compensation under such circumstances, or, perhaps more properly speaking, to fix a maximum beyond which any charge made would be unreasonable. Undoubtedly, in mere private contracts, relating to matters in which the public has no interest, what is reasonable must be ascertained judicially. But this is because the legislature has no control over such a contract. So, too, in matters which do effect the public interest, and as to which legislative control may be exercised, if there are no statutory regulations upon the subject, the courts must determine what is reasonable. The controlling fact is the power to regulate at all. If that exists, the right to establish the maximum of charge, as one of the means of regulation, is implied.

*   *   *

We know that this is a power which may be abused; but that is no argument against its existence. For protection against abuses by legislatures the people must resort to the polls, not to the courts.

Substantive Due Process in the State Courts

In re Jacobs
98 N.Y. 98 (1885)

The New York Court of Appeals was in the forefront among the state courts in the development of substantive due process. In this opinion, Judge Robert Earl touched on all the elements of the doctrine as it would be fully developed in the next generation. The court's Social Darwinian assumptions led it to substitute its own concepts of desirable public policy for the legislature's.

The relator Jacobs was arrested on the 14th day of May, 1884, [for violating] "An act to improve the public health by prohibiting the manufacture of cigars and preparation of tobacco in any form in tenement-houses in certain cases, and regulating the use of tenement-houses in certain cases."

*   *   *

What does this act attempt to do? In form, it makes it a crime for a cigarmaker in New York and Brooklyn . . . to carry on a perfectly lawful trade in his own home. Whether he owns the tenement-house or has hired a room therein for the purpose of prosecuting his trade, he cannot manufacture therein his own tobacco into cigars for his own use or for sale, and he will become a criminal for doing that which is perfectly lawful outside of the two cities named—everywhere else, so far as we are able to learn, in the whole world. He must either abandon the trade by which he earns a livelihood for himself and family, or, if able, procure a room elsewhere, or hire himself out to one who has a room upon such terms as, under the fierce competition of trade and the inexorable laws of supply and demand, he may be able to obtain from his employer. He may choose to do his work where he can have the supervision of his family and their help, and such choice is denied him. He may choose to work for himself rather than for a taskmaster, and he is left without freedom of choice. He may desire the advantage of cheap production in consequence of his cheap rent and family help, and of this he is deprived. In the unceasing struggle for success and existence which pervades all societies of men, he may be deprived of that which will enable him to maintain his hold, and to survive. . . . It is therefore, plain that this law interferes with the profitable and free use of his property by the owner or lessee of a tenement-house who is a cigarmaker, and trammels him in the application of his industry and the disposition of his labor, and thus, in a strictly legitimate sense, it arbitrarily deprives him of his property and of some portion of his personal liberty.

The constitutional guaranty that no person shall be deprived of his property without due process of law may be violated without the physical taking of property for public or private use. Property may be destroyed, or its value may be annihilated; it is owned and kept for some useful purpose and it has no value unless it can be used. Its capability for enjoyment and adaptability to some use are essential characteristics and attributes without which property cannot be conceived; and hence any law which destroys it or its value, or takes away any of its essential attributes, deprives the owner of his property.

The constitutional guaranty would be of little worth, if the legislature could, without compensation, destroy property or its value, deprive the owner of its use, deny him the right to live in his own house, or to work at any lawful trade therein. If the legislature has the power under the Constitution to prohibit the prosecution of one lawful trade in a tenement-house, then it may prevent the prosecution of all trades therein.

*   *   *

So, too, one may be deprived of his liberty and his constitutional rights thereto violated without the actual imprisonment or restraint of his person. Liberty, in its broad sense as understood in this country, means the right, not only of freedom from actual servitude, imprisonment or restraint, but the right of one to use his faculties in all lawful ways, to live and work where he will, to earn his livelihood in any lawful calling, and to pursue any lawful trade or avocation. All laws, therefore, which impair or trammel these rights, which limit one in his choice of a trade or profession, or confine him to work or live in a specified locality, or exclude him from his own house, or restrain his otherwise lawful movements (except as such laws may be passed in the exercise by the legislature of the police power, which will be noticed later), are infringements upon his fundamental rights of liberty, which are under constitutional protection.

*   *   *

But the claim is made that the legislature could pass this act in the exercise of the police power which every sovereign State possesses. That power is very broad and comprehensive, and is exercised to promote the health, comfort, safety and welfare of society. . . . Under it the conduct of an individual and the use of property may be regulated so as to interfere, to some extent, with the freedom of the one and the enjoyment of the other; and in cases of great emergency engendering overruling necessity, property may be taken or destroyed without compensation, and without what is commonly called due process of law. The limit of the power cannot be accurately defined and the courts have not been able or willing definitely to circumscribe it. But the power, however broad and extensive, is not above the Constitution.

*   *   *

These citations are sufficient to show that the police power is not without limitations, and that in its exercise the legislature must respect the great fundamental rights guaranteed by the Constitution. If this were otherwise, the power of the legislature would be practically without limitation. In the assumed exercise of the police power in the interest of the health, the welfare or the safety of the public, every right of the citizen might be invaded and every constitutional barrier swept away.

Generally it is for the legislature to determine what laws and regulations are needed to protect the public health and secure the public comfort and safety, and while its measures are calculated, intended, convenient and appropriate to accomplish these ends, the exercise of its discretion is not subject to review by the courts. But they must have some relation to these ends. Under the mere guise of police regulations, personal rights and private property cannot be arbitrarily invaded, and the determination of the legislature is not final or conclusive. If it passes an act ostensibly for the public health, and thereby destroys or takes away the property of a citizen, or interferes with his personal liberty, then it is for the courts to scrutinize the act and see whether it really relates to and is convenient and appropriate to promote health.

It is plain that this is not a health law, and that it has no relation whatever to the public health. Under the guise of promoting the public health the legislature might as well have banished cigarmaking from all the cities of the State, or confined it to a single city or town, or have placed under a similar ban the trade of a baker, of a tailor, of a shoemaker, of a woodcarver, or of any other of the innocuous trades carried on by artisans in their own homes. The power would have been the same, and its exercise, so far as it concerns fundamental constitutional rights, could have been justified by the same arguments. Such legislation may invade one class of rights to-day and another tomorrow, and if it can be sanctioned under the Constitution, while far removed in time we will not be far away in practical statesmanship from those ages when governmental prefects supervised the building of houses, the rearing of cattle, the sowing of seed and the reaping of grain, and governmental ordinances regulated the movements and labor of artisans, the rate of wages, the price of food, the diet and clothing of the people, and a large range of other affairs long since in all civilized lands regarded as outside of governmental functions. Such governmental interferences disturb the normal adjustments of the social fabric, and usually derange the delicate and complicated machinery of industry and cause a score of ills while attempting the removal of one.

Note: A Specter Haunting the Courts

Conservative jurists readily voiced the fears that lay behind their doctrinal innovations limiting legislative power. Judge Rufus Peckham of the New York Court of Appeals, dissenting in a case that upheld the constitutionality of legislative regulation of grain-warehouse rates, wrote bluntly about the ideological impetus behind the new substantive due process adjudication:

> To uphold legislation of this character is to provide the most frequent opportunity for arraying class against class; and, in addition to the ordinary competition that exists throughout all industries, a new competition will be introduced, that of competition for the possession of the government, so that legislative aid may be given to the class in possession thereof in its contests with rival classes or interests in all sections and corners of the industrial world. . . .
>
> In my opinion the court should not strain after holding such species of legislation constitutional. It is so plain an effort to interfere with what seems to me the most sacred rights of property and the individual's liberty of contract that no special intendment in its favor should be indulged in.
>
> *   *   *
>
> The legislation under consideration is not only vicious in its nature, communistic in its tendency, and, in my belief, wholly inefficient to permanently obtain the result aimed at, but, for the reasons already given, it is an illegal effort to interfere with the lawful privilege of the individual to seek and obtain such compensation as he can for the use of his own property, where he neither asks nor receives from the sovereign power any special right or immunity not given to and possessed by every other citizen, and where he has not devoted his property to any public use, within the meaning of the law.[7]

Note: Substantive Due Process and Corporations

Before the Civil War, it was doubtful that corporations could claim the protection of the Fifth Amendment's due process clause. The United States Supreme Court had held that corporations were not "Citizens" within the meaning of the privileges-and-immunities clause of Article IV, Section 2. There is no evidence in the debates preceding adoption of the Fourteenth Amendment that its framers in Congress intended its due process clause to apply to corporations, although for a time some scholars suggested that there had been a conspiracy among congressional Republicans to have it thus apply. That far-fetched notion was exploded more than a generation ago and may be consigned to the attic of defunct conspiracy theories.

In oral arguments before the Supreme Court in 1886, counsel began to make the point that corporations were now protected by the Fourteenth Amendment. Chief Justice Morrison R. Waite cut him off, stating that

> the Court does not wish to hear argument on the question whether the provision in the Fourteenth Amendment to the Constitution, which forbids a State to deny any person within its jurisdiction the equal protection of the laws, applies to these corporations. We are all of the opinion that it does.[8]

Seldom has so momentous a decision been made so offhandedly. Thereafter, corporations enjoyed the full protection of the due process and equal protection clauses. However, there was a historical irony in this. Since corporations were now positioned to reap the benefits of the substantive due process era, the real beneficiaries of the Fourteenth Amendment's Section 1 (the freed black people whom Congress explicitly intended to help) were relegated to a nether region outside the bounds of the amendment's protection.

Note: The Labor Injunction

Since 1883, federal and state judges had been expanding the use of injunctions to break strikes and labor unions, despite legislative attempts to restrict the innovation. The labor injunction was an especially sinister and powerful device. It worked as follows: a United States attorney, often acting at the behest of colleagues in private practice who represented employers, would forum-shop to find a judge hostile to labor unions and would request an injunction to stop all activities in connection with a strike, including those that after World War I would be considered to be protected by the First Amendment. (In the late nineteenth century, the First Amendment had not yet assumed the prominent place that it occupies today in the protection of the freedom of speech, press, and association. If not a dead letter, it was at most dormant.) The judge would sometimes hold hearings in camera, virtually ensuring a secret proceeding. The proceedings themselves would be *ex parte*, meaning that the union, its members, and their attorneys were not permitted to participate. When some union member violated the injunction, even by doing something protected by the First Amendment, such as distributing leaflets, he would immediately be jailed, and his union massively fined. At no point in the proceeding would a jury, grand or petit, be empaneled. Thus workers were sent to prison as a result of proceedings stripped of all the traditional Anglo-American guarantees of procedural due process. This, of course, was one of the most attractive features of the labor injunction to lawyers representing industry.

Federal Police Power and Labor

In re Debs
154 U.S. 564 (1895)

Debs illustrates the United States Supreme Court's differential attitude toward the problem of federal power and its opportunistic abandonment of consistency when presented with an opportunity to strike a blow at labor unions. The Debs *case grew out of the Pullman strike of 1894, which had halted the operations of all railroads running through Chicago. President Grover Cleveland, a conservative Democrat, sent federal troops to Chicago to break the strike, while his attorney general, Richard Olney (a railroad lawyer before he assumed public office), sought an injunction against the American Railway Union and its president, Eugene V. Debs. Debs was held in contempt for violation of the injunction, and this opinion resulted from his appeal.*

The Supreme Court produced its Debs *opinion in the same term as* Knight, *excerpted immediately below. Comparison of the two is instructive; at first glance, the reader would not believe that the same Court issued both. To strike down federal regulatory power that impeded corporations, the Court in* Knight *embraced a restrictive view of the federal commerce power, while in* Debs, *to smash a union, the Court adopted a broad and comprehensive posture toward the commerce authority.*

The case presented by the bill is this: The United States, finding that the interstate transportation of persons and property, as well as the carriage of the mails, is forcibly obstructed, and that a combination and conspiracy exists to subject the control of such transportation to the will of the conspirators, applied to one of their courts, sitting as a court of equity, for an injunction to restrain such obstruction and prevent carrying into effect such conspiracy. Two questions of importance are presented: First. Are the relations of the general government to interstate commerce and the transportation of the mails such as authorize a direct interference to prevent a forcible obstruction thereof? Second. If authority exists, as authority in governmental affairs implies both power and duty, has a court of equity jurisdiction to issue an injunction in aid of the performance of such duty?

First. What are the relations of the general government to interstate commerce and the transportation of the mails? They are those of direct supervision, control and management. While under the dual system which prevails with us the powers of government are distributed between the State and the Nation, and while the latter is properly styled a government of enumerated powers, yet within the limits of such enumeration it has all the attributes of sovereignty, and, in the exercise of those enumerated powers, acts directly upon the citizen, and not through the intermediate agency of the State.

As, under the Constitution, power over interstate commerce and the transportation of the mails is vested in the national government, and Congress by virtue of such grant has assumed actual and direct control, it follows that the national government may prevent any unlawful and forcible interference therewith. But how shall this be accomplished? Doubtless, it is within the competency of Congress to prescribe by legislation that any interference with these matters shall be offences against the United States, and prosecuted and punished by indictment in the proper courts. But is that the only remedy? Have the vast interests of the nation in interstate commerce, and in the transportation of the mails, no other protection than lies in the possible punishment of those who interfere with it? To ask the question is to answer it.

But there is no such impotency in the national government. The entire strength of the nation may be used to enforce in any part of the land the full and free exercise of all national powers and the security of all rights entrusted by the Constitution to its care. The strong arm of the national government may be put forth to brush away all obstructions to the freedom of interstate commerce or the transportation of the mails. If the emergency arises, the army of the Nation and all its miltia, are at the service of the Nation to compel obedience to its laws.

But passing to the second question, is there no other alternative than the use of force on the part of the executive authorities whenever obstructions arise to the freedom of interstate commerce or the transportation of the mails? Is the army the only instrument by which rights of the public can be enforced and the peace of the nation preserved? Grant that any public nuisance may be forcibly abated either at the instance of the authorities, or by an individual suffering private damage there-from, the existence of this right of forcible abatement is not inconsistent with nor does it destroy the right of appeal in an orderly way to the courts for a judicial determination, and an exercise of their powers by writ of injunction and otherwise to accomplish the same result.

So, in the case before us, the right to use force does not exclude the right of appeal to the courts for a judicial determination and for the exercise of all their powers of prevention. Indeed, it is more to the praise than to the blame of the government, that, instead of determining for itself questions of right and wrong on the part of these petitioners and their associates and enforcing that determination by the club of the policeman and the bayonet of the soldier, it submitted all those questions to the peaceful determination of judicial tribunals, and invoked their consideration and judgment as to the measure of rights and powers and the correlative obligations of those against whom it made complaint. And it is equally to the credit of the latter that the judgment of those tribunals was by the great body of them respected, and the troubles which threatened so much disaster terminated.

We have given to this case the most careful and anxious attention, for we realize that it touches closely questions of supreme importance to the people of this country. Summing up our conclusions, we hold that the government of the United States is one having jurisdiction over every foot of soil within its territory, and acting directly upon each citizen; that while it is a government of enumerated powers, it has within the limits of those powers all the attributes of sovereignty; that to it is committed power over interstate commerce and the transmission of the mail; that the powers thus conferred upon the national government are not dormant, but have been assumed and put into practical exercise by the legislation of Congress; that in the exercise of those powers it is competent for the nation to remove all obstructions upon highways, natural or artificial, to the passage of interstate commerce or the carrying of the mail; that while it may be competent for the government (through the executive branch and in the use of the entire executive power of the nation) to forcibly remove all such obstructions, it is equally within its competency to appeal to the civil courts for an inquiry and determination as to the existence and character of any alleged obstructions, and if such are found to exist, or threaten to occur, to invoke the powers of those courts to remove or restrain such obstructions; that the jurisdiction of courts to interfere in such matters by injunction is one recognized from ancient times and by indubitable authority; that such jurisdiction is not ousted by the fact that the obstructions are accompanied by or consist of acts in themselves violations of the criminal law; that the proceeding by injunction is of a civil character, and may be enforced by proceedings in contempt; that such proceedings are not in execution of the criminal laws of the land; that the penalty for a violation of injunction is no substitute for and no defence to a prosecution for any criminal offences committed in the course of such violation; that the complaint filed in this case clearly showed an existing obstruction of artificial highways for the passage of interstate commerce and the transmission of the mail—an obstruction not only temporarily existing, but threatening to continue; . . . and, finally, that, the Circuit Court, having full jurisdiction in the premises, its finding of the fact of disobedience is not open to review on habeas corpus in this or any other court.

Federal Police Power Under the Commerce Clause

United States v. *E.C. Knight & Co.*
156 U.S. 1 (1895)

The Knight *case was a curiosity. Together with a clutch of other opinions handed down in the mid-1890s—In re* Debs *(1895), the* Income Tax Cases *(1895), and* Plessy v. Ferguson *(1896)—it marked the triumph of conservative constitutionalism and what its sponsors hoped would be a fatal blow to radicalism in all its forms.* Knight *did in fact realize the hopes of its enthusiasts, enduring into the 1930s as an impediment to the exercise of the federal police power. Its direct–indirect distinction, contrived though it was, was equally long-lived.* Knight *was a showcase of the formalist mentality: its majority persuaded themselves that a company that controlled the production of more than 90 percent of the sugar consumed in the United States did not directly affect interstate commerce. It also reflected a concept of federalism that had died with the Civil War, lending Chief Justice Melville W. Fuller's words a distinctly out-of-touch quality.*

Yet the holding of the case, which dealt with the application of the new Sherman Anti-Trust Act, had little impact in that area. Knight *scarcely deflected antitrust enforcement by the executive branch, at most delaying realization of the promise of the act by less than a decade. Its vision of Congress's commerce power was at odds with its contemporary, the* Debs *opinion, and the Court ignored its strictures freely before World War I in those cases where it approved of the exercise of national regulatory power.*

By the purchase of the stock of the four Philadelphia refineries, with shares of its own stock, the American Sugar Refining Company acquired nearly complete control of the manufacture of refined sugar within the United States. The bill charged that the contracts under which these purchases were made constituted combinations in restraint of trade, and that in entering into them the defendants combined and conspired to restrain the trade and commerce in refined sugar among the several States and with foreign nations, contrary to the [Sherman Anti-Trust Act.]

The fundamental question is whether conceding that the existence of a monopoly in manufacture is established by the evidence, that monopoly can be directly suppressed under the act of Congress in the mode attempted by this bill.

It cannot be denied that the power of a State to protect the lives, health, and property of its citizens, and to preserve good order and the public morals, "the power to govern men and things within the limits of its dominion," is a power originally and always belonging to the States, not surrendered by them to the general government, nor directly restrained by the Constitution of the United States, and essentially exclusive.

The argument is that the power to control the manufacture of refined sugar is a monopoly over a necessary of life, to the enjoyment of which by a large part of the population of the United States interstate commerce is indispensible, and that, therefore, the general government in the exercise of the power to regulate commerce may repress such monopoly directly and set aside the instruments which have created it. But this argument cannot be confined to necessaries of life merely, and must include all articles of general consumption. Doubtless the power to control the manufacture of a given thing involves in a certain sense the control of its disposition, but this is a secondary and not the primary sense; and although the exercise of that power may result in bringing the operation of commerce into play, it does not control it, and affects it only incidentally and indirectly. Commerce succeeds to manufacture, and is not a part of it. The power to regulate commerce is the power to prescribe the rule by which commerce shall be governed, and is a power independent of the power to suppress monopoly. But it may operate in repression of monopoly whenever that comes within the rules by which commerce is governed or whenever the transaction is itself a monopoly of commerce.

It is vital that the independence of the commercial power and of the police power, and the delimitation between them, however sometimes perplexing, should always be recognized and observed, for while the one furnishes the strongest bond of union, the other is essential to the preservation of the autonomy of the States as required by our dual form of government; and acknowledged evils, however grave and urgent they may appear to be, had better be borne, than the risk be run, in the effort to suppress them, of more serious consequences by resort to expedients of even doubtful constitutionality.

Contracts, combinations, or conspiracies to control domestic enterprise in manufacture, agriculture, mining, production in all its forms, or to raise or lower prices or wages, might unquestionably tend to restrain external as well as domestic trade, but the restraint would be an indirect result, however inevitable and whatever its extent, and such result would not necessarily determine the object of the contract, combination, or conspiracy.

It was in the light of well-settled principles that the act of July 2, 1890, was framed. Congress did not attempt thereby to assert the power to deal with monopoly directly as such; or to limit and restrict the rights of corporations created by the States or the citizens of the States in the acquisition, control, or disposition of property; or to regulate or prescribe the price or prices at which such property or the products thereof should be sold; or to make criminal the acts of persons in the acquisition and control of property which the States of their residence or creation sanctioned or permitted. Aside from the provisions applicable where Congress might exercise municipal power, what the law struck at was combinations, contracts, and conspiracies to monopolize trade and commerce among the several States or with foreign nations; but the contracts and acts of the defendants related exclusively to the acquisition of the Philadelphia refineries and the business of sugar refining in Pennsylvania, and bore no direct relation to commerce between the States or with foreign nations. . . .

Liberty of Contract

Allgeyer v. *Louisiana*
165 U.S. 578 (1897)

Although useful for harassing labor organizations, the doctrine of substantive due process required some refinement to provide a judicial weapon against legislative efforts to enact statutes protecting the interests of workers. Fittingly enough, it was Rufus Peckham, now elevated to the United States Supreme Court, who hit on the needed improvement. Allgeyer *did not directly implicate unions or workers; it involved a statute that regulated the writing of insurance contracts by out-of-state firms. But Peckham articulated a doctrine of such abstract scope that it could be applied to labor relations as well.*

Liberty of contract became the basis of some of the twentieth century's most mischievous decisions until it was repudiated in 1937. Due process has taken on a second life in our own time in abortion cases, but liberty of contract still lies mouldering in its grave, despite the efforts of some modern conservatives to revive it as an inhibition on state regulatory power.

The Supreme Court of Louisiana says that the act of writing within that State, the letter of notification, was an act therein done to effect an insurance on property then in the State, in a marine insurance company which had not complied with its laws, and such act was, therefore, prohibited by the statute. As so construed we think the statute is a violation of the Fourteenth Amendment of the Federal Constitution, in that it deprives the defendants of their liberty without due process of law. The statute which forbids such acts does not become due process of law, because it is inconsistent with the provisions of the Constitution of the Union. The liberty mentioned in that amendment means not only the right of the citizen to be free from the mere physical restraint of his person, as by incarceration, but the term is deemed to embrace the right of the citizen to be free in the enjoyment of all his faculties; to be free to use them in all lawful ways; to live and work where he will; to earn his livelihood by any lawful calling; to pursue any livelihood or avocation, and for that purpose to enter into all contracts which may be proper, necessary and essential to his carrying out to a successful conclusion the purposes above mentioned.

Has not a citizen of a State, under the provisions of the Federal Constitution above mentioned, a right to contract outside the State for insurance on his property—a right of which state legislation cannot deprive him?

*   *   *

The act done within the limits of the State under the circumstances of this case and for the purpose therein mentioned, we hold a proper act, one which the defendants were at liberty to perform and which the state legislature had no right to prevent, at least with reference to the Federal Constitution. To deprive the citizen of such a right as herein described without due process of law is illegal. Such a statute as this in question is not due process of law, because it prohibits an act which under the Federal Constitution the defendants had a right to perform. This does not interfere in any way with the acknowledged right of the State to enact such legislation in the legitimate exercise of its police or other powers as to it may seem proper. In the exercise of such right, however, care must be taken not to infringe upon those other rights of the citizen which are protected by the Federal Constitution.

In the privilege of pursuing an ordinary calling or trade and of acquiring, holding and selling property must be embraced the right to make all proper contracts in relation thereto, and although it may be conceded that this right to contract in relation to persons or property or to do business within the jurisdiction of the State may be regulated and sometimes prohibited when the contracts or business conflict with the policy of the State as contained in its statutes, yet the power does not and cannot extend to prohibiting a citizen from making contracts of the nature involved in this case outside of the limits and jurisdiction of the State, and which are also to be performed outside such jurisdiction; . . .

Judicial Paternalism

Holden v. *Hardy*
169 U.S. 366 (1898)

Holden *provided the United States Supreme Court, in a Janus-like manner, an occasion to display its other face toward labor—paternalism. The progressive temper of Justice Henry B. Brown's opinion demonstrates the Court's inconsistent approach to labor cases, especially because it was handed down shortly after* Allgeyer. *Those two cases stand as sources of two inconsistent streams of precedent, the one permissive toward legislation protecting workers, the other hostile.* Holden *is remarkable in another respect. Justice Brown here accepted the heretical idea that employer and employee do not stand on an equal bargaining footing, a potentially fatal blow to liberty of contract. This case involved a challenge to the Utah Smelter Acts, excerpted earlier in this chapter.*

An examination of both these classes of cases under the Fourteenth Amendment will demonstrate that, in passing upon the validity of state legislation under that amendment, this court has not failed to recognize the fact that the law is, to a certain extent, a progressive science; that in some of the States' methods of procedure, which at the time the Constitution was adopted were deemed essential to the protection and safety of the people, or to the liberty of the citizen, have been found to be no longer necessary; that restrictions which had formerly been laid upon the conduct of individuals, or of classes of individuals, had proved detrimental to their interests; while, upon the other hand, certain other classes of persons, particularly those engaged in dangerous or unhealthful employments, have been found to be in need of additional protection.

*   *   *

The present century has originated legal reforms of no less importance. The whole fabric of special pleading, once thought to be necessary to the culmination of the real issue between the parties, has crumbled to pieces. The ancient tenures of real estate have been largely swept away, and land is now transferred almost as easily and cheaply as personal property. Married women have been emancipated from the control of their husbands and placed upon a practical equality with them with respect to the acquisition, possession and transmission of property. Imprisonment for debt has been abolished. Exemptions from execution have been largely added to, and in most of the States homesteads are rendered incapable of seizure and sale upon forced process. [These examples] are mentioned only for the purpose of calling attention to the probability that other changes of no less importance may be made in the future, and that while the cardinal principles of justice are immutable, the methods by which justice is administered are subject to constant fluctuation, and that the Constitution of the United States, which is necessarily and to a large extent inflexible and exceedingly difficult of amendment, should not be so construed as to deprive the States of the power to so amend their laws as to make them conform to the wishes of the citizens as they may deem best for the public welfare without bringing them into conflict with the supreme law of the land.

Of course, it is impossible to forecast the character or extent of these changes, but in view of the fact that from the day Magna Charta was signed to the present moment, amendments to the structure of the law have been made with increasing frequency, it is impossible to suppose that they will not continue, and the law be forced to adapt itself to new conditions of society, and, particularly, to the new relations between employers and employees, as they arise.

*   *   *

This right of contract, however, is itself subject to certain limitations which the State may lawfully impose in the exercise of its police powers. While this power is inherent in all governments, it has doubtless been greatly expanded in its application during the past century, owing to an enormous increase in the number of occupations which are dangerous, or so far detrimental to the health of employees as to demand special precautions for their well-being and protection, or the safety of adjacent property.

*   *   *

But if it be within the power of a legislature to adopt such means for the protection of the lives of its citizens, it is difficult to see why precautions may not also be adopted for the protection of their health and morals. It is as much for the interest of the State that the public health should be preserved as that life should be made secure. With this end in view quarantine laws have been enacted in most if not all of the States; insane asylums, public hospitals and institutions for the care and education of the blind established; and special measures taken for the exclusion of infected cattle, rags and decayed fruit. In other States laws have been enacted limiting the hours during which women and children shall be employed in factories; and while their constitutionality, at least as applied to women, has been doubted in some of the States, they have been generally upheld.

*   *   *

Upon the principles above stated, we think the act in question may be sustained as a valid exercise of the police power of the State. The enactment does not profess to limit the hours of all workmen, but merely those who are employed in underground mines, or in the smelting, reduction or refining of ores or metals. These employments, when too long pursued, the legislature has judged to be detrimental to the health of the employees, and, so long as there are reasonable grounds for believing that this is so, its decision upon this subject cannot be reviewed by the Federal courts.

The legislature has also recognized the fact, which the experience of legislators in many States has corroborated, that the proprietors of these establishments and their operatives do not stand upon an equality, and that their interests are, to a certain extent, conflicting. The former naturally desire to obtain as much labor as possible from their employees, while the latter are often induced by the fear of discharge to conform to regulations which their judgment, fairly exercised, would pronounce to be detrimental to their health or strength. In other words, the proprietors lay down the rules and the laborers are practically constrained to obey them. In such cases self-interest is often an unsafe guide, and the legislature may properly interpose its authority.

It may not be improper to suggest in this connection that although the prosecution in this case was against the employer of labor, who apparently under the statute is the only one liable, his defence is not so much that his right to contract has been infringed upon, but that the act works as a peculiar hardship to his employees, whose right to labor as long as they please is alleged to be thereby violated. The argument would certainly come with better grace and greater cogency from the latter class. But the fact that both parties are of full age and competent to contract does not necessarily deprive the State of the power to interefere where the parties do not stand upon an equality, or where the public health demands that one party to the contract shall be protected against himself.

We are of opinion that the act in question was a valid exercise of the police power of the State, and the judgments of the Supreme Court of Utah are, therefore,

Affirmed.

Substantive Due Process in Nonlabor Cases

Champion v. *Ames*
188 U.S. 321 (1903)

Powerful as the doctrine of substantive due process was in labor cases, its impact in other areas was spotty because it was not backed up by the animosity that judges felt toward labor unions. With its grip thus somewhat enfeebled, substantive due process could sometimes be overridden by competing policy considerations. Thus the phenomenon noted in the labor cases, two inconsistent streams of precedent, was even more pronounced in nonlabor cases. This proved an embarrassment to the Court and to claims for the rule of law, since the Court oscillated between accepting regulatory legislation, as it did early in the twentieth century, and then condemning it, as it did in the 1920s. Eventually, the inconsistency would somehow have to be reconciled, rationalized, or eliminated.

The case excerpted below, popularly known as the Lottery Case, *was the first major decision in the twentieth century that sustained the federal police power. It was notable for Justice John M. Harlan's insistence that the power to regulate commerce included the power to prohibit entirely the shipment of an article, thus destroying commerce in it, and for his sweeping assertion that Congress could regulate for the protection of the people's morals.*

The appellant insists that the carrying of lottery tickets from one State to another State by an express company engaged in carrying freight and packages from State to State, although such tickets may be contained in a box or package, does not constitute, and cannot by any act of Congress be legally made to constitute, commerce among States within the meaning of the clause of the Constitution of the United States providing that Congress shall have power "to regulate commerce with foreign nations, and among the several States, and with the Indian tribes;" consequently, that Congress cannot make it an offence to cause such tickets to be carried from one State to another.

The questions presented by these opposing contentions are of great moment, and are entitled to receive, as they have received, the most careful consideration.

What is the import of the word "commerce" as used in the Constitution? It is not defined by that instrument. Undoubtedly, the carrying from one State to another by independent carriers of things or commodities that are ordinary subjects of traffic, and which have in themselves a recognized value in money, constitutes interstate commerce. But does not commerce among the several States include something more? Does not the carrying from one State to another, by independent carriers, of lottery tickets that entitle the holder to the payment of a certain amount of money therein specified also constitute commerce among States?

*   *   *

Commerce among the States embraces navigation, intercourse, communication, traffic, the transit of persons, and the transmission of messages by telegraph. They also show that the power to regulate commerce among the several States is vested in Congress as absolutely as it would be in a single government, having in its constitution the same restrictions on the exercise or the power as are found in the Constitution of the United States; that such power is plenary, complete in itself, and may be exerted by Congress to its utmost extent, subject only to such limitations as the Constitution imposes upon the exercise of the powers granted by it; and that in determining the character of the regulations to be adopted Congress has a large discretion which is not to be controlled by the courts, simply because, in their opinion, such regulations may not be the best or most effective that could be employed.

*   *   *

We are of opinion that lottery tickets are subjects of traffic and therefore are subjects of commerce, and the regulation of the carrying of such tickets from State to State, at least by independent carriers, is a regulation of commerce among the several States.

*   *   *

We have said that the carrying from State to State of lottery tickets constitutes interstate commerce, and that the regulation of such commerce is within the power of Congress under the Constitution. Are we prepared to say that a provision which in, in effect, a prohibition of the carriage of such articles from State to State is not a fit or appropriate mode for the regulation of that particular kind of commerce? If lottery traffic, carried on through interstate commerce, is a matter of which Congress may take cognizance and over which its power may be exerted, can it be possible that it must tolerate the traffic, and simply regulate the manner in which it may be carried on? Or may not Congress, for the protection of the people of all the States, and under the power to regulate interstate commerce, devise such means, within the scope of the Constitution, and not prohibited by it, as will drive that traffic out of commerce among the States?

If a State when considering legislation for the suppression of lotteries within its own limits, may properly take into view the evils that inhere in the raising of money, in that mode, why may not Congress, invested with the power to regulate commerce among the several States, provide that such commerce shall not be polluted by the carrying of lottery tickets from one State to another? In this connection it must not be forgotten that the power of Congress to regulate commerce among the States is plenary, is complete in itself, and is subject to no limitations except such as may be found in the Constitution. What provision in that instrument can be regarded as limiting the exercise of the power granted? What clause can be cited which, in any degree, countenances the suggestion that one may, of right, carry or cause to be carried from one State to another that which will harm the public morals? We cannot think of any clause of that instrument that could possibly be invoked by those who assert their right to send lottery tickets from State to State except the one providing that no person shall be deprived of his liberty without due process of law. But surely it will not be said to be a part of one's liberty, as recognized by the supreme law of the land, that he shall be allowed to introduce into commerce among the States an element that will be confessedly injurious to the public morals.

If it be said that the 1895 [act] is inconsistent with the Tenth Amendment, reserving to the States respectively or to the people the powers not delegated to the United States, the answer is that the power to regulate commerce among the States has been expressly delegated to Congress.

*   *   *

The judgment is

Affirmed.

Mr. Chief Justice Fuller, with whom concur Mr. Justice Brewer, Mr. Justice Shiras and Mr. Justice Peckham, dissenting.

The Apogee of Substantive Due Process

Lochner v. *New York*
198 U.S. 45 (1905)

Lochner stands as the classic substantive due process and liberty of contract case. Justice Peckham's majority opinion is widely condemned today by conservatives and liberals alike, but a lively debate persists on why Peckham's opinion is so firmly repudiated. Justice Holmes's dissent, a classic that contains some of his most frequently quoted aphorisms, insisted that it was not for judges to weigh the justifications for legislative policy-making.

The indictment, it will be seen, charges that the plaintiff in error violated the one hundred and tenth section of article 8, chapter 415, of the Laws of 1897, known as the labor law of the State of New York, in that he wrongfully and unlawfully required and permitted an employee working for him to work more than sixty hours in one week.

*   *   *

The statute necessarily interferes with the right of contract between the employer and employees, concerning the number of hours in which the latter may labor in the bakery of the employer. The general right to make a contract in relation to his business is part of the liberty of the individual protected by the Fourteenth Amendment of the Federal Constitution. Under that provision no State can deprive any person of life, liberty or property without due process of law. The right to purchase or to sell labor is part of the liberty protected by this amendment, unless there are circumstances which exclude the right. There are, however, certain powers, existing in the sovereignty of each State in the Union, somewhat vaguely termed police powers, the exact description and limitation of which have not been attempted by the courts. Those powers, broadly stated and without, at present, any attempt at a more specific limitation, relate to the safety, health, morals and general welfare of the public. Both property and liberty are held on such reasonable conditions as may be imposed by the governing power of the State in the exercise of those powers, and with such conditions the Fourteenth Amendment was not designed to interfere.

*   *   *

Therefore, when the State, by its legislature, in the assumed exercise of its police powers, has passed an act which seriously limits the right to labor or the right of contract in regard to their means of livelihood between persons who are sui juris (both employer and employee), it becomes of great importance to determine which shall prevail—the right of the individual to labor for such time as he may choose, or the right of the State to prevent the individual from laboring or from entering into any contract to labor, beyond a certain time prescribed by the State.

*   *   *

It must, of course, be conceded that there is a limit to the valid exercise of the police power by the State. There is no dispute concerning the general proposition. Otherwise the Fourteenth Amendment would have no efficacy and legislatures of the States would have unbounded power, and it would be enough to say that any piece of legislation was enacted to conserve the morals, the health or the safety of the people; such legislation would be valid, no matter how absolutely without foundation the claim might be. The claim of the police power would be a mere pretext—become another and delusive name for the supreme sovereignty of the State to be exercised free from constitutional restraint. This is not contended for. In every case that comes before this court, therefore, where legislation of this character is concerned and where the protection of the Federal Constitution is sought, the question necessarily arises: Is this a fair, reasonable and appropriate exercise of the police power of the State, or is it an unreasonable, unnecessary and arbitrary interference with the right of the individual to his personal liberty or to enter into those contracts in relation to labor which may seem to him appropriate or necessary for the support of himself and his family? Of course the liberty of contract relating to labor includes both parties to it. The one has as much right to purchase as the other to sell labor.

This is not a question of substituting the judgment of the court for that of the legislature. If the act is within the power of the State it is valid, although the judgment of the court might be totally opposed to the enactment of such a law. But the question would still remain: Is it within the police power of the State? and that question must be answered by the court.

The question whether this act is valid as a labor law, pure and simple, may be dismissed in a few words. There is no reasonable ground for interfering with the liberty of person or the right of free contract, by determining the hours of labor, in the occupation of a baker. There is no contention that bakers as a class are not equal in intelligence and capacity to men in other trades or manual occupations, or that they are not able to assert their rights and care for themselves without the protecting arm of the State, interfering with their independence of judgment and of action. They are in no sense wards of the State. Viewed in the light of a purely labor law, with no reference whatever to the question of health, we think that a law like the one before us involves neither the safety, the morals nor the welfare of the public, and that the interest of the public is not in the slightest degree affected by such an act. The law must be upheld, if at all, as a law pertaining to the health of the individual engaged in the occupation of a baker. It does not affect any other portion of the public than those who are engaged in that occupation. Clean and wholesome bread does not depend upon whether the baker works but ten hours per day or only sixty hours a week. The limitation of the hours of labor does not come within the police power on that ground.

It is a question of which of two powers or rights shall prevail—the power of the State to legislate or the right of the individual to liberty of person and freedom of contract. The mere assertion that the subject relates though but in a remote degree to the public health does not necessarily render the enactment valid. The act must have a more direct relation, as a means to an end, and the end itself must be appropriate and legitimate, before an act can be held to be valid which interferes with the general right of an individual to be free in his person and in his power to contract in relation to his own labor.

*   *   *

We think the limit of the police power has been reached and passed in this case. There is, in our judgment, no reasonable foundation for holding this to be necessary or appropriate as a health law to safeguard the public health or the health of the individuals who are following the trade of a baker. If this statute be valid, and if, therefore, a proper case is made out in which to deny the right of an individual, sui juris, as employer or employee, to make contracts for the labor of the latter under the protection of the provisions of the Federal Constitution, there would seem to be no length to which legislation of this nature might not go.

We do not believe in the soundness of the views which uphold this law. On the contrary, we think that such a law as this, although passed in the assumed exercise of the police power, and as relating to the public health, or the health of the employees named, is not within that power, and is invalid. The act is not, within any fair meaning of the term, a health law, but is an illegal interference with the rights of individuals, both employers and employees, to make contracts regarding labor upon such terms as they may think best, or which they may agree upon with the other parties to such contracts. Statutes of the nature of that under review, limiting the hours in which grown and intelligent men may labor to earn their living, are mere meddlesome interferences with the rights of the individual, and they are not saved from condemnation by the claim that they are passed in the exercise of the police power and upon the subject of the health of the individual whose rights are interfered with, unless there be some fair ground, reasonable in and of itself, to say that there is material danger to the public health or to the health of the employees, if the hours of labor are not curtailed.

*   *   *

It is impossible for us to shut our eyes to the fact that many of the laws of this character, while passed under what is claimed to be the police power for the purpose of protecting the public health or welfare, are, in reality, passed from other motives. We are justified in saying so when, from the character of the law and the subject upon which it legislates, it is apparent that the public health or welfare bears but the most remote relation to the law. The purpose of a statute must be determined from the natural and legal effect of the language employed; and whether it is or is not repugnant to the Constitution of the United States must be determined from the natural effect of such statutes when put into operation, and not from their proclaimed purpose.

*   *   *

It is manifest to us that the limitation of the hours of labor as provided for in this section of the statute under which the indictment was found, and the plaintiff in error convicted, has no such direct relation to and no such substantial effect upon the health of the employee, as to justify us in regarding the section as really a health law. It seems to us that the real object and purpose were simply to regulate the hours of labor between the master and his employees (all being men, sui juris), in a private business, not dangerous in any degree to morals or in any real and substantial degree, to the health of the employees. Under such circumstances the freedom of master and employe to contract with each other in relation to their employment, and in defining the same, cannot be prohibited or interfered with, without violating the Federal Constitution.

Reversed.

Mr. Justice Holmes dissenting.

I regret sincerely that I am unable to agree with the judgment in this case, and that I think it my duty to express my dissent.

This case is decided upon an economic theory which a large part of the country does not entertain. If it were a question whether I agreed with that theory, I should desire to study it further and long before making up my mind. But I do not conceive that to be my duty, because I strongly believe that my agreement or disagreement has nothing to do with the right of a majority to embody their opinions in law. It is settled by various decisions of this court that state constitutions and state laws may regulate life in many ways which we as legislators might think as injudicious or if you like as tyrannical as this, and which equally with this interfere with the liberty to contract. Sunday laws and usury laws are ancient examples. A more modern one is the prohibition of lotteries. The liberty of the citizen to do as he likes so long as he does not interfere with the liberty of others to do the same, which has been a shibboleth for some well-known writers, is interfered with by school laws, by the Post Office, by every state or municipal institution which takes his money for purposes thought desirable, whether he likes it or not. The Fourteenth Amendment does not enact Mr. Herbert Spencer's Social Statics.

*   *   *

Some of these laws embody convictions or prejudices which judges are likely to share. Some may not. But a constitution is not intended to embody a particular economic theory, whether of paternalism and the organic relation of the citizen to the State or of laissez faire. It is made for people of fundamentally different views, and the accident of our finding certain opinions natural and familiar or novel and even shocking ought not to conclude our judgment upon the question whether statutes embodying them conflict with the Constitution of the United States.

General propositions do not decide concrete cases. The decision will depend on a judgment or intuition more subtle than any articulate major premise. But I think that the proposition just stated, if it is accepted, will carry us far toward the end. Every opinion tends to become a law. I think that the word liberty in the Fourteenth Amendment is perverted when it is held to prevent the natural outcome of a dominant opinion, unless it can be said that a rational and fair man necessarily would admit that the statute proposed would infringe fundamental principles as they have been understood by the traditions of our people and our law. It does not need research to show that no such sweeping condemnation can be passed upon the statute before us. A reasonable man might think it a proper measure on the score of health.

Paternalism and the Female Worker

<h2 style="text-align:center">Muller v. Oregon
208 U.S. 412 (1908)</h2>

This case presents a curious blend of realistic, antiformalist reasoning and patriarchal assumptions. Justice David J. Brewer, one of the most formalist of the judges on the Court of that era, warmly embraced both the substance and the technique of the Brandeis brief (excerpted in Chapter 9), probably because its content was compatible with judges' assumptions about the place of women in society. Nonetheless, Muller's *result was consistent with* Lochner, *which by its express language was limited to adult males.*

On February 19, 1903, the legislature of the State of Oregon passed an act (Session Laws, 1903, p. 148), the first section of which is in these words:

"SEC. 1.   That no female (shall) be employed in any mechanical establishment, or factory, or laundry in this State more than ten hours during any one day."

*   *   *

It is the law of Oregon that women, whether married or single, have equal contractual and personal rights with men.

*   *   *

It thus appears that, putting to one side the elective franchise, in the matter of personal and contractual rights [women] stand on the same plane as the other sex. Their rights in these respects can no more be infringed than the equal rights of their brothers.

In patent cases counsel are apt to open the argument with a discussion of the state of the art. It may not be amiss, in the present case, before examining the constitutional question, to notice the course of legislation as well as expressions of opinion from other than judicial sources. In the brief filed by Mr. Louis D. Brandeis, for the defendant in error, is a very copious collection of all these matters, an epitome of which is found in the margin.

The legislation and opinions referred to in the margin may not be, technically speaking, authorities, and in them is little or no discussion of the constitutional question presented to us for determination, yet they are significant of a widespread belief that woman's physical structure, and the functions she performs in consequence thereof, justify special legislation restricting or qualifying the conditions under which she should be permitted to toil. Constitutional questions, it is true, are not settled by even a consensus of present public opinion, for it is the peculiar value of a written constitution that it places in unchanging form limitations upon legislative action, and thus gives a permanence and stability to popular government which otherwise would be lacking. At the same time, when a question of fact is debatable, and the extent to which a special constitutional limitation goes is affected by the truth in respect to that fact, a widespread and long continued belief concerning it is worthy of consideration. We take judicial cognizance of all matters of general knowledge.

It is undoubtedly true, as more than once declared by this court, that the general right to contract in relation to one's business is part of the liberty of the individual, protected by the Fourteenth Amendment to the Federal Constitution; yet it is equally well settled that this liberty is not absolute and extending to all contracts, and that a State may, without conflicting with the provisions of the Fourteenth Amendment, restrict in many respects the individual's power of contract.

*   *   *

That woman's physical structure and the performance of maternal functions place her at a disadvantage in the struggle for subsistence is obvious. This is especially true when the burdens of motherhood are upon her. Even when they are not, by abundant testimony of the medical fraternity continuance for a long time on her feet at work, repeating this from day to day, tends to injurious effects upon the body, and as healthy mothers are essential to vigorous offspring, the physical well-being of woman becomes an object of public interest and care in order to preserve the strength and vigor of the race.

Still again, history discloses the fact that woman has always been dependent upon man. He established his control at the outset by superior physical strength, and this control in various forms, with diminishing intensity, has continued to the present. As minors, though not to the same extent, she has been looked upon in the courts as needing especial care that her rights may be preserved. Education was long denied her, and while now the doors of the school room are opened and her opportunities for acquiring knowledge are great, yet even with that and the consequent increase of capacity for business affairs it is still true that in the struggle for subsistence she is not an equal competitor with her brother. Though limitations upon personal and contractual rights may be removed by legislation, there is that in her disposition and habits of life which will operate against a full assertion of those rights. She will still be where some legislation to protect her seems necessary to secure a real equality of right. Doubtless there are individual exceptions, and there are many respects in which she has an advantage over him; but looking at it from the viewpoint of the effort to maintain an independent position in life, she is not upon an equality. Differentiated by these matters from the other sex, she is properly placed in a class by herself, and legislation designed for her protection may be sustained, even when like legislation is not necessary for men and could not be sustained. It is impossible to close one's eyes to the fact that she still looks to her brother and depends upon him. Even though all restrictions on political, personal and contractual rights were taken away, and she stood, so far as statutes are concerned, upon an absolutely equal plane with him, it would still be true that she is so constituted that she will rest upon and look to him for protection; that her physical structure and a proper discharge of her maternal functions—having in view not merely her own health, but the well-being of the race—justify legislation to protect her from the greed as well as the passion of man. The limitations which this statute places upon her contractual powers, upon her right to agree with her employer as to the time she shall labor, are not imposed solely for her benefit, but also largely for the benefit of all. Many words cannot make this plainer. The two sexes differ in structure of body, in the functions to be performed by each, in the amount of physical strength, in the capacity for long-continued labor, particularly when done standing, the influence of vigorous health upon the future well-being of the race, the self-reliance which enables one to assert full rights, and in the capacity to maintain the struggle for subsistence. This difference justifies a difference in legislation and upholds that which is designed to compensate for some of the burdens which rest upon her.

For these reasons, and without questioning in any respect the decision in Lochner v. New York, we are of the opinion that it cannot be adjudged that the act in question is in conflict with the Federal Constitution, so far as it respects the work of a female in a laundry, and the judgment of the Supreme Court of Oregon is

Affirmed.

The *Danbury Hatters Case*

Loewe v. Lawlor
208 U.S. 274 (1908)

This opinion by Chief Justice Fuller demonstrated the Court's double standard in commerce clause cases, expanding federal power when the result was to harass union organization, but constricting it when the subject was the regulation of a corporation. Most of this opinion, excluded from this excerpt, consisted of scissors-and-paste excerpts from other opinions, none of them responsive to the issues presented in the case. To Fuller, it seemed obvious and beyond the need for reasoning that union organization violated the Sherman Anti-Trust Act. He saw no need to try to distinguish the outcome here from the Knight *case.*

This was an action brought in the Circuit Court of the District of Connecticut under the Anti-Trust Act claiming threefold damages for injuries inflicted on plaintiffs by a combination or conspiracy declared to be unlawful by the act.

*　　*　　*

In our opinion, the combination described in the declaration is a combination "in restraint of trade or commerce among the several States," in the sense in which those words are used in the act, and the action can be maintained accordingly.

And that conclusion rests on many judgments of this court, to the effect that the act prohibits any combination whatever to secure action which essentially obstructs the free flow of commerce between the States, or restricts, in that regard, the liberty of a trader to engage in business.

*　　*　　*

The averments here are that there was an existing interstate traffic between plaintiffs and citizens of other States, and that for the direct purpose of destroying such interstate traffic defendants combined not merely to prevent plaintiffs from manufacturing articles then and there intended for transportation beyond the State, but also to prevent the vendees from reselling the hats which they had imported from Connecticut, or from further negotiating with plaintiffs for the purchase and interstate transportation of such hats from Connecticut to the various places of destination. So that, although some of the means whereby the interstate traffic was to be destroyed were acts within a State, and some of them were in themselves as a part of their obvious purpose and effect beyond the scope of Federal authority, still, as we have seen, the acts must be considered as a whole, and the plan is open to condemnation, notwithstanding a negligible amount of intrastate business might be affected in carrying it out. If the purposes of the combination were, as alleged, to prevent any interstate transportation at all, the fact that the means operated at one end before physical transportation commenced and at the other end after the physical transportation ended was immaterial.

Nor can the act in question be held inapplicable because defendants were not themselves engaged in interstate commerce. The act made no distinction between classes. It provided that "every" contract, combination or conspiracy in restraint of trade was illegal. The records of Congress show that several efforts were made to exempt, by legislation, organizations of farmers and laborers from the operation of the act and that all these efforts failed, so that the act remained as we have it before us.

Workers' Compensation and Substantive Due Process

Ives v. *South Buffalo Railway Co.*
201 N.Y. 271 (1911)

This opinion embodied the last spasm of substantive due process in the state courts. It shocked the country, disturbing the sense of justice of even so conservative a figure as President William Howard Taft, who condemned it as "retro-

*grade." It had no long-term effect in impeding the universal adoption of workers'
compensation, in part because its beneficiaries, the corporations, desired the
advantages that workers' compensation systems provided them.*

The statute struck down here was the pioneering New York Worker's Compensation Act of 1910, excerpted in this chapter.

The statute, judged by our common-law standards, is plainly revolutionary. Its central and controlling feature is that every employer who is engaged in any of the classified industries shall be liable for any injury to a workman arising out of and in the course of the employment by "a necessary risk or danger of the employment or one inherent in the nature thereof; . . . provided that the employer shall not be liable in respect of any injury to the workman which is caused in whole or in part by the serious and willful misconduct of the workman." This rule of liability, stated in another form, is that the employer is responsible to the employee for every accident in the course of employment, whether the employer is at fault or not, and whether the employee is at fault or not, except when the fault of the employee is so grave as to constitute serious and willful misconduct on his part. The radical character of this legislation is at once revealed by contrasting it with the rule of the common law, under which the employer is liable for injuries to his employee only when the employer is guilty of some act or acts of negligence which caused the occurrence out of which the injuries arise, and then only when the employee is shown to be free from any negligence which contributes to the occurrence.

This quoted summary of the report of the commission to the legislature, which clearly and fairly epitomizes what is more fully set forth in the body of the report, is based upon a most voluminous array of statistical tables, extracts from the works of philosophical writers and the industrial laws of many countries, all of which are designed to show that our own system of dealing with industrial accidents is economically, morally and legally unsound. Under our form of government, however, courts must regard all economic, philosophical and moral theories, attractive and desirable though they may be, as subordinate to the primary question whether they can be moulded into statutes without infringing upon the letter or spirit of our written constitutions. In that respect we are unlike any of the countries whose industrial laws are referred to as models for our guidance. Practically all of these countries are so called constitutional monarchies in which, as in England, there is no written constitution, and the Parliament or law-making body is supreme. In our country the Federal and State Constitutions are the charters which demark the extent and the limitations of legislative power; and while it is true that the rigidity of a written constitution may at times prove to be a hindrance to the march of progress, yet more often its stability protects the people against the frequent and violent fluctuations of that which, for want of a better name, we call public opinion.

*   *   *

This legislation is challenged as void under the fourteenth amendment to the Federal Constitution and under section 6, article 1 of our State Constitution, which guarantee all persons against deprivation of life, liberty or property without due process of law.

*   *   *

. . . It is conceded that this is a liability unknown to the common law and we think it plainly constitutes a deprivation of liberty and property under the Federal and State Constitutions, unless its imposition can be justified under the police power which will be discussed under a separate head. In arriving at this conclusion we do not overlook the cogent economic and sociological arguments which are urged in support of the statute. There can be no doubt as to the theory of this law. It is based upon the proposition that the inherent risks of an employment should in justice be placed upon the shoulders of the employer, who can protect himself against loss by insurance and by such an addition to the price of his wares as to cast the burden ultimately upon the consumer; that indemnity to an injured employee should be as much a charge upon the business as the cost of replacing or repairing disabled or defective machinery, appliances or tools; that, under our present system, the loss falls immediately upon the employee who is almost invariably unable to bear it, and ultimately upon the community which is taxed for the support of the indigent; and that our present system is uncertain, unscientific and wasteful, and fosters a spirit of antagonism between employer and employee which it is to the interest of the state to remove. We have already admitted the strength of this appeal to a recognized and widely prevalent sentiment, but we think it is an appeal which must be made to the people and not to the courts. The right of property rests not upon philosophical or scientific speculations nor upon the commendable impulses of benevolence or charity, nor yet upon the dictates of natural justice. The right has its foundation in the fundamental law. That can be changed by the people, but not by legislatures. In a government like ours theories of public good or necessity are often so plausible or sound as to command popular approval, but courts are not permitted to forget that the law is the only chart by which the ship of state is to be guided. Law as used in this sense means the basic law and not the very act of legislation which deprives the citizen of his rights, privileges and property. Any other view would lead to the absurdity that the Constitutions protect only those rights which the legislatures do not take away. If such economic and sociologic arguments as are here advanced in support of this statute can be allowed to subvert the fundamental idea of property, then there is no private right entirely safe, because there is no limitation upon the absolute discretion of legislatures, and the guarantees of the Constitution are a mere waste of words.

In its final and simple analysis that is taking the property of A and giving it to B, and that cannot be done under our Constitutions.

*   *   *

If we are warranted in concluding that the new statute violates private right by taking the property of one and giving it to another without due process of law, that is really the end of this case. But the auspices under which this legislation was enacted, no less than its intrinsic importance, entitle its advocates to the fullest consideration of every argument in its support, and we, therefore, take up the discussion of the police power under which this law is sought to be justified. The police power is, of course, one of the necessary attributes of civilized government. In its most comprehensive sense it embraces the whole system by which the state seeks to preserve the public order, to prevent offenses against the law, to insure to citizens in their intercourse with each other the enjoyment of their own so far as is reasonably consistent with a like enjoyment of rights by others. Under it persons and property are subjected to all kinds of restraints and burdens in order to secure the general comfort, health and prosperity of the state. But it is a power which is always subject to the Constitution, for in a constitutional government limitation is the abiding principle, exhibited in its highest form in the Constitution as the deliberative judgment of the people, which moderates every claim of right and controls every use of power.

*   *   *

In order to sustain legislation under the police power the courts must be able to see that its operation tends in some degree to prevent some offense or evil, or to preserve public health, morals, safety and welfare. If it discloses no such purpose, but is clearly calculated to invade the liberty and property of private citizens, it is plainly the duty of the courts to declare it invalid, for legislative assumption of the right to direct the channel into which the private energies of the citizen may flow, or legislative attempt to abridge or hamper the right of the citizen to pursue, unmolested and without reasonable regulation, any lawful calling or avocation which he may choose, has always been condemned under our form of government.

Note: Child Labor

If there was one subject of public administration (aside from the domain of sexual morality) on which nearly all Americans could reach a consensus in the early twentieth century, it would have been child labor. Few Americans any longer concurred with Alexander Hamilton's 1793 enthusiasm for putting children to work in factories; the stunting effects on their physical and intellectual development were too obvious. As the *Lottery Case* demonstrated, moral consensus sometimes easily overrode constitutional scruples in cases involving the federal police power. Congress had little difficulty in wielding its commerce power to destroy interstate traffic in the products of child labor.

Thus it came as an unpleasant surprise when the United States Supreme Court struck down the first Child Labor Act on states'-rights, Tenth Amendment grounds in *Hammer* v. *Dagenhart* (1918).[9] Justice William R. Day's opinion relied on the formalistic distinctions that had characterized the *Knight* opinion, as well as antebellum ideas of federalism that had been mouldering away after 1865:

> The thing intended to be accomplished by this statute is the denial of the facilities of interstate commerce to those manufacturers in the States who employ children within the prohibited ages. The act in its effect does not regulate transportation among the States, but aims to standardize the ages at which children may be employed in mining and manufacturing within the States. The goods shipped are of themselves harmless.
>
> The grant of power to Congress over the subject of interstate commerce was to enable it to regulate such commerce, and not to give it authority to control the States in their exercise of the police power over local trade and manufacture.
>
> The grant of authority over a purely federal matter was not intended to destroy the local power always existing and carefully reserved to the States in the Tenth Amendment to the Constitution.
>
> The maintenance of the authority of the States over matters purely local is as essential to the preservation of our institutions as is the conservation of the supremacy of the federal power in all matters entrusted to the Nation by the Federal Constitution.

In interpreting the Constitution it must never be forgotten that the Nation is made up of States to which are entrusted the powers of local government. And to them and to the people the powers not expressly delegated to the National Government are reserved.

Finding itself thwarted by the Supreme Court in its commerce clause initiative, Congress turned to its taxing powers and levied a prohibitive excise tax on the products of child labor. The new Chief Justice of the United States, William Howard Taft, disposed of this effort as easily as the earlier one, inventing another artificial distinction to suit the occasion, in *Bailey* v. *Drexel Furniture* (1922):

A court must be blind not to see that the so-called tax is imposed to stop the employment of children within the age limits prescribed. Its prohibitory and regulatory effect and purpose are palpable. All others can see and understand this. How can we properly shut our minds to it?

Grant the validity of this law, and all that Congress would need to do, hereafter, in seeking to take over to its control any one of the great number of subjects of public interest, jurisdiction of which the States have never parted with, and which are reserved to them by the Tenth Amendment, would be to enact a detailed measure of complete regulation of the subject and enforce it by a so-called tax upon departures from it. To give such magic to the word "tax" would be to break down all constitutional limitation of the powers of Congress and completely wipe out the sovereignty of the States.[10]

Frustrated by the Supreme Court's unexpected and intransigent attitude to its efforts to eliminate the evils of child labor, Congress in 1924 turned to the ultimate weapon, constitutional amendment. It sent the following amendment out to the states:

Section 1. The Congress shall have power to limit, regulate, and prohibit the labor of persons under 18 years of age.
Section 2. The power of the several States is unimpaired by this article except that the operation of State laws shall be suspended to the extent necessary to give effect to legislation enacted by Congress.

Although ratified by twenty-eight states, the amendment has never received enough endorsements to become part of the Constitution. Nevertheless, Americans in the 1930s widely but erroneously believed that it had been ratified, so heartfelt was their opposition to child labor. Congress did not annex a seven-year expiration condition to the amendment, as it has to all subsequent amendments, so technically the amendment is still outstanding and could be ratified by the states. Modern developments in constitutional doctrine have rendered that unnecessary.

8

Total War, Civil Liberties, and Civil Rights

Individual Rights in a Changing Culture

From 1900 to 1950, the culture, economy, and demography of the United States changed dramatically. Immigration, internal migration, industrialization, urbanization, and war altered the face of America and the nation's role in world affairs. This substantial transformation of the society affected law and legal culture. The locus of legal change shifted from the state courts to the federal courts. Similarly, political power moved from Congress to the executive branch and increasingly to the courts; the membership of the bench and bar also changed to reflect some, but not all, of the changes in the population.

Massive immigration from 1880 to 1924 altered the culture. In 1850, America was a nation largely populated by Protestants of Anglo-Saxon and northern European origin, pockets of Irish Catholics, and slaves of African origin. By World War I, the nation looked and sounded like a different place. Millions of Catholics and Jews destroyed the Protestant hegemony of an earlier age. Immigrants from eastern and southern Europe, the Middle East, and the Far East similarly undermined the dominance of northern European culture. In 1924, in a futile attempt to preserve a Protestant America that no longer existed, Congress established strict immigration quotas, virtually stopping immigration from much of the world. This law symbolized the tension between the America of the nineteenth century and the nation that had emerged in the twentieth century.

Almost as dramatic as immigration was the movement of people within the United States. The western frontier disappeared before 1900. The last two contiguous territories became states in 1912. But if the age of the western frontier was over, the age of the urban frontier had just begun. Although some western farming and mining regions were dominated by immigrants, most newcomers from Europe and Asia moved to cities. Starting with World War I, they were joined by the movement of southern blacks into cities. In 1900, the problem of race relations was confined to the South for blacks and whites, and to the West Coast for Asians and whites. The migration of blacks out of the South increased rapidly during the Depression and World War II and expanded even more rapidly after 1945.

These new people flooded into American cities, providing laborers for expanding industries. The nexus of law and economics in this period is dealt with in Chapter 7 of this book. But immigration, industrialization, and urbanization also affected non-economic aspects of legal culture. In response to these changes, radical movements emerged that rejected the social and economic order of the day. The repression of these movements during and after World War I forced lawyers and jurists to consider seriously, for the first time since the Civil War, the place of radical dissent in American legal and political culture. The changing population also affected the legal profession. The children of immigrants looked to law as a way to rise in American society; more established lawyers feared that attorneys from these new groups would alter the "club" that the bar had become. The established bar objected to the social values of lawyers from immigrant families, who more often supported labor unions, poor people, and progressive reform. They also feared the competition of the hard-working, upwardly mobile immigrants and their children. Two results of this growing antagonism were new educational requirements for admission to the bar or to law schools and attempts by the organized bar to destroy law schools that catered to immigrants and blacks. The segregation of the American Bar Association and the ABA's opposition to the nomination of Louis Brandeis, the first Jew to serve on the United States Supreme Court, symbolized the tension in the profession between the old and the new.

The two world wars had an enormous impact on society and thus on law. During the wars, Congress increasingly regulated economic activities, conscripted civilians for military service, and limited free speech, while continuing to expand programs and budgets. The presidency became even more powerful, as Congress gradually, and sometimes almost gleefully, relinquished power to the chief executive. The president soon came to command bloated bureaucracies, enormous resources, and gigantic armies. From 1917 to 1920, the executive branch used wartime powers to crush radicals and labor organizers under the banner of patriotism. The wartime experience revealed that liberties were easily ignored or trampled on. For these reasons, civil liberties emerged from the wartime experience as an important legal issue. More durable than the repressive statutes were the ideas set forth in dissenting opinions by United States Supreme Court Justices Louis Brandeis and Oliver Wendell Holmes, Jr. More durable than the repressive prosecutions of Attorney General A. Mitchell Palmer and New York's Lusk Committee in 1919 to 1920 was the American Civil Liberties Union (ACLU), organized to protect the political and civil liberties of all Americans, regardless of their ideology. Starting in the 1930s, the ACLU developed into one of the most important litigation-oriented organizations in the country.

The two wars, the Depression, and black migration out of the South led to heightened racial consciousness. At the beginning of this period, black rights were at their lowest point since 1866. Lynchings were common and increased dramatically during World War I. Black veterans, who fought to "make the world safe for Democracy," were disinclined to accepted second-class citizenship at home. When these veterans returned from France, they found an organization ready to serve their needs. The National Association for the Advancement of Colored People (NAACP), organized in 1909, took the lead in fighting for civil rights through lobbying and litigation. Victories were few at first, but gradually the organization convinced the United States Supreme Court to breathe new life into the moribund Civil War Amendments.

The NAACP began with a battery of upper-class white lawyers, inheritors of the abolitionist tradition and a sense of noblesse oblige toward blacks. Gradually black attorneys, led by Charles Hamilton Houston and William Hastie of Howard Law School and their brilliant protégé Thurgood Marshall, began to represent black litigants at the local, state, and federal levels. Just the sight of a black attorney arguing for civil rights in the rural South or before the United States Supreme Court was a victory of sorts. More substantive victories came later. When soldiers returned from the war against racism and hate in Europe and Japan, the war against segregation and prejudice at home would begin in earnest. Within a decade, the arguments of Thurgood Marshall, like Joshua's trumpets, began to destroy the walls of segregation. Unfortunately, the prejudices behind those walls proved more durable than many lawyers or judges expected.

The kinds of changes brought about by ACLU and NAACP litigation were possible because of fundamental changes in American constitutional law. At the same time, these two organizations, along with other litigators, helped change the meaning of the nation's Constitution. At the beginning of this period, the United States Supreme Court played a minor role in the development of law. Few legal issues raised federal questions. By mid-century, almost anything could raise a federal question. The states had become subordinate to the national government, and important legal changes increasingly came from the Supreme Court, rather than from state courts. Legislatures at the state and federal levels also mattered less. At the national level, presidential power grew, while the power of Congress diminished.

In 1900, individual rights—civil liberties, civil rights, criminal due process—were generally the domain of the states, which treated their residents and citizens pretty much as they wished. By 1950, the Supreme Court was dramatically altering the relationship between the states and the people. Supreme Court decisions in the 1930s and 1940s set the stage for a massive revolution of rights in the 1950s and 1960s, and for the intervention of federal legislation in areas that, since the end of Reconstruction, had been the domain of the states.

Technology meanwhile restructured American life and the law. Race relations changed as public transportation made internal migration easier and cheaper and as newspapers and radio made all Americans feel closer together. The concept of states' rights began to crumble as the borders between states became more artificial. Technology also meant that people could more easily lose their privacy. In criminal law, the telephone and the wiretap forced judges to rethink the concept of "search" as defined in the Bill of Rights. Telephones, high-speed printing presses, and photography made it more difficult for people—be they common or prominent—to retain their privacy.

LOUIS D. BRANDEIS AND SAMUEL D. WARREN
"The Right to Privacy"
1890

After his marriage to Mabel Bayard, the daughter of Senator Thomas Bayard, newspaper gossip columns plagued Samuel D. Warren, the former law partner of Louis D. Brandeis. This problem led to their seminal Harvard Law Review *article "The Right to Privacy." Brandeis hoped the article would "make more people see that invasions of privacy" should not be tolerated. According to the* Columbia Law Review, *this enormously influential article "enjoyed the unique distinction of having initiated and theoretically outlined a new field of jurisprudence" by setting the stage for the protection "against the use of one's personality for private gain by others, or to feed a prurient curiosity." The article also pointed the way to a second subfield of law, the tort of emotional distress, whether caused by negligence or intention.*

In addition, the article illustrates the crucial changes taking place in American society, as photography, new forms of journalism, and urbanization intruded on the lives of individuals. The article helps explain the need for new legal theories to protect individual rights in the changing society of industrial America. Critical to this is Brandeis's assertion of "the right to be let alone." The articulation of this right lay the foundation for the evolution of a right to privacy in both common law and constitutional law.

That the individual shall have full protection in person and in property is a principle as old as the common law; but it has been found necessary from time to time to define anew the exact nature and extent of such protection. Political, social, and economic changes entail the recognition of new rights, and the common law, in its eternal youth, grows to meet the demands of society. Thus, in very early times, the law gave a remedy only for physical interference with life and property. . . . The "right to life" served only to protect the subject from battery in its various forms; liberty meant freedom from actual restraint; and the right to property secured to the individual his lands and his cattle. Later, there came a recognition of man's spiritual nature, of his feelings and his intellect. Gradually the scope of these legal rights broadened; and now the right to life has come to mean the right to enjoy life,—the right to be let alone; the right to liberty secures the exercise of extensive civil privileges; and the term "property" has grown to comprise every form or possession—intangible, as well as tangible.

*   *   *

Recent inventions and business methods call attention to the next step which must be taken for the protection of the person, and for securing to the individual what Judge Cooley calls the right "to be let alone." Instantaneous photographs and newspaper enterprise have invaded the sacred precincts of private and domestic life; and numerous mechanical devices threaten to make good the prediction that "what is whispered in the closet shall be proclaimed from the house-tops." For years there has been a feeling that the law must afford some remedy for the unauthorized circulation of portraits of private persons and the evil of the invasion of privacy by the newspapers . . . and the question whether our law will recognize and protect the right to privacy . . . must soon come before our courts for consideration.

Of the desirability—indeed of the necessity—of some such protection, there can, it is believed, be no doubt. The press is overstepping in every direction the obvious bounds of propriety and of decency. Gossip is no longer the resource of the idle and of the vicious, but has become a trade, which is pursued with industry as well as effrontery. To satisfy a prurient taste the details of sexual relations are spread broadcast in the columns of the daily papers. To occupy the indolent, column upon column is filled with idle gossip, which can only be procured by intrusion upon the domestic circle. The intensity and complexity of life, attendant upon advancing civilization, have rendered necessary some retreat from the world, and man, under the refining influence of culture, has become more sensitive to publicity, so that solitude and privacy have become more essential to the individual; but modern enterprise and invention have, through invasions upon his privacy, subjected him to mental pain and distress, far greater than could be inflicted by mere bodily injury. . . . In this, as in other branches of commerce, the supply creates the demand. Each crop of unseemly gossip, thus harvested, becomes the seed of more, and, in direct proportion to its circulation, results in a lowering of social standards and of morality. Even gossip apparently harmless, when widely and persistently circulated, is potent for evil. . . . It belittles by inverting the relative importance of things, thus dwarfing the thoughts and aspirations of a people. When personal gossip attains the dignity of print, and crowds the space available for matters of real interest to the community, what wonder that the ignorant and thoughtless mistake its relative importance. Easy of comprehension, appealing to that weak side of human nature which is never wholly cast down by the misfortunes and frailties of our neighbors, no one can be surprised that it usurps the place of interest in brains capable of other things. Triviality destroys at once robustness of thought and delicacy of feelings. No enthusiasm can flourish, no generous impulse can survive under its blighting influence.

*　　*　　*

The common law secures to each individual the right of determining, ordinarily, to what extent his thoughts, sentiments, and emotions shall be communicated to others. Under our system of government, he can never be compelled to express them (except when upon the witness stand); and even if he has chosen to give them expression, he generally retains the power to fix the limits of the publicity which shall be given them. . . . [T]his right does not depend upon the particular method of expression adopted. . . . Neither does the existence of the right depend upon the nature or value of the thought or emotion, nor upon the excellence of the means of expression. The same protection is accorded to a casual letter or an entry in a diary and to the most valuable poem or essay, to a botch or daub and to a masterpiece. In every such case the individual is entitled to decide whether that which is his shall be given to the public. No other has the right to publish his productions in any form, without his consent. This right is wholly independent of the material on which, or the means by which, the thought, sentiment, or emotion is expressed. It may exist independently of any corporeal being, as in words spoken, a song sung, a drama acted. Or if expressed on any material, as a poem in writing, the author may have parted with the paper, without forfeiting any proprietary right in the composition itself. The right is lost only when the author himself communicates his production to the public—in other words, publishes it. It is entirely independent of the copyright laws, and their extension into the domain of art. The aim of those statutes is to secure to the author, composer, or artist the entire profits arising from publication; but the common-law protection enables him to control absolutely the act of publication, and in . . . his own discretion, to decide whether there shall be any publication at all. The statutory right is of no value, unless there is a publication.

What is the nature, the basis, of this right to prevent the publication of manuscripts or works of art? It is stated to be the enforcement of a right of property; and no difficulty arises in accepting this view, so long as we have only to deal with the reproduction of literary and artistic compositions. . . . But where the value of the production is found not in the right to take the profits arising from publication, but in the peace of mind or the relief afforded by the ability to prevent any publication at all, it is difficult to regard the right as one of property, in the common acceptation of that term. . . . A man writes a dozen letters to different people. No person would be permitted to publish a list of the letters written. If the letters or the contents of the diary were protected as literary compositions, the scope of the protection afforded should be the same secured to a published writing under the copyright law. But the copyright law would not prevent an enumeration of the letters, or the publication of some of the facts contained therein. The copyright of a series of paintings or etchings would prevent a reproduction of the paintings as pictures; but it would not prevent a publication of a list or even a description of them. Yet in the famous case of *Prince Albert v. Strange*, the court held that the common-law rule prohibited not merely the reproduction of the etchings which the plaintiff and Queen Victoria had made for their own pleasure, but also "the publishing (at least by printing or writing), though not by copy or resemblance, a description of them, whether more or less limited or summary, whether in the form of a catalogue or otherwise." . . .

These considerations lead to the conclusion that the protection afforded to thoughts, sentiments, and emotions, expressed through the medium of writing or of the arts, so far as it consists in preventing publication, is merely an instance of the enforcement of the more general right of the individual to be let alone. It is like the right not to be assaulted or beaten, the right not to be imprisoned, the right not to be maliciously prosecuted, the right not to be defamed. . . . The principle which protects personal writings and all other personal productions, not against theft and physical appropriation, but against publication in any form, is in reality not the principle of private property, but that of an inviolate personality.

If we are correct in this conclusion, the existing law affords a principle which may be invoked to protect the privacy of the individual from invasion either by the too enterprising press, the photographer, or the possessor of any other modern device for recording or reproducing scenes or sounds. For the protection afforded is not confined by the authorities to those cases where any particular medium or form of expression has been adopted, nor to products of the intellect. The same protection is afforded to emotions and sensations expressed in a musical composition or other work of art as to a literary composition; and words spoken, a pantomime acted, a sonata performed, is no less entitled to protection than if each had been reduced to writing. . . . If, then, the decisions indicate a general right to privacy for thoughts, emotions, and sensations, these should receive the same protection, whether expressed in writing, or in conduct, in conversation, in attitudes, or in facial expression.

      *   *   *

If the invasion of privacy constitutes a legal *injuria*, the elements for demanding redress exist, since already the value of mental suffering, caused by an act wrongful in itself, is recognized as a basis for compensation.

The right of one who has remained a private individual, to prevent his public portraiture, presents the simplest case for such extension; the right to protect one's self from pen portraiture, from a discussion by the press of one's private affairs, would be a more important and far-reaching one. If casual and unimportant statements in a letter, if handiwork, however inartistic and valueless, if possessions of all sorts are protected not only against reproduction, but against description and enumeration, how much more should the acts and sayings of a man in his social and domestic relations be guarded from ruthless publicity. If you may not reproduce a woman's face photographically without her consent, how much less should be tolerated the reproduction of her face, her form, and her actions, by graphic descriptions colored to suit a gross and depraved imagination.

*   *   *

It remains to consider what are the limitations of this right to privacy. . . .

1. The right to privacy does not prohibit any publication of matter which is of public or general interest.

In determining the scope of this rule, aid would be afforded by the analogy, in the law of libel and slander, of cases which deal with the qualified privilege of comment and criticism on matters of public and general interest. . . . The design of the law must be to protect those persons with whose affairs the community has no legitimate concern, from being dragged into an undesirable and undesired publicity and to protect all persons, whatsoever; their position or station, from having matters which they may properly prefer to keep private, made public against their will. It is the unwarranted invasion of individual privacy which is reprehended, and to be, so far as possible, prevented. . . . There are persons who may reasonably claim as a right, protection from the notoriety entailed by being made the victims of journalistic enterprise. There are others who, in varying degrees, have renounced the right to live their lives screened from public observation. . . . Peculiarities of manner and person, which in the ordinary individual should be free from comment, may acquire a public importance, if found in a candidate for political office. . . . To publish of a modest and retiring individual that he suffers from an impediment in his speech or that he cannot spell correctly, is an unwarranted . . . infringement of his rights, while to state and comment on the same characteristics found in a would-be congressman could not be regarded as beyond the pale of propriety.

*   *   *

In general, then, the matters of which the publication should be repressed may be described as those which concern the private life, habits, acts, and relations of an individual, and have no legitimate connection with his fitness for a public office which he seeks or for which he is suggested, or for any public or quasi public position which he is suggested, and have no legitimate relation to or bearing upon any act done by him in a public or quasi public capacity. . . . Some things all men alike are entitled to keep from popular curiosity, whether in public life or not, while others are only private because the persons concerned have not assumed a position which makes their doings legitimate matters of public investigation.

2. The right to privacy . . . is not invaded by any publication made in a court of justice, in legislative bodies, or the committees of those bodies; in municipal

assemblies, or the committees of such assemblies, or practically by any communication made in any other public body, municipal or parochial, or in any body quasi public, like the large voluntary associations formed for almost every purpose of benevolence, business, or other general interest; and (at least in many jurisdictions) reports of any such proceedings would in some measure be accorded a like privilege. . . .

*　　*　　*

5.   The truth of the matter published does not afford a defense. . . . It is not for injury to the individual's character that redress or prevention is sought, but for injury to the right of privacy. For the former, the law of slander and libel provides perhaps a sufficient safeguard. The latter implies the right not merely to prevent inaccurate portrayal of private life, but to prevent its being depicted at all.

6.   The absence of "malice" in the publisher does not afford a defence.

Personal ill-will is not an ingredient of the offence, any more than in an ordinary case of trespass to person or to property. . . . The invasion of the privacy that is to be protected is equally complete and equally injurious, whether the motives by which the speaker or writer was actuated are, taken by themselves, culpable or not. . . . Viewed as a wrong to the individual, this rule is the same pervading the whole law of torts, by which one is held responsible for his intentional acts, even though they are committed with no sinister intent; and viewed as a wrong to society, it is the same principle adopted in a large category of statutory offences.

*　　*　　*

. . . [T]he protection of society must come mainly through a recognition of the rights of the individual. Each man is responsible for his own acts and omissions only. If he condones what he reprobates, with a weapon at hand equal to his defence, he is responsible for the results. If he resists, public opinion will rally to his support. Has he then such a weapon? It is believed that the common law provides him with one, forged in the slow fire of the centuries, and to-day fitly tempered to his hand. The common law has always recognized a man's house as his castle, impregnable, often, even to its own officers engaged in the execution of its commands. Shall the courts thus close the front entrance to constituted authority, and open wide the back door to idle or prurient curiosity?

World War I and Civil Liberties

World War I stimulated an enormous expansion of federal power. Military procurement, the draft, and opposition to the war led to a new and unprecedented role for the federal government in the economy and to a "pattern of repression" previously unknown in American history. Out of this repression emerged modern civil liberties.

Wartime laws permanently altered the federal government's role in the economy. The war allowed the Wilson administration to "rationalize" the economy along progressive lines, affecting areas of the economy previously unregulated or ineffectively regulated by the states. Congress created numerous bureaucracies, such as the Office of Food Administration and the War Industries Board, to regulate almost all aspects of manufacturing and commerce. The Lever Act (1917) allowed the president to regulate food and fuel prices, to seize and operate mines and factories, to limit liquor production, and to "commandeer" any "distilled spirits . . . for redistillation" and use "in the manufacture of munitions and other military and hospital supplies." The Wartime Prohibition Act (1918) temporarily stopped the sale of liquor. Another act established rent control in Washington, D.C. The prewar Army Appropriation Act (1916) allowed wartime seizure of the railroads. When these laws were challenged, the Supreme Court upheld them. Although emergency acts, these laws set the stage for more far-reaching economic regulation of the modern era.

The government also sought to regulate the ideas, thoughts, sympathies, and actions of the American people. World War I was not universally popular, and even some members of Congress opposed the declaration of war. This opposition to the war led to intense repression. One lasting result of the war was the emergence of the government's power to restrict freedom of expression through various statutes. The Espionage Act of 1917 punished spying and communicating with the enemy and allowed $10,000 fines and twenty-year jail terms for anyone who made

> false statements with intent to interfere with the operation of success of the military or naval forces of the United States or to promote the success of its enemies and who-ever . . . cause or attempt to cause insubordination, disloyalty, mutiny, or refusal of duty, in the military . . . or shall willfully obstruct the recruiting or enlisted service of the United States.

The act also allowed the post office to prohibit from the mails any publication deemed dangerous, seditious, or treasonous. Without defining these terms, postal officials banned such publications as the *New York Times* and the *Saturday Evening Post*, as well as numerous pacifist, radical, socialist, religious, and antiwar publications. The Supreme Court upheld this law in *Schenck v. United States* (1919).

The Sedition Act of 1918 (technically an amendment to the Espionage Act) stipulated the same punishments as the 1917 act for anyone who might

> utter, print, write or publish any disloyal profane, scurrilous, or abusive language about the form of government of the United States, or the Constitution . . . or the military or naval forces . . . or the flag . . . or the uniform of the Army or Navy . . . or any language intended to bring the form of the government of the United States . . . into contempt, scorn, contumely, or disrepute.

The law also punished anyone who

> by utterance, writing, printing, publication, or language spoken, urge, incite or advocate any curtailment of production in this country of any thing or things, product or products, necessary or essential to the prosecution of the war . . . with intent to cripple or hinder the United States in the prosecution of the war, and whoever shall willfully advocate, teach, defend, or suggest the doing of any of the acts or things in this section . . . and whoever shall by word or act support or favor the cause of any country with which the United States is at war.

The law also provided for the immediate dismissal of any federal employee who "utters any unpatriotic or disloyal language, or who, in an abusive and violent manner criticizes the Army or Navy or the flag of the United States." The Supreme Court affirmed the constitutionality of this law in *Abrams v. United States* (1919).

The Suppression of Dissent During World War I

The Espionage Act and the Sedition Act helped create a climate of fear, hostility, and repression during the war. Throughout the nation, free speech was virtually impossible for those who did not support the war. At the local, state, and federal level, legislators, police, and the "people" suppressed opponents of the war. The sheer variety of repression described below by historian Paul Murphy suggests the nature of the problem of civil liberties during wartime.

PAUL MURPHY

World War I and the Origins of Civil Liberties in the United States
1979

Any empirically precise analysis of public reaction to the whole national pattern of repression is impossible. Attitudinal surveys were not carried out at the time, nor were public opinion polls taken. Impressionistic and anecdotal evidence, however, tends to suggest a number of things. By and large, the country's collective political conscience regarding civil liberties was not sufficiently well developed to make a meaningful general response. By and large the public was less likely to react to the steady expansion of the government's formal repressive policies and mechanisms than to specific episodes and outrages with which they could identify in a highly personalized way. Regrettably, for the scholar, little satisfactory documentation remains which affords any accurate contemporary group response to the wide range of nationally reported episodes which punctuated the war period. Reciting some of the more colorful, however, affords a flavor of wartime behavior. Consider the following:

- Beethoven's music was banned in Pittsburgh for the duration of the war.
- J. M. Ellis, a black Baptist preacher, was beaten by a mob at Newport, Arkansas, for alleged treasonable utterances which were regarded as unproved by a grand jury after he had been kept in jail for ninety-six days.
- Aliens were barred from holding licenses and permits to do business within the city limits of Cleveland, Ohio.

*   *   *

- At Marysville, Nebraska, a mob broke into a school, removed all books and material either written in German or about Germany, including Bibles in German, piled them outside and burned them.
- In Detroit, Louis Rafelburge, who was said to have made unfavorable remarks about the Red Cross, was taken from his home in his night clothes, given a haircut and had his mustache trimmed by members of a mob which for a while threatened to duck him in the river.
- After being tarred and feathered, George Koetzer, a brewery worker of San Jose, California, was chained to a brass cannon in the city park. He was charged with having made pro-German remarks.

- Clarence Nesbitt, of Thetford Township, Michigan, was tarred and feathered by a group of men who were displeased because he bought only $1,500 worth of Liberty Bonds instead of the $3,000 that they thought he ought to have purchased.
- The Austrian-born violinist, Fritz Kreisler, and the famous Swiss-born conductor of the Boston Symphony, Dr. Karl Muck, were denied access to American music halls.
- In Columbus, Ohio, school teachers were required to meet after school to paste in school music books blank sheets of paper covering "The Watch on the Rhine" and "The Lorelei."

*   *   *

- Victor Berger, Milwaukee Socialist editor, whose newspaper the *Milwaukee Leader*, was indicted for violating the Espionage Act, was denied his seat, with only one dissenting vote, following election to the House of Representatives. One congressman summarized the opposition position, "The one and only issue in this case is that of Americanism."

*   *   *

- In Montana, Ves Hall was arrested and charged with espionage for having stated that he would not go to war, that Germany would win, that President Wilson was crooked, and that the war was being fought for the benefit of Wall Street millionaires.
- John White, an Ohio farmer, was sentenced to twenty-one months in the penitentiary for stating that soldiers in American camps "were dying off like flies" and that the "murder of innocent women and children by German soldiers was no worse than the United States' soldiers did in the Philippines."
- In Texas, three organizers of the Non-Partisan League were arrested and jailed for disloyalty. When M. M. Offut, state office manager, protested, he was seized and had his hair and beard cut off with sheep shears before he was driven out of town. The three men were taken by a mob and given a severe whipping. The *Greenville* (Texas) *Banner* stated that this was evidence that "Americanism is not to be tampered with around Mineola."
- A Minnesota man was arrested under the Minnesota Espionage Act for criticizing women knitting socks for soldiers, in stating, "No soldier ever sees these socks."

*   *   *

- Women in charge of the Emergency Peace Federation, headquartered in Washington, D.C., were ordered by militiamen to close the office and "beat it," or they would be "raided and raped."
- Six farmers in Texas were horsewhipped because they had not subscribed to the Red Cross.
- George Maynard of Medford, Oregon, a member of the International Bible Students' Association, had an iron cross painted on his chest, and was driven out of town.

- In Baltimore, the day before Wilson's war message, rioters broke up a meeting at which David Starr Jordan, president of Stanford University, was to talk under the auspices of the American Union against Militarism, chanting "We'll hang Dave Jordan to a sour apple tree." The *New York Times* noted that the mob was led by "men socially prominent," including "college professors, students, bankers, and lawyers."
- The producer of a film *The Spirit of '76* which dealt exclusively with the American Revolution but showed scenes unflattering to the British army, was convicted of attempting to cause insubordination in the armed forces of the United States and sentenced to prison for ten years.
- D. T. Blodgett was sentenced to twenty years in prison for circulating a pamphlet urging the voters of Iowa not to re-elect a congressman who had voted for conscription.
- Twenty-seven South Dakota farmers were convicted for sending a petition to the government objecting to the draft quota for their county and calling the war a "capitalist's war."

Censorship During World War I

Shortly after the adoption of the Espionage Act of 1917, the post office began to censor radical publications. In July, *The Masses*, a socialist monthly, sought an injunction to prevent the post office from refusing to deliver the magazine. In *Masses Publishing Co. v. Patten* (1917), Federal District Judge Learned Hand warned that "one may not counsel or advise others to violate the law as it stands." He recognized that

> words are not only the keys of persuasion, but the triggers of action, and those which have no purport but to counsel the violation of law cannot by any latitude of interpretation be a part of that public opinion which is the final source of government in a democratic state.

But Hand warned that suppression was acceptable only under narrow circumstances. He rejected suppression of a publication for "abuse and criticism of the existing law, or of the policies of the war." Merely "hostile criticism" that might, in some remote way, "cause" dissatisfaction with the government or the military did not justify censorship. He asserted that to "assimilate" legitimate agitation

> with direct incitement to violent resistance, is to disregard the tolerance of all methods of political agitation which in normal times is a safeguard of free government. The distinction is not a scholastic subterfuge, but a hard-bought acquisition in the fight for freedom. . . . If one stops short of urging upon others . . . to resist the law, it seems to me one should not be held to have attempted to cause its violation. If that be not the test, I can see no escape from the conclusion that under this section every political agitation which can be shown to be apt to create a seditious temper is illegal.

Hand held that the post office could not prohibit *The Masses* from the mails. Hand's test was whether the publication directly advocated violation of the law. Had Hand's test been applied nationally, the war might have passed with relatively few prosecutions for dissent and with much free discussion of the war and its merits. But Hand was overruled by the Court of Appeals, and in the *Schenck case* the United States Supreme Court articulated a more open-ended test of freedom of expression.

Schenck v. *United States*
249 U.S. 47 (1919)

Schenck was the first Supreme Court case to interpret the First Amendment's speech and press clauses. In upholding Socialist party General Secretary Charles Schenck's conviction under the Espionage Act for having attempted to obstruct the draft by printing, and mailing to draft-age men, 15,000 antiwar leaflets, Justice Oliver Wendell Holmes, Jr., set out the "clear and present danger test," which dominated First Amendment jurisprudence for the next half-century. Holmes developed this test through common-law reasoning, rather than relying on precedent.

The document in question upon its first printed side recited the first section of the Thirteenth Amendment, said that the idea embodied in it was violated by the Conscription Act and that a conscript is little better than a convict. In impassioned language it intimated that conscription was despotism in its worst form and a monstrous wrong against humanity in the interest of Wall Street's chosen few. It said "Do not submit to intimidation," but in form at least confined itself to peaceful measures such as a petition for the repeal of the act. The other . . . side of the sheet was headed "Assert Your Rights." It stated reasons for alleging that any one violated the Constitution when he refused to recognize "your right to assert your opposition to the draft," and went on "If you do not assert and support your rights, you are helping to deny or disparage rights which it is the solemn duty of all citizens and residents of the United States to retain." It described the arguments on the other side as coming from cunning politicians and a mercenary capitalist law as helping to support an infamous conspiracy. It denied the power to send our citizens away to foreign shores to shoot up the people of other lands, and added that words could not express the condemnation such cold-blooded ruthlessness deserves, &c., &c., winding up "You must do your share to maintain, support and uphold the rights of the people of this country." Of course the document would not have been sent unless it had been intended to have some effect, and we do not see what effect it could be expected to have upon persons subject to the draft except to influence them to obstruct the carrying of it out. The defendants do not deny that the jury might find against them on this point.

But it is said, suppose that was the tendency of this circular, it is protected by the First Amendment. . . . Two of the strongest expressions are said to be quoted respectively from well-known public men. It well may be that the prohibition of laws abridging the freedom of speech is not confined to previous restraints, although to prevent them may have been the main purpose. . . . We admit that in many places and in ordinary times the defendants in saying all that was said in the circular would have been within their constitutional rights. But the character of every act depends upon the circumstances in which it is done. The most stringent protection of free speech would not protect a man in falsely shouting fire in a theatre and causing a panic. It does not even protect a man from an injunction against uttering words that may have all the effect of force. The question in every case is whether the words used are used in such circumstances and are of such a nature as to create a clear and present danger that they will bring about the substantive evils that Congress has a right to prevent. It is a question of proximity and degree. When a nation is at war many things that might be said in time of peace are such a hindrance to its effort that their utterance will not be endured so long as men fight and that no Court could regard them as protected by any constitutional right. It seems to be admitted that if an actual obstruction of the recruiting service were proved, liability for words that produced that effect might be enforced. The statute of 1917 . . . punishes conspiracies to obstruct as well as actual obstruction. If the act, (speaking, or circulating a paper,) its tendency and the intent with which it is done are the same, we perceive no ground for saying that success alone warrants making the act a crime. . . .

Note: *Debs* v. *United States*, 249 U.S. 211 (1919)

A week after the Court decided *Schenck*, Justice Holmes upheld the Espionage Act conviction of Eugene V. Debs. This case was particularly troublesome because as the Socialist party candidate for president in 1912, Debs had captured nearly a million votes. Debs was convicted for a speech in which he had attacked militarism, war, and the draft. At his trial, Debs bravely declared: "I have been accused of obstructing the war. I admit it. Gentlemen, I abhor war. I would oppose the war if I stood alone." Debs spent the rest of the war in federal prison. In 1920, he ran for president from prison, getting over 900,000 votes, in the face of a massive "red scare," which led to the arrest of thousands of socialists, labor organizers, and others viewed as "radical" by the Wilson administration.

Abrams et al. v. *United States*
250 U.S. 616 (1919)

Abrams and his co-defendants printed leaflets condemning American intervention in the Russian Revolution, which they "distributed" by throwing out of a window onto a New York City street. The pamphlet called President Wilson "Our Kaiser," and accused him of being "too much of a coward to come out openly and say: 'We capitalistic nations cannot afford to have a proletarian republic in Russia.'" The pamphlet urged a general strike to protest the "barbaric intervention" in the Russian Revolution. Justice John H. Clarke, writing for a 7 to 2 majority, dismissed Abrams's First Amendment claims with a swift reference to Schenck *and sustained the conviction under the Sedition Act, on the theory that "men must be held to have intended, and to be accountable for, the effects which their acts were likely to produce." Clark declared that "the obvious effect" of the leaflet "would be to persuade persons . . . not to work in ammunition factories, where their work would produce 'bullets, bayonets, cannon' and other munitions," and this would affect the war against Germany as well as the American Expeditionary Force in Russia.*

Mr. Justice Holmes dissenting.

This indictment is founded wholly upon the publication of two leaflets. . . .

The first of these leaflets says that the President's cowardly silence about the intervention in Russia reveals the hypocrisy of the plutocratic gang in Washington. It intimates that "German militarism combined with allied capitalism to crush the Russian revolution"—goes on that the tyrants of the world fight each other until they see a common enemy-working class enlightenment, when they combine to crush it; and that now militarism and capitalism combined, though not openly, to crush the Russian revolution. It says that there is only one enemy of the workers of the world and that is capitalism; that it is a crime for workers of America, &c., to fight the workers' republic of Russia, and ends "Awake! Awake, you Workers of the World! Revolutionists." A note adds "It is absurd to call us pro-German. We hate and despise German militarism more than do you hypocritical tyrants. We have more reasons for denouncing German militarism than has the coward of the White House."

The other leaflet, headed "Workers—Wake Up," with abusive language says that America together with the Allies will march for Russia to help the Czecko-Slovaks in their struggle against the Bolsheviki, and that this time the hypocrites shall not fool the Russian emigrants and friends of Russia in America. It tells the Russian emigrants that they now must spit in the face of the false military propaganda by which their sympathy and help to the prosecution of the war have been called forth and says that with the money they have lent or are going to lend "they will make bullets not only for the Germans but also for the Workers Soviets of Russia," and further, "Workers in the ammunition factories, you are producing bullets, bayonets, cannon, to murder not only the Germans, but also your dearest, best, who are in Russia and are fighting for freedom." It then appeals to the same Russian emigrants at some length not to consent to the "inquisitionary expedition to Russia," and says that the destruction of the Russian revolution is "the politics of the march to Russia." The leaflet winds up by saying "Workers, our reply to this barbaric intervention has to be a general strike!," and after a few words on the spirit of revolution, exhortations not to be afraid, and some usual tall talk ends "Woe unto those who will be in the way of progress. Let solidarity live! The Rebels."

No argument seems to me necessary to show that these pronunciamentos in no way attack the form of government of the United States. . . . [I]t seems too plain to be denied that the suggestion to workers in the ammunition factories that they are producing bullets to murder their dearest, and the further advocacy of a general strike, both in the second leaflet, do urge curtailment of production of things necessary to the prosecution of the war within the meaning of the [Espionage] Act. . . .

But to make the conduct criminal that statute requires that it should be "with intent by such curtailment to cripple or hinder the United States in the prosecution of the war." It seems to me that no such intent is proved.

*   *   *

It seems to me that this statute must be taken to use its words in a strict and accurate sense. They would be absurd in any other. A patriot might think that we were wasting money on aeroplanes, or making more cannon of a certain kind than we needed, and might advocate curtailment with success, yet even if it turned out that the curtailment hindered and was thought by other minds to have been obviously likely to hinder the United States in the prosecution of the war, no one would hold such conduct a crime. I admit that my illustration does not answer all that might be said but it is enough to show what I think and to let me pass to a more important aspect of the case. I refer to the First Amendment to the Constitution that Congress shall make no law abridging the freedom of speech.

I never have seen any reason to doubt that the questions of law that alone were before this Court in the cases of *Schenck*, *Frohwerk* and *Debs* were rightly decided. I do not doubt for a moment that by the same reasoning that would justify punishing persuasion to murder, the United States constitutionally may punish speech that produces or is intended to produce a clear and imminent danger that it will bring about forthwith certain substantive evils that the United States constitutionally may seek to prevent. The power undoubtedly is greater in time of war than in time of peace because war opens dangers that do not exist at other times.

But as against dangers peculiar to war, as against others, the principle of the right to free speech is always the same. It is only the present danger of immediate evil or an intent to bring it about that warrants Congress in setting a limit to the expression of opinion where private rights are not concerned. Congress certainly cannot forbid all effort to change the mind of the country. Now nobody can suppose that the surreptitious publishing of a silly leaflet by an unknown man, without more, would present any immediate danger that its opinions would hinder the success of the government arms or have any appreciable tendency to do so. . . .

I do not see how anyone can find the intent required by the statute in any of the defendants' words. The second leaflet is the only one that affords even a foundation for the charge, and there, without invoking the hatred of German militarism expressed in the former one, it is evident from the beginning to the end that the only object of the paper is to help Russia and stop American intervention there against the popular government—not to impede the United States in the war that it was carrying on. To say that two phrases taken literally might import a suggestion of conduct that would have interference with the war as an indirect and probably undesired effect seems to me by no means enough to show an attempt to produce that effect.

*   *   *

In this case sentences of twenty years imprisonment have been imposed for the publishing of two leaflets that I believe the defendants had as much right to publish as the Government has to publish the Constitution of the United States now vainly invoked by them. Even if I am technically wrong and enough can be squeezed from these poor and puny anonymities to turn the color of legal litmus paper; I will add, even if what I think the necessary intent were shown; the most nominal punishment seems to me all that possibly could be inflicted, unless the defendants are to be made to suffer not for what the indictment alleges but for the creed that they avow— a creed that I believe to be the creed of ignorance and immaturity when honestly held, as I see no reason to doubt that it was held here, but which, although made the subject of examination at the trial, no one has a right even to consider in dealing with the charges before the Court.

Persecution for the expression of opinions seems to me perfectly logical. If you have no doubt of your premises or your power and want a certain result with all your heart you naturally express your wishes in law and sweep away all opposition. To allow opposition by speech seems to indicate that you think the speech impotent, as when a man says that he has squared the circle, or that you do not care whole-heartedly for the result, or that you doubt either your power or your premises. But when men have realized that time has upset many fighting faiths, they may come to believe even more than they believe the very foundations of their own conduct that the ultimate good desired is better reached by free trade in ideas—that the best test of truth is the power of the thought to get itself accepted in the competition of the market, and that truth is the only ground upon which their wishes safely can be carried out. That at any rate is the theory of our Constitution. It is an experiment, as all life is an experiment. Every year if not every day we have to wager our salvation upon some prophecy based upon imperfect knowledge. While that experiment is part of our system I think that we should be eternally vigilant against attempts to check the expression of opinions that we loathe and believe to be fraught with death, unless they so imminently threaten immediate interference with the lawful and pressing purposes of the law that an immediate check is required to save the country. I wholly disagree with the argument of the Government that the First Amendment left the common law as to seditious libel in force. History seems to me against the notion. I had conceived that the United States through many years had shown its repentance for the Sedition Act of 1798, by repaying fines that it imposed. Only the emergency that makes it immediately dangerous to leave the correction of evil counsels to time warrants making any exception to the sweeping command, "Congress shall make no law . . . abridging the freedom of speech." Of course I am speaking only of expressions of opinion and exhortations, which were all that were uttered here, but I regret that I cannot put into more impressive words my belief that in their conviction upon this indictment the defendants were deprived of their rights under the Constitution of the United States.

Mr. Justice Brandeis concurs with the foregoing opinion.

Note: The *Abrams* Dissent

Justice Holmes's *Abrams* dissent has been called the "most eloquent and moving defense of free speech since Milton's *Areogpagitica*." Here Holmes laid out a theory of freedom of speech in a democracy that would eventually be adopted by the Supreme Court. Nevertheless, the change from *Schenck* to *Abrams* is puzzling. Despite his ringing defense of free speech, Holmes endorsed his *Schenck* opinion, while appearing to modify his test. Is the test in *Abrams* different from that in *Schenck*? Is this a change of position or merely the application of different facts to the same test?

Radicals and Civil Liberties

At the end of World War I, Americans faced rampant inflation and unemployment. Returning soldiers found it difficult to find jobs, while workers in defense-related industries were laid off or fired. Socialists saw an opportunity to increase their following. They were heartened by the Communist revolution in Russia in 1917 and by the strength of socialism in other European countries, including Germany. For many American radicals, the age of revolution seemed at hand. Most members of the old Socialist party split from that organization to form what evolved into the American Communist party.

Conservatives also thought the revolution was at hand, and they were not pleased. On January 2, 1920, United States Attorney General A. Mitchell Palmer launched a nationwide preemptive strike against radicals, arresting over 4,000 people, mostly members of the Socialist party or the Industrial Workers of the World (IWW). These raids were conducted without warrants and with little regard for due process. Thousands were incarcerated in overcrowded jails for months.

What Palmer did on the national scale, others accomplished at the state and local levels. Even before the Palmer raids began, the New York legislature, through the Lusk Committee, began to investigate radicals in that state. "Investigation" for the Lusk Committee meant police raids on the offices of radical organizations and arrests of members. The New York Assembly also refused to seat five legally elected socialists.

Most of the radicals jailed by state and federal authorities were eventually pardoned, although many were deported or died in jail. The survivors left prison with their lives shattered. For most, their only crime was believing in the wrong ideology and joining the wrong organizations.

By mid-decade, the "red scare" had run its course, leaving the IWW virtually destroyed, the Communist party decimated, and the Socialist party no longer able to garner much electoral support. Americans of the 1920s turned from mass hysteria over radicalism to the mass excesses of the Jazz Age. Prohibition, gangsters, and conspicuous consumption occupied the public's mind. While huge raids on radicals ceased, the 1920s remained a dangerous decade for Americans with radical ideas. Although the courts rarely protected civil liberties, hints of a more tolerant future could be found in the prophetic dissents of Justices Oliver Wendell Holmes, Jr., and Louis Brandeis, and in the recognition by the Supreme Court that the Fourteenth Amendment made the First Amendment applicable to the states.

Note: Civil Liberties and Fourteenth Amendment Incorporation

The Fourteenth Amendment prohibits state infringements of due process with expansive language, which the late-nineteenth-century Court had turned into a shield for business interests. From 1884 to 1908, the United States Supreme Court refused to use the due process clause of the Fourteenth Amendment to make various provisions of the Bill of Rights applicable to the states. *Hurtado* v. *California* (1884) upheld a California murder conviction without a grand jury indictment. In *Maxwell* v. *Dow* (1900), the Court upheld a Utah conviction of the bank-robbing desperado "Gunplay" Maxwell by an eight-man jury (instead of the traditional twelve-man jury). In *Twining* v. *New Jersey* (1908), the Court rejected a claim that the due process clause of the Fourteenth Amendment and the Fifth Amendment protected Twining, a corrupt bank officer, against self-incrimination in a state trial. Justice William H. Moody concluded that the protection against self-incrimination was neither a "fundamental" right nor necessary for due process. In reaching this decision, however, the Court opened the door to future applications of the Bill of Rights to the states through the Fourteenth Amendment, noting that "some of the personal rights safeguarded by the first eight Amendments against national action may also be safeguarded against state action, because a denial of them would be a denial of due process of law."

The connection between civil liberties and property continued after World War I. After the war, Nebraska prohibited teaching foreign languages to children who had not "successfully passed the eighth grade." This act was aimed at the state's large German-speaking community. In *Meyer* v. *Nebraska* (1922), the Court reversed the conviction of a German instructor at a German Lutheran parochial school. The Court held that the Nebraska law deprived citizens of their "liberty, or property, without due process of law" because the Fourteenth Amendment protected

> the right of the individual to contract, to engage in any of the common occupations of life, to acquire useful knowledge, to marry, establish a home and bring up children, to worship God according to the dictates of his own conscience, and generally to enjoy those privileges long recognized at common law as essential to the orderly pursuit of happiness of free men.

This decision did not incorporate First Amendment protections of religious liberty through the Fourteenth Amendment. Rather, it applied the conservative doctrine found in *Lochner* v. *New York* (1905) and other cases that the state "under the guise of protecting the public interest" could not interfere with the liberty of contract and the common-law rights of parents to raise their children. In *Pierce* v. *Society of the Sisters* (1925), the Court reaffirmed the doctrine in *Meyer* by striking down Oregon's prohibition on private schools. The Court found that

> the fundamental theory of liberty upon which all governments in this Union repose excludes any general power of the state to standardize its children by forcing them to accept instruction from public teachers only. The child is not the mere creature of the state; those who nurture him and direct this destiny have the right . . . to recognize and prepare him [for life].

In addition, the Court held that the Society of Sisters and other owners of private schools had a property right in their schools that the state could not arbitrarily take from them. Thus the Court permanently enjoined enforcement of the Oregon law.

Seven days after deciding *Pierce*, the Court began the incorporation of the Bill of Rights to the states in *Gitlow* v. *New York* (1925). Gitlow, a Communist party leader, had been convicted of violating New York's criminal anarchy law. On appeal, Gitlow argued that his conviction violated his First Amendment rights because he never constituted a "clear and present danger" that the state could legitimately suppress. The conservative Taft Court rejected Gitlow's arguments about the nature of free speech in a democracy, but did accept Gitlow's theoretical point: that the Fourteenth Amendment prohibited the states from abridging First Amendment rights. Casually and almost without any careful thought, the Court reversed over fifty years of precedent with a simple statement: "For present purposes we may and do assume that freedom of speech and of the press—which are protected by the First Amendment from abridgment by Congress—are among the fundamental personal rights 'liberties' protected by the due process clause of the Fourteenth Amendment from impairment by the States,"

Gitlow thus became a major watershed in American legal and constitutional history. After *Gitlow*, most of the Bill of Rights would be gradually incorporated, through the Fourteenth Amendment, to apply to the states. This held both for politically sensitive cases tied to freedom of expression and for run-of-the-mill criminal cases involving search and seizure, arrest, and trial. *Gitlow* began an era when almost all public law, and a good deal of private law, would come under federal jurisdiction through the Fourteenth Amendment and the Bill of Rights.

Whitney v. *California*
274 U.S. 357 (1927)

A California court found Whitney in violation of the state's Criminal Syndicalism Act because of her membership in the Communist Labor Party of America. Because at trial Whitney failed to assert a right to freedom of speech under the First and Fourteenth Amendments, the Supreme Court unanimously held that no federal question had been properly raised. Justice Brandeis, joined by Justice Holmes, concurred in the technical result of the case with one of the most eloquent defenses of freedom of expression in American legal history.

This Court has not yet fixed the standard by which to determine when a danger shall be deemed clear; how remote the danger may be and yet be deemed present; and what degree of evil shall be deemed sufficiently substantial to justify resort to abridgment of free speech and assembly as the means of protection. To reach sound conclusions on these matters, we must bear in mind why a State is, ordinarily, denied the power to prohibit dissemination of social, economic and political doctrine which a vast majority of its citizens believes to be false and fraught with evil consequence.

Those who won our independence believed that the final end of the State was to make men free to develop their faculties; and that in its government the deliberative forces should prevail over the arbitrary. They valued liberty both as an end and a means. They believed liberty to be the secret of happiness and courage to be the secret of liberty. They believed that freedom to think as you will and to speak as you think are means indispensable to the discovery and spread of political truth; that without free speech and assembly discussion would be futile; that with them, discussion affords ordinarily adequate protection against the dissemination of noxious doctrine; that the greatest menace to freedom is an inert people; that public discussion is a political duty; and that this should be a fundamental principle of the American government. They recognized the risks to which all human institutions are subject. But they knew that order cannot be secured merely through fear of punishment for its infraction; that it is hazardous to discourage thought, hope and imagination; that fear breeds repression; that repression breeds hate; that hate menaces stable government; that the path of safety lies in the opportunity to discuss freely supposed grievances and proposed remedies; and that the fitting remedy for evil counsels is good ones. Believing in the power of reason as applied through public discussion, they eschewed silence coerced by law—the argument of force in its worst form. Recognizing the occasional tyrannies of governing majorities, they amended the Constitution so that free speech and assembly should be guaranteed.

Fear of serious injury cannot alone justify suppression of free speech and assembly. Men feared witches and burnt women. It is the function of speech to free men from the bondage of irrational fears. To justify suppression of free speech there must be reasonable ground to fear that serious evil will result if free speech is practiced. There must be reasonable ground to believe that the danger apprehended is imminent. There must be reasonable ground to believe that the evil to be prevented is a serious one. Every denunciation of existing law tends in some measure to increase the probability that there will be violation of it. Condonation of a breach enhances the probability. Expressions of approval add to the probability. Propagation of the criminal state of mind by teaching syndicalism increases it. Advocacy of law-breaking heightens it still further. But even advocacy of violation, however reprehensible morally, is not a justification for denying free speech where the advocacy falls short of incitement and there is nothing to indicate that the advocacy would be immediately acted on. The wide difference between advocacy and incitement, between preparation and attempt, between assembling and conspiracy, must be borne in mind. In order to support a finding of clear and present danger it must be shown either that immediate serious violence was to be expected or was advocated, or that the past conduct furnished reason to believe that such advocacy was then contemplated.

Those who won our independence by revolution were not cowards. They did not fear political change. They did not exalt order at the cost of liberty. To courageous, self-reliant men, with confidence in the power of free and fearless reasoning applied through the processes of popular government, no danger flowing from speech can be deemed clear and present, unless the incidence of the evil apprehended is so imminent that it may befall before there is opportunity for full discussion. If there be time to expose through discussion the falsehood and fallacies, to avert the evil by the processes of education, the remedy to be applied is more speech, not enforced silence. Only an emergency can justify repression. Such must be the rule if authority is to be reconciled with freedom. Such, in my opinion, is the command of the Constitution. It is therefore always open to Americans by showing that there was no emergency justifying it.

Moreover, even imminent danger cannot justify resort to prohibition of these functions essential to effective democracy, unless the evil apprehended is relatively serious. Prohibition of free speech and assembly is a measure so stringent that it would be inappropriate as the means for averting a relatively trivial harm to society. A police measure may be unconstitutional merely because the remedy, although effective as means of protection, is unduly harsh or oppressive. Thus, a State might, in the exercise of its police power, make any trespass upon the land of another a crime, regardless of the results or of the intent or purpose of the trespasser. It might, also, punish an attempt, a conspiracy, or an incitement to commit the trespass. But it is hardly conceivable that this Court would hold constitutional a statute which punished as a felony the mere voluntary assembly with a society formed to teach that pedestrians had the moral right to cross unenclosed, unposted, waste lands and to advocate their doing so, even if there was imminent danger that advocacy would lead to a trespass. The fact that speech is likely to result in some violence or in destruction of property is not enough to justify its suppression. There must be the probability of serious injury to the State. Among free men, the deterrents ordinarily to be applied to prevent crime are education and punishment for violations of the law, not abridgment of the rights of free speech and assembly.

World War II and Legal Developments

World War I unleashed unprecedented hysteria, undermining civil liberties in the nation. This hysteria was partly a result of the mixed feelings Americans had about the war. Many Americans opposed the war or at least doubted that a war in Europe was an American concern. The uncertain causes of the war and the weakness of support for the war partly explain the aggressive suppression of opposition to the war.

The situation was different at the beginning of World War II. In the 1930s, the United States had aided China in its war against Japan and openly sided with Britain in the war against Germany. Although isolationism had been a powerful force in the 1930s, the surprise bombing of Pearl Harbor united Americans as few events have. During this war there were, with one gigantic exception, few attacks on civil liberties. Some American fascists were tried,[1] but unlike World War I, during World War II, Americans tolerated dissent and conscientious objectors. In the flag salute cases, the Court finally recognized the importance of protecting minority rights, even during wartime.

The great exception to this trend was the forcible incarceration of approximately 112,000 Japanese-Americans in what were euphemistically called "relocation centers" or "internment camps." Two-thirds of these people were American citizens of Japanese ancestry. The rest were mostly aged immigrants who had lived in the United States for decades, but, because of racist naturalization laws, were not allowed to become citizens.

The Flag Salute Cases

In 1936, school officials in Minersville, Pennsylvania, expelled Lillian and William Gobitis for refusing to salute the flag. As Jehovah's Witnesses, the Gobitis family believed that saluting a flag violated biblical injunctions against worshiping graven images. In *Minersville School District* v. *Gobitis* (1940), the Court ruled 8 to 1 (Justice Harlan Stone dissenting) in favor of the school district. Writing for the Court, Justice Felix Frankfurter argued that saluting the flag "promot[ed] . . . national cohesion," and this was "an interest inferior to none in the hierarchy of legal values." Frankfurter thought that "National unity" was "the basis of national security," and he was unwilling "to deny the legislature the right to select appropriate means for its attainment."

Frankfurter personally opposed the forced flag salute, but he thought the courts ought not interfere with the legitimate goal of instilling patriotism in children and the reasonable method of saluting the flag. He suggested that

> where all effective means of inducing political changes are left free from interference, education in the abandonment of foolish legislation is itself a training in liberty. To fight

out the wise use of legislative authority in the forum of public opinion and before legislative assemblies rather than to transfer such a context to the judicial arena, serves to vindicate the self-confidence of a free people.

West Virginia State Board of Education
v. Barnette
319 U.S. 624 (1943)

Immediately after Gobitis, *Jehovah's Witnesses faced widespread suppression and violence at the hands of mobs, vigilantes, and even police officials. In 1942, West Virginia's State Board of Education required that all teachers and students "participate in the salute honoring the Nation represented by the Flag." Refusal to salute the flag was considered "insubordination," which led to expulsion of the children and subjected their parents to up to $50 fines and up to thirty days in jail. The Barnette children, who were Jehovah's Witnesses, challenged the law after they were subjected to its penalties. A federal district court enjoined the enforcement of the law, and the Board of Education appealed to the United States Supreme Court, relying on* Gobitis.

Mr. Justice Jackson delivered the opinion of the Court.

* * *

As the present Chief Justice [Stone] said in dissent in the *Gobitis* case, the State may "require teaching by instruction and study of all in our history and in the structure and organization of our government, including the guaranties of civil liberty, which tend to inspire patriotism and love of country." Here, however, we are dealing with a compulsion of students to declare a belief. They are not merely made acquainted with the flag salute so that they may be informed as to what it is or even what it means. The issue here is whether this slow and easily neglected route to aroused loyalties constitutionally may be short-cut by substituting compulsory salute and slogan. This issue is not prejudiced by the Court's previous holding that where a State, without compelling attendance, extends college facilities to pupils who voluntarily enroll, it may prescribe military training as part of the course without offense to the Constitution. It was held that those who take advantage of its opportunities may not on ground of conscience refuse compliance with such conditions. *Hamilton* v. *Regents*. In the present case attendance is not optional. . . .

There is no doubt that the flag salute is a form of utterance. Symbolism is a primitive but effective way of communicating ideas. The use of an emblem or flag to symbolize some system, idea, institution, or personality, is a short cut from mind to mind. Causes and nations, political parties, lodges and ecclesiastical groups seek to knit the loyalty of their followings to a flag or banner, a color or design. The State announces rank, function, and authority through crowns and maces, uniforms and black robes; the church speaks through the Cross, the Crucifix, the altar and shrine, and clerical raiment. Symbols of State often convey political ideas just as religious symbols come to convey theological ones. Associated with many to these symbols are appropriate gestures of acceptance or respect: a salute, a bowed or bared head, a bended knee. A person gets from a symbol the meaning he puts into it, and what is one man's comfort and inspiration is another's jest and scorn.

Over a decade ago Chief Justice Hughes led this Court in holding that the display of a red flag as a symbol of opposition by peaceful and legal means to organized government was protected by the free speech guaranties of the Constitution. *Stromberg* v. *California*. Here it is the State that employs a flag as a symbol of adherence to government as presently organized. It requires the individual to communicate by word and sign his acceptance of the political ideas it thus bespeaks. Objection to this form of communication when coerced is an old one, well known to the framers of the Bill of Rights.

It is also to be noted that the compulsory flag salute and pledge requires affirmation of a belief and an attitude of mind. . . . It is now a commonplace that censorship or suppression of expression of opinion is tolerated by our Constitution only when the expression presents a clear and present danger of action of a kind the State is empowered to prevent and punish. It would seem that involuntary affirmation could be commanded only on even more immediate and urgent grounds than silence. But here the power of compulsion is invoked without any allegation that remaining passive during a flag salute ritual creates a clear and present danger that would justify an effort even to muffle expression. To sustain the compulsory flag salute we are required to say that a Bill of Rights guards the individual's right to speak his own mind, left it open to public authorities to compel him to utter what is not in his mind.

*   *   *

The *Gobitis* decision, however, *assumed* . . . that power exists in the State to impose the flag salute discipline upon school children in general. The Court only examined and rejected a claim based on religious beliefs of immunity from an unquestioned general rule. The question which underlies the flag salute controversy is whether such a ceremony so touching matters of opinion and political attitude may be imposed upon the individual by official authority under powers committed to any political organization under our Constitution. We examine rather than assume existence of this power and . . . re-examine specific grounds assigned for the *Gobitis* decision.

1.   It was said [in Frankfurter's *Gobitis* opinion] that the flag-salute controversy confronted the Court with "the problem which Lincoln cast in memorable dilemma: 'Must a government of necessity be too *strong* for the liberties of its people, or too *weak* to maintain its own existence?' and that the answer must be in favor of strength."

We think issues may be examined free of pressure or restraint growing out of such considerations.

It may be doubted whether Mr. Lincoln would have thought that the strength of government to maintain itself would be impressively vindicated by our confirming power of the State to expel a handful of children from school. Such oversimplification, so handy in political debate, often lacks the precision necessary to postulates of judicial reasoning. If validly applied to this problem, the utterance cited would resolve every issue of power in favor of those in authority and would require us to override every liberty thought to weaken or delay execution of their policies.

Government of limited power need not be anemic government. Assurance that rights are secure tends to diminish fear and jealousy of strong government, and by making us feel safe to live under it makes for its better support. Without promise of a limiting Bill of Rights it is doubtful if our Constitution could have mustered enough strength to enable its ratification. To enforce those rights today is not to choose weak government over strong government. It is only to adhere as a means of strength to individual freedom of mind in preference to officially disciplined uniformity for which history indicates a disappointing and disastrous end.

2.   It was also considered in the *Gobitis* case that functions of educational officers in States, counties and school districts were such that to interfere with their authority "would in effect make us the school board for the country."

*   *   *

Such Boards are numerous and their territorial jurisdiction often small. But small and local authority may feel less sense of responsibility to the Constitution, and agencies of publicity may be less vigilant in calling it to account. The action of Congress in making flag observance voluntary and respecting the conscience of the objector in a matter so vital as raising the Army contrasts sharply with these local regulations in matters relatively trivial to the welfare of the nation. There are village tyrants as well as village Hampdens, but none who acts under color of law is beyond reach of the Constitution.

3.   The *Gobitis* opinion reasoned that this is a field "where courts possess no marked . . . competence," that it is committed to the legislatures as well as the courts to guard cherished liberties and that it is constitutionally appropriate to "fight out the wise use of legislative authority in the forum of public opinion and before legislative assemblies rather than to transfer such a contest to the judicial arena. . . ."

The very purpose of a Bill of Rights was to withdraw certain subjects from the vicissitudes of political controversy, to place them beyond the reach of majorities and officials and to establish them as legal principles to be applied by the courts. One's right to life, liberty, and property, to free speech, a free press, freedom of worship and assembly, and other fundamental rights may not be submitted to vote; they depend on the outcome of no elections.

4.   Lastly, and this is the very heart of the *Gobitis* opinion, it reasons that "National unity is the basis of national security," that the authorities have "the right to select appropriate means for its attainment," and hence reaches the conclusion that such compulsory measures toward "national unity" are constitutional. Upon the verity of this assumption depends our answer in this case.

*   *   *

Struggles to coerce uniformity of sentiment in support of some end thought essential to their time and country have been waged by many good as well as by evil men. Nationalism is a relatively recent phenomenon but at other times and places the ends have been racial or territorial security, support of a dynasty or regime, and particular plans for saving souls. As . . . moderate methods to attain unity have failed, those bent on its accomplishment must resort to an ever-increasing severity. . . . Ultimate futility of such attempts to compel coherence is the lesson of every such effort from the Roman drive to stamp out Christianity as a disturber of its pagan unity, the Inquisition, as a means to religious and dynastic unity, the Siberian exiles as a means to Russian unity, down to the fast failing efforts of our present totalitarian enemies. Those who begin coercive elimination of dissent soon find themselves exterminating dissenters. Compulsory unification of opinion achieves only the unanimity of the graveyard.

It seems trite but necessary to say that the First Amendment to our Constitution was designed to avoid these ends by avoiding these beginnings. There is no mysticism in the American concept of the State or of the nature or origin of its authority. We set up government by consent of the governed, and the Bill of Rights denies those in power any legal opportunity to coerce that consent. Authority here is to be controlled by public opinion, not public opinion by authority.

The case is made difficult not because the principles of its decision are obscure but because the flag involved is our own. Nevertheless, we apply the limitations of the Constitution with no fear that freedom to be intellectually and spiritually diverse or even contrary will disintegrate the social organization. To believe that patriotism will not flourish if patriotic ceremonies are voluntary and spontaneous instead of a compulsory routine is to make an unflattering estimate of the appeal of our institutions to free minds. We can have intellectual individualism and the rich cultural diversities that we owe to exceptional minds only at the price of occasional eccentricity and abnormal attitudes. When they are so harmless to others or to the State as those we deal with here, the price is not too great. But freedom to differ is not limited to things that do not matter much. That would be a mere shadow of freedom. The test of its substance is the right to differ as to things that touch the heart of the existing order.

If there is any fixed star in our constitutional constellation, it is that no official, high or petty, can prescribe what shall be orthodox in politics, nationalism, religion, or other matters of opinion or force citizens to confess by word or act their faith therein. If there are any circumstances which permit an exception, they do not now occur to us.

We think the action of the local authorities in compelling the flag salute and pledge transcends constitutional limitations on their power and invades the sphere of intellect and spirit which it is the purpose of the First Amendment to our Constitution to reserve from all official control.

The decision of this Court in *Minersville School District* v. *Gobitis . . .* [is] overruled, and the judgment enjoining enforcement of the West Virginia Regulation is Affirmed.

Mr. Justice Frankfurter, dissenting:

One who belongs to the most vilified and persecuted minority in history is not likely to be insensible to the freedoms guaranteed by our Constitution. Were my purely personal attitude relevant I should wholeheartedly associate myself with the general libertarian views in the Court's opinion, representing as they do the thought and action of a lifetime. But as judges we are neither Jew nor Gentile, neither Catholic nor agnostic. We owe equal attachment to the Constitution and are equally bound by our judicial obligations whether we derive our citizenship from the earliest or the latest immigrants to these shores. As a member of this Court I am not justified in writing my private notions of policy into the Constitution, no matter how deeply I may cherish them or how mischievous I may deem their disregard. The duty of a judge who must decide which of two claims before the Court shall prevail, that of a State to enact and enforce laws within its general competence or that of an individual to refuse obedience because of the demands of his conscience, is not that of the ordinary person. It can never be emphasized too much that one's own opinion about the wisdom or evil of a law should be excluded altogether when one is doing one's duty on the bench. The only opinion of our own even looking in that direction that is material is our opinion whether legislators could in reason have enacted such a law. In the light of all the circumstances, including the history of this question in this Court, it would require more daring than I possess to deny that reasonable legislators could have taken the action which is before us for review. Most unwillingly, therefore, I must differ from my brethren with regard to legislation like this. I cannot bring my mind to believe that the "liberty" secured by the Due Process Clause gives this Court authority to deny to the State of West Virginia the attainment of that which we all recognize as a legitimate legislative end, namely, the promotion of good citizenship, by employment of the means here chosen.

*   *   *

That claims are pressed on behalf of sincere religious convictions does not of itself establish their constitutional validity. Nor does waving the banner of religious freedom relieve us from examining into the power we are asked to deny the states. Otherwise the doctrine of separation of church and state, so cardinal in the history of this nation and for the liberty of our people, would mean not the disestablishment of a state church but the establishment of all churches and of all religious groups.

The subjection of dissidents to the general requirement of saluting the flag, as a measure conducive to the training of children in good citizenship, is very far from . . . exacting obedience to general laws that have offended deep religious scruples. Compulsory vaccination . . . food inspection regulations . . . the obligation to bear arms . . . testimonial duties . . . compulsory medical treatment . . . these are but illustrations of conduct that has often been compelled in the enforcement of legislation of general applicability even though the religious consciences of particular individuals rebelled at the exaction.

Law is concerned with external behavior and not with the inner life of man. It rests in large measure upon compulsion. Socrates lives in history partly because he gave his life for the conviction that duty of obedience to secular law does not presuppose consent to its enactment or belief in its virtue. The consent upon which free government rests is the consent that comes from sharing in the process of making and unmaking laws. . . . The individual conscience may profess what faith it chooses. . . . [B]ut it cannot thereby restrict community action through political organs in matters of community concern, so long as the action is not asserted in a discriminatory way either openly or by stealth. One may have the right to practice one's religion and at the same time owe the duty of formal obedience to laws that run counter to one's beliefs. . . .

*   *   *

The flag salute exercise has no kinship whatever to the oath tests so odious in history. For the oath test was one of the instruments for suppressing heretical beliefs. Saluting the flag suppresses no belief nor curbs it. Children and their parents may believe what they please, avow their belief and practice it. It is not even remotely suggested that the requirement for saluting the flag involves the slightest restriction against the fullest opportunity on the part both of the children and of their parents to disavow as publicly as they choose to do so the meaning that others attach to the gesture of salute. All channels of affirmative free expression are open to both children and parents. Had we before us any act of the state putting the slightest curbs upon such free expression, I should not lag behind any member of this Court in striking down such an invasion of the right to freedom of thought and freedom of speech protected by the Constitution.

*　　*　　*

One's conception of the Constitution cannot be severed from one's conception of a judge's function in applying it. . . . Our system is built on the faith that men set apart for this special function, freed from the influences of immediacy and from the deflections of worldly ambition, will become able to take a view of longer range than the period of responsibility entrusted to Congress and legislatures. We are dealing with matters as to which legislators and voters have conflicting views. Are we as judges to impose our strong convictions on where wisdom lies? That which three years ago had seemed . . . to lie within permissible areas of legislation is now outlawed by the deciding shift of opinion of two Justices. What reason is there to believe that they or their successors may not have another view a few years hence? Is that which was deemed to be of so fundamental a nature as to be written into the Constitution to endure for all times to be the sport of shifting winds of doctrine? Of course, judicial opinions, even as to questions of constitutionality, are not immutable. As has been true in the past, the Court will from time to time reverse its position. But I believe that never before these Jehovah's Witnesses cases . . . has this Court overruled decisions so as to restrict the powers of democratic government. Always heretofore, it has withdrawn narrow views of legislative authority so as to authorize what formerly it had denied.

*　　*　　*

Of course patriotism can not be enforced by the flag salute. But neither can the liberal spirit be enforced by judicial invalidation of illiberal legislation. Our constant preoccupation with the constitutionality of legislation rather than with its wisdom tends to preoccupation of the American mind with a false value. The tendency of focusing attention on constitutionality is to make constitutionality synonymous with wisdom, to regard a law as all right if it is constitutional. Such an attitude is a great enemy of liberalism. Particularly in legislation affecting freedom of thought and freedom of speech much which should offend a free-spirited society is constitutional. Reliance for the most precious interests of civilization, therefore, must be found outside of their vindication in courts of law. Only a persistent positive translation of the faith of a free society into the convictions and habits and actions of a community is the ultimate reliance against unabated temptations to fetter the human spirit.

The Japanese Internment

Shortly after the attack on Pearl Harbor, General John DeWitt, head of the Western Defense Command, argued for military control of the 112,000 West Coast Japanese-Americans, three-quarters of whom were citizens. His erroneous reports of sabotage in California and off-shore Japanese naval activity added to a growing hysteria. "To hell with habeas corpus," one newspaper columnist said, in arguing for "concentration camps" for Japanese-Americans. Republican Congressman Leland Ford urged that any "Japanese, whether citizens or not" would prove he is "patriotic" by "permitting himself to be placed in a concentration camp."[2]

Attorney General Francis Biddle resisted any mass evacuation of American citizens on the grounds that such a procedure would violate their constitutional rights. However, Biddle was outmaneuvered by Assistant Attorney General Tom Clark, who favored an internment, and by Assistant Secretary of War John J. McCloy. When Biddle opposed military evacuation of civilians, McCloy told the attorney general, "You are putting a Wall Street lawyer in a helluva box, but if it is a question of the safety of the country [or] the constitution . . . why the constitution is just a scrap of paper to me."[3]

Note: Executive Order—No. 9066

On February 19, 1942, acting in his capacity as commander-in-chief under authority granted by the Espionage Act of 1917 and various acts passed in 1940 and 1941, President Franklin D. Roosevelt issued Executive Order—No. 9066, allowing the exclusion of civilians from "military areas." Declaring "that the successful prosecution of the war requires every possible protection against espionage and against sabotage," Roosevelt authorized

> the Secretary of War and the Military Commanders who he may from time to time designate . . . to prescribe military areas in such places and of such extent as [they] . . . may determine, from which any or all persons may be excluded and with respect to which, the right of any person to enter, remain in, or leave shall be subject to whatever restrictions the Secretary of War or the appropriate Military Commander may impose in his discretion.

Roosevelt ordered the Secretary of War "to provide for residents of any such area who are excluded therefrom, such transportation, food, shelter, and other accommodations as may be necessary." All other executive departments and federal agencies were ordered to assist the Secretary of War or the said military commanders in carrying out this Executive Order, including the furnishing of medical aid, hospitalization, food, clothing, transportation, use of land, shelter, and other supplies, equipment, utilities, facilities, and services."

In March, President Roosevelt signed Executive Order—No. 9102, creating the War Relocation Authority. On March 24, General DeWitt imposed a nighttime curfew on all persons of Japanese ancestry. On March 27, DeWitt prohibited Japanese-Americans from moving away from where they lived. Starting on March 24 and continuing through May, General DeWitt issued a series of "Civilian Exclusion Orders" requiring Japanese-Americans to report to civilian control centers, from which they were removed to internment camps.

Hirabayashi v. United States
320 U.S. 81 (1943)

In May 1942, Gordon Hirabayashi, an American citizen of Japanese ancestry and a senior at the University of Washington, refused to obey a curfew imposed on Japanese-Americans and to report to the civilian control station where his "presence" was "required" as "a preliminary step to the exclusion from that area of persons of Japanese ancestry." Hirabayashi believed that if he obeyed these orders, "he would be waiving his rights as an American citizen." Although the Court unanimously justified the curfew as a military necessity, Justice Frank Murphy's concurrence indicates the Court's fragile unanimity.

Mr. Chief Justice Stone delivered the Opinion of the Court.

*   *   *

The challenged orders were defense measures for the avowed purpose of safeguarding the military area in question, at a time of threatened air raids and invasion by the Japanese forces, from the danger of sabotage and espionage. As the curfew was made applicable to citizens residing in the area only if they were of Japanese ancestry, our inquiry must be whether in the light of all the facts and circumstances there was any substantial basis for the conclusion . . . that the curfew as applied was a protective measure necessary to meet the threat of sabotage and espionage which would substantially affect the war effort and which might reasonably be expected to aid a threatened enemy invasion. The alternative which appellant insists must be accepted is for the military authorities to impose the curfew on all citizens within the military area, or on none. In a case of threatened danger requiring prompt action, it is a choice between inflicting obviously needless hardship on the many, or sitting passive and unresisting in the presence of the threat. We think that constitutional government, in time of war, is not so powerless and does not compel so hard a choice if those charged with the responsibility of our national defense have reasonable ground for believing that the threat is real.

*   *   *

But appellant insists that the exercise of the power is inappropriate and unconstitutional because it discriminates against citizens of Japanese ancestry. . . .

Distinctions between citizens solely because of their ancestry are by their very nature odious to a free people whose institutions are founded upon the doctrine of equality. For that reason, legislative classification or discrimination based on race alone has often been held to be a denial of equal protection. . . .

We may assume that these considerations would be controlling here were it not for the fact that the danger of espionage and sabotage, in time of war and of threatened invasion, calls upon the military authorities to scrutinize every relevant fact bearing on the loyalty of populations in the danger areas. Because racial discriminations are in most circumstances irrelevant and therefore prohibited, it by no means follows that, in dealing with the perils of war, Congress and the Executive are wholly precluded from taking into account those facts and circumstances which are relevant to measures for our national defense and for the successful prosecution of the war, and which may in fact place citizens of one ancestry in a different category from others. . . . The adoption by Government, in the crisis of war and of threatened invasion, of measures for the public safety, based upon the recognition of facts and circumstances which indicate that a group of one national extraction may menace that safety more than others, is not wholly beyond the limits of the Constitution and is not to be condemned merely because in other and in most circumstances racial distinctions are irrelevant. . . .

*   *   *

Mr. Justice Murphy, concurring:

Distinctions based on color and ancestry are utterly inconsistent with our traditions and ideals. They are at variance with the principles for which we are now waging war. We cannot close our eyes to the fact that for centuries the Old World has been torn by racial and religious conflicts and has suffered the worst kind of anguish because of inequality of treatment for different groups. There was one law for one and a different law for another. Nothing is written more firmly into our law than the compact of the Plymouth voyagers to have just and equal laws. To say that any group cannot be assimilated is to admit that the great American experiment has failed, that our way of life has failed when confronted with the normal attachment of certain groups to the lands of their forefathers. As a nation we embrace many groups, some of them among the oldest settlements in our midst, which have isolated themselves for religious and cultural reasons.

Today is the first time, so far as I am aware, that we have sustained a substantial restriction of the personal liberty of citizens of the United States based upon the accident of race or ancestry. Under the curfew order here challenged no less than 70,000 American citizens have been placed under a special ban and deprived of their liberty because of their particular raciai inheritance. In this sense it bears a melancholy resemblance to the treatment accorded to members of the Jewish race in Germany and in other parts of Europe. The result is the creation in this country of two classes of citizens for purposes of a critical and perilous hour—to sanction discrimination between groups of United States citizens on the basis of ancestry. In my opinion this goes to the very brink of constitutional power.

Korematsu v. *United States*
323 U.S. 214 (1944)

Fred Korematsu was a native Californian of Japanese ancestry. After the bombing of Pearl Harbor, he volunteered for the army, but was rejected for health reasons. He then studied welding and obtained a defense-industry job. In May 1942, he had a good job and a Caucasian girlfriend unaffected by the relocation. He tried to avoid relocation by claiming to be of Mexican ancestry. In June, he was arrested for violating the exclusion orders.

Korematsu is usually read because of Justice Hugo Black's assertion that racial restrictions are "immediately suspect" and should be given "the most rigid scrutiny." This is the only case in which the Supreme Court applied the "rigid scrutiny" test to a racial restriction and upheld the challenged law. Korematsu is also important for the dissents challenging the majority's deference to the military's handling of civilian matters.

Mr. Justice Black delivered the opinion of the Court.

*   *   *

It should be noted, to begin with, that all legal restrictions which curtail the civil rights of a single racial group are immediately suspect. That is not to say that all such restrictions are unconstitutional. It is to say that courts must subject them to the most rigid scrutiny. Pressing public necessity may sometimes justify the existence of such restrictions; racial antagonism never can.

*   *   *

In the light of the principles we announced in the *Hirabayashi* case, we are unable to conclude that it was beyond the war power of Congress and the Executive to exclude those of Japanese ancestry from the West Coast war area at the time they did. True, exclusion from the area in which one's home is located is a far greater deprivation than constant confinement to the home from 8:00 p.m. to 6:00 a.m. Nothing short of apprehension by the proper military authorities of the gravest imminent danger to the public safety can constitutionally justify either. But exclusion from a threatened area, no less than curfew, has a definite and close relationship to the prevention of espionage and sabotage. The military authorities, charged with the primary responsibility of defending our shores, concluded that curfew provided inadequate protection and ordered exclusion. They did so, as pointed out in our *Hirabayashi* opinion, in accordance with Congressional authority to the military to say who should, and who should not, remain in the threatened areas.

*   *   *

Like curfew, exclusion of those of Japanese origin was deemed necessary because of the presence of an unascertained number of disloyal members of the group, most of whom we have no doubt were loyal to this country. It was because we could not reject the finding of the military authorities that it was impossible to bring about an immediate segregation of the disloyal from the loyal that we sustained the validity of the curfew order as applying to the whole group. In the instant case, temporary exclusion of the entire group was rested by the military on the same ground. The judgment that exclusion of the whole group was for the same reason a military imperative answers the contention that the exclusion was in the nature of group punishment based on antagonism to those of Japanese origin. That there were members of the group who retained loyalties to Japan has been confirmed by investigations made subsequent to the exclusion. Approximately five thousand American citizens of Japanese ancestry refused to swear unqualified allegiance to the United States and to renounce allegiance to the Japanese Emperor, and several thousand evacuees requested repatriation to Japan.

We uphold the exclusion order as of the time it was made and when the petitioner violated it. . . . In doing so, we are not unmindful of the hardships imposed by it upon a large group of American citizens. . . . But hardships are part of war, and war is an aggregation of hardships. All citizens alike, both in and out of uniform, feel the impact of war in greater or lesser measure. Citizenship has its responsibilities as well as its privileges, and in time of war the burden is always heavier. Compulsory exclusion of large groups of citizens from their homes, except under circumstances of direst emergency and peril, is inconsistent with our basic governmental institutions. But when under conditions of modern warfare our shores are threatened by hostile forces, the power to protect must be commensurate with the threatened danger.

*   *   *

We are . . . being asked to pass . . . upon the whole subsequent detention program in both assembly and relocation centers, although the only issues framed at the trial related to petitioner's remaining in the prohibited area in violation of the exclusion order. Had petitioner here left the prohibited area and gone to an assembly center we cannot say either as a matter of fact or law that . . . [it] would have resulted in his detention in a relocation center. Some who did report to the assembly center were not sent to relocation centers, but were released upon condition that they remain outside the prohibited zone. . . . The lawfulness of one [order] does not necessarily determine the lawfulness of the others. This is made clear when we analyze the requirements of the separate provisions of the separate orders . . . that those of Japanese ancestry (1) depart from the area; (2) report to and temporarily remain in an assembly center; (3) go under military control to a relocation center there to remain for an indeterminate period until released conditionally or unconditionally by the military authorities. Each of these requirements . . . imposed distinct duties in connection with the separate steps in a complete evacuation program. . . .

                              *   *   *

Since the petitioner has not been convicted of failing to report or to remain in an assembly or relocation center, we cannot in this case determine the validity of those separate provisions of the order. It is sufficient here for us to pass upon the order which petitioner violated. . . . It will be time enough to decide the serious constitutional issues which petitioner seeks to raise when an assembly or relocation order is applied or is certain to be applied to him, and we have its terms before us.

                              *   *   *

It is said that we are dealing here with the case of imprisonment of a citizen in a concentration camp solely because of his ancestry, without evidence or inquiry concerning his loyalty and good disposition towards the United States. Our task would be simple, our duty clear, were this a case involving the imprisonment of a loyal citizen in a concentration camp because of racial prejudice. Regardless of the true nature of the assembly and relocation centers—and we deem it unjustifiable to call them concentration camps with all the ugly connotations that term implies—we are dealing specifically with nothing but an exclusion order. To cast this case into outlines of racial prejudice, without reference to the real military dangers which were presented, merely confuses the issue. Korematsu was not excluded from the Military Areas because of hostility to him or his race. He *was* excluded because we are at war with the Japanese Empire, because the properly constituted military authorities feared an invasion of our West Coast and felt constrained to take proper security measures, because they decided that the military urgency of the situation demanded that all citizens of Japanese ancestry be segregated from the West Coast temporarily, and finally, because Congress, reposing its confidence in this time of war in our military leaders—as inevitably it must—determined that they should have the power to do just this. There was evidence of disloyalty on the part of some, the military authorities considered that the need for action was great, and time was short. We cannot—by availing ourselves of the calm perspective of hindsight—now say that at that time these actions were unjustified.

                                                            Affirmed.

Mr. Justice Roberts.

    I dissent. . . .

    This is not a case of keeping people off the streets at night as was *Hiraba-*

yashi. . . . On the contrary, it is the case of convicti..g a citizen as a punishment for not submitting to imprisonment in a concentration camp . . . solely because of his ancestry, without evidence or inquiry concerning his loyalty. . . .

*   *   *

The petitioner . . . according to the uncontradicted evidence, is a loyal citizen of the nation.

*   *   *

[Here Roberts presented the chronology of events leading to Korematsu's arrest. Under DeWitt's order of March 27, Korematsu was "prohibited from leaving" Military Area 1. Under DeWitt's Order of May 3, all Japanese-Americans were excluded from Military Area 1 and required to report to a civil control station "for instructions to go to an Assembly Center." Roberts concluded that "the obvious purpose of the orders . . . was to drive all citizens of Japanese ancestry into Assembly Centers."]

The predicament in which the petitioner thus found himself was this: He was forbidden, by Military Order, to leave the zone in which he lived; he was forbidden, by Military Order, after a date fixed, to be found within that zone unless he were in an Assembly Center located in that zone. General DeWitt's report to the Secretary of War . . . makes it entirely clear . . . that an Assembly Center was a euphemism for a prison. No person within such a center was permitted to leave except by Military Order.

In the dilemma that he dare not remain in his home, or voluntarily leave the area, without incurring criminal penalties, and that the only way he could avoid punishment was to go to an Assembly Center and submit himself to military imprisonment, the petitioner did nothing.

*   *   *

We cannot shut our eyes to the fact that had the petitioner attempted to . . . leave the military area in which he lived he would have been arrested and tried and convicted. . . . The two conflicting orders, one which commanded him to stay and the other which commanded him to go, were nothing but a cleverly devised trap to accomplish the real purpose of the military authority, which was to lock him up in a concentration camp. The only course by which the petitioner could avoid arrest and prosecution was to go to that camp according to instructions to be given him when he reported at a Civil Control Center. We know that is the fact. Why should we set up a figmentary and artificial situation instead of addressing ourselves to the actualities of the case?

*   *   *

Mr. Justice Murphy, dissenting.

This exclusion of "all persons of Japanese ancestry, both alien and non-alien," from the Pacific Coast area on a plea of military necessity in the absence of martial law ought not to be approved. Such exclusion goes over "the very brink of constitutional power" and falls into the ugly abyss of racism.

In dealing with matters relating to the prosecution and progress of a war, we must accord great respect and consideration to the judgments of the military authorities who are on the scene and who have full knowledge of the military facts. . . .

At the same time, however, it is essential that there be definite limits to military discretion, especially where martial law has not been declared. Individuals must not be left impoverished of their constitutional rights on a plea of military necessity that has neither substance nor support. Thus. . . the military claim must subject itself to the judicial process of having its reasonableness determined and its conflicts with other interests reconciled. . . .

*   *   *

That this forced exclusion was the result in good measure of this erroneous assumption of racial guilt rather than bona fide military necessity is evidenced by the Commanding General's Final Report on the evacuation. . . . In it he refers to all individuals of Japanese descent as "subversive," as belonging to "an enemy race" whose "racial strains are undiluted," and as constituting "over 112,000 potential enemies . . . at large today". . . . In support of this blanket condemnation of all persons of Japanese descent, however, no reliable evidence is cited to show that such individuals were generally disloyal, or . . . constitute[d] a special menace to defense installations or war industries, or had otherwise by their behavior furnished reasonable ground for their exclusion as a group.

Justification for the exclusion is sought, instead, mainly upon questionable racial and sociological grounds not ordinarily within the realm of expert military judgment, supplemented by certain semi-military conclusions drawn from an unwarranted use of circumstantial evidence. Individuals of Japanese ancestry are condemned because they are said to be "a large, unassimilated, tightly knit racial group, bound to an enemy nation by strong ties of race, culture, custom and religion." They are claimed to be given to "emperor worshipping ceremonies" and to "dual citizenship." Japanese language schools and allegedly pro-Japanese organizations are cited as evidence of possible group disloyalty, together with facts as to certain persons being educated and residing at length in Japan. . . .

The main reasons relied upon by those responsible for the forced evacuation . . . [are] largely an accumulation of much of the misinformation, half-truths and insinuations that for years have been directed against Japanese Americans by people with racial and economic prejudices—the same people who have been among the foremost advocates of the evacuation. A military judgment based upon such racial and sociological considerations is not entitled to the great weight ordinarily given the judgments based upon strictly military considerations. Especially is this so when every charge relative to race, religion, culture, geographical location, and legal and economic status has been substantially discredited by independent studies made by experts in these matters.

No adequate reason is given for the failure to treat these Japanese Americans on an individual basis by holding investigations and hearings to separate the loyal from the disloyal, as was done in the case of persons of German and Italian ancestry. It is asserted merely that the loyalties of this group "were unknown and time was of the essence." Yet nearly four months elapsed after Pearl Harbor before the first exclusion order was issued; nearly eight months went by until the last order was issued; and the last of these "subversive" persons was not actually removed until almost eleven months had elapsed. Leisure and deliberation seem to have been more of the essence than speed. And the fact that conditions were not such as to warrant a declaration of martial law adds strength to the belief that the factors of time and military necessity were not as urgent as they have been represented to be.

Moreover, there was no adequate proof that the Federal Bureau of Investigation and the military and naval intelligence services did not have the espionage and sabotage situation well in hand during this long period. Nor is there any denial of the fact that not one person of Japanese ancestry was accused or convicted of espionage or sabotage after Pearl Harbor while they were still free, a fact which is some evidence of the loyalty of the vast majority of those individuals and of the effectiveness of the established methods of combating these evils. It seems incredible that under these circumstances it would have been impossible to hold loyalty hearings for the mere 112,000 persons involved—or at least for the 70,000 American citizens—especially when a large part of this number represented children and elderly men and women. . . .

I dissent, therefore, from this legalization of racism. Racial discrimination in any form and in any degree has no justifiable part whatever in our democratic way of life. It is unattractive in any setting but it is utterly revolting among a free people who have embraced the principles set forth in the Constitution of the United States. All residents of this nation are kin in some way by blood or culture to a foreign land. Yet they are primarily and necessarily a part of the new and distinct civilization of the United States. They must accordingly be treated at all times as the heirs of the American experiment and as entitled to all the rights and freedoms guaranteed by the Constitution.

Mr. Justice Jackson, dissenting.

Korematsu was born on our soil, of parents born in Japan. The Constitution makes him a citizen of the United States by nativity and a citizen of California by residence. No claim is made that he is not loyal to this country. There is no suggestion that apart from the matter involved here he is not law-abiding and well disposed. Korematsu, however, has been convicted of an act not commonly a crime. It consists merely of being present in the state whereof he is a citizen, near the place where he was born, and where all his life he has lived.

Even more unusual is the series of military orders which made this conduct a crime. They forbid such a one to remain, and they also forbid him to leave. They were so drawn that the only way Korematsu could avoid violation was to give himself up to the military authority. This meant submission to custody, examination, and transportation out of the territory, to be followed by indeterminate confinement in detention camps.

A citizen's presence in the locality, however, was made a crime only if his parents were of Japanese birth. Had Korematsu been one of four—the others being, say, a German alien enemy, an Italian alien enemy, and a citizen of American-born ancestors, convicted of treason but out on parole—only Korematsu's presence would have violated the order. The difference between their innocence and his crime would result, not from anything he did, said or thought, different than they, but only in that he was born of different racial stock.

Now, if any fundamental assumption underlies our system, it is that guilt is personal and not inheritable. Even if all of one's antecedents had been convicted of treason, the Constitution forbids its penalties to be visited upon him, for it provides that "no attainder of treason shall work corruption of blood, or forfeiture except during the life of the person attainted." But here is an attempt to make an otherwise innocent act a crime merely because this prisoner is the son of parents as to whom he had no choice, and belongs to a race from which there is no way to resign. . . .

*   *   *

. . . [A] judicial construction of the due process clause that will sustain this order is a far more subtle blow to liberty than the promulgation of the order itself. A military order, however unconstitutional, is not apt to last longer than the military emergency. Even during that period a succeeding commander may revoke it all. But once a judicial opinion rationalizes such an order to show that it conforms to the Constitution, or rather rationalizes the Constitution to show that the Constitution sanctions such an order, the Court for all time has validated the principle of racial discrimination in criminal procedure and of transplanting American citizens. The principle then lies about like a loaded weapon ready for the hand of any authority that can bring forward a plausible claim of an urgent need. Every repetition imbeds that principle more deeply in our law and thinking and expands it to new purposes. All who observe the work of courts are familiar with what Judge Cardozo described as "the tendency of a principle to expand itself to the limit of its logic." A military commander may overstep the bounds of constitutionality, and it is an incident. But if we review and approve, that passing incident becomes the doctrine of the Constitution. There it has a generative power of its own, and all that it creates will be in its own image. . . .

*   *   *

I should hold that a civil court cannot be made to enforce an order which violates constitutional limitations even if it is a reasonable exercise of military authority. The courts can exercise only the judicial power, can apply only law, and must abide by the Constitution, or they cease to be civil courts and become instruments of military policy.

Of course the existence of a military power resting on force, so vagrant, so centralized, so necessarily heedless of the individual, is an inherent threat to liberty. But I would not lead people to rely on this Court for a review that seems to me wholly delusive. The military reasonableness of these orders can only be determined by military superiors. If the people ever let command of the war power fall into irresponsible and unscrupulous hands, the courts wield no power equal to its restraint. The chief restraint upon those who command the physical forces of the country, in the future as in the past, must be their responsibility to the political judgments of their contemporaries and to the moral judgments of history.

My duties as a justice as I see them do not require me to make a military judgment as to whether General DeWitt's evacuation and detention program was a reasonable military necessity. I do not suggest that the courts should have attempted to interfere with the Army in carrying out its task. But I do not think they may be asked to execute a military expedient that has no place in law under the Constitution. I would reverse the judgment and discharge the prisoner.

Note: *Ex parte Endo*, 323 U.S. 273 (1944)

On the same day it upheld Korematsu's conviction, a unanimous Court ordered the release of Mitsuye Endo from the War Relocation Center at Topaz, Utah. Endo claimed she was a "loyal and law-abiding citizen of the United States, that no charge has been made against her, and that she is being unlawfully . . . confined in the Relocation Center under armed guard and held there against her will." The government did not dispute her loyalty or claim a right to "detain citizens against whom no charges of disloyalty or subversiveness have been made for a period longer than that necessary to separate the loyal from the disloyal and to provide the necessary guidance for relocation." But the government argued that "a planned and orderly relocation was essential to the success of the evacuation program" and that an immediate release of Endo and others would lead to "a dangerously disorderly migration of unwanted people to unprepared communities," which would result in "hardship and disorder."

Speaking for a unanimous Court, Justice William O. Douglas rejected these arguments. Douglas asserted:

> Loyalty is a matter of the heart and mind, not of race, creed, or color. He who is loyal is by definition not a spy or a saboteur. When the power to detain is derived from the power to protect the war effort against espionage and sabotage, detention which has no relationship to that objective is unauthorized.

Civil Liberties and Criminal Justice in Crisis Times

The first four decades of the twentieth century were marked by a rapid rise in crime and important changes in the criminal justice system. Millions of immigrants and their children swelled the nation's population from the 1880s to World War I and account for an absolute rise in the crime rate. As historian Mark Haller notes, crime provided a "means of social mobility for persons of marginal social and economic position in society."[4]

Reform legislation regulating prostitution, narcotics, labor, and manufacturing created new federal and state crimes. The most important "reform" to affect crime was Prohibition, which created the conditions for popular illegal behavior and the development of organized crime. It is estimated that between 1923 and 1926 in Chicago alone, over 375 people were killed by gangsters or the police. Prohibition strengthened organized crime while weakening police departments and state and local governments. Police and political corruption grew from the dollars earned through organized criminal activity. This activity soon spread to organized prostitution, gambling, extortion, and numerous other criminal activities.

Changes in constitutional law led to a rethinking of criminal law. By the end of the 1930s, the selective incorporation of the Bill of Rights had affected many of the due process and criminal procedure provisions of the Constitution. Equally important, the changing nature of crime and technological developments led to troublesome constitutional questions. For example, *Olmstead* v. *United States* (1928) raised the question whether the Fourth Amendment prohibited a warrantless wiretap.

The Emergence of Criminal Due Process

The Fourth, Fifth, Sixth, and Eighth Amendments collectively guarantee that persons accused of crimes will have fair trials. Between World War I and World War II, a small revolution in criminal due process took place as the Supreme Court took steps to guarantee reasonably fair criminal trials in federal courts. This modern redefinition of what constituted due process began with *Weeks* v. *United States*.

Weeks v. *United States*
232 U.S. 383 (1914)

Weeks was convicted of violating a federal law prohibiting the selling of lottery tickets through the mail. He appealed, asserting that his house was searched without a warrant, his property was illegally seized, and he was arrested without a warrant. Justice William R. Day delivered the opinion of the Court.

. . . [T]he question presented involves . . . the duty of the court with reference to the motion made by the defendant for the return of certain letters, as well as other papers, taken from his room by the United States marshal, who, without authority of process . . . visited the room of the defendant for the declared purpose of obtaining additional testimony to support the charge against the accused, and having gained admission to the house took . . . certain letters written to the defendant, tending to show his guilt. These letters were placed in the control of the District Attorney and were subsequently produced by him and offered in evidence against the accused at the trial. The defendant contends that such appropriation of his private correspondence was in violation of rights secured to him by the . . . Fourth Amendment, which provides:

"The right of the people to be secure in their persons, houses, papers, and effects, against unreasonable searches and seizures, shall not be violated, and no warrants shall issue, but upon probable cause, supported by oath or affirmation and particularly describing the place to be searched, and the persons or things to be seized."

The history of this Amendment is given with particularity in the opinion of Mr. Justice Bradley, speaking for the court in *Boyd* v. *United States* [1885]. As was there shown, it took its origin in the determination of the framers of the Amendments to the Federal Constitution to provide for that instrument a Bill of Rights, securing to the American people, among other things, those safeguards which had grown up in England to protect the people from unreasonable searches and seizures, such as were permitted under the general warrants issued under authority of the Government by which there had been invasions of the home and privacy of the citizens and the seizure of their private papers in support of charges, real or imaginary, made against them. Such practices had also received sanction under warrants and seizures under the so-called writs of assistance, issued in the American colonies. Resistance to these practices had established the principle which was enacted into the fundamental law in the Fourth Amendment, that a man's house was his castle and not to be invaded by any general authority to search and seize his goods and papers. Judge Cooley, in his *Constitutional Limitations* . . . said: "The maxim that 'every man's house is his castle,' is made a part of our constitutional law in the clauses prohibiting unreasonable searches and seizures, and has always been looked upon as of high value to the citizen." "Accordingly," says Lieber in . . . *Civil Liberty and Self-Government* . . . "no man's house can be forcibly opened, or he or his goods be carried away after it has thus been forced, except in cases of felony, and then the sheriff must be furnished with a warrant, and take great care lest he commit a trespass. This principle is jealously insisted upon." In *Ex parte Jackson* this court recognized the principle of protection as applicable to letters and sealed packages in the mail, and held that . . . such matter could only be opened and examined upon warrants issued on oath or affirmation particularly describing the thing to be seized, "as is required when papers are subjected to search in one's own household."

In the *Boyd Case* . . . Mr. Justice Bradley said:

"The principles laid down in this opinion affect the very essence of constitutional liberty and security. They reach farther than the concrete form of the case then before the court, with its adventitious circumstances; they apply to all invasions on the part of the government and its employees of the sanctity of a man's home and the privacies of life. It is not the breaking of his doors, and the rummaging of his drawers, that constitutes the essence of the offence; but it is the invasion of his indefeasible right of personal liberty and private property, where that right has never been forfeited by his conviction of some public offence,—it is the invasion of this sacred right which underlies and constitutes the essence of Lord Camden's judgment [in *Entick* v. *Carrington*]."

*   *   *

The effect of the Fourth Amendment is to put the courts of the United States and Federal officials . . . under limitations and restraints as to the exercise of such power and authority, and to forever secure the people, their persons, houses, papers and effects against all unreasonable searches and seizures under the guise of law. This protection reaches all alike, whether accused of crime or not, and the duty of giving to it force and effect is obligatory upon all entrusted under our Federal system with the enforcement of the laws. The tendency of those who execute the criminal laws of the country to obtain conviction by means of unlawful seizures and enforced confessions . . . should find no sanction in the judgments of the courts which are charged at all times with the support of the Constitution and to which people of all conditions have a right to appeal for the maintenance of such fundamental rights.

*   *   *

The case [before the Court] . . . involves the right of the court in a criminal prosecution to retain for the purposes of evidence the letters and correspondence of the accused, seized in his house in his absence and without his authority, by a United States marshal holding no warrant for his arrest and none for the search of his premises. The accused . . . made timely application to the court for an order for the return of these letters, as well as other property. This application was denied, the letters retained and put in evidence. . . . If letters and private documents can thus be seized and held and used in evidence against a citizen accused of an offense, the protection of the Fourth Amendment declaring his right to be secure against such searches and seizures is of no value, and . . . might as well be stricken from the Constitution. The efforts of the courts and their officials to bring the guilty to punishment, praiseworthy as they are, are not to be aided by the sacrifice of those great principles established by years of endeavor and suffering which have resulted in their embodiment in the fundamental law of the land. The United States Marshal could only have invaded the house of the accused when armed with a warrant issued as required by the Constitution, upon sworn information and describing with reasonable particularity the thing for which the search was to be made. Instead, he acted without sanction of law, doubtless prompted by the desire to bring further proof to the aid of the Government, and under color of his office undertook to make a seizure of private papers in direct violation of the constitutional prohibition against such action. Under such circumstances, without sworn information and particular description, not even an order of court would have justified such procedure, much less was it within the authority of the United States Marshal to thus invade the house and privacy of the accused. In *Adams* v. *New York* this court said that the Fourth Amendment was intended to secure the citizen in person and property against unlawful invasion of the sanctity of his home by officers of the law acting under legislative or judicial sanction. . . . To sanction such proceedings would be to affirm by judicial decision a manifest neglect if not an open defiance of the prohibitions of the Constitution, intended for the protection of the people against such unauthorized action.

*　　　　*　　　　*

It results that the judgment of the court below must be reversed, and the case remanded for further proceedings in accordance with this opinion.

Olmstead v. *United States*
277 U.S. 438 (1928)

Olmstead, a Prohibition-era bootlegger in Seattle, Washington, with fifty employees and annual sales of over $2 million, was convicted on evidence "largely obtained by intercepting messages on the telephones of the conspirators by four federal prohibition officers." In upholding the conviction, Chief Justice William Howard Taft noted that the wiretaps "were made without trespass upon any property of the defendants. They were made in the basement of the large office building. The taps from house lines were made in the streets near the houses." Taft acknowledged that the "historical purpose of the Fourth Amendment . . . was to prevent the use of governmental force to search a man's house, his person, his papers and his effects; and to prevent their seizure against his will." But, Taft argued, "the Amendment does not forbid what was done here. There was no searching. There was no seizure. The evidence was secured by the use of the sense of hearing and that only. There was no entry of the houses or offices of the defendants." Taft found that "the language of the Fourth Amendment can not be extended and expanded to include telephone wires reaching to the whole world from the defendant's house or office." He argued that the wires were "not part of his house or office any more than are the highways along which they are stretched. Taft noted that wiretaps were illegal under Washington law but did not believe this barred federal agents from using them in the absence of congressional action.

Mr. Justice Louis Brandeis dissenting:

*　　　　*　　　　*

The Government makes no attempt to defend the methods employed by its officers. Indeed, it concedes that if wire-tapping can be deemed a search and seizure within the Fourth Amendment, such wire-tapping . . . was an unreasonable search and seizure, and that the evidence thus obtained was inadmissible. But it relies on the language of the Amendment; and it claims that the protection given thereby cannot properly be held to include a telephone conversation.

* * *

When the Fourth and Fifth Amendments were adopted, "the form that evil had theretofore taken," had been necessarily simple. Force and violence were then the only means known to man by which a Government could directly effect self-incrimination. It could compel the individual to testify—a compulsion effected, if need be, by torture. It could secure possession of his papers and other articles incident to his private life—a seizure effected, if need be, by breaking and entry. Protection against such invasion of "the sanctities of a man's home and the privacies of life" was provided in the Fourth and Fifth Amendments by specific language. *Boyd* v. *United States*. But "time works changes, brings into existence new conditions and purposes." Subtler and more far-reaching means of invading privacy have become available to the Government. Discovery and invention have made it possible for the Government, by means far more effective than stretching upon the rack, to obtain disclosure in court of what is whispered in the closet.

Moreover, "in the application of a constitution, our contemplation cannot be only of what has been but of what may be." The progress of science in furnishing the Government with means of espionage is not likely to stop with wire-tapping. Ways may some day be developed by which the Government, without removing papers from secret drawers, can reproduce them in court, and by which it will be enabled to expose to a jury the most intimate occurrences of the home. Advances in the psychic and related sciences may bring means of exploring unexpressed beliefs, thoughts and emotions. "That places the liberty of every man in the hands of every petty officer" was said by James Otis of much lesser intrusions than these. To Lord Camden, a far slighter intrusion seems "subversive of all the comforts of society." Can it be that the Constitution affords no protection against such invasions of individual security.

* * *

Decisions of this Court applying the principle of the *Boyd* case have settled these things. Unjustified search and seizure violates the Fourth Amendment, whatever the character of the paper; whether the paper when taken by the federal officers was in the home, in an office or elsewhere; whether the taking was effected by force, by fraud, or in the orderly process of a court's procedure. From these decisions, it follows necessarily that the Amendment is violated by the officer's reading the paper without a physical seizure, without his even touching it; and that use, in any criminal proceeding, of the contents of the paper so examined—as where they are testified to by a federal officer who thus saw the document . . . any such use constitutes a violation of the Fifth Amendment.

. . . The makers of our Constitution undertook to secure conditions favorable to the pursuit of happiness. They recognized the significance of man's spiritual nature, of his feelings and of his intellect. They knew that only a part of the pain, pleasure and satisfactions of life are to be found in the material things. They sought to protect Americans in their beliefs, their thoughts, their emotions and their sensations. They conferred, as against the Government, the right to be let alone—the most comprehensive of rights and the right most valued by civilized men. To protect that right, every unjustifiable intrusion by the Government upon the privacy of the individual, whatever the means employed, must be deemed a violation of the Fourth Amendment. And the use, as evidence in a criminal proceeding, of facts ascertained by such intrusion, must be deemed a violation of the Fifth.

Applying to the Fourth and Fifth Amendments the established rule of construction, the defendants' objections to the evidence by wire-tapping must, in my opinion be sustained. It is, of course, immaterial where the physical connection with the telephone wires leading into the defendants' premises was made. And it is also immaterial that the intrusion was in aid of law enforcement. Experience should teach us to be most on our guard to protect liberty when the Government's purposes are beneficent. Men born to freedom are naturally alert to repel invasion of their liberty by evil-minded rulers. The greatest dangers to liberty lurk in insidious encroachment by men of zeal, well-meaning but without understanding.

Independently of the constitutional question, I am of opinion that the judgment should be reversed. By the laws of Washington, wire-tapping is a crime. To prove its case, the Government was obliged to lay bare the crimes committed by its officers on its behalf. A federal court should not permit such a prosecution to continue. . . .

*   *   *

When these unlawful acts were committed, they were crimes only of the officers individually. The Government was innocent . . . for no federal official is authorized to commit a crime on its behalf. When the Government, having full knowledge, sought, through the Department of Justice, to avail itself of the fruits of these acts in order to accomplish its own ends, it assumed moral responsibility for the officers' crimes. And if this Court should permit the Government, by means of its officers' crimes, to effect its purpose of punishing the defendants, there would seem to be present all the elements of a ratification. If so, the Government itself would become a lawbreaker.

. . . The governing principle has long been settled. It is that a court will not redress a wrong when he who invokes its aid has unclean hands. The maxim of unclean hands comes from courts of equity. But the principle prevails also in courts of law. Its common application is in civil actions between private parties. Where the Government is the actor, the reasons for applying it are even more persuasive. Where the remedies invoked are those of the criminal law, the reasons are compelling.

The door of a court is not barred because the plaintiff has committed a crime. The confirmed criminal is as much entitled to redress as his most virtuous fellow citizen; no record of crime, however long, makes one an outlaw. The court's aid is denied only when he who seeks it has violated the law in connection with the very transaction as to which he seeks legal redress. Then aid is denied despite the defendant's wrong. It is denied in order to maintain respect for law; in order to promote confidence in the administration of justice; in order to preserve the judicial process from contamination. The rule is one, not of action, but of inaction. . . . A defense may be waived. It is waived when not pleaded. But the objection that the plaintiff comes with unclean hands will be taken by the court itself. It will be taken despite the wish to the contrary of all the parties to the litigation. The court protects itself.

Decency, security and liberty alike demand that government officials shall be subjected to the same rules of conduct that are commands to the citizen. In a government of laws, existence of the government will be imperilled if it fails to observe the law scrupulously. Our Government is the potent, the omnipresent teacher. For good or for ill, it teaches the whole people by its example. Crime is contagious. If the Government becomes a lawbreaker, it breeds contempt for law; it invites every man to become a law unto himself; it invites anarchy. To declare that in the administration of the criminal law the end justifies the means—to declare that the Government may commit crimes in order to secure the conviction of a private criminal—would bring terrible retribution. Against that pernicious doctrine this Court should resolutely set its face.

Note: Prohibition and the Law

Olmsted can be seen as a "Prohibition case" as well as a criminal law case. *Olmsted* reminds us of the dangers to civil liberties from the suppression of vice and other "victimless crimes." The Eighteenth Amendment prohibited the manufacture, importation, and sale of "intoxicating liquors." In *Rhode Island* v. *Palmer* (1920), New Jersey, Rhode Island, individuals, and companies argued that the amendment had not been properly passed by Congress or properly ratified, that it violated the sovereignty of the states, and that its enforcement clause ("The Congress and the several States shall have concurrent power to enforce this article") empowered the states to allow liquor within their jurisdiction. The Court rejected these contentions, but gave no rationale for its holding and offered no "opinion" as such. Instead, Justice Willis Van Devanter "announced the conclusions of the court" upholding Prohibition.

America's experiment with Prohibition was short-lived but, in terms of law enforcement, extremely costly. While per capita alcohol consumption dropped, the crime rate rose as criminal organizations expanded to satisfy the nation's thirst for drink. Prohibition's legacy includes the institutionalization of the FBI as a national police force and the entrenchment of organized crime throughout the nation.

Crime in the Cities

The rapid growth of cities after the Civil War was accompanied by an appallingly high crime rate. In the first third of the twentieth century, few people pondered the causes of crime, such as poverty, discrimination against ethnic and racial minorities, and of course Prohibition, which instantly converted millions of Americans into "criminals" when they drank a beer. Prohibition also created huge opportunities for criminals to make large profits and have the support of millions of Americans who were anxious to obtain prohibited liquor.

ROSCOE POUND AND FELIX FRANKFURTER
Criminal Justice in Cleveland
1922

Progressive reformers believed that crime might be stopped through improved training of local police, more efficient courts, and an eradication of political corruption. Illustrative of the problem of urban crime and the progressive re-

sponse to it, Criminal Justice in Cleveland *was written by a team of eleven legal scholars hired by a civic foundation to thoroughly examine the criminal justice system in Cleveland.*

A cursory examination of the problem of crime in Cleveland produces some startling facts. For the year 1920 Cleveland, with approximately 800,000 population, had six times as many murders as London, with 8,000,000 population. For every robbery or assault with intent to rob committed during this same period in London there were 17 such crimes committed in Cleveland. Cleveland had as many murders during the first three months of the present year as London had during all of 1920. . . . There are more robberies and assaults to rob in Cleveland every year than in all England, Scotland, and Wales put together. In 1919 there were 2,327 automobiles stolen in Cleveland; in London there were 290; in Liverpool, 10.

Comparisons of this kind between Cleveland, on the one hand, and European cities, on the other, could be almost indefinitely extended. . . . And yet, compared with other American cities, Cleveland's record does not show to any special disadvantage. For the first quarter of 1921 there were four more murders committed in Detroit than in Cleveland, and nearly twice as many automobiles stolen in Detroit. During the first three months of 1921 St. Louis had 481 robberies, while Cleveland had 272; for the same period complaints of burglary and housebreaking in St. Louis numbered 1,106, as compared to 565 such complaints in Cleveland. For this same period the number of murders in Buffalo, a much smaller city, equaled those in Cleveland, and burglaries, housebreakings, and larcenies were almost as numerous. In 1919 Chicago, more than three times the size of Cleveland, had 293 murders and manslaughters, compared with Cleveland's 55, so that the ratio was easily two to one in Cleveland's favor; the 1920 statistics of the two cities show an even better proportion for Cleveland.

On the other side of the scale, for the first three months of the present year Cleveland had more than twice the number of robberies and assaults to rob that Detroit had, and a similar large proportion of burglaries and housebreakings. During this period there were 296 automobiles stolen in St. Louis, as against 446 in Cleveland. Cleveland is approximately three times larger than Toledo, and yet in 1920 Cleveland had 87 murders, while Toledo had only 11.

Another basis of comparison is between the crime statistics of Cleveland in 1921 and Cleveland in former years. For the first six months of 1921, the period in which this survey was carried on, the number of murders committed in Cleveland was 15. For the same period in 1920 the number of murders was 30. . . . The following figures show the average number of complaints for the first quarter of each of the four years from 1917 to 1920 inclusive, classified according to four outstanding crimes:

Robbery and assault to rob	283
Burglary and larceny	418
Murder	17
Automobiles driven away	361

The following figures give the number of complaints of the same crimes for the first quarter of 1921:

Robbery and assault to rob	272
Burglary and larceny	265
Murder	6
Automobiles driven away	446

Obviously, there has been some improvement within the last four years.

All in all, crime conditions are no more vicious in Cleveland than they are in other American cities. . . . In this respect, therefore, Cleveland's problem is the problem of America, for the same causes that are maintaining the high crime rate of Chicago, St. Louis, New York, Detroit, and San Francisco are operating here.

What are these causes? Here we can only hint at some of the deeper social and economic causes. The lack of homogeneity in our population and its increasing instability, the absence of settled habits and traditions of order, the breakdown of the administration of criminal law in the United States, and the many avenues by which offenders can escape punishment, our easy habit of passing laws which do not represent community standards or desires, our lack of cohesive industrial organization, our distrust of experts in the management of governmental enterprises—all these are undoubtedly contributing factors.

But there is another factor, still more potent: police machinery in the United States has not kept pace with modern demands. It has developed no effective technique to master the burden which modern social and industrial conditions impose. Clinging to old traditions, bound by old practices which business and industry long ago discarded, employing a personnel poorly adapted to its purposes, it grinds away on its perfunctory task without self-criticism, without imagination, and with little initiative.

Civil Rights and Racial Justice

In 1954, the Supreme Court initiated a revolution in American law and culture in *Brown* v. *Board of Education of Topeka*. Much of American legal history can be phrased in terms of pre-*Brown* and post-*Brown*. Legalized racial discrimination, which had been developing for 300 years, disappeared within 25 years after *Brown*.

Revolutionary though it was, *Brown* did not emerge full-blown from the pen of Chief Justice Earl Warren. *Brown* was the culmination of case law that had been developing throughout the century. Successful challenges to discrimination in political institutions, public education, and law enforcement laid the foundation for *Brown*. This foundation for a civil rights revolution was laid by black and white attorneys, usually working under the auspices of the NAACP Legal Defense and Education Fund and tied to initiatives taken by the faculty and students at Howard Law School. These cases suggest the way in which the Supreme Court began to reverse the long pattern of legalized discrimination in most American institutions.

The civil rights litigation from World War I to *Brown* did more than undermine segregation and set the stage for the civil rights revolution of the 1950s and 1960s. This litigation also initiated an era of legal activism, as reformers turned to the courts to gain new rights and reform society. This perhaps is the most dramatic change of the era. Before the mid-1930s, reformers generally feared courts, which tended to overturn progressive legislation. By the 1950s, reformers, led by the civil rights movement, saw the federal judiciary as an ally in battles against discrimination, unfair police methods, corrupt and old-fashioned political practices, and reactionary state legislatures. Activists, from environmental reformers to women's rights advocates, turned to the courts to change laws and protect rights. The civil rights litigation of the 1930s and 1940s thus turned out to be the harbinger of the future.

Race and the Franchise

The Fifteenth Amendment prohibited racial discrimination in voting, but in *United States* v. *Reese* (1876), the Supreme Court severely limited Congress's enforcement power, holding that the amendment did "not confer the right of suffrage upon anyone." In *Williams* v. *Mississippi* (1898), the Court upheld literacy tests and poll taxes for voters. Through these and other methods, the South effectively disfranchised blacks.

Literacy tests had the disadvantage of also disfranchising uneducated whites. Ingenious southern legislators solved this problem through "grandfather clauses," which allowed the direct descendants of pre-1866 voters to vote without taking literacy tests, thus permitting illiterate whites to vote while disfranchising most blacks. The first twentieth-century United States Supreme Court victory for blacks came in *Guinn* v. *United States* (1915), when the Court struck down Oklahoma's "grandfather clause." Solicitor General John W. Davis successfully argued this case. Ironically, some forty years later Davis would defend South Carolina and segregation in *Brown* v. *Board of Education* (1954).

Partly in response to *Guinn*, in 1923 Texas prohibited blacks from participating in the Democratic party primary. Blacks could still vote in the general election, but the "white primary" barred them from effective political participation because at this time the Democratic candidate invariably won the general election. In *Nixon* v. *Herndon* (1927) and *Nixon* v. *Condon* (1932), the United States Supreme Court found that the Texas laws violated the equal protection clause of the Fourteenth Amendment because the Democratic party acted under state sanction. But the "Democrats of Texas were nothing if not resourceful." A state convention called without the benefit of enabling legislation limited participation in Democratic primaries to " 'all white citizens' qualified to vote under the state Constitution and laws."[5] In *Grovey* v. *Townsend* (1935), the Supreme Court upheld this version of the white primary because it did not involve "state action." Once again, black Texans were effectively barred from politics.

In *United States* v. *Classic* (1941), the Supreme Court affirmed the federal election fraud convictions of Louisiana officials who had failed to count the ballots of *whites* in a congressional primary. The Court held that a congressional primary could be regulated by Congress. The *Classic* decision, combined with the appointment of new, liberal Justices, set the stage for *Smith* v. *Allright* (1944), in which Thurgood Marshall argued against the white primary. The Texas Democratic party failed to send counsel, confident that the Court would uphold the *Grovey* precedent. Associate

Justice Stanley Reed of Kentucky spoke for an 8 to 1 majority, which finally ended the white primary.

Reed relied on the earlier *Nixon* cases and the *Classic* case to overrule *Grovey*. Justice Reed concluded that

> it may now be taken as a postulate that the right to vote in such a primary for the nomination of candidates without discrimination by the State, like the right to vote in a general election, is a right secured by the Constitution. By the terms of the Fifteenth Amendment that right may not be abridged by any State on account of race. Under our Constitution the great privilege of the ballot may not be denied a man by the State because of his color.

This decision led the Court to reevaluate its position in *Grovey* in an unusually blunt way.

> The privilege of membership in a party may be, as this Court said in *Grovey v. Townsend*, no concern of a State. But when, as here, that privilege is also the essential qualification for voting in a primary to select nominees for a general election, the State makes the action of the party the action of the State. In reaching this conclusion we are not unmindful of the desirability of continuity of decision in constitutional questions. However, when convinced of former error, this Court has never felt constrained to follow precedent. In constitutional questions, where correction depends upon amendment and not upon legislative action this Court throughout its history has freely exercised its power to reexamine the basis of its constitutional decisions. This has long been accepted practice, and this practice has continued to this day. This is particularly true when the decision believed erroneous is the application of a constitutional principle rather than an interpretation of the Constitution to extract the principle itself. Here we are applying, contrary to the recent decision in *Grovey v. Townsend*, the well-established principle of the Fifteenth Amendment, forbidding the abridgement by a State of a citizen's right to vote. *Grovey v. Townsend* is overruled.

Race and Education

In *Plessy* v. *Ferguson* (1896), the United States Supreme Court had upheld the concept of "separate but equal" in public facilities. In *Cumming* v. *Board of Education of Richmond* (1899), the Court refused to order a Georgia school district to dismantle a white high school when the district failed to provide a similar school for blacks. Since the case did not directly present the question of segregated education, the Court did not directly address it. In *Berea College* v. *Kentucky* (1908), the Court once again dodged the constitutionality of segregated schools. The Court upheld Kentucky's prohibition on integrated classes at this state-chartered private school on the grounds that the state retained the right to amend the college's corporate charter.

Gong Lum v. *Rice* (1927) was the last major Supreme Court decision to uphold segregated schools. Mississippi's 1890 Constitution provided that "separate schools shall be maintained for children of the white and colored races." Gong Lum, a Chinese-American, tried to register his daughter at the only public high school in her district, which was solely for whites. Officials determined she was "colored" and rejected her. Gong Lum did not challenge the concept of segregation per se, but only its application to his daughter. In upholding the Mississippi school officials' right to assign students as they wished, Chief Justice William Howard Taft noted that they were obligated to provide schools for all children, regardless of their race. A decade later, the Court took its first tentative step toward school integration.

Missouri ex rel. Gaines v. Canada
305 U.S. 337 (1938)

Lloyd Gaines was denied admission to the University of Missouri School of Law solely because of his race. The state offered to pay his tuition at the public law schools in adjacent states. Gaines refused this offer, arguing that he had a constitutional right to a legal education in the state where he lived. Chief Justice Charles Evans Hughes wrote the majority opinion, vindicating Gaines's claim.

In answering petitioner's contention that this discrimination constituted a denial of his constitutional right, the state court has fully recognized the obligation of the State to provide negroes with advantages for higher education substantially equal to the advantages afforded to white students. The State has sought to fulfill that obligation by furnishing equal facilities in separate schools, a method the validity of which has been sustained by our decisions. Respondents' counsel have appropriately emphasized the special solicitude of the State for the higher education of negroes as shown in the establishment of Lincoln University, a state institution well conducted on a plane with the University of Missouri so far as the offered courses are concerned. It is said that Missouri is a pioneer in that field and is the only State in the Union which has established a separate university for negroes on the same basis as the state university for white students. But, commendable as is that action, the fact remains that instruction in law for negroes is not now afforded by the State, either at Lincoln University or elsewhere within the State, and that the State excludes negroes from the advantages of the law school it has established at the University of Missouri.

It is manifest that this discrimination if not relieved . . . would constitute a denial of equal protection. . . .

The Supreme Court of Missouri in the instant case has . . . [argued] (1) that in Missouri . . . there is "a legislative declaration of a purpose to establish a law school for negroes at Lincoln whenever necessary or practical"; and (2) that, "pending the establishment of such a school, adequate provision has been made for the legal education of negro students in recognized schools outside of this State."

As to the first ground, it appears that the policy of establishing a law school at Lincoln University has not yet ripened into an actual establishment, and it cannot be said that a mere declaration of purpose, still unfulfilled, is enough. The provision for legal education at Lincoln is at present entirely lacking. Respondents' counsel urge that if, on the date when petitioner applied for admission to the University of Missouri, he had instead applied to the curators of Lincoln University it would have been their duty to establish a law school; that this "agency of the State," to which he should have applied, was "specifically charged with mandatory duty to furnish him what he seeks." . . .

*   *   *

The state court has not held that it would have been the duty of the curators to establish a law school at Lincoln University for the petitioner on his application. Their duty, as the court defined it, would have been either to supply a law school at Lincoln University . . . or to furnish him the opportunity to obtain his legal training in another State. . . . Thus the law left the curators free to adopt the latter course. The state court has not ruled or intimated that their failure or refusal to establish a law school for a very few students, still less for one student, would have been an abuse of the discretion with which the curators were entrusted. . . .

The state court stresses the advantages that are afforded by the law schools of the adjacent States,—Kansas, Nebraska, Iowa and Illinois,—which admit non-resident negroes. The court considered that these were schools of high standing where one desiring to practice law in Missouri can get "as sound, comprehensive, valuable legal education" as in the University of Missouri; that the system of education in the former is the same as that in the latter and is designed to give the students a basis for the practice of law in any State where the Anglo-American system of law obtains; that the law school of the University of Missouri does not specialize in Missouri law and that the course of study and the case books used in the five schools are substantially identical. Petitioner insists that for one intending to practice in Missouri there are special advantages in attending a law school there, both in relation to the opportunities for the particular study of Missouri law and for the observation of the local courts, and also in view of the prestige of the Missouri law school among the citizens of the State, his prospective clients. . . .

We think that these matters are beside the point. The basic consideration is not as to what sort of opportunities other States provide, or whether they are as good as those in Missouri, but as to what opportunities Missouri itself furnishes to white students and denies to negroes solely upon the ground of color. The admissibility of laws separating the races in the enjoyment of privileges afforded by the State rests wholly upon the equality of the privileges which the laws give to the separated groups within the State. The question here is not of a duty of the State to supply legal training, or of the quality of the training which it does supply, but of its duty when it provides such training to furnish it to the residents of the State upon the basis of an equality of right. By the operation of the laws of Missouri a privilege has been created for white law students which is denied to negroes by reason of their race. The white resident is afforded legal education within the State; the negro resident having the same qualifications is refused it there and must go outside the State to obtain it. That is a denial of the equality of legal right to the enjoyment of the privilege which the State has set up, and the provision for the payment of tuition fees in another State does not remove the discrimination.

The equal protection of the law is "a pledge of the protection of equal laws." *Yick Wo* v. *Hopkins*. Manifestly, the obligation of the State to give the protection of equal laws can be performed only where its laws operate, that is, within its own jurisdiction. It is there that the equality of legal right must be maintained. That obligation is imposed by the Constitution upon the States severally as governmental entities,—each responsible for its own laws establishing the rights and duties of persons within its borders. It is an obligation the burden of which cannot be cast by one State upon another, and no State can be excused from performance by what another State may do or fail to do. That separate responsibility of each State within its own sphere is of the essence of statehood maintained under our dual system. We find it impossible to conclude that what otherwise would be an unconstitutional discrimination, with respect to the legal right to the enjoyment of opportunities within the State, can be justified by requiring resort to opportunities elsewhere. That resort may mitigate the inconvenience of the discrimination but cannot serve to validate it.

*   *   *

Here, petitioner's right was a personal one. It was as an individual that he was entitled to the equal protection of the laws, and the State was bound to furnish him within its borders facilities for legal education substantially equal to those which the State there afforded for persons of the white race. . . .

Note: Beyond *Gaines*

Gaines did not require integrated education. It left the states the option of building separate law schools and graduate schools. Not until *Sweatt* v. *Painter* (1950) would the Supreme Court hold that segregation in graduate and professional schools, such as law schools, was unconstitutional. Nevertheless, *Gaines* was a major civil rights victory because, for the first time, the United States Supreme Court required that a state actually provide "equal" facilities along with "separate" ones.

Racial Justice and Criminal Law

From the earliest period of American history, race and racial discrimination have been connected to the criminal justice system. Some of the very first enslaved blacks were initially runaway servants whose punishment for escaping was lifetime servitude. Throughout the antebellum period, the South maintained special criminal codes for blacks. After the Civil War, formal equality existed in criminal codes, but discrimination in enforcement was the rule. Before 1950, the vast majority of blacks lived in the South, where they faced a criminal justice system designed to keep them at the bottom of the social structure.

In the 1930s, the United States Supreme Court began to provide some due process protections for southern blacks. The worst excesses of police brutality and kangaroo-court justice were declared unconstitutional. But the dictates of the High Court filtered down slowly, if at all, to local police departments.

In addition to formal law, informal "lynch law" remained an all-too-common method of repressing blacks. It was not uncommon for police officials to aid lynchers or even take part in clandestine murders. Between 1889 and 1941, the nation recorded 3,700 lynchings. Some were politically motivated, such as radical union members lynched in the West or the German-American lynched in Illinois in 1918 for "disloyal remarks." Others were against ethnic groups, such as the mob killing of eleven Italian immigrants in New Orleans in 1891 and the anti-Semitic murder of Leo Frank in Georgia in 1915. Sometimes whites were lynched for less dramatic reasons, such as horse stealing.

Although there was at least 1 lynching in all but five states between 1889 and 1918, most lynchings—over 2,900—took place in the South, where the overwhelming majority of the victims were black. Despite the myths, only 16 percent of southern black victims were accused of interracial rape or other sex-related crimes. Many black victims were accused of murder and assault, but others were lynched for "creating a disturbance," "stealing hogs," "aiding a colored man to escape," "disagreement with a white man," "writing a letter to a white woman," "miscegenation," "mistaken identity," "bad reputation," "insulting" whites, or "giving evidence" at the trials of whites. Often the cause was determined to be simply "race prejudice."[6]

Opposition from the NAACP and southern white civic organizations, such as the Commission on Interracial Cooperation and the Association of Southern Women for the Prevention of Lynching, eventually undermined public support for lynching. During World War II, the rate of lynchings dropped, but in the 1950s and 1960s lynchings and racially motivated murders became more common, as some Southerners responded to the civil rights movement with extreme violence. The most infamous incident was the torture murders of three civil rights workers—two whites and a black—in Philadelphia, Mississippi, in 1964.

JAMES HARMON CHADBOURN
"Lynching and the Administration of Justice"
1933

This introductory chapter to the book Lynching and the Law *sets out some of the sociological and legal analyses of the antilynching movement. The fact that this book was written by a southern white, and published by the University of North Carolina Press, indicates that the southern establishment regarded lynching as a problem. Also significant is Chadbourn's positive reference to* Rope and Faggot, *a study of lynching written by Walter White, the head of the NAACP. Despite the antilynching attitude among many educated Southerners, senators from the South continued to oppose any federal legislation to ban lynching.*

THE AMOUNT of study given today to the problem of lynching is evidence that the public conscience has been awakened by the 3,753 lynchings between 1889 and 1932. Witness, for example, the reports of the Southern Commission on the Study of Lynching; Walter White's penetrating book, *Rope and Faggot.* . . .

*   *   *

Thanks to the pioneer record-keeping of *The Chicago Tribune,* begun in 1889, later taken up and amplified by Tuskegee Institute and the National Association for the Advancement of Colored People, certain elemental statistics are available. These are: number of occurrences, location, race and sex of the lynched person, inciting offense or event, and the manner of killing. . . . We have been shown the proportion between the various offenses, manners of killing, men and women, Negroes and whites; the proportions of occurrences by sections of the country . . . the proportions according to total and race populations by counties, states, and sections; and finally, the proportions according to months of the year and days of the week.

We have been carried beyond the laboratory of the statistician by the findings of the Southern Commission. The basis of its information is a series of painstaking case studies of the lynchings in 1930 made by trained investigators working in the field. Common threads of economic and social factors have thus been found woven into the pattern of the typical 1930 lynching community.

It is a rural Southern county characterized in general by social and economic decadence. For example, it is below the state average in per capita tax valuation, bank deposits, income from farm and factory, income tax returns, and ownership of automobiles. Educational facilities are also below the state average. The church membership is seventy five per cent Southern Baptist and Methodist. There is generally prevalent a supposed necessity for protecting white women against sex crimes by the Negroes. All these, plus emotional and recreational starvation and a fear of economic domination by enterprising Negroes, create the complex of "keeping the nigger in his place." Periodic lynchings are the result.

*　　　　*　　　　*

Lynching is often interpreted as a protest against the inefficiency of courts as agencies for the punishment of crime. As far back as 1893, the Georgia Bar Association resolved that "the reason, or at least one great reason, why lynchings occur is because there is a distrust, and a constantly growing distrust, in the promptness and efficiency of the law." In later years the same idea has been constantly reiterated, along with its obvious corollary that "the remedy for lynching is to restore the confidence of society in the just, prompt, and efficient trial and punishment of criminals."

*　　　　*　　　　*

An examination of available data from this standpoint brings forth some significant facts. In some cases a person has been lynched during the course of, or after, the completion of legal proceedings against him. While of course no amount of judicial malpractice in such cases affords a valid excuse for lynching, such cases should be examined to determine whether it was present. If it was, then one of the probable incentives for lynchings can be identified and possibly corrected.

Not judicial error, but executive clemency, seems to have occasioned most of the lynchings which occurred during or after completion of the legal process. This was true in Georgia's *cause célèbre*—the case of Leo Frank. Similar are the cases . . . in Angleton, Texas, [and] . . . Crawfordsville, Georgia. . . . A stay of execution by the Supreme Court in Mississippi had the same effect . . . and the same was true of the filing of a motion for an appeal [in] . . . Louisiana. . . .

*　　　　*　　　　*

[Here Chadbourn discussed cases in which blacks were lynched after they were paroled or had served their sentences.]

A protest against the way in which legal processes operated can perhaps be discerned in these cases. But who can say whether the pardons, the stay of execution, or the light sentences were improper?

In some cases, moreover, there is not even the suspicion of judicial malpractice. Cases are on record where lynchings have followed in the face of extreme sentences. In 1916 a Negro in Waco, Texas, killed a white woman. He was carried to Dallas for safekeeping. There an agreement was made between a part of the Waco community, the local authorities, and the Negro that he would be promptly tried, that he would waive his right to seek change of venue and to appeal, and that he would be protected from lynch law. On this agreement he was brought back. In a courtroom seating 500 there were 1500, with 2000 outside. As the jurors were called, members of the crowd yelled, "We don't need any jury!" After a hurried trial, the jury deliberated three minutes and returned a verdict of guilty. The defendant was sentenced to hang in a few hours. There was a pause of a full minute while the judge made the entry: "Jury verdict of guilty." Meanwhile the court stenographer . . . slipped back of the sheriff and out of the room. The sheriff followed him. The silence was broken as a tall Waco citizen, driver of a brewery truck, yelled to the crowd, "Get the nigger!" A gruesome burning at the stake followed.

*   *   *

These sample cases . . . leave one in some doubt . . . that sometimes . . . lynching is an expression of distrust in the efficacy of legal processes in the given case. But whether there was some ground for the distrust, in that the particular case was mishandled, an investigator is at a loss to say. Yet this expression of distrust is not an invariable condition in all lynchings. In [many cases] . . . the lynchers could have had no ground for dissatisfaction with the operation of orderly legal processes. In a word, in the case of a person who is lynched during or after trial, the evidence of a correlation between the judicial handling of his case and the lynching is contradictory and inconclusive. It can scarcely be said . . . [that] we can identify judicial inefficiency as a major factor in these lynchings.

*   *   *

It should be remembered, moreover, that most victims of lynching are Negroes. The evidence is convincing that Negroes who are tried for serious crimes in lynching communities are more drastically punished than are whites similarly circumstanced. Professor Brearley estimates that in South Carolina for the period 1920–1926, 64.1 percent of the Negroes charged with murder or manslaughter were found guilty, while the similar percentage for whites was 31.7. In regard to the severity of the punishment inflicted on Negroes, he says:

"Further evidence that the Negro is more severely punished than is the white person is presented by the 1910 census of prisoners. At this time Negroes constituted only 10.69 per cent of the total population of the United States but they received 56.0 per cent of the grave homicide sentences and 49.1 per cent of the lesser homicide sentences in the United States. In the South the Negroes provided 74.4 per cent of those sentenced for grave homicide during the year 1910 and 67.6 per cent of those committed for lesser homicides. During the same year the average sentence for those punished by imprisonment without fine and by definite sentences was 5.2 months for the whites and 17.4 months for the Negroes." . . .

Dr. Raper finds that. . . .

"Data secured from the superintendents of state prison systems and wardens of penitentiaries of Southern States for the eighteenth-month period ending July 1, 1931, demonstrate conclusively that Negro criminals brought before the courts are not dealt with leniently. In ten Southern States, of the eighty-one executions, thirteen were white—all convicted of murder—and sixty-eight were Negroes: fifty-seven murderers, eight rapists, and three burglars. During the same period, in twelve states, of 669 life sentences imposed, 199 were whites: 192 murders, six rapists, and one burglar; of the 470 Negroes, 425 were convicted of murder, twenty of rape, and twenty-five of burglary and other offenses. For minor offenses, too, the sentences for Negroes were often greater than for whites."

Note: Lynching and Federal Law

In the 1930s, northern Democrats and civil rights organizations worked for the passage of a federal antilynching bill. In 1937, such a bill passed the House, but filibusters led by Senators Tom Connally of Texas and Theodore K. Bilbo of Mississippi killed the bill. Although President Roosevelt expressed his support for the bill, he never worked for its passage. Some New Deal policies, especially the creation of the Civilian Conservation Corps (CCC), may have helped end lynching by removing to the CCC camps "actual and potential lynchers from the environment which favored mob violence." The military draft before and during World War II also led to a decline in lynching.

Note: Black Rights, Southern Justice, and the Supreme Court

In the 1930s and 1940s, the Supreme Court and the executive branch of the federal government began to intervene on behalf of blacks who were denied fair trials in the Deep South.

The *Scottsboro Cases*. In 1931 nine black youths, the Scottsboro Boys, were convicted of rape in Alabama on the basis of perjured testimony at a circus trial. Their convictions were overturned in *Powell* v. *Alabama* (1932) because they had been denied adequate counsel. They were retried, and in *Norris* v. *Alabama* (1935), their convictions were again reversed because of the "long continued, systematic and arbitrary exclusion of qualified negro [*sic*] citizens from service on juries. . . ." The Court forced Alabama officials to place the names of blacks on the jury roles. All the Scottsboro Boys were subsequently convicted by all-white juries that were chosen from an integrated pool of jurors.

Brown v. *Mississippi* (1936). Ed Brown was convicted of murder based on a confession he gave after police officers "hanged him by a rope to the limb of a tree, and, having let him down, they hung him again, and when he was let down the second time, and he still protested his innocence, he was tied to a tree and whipped. . . ." Declaring that "the rack and torture chamber may not be substituted for the witness stand," the Supreme Court reversed the conviction "for want of the essential elements of due process. . . ."

Screws v. *United States* (1945). This case involved what Justice William O. Douglas described as "a shocking and revolting episode in law enforcement." After arresting Robert Hall, a black accused of theft, Claude Screws, a Georgia sheriff, and two deputies "began beating him with their fists and with a solid-bar blackjack about eight inches long and weighing two pounds. . . ." After some thirty minutes of this treatment, Hall died. Screws was convicted under a modern version of the Civil Rights Act of 1866. This law, as the dissenters noted, had been "a dead letter" since Reconstruction. A sharply divided Supreme Court upheld the constitutionality of the law and the prosecution, but ordered a new trial on narrowly technical grounds. *Screws* indicates the beginning of federal protection of the civil rights of blacks against the violence of southern law enforcement.

9

The Rise of Legal Liberalism, Economic Reform, and the New Deal 1900–1945

Momentous events between World Wars I and II reshaped American legal culture. The most important of these was the Great Depression, which followed the Wall Street panic of November 1929. The Depression was an economic scourge of mammoth proportions; it spread with devastating impact over not just the American but the world economy. By the late 1920s, the ups and downs of the business cycle were a routine feature of American life, but at no time in the past had the economy plunged so low and then remained there. Unemployment soared, rising to almost one-quarter of the labor force in 1933, a twentieth-century high. Banks failed in record numbers. Between 1929 and 1932, 5,000 banks closed their doors, and the life savings of millions of Americans evaporated.

The Great Depression called into question the optimistic and laissez-faire attitudes that had characterized post–Civil War America. The idea that voluntary rather than governmental regulation was best seemed debatable when so many people suffered. Moreover, the economic pall fell over not just poor blacks and whites, but also the aspiring middle class, with its faith in the idea that economic well-being flowed from personal virtue and that government had a limited role in promoting the collective social welfare. Socialist leaders, such as Norman Thomas, urged radical collectivist solutions to the problems of building economic confidence and alleviating human suffering. Others, like William Dudley Pelly, called for the restoration of democracy, Christianity, and free enterprise through an American brand of fascism.

The New Deal of President Franklin Delano Roosevelt, who swept to victory in 1932, emerged as the consensus, middle-of-the-road approach to the problems of economic collapse. Critics on both the right and the left challenged the New Deal, believing that while FDR was a decent and well-meaning man he was squandering an opportunity to fundamentally transform American life. Although the New Deal did not offer any fundamental reshuffling of American government and society, it did bring about broad changes, many of which involved the legal culture. The Great Depression, after all, was as much a legal as an economic crisis, one that was magnified by the simple fact that the American economy since the Civil War had developed a national market structure that the states were increasingly unable to deal with alone.

Alleviating human suffering and restoring economic confidence, therefore, required a degree of governmental involvement in the day-to-day lives of Americans that raised unprecedented questions about the protection of individual property interests, the separation of powers among the three branches, and the proper relationship between the states and the federal government. Property rights, separation of powers, social welfare, and federalism emerged as central concerns in the legal history of these years. The national programs associated with FDR's presidency became the center of these concerns, although many of the same issues were raised by "little" New Deal programs in the states.

These issues were given even greater currency since the intellectual context in which they occurred was itself rapidly developing. The mechanical legal scientism of Christopher Columbus Langdell faced new challenges, especially with the advent of social science as a legitimate method of organizing human knowledge. The social sciences relied on a scientific method that invested great credibility in empirical evidence as opposed to the supposedly immutable doctrines of Langdell. The result was a more empirical and experimental attitude toward the problems and assumptions of the learned disciplines. Psychology, economics, anthropology, and political science, for example, applied social science techniques in ways that placed human behavior within a functional social context.

The social science revolution, which was firmly connected to the Progressive legacy of efficiency and rationality in government, had important implications for the relationship between law and public policy. The Langdellian scheme of legal education stressed a priori assumptions. The genius of his "science of the law" was that it gave fixed and supposedly objective principles to guide succeeding generations. The social sciences enfeebled these basic assumptions by demonstrating that for human knowledge to be valid it had to be based on empirical evidence. That meant, as Edward A. Purcell, Jr., has argued, that all "knowledge was necessarily tentative and subject to change."[1] The implication was quite clear: the new methods administered a heavy dose of ethical relativism to a legal system that prided itself on moral certainties supported by Langdellian legal science. Social science dealt with only objective facts and was morally neutral. Thus social science could not tell civilization how it should act; it could help only in understanding the circumstances in which such judgments had to be made.

The methods of social science, the moral relativism that accompanied it, and the economic stress of the Great Depression combined to reshape the legal culture. The traditional objective notion of the late nineteenth century held that judicial decisions were based on rules and precedents defined historically and applied mechanically. When placed in the context of the Progressive theory of lawmaking by administrative agencies, the social sciences held forth new hope of adapting law to particular social exigencies. The result was a growing attention to the ways in which social science could "improve" the decisions made according to the rule of law. Two of the most important consequences of these developments were Sociological Jurisprudence, which had its roots in the Progressive era, and Legal Realism, which flourished in the 1920s and 1930s. Sociological Jurisprudence and Legal Realism increasingly conflicted with not just the legal science of Langdell, but also each other. The sociological jurisprudents, such as Roscoe Pound and Louis Brandeis, persisted in a view of law that stressed moral and ethical beliefs. Law might be flexible, but it was—and should be—value laden. At the same time, Legal Realists rejected such notions and increasingly drifted into ethical relativism.

The economic crisis of the Great Depression propelled these trends toward the formulation of legal liberalism, the dominant value of modern American legal culture. It fused the social reformist and administrative-law impulses of Progressivism, the relativism and instrumentalism of Legal Realism and Sociological Jurisprudence, and the regulatory responsibility of the state that marked the New Deal. Traditional liberalism had held the individual paramount and feared the active state. The new liberalism reversed that pattern; it emphasized that the state had a positive duty, through administrative agencies, courts, and legislatures, to promote the public interest by encouraging social and economic justice. The emphasis, however, was always on harmony and stability among contending interests; the object of the new liberal state was neither to redistribute wealth significantly nor to guarantee fully that every person should be put in the same condition as every other. Classical notions of laissez faire, which had never fully characterized the American historical experience, withered but did not die, and in the decades after the New Deal, legal liberal culture flourished until it came under sustained attack beginning in the 1960s from both the political right and left.

Sociological Jurisprudence, the American Law Institute, and Legal Realism

Progressive reformers during the late nineteenth and early twentieth centuries brought the institutions of American law under attack. They cast the judiciary as unresponsive to the social demands of industrialization, urbanization, and immigration; they charged that administrative and regulatory agencies were little more than tools of the regulated; and they condemned legislatures as the agencies of the wealthy. Many Progressives, for example, in pushing for the direct election of United States senators, portrayed the upper house of Congress as a millionaires' club.

Yet the generation of Americans who came into public life in the first third of the twentieth century disagreed about how law was to respond to social change, with resulting diversity in the legal culture. Sociological Jurisprudence, the American Law Institute, and Legal Realism offered their distinctive and often competing solutions to the new problems of the age.

OLIVER WENDELL HOLMES, JR.

"Law and the Court"

1913

President Theodore Roosevelt appointed Oliver Wendell Holmes, Jr., to the Supreme Court in 1902, where he served until his retirement in 1932 at age ninety. Holmes was in many ways a transitional figure between the strict legal scientism of Langdell, with whom he disagreed sharply while serving on the Harvard Law School faculty, and the Legal Realists. Holmes was a great skeptic; he believed

*that the common law was not "a brooding omnipresence in the sky," but the
reflection of historically contingent choices. Each generation, he concluded, had
to come to terms with the law. On balance, his conservative, property-oriented
colleagues on the high bench had failed to do so, and they had brought public
ridicule on themselves by failing to appreciate the limits of their authority.
Holmes argued that once the legislature had spoken, unless an act was palpably
unconstitutional, the courts should not intervene. He also insisted that new forms
of learning, especially the social sciences, could illuminate legal controversies.
As the essay below suggests, Holmes doubted that judges alone had the capacity
to deal with the great issues of the Progressive era.*

[I] turn to the Court to which for ten now accomplished years it has been my
opportunity to belong. We are very quiet there, but it is the quiet of a storm centre,
as we all know. Science has taught the world skepticism and has made it legitimate
to put everything to the test of proof. Many beautiful and noble reverences are
impaired, but in these days no one can complain if any institution, system, or belief
is called on to justify its continuance in life. Of course we are not excepted and have
not escaped. Doubts are expressed that go to our very being. Not only are we told
that when John Marshall pronounced an Act of Congress unconstitutional in *Marbury* v. *Madison* he usurped a power that the Constitution did not give, but we are
told that we are the representatives of a class—a tool of the money power. I get
letters, not always anonymous, intimating that we are corrupt. Well, gentlemen, I
admit that it makes my heart ache. It is very painful, when one spends all the
energies of one's soul in trying to do good work, with no thought but that of solving
a problem according to the rules by which one is bound, to know that many see
sinister motives and would be glad of evidence that one was consciously bad. But
we must take such things philosophically and try to see what we can learn from
hatred and distrust and whether behind them there may not be some germ of
inarticulate truth.

The attacks upon the Court are merely an expression of the unrest that seems to
wonder vaguely whether law and order pay. When the ignorant are taught to doubt
they do not know what they safely may believe. And it seems to me that at this time
we need education in the obvious more than investigation of the obscure. I do not
see so much immediate use in committees on the high cost of living and inquiries
how far it is due to the increased production of gold, how far to the narrowing of
cattle ranges and the growth of population, how far to the bugaboo, as I do in
bringing home to people a few social and economic truths.

                        *   *   *

I should like to see it brought home to the public that the question of fair prices
is due to the fact that none of us can have as much as we want of all the things we
want; that as less will be produced than the public wants, the question is how much
of each product it will have and how much go without; that thus the final competition is between the objects of desire, and therefore between the producers of those
objects; that when we oppose labor and capital, labor means the group that is selling
its product and capital all the other groups that are buying it. The hated capitalist is

simply the mediator, the prophet, the adjuster according to his divination of the future desire. If you could get that believed, the body of the people would have no doubt as to the worth of law.

That is my outside thought on the present discontents. As to the truth embodied in them, in part it cannot be helped. It cannot be helped, it is as it should be, that the law is behind the times. I told a labor leader once that what they asked was favor, and if a decision was against them they called it wicked. The same might be said of their opponents. It means that the law is growing. As law embodies beliefs that have triumphed in the battle of ideas and then have translated themselves into action, while there still is doubt, while opposite convictions still keep a battle front against each other, the time for law has not come; the notion destined to prevail is not yet entitled to the field. It is a misfortune if a judge reads his conscious or unconscious sympathy with one side or the other prematurely into the law, and forgets that what seem to him to be first principles are believed by half his fellow men to be wrong. I think that we have suffered from this misfortune, in State courts at least, and that this is another and very important truth to be extracted from the popular discontent. When twenty years ago a vague terror went over the earth and the word socialism began to be heard, I thought and still think that fear was translated into doctrines that had no proper place in the Constitution or the common law. Judges are apt to be naif, simple-minded men, and they need something of Mephistopheles. We too need education in the obvious—to learn to transcend our own convictions and to leave room for much that we hold dear to be done away with short of revolution by the orderly change of law.

I have no belief in panaceas and almost none in sudden ruin. I believe with Montesquieu that if the chance of a battle—I may add, the passage of a law—has ruined a state, there was a general cause at work that made the state ready to perish by a single battle or a law. Hence I am not much interested one way or the other in the nostrums now so strenuously urged. I do not think the United States would come to an end if we lost our power to declare an Act of Congress void. I do think the Union would be imperiled if we could not make that declaration as to the laws of the several States. For one in my place sees how often a local policy prevails with those who are not trained to national views and how often action is taken that embodies what the Commerce Clause was meant to end. But I am not aware that there is any serious desire to limit the Court's power in this regard. For most of the things that properly can be called evils in the present state of the law I think the main remedy, and for the evils of public opinion, is for us to grow more civilized.

If I am right it will be a slow business for our people to reach rational views, assuming that we are allowed to work peaceably to that end. But as I grow older I grow calm. If I feel what are perhaps an old man's apprehensions, that competition from new races will cut deeper than working men's disputes and will test whether we can hang together and can fight; if I fear that we are running through the world's resources at a pace that we cannot keep; I do not lose my hopes. I do not pin my dreams for the future to my country or even to my race. I think it probable that civilization somehow will last as long as I care to look ahead—perhaps with smaller numbers, but perhaps also bred to greatness and splendor by science. I think it not improbable that man, like the grub that prepares a chamber for the winged thing it never has seen but is to be—that man may have cosmic destinies that he does not understand. And so beyond the vision of battling.

Note: Oliver Wendell Holmes, Jr., and Judging

Holmes believed that practical considerations rooted in underlying social needs and conflicts ultimately shaped the course of the law. Hence, lawmakers could resist such trends on only a temporary basis by appealing to abstract logic and deductive reasoning, the foundation on which Langdell rested his vaunted method. Nor did Holmes assume that there were moral and social absolutes; instead, judges articulated the law based on their perceptions and sentiments. The lawyer's job was to predict their behavior and to advise clients accordingly. Thus Holmes spoke for a practical legal science, one tailored to the behavioral insights of the new social sciences.

The excerpt from Holmes also points to the growing emphasis on the commerce power as a means of uniting the island economic communities that had so characterized nineteenth-century America. The commerce clause of the Constitution had a controversial history, but it became even more important in the early twentieth century as Progressive reformers enlisted it in an attempt to impose some national order on the economy. Holmes had been at the forefront in sketching broader regulatory authority for the government under the commerce power. His famous decision in *Swift & Co.* v. *United States* (1905) enunciated the "stream of commerce doctrine," which affirmed the power of Congress to regulate commerce even in individual states as long as it was part of the broader current of national commerce.

Holmes also pushed then-current understanding of judging toward a greater sense of the individual jurist rather than the logic of the law itself. What judges did made a difference; they were not mindless, mechanical operators of an autonomous, logical body of rules. By the beginning of the twentieth century, therefore, legal reformers, most notably John Chipman Gray, a professor of law at Harvard, and Louis D. Brandeis, a Boston lawyer and future justice of the Supreme Court, argued that judges had to pay attention to the probable social results of their decisions.

LOUIS D. BRANDEIS
"Brief for the Defendant in Error,"
Muller v. *Oregon*
October Term, 1907

Louis D. Brandeis, a Boston lawyer, was known in the early twentieth century as the "people's attorney" because of his prominent role in advocating public-interest causes. Brandeis employed litigation to press his social agenda, loading his briefs with a maximum of sociological evidence and a minimum of logical argumentation. The Muller *arguments became the best known example of the "Brandeis brief." These arguments were especially important because earlier the Supreme Court had decided* Lochner v. New York *(1905) (see Chapter 7). The Justices in that case overturned a New York State law that limited the number of hours men were permitted to work in bakeries. The* Lochner *majority relied on the concept of freedom to contract, claiming that this right existed in the due process clause of the Fourteenth Amendment and "protected" employees from having state legislatures deny their "freedom" to work twelve, fourteen, or even sixteen hours a day. The Court in* Muller *was asked to consider whether an Oregon statute passed in 1903 that provided that "no female [shall] be employed in any mechanical establishment or factory or laundry . . . more than ten hours during any one day" violated the same due process provision of the Fourteenth Amendment.*

THE WORLD'S EXPERIENCE UPON WHICH THE LEGISLATION
LIMITING THE HOURS OF LABOR FOR WOMEN IS BASED

I. The Dangers of Long Hours

A. Causes
(1) Physical Differences Between Men and Women

The dangers of long hours for women arise from their special physical organization taken in connection with the strain incident to factory and similar work.

Long hours of labor are dangerous for women primarily because of their special physical organization. In structure and function women are differentiated from men. Besides these anatomical and physiological differences, physicians are agreed that women are fundamentally weaker than men in all that makes for endurance: in muscular strength, in nervous energy, in the powers of persistent attention and application. Overwork, therefore, which strains endurance to the utmost, is more disastrous to the health of women than of men, and entails upon them more lasting injury.

Report of Select Committee on Shops Early Closing Bill, British House of Commons, 1895.

Dr. Percy Kidd, physician in Brompton and London Hospitals:

The most common effect I have noticed of the long hours is general deterioration of health; very general symptoms which we medically attribute to over-action, and debility of the nervous system; that includes a great deal more than what is called nervous disease, such as indigestion, constipation, a general slackness, and a great many other indefinite symptoms.

Are those symptoms more marked in women than in men?

I think they are much more marked in women. I should say one sees a great many more women of this class than men; but I have seen precisely the same symptoms in men, I should not say in the same proportion, because one has not been able to make anything like a statistical inquiry. There are other symptoms, but I mention those as being the most common. Another symptom especially among women is anemia, bloodlessness or pallor, that I have no doubt is connected with long hours indoors.

Report of the Maine Bureau of Industrial and Labor Statistics, 1888.

Let me quote from Dr. Ely Van der Warker (1875):

Woman is badly constructed for the purposes of standing eight or ten hours upon her feet. I do not intend to bring into evidence the peculiar position and nature of the organs contained in the pelvis, but to call attention to the peculiar construction of the knee and the shallowness of the pelvis, and the delicate nature of the foot as part of a sustaining column. The knee joint of woman is a sexual characteristic. Viewed in front and extended, the joint in but a slight degree interrupts the gradual taper of the thigh into the leg. Viewed in a semi-flexed position, the joint forms a smooth ovate spheroid. The reason of this lies in the smallness of the patella in front, and the narrowness of the articular surfaces of the tibia and femur, and which in man form the lateral prominences, and thus is much more perfect as a sustaining column than that of a woman. The muscles which keep the body fixed upon the thighs in the erect position labor under the disadvantage of shortness of purchase, owing to the short distance, compared to that of man, between the crest of the ilium and the great trochanter of the femur, thus giving to man a much larger purchase in the leverage existing between the trunk and the extremities. Comparatively the foot is less able to sustain weight than that of man, owing to its shortness and the more delicate formation of the tarsus and metatarsus.

Report of the Massachusetts Bureau of Labor Statistics, 1875.

A "lady operator," many years in the business, informed us: "I have had hundreds of lady compositors in my employ, and they all exhibited, in a marked manner, both in the way they performed their work and in its results, the difference in physical ability between themselves and men. They cannot endure the prolonged close attention and confinement which is a great part of type-setting. I have few girls with me more than two or three years at a time; they must have vacations, and they break down in health rapidly. I know no reason why a girl could not set as much type as a man, if she were as strong to endure the demand on mind and body."

Report of the Nebraska Bureau of Labor and Industrial Statistics, 1901–1902.

They (women) are unable, by reason of their physical limitations, to endure the same hours of exhaustive labor as may be endured by men without injury to their health would wreck the constitution and destroy the health of women, and render them incapable of bearing their share of the burdens of the family and the home. The State must be accorded the right to guard and protect women as a class against such a condition, and the law in question to that extent conserves the public health and welfare.

In strength as well as in rapidity and precision of movement women are inferior to men. This is not a conclusion that has ever been contested. It is in harmony with all the practical experience of life. It is perhaps also in harmony with the results of those investigators . . . who have found that, as in the blood of women, so also in their muscles, there is more water than in those of men. To a very great extent it is a certainty, a matter of difference in exercise and environment. It is probably, also, partly a matter of organic constitution.

The motor superiority of men, and to some extent of males generally, is, it can scarcely be doubted, a deep-lying fact. It is related to what is most fundamental in men and in women, and to their whole psychic organization.

There appears to be a general agreement that women are more docile and amenable to discipline; that they can do light work equally well; that they are steadier in some respects; but that, on the other hand, they are often absent on account of slight indisposition, and they break down sooner under strain.

*   *   *

It has been estimated that out of every one hundred days women are in a semi-pathological state of health for from fourteen to sixteen days. The natural congestion of the pelvic organs during menstruation is augmented and favored by work on sewing machines and other industrial occupations necessitating the constant use of the lower part of the body. Work during these periods tends to induce chronic congestion of the uterus and appendages, and dysmenorrhea and flexion of the uterus are well known affections of working girls.

VII. Laundries

The specific prohibition in the Oregon Act of more than ten hours' work in laundries is not an arbitrary discrimination against that trade. Laundries would probably not be included under the general terms of "manufacturing" or "mechanical establishments"; and yet the special dangers of long hours in laundries, as the business is now conducted, present strong reasons for providing a legal limitation of the hours of work in that business.

Dangerous Trades. Thomas Oliver, Medical Expert on Dangerous Trades Committees of the Home Office. 1902.

Chapter XLVII. Laundry Workers.

It is perhaps difficult to realize that the radical change which has everywhere transformed industrial conditions has already affected this occupation (laundry work) also, and that for good or for evil the washerwoman is passing under the influences which have so profoundly modified the circumstances of her sister of the spinning-wheel and the sewing needle. When the first washing machine and ironing roller were applied to this occupation, alteration in the conditions became as much a foregone conclusion as it did in the case of the textile or the clothing manufactures, when the spinning frame, the power loom, or the sewing machine appeared.

Meanwhile, few industries afford at the present time a more interesting study. From a simple home occupation it is steadily being transformed by the application of power-driven machinery and by the division of labor into a highly organized factory industry, in which complicated labor-saving contrivances of all kinds play a prominent part. The tremendous impetus in the adoption of machinery, and the consequent modification of the system of employment so striking in the large laundries, is not greater than the less obvious but even more important development in the same direction among small laundries. Indeed the difference is rapidly becoming one of degree only. In the large laundries may be found perhaps more machinery and a greater number of the newest devices, but the fundamental change has affected all alike.

*   *   *

D. Bad Effect upon Morals

Report of British Chief Inspector of Factories and Workshops, 1900.

One of the most unsatisfactory results of the present system of lack of working hours in laundries is the unfortunate moral effect on the women and girls. . . .

Women who are employed at arduous work till far into the night are not likely to be
early risers nor given to punctual attendance in the mornings, and workers who on
one or two days in the week are dismissed to idleness or to other occupations, while
on the remaining days they are expected to work for abnormally long hours, are not
rendered methodical, industrious, or dependable workers by such an unsatisfactory
training. The self-control and good habits engendered by a regular and definite
period of moderate daily employment, which affords an excellent training for the
young worker in all organized industries, is sadly lacking, and, instead, one finds
periods of violent over-work alternating with hours of exhaustion. The result is the
establishment of a kind of "vicious circle"; bad habits among workers make compliance by their employers with any regulation as to hours very difficult while a lack
of loyal adherence to reasonable hours of employment by many laundry occupiers
increases the difficulty for those who make the attempt in real earnestness.

The American Law Institute

ELIHU ROOT
"Report of the Committee," American Law Institute
1923

*Elihu Root was one of the nation's most successful early-twentieth-century Wall
Street lawyers. In short, he was the establishment, and the American Law Institute (ALI), which was founded in Washington, D.C., in 1923, was the establishment's response to the flux and uncertainty in the law. Root's "Report," which
was presented to the organizational meeting of the ALI, broadly outlined the
institute's goal of adding greater precision to the administration of justice.*

I have been requested by the Committee to make a brief statement in explanation of
the proceedings which bring us to the point where we are now. Most of you know
that for many years we have been talking in the American Bar Association and in
many State Bar Associations about the increasing complexity and confusion of the
substantive law which is applied in all our states and in the Federal courts. . . . It
was apparent that the confusion, the uncertainty, was growing worse from year to
year. It was apparent that the vast multitude of decisions which our practitioners are
obliged to consult was reaching a magnitude which made it impossible in ordinary
practice to consult them. It was apparent that whatever authority might be found for
one view of the law upon any topic, other authorities could be found for a different
view upon the same topic. The great number of books, the enormous amount of
litigation, the struggles of the courts to avoid too strict an application of the rule of
state decision, the fact that the law had become so vast and complicated that the
conditions of ordinary practice and ordinary judicial duty made it impossible to
make adequate examinations—all these had tended to create a situation where the
law was becoming guesswork.

You will find in the paper which has been distributed the statement that a count made in 1917 showed 175,000 pages of reported decisions in the United States, as against 7,000 in Great Britain. Three years before I had a count made in the Library of Congress. . . . It showed that during the five years preceding 1914 over 62,000 statutes had been passed and included in the printed volumes of laws in the United States, and that during the same five years over 65,000 decisions of courts of last resort had been delivered and included in the printed volumes of reports. And still it goes on.

It was evident that the time would presently come, unless something were done, when courts would be forced practically to decide cases not upon authority but upon the impression of the moment, and that we should ultimately come to the law of the Turkish Kadi, where a good man decides under good impulses and a bad man decides under bad impulses, as the case may be; and that our law, as a system, would have sunk below the horizon, and the basis of our institutions would have disappeared.

The result of the conference was first to consider an attempt to secure a great meeting of representatives of the bar from all over the country, and then the suggestion was made that the meeting would have nothing to do of practical effect, because they would have nothing to work on, and that they would be driven to appoint a committee to study the subject and to report upon . . . this problem.

Accordingly, such a committee was got together. They secured funds, they employed competent and experienced assistants, and for nearly a year the work has been conducted, and the result of the work is this report. . . . The idea of the report is that if we can get a statement of the law so well done as to be generally acceptable and made the basis for judicial consideration, we will have accomplished at the outset a very great advance.

We recall the part played in judicial decisions by what Judge Story said, not only in his decisions, but in his textbooks and in his writings; the part played in judicial decision by what Chancellor Kent said in his great work. To take recent instances, take the work on equity written by John Norton Pomeroy. I have not followed the reports closely enough to know whether it still continues, but for a good many years after the publication of that work the courts quoted what he said with practically the effect with which they would have quoted a great judicial decision.

There is a work now which is playing the same part, Mr. Samuel Williston's work on contracts, which is being quoted in the same way.

Now, if you can have the law systematically, scientifically stated, the principles stated by competent men, giving their discussions of the theories upon which their statements are based, giving a presentation and discussion of all the judicial decisions upon which their statements are based, and if such a statement can be revised and criticized and tested by a competent group of lawyers of eminence, and when their work is done if their conclusions can be submitted to the bar that we have here, if that can be done when the work is completed, we will have a statement of the common law of America which will be the prima facie basis on which judicial action will rest; and any lawyer, whose interest in litigation requires him to say that a different view of the law shall be taken, will have upon his shoulders the burden to overturn the statement.

Instead of going back through ten thousand cases it will have been done for him;

there will be not a conclusive presumption but a practical prima facie statement upon which, unless it is overturned, judgment may rest.

If such a thing is done it will tend to assert itself and to confirm itself and to gather authority as time goes on. Of course it cannot be final, for times are continually changing and new conditions arise, and there will have to be revision after revision; but we will have dealt with the past and will have gotten this old man of the sea off our shoulders in a great measure.

It is a great work. It is a work before which anyone might well become discouraged. Unless the work can be done greatly it is worthless. It is of no use to produce another digest, another cyclopedia. That kind of work is being done admirably. It is no use to duplicate the work of the West Publishing Company, which has done so well. It must be so done as to carry authority, as to carry conviction of impartial judgment upon the most thorough scientific investigation and tested accuracy of statement.

Can it be done? If it cannot, why we must go on through this swamp of decisions with consequences which we cannot but dread. The great work of the Roman law had imperial power behind it; Theodosius and Justinian could command and all the resources of a great empire responded. In the simpler and narrower work of the Code Napoleon, again, imperial will put motive power behind the enterprise. What have we? No legislature, no Congress can command; no individual can do the work. Men who come and go, who spend a little time from their ordinary occupations, and go, cannot accomplish it.

Means must be raised for an adequate force, for continuous application. Participation in the enterprise must be deemed highly honorable. Selection for participation must be deemed to confer distinction, it must be recognized as a great and imperative public service. How can it be done? It can be done only if the public opinion of the American democracy recognizes the need of the service, and that public opinion you here today represent and can awaken and direct.

That is why the Committee solicited your attendance here, to ask you whether you will put all that you represent behind the undertaking, so that the American democracy may be behind it.

Note: The American Law Institute and the Restatements

Since certainty in the law was the major concern of the ALI, its major contribution was the publication of restatements of the law. These restatements summarized the law in a major field (contract, tort, and such) and reorganized it along symmetrical lines. The first restatement appeared in 1932 with the publication of Samuel Williston's volumes on the law of contracts. Although the restatements never attained the level of prestige projected for them by the ALI, they were important contributions to the ongoing effort to organize knowledge about the law. The restatements foundered in part because of the Great Depression, which dried up foundation funds that had supported the research and publication effort, and forced the ALI to scrap all but a few projects. By 1945 the ALI had published only eight restatements, and those functioned more as research tools than as the sources of legal authority Root and others had envisaged.

Legal Realism

JEROME FRANK
Law and the Modern Mind
1936

The most controversial stream of legal reform flowed not out of the ALI or Sociological Jurisprudence, but from Legal Realism. Composed of legal educators mostly at Yale and Columbia universities, this movement expanded on Holmes's original insight into the relationship between law and social change, took seriously the idea that judges' actions grew from their own innate personality traits, and insisted that the words of the law had always to be measured against the behavior of persons operating under them. The Realists' adoption of a behavioral perspective and their belief that not a single set of moral values could reign permanently, since society was always in flux, introduced a strong sense of ethical relativism into legal culture at the very time in which the Great Depression placed enormous demands on it for change. The following excerpt from Jerome Frank, a Yale law professor, member of the New Deal bureaucracy in Washington, and subsequently United States Court of Appeals Judge for the Second Circuit, underscores the Realists' skepticism about precedent and the powerful psychological forces that shaped a judge's decision making.

Lawyers and judges purport to make large use of precedents; that is, they purport to rely on the conduct of judges in past cases as a means of procuring analogies for action in new cases. But since what was actually decided in the earlier cases is seldom revealed, it is impossible, in a real sense, to rely on these precedents. What the courts in fact do is to manipulate the language of former decisions. They could approximate a system of real precedents only if the judges, in rendering those former decisions, had reported with fidelity the precise steps by which they arrived at their decisions. The paradox of the situation is that, granting there is value in a system of precedents, our present use of illusory precedents makes the employment of real precedents impossible.

The decision of a judge after trying a case is the product of a unique experience. "Of the many things which have been said of the mystery of the judicial process," writes [Hessel] Yntema, "the most salient is that decision is reached after an emotive experience in which principles and logic play a secondary part. The function of juristic logic and the principles which it employs seem to be like that of language, to describe the event which has already transpired. These considerations must reveal to us the impotence of general principles to control decision. Vague because of their generality, they mean nothing save what they suggest in the organized experience of one who thinks them, and, because of their vagueness, they only remotely compel the organization of that experience. The important problem . . . is not the formulation of the rule but the ascertainment of the cases to which, and the extent to which, it applies. And this, even if we are seeking uniformity in the administration of justice, will lead us again to circumstances of the concrete case. . . .The reason why the general principle cannot control is because it does not inform. . . .It should be obvious that when we have observed a recurrent phenomenon in the decisions of the courts, we may appropriately express the classification in a rule. But the rule will be only a mnemonic device, a useful but hollow diagram of what has been. It will be intelligible only if we relive again the experience of the classifier."

The rules a judge announces when publishing his decision are, therefore, intelligible only if one can relive the judge's unique experience while he was trying the case—which, of course, cannot be done. One cannot even approximate that experience as long as opinions take the form of abstract rules applied to facts formally described. Even if it were desirable that, despite its uniqueness, the judge's decision should be followed, as an analogy, by other judges while trying other cases, this is impossible when the manner in which the judge reached his judgment in the earlier case is most inaccurately reported, as it now is. You are not really applying his decision as a precedent in another case unless you can say, in effect, that, having relived his experience in the earlier case, you believe that he would have thought his decision applicable to the facts of the latter case. And as opinions are now written it is impossible to guess what the judge did experience in trying a case. The facts of all but the simplest controversies are complicated and unlike those of any other controversy; in the absence of a highly detailed account by the judge of how he reacted to the evidence, no other person is capable of reproducing his actual reactions. The rules announced in his opinions are therefore often insufficient to tell the reader why the judge reached his decision.

[T]he "personal bent of the judge" to some extent affects his decisions. But this "personal bent," . . . is a factor only in the selection of new rules for unprovided cases. However, in a profound sense the unique circumstances of almost any case make it an "unprovided case" where no well-established rule "authoritatively" compels a given result. The uniqueness of the facts and of the judge's reaction thereto is often concealed because the judge so states the facts that they appear to call for the application of a settled rule. But that concealment does not mean that the judge's personal bent has been inoperative or that his emotive experience is simple and reproducible.

[Herman] Oliphant has argued that the courts have been paying too much attention to the language of prior cases and that the proper use of the doctrine of following the precedents should lead courts to pay more attention to what judges in earlier cases have decided as against what they have said in their opinions. It may be true that in a limited number of simple cases we can guess what the judge believed to be the facts, and therefore can guess what facts, in any real sense, he was passing on. But usually there are so many and such diverse factors in the evidence which combine in impelling the judge's mind to a decision, that what he decided is unknown—except in the sense that he gave judgment for A, or sent B to prison for ten years, or enjoined C from interfering with D.

At any rate, that will be true while the present method of reporting and deciding cases is adhered to. If and when we have judges trained to observe their own mental processes and such judges with great particularity set forth in their opinions all the factors which they believe led to their conclusions, a judge in passing on a case may perhaps find it possible, to some considerable extent, intelligently to use as a control or guide, the opinion of another judge announced while passing on another case. But as matters stand, reliance on precedents is illusory because judges can seldom tell precisely what has been theretofore decided.

What has just been said is not intended to mean that most courts arrive at their conclusions arbitrarily or apply a process of casuistical deception in writing their opinions. The process we have been describing involves no insincerity or duplicity. The average judge sincerely believes that he is using his intellect as "a cold logic engine" in applying rules and principles derived from the earlier cases to the objective facts of the case before him.

A satirist might indeed suggest that it is regrettable that the practice of precedent-mongering does not involve conscious deception, for it would be comparatively easy for judges entirely aware of what they were doing, to abandon such conscious deception and to report accurately how they arrived at their decisions. Unfortunately, most judges have no such awareness. Worse than that, they are not even aware that they are not aware. Judges Holmes, Cardozo, Hand, Hutcheson, Lehman and a few others have attained the enlightened state of awareness of their unawareness. A handful of legal thinkers off the bench have likewise come to the point of ignorance of all of us as to just how decisions, judicial or otherwise, are reached. Until many more lawyers and judges become willing to admit that ignorance which is the beginning of wisdom and from that beginning work forward painstakingly and consciously, we shall get little real enlightenment on that subject.

Note: Legal Realism

Frank's contribution to Legal Realism involved more than *Law and the Modern Mind*, which became the most provocative statement of the movement's position. He was also an intellectual prod to his Yale colleague Karl N. Llewellyn, who wrote "Some Realism About Realism—Responding to Dean [Roscoe] Pound," *Harvard Law Review* (1931). The essay became a landmark in twentieth-century legal thought because it succeeded in summing up the essential nature of Legal Realism while pointing to the open and dynamic legal culture that emerged from the New Deal era. Llewellyn himself was involved in the American Law Institute, and after World War II, he published under its auspices the model Uniform Commercial Code.

Realists, however, regularly quarreled with one another from the movement's beginning, a development that dissipated much of its energies in theoretical hair splitting. In the case of Llewellyn, for example, his essay took direct aim at Dean Roscoe Pound of Harvard, one of the early advocates of Sociological Jurisprudence. Llewellyn argued that the way Realists examined the law was more significant than any particular values that analysis might reveal. Truth, for the Realists, was based on empirically established facts that yielded necessarily tentative and relative hypotheses. This approach meant that the Realists had difficulty articulating a consistent ethical and moral position; instead, with each situation a different set of facts influenced the course of the law. It was this relativism against which Pound reacted. The differences within the legal community only sharpened during the late 1930s and the 1940s with the rise and ultimate defeat of Nazism. Catholic legal educators in particular reasserted the view that human reason could discover certain universal principles of justice by analyzing philosophically the nature of reality. Such an analysis, they claimed, promised to yield not only a consistent rule of law but one rooted in moral principles.

The Realists did score one impressive victory. They stressed the virtues of an instrumental as opposed to a formalistic approach to social change through law at a time when the nation reeled under the weight of the Great Depression. The pragmatism and instrumentalism of the New Deal complemented the result-oriented and behavioral approach of Legal Realism, although the specific theories of Legal Realists seldom directly influenced the conduct of New Deal policy makers. Rather, the contribution was one of tone as squads of lawyers educated in the visions of Legal Realism and Sociological Jurisprudence arrived in Washington to administer the New Deal.

The New Deal and the Rise of Legal Liberalism

The Great Depression raised profound questions about the relationship of government to the economy and of the nation to the states, questions made critical in the legal culture by the Legal Realists' pronouncements about the instrumental character of law. Classical nineteenth-century liberalism stressed the passive rather than the active role of government. According to laissez-faire ideology, a government that governed least governed best. Unrestrained market forces were the fairest and most efficient means of deciding between winners and losers in life's economic race. Of course, government was never altogether passive; the states had bequeathed a rich tradition of governmental involvement in the economy that stretched back to the colonial era. These efforts had modest redistributional consequences; there was no broad consensus in favor of the idea that government at any level should provide for individual economic security. Moreover, what governmental activity did take place stressed promotion more than regulation. In the late nineteenth and early twentieth centuries, however, Progressive reformers pressed successfully for a shift from promotion to regulation. The purpose of the new regulatory state was to restore both business efficiency and economic justice by substituting administrative expertise for the traditional distributional scheme of political parties. Even big business found much to applaud in this regulatory movement, since it promised to replace cut-throat competition with predictable market relations. The Great Depression, then, merely hastened, albeit in dramatic fashion, a shift in the underlying character of liberalism.

The critical issue in the 1930s, therefore, was not whether government should intervene but the method of its intervention. During the previous decade, the direct role of the federal government in the economy declined. The Progressive insistence on an efficient and orderly economy did persist in such government-sponsored activities as the trade association movement. The administration of Republican President Herbert Hoover (1929–1933), for example, expected government to create the circumstances in which private individuals and groups would police themselves. With the Depression, however, this cheery vision of an economy founded on voluntary controls faded. In its place came the New Deal.

Democratic President Franklin D. Roosevelt, who came into office in 1933, masterminded the New Deal. One of the keystones of his program was greater involvement by the national government in the national economy. The alphabet soup of New Deal programs was controversial because it broke down the traditional scheme of federalism, raised the specter of a growing administrative state, and embraced certain social-welfare assumptions, the most significant of which was the belief that government had a positive duty to provide for the well-being of each citizen. The New Deal seems relatively benign today, in large measure because we have come to accept most of its tenets. But in the 1930s, with the nation shocked by an economic earthquake, it seemed a good deal more far-reaching, even revolutionary, to its detractors. The New Deal encountered its stiffest test before the Supreme Court, whose justices questioned the notion of emergency powers (on which much of FDR's and the Democratic Congress's actions rested), the delegation by Congress of its authority to administrative agencies, and the intervention by the national government in matters previously the domain of the states.

There were, as well, plenty of "little" New Deals in the states. There lawmakers passed a host of relief and regulatory measures that reflected, even though they seldom drew directly from, the instrumental vision of law proffered by the Legal Realists. Many of these state measures were also tested before the Supreme Court, where, like federal legislation, they came into collision with constitutional doctrines and judicial attitudes of another era.

The State and Federal Legislative Response

Economic panics and financial contractions were nothing new in American history; the Great Depression was only one more phase of the business cycle. Demands by debtors for relief had accompanied every downturn. State efforts to provide relief collided with the federal constitutional guarantee that no state could impair contracts. For example, Minnesota in 1933 passed the Mortgage Moratorium Law, which delayed foreclosures on real property, doing so with the hope that debtors might be able to regain their economic footing, repay their debts, and return to normal economic conduct. Unhappy creditors challenged such laws, arguing that protection of contracts was most important when economic conditions were most difficult.

The Minnesota law was only one of many measures passed by the states to deal with the hardships created by the Depression. New Jersey passed legislation adjusting insurance rates; Oklahoma decided to regulate the price of ice. Lawmakers in every state believed that the economic crisis warranted these measures.

Restoration of the moribund economy was the most important task before Roosevelt's administration and Congress. During his first one hundred days in office, FDR enjoyed broad support in Congress as well as in the business community, which realized that something had to be done to restore economic confidence. The President declared a four-day national bank holiday and suspended the payment of private debts in gold. He also successfully urged Congress to pass the Federal Securities Act (which required full disclosure to investors of information about new securities and established a new agency, the Securities and Exchange Commission, to oversee Wall Street) and the Glass-Steagall Act (which created the Federal Deposit Insurance Corporation to guarantee bank deposits up to $2,500), to create the Tennessee Valley

Authority (an independent public corporation to produce and sell electric power and nitrogen fertilizer as a way of promoting economic development in the poverty-stricken Tennessee River Valley), and to pass the Agricultural Adjustment Act (which subsidized farmers for not growing crops on the theory that as the supply of agricultural commodities declined, their value would increase).

The National Industrial Recovery Act of 1933 was only one of several measures that FDR's administration supported, but its commitment to economic planning, based on administrative decision making, was the heart of the so-called First New Deal. The preamble read something like a lawyer's brief, making the ingenious but questionable argument that since the Great Depression had placed burdens on interstate commerce, Congress could regulate vast areas of business and labor that it had previously left untouched. The measure was also a grab bag of political offerings; everybody got something. Business received authority to draft codes that were exempt from anti-trust laws; labor received, under Section 7(a), the right to bargain collectively and to have minimum wages and maximum hours, and those out of work were promised public works. The law established the National Recovery Administration (NRA) to facilitate code drafting and granted to the president authority to impose codes on any recalcitrant industry. Once the president approved a code, it had the force of law. In sum, the measure not only broke down many of the traditional lines blocking government involvement in the economy, but also delegated significant authority from Congress to the president and through him to an administrative agency. In this way, the New Deal built on the mobilization experience of World War I and the Progressive belief in rational administration. The emerging social-welfare state envisioned in the "First New Deal," therefore, relied on authority delegated by Congress to administrative bodies.

Despite the rich harvest of legislation and the rapid growth of the new administrative network in Washington, the Great Depression persisted. The economy did revive somewhat in 1934, giving the NRA an illusion of success, but by 1935 unemployment still stood at around 20 percent. The persistence of the Depression only deepened the sense of urgency and unease with government. FDR responded to a seeming failure of the "First New Deal" by embarking on an even more aggressive legislative campaign. This "Second New Deal" involved far-reaching legislation that brought even greater penetration by the national government through administrative authority into the day-to-day lives of the citizenry. For example, the National Labor Relations Act (also known as the Wagner Act) of 1935 bolstered labor's position by guaranteeing two of its most important long-term goals: the rights to unionize and to bargain collectively. The Social Security Act of 1935 established a vast system that provided a modest cushion for most Americans against unemployment, dependency, and old age. These and many other measures permanently affected American society; they were bold (but not radical) experiments that summoned federal legal authority to reshape certain underlying economic and social relationships. Even FDR's harshest critics agree today that he continued to deal from the same deck as Theodore Roosevelt, Woodrow Wilson, and even Herbert Hoover. His New Deal adjusted the system of American business enterprise to new realities by making certain economic practices, previously considered private, matters of public oversight.

While these New Deal measures have become the essence of the modern liberal, social-welfare state, they initially stirred great constitutional controversy. Congress passed the legislation of the "First New Deal" in great haste and often with sloppy wording. FDR gave the committee charged with writing the NRA one week to overhaul the nation's business structure.

The Supreme Court and the New Deal

The Hundred Days brought enormous excitement to the nation and with it a sense of hope for economic revival. An almost electric charge existed in Washington, and the new lawyers that piled into the New Deal administrative agencies did much to revive spirits. Roosevelt attracted into government bright young lawyers from some of the nation's most prestigious law schools. Legal Realist Jerome Frank, for example, became general counsel for the Agricultural Adjustment Agency. "I am—I make no secret of it—a reformer," Frank proudly admitted.[2] William O. Douglas, who had studied law at Columbia and believed that it was more a social science than a profession, became at age thirty-six the chief enforcement officer on the newly created Securities and Exchange Commission. And so it went—bright, aggressive, young lawyers seeking to remake the constitutional order through administrative and legal posts in a government dedicated to restoring the nation's economic health.

The justices of the High Court, however, took exception to much of the legislative enthusiasm of the New Deal, as it manifested itself both in Washington and in the states—with the result that the president and the justices were at odds with one another. In *New State Ice Company* v. *Liebman* (1932), for example, the Court struck down an Oklahoma statute as a violation of the principle that a state could regulate only those businesses "affected with a public interest." The justices concluded that the Oklahoma lawmakers had improperly invoked their police powers to foster an economic monopoly.

The nearly desperate circumstances surrounding the passage of the Minnesota Mortgage Moratorium Law seem to have influenced the justices. More than one-half of the citizens of Minnesota lived on farms, and they simply could not make ends meet. In the fall and winter of 1932, for example, corn was quoted as low as 8 cents per bushel, oats at 2 cents and wheat at 29 cents per bushel, eggs at 7 cents per dozen, and butter at 10 cents per pound. Moreover, mining, the state's second most important economic activity, was left reeling. The production of iron ore fell to less than 15 percent of normal production. The justices, in *Home Building and Loan Association* v. *Blaisdell* (1934), voted 5 to 4 to sustain the Minnesota law on the grounds that it was a proper emergency act that merely extended the period of redemption between foreclosure and sale of the farm, giving farmers a greater amount of time to raise money. The law did not cancel any outstanding debt; it simply adjusted the remedy available under the law. Chief Justice Charles Evans Hughes wrote for the majority that

> [w]hile emergency does not create power, emergency may furnish the occasion for the exercise of power. . . . The constitutional question presented in the light of an emergency is whether the power possessed embraces the particular conditions.
>
> When the provisions of the Constitution, in grant or restriction, are specific, so particularized as not to admit of construction, no question is presented. . . . But where

constitutional grants and limitations of power are set forth in general clauses, which afford a broad outline, the process of construction is essential to fill in the details. That is true of the contract clause. . . .

But full recognition of the occasion and general purpose of the clause does not suffice to fix its precise scope. Nor does an examination of the details of prior legislation in the States yield criteria which can be considered controlling. To ascertain the scope of the constitutional prohibition we examine the course of judicial decisions in its application. These put it beyond question that the prohibition is not an absolute one and is not to be read with literal exactness like a mathematical formula.

The New Dealers ignored many traditional limits of authority between the states and the nation, extended the commerce and taxing powers in novel ways, and invoked a constitutional theory of emergency powers to rationalize what they did. They were pragmatic and determined to end the Depression, but they were often impatient with prevailing constitutional rules.

The Supreme Court was not. The result was a collision between the justices, who saw their responsibility as remaining faithful to the Constitution as they understood it, and the administration, which charged that the Court was indifferent to the plight of millions of Americans. The administration's task of defending itself legally was made all the more difficult by its limited resources and internal bickering. Attorney General Homer Cummings, for example, expected that his office would represent the administration in every proceeding brought before the Supreme Court; at the same time, the chief counsels and heads of the various New Deal agencies wanted to protect their own turf. Moreover, many of the Department of Justice lawyers, who came from a different generation than the young New Dealers, were not only hostile to their youthful and exuberant colleagues but critical of much of the New Deal legislation. Even if there had been no infighting, the novel constitutional grounds on which the New Deal rested guaranteed close scrutiny by the High Court.

That scrutiny was ensured by the composition of the Court. The conservative wing of the Court was composed of the Four Horsemen, named after the Four Horsemen of the Apocalypse. Justices Willis Van Devanter, James McReynolds, George Sutherland, and Pierce Butler consistently voted together and against the New Deal. On the other wing were three generally liberal justices: Benjamin N. Cardozo, Louis D. Brandeis, and Harlan Fiske Stone. Between these two wings, on what was a highly contentious Court, rested the swing votes of Chief Justice Charles Evans Hughes and Justice Owen J. Roberts.

Schechter v. United States
295 U.S. 495 (1935)

Initially, the Supreme Court accepted some New Deal measures. The justices gave a favorable reading to two important state Depression laws. In Home Building and Loan Association v. *Blaisdell (1934), they sustained the Minnesota Mortgage Moratorium Law, and in* Nebbia v. *New York (1934), they upheld a New York law regulating the price of milk. In both instances, the Court had split 5 to 4. But when the Court began in December 1934 to hear cases involving hastily drawn "First New Deal" legislation, the administration quickly realized that it*

*was headed for trouble. Two of the main components of its program—the Nation-
al Industrial Recovery Act (NIRA) and the Agricultural Adjustment Act—came
under withering and ultimately fatal constitutional inspection. In* Schechter v.
United States, *the so-called sick-chicken case, the Court had to determine whether the live-poultry code of the NIRA was an unconstitutional regulation of intra-*
state *commerce and an excessive delegation of legislative power to the president.*

Mr. Chief Justice Hughes delivered the opinion of the Court.

    A. L. A. Schechter Poultry Corporation and Schechter Live Poultry Market are
corporations conducting wholesale poultry slaughterhouse markets in Brooklyn,
New York City. Joseph Schechter operated the latter corporation and also guaranteed
the credits of the former corporation which was operated by Martin, Alex and Aaron
Schechter. Defendants ordinarily purchase their live poultry from commission men
at the West Washington Market in New York City or at the railroad terminals serving
the City, but occasionally they purchase from commission men in Philadelphia.
They buy the poultry for slaughter and resale. After the poultry is trucked to their
slaughterhouse markets in Brooklyn, it is there sold, usually within twenty-four
hours, to retail poultry dealers and butchers who sell directly to consumers. The
poultry purchased from defendants is immediately slaughtered, prior to delivery, by
Schochtim [slaughterers working under Orthodox Jewish law and ritual to provide
kosher meat] in defendants' employ. Defendants do not sell poultry in interstate
commerce.

    The "Live Poultry Code" was promulgated under [Section] 3 of the National
Industrial Recovery Act. That section . . . authorizes the President to approve
"codes of fair competition." Such a code may be approved for a trade or industry,
upon application by one or more trade or industrial associations or groups, if the
President finds (1) that such associations or groups "impose no inequitable restrictions on admission to membership therein and are truly representative," and (2) that
such codes are not designed "to promote monopolies or to eliminate or oppress
small enterprises and will not operate to discriminate against them, and will tend to
effectuate the policy" of Title I of the Act. Such codes "shall not permit monopolies
or monopolistic practices." As a condition of his approval, the President may
"impose such conditions (including requirements for the making of reports and the
keeping of accounts) for the protection of consumers, competitors, employees, and
others, and in furtherance of the public interest, and may provide such exceptions to
and exemptions from the provisions of such code as the President in his discretion
deems necessary to effectuate the policy herein declared." Where such a code has
not been approved, the President may prescribe one, either on his own motion or on
complaint. Violation of any provision of a code (so approved or prescribed) "in any
transaction in or affecting interstate or foreign commerce" is made a misdemeanor
punishable by a fine of not more than $500 for each offense, and each day the
violation continues to be deemed a separate offense.

                *   *   *

    First.   Two preliminary points are stressed by the Government with respect to
the appropriate approach to the important questions presented. We are told that the
provision of the statute authorizing the adoption of codes must be viewed in the light

of the grave national crisis with which Congress was confronted. Undoubtedly, the conditions to which power is addressed are always to be considered when the exercise of power is challenged. Extraordinary conditions may call for extraordinary remedies. But the argument necessarily stops short of an attempt to justify action which lies outside the sphere of constitutional authority. Extraordinary conditions do not create or enlarge constitutional power. The Constitution established a national government with powers deemed to be adequate, as they have proved to be both in war and peace, but these powers of the national government are limited by the constitutional grants. Those who act under these grants are not at liberty to transcend the imposed limits because they believe that more or different power is necessary. Such assertions of extra-constitutional authority were anticipated and precluded by the explicit terms of the Tenth Amendment,—"the powers not delegated to the United States by the Constitution, nor prohibited by it to the States, are reserved to the States respectively, or to the people."

Second.   The question of the delegation of legislative power.

*   *   *

[W]e turn to the Recovery Act to ascertain what limits have been set to the exercise of the President's discretion. First, the President, as a condition of approval, is required to find that the trade or industrial associations or groups which propose a code, "impose no inequitable restrictions on admission to membership" and are "truly representative." That condition, however, relates only to the status of the initiators of the new laws and not to the permissible scope of such laws. Second, the President is required to find that the code is not "designed to promote monopolies or to eliminate or oppress small enterprises and will not operate to discriminate against them." And, to this is added a proviso that the code "shall not permit monopolies or monopolistic practices." But these restrictions leave virtually untouched the field of policy envisaged by section one, and, in that wide field of legislative possibilities, the proponents of a code, refraining from monopolistic designs, may roam at will and the President may approve or disapprove their proposals as he may see fit. That is the precise effect of the further finding that the President is to make—that the code "will tend to effectuate the policy of this title." While this is called a finding, it is really but a statement of an opinion as to the general effect upon the promotion of trade or industry of a scheme of laws. These are the only findings which Congress has made essential in order to put into operation a legislative code having the aims described in the "Declaration of policy."

Nor is the breadth of the President's discretion left to the necessary implications of this limited requirement as to his findings. As already noted, the President in approving a code may impose his own conditions, adding to or taking from what is proposed, as "in his discretion" he thinks necessary "to effectuate the policy" declared by the Act. Of course, he has no less liberty when he prescribes a code on his own motion or on complaint, and he is free to prescribe one if a code has not been approved. The Act provides for the creation by the President of administrative agencies to assist him, but the action or reports of such agencies, or of his other assistants,—their recommendations and findings in relation to the making of codes—have no sanction beyond the will of the President, who may accept, modify or reject them as he pleases. Such recommendations or findings in no way limit the authority which 3 undertakes to vest in the President with no other conditions than those there specified. And this authority relates to a host of different trades and industries, thus extending the President's discretion to all the varieties of laws which he may deem to be beneficial in dealing with the vast array of commercial and industrial activities throughout the country.

Such a sweeping delegation of legislative power finds no support in the decisions upon which the Government especially relies.

*   *   *

Third.   The question of the application of the provisions of the Live Poultry Code to intrastate transactions. Although the validity of the codes (apart from the question of delegation) rests upon the commerce clause of the Constitution, 3(a) is not in terms limited to interstate and foreign commerce. From the generality of its terms, and from the argument of the Government at the bar, it would appear that 3(a) was designed to authorize codes without that limitation. But under 3(f) penalties are confined to violations of a code provision "in any transaction in or affecting interstate or foreign commerce." This aspect of the case presents the question whether the particular provisions of the Live Poultry Code, which the defendants were convicted for violating and for having conspired to violate, were within the regulating power of Congress.

These provisions relate to the hours and wages of those employed by defendants in their slaughterhouses in Brooklyn and to the sales there made to retail dealers and butchers. The undisputed facts thus afford no warrant for the argument that the poultry handled by defendants at their slaughterhouse markets was in a "current" or "flow" of interstate commerce and was thus subject to congressional regulation. . . .

Did the defendants' transactions directly "affect" interstate commerce so as to be subject to federal regulations? The power of Congress extends not only to the regulation of transactions which are part of interstate commerce, but to the protection of that commerce from injury. It matters not that the injury may be due to the conduct of those engaged in intrastate operations.

*   *   *

In determining how far the federal government may go in controlling intrastate transactions upon the ground that they "affect" interstate commerce, there is a necessary and well-established distinction between direct and indirect effects. The precise line can be drawn only as individual cases arise, but the distinction is clear in principle. Direct effects are illustrated by the railroad cases we have cited, e.g., the effect of failure to use prescribed safety appliances on railroads which are the highways of both interstate and intrastate commerce, injury to an employee engaged in interstate transportation by the negligence of an employee engaged in an intrastate movement, the fixing of rates for intrastate transportation which unjustly discriminate against interstate commerce. But where the effect of intrastate transactions upon interstate commerce is merely indirect, such transactions remain within the domain of state power. If the commerce clause were construed to reach all enterprises and transactions which could be said to have an indirect effect upon interstate commerce, the federal authority would embrace practically all the activities of the people and the authority of the State over its domestic concerns would exist only by sufferance of the federal government. In deed, on such a theory, even the development of the State's commercial facilities would be subject to federal control.

The question of chief importance relates to the provisions of the Code as to the hours and wages of those employed in defendants' slaughterhouse markets. It is plain that these requirements are imposed in order to govern the details of defendants' management of their local business. The persons employed in slaughtering and selling in local trade are not employed in interstate commerce. Their hours and wages have no direct relation to interstate commerce. The question of how many hours these employees should work and what they should be paid differs in no essential respect from similar questions in other local businesses which handle commodities brought into a State and there dealt in as a part of its internal commerce. This appears from an examination of the considerations urged by the Government with respect to conditions in the poultry trade. Thus, the Government argues that hours and wages affect prices; that slaughterhouse men sell at a small margin above operating costs; that labor represents 50 to 60 percent of these costs; that a slaughterhouse operator paying lower wages or reducing his cost by exacting long hours of work, translates his saving into lower prices; that this results in demands for a cheaper grade of goods; and that the cutting of prices brings about a demoralization of the price structure. Similar conditions may be adduced in relation to other business.

*   *   *

It is not the province of the Court to consider the economic advantages or disadvantages of such a centralized system. It is sufficient to say that the Federal Constitution does not provide for it. Our growth and development have called for wide use of the commerce power of the federal government in its control over the expanded activities of commerce, and in protecting that commerce from burdens, interferences, and conspiracies to restrain and monopolize it. But the authority of the federal government may not be pushed to such an extreme as to destroy the distinction, which the commerce clause itself establishes, between commerce "among the several States" and the internal concerns of a State. The same answer must be made to the contention that is based upon the serious economic situation which led to the passage of the Recovery Act,—the fall in prices, the decline in wages and employment, and the curtailment of the market for commodities. Stress is laid upon the great importance of maintaining wage distributions which would provide the necessary stimulus in starting "the cumulative forces making for expanding commercial activity." Without in any way disparaging this motive, it is enough to say that the recuperative efforts of the federal government must be made in a manner consistent with the authority granted by the Constitution.

We are of the opinion that the attempt through the provisions of the Code to fix the hours and wages of employees of defendants in their intrastate business was not a valid exercise of federal power.

United States v. *Butler*
297 U.S. 1 (1936)

The Agricultural Adjustment Act was designed to raise agricultural prices by limiting crop production. The AAA established a processing tax to fund crop subsidies and soil restrictions. Where the NIRA had relied on the commerce power, the AAA depended on the taxing power for its constitutional authority. Critics complained that the government had taken on the unconstitutional task of controlling agriculture and that the tax was an integral part of this unconstitutional plan. The government insisted that it could not be challenged in its taxing authority, basing its view on Frothingham v. Mellon *(1923). The Court held in* Frothingham *that taxpayers had no standing to question how the federal government spent its tax revenues. The conservatives on the Court, in a part of the decision not reprinted below, disposed of this precedent.*

Justice Roberts for the majority.

It is inaccurate and misleading to speak of the exaction from processors prescribed by the challenged act as a tax, or to say that as a tax it is subject to no infirmity. A tax, in the general understanding of the term, and as used in the Constitution, signifies an exaction for the support of the Government. The word has never been thought to connote the expropriation of money from one group for the benefit of another. . . . But manifestly no justification for it can be found unless as an integral part of such regulation. The exaction cannot be wrested out of its setting, denominated an excise for raising revenue and legalized by ignoring its purpose as a mere instrumentality for bringing about a desired end. To do this would be to shut our eyes to what all others than we can see and understand. . . .

We conclude that the act is one regulating agricultural production; that the tax is a mere incident of such regulation and that the respondents have standing to challenge the legality of the exaction.

The Government asserts that even if the respondents may question the propriety of the appropriation embodied in the statute their attack must fail because Article I, [Section] 8 of the Constitution authorizes the contemplated expenditure of the funds raised by the tax. This contention presents the great and the controlling question in the case. . . .

There should be no misunderstanding as to the function of this court in such a case. It is sometimes said that the court assumes a power to overrule or control the action of the people's representatives. This is a misconception. The Constitution is the supreme law of the land ordained and established by the people. All legislation must conform to the principles it lays down. When an act of Congress is appropriately challenged in the courts as not conforming to the constitutional mandate the judicial branch of the Government has only one duty,—to lay the article of the Constitution which is invoked beside the statute which is challenged and to decide whether the latter squares with the former. All the court does, or can do, is to announce its considered judgment upon the question. The only power it has, if such it may be called, is the power of judgment. This court neither approves nor condemns any legislative policy. Its delicate and difficult office is to ascertain and declare whether the legislation is in accordance with, or in contravention of, the provisions of the Constitution; and, having done that, its duty ends.

The clause thought to authorize the legislation,—the first,—confers upon the Congress power "to lay and collect Taxes, Duties, Imposts and Excises, to pay the Debts and provide for the common Defense and general Welfare of the United States. . . ." It is not contended that this provision grants power to regulate agricultural production upon the theory that such legislation would promote the general welfare. The Government concedes that the phrase "to provide for the general welfare" qualifies the power "to lay and collect taxes." The view that the clause grants power to provide for the general welfare, independently of the taxing power, has never been authoritatively accepted. . . . The true construction undoubtedly is that the only thing granted is the power to tax for the purpose of providing funds for payment of the nation's debts and making provision for the general welfare.

Nevertheless the Government asserts that warrant is found in this clause for the adoption of the Agricultural Adjustment Act. The argument is that Congress may appropriate and authorize the spending of moneys for the "general welfare"; that the phrase should be liberally construed to cover anything conducive to national welfare; that decision as to what will promote such welfare rests with Congress alone, and the courts may not review its determination; and finally that the appropriation under attack was in fact for the general welfare of the United States.

Since the foundation of the Nation sharp differences of opinion have persisted as to the true interpretation of the phrase. Madison asserted it amounted to no more than a reference to the other powers enumerated in the subsequent clauses of the same section; that, as the United States is a government of limited and enumerated powers, the grant of power to tax and spend for the general national welfare must be confined to the enumerated legislative fields committed to the Congress. In this view the phrase is mere tautology, for taxation and appropriation are or may be necessary incidents of the exercise of any of the enumerated legislative powers. Hamilton, on the other hand, maintained the clause confers a power separate and distinct from those later enumerated, is not restricted in meaning by the grant of them, and Congress consequently has a substantive power to tax and to appropriate, limited only by the requirement that it shall be exercised to provide for the general welfare of the United States. Each contention has had the support of those whose views are entitled to weight. . . .

We are not now required to ascertain the scope of the phrase "general welfare of the United States" or to determine whether an appropriation in aid of agriculture falls within it. Wholly apart from that question, another principle embedded in our Constitution prohibits the enforcement of the Agricultural Adjustment Act. The act invades the reserved rights of the states. It is a salutary plan to regulate and control agricultural production, a matter beyond the powers delegated to the federal government. The tax, the appropriation of the funds raised, and the direction for their disbursement, are but parts of the plan. They are but means to an unconstitutional end.

From the accepted doctrine that the United States is a government of delegated powers, it follows that those not expressly granted, or reasonably to be implied from such as are conferred, are reserved to the states or to the people. To forestall any suggestion to the contrary, the Tenth Amendment was adopted. The same proposition, otherwise stated, is that powers not granted are prohibited. None to regulate agricultural production is given, and therefore legislation by Congress for that purpose is forbidden.

It is an established principle that the attainment of a prohibited end may not be accomplished under the pretext of the exertion of powers which are granted.

                    *   *   *

Congress could not, under the pretext of raising revenue, lay a tax on processors who refuse to pay a certain price for cotton, and exempt those who agree so to do, with the purpose of benefiting producers.

If the taxing power may not be used as the instrument to enforce a regulation of matters of state concern with respect to which the Congress has no authority to interfere, may it, as in the present case, be employed to raise the money necessary to purchase a compliance which the Congress is powerless to command?

The Government asserts that whatever might be said against the validity of the plan if compulsory, it is constitutionally sound because the end is accomplished by voluntary cooperation. There are two sufficient answers to the contention. The regulation is not in fact voluntary. The farmer, of course, may refuse to comply, but the price of such refusal is the loss of benefits. The amount offered is intended to be sufficient to exert pressure on him to agree to the proposed regulation. The power to confer or withhold unlimited benefits is the power to coerce or destroy.

Congress has no power to enforce its commands on the farmer to the ends sought by the Agricultural Adjustment Act. It must follow that it may not indirectly accomplish those ends by taxing and spending to purchase compliance. . . . It does not help to declare that local conditions throughout the nation have created a situation of national concern; for this is but to say that whenever there is a widespread similarity of local conditions, Congress may ignore constitutional limitations upon its own powers and usurp those reserved to the states. If, in lieu of compulsory regulation of subjects within the states' reserved jurisdiction, which is prohibited, the Congress could invoke the taxing and spending power as a means to accomplish the same end, Article I would become the instrument for total subversion of the governmental powers reserved to the individual states.

If the act before us is a proper exercise of the federal taxing power, evidently the regulation of all industry throughout the United States may be accomplished by similar exercises of the same power. It would be possible to exact money from one branch of an industry and pay it to another branch in every field of activity which lies within the province of the states. The mere threat of such a procedure might well induce the surrender of rights and the compliance with federal regulation as the price of continuance in business.

We have held in *Schechter Poultry Corp.* v. *United States*, that Congress has no power to regulate wages and hours of labor in a local business. If the petitioner is right, this very end may be accomplished by appropriating money to be paid to employers from the federal treasury under contracts whereby they agree to comply with certain standards fixed by federal law or by contract.

Until recently no suggestion of the existence of any such power in the Federal Government has been advanced. The expressions of the framers of the Constitution, the decisions of this court interpreting that instrument, and the writings of great commentators will be searched in vain for any suggestion that there exists in the clause under discussion or elsewhere in the Constitution, the authority whereby every provision and every fair implication from that instrument may be subverted, the independence of the individual states obliterated, and the United States converted into a central government exercising uncontrolled police power in every state of the Union, superseding all local control or regulation of the affairs or concerns of the states.

Since, as we have pointed out, there was no power in the Congress to impose the contested exaction, it could not lawfully ratify or confirm what an executive officer had done in that regard. Consequently the Act of 1935 does not affect the rights of the parties.

The judgment is

Affirmed.

Mr. Justice Stone, dissenting.

I think the judgment should be reversed.

That the governmental power of the purse is a great one is not now for the first time announced. Every student of the history of government and economics is aware of its magnitude and of its existence in every civilized government. Both were well understood by the framers of the Constitution when they sanctioned the grant of the spending power to the federal government, and both were recognized by Hamilton and Story, whose views of the spending power as standing on a parity with the other powers specifically granted, have hereto been generally accepted.

The suggestion that it must now be curtailed by judicial fiat because it may be abused by unwise use hardly rises to the dignity of argument. So may judicial power be abused.

A tortured construction of the Constitution is not to be justified by recourse to extreme examples of reckless congressional spending which might occur if courts could not prevent—expenditures which, even if they could be thought to effect any national purpose, would be possible only by action of a legislature lost to all sense of public responsibility. Such suppositions are addressed to the mind accustomed to believe that it is the business of courts to sit in judgment on the wisdom of legislative action. Courts are not the only agency of government that must be assumed to have capacity to govern. Congress and the courts both unhappy may falter or be mistaken in the performance of their constitutional duty. But interpretation of our great charter of government which proceeds on any assumption that the responsibility for the preservation of our institutions is the exclusive concern of any one of the three branches of government, or that it alone can save them from destruction is far more likely, in the long run, "to obliterate the constituent members" of "an indestructible union of indestructible states" than the frank recognition that language, even of a constitution, may mean what it says: that the power to tax and spend includes the power to relieve a nationwide economic maladjustment by conditional gifts of money.

FDR's Court-Packing Plan

By the presidential election of 1936, the Supreme Court had overturned or significantly limited all the major parts of the "First New Deal," and the justices were about to tackle the new stream of laws that encompassed the "Second New Deal." Roosevelt won a landslide victory in 1936 over his Republican opponent, Alfred Landon, and he intended to start his second term by taking on his last significant adversary—the Supreme Court. Roosevelt was especially frustrated because during his first term no vacancies had occurred on the high bench. Critics complained that the justices were too old and out of touch with the times to render decisions during a period of such great national crisis. The newspaper columnists Drew Pearson and Robert S. Allen in 1936 wrote an exposé of the Court, and the public fastened its title, *The Nine Old Men*, on the justices. The description was disingenuous; the oldest member of the Court, Louis D. Brandeis, while thoroughly independent, was also a member of the Court's liberal wing.

FRANKLIN ROOSEVELT

Fireside Chat on the "Court-Packing" Bill
March 9, 1937

This radio address by President Roosevelt was his strongest effort to garner public support for his "court-packing" plan. It came at a time when FDR enjoyed enormous popular support, as his victory at the polls only a few months before had demonstrated. The Judiciary Reorganization Bill, however, stirred public anxiety because it seemed to place political considerations above the rule of law. The measure also divided the Democratic party, gave conservative Republicans an issue on which they successfully attacked the president for the first time, and raised in dramatic fashion one of the most important constitutional issues of the New Deal—separation of powers.

Tonight, sitting at my desk in the White House, I make my first radio report to the people in my second term of office. . . .

In 1933 you and I knew that we must never let our economic system get completely out of joint again—that we could not afford to take the risk of another great depression.

We also become convinced that the only way to avoid a repetition of those dark days was to have a government with power to prevent and to cure the abuses and the inequalities which had thrown that system out of joint.

The American people have learned from the depression. For in the last three national elections an overwhelming majority of them voted a mandate that the Congress and the President begin the task of providing that protection—not after long years of debate, but now.

The Courts, however, have cast doubts on the ability of the elected Congress to protect us against catastrophe by meeting squarely our modern social and economic conditions.

We are at a crisis, a crisis in our ability to proceed with that protection. . . .

I want to talk with you very simply tonight about the need for present action in this crisis—the need to meet the unanswered challenge of one-third of a Nation ill-nourished, ill-clad, ill-housed.

Last Thursday I described the American form of Government as a three-horse team provided by the Constitution to the American people so that their field might be plowed. The three horses are, of course, the Congress, the Executive and the Courts. Two of the horses, the Congress and the Executive, are pulling in unison today; the third is not. Those who have intimated that the President of the United

States is trying to drive that team, overlook the simple fact that the President, as Chief Executive, is himself one of the horses.

It is the American people themselves who are in the driver's seat. It is the American people themselves who want the furrow plowed.

It is the American people themselves who expect the third horse to pull in unison with the other two.

I hope that you have re-read the Constitution of the United States in these past few weeks. Like the Bible, it ought to be read again and again.

It is an easy document to understand when you remember that it was called into being because the Articles of Confederation under which the original thirteen States tried to operate after the Revolution showed the need of a National Government with power enough to handle national problems. In its Preamble, the Constitution states that it was intended to form a more perfect Union and promote the general welfare; and the powers given to the Congress to carry out those purposes can best be described by saying that they were all the powers needed to meet each and every problem which then had a national character and which could not be met by merely local action.

But the framers went further. Having in mind that in succeeding generations many other problems then undreamed of would become national problems, they gave to the Congress the ample broad powers "to levy taxes . . . and provide for the common defense and general welfare of the United States."

That, my friends, is what I honestly believe to have been the clear and underlying purpose of the patriots who wrote a Federal Constitution to create a National Government with national power, intended as they said, "to form a more perfect union . . . for ourselves and our posterity."

For nearly twenty years there was no conflict between the Congress and the Court. Then in 1803, Congress passed a statute which the Court said violated an express provision of the Constitution. The Court claimed the power to declare it unconstitutional and did so declare it. But a little later the Court itself admitted that it was an extraordinary power to exercise and through Mr. Justice Washington laid down this limitation upon it. He said: "It is but a decent respect due to the wisdom, the integrity and the patriotism of the Legislative body, by which any law is passed, to presume in favor of its validity until its violation of the Constitution is proved beyond all reasonable doubt."

But since the rise of the modern movement for social and economic progress through legislation, the Court has more and more often and more and more boldly asserted a power to veto laws passed by the Congress and by State Legislatures in complete disregard of this original limitation, which I have just read.

In the last four years the sound rule of giving statutes the benefit of all reasonable doubt has been cast aside. The Court has been acting not as a judicial body, but as a policy-making body.

The Court, in addition to the proper use of its judicial functions, has improperly set itself up as a third House of the Congress—a super-legislature, as one of the Justices has called it—reading into the Constitution words and implications which are not there, and which were never intended to be there.

We have, therefore, reached the point as a Nation where we must take action to save the Constitution from the Court, and the Court from itself. We must find a way to take an appeal from the Supreme Court to the Constitution itself. We want a Supreme Court which will do justice under the Constitution—not over it. In our Courts we want a government of laws and not of men.

I want—as all Americans want—an independent judiciary as proposed by the framers of the Constitution. That means a Supreme Court that will enforce the Constitution as written—that will refuse to amend the Constitution by the arbitrary exercise of judicial power—amendment, in other words, by judicial say-so. It does not mean a judiciary so independent that it can deny the existence of facts which are universally recognized.

What is my proposal? It is simply this: Whenever a Judge or Justice of any Federal Court has reached the age of seventy and does not avail himself of the opportunity to retire on a pension, a new member shall be appointed by the President then in office, with the approval, as required by the Constitution, of the Senate of the United States.

That plan has two chief purposes. By bringing into the Judicial system a steady and continuing stream of new and younger blood, I hope, first, to make the administration of all Federal justice, from the bottom to the top, speedier and, therefore, less costly; secondly, to bring to the decision of social and economic problems younger men who have had personal experience and contact with modern facts and circumstances under which average men have to live and work. This plan will save our national Constitution from hardening of the judicial arteries.

*   *   *

Those opposing this plan have sought to arouse prejudice and fear by crying that I am seeking to "pack" the Supreme Court and that a baneful precedent will be established.

What do they mean by the words "packing the Supreme Court"?

Let me answer this question with a bluntness that will end all honest misunderstanding of my purposes.

If by that phrase "packing the Court" it is charged that I wish to place on the bench spineless puppets who would disregard the law and would decide specific cases as I wished them to be decided, I make this answer—that no President fit for this office would appoint, and no Senate of honorable men fit for their office would confirm, that kind of appointees to the Supreme Court.

But if by that phrase the charge is made that I would appoint and the Senate would confirm Justices worthy to sit beside present members of the Court who understand modern conditions—that I will appoint Justices who will not undertake to override the judgment of the Congress on legislative policy—that I will appoint Justices who will act as Justices and not as legislators—if the appointment of such Justices can be called "packing the Court," then I say that I, and with me the vast majority of the American people, favor doing just that thing—now.

*   *   *

So, I now propose that we establish by law an assurance against any . . . ill-balanced Court in the future. I propose that hereafter, when a Judge reaches the age of seventy, a new and younger Judge shall be added to the Court automatically. In this way I propose to enforce a sound public policy by law instead of leaving the composition of our Federal Courts, including the highest, to be determined by chance or the personal decision of individuals.

*   *   *

Like all lawyers, like all Americans, I regret the necessity of this controversy. But the welfare of the United States, and indeed of the Constitution itself, is what we all must think about first. Our difficulty with the Court today rises not from the Court as an institution but from human beings within it. We cannot yield our constitutional destiny to the personal judgment of a few men who, being fearful of the future, would deny us the necessary means of dealing with the present.

This plan of mine is no attack on the Court; it seeks to restore the Court to its rightful and historic place in our system of Constitutional Government and to have it resume its high task of building anew on the Constitution "a system of living law." The Court itself can best undo what the Court has done. . . .

Note: The Fate of FDR's Court-Packing Plan

Roosevelt cloaked his court-packing scheme in the rhetoric of judicial reform. More judges were required to clear the dockets of the lower federal courts. While the dockets of the lower federal courts had expanded dramatically in the twentieth century, Chief Justice Hughes testified before Congress that more members of the High Court would only slow its work. In the final analysis, the president attempted to pull every possible lever to make his proposal, which was blatantly political, work by appealing to those interests with grievances against the courts. For example, Roosevelt and his attorney general, Homer Cummings, sought labor support by stressing that Democratic appointees to the lower courts would curtail the practice of federal judges issuing injunctions against workers engaged in strikes and lockouts. To this extent, FDR's proposal for new blood on the federal courts confirmed one of the basic assumptions of the Legal Realists: judges protected the interests with which they were associated.

The Judiciary Reorganization Bill, while probably doomed from the outset, suffered from some back luck. Senator Joseph T. Robinson, the Senate floor manager for the bill and a strong ally of the president, died during the summer debate over the measure. The Court itself also seemingly influenced the outcome; at least some historians believe that a few of the justices read the election returns.

The Retreat from Economic Substantive Due Process

West Coast Hotel v. *Parrish*
300 U.S. 379 (1937)

This case involved a Washington State minimum wage law that applied exclusively to women. The Court had previously dealt with such matters and had sharply limited the authority of the states and Congress to pass such legislation. As late as June 1936, for example, the justices in Morehead v. *New York ex rel.* Tipaldo *overturned by a 5 to 4 vote a model New York State minimum wage law.*

Justice George Sutherland rested his majority opinion on the leading precedent,
Adkins v. Children's Hospital *(1923). The justices in that case had invalidated a
Washington, D.C., minimum wage law as a violation of the due process clause of
the Fifth Amendment. The* West Coast Hotel *case involved similar concerns with
substantive due process of law and freedom to contract as they arose under the
Fourteenth Amendment. The decision, coming as it did on the heels of FDR's
court-packing plan, also clearly signaled the Court's acceptance of the main
features of the New Deal.*

Mr. Chief Justice Hughes delivered the opinion of the Court.

This case presents the question of the constitutional validity of the minimum
wage law of the State of Washington.

*   *   *

The appellant conducts a hotel. The appellee Elsie Parrish was employed as a
chambermaid and (with her husband) brought this suit to recover the difference
between the wages paid her and the minimum wage fixed pursuant to the state law.
The minimum wage is $14.50 per week of 48 hours. The appellant challenged the act
as repugnant to the due process clause of the Fourteenth Amendment of the Constitution of the United States. The Supreme Court of the State, reversing the trial court,
sustained the statute and directed judgment for the plaintiffs. The case is here on
appeal.

*   *   *

The principle which must control our decision is not in doubt. The constitutional
provision invoked is the due process clause of the Fourteenth Amendment governing
the States, as the due process clause invoked in the *Adkins* case governed Congress.
In each case the violation alleged by those attacking minimum wage regulation for
women is deprivation of freedom of contract. What is this freedom? The Constitution does not speak of freedom of contract. It speaks of liberty and prohibits the
deprivation of liberty without due process of law. In prohibiting that deprivation the
Constitution does not recognize an absolute and uncontrollable liberty. Liberty in
each of its phases has its history and connotation. But the liberty safeguarded is
liberty in a social organization which requires the protection of law against the evils
which menace the health, safety, morals and welfare of the people. Liberty under
the Constitution is thus necessarily subject to the restraints of due process, and
regulation which is reasonable in relation to its subject and is adopted in the interests
of the community is due process.

This essential limitation of liberty in general governs freedom of contract in
particular.

This power under the [Fourteenth Amendment to the] Constitution to restrict
freedom of contract has had many illustrations. That it may be exercised in the
public interest with respect to contracts between employer and employee is
undeniable.

In dealing with the relation of employer and employed, the legislature has
necessarily a wide field of discretion in order that there may be suitable protection
of health and safety, and that peace and good order may be promoted through
regulations designed to insure wholesome conditions of work and freedom from
oppression.

The point that has been strongly stressed that adult employees should be deemed competent to make their own contracts was decisively met nearly forty years ago in *Holden* v. *Hardy*, supra, where we pointed out the inequality in the footing of the parties.

It is manifest that this principle is peculiarly applicable in relation to the employment of women in whose protection the State has a special interest. That phase of the subject received elaborate consideration in *Muller* v. *Oregon* (1908) where the constitutional authority of the State to limit the working hours of women was sustained.

*   *   *

We think that the decision in the *Adkins* case was a departure from the true application of the principles governing the regulation by the State of relation of employer and employed.

With full recognition of the earnestness and vigor which characterizes the prevailing opinion in the *Adkins* case, we find it impossible to reconcile that ruling with these well-considered declarations. What can be closer to the public interest than the health of women and the protection from unscrupulous and overreaching employers? And if the protection of women is a legitimate end of the exercise of state power, how can it be said that the requirement of the payment of a minimum wage fairly fixed in order to meet the very necessities of existence is not an admissible means to that end? The legislature of the State was clearly entitled to consider the situation of women in employment, the fact that they are in the class receiving the least pay, that their bargaining power is relatively weak, and that they are the ready victims of those who would take advantage of their necessitous circumstances. The legislature was entitled to adopt measures to reduce the evils of the "sweating system," the exploiting of workers at wages so low as to be insufficient to meet the bare cost of living, thus making their very helplessness the occasion of a most injurious competition. The legislature had the right to consider that its minimum wage requirements would be an important aid in carrying out its policy of protection. The adoption of similar requirements by many States evidences a deep-seated conviction both as to the presence of the evil and as to the means adapted to check it. Legislative response to that conviction cannot be regarded as arbitrary or capricious, and that is all we have to decide. Even if the wisdom of the policy be regarded as debatable and its effects uncertain, still the legislature is entitled to its judgment.

There is an additional and compelling consideration which recent economic experience has brought into a strong light. The exploitation of a class of workers who are in an unequal position with respect to bargaining power and are thus relatively defenseless against the denial of a living wage is not only detrimental to their health and well being but casts a direct burden for their support upon the community. What these workers lose in wages the taxpayers are called upon to pay. The bare cost of living must be met. We may take judicial notice of the unparalleled demands for relief which arose during the recent period of depression and still continue to an alarming extent despite the degree of economic recovery which has been achieved. It is unnecessary to cite official statistics to establish what is of common knowledge through the length and breadth of the land. While in the instant case no factual brief has been presented, there is no reason to doubt that the State of

Washington has encountered the same social problem that is present elsewhere. The community is not bound to provide what is in effect a subsidy for unconscionable employers. The community may direct its law-making power to correct the abuse which springs from their selfish disregard of the public interest. The argument that the legislation in question constitutes an arbitrary discrimination, because it does not extend to men, is unavailing. This Court has frequently held that the legislative authority, acting within its proper field, is not bound to extend its regulation to all cases which it might possibly reach. The legislature "is free to recognize degrees of harm and it may confine its restrictions to those classes of cases where the need is deemed to be clearest." If "the law presumably hits the evil where it is most felt, it is not to be overthrown because there are other instances to which it might have been applied." There is no "doctrinaire requirement" that the legislation should be couched in all embracing terms. . . . This familiar principle has repeatedly been applied to legislation which singles out women, and particular classes of women, in the exercise of the State's protective power. Their relative need in the presence of the evil, no less than the existence of the evil itself, is a matter for the legislative judgment.

Our conclusion is that the case of *Adkins v. Children's Hospital* should be, and it is, overruled. The judgment of the Supreme Court of the State of Washington is
Affirmed.

Mr. Justice Sutherland, dissenting:

Under our form of government, where the written Constitution, by its own terms, is the supreme law, some agency, of necessity, must have the power to say the final word as to the validity of a statute assailed as unconstitutional. The Constitution makes it clear that the power has been entrusted to this court when the question arises in a controversy within its jurisdiction; and so long as the power remains there, its exercise cannot be avoided without betrayal of the trust.

*   *   *

It is urged that the question involved should now receive fresh consideration, among other reasons, because of the "economic conditions which have super-vened"; but the meaning of the Constitution does not change with the ebb and flow of economic events. We frequently are told in more general words that the Constitution must be construed in the light of the present. If by that it is meant that the Constitution is made up of living words that apply to every new condition which they include, the statement is quite true. But to say, if that be intended, that the words of the Constitution mean today what they did not mean when written—that is, that they do not apply to a situation now to which they would have applied—then is to rob that instrument of the essential element which continues it in force as the people have made it until they, and not their official agents, have made it otherwise.

The judicial function is that of interpretation; it does not include the power of amendment under the guise of interpretation. To miss the point of difference between the two is to miss all that the phrase "supreme law of the land" stands for and to convert what was intended as inescapable and enduring mandates into mere moral reflections.

If the Constitution, intelligently and reasonably construed in the light of these principles, stands in the way of desirable legislation, the blame must rest upon that instrument, and not upon the court for enforcing it according to its terms. The remedy in that situation—and the only true remedy—is to amend the Constitution.

Note: The Decline of Substantive Due Process

Historians and observers of the Court have frequently described the decision in *West Coast Hotel* as a "switch in time that saved nine." There is no doubt that the Court changed direction, and the justices' determination to overrule their earlier holding in *Adkins* underscored their serious purpose. The Court subsequently indicated that its behavior in *West Coast Hotel* was no fluke. Two weeks later, it decided *National Labor Relations Board* v. *Jones & Laughlin Steel Company*, in which Chief Justice Hughes used Holmes's "stream of commerce" theory to sustain the constitutionality of the Wagner Act. On May 24, 1937, the justices upheld the Social Security Act in *Stewart Machine Company* v. *Davis*, a decision that repudiated Roberts's narrow view of the taxing power in *Butler* (1936). In a companion case, *Helvering* v. *Davis* (1937), Justice Cardozo actually cited Roberts as authority to sketch an expansive view of the general welfare clause in support of the old-age tax and benefits provisions of the Social Security Act. While the justices did not formally abandon substantive due process in economic regulatory cases until *Ferguson* v. *Skrupa* (1963), there was no doubt that they had retreated from the business of trying to regulate business.

Ordered Liberty, Preferred Positions, and Selective Incorporation

While the Supreme Court had removed itself from matters of economic regulation after 1937, its influence over American life grew, not diminished. Almost immediately, the justices began to build a new line of cases involving civil liberties and civil rights. To do so, the justices had to reconsider the scope of the Fourteenth Amendment as it applied to the Bill of Rights. The problem before the Court became the extent to which the Fourteenth Amendment had incorporated—that is, made a part of—the Bill of Rights guarantees. Such a matter was crucial, since the Court had historically taken the position that the Bill of Rights applied against only the states and not the national government. The Roosevelt Court appointees (and their successors) never agreed on the matter, however; the result was a continuing debate about the power of the Court to provide national protection for civil liberties and civil rights.

Palko v. Connecticut
302 U.S. 219 (1937)

Palko was convicted initially of second-degree murder, after which the prosecutor took the unusual step of appealing and winning a new trial. At the second trial, Palko was convicted, this time for first-degree murder, and was sentenced to death. He claimed that the second trial amounted to double jeopardy, in violation of the Fifth Amendment, which his counsel argued applied to the states through the Fourteenth Amendment.

Mr. Justice Cardozo delivered the opinion of this Court:

We have said that in appellant's view the Fourteenth Amendment is to be taken as embodying the prohibitions of the Fifth. His thesis is even broader. Whatever would be a violation of the original bill of rights (Amendments I to VIII) if done by the federal government is now equally unlawful by force of the Fourteenth Amendment if done by a state. There is no such general rule.

The Fifth Amendment provides, among other things, that no person shall be held to answer for a capital or otherwise infamous crime unless on presentment or indictment of a grand jury. This court held that, in prosecutions by a state, presentment or indictments by a grand jury may give way to informations at the instance of a public officer. . . .

*   *   *

On the other hand, the due process clause of the Fourteenth Amendment may make it unlawful for a state to abridge by its statutes the freedom of speech which the First Amendment safeguards against encroachment by the Congress, or the like freedom of the press, or the free exercise of religion, or the right of peaceable assembly, without which speech would be unduly trammeled, or right of one accused of crime to the benefit of counsel. In these and other situations immunities that are valid as against the federal government by force of the specific pledges of particular amendments have been found to be implicit in the concept of ordered liberty, and thus, through the Fourteenth Amendment, become valid as against the states.

The line of division may seem to be wavering and broken if there is a hasty catalogue of the cases on the one side and the other. Reflection and analysis will induce a different view. There emerges the perception of a rationalizing principle which gives to discrete instances a proper order and coherence. The right to trial by jury and the immunity from prosecution except as the result of an indictment may have value and importance. Even so, they are not of the very essence of a scheme of ordered liberty. To abolish them is not to violate a "principle of justice so rooted in the traditions and conscience of our people as to be ranked as fundamental". . . . Few would be so narrow or provincial as to maintain that a fair and enlightened system of justice would be impossible without them. What is true of jury trials and indictments is true also, as the cases show, of the immunity from compulsory self-incrimination. . . . This too might be lost, and justice still be done. Indeed, today as in the past there are students of our penal system who look upon the immunity as a mischief rather than a benefit, and who would limit its scope, or destroy it altogether. No doubt there would remain the need to give protection against torture, physical or mental.

Justice, however, would not perish if the accused were subject to a duty to respond to orderly inquiry. The exclusion of these immunities and privileges from the privileges and immunities protected against the action of the states has not been arbitrary or casual. It has been dictated by a study and appreciation of the meaning, the essential implications, of liberty itself.

We reach a different plane of social and moral values when we pass to the privileges and immunities that have been taken over from the earlier articles of the federal bill of rights and brought within the Fourteenth Amendment by a process of absorption. These in their origin were effective against the federal government alone. If the Fourteenth Amendment has absorbed them, the process of absorption has had its source in the belief that neither liberty nor justice would exist if they were sacrificed. . . . This is true, for illustration, of freedom of thought, and speech. Of that freedom one may say that it is the matrix, the indispensable condition, of nearly every other form of freedom. With rare aberrations a pervasive recognition of that truth can be traced in our history, political and legal. So it has come about that the domain of liberty, withdrawn by the Fourteenth Amendment from encroachment by the states, has been enlarged by latter-day judgments to include liberty of the mind as well as liberty of action. The extension became, indeed, a logical imperative when once it was recognized, as long ago it was, that liberty is something more than exemption from physical restraint, and that even in the field of substantive rights and duties the legislative judgment, if oppressive and arbitrary, may be overridden by the courts. . . . Fundamental too in the concept of due process, and so in that of liberty, is the thought that condemnation shall be rendered by after trial. . . . The hearing, moreover, must be a real one, not a sham or a pretense. For that reason, ignorant defendants in a capital case [*Powell* v. *Alabama*] were held to have been condemned unlawfully when in truth, though not in form, they were refused the aid of counsel. . . . The decision did not turn upon the fact that the benefit of counsel would have been guaranteed to the defendants by the provisions of the Sixth Amendment if they had been prosecuted in a federal court. The decision turned upon the fact that in the particular situation laid before us in the evidence the benefit of counsel was essential to the substance of a hearing.

Note: *Carolene Products* and Preferred Positions

Cardozo's opinion in *Palko* was one of the most important in the history of twentieth-century civil liberties. He concluded that the Fourteenth Amendment did not automatically incorporate the entire Bill of Rights. Some parts of it were incorporated; other parts were not. The difficult question, of course, became which ones. What Cardozo said was that those rights essential to the maintenance of "ordered liberty" and "so rooted in the traditions . . . of our people as to be ranked as fundamental" were incorporated. Cardozo, therefore, adopted a doctrine of "selective incorporation" through which the Court became a powerful arbitrator of what was a fundamental right.

A year later, the Court took another decisive step in shaping the future agenda of civil liberties and civil rights. In *United States* v. *Carolene Products* (1938), Justice Harlan F. Stone seized on a minor piece of federal regulatory legislation passed well before the New Deal to make an important point about what rights the Court believed to be fundamental and to mark a new direction in the Court's agenda. Stone warned legislators that thenceforth the Court was going to devote greater attention to the operation of legislation that affected individual noneconomic rights, especially those rights necessary to the full functioning of the political process. Thus while the Court asserted a theory of judicial restraint and deference on matters of economic regulation, it indicated a willingness to become active in protecting individual rights in the political process. The social scientific rationale behind judicial restraint in matters of economic regulatory legislation was turned to support increasingly active intervention by the Court in noneconomic matters.

Footnote 4:
United States v. Carolene Products Co.
304 U.S. 144 (1938)

Almost ignored at the time, Justice Stone's footnote 4 became the opening constitutional wedge in the most important feature of post-1937 legal liberalism— civil rights and civil liberties.

Mr. Justice Stone delivered the opinion of the Court.

4. There may be narrower scope for operation of the presumption of constitutionality when legislation appears on its face to be within a specific prohibition of the Constitution, such as those of the first ten amendments, which are deemed equally specific when held to be embraced within the Fourteenth.

It is unnecessary to consider now whether legislation which restricts those political processes which can ordinarily be expected to bring about repeal of undesirable legislation, is to be subjected to more exacting judicial scrutiny under the general prohibitions of the Fourteenth Amendment than are most other types of legislation. The present statutory findings affect appellee no more than the reports of the Congressional committees; and since in the absence of the statutory findings they would be presumed, their incorporation in the statute is no more prejudicial than surplusage.

Where the existence of a rational basis for legislation whose constitutionality is attacked depends upon facts beyond the sphere of judicial notice, such facts may properly be made the subject of judicial inquiry . . . and the constitutionality of a statute predicated upon the existence of a particular state of facts may be challenged by showing to the court that those facts have ceased to exist. . . . Similarly we recognize that the constitutionality of a statute, valid on its face, may be assailed by proof of facts tending to show that the statute as applied to a particular article is without support in reason because the article, although within the prohibited class, is so different from others of the class as to be without the reason for the prohibition, though the effect of such proof depends on the relevant circumstances of each case, as for example the administrative difficulty of excluding the article from the regulated class. But by their very nature such inquiries, where the legislative judgment is drawn in question, must be restricted to the issue whether any state of facts either known or which could reasonably be assumed affords support for it. Here the demurrer challenges the validity of the statute on its face and it is evident from all the considerations presented to Congress, and those of which we may take judicial notice, that the question is at least debatable whether commerce in filled milk should be left unregulated, or in some measure restricted, or wholly prohibited. As that decision was for Congress, neither the finding of a court arrived at by weighing the evidence, nor the verdict of a jury can be substituted for it. . . .

Nor need we enquire whether similar considerations enter into the review of statutes directed at particular religious, . . . national . . . or racial minorities, . . .

whether prejudice against discrete and insular minorities may be a special condition, which tends seriously to curtail the operation of those political processes ordinarily to be relied upon to protect minorities, and which may call for a correspondingly more searching judicial inquiry.

The Limits of Federal Judicial Power

In *Swift* v. *Tyson* (1842), Supreme Court Justice Joseph Story had developed the concept of a federal common law of commerce. Story had done so in the belief that only through a general, national law of commerce would it be possible for the nation to grow economically. The pro-business federal courts invoked Story's opinion in *Swift* where commercial cases were in diversity—that is, where citizens of different states were involved. By the 1930s, however, most states had revised their commercial law to fit national practices, since doing so was clearly to the advantage of businesses in every state. But many businesses, hoping to find a friendlier forum in the federal courts, continued to manufacture diversity cases in order to avoid the state courts. Not only did these suits add to the already clogged dockets of the federal courts, but they seriously undermined the authority of the individual states. On the Supreme Court, Justice Louis Brandeis campaigned relentlessly to overturn *Swift*, finally succeeding in securing a majority of the justices in *Erie Railroad Co.* v. *Tompkins* (1938).

Note: The Fate of *Erie*

The *Erie* decision was seemingly a turning point in the history of the federal courts, since it appeared to return to the states significant control over commercial law. But Brandeis's hopes proved wistful. For example, the same day that Brandeis gave his opinion, the Court also held in *Hinderliter* v. *La Plata River Co.* that there was a federal common law that regulated the division of water between states and that the interpretation of that law rested exclusively with the federal courts. Moreover, Brandeis had expected that state law would apply as long as a federal statute did not exist, but the Supreme Court itself in 1941 took the step of holding that federal law applied where a procedural issue was raised, while state law would apply where a substantive question was involved. But

> the line between procedural and substantive law could not always be easily determined. . . . Although *Erie* remains the law, so many exceptions and explanations have been created that . . . we have in essence adopted a neo-Swiftian doctrine under which federal courts always apply federal law unless there is a compelling reason to use state law—just the opposite of what Brandeis had hoped to accomplish.[3]

10

The Tensions of Contemporary Law
and Society
1945–1987

World War II was a major turning point in American history, the consequences of which rippled through the legal culture. The United States emerged from the war as the world's greatest power, but the exercise of its economic and military might brought it into conflict with Communist powers in the Soviet Union and China. America, especially during the administrations of Presidents Harry S. Truman (1945–1953) and Dwight D. Eisenhower (1953–1961), became mired in an ideological Cold War. From time to time, however, the Cold War turned hot, as in Korea from 1950 to 1954 and in Vietnam from 1964 to 1973. The atmosphere of domestic politics became so permeated with fears of a supposed Communist threat that much of the emergency wartime legislation passed between 1941 and 1945 remained on the books well into the 1970s. With the nation on a permanent war footing, a consensus initially emerged that the United States was a uniquely free, moral society and a political democracy. But it was more a fear of foreign political ideologies (notably Communism), the possibility of nuclear warfare, and the loss of American influence throughout the world that promoted this consensus. From a constitutional perspective, the atmosphere of fear was hostile to traditional American values, such as political dissent, freedom of association, and separation of powers.

World War II also had important economic consequences. FDR's New Deal programs had only limited success at restoring national prosperity; the four years of conflict following Pearl Harbor, however, provided the economic foundation for postwar prosperity. Technological innovations, accumulated savings from wartime wages, the G.I. Bill, and housing loans from the Veterans Administration fueled four decades of unparalleled economic growth. Yet the resulting economic prosperity was not evenly distributed; the top 10 percent of Americans steadily gained a larger and larger percentage of the nation's total wealth.

The war resulted in another change. For blacks and women, wartime conditions provided a glimpse of economic opportunities that, once enjoyed, were not easily forgotten when the conflict ended. The wartime emergency generated tremendous pressures for manpower, and blacks participated in the armed services to a degree unknown since the Civil War. Blacks who stayed at home found their services much in demand as well, and they gained access to manufacturing jobs previously denied them. The wartime economy also brought women in unprecedented numbers into manufacturing, service, and supervisory roles long closed to them. The legendary "Rosie the Riveter" symbolized the heightened gender diversity of the American labor force.

World War II also had important structural implications for the American constitutional system. In order to fight the conflict, the government continued the process of greater and greater centralization of decision making and increased reliance on an ever-expanding administrative network, one that far surpassed in size and ambition anything attempted during World War I or the New Deal. Indeed, many New Deal lawyers of the 1930s went into service in the wartime federal government and then, after 1945, entered into lucrative practices in the nation's capital, where administrative and regulatory law emerged as a distinct body of authority governing such matters as labor relations, telecommunications, the environment, and transportation. The regulatory bureaucracy in Washington became a kind of fourth branch of government that in theory placed expertise ahead of partisan necessity in decision making.

The full implications of the changes wrought by the war appeared during the next four decades. The political consensus of the 1950s, for example, crumbled under the weight of the civil rights and antiwar movements of the mid-1960s and early 1970s. The nonviolent tactics developed by black leaders, such as the Reverend Martin Luther King, Jr., became part of the protest arsenal of antiwar activists. Many Americans lumped hippies, civil rights advocates, and antiwar protesters in the same lot. The so-called silent majority, while troubled by the war in Southeast Asia and lingering social inequality, also clung to traditional values of hard work, the nuclear family, good manners, and patriotism.

An underlying demographic shift further abetted social discontent. Following the end of World War II, Americans married and reproduced at levels not seen since the nineteenth century. The result was a population cohort that moved like a large mass being digested by a snake. At the height of this baby boom in the mid-1950s, the average family had more than three children. This generation not only created strong demands for education, employment, and such, but also ushered in a new crime wave. The ranks of the most crime-prone age group, those between fifteen and twenty-four, swelled by more than a million persons a year during the 1960s. And the great urban race riots from 1964 to 1968 brought increasingly strident demands for improvements in the criminal justice system. Americans were divided over whether the issues should be attacked by addressing the social pathology of crime (poverty, hunger, broken families, and such) or by implementing get-tough measures intended to deter crime and, once it occurred, mete out appropriate retributive punishments. Under such circumstances, the rights of the accused became a major public law issue.

Behind these events lay mounting pressures for change from groups previously considered to be on the margins of law, society, and politics. Minority groups became impatient with business as usual and with traditional political solutions. Blacks and feminist leaders, for example, attacked entrenched race and gender discrimination, although they did so with different degrees of success and with the realization that race and gender, as defining categories, cut quite differently across American life.

They were joined by environmentalists and consumer-rights advocates, both of whom denounced long-standing practices that defiled the environment and permitted dangerous goods and shoddy practices in the marketplace. While these groups differed from one another, they shared the belief that the scheme of legal liberalism forged by the New Deal offered the means by which to restore balance in the environment, the economy, and society.

These groups pursued special-interest litigation in an effort to achieve through the legal process what they had not realized through politics. As Lawrence M. Friedman has observed, their efforts symbolized the emergence in the mid-1960s of a general "expectation of justice" and an accompanying "general expectation of recompense" for wrongs of every nature.[1] The Supreme Court, with its agenda switched from the economic regulatory issues of the New Deal era to matters of civil liberties and civil rights, emerged at the center of this quest for "total justice." The justices' decisions, especially during the period from 1954 to 1969 when Earl Warren presided over the Court, became a source of continuing controversy. Political and legal conservatives believed that the Court, in its quest to give greater emphasis to equality and political openness, had usurped authority over matters, such as criminal justice, that properly belonged to the states and had set itself up as a quasi-legislative body.

The documents in this chapter deal with many of the resulting tensions over law in contemporary society. We begin with an examination of how "rights consciousness" has permeated private and public law, turn to the implications of the rise of the administrative state, then probe the crisis over the roles of the president and Congress, and explore the delivery of legal services in a pluralistic society. We conclude with an examination of the two predominant intellectual challenges to the culture of legal liberalism in the post–World War II era: the Law and Economics and the Critical Legal Studies movements.

The Liberal State: Private Law, Rights Consciousness, and Economic Equality

Legislative activism emerged as one of the significant new features of the post–World War II legal order. A single fat volume of statutes in the early nineteenth century could encompass all the laws of a state. By the 1980s, a whole book shelf was often necessary. In this new "age of statutes," legislators intervened in relationships that common-law judges had historically regulated. More legislation also meant that the task of judges increasingly became one of construing statutes and administrative regulations and not just elaborating on common-law doctrines. But the character of disputes raised through the common law also changed. In the trial courts, a pronounced shift occurred from civil to criminal matters, and on the civil side there was a smaller proportion of cases that involved market transactions (e.g., contract, property, debt collection) and a greater number of cases concerning tort and family issues. The traditional lines that demarcated private law categories blurred, leading to the creation of protean bodies of new law, such as administrative law and products liability, that gave judges extensive new policy-making authority.

The "New" Property and New Property Rights

The New Deal ushered in the welfare state, which included the concept of entitlement. An entitlement is a claim that a person has on some benefit distributed by the government, such as a parent's claim to payments under the federal Aid to Families with Dependent Children program. Considered as a property concept, it differs from traditional kinds of property in that the claimant ("owner") does not have legal "title" to a tangible or an intangible object of real or personal property; instead, he or she has a claim against a benefit program. Thus the federal government particularly, but also state governments, became sources of wealth. This so-called new property was invariably legislatively created in the form, for example, of social security, unemployment, and welfare benefits, but it also included licenses and franchises given by the government to private individuals. Administrative bureaucracies typically regulated the distribution of this new property, although in the 1960s and 1970s aggrieved plaintiffs frequently asked the courts to overturn administrative decisions on the grounds that this new property should be as securely protected as had been the traditional concept of property. Liberal public-interest lawyers claimed that the High Court should shield the recipients of these entitlements from the capricious activities of the bureaucratic state by granting certain of them (the poor, veterans, unwed mothers, dependent children) constitutional protections. Counsel for the government, however, argued that such entitlements were mere grants made at the discretion of the government and that entitlement required no new special constitutional protections.

Even in traditional areas of property law, broad changes occurred. Recall that during the nineteenth century, the inviolability of private property was challenged by the emerging police-power doctrine, which permitted government to take a greater and greater role in placing community interests above the ambitions of individual property owners. In some instances, nineteenth-century state legislatures had actually "lent" the eminent domain power to private businesses. But laissez-faire ideology also structured legal approaches to property; legislative efforts at the end of the century to control the emerging corporate structure through regulation were often met with judicial hostility. The New Deal Court, however, in enunciating its "preferred positions" doctrine in *United States* v. *Carolene Products* (1938), abandoned laissez-faire constitutionalism and deferred to legislative judgments involving regulation of property. The judicial scrutiny of economic regulation became purely nominal. Yet the tension between private enjoyment of property and public regulation of it, in the name of the community, became more, not less, troublesome in the post–World War II period. The same was true in zoning and landlord–tenant law, as the following materials suggest.

Lionshead Lake, Inc. v. *Wayne Tp.*
10 N.J. 165

Zoning laws after World War II went hand-in-hand with suburban development. The automobile opened the countryside; low land values put housing within the reach of many people, and the suburbs offered prosperous middle-class and well-

to-do persons a refuge from the inner city. City and county officials quickly learned that through zoning regulations they could enhance the value of their communities by restricting the access of undesirable persons. This celebrated case deals with one such "snob" zoning ordinance in New Jersey.

The opinion of the court was delivered by VANDERBILT, C. J.

The plaintiff, the owner and developer of a large tract of land in the defendant township, commenced this action . . . challenging the validity of the defendant's zoning ordinance in fixing the minimum size of dwellings and in placing certain of its properties in a residential district. . . .

The Township of Wayne is the most extensive municipality in Passaic County. It covers 25.34 square miles in comparison with the 23.57 square miles of Newark. It has a population of 11,815 in comparison with Newark's 437,857. Only 12% of the total area of the township has been built up. Included within its borders are several sizable lakes . . . and as a result a considerable number of its residences have been built for summer occupancy only. Although a political entity it is in fact a composite of about a dozen widely scattered residential communities, varying from developments like the plaintiff's where the average home costs less than $10,000, to more expensive sections where the homes cost from $35,000 to $75,000. It has but little business or industry.

On July 12, 1949, four years after the plaintiff had commenced the development of its Lionshead Lake properties and after over a hundred houses had been constructed there, the defendant adopted a revised zoning ordinance dividing the entire township into four districts; resident districts A and B, a business district and an industrial district, the last two comprising but a very small proportion of the township's total area. In section 3 of the ordinance pertaining to residence A districts it was provided that:

"(d) Minimum Size of Dwellings:

"Every dwelling hereafter erected or placed in a Residence A District shall have a living-floor space, as herein defined.

"of not less than 768 square feet for a one story dwelling:

"of not less than 1000 square feet for a two story dwelling having an attached garage;

"of not less than 1200 square feet for a two story dwelling not having an attached garage."

These minimum size requirements for dwellings were made applicable . . . throughout the entire township.

Within the entire township only about 70% of all the existing dwellings meet the minimum requirements of the ordinance; in some sections of the township as few as 20% of the existing dwellings comply with the ordinance requirements, in others (among them the plaintiff's Lionshead Lake development) only about 50% are above the prescribed minimum, while in other areas the percentage of compliance is far greater, reaching 100% in some of the more exclusive sections. The low percentage of compliance in certain areas is not particularly significant, however, for the reason that the township is as yet substantially undeveloped. [This court] has held that so long as the zoning ordinance was reasonably designed, by whatever means, to further the advancement of a community as a social, economic, and political unit, it is in the general welfare and therefore a proper exercise of the zoning power. The underlying question before us is whether in the light of these constitutional and legislative provisions the zoning ordinance of the defendant township is arbitrary and unreasonable. That question, moreover, must be answered in the light of the facts of this particular case. We must bear in mind, finally, that a zoning ordinance is not like the law of the Medes and Persians; variances may be permitted, the zoning ordinance may be amended, and if the ordinance proves unreasonable in operation it may be set aside at any time.

*   *   *

The Township of Wayne is still for the most part a sparsely settled countryside with great natural attractions in its lakes, hills and streams, but obviously it lies in the path of the next onward wave of suburban development. Whether that development shall be "with a view of conserving the value of property and encouraging the most appropriate use of land throughout such municipality" and whether it will "prevent the overcrowding of land or buildings" and "avoid undue concentration of population" depends in large measure on the wisdom of the governing body of the municipality as expressed in its zoning ordinance. It requires as much official watchfulness to anticipate and prevent suburban blight as it does to eradicate city slums.

Has a municipality the right to impose minimum floor area requirements in the exercise of its zoning powers? Much of the proof adduced by the defendant township was devoted to showing that the mental and emotional health of its inhabitants depended on the proper size of their homes. We may take notice without formal proof that there are minimums in housing below which one may not go without risk of impairing the health of those who dwell therein. One does not need extensive experience in matrimonial causes to become aware of the adverse effect of overcrowding on the well-being of our most important institution, the home. Moreover, people who move into the country rightly expect more land, more living room, indoors and out, and more freedom in their scale of living than is generally possible in the city. City standards of housing are not adaptable to suburban areas and especially to the upbringing of children. But quite apart from these considerations of public health which cannot be overlooked, minimum floor-area standards are justified on the ground that they promote the general welfare of the community and, as we have seen in *Schmidt v. Board of Adjustment of the City of Newark*, the courts in conformance with the constitutional provisions and the statutes hereinbefore cited take a broad view of what constitutes general welfare. The size of the dwellings in any community inevitably affects the character of the community and does much to determine whether or not it is a desirable place in which to live. It is the prevailing view in municipalities throughout the State that such minimum floor-area standards are necessary to protect the character of the community. . . . In the light of the Constitution and of the enabling statutes, the right of a municipality to impose minimum floor-area requirements is beyond controversy.

*   *   *

The zoning powers of municipalities have been extended by Art. IV, Sec. VI, par. 2 of the Constitution of 1947:

"The Legislature may enact general laws under which municipalities, other than counties, may adopt zoning ordinances limiting and restricting to specified districts and regulating therein, buildings and structures, according to their construction, and the nature and extent of their use, *and the nature and extent of the uses of land*, and the exercise of such authority shall be deemed to be within the police power of the State. Such laws shall be subject to repeal or alteration by the Legislature."

*   *   *

When the enabling zoning statutes . . . are read in the light of the constitutional mandate to construe them liberally, there can be no doubt that a municipality has the power by a suitable zoning ordinance to impose minimum living-floor space requirements for dwellings.

*   *   *

Thus not only has the Constitution conferred on the Legislature very broad powers to pass enabling acts with respect to zoning but the Legislature in a like effort to make effective its constitutional power in this respect has given the municipalities similar broad powers expressed in considerably greater detail than in the Constitution. To the traditional presumption with respect to the validity of every legislative act there has been added, moreover, the constitutional mandate to construe such legislation liberally in favor of the municipalities.

*   *   *

We are bound by these changes in our organic law and . . . in the light of all of the surrounding circumstances the minimum floor-area requirements are reasonable. . . . If some such requirements were not imposed there would be grave danger in certain parts of the township, particularly around the lakes which attract summer visitors, of the erection of shanties which would deteriorate land values generally to the great detriment of the increasing number of people who live in Wayne Township the year round. The minimum floor area requirements imposed by the ordinance are not large for a family of normal size. Without some such restrictions there is always the danger that after some homes have been erected giving a character to a neighborhood others might follow which would fail to live up to the standards thus voluntarily set. This has been the experience in many communities and it is against this that the township has sought to safeguard itself within limits which seem to us to be altogether reasonable. . . .

The judgment on the first count of the plaintiff's complaint is reversed.

OLIPHANT, J. (dissenting)

I find I must dissent from the philosophy and the result arrived at in the majority opinion. Zoning has its purposes, but as I conceive the effect of the majority opinion precludes individuals in those income brackets who could not pay between $8,500 and $12,000 for the erection of a house on a lot from ever establishing a residence in this community as long as the 768 square feet of living space is the minimum requirement in the zoning ordinance. A zoning provision that can produce this effect certainly runs afoul of the fundamental principles of our form of government. It places an unnecessary and severe restriction upon the alienation of real estate. It is not necessary, it seems to me, in order to meet any possible threat to the general health and welfare of the community.

*   *   *

While zoning regulations may legitimately be imposed in the district to serve the general welfare by "conserving the value of property and encouraging the most appropriate uses of land," such regulations are wholly unreasonable and beyond the zoning power and an unwarranted interference with private property rights if they are designed or operate to change completely, for better or for worse, the very character of the district. Any regulation imposed must bear a reasonable relation to the particular area subject thereto. Insofar as the minimum living floor space requirements of the ordinance under review apply to the entire community and to the plaintiff's properties in particular, they are clearly arbitrary and capricious and were very properly set aside by the trial court as an abuse of the zoning power.

My views on this particular phase of zoning do not prohibit minimum floor space in a house in particular districts or a proper correlation of minimum floor space in the house and the area of the lot or lots in question, but I cannot agree with the majority when they state with respect to this minimum square footage requirements that "whether it will 'prevent the overcrowding of land or buildings' and 'avoid undue concentration of population' depends in large measure on the wisdom of the governing body of the municipality." This is clearly indicative of a lack of standard with respect to this particular phase of zoning in the Zoning Act itself and it assumes that the discretion of the zoning board or governing body of a municipality amounts to wisdom. . . .

Note: Zoning and Entitlement

The authority to zone derived from the police powers of the states, which usually delegated it to municipalities. New York City passed the first comprehensive zoning plan in 1916, and it subsequently became a model for the rest of the nation. The Supreme Court a decade later, in *Village of Euclid* v. *Ambler Realty Co.* (1926), upheld local zoning control as a rational extension of traditional public-nuisance law. Justice George Sutherland, speaking for the Court, made the point that zoning laws had the added advantage of alerting all owners before the fact of what they could and could not do with their property.

Proponents of the Law and Economics school insist that zoning and, more generally, all forms of property regulation are economically inefficient because public officials are far less likely than rationally acting private individuals to maximize the use and derive the greatest wealth from land. In *Nollan* v. *California Coastal Commission* (1987), the Supreme Court indicated that it will give increased scrutiny to takings carried out by *regulatory* bodies. In that case, Justice Antonin Scalia's opinion for the Court held that the California Coastal Commission could not, without paying compensation, condition the grant of permission to rebuild a property owner's house on the transfer to the public of an easement across beachfront property that would allow the public access to the beach.

The Supreme Court in *Dandridge* v. *Williams et al.* (1969) refused to adopt the position that entitlements were matters of rights. While the Court, responding to congressional legislation, has accepted greater judicial intervention to examine the conduct of bureaucratic and regulatory officials, it has also permitted them significant discretion in deciding whether particular individuals can receive certain entitlement. Hence, at the same time that public officials have made greater inroads on the enjoyment of private property, they have withstood significant challenges to their authority to distribute the so-called new property. The Court, however, held in *Goldberg* v. *Kelly* (1970) that state welfare agencies must afford a recipient of public-assistance payments an evidentiary hearing prior to termination. Failure to do so violates the due process clause of the Fourteenth Amendment in a procedural, not a substantive, sense.

Contract

In the nineteenth century, contract became the most important category of private law because it stressed such "classical" elements as the importance of caveat emptor, consideration, and mutuality of bargaining. But in the twentieth century, the weight of the Legal Realist movement combined with the rise of a mass consumer economy to undermine the once dominant role of contract. The attack on the entire idea of contract became so ferocious that Yale Law School professor Grant Gilmore in 1974 proclaimed its demise in a widely influential book, *The Death of Contract*. Gilmore argued that expansive concepts of tort law had rendered contract ideals meaningless.

Gilmore's obituary for contract law was premature, since contract continues to have vitality in sustaining important social and economic relationships. Yet legal commentators, judges, and legislators have significantly reshaped it. They have done so by promoting two concepts: reliance and unconscionability. Together, these concepts have circumscribed unrestrained bargaining among private parties.

Williams v. *Walker-Thomas Furniture Company*
350 F.2d 445 (1965)

This case involved the question of whether an equitable doctrine of unconscionability covered by Section 2-302 of the Uniform Commercial Code, as adopted by Congress for the District of Columbia, should prevail over a traditional commitment to a meeting of minds between bargaining parties. The case has a number of social and economic permutations as well. For example, should ghetto merchants be given greater leeway, in view of their customer base, to protect their property interests through tougher contract terms than would be the case in an affluent suburb? What impact might the Williams *decision be expected to have on the availability and prices of consumer goods in poor urban neighborhoods? Indeed, should judges take such matters into consideration?*

J. SKELLY WRIGHT, Circuit Judge:

Appellee, Walker-Thomas Furniture Company, operates a retail furniture store in the District of Columbia. During the period from 1957 to 1962 each appellant in these cases purchased a number of household items from Walker-Thomas, for which payment was to be made in installments. The terms of each purchase were contained in a printed form contract which set forth the value of the purchased item and purported to lease the item to appellant for a stipulated monthly rent payment. The contract then provided, in substance, that title would remain in Walker-Thomas until the total of all the monthly payments made equated the stated value of the item, at which time appellants could take title. In the event of a default in the payment of any monthly installment, Walker-Thomas could repossess the item.

The contract further provided that "the amount of each periodical installment payment to be made by [purchaser] to the Company under this present lease shall be inclusive of and not in addition to the amount of each installment payment to be made by [purchaser] under such prior leases, bills or accounts; *and all payments now and hereafter made by [purchaser] shall be credited pro rata on all outstanding leases, bills and accounts* due the Company by [purchaser] at the time each such payment is made." [Emphasis added.] The effect of this rather obscure provision was to keep a balance due on every item purchased until the balance due on all items, whenever purchased, was liquidated. As a result, the debt incurred at the time of purchase of each item was secured by the right to repossess all the items previously purchased by the same purchaser, and each new item purchased automatically became subject to a security interest arising out of the previous dealings.

On May 12, 1962, appellant purchased an item described as Daveno, three tables, and two lamps, having a total stated value of $391.10. Shortly thereafter, she defaulted on her monthly payments and appellee sought to replevy all the items purchased since the first transaction in 1958. Similarly, on April 17, 1962, appellant Williams bought a stereo set of stated value of $514.95. She too defaulted shortly thereafter, and appellee sought to replevy all the items purchased since December, 1957. . . .

Appellants' principal contention, rejected by both the trial and the appellate courts below, is that these contracts, or at least some of them, are unconscionable and, hence, not enforceable. In its opinion . . . the District of Columbia Court of Appeals reject[ed] this contention.

                              *   *   *

We do not agree that the court lacked the power to refuse enforcement to contracts found to be unconscionable. In other jurisdictions, it has been held as a matter of common law that unconscionable contracts are not enforceable. While no decision of this court so holding has been found, the notion that an unconscionable bargain should not be given full enforcement is by no means novel. . . . Since we have never adopted or rejected such a rule, the question here presented is actually one of the first impression.

Congress has recently enacted the Uniform Commercial Code, which specifically provides that the court may refuse to enforce a contract which it finds to be unconscionable at the time it was made. . . . The enactment of this section, which occurred subsequent to the contracts here in suit, does not mean that the common law of the District of Columbia was otherwise at the time of enactment, nor does it preclude the court from adopting a similar rule in the exercise of its powers to develop the common law for the District of Columbia. In fact, in view of the absence of prior authority on the point, we consider the congressional adoption of section 2-302 persuasive authority for following the rationale of the cases from which the section is explicitly derived. Accordingly, we hold that where the element of unconscionability is present at the time a contract is made, the contract should be enforced.

Unconscionability has generally been recognized to include an absence of meaningful choice on the part of one of the parties together with contract terms which are unreasonably favorable to the other party. Whether a meaningful choice is present in a particular case can only be determined by consideration of all the circumstances surrounding the transaction. In many cases the meaningfulness of the choice is negated by a gross inequality of bargaining power. The manner in which the contract was entered into is also relevant to this consideration. Did each party to the contract, considering his obvious education or lack of it, have a reasonable opportunity to understand the terms of the contract, or were the important terms hidden in a maze of fine print and minimized by deceptive sales practices? Ordinarily, one who signs an agreement without full knowledge of its terms might be held to assume the risk that he has entered a one-sided bargain. But when a party of little bargaining power, and hence little real choice, signs a commercially unreasonable contract with little or no knowledge of its terms, it is hardly likely that his consent, or even an objective manifestation of his consent, was ever given to all the terms. In such a case the usual rule that the terms of the agreement are not to be questioned should be abandoned and the court should consider whether the terms of the contract are so unfair that enforcement should be withheld.

In determining reasonableness or fairness, the primary concern must be with the terms of the contract considered in light of the circumstances existing when the contract was made. The test is not simple, nor can it be mechanically applied. The terms are to be considered "in light of the general commercial background and the commercial needs of the particular trade or case." Corbin suggests the test as being whether the terms are "so extreme as to appear unconscionable according to the mores and business practices of the time and place." . . . We think this formulation correctly states the test to be applied in those cases where no meaningful choice was exercised upon entering the contract.

Because the trial court and the appellate court did not feel that enforcement could be refused, no findings were made on the possible unconscionability of the contracts in these cases. Since the record is not sufficient for our deciding the issue as a matter of law, the cases must be remanded to the trial court for further proceedings.

So ordered.

Torts

In the nineteenth century, tort law emphasized fault and the establishment of blameworthiness; in the twentieth century, especially in the post–World War II era, it has stressed compensation for injured persons. This shift in tort law has placed the costs of accidents and their prevention on the party to whom it was most bearable. Legal scholars, however, have differed radically on the wisdom of this development. Richard Posner and Richard Epstein, both associated with the Law and Economics movement, have protested that placing the costs of accidents on those businesses and persons with the deepest pockets only drives up the cost of goods and services without providing any significant deterrent against future recklessness. Yale Law School professor Guido Calabresi, on the contrary, insists that spreading the costs of accidents over those best able to pay makes good moral sense.

As a matter of historical development, modern tort law would be unthinkable without liability insurance. Through premiums paid by many policyholders, insurance companies spread the costs of accidents while making a profit. Insurance has social utility in another way because it permits businesses to develop and individuals to use new, complex technologies under a protective umbrella. The modern transportation system depends on automobile insurance.

Yet an extraordinary degree of controversy has plagued both modern tort law and liability insurance. The rising costs of all kinds of liability insurance sparked demands for reform of the system in the 1960s and again in the 1980s. The most prominent of these legislatively imposed reforms has been "no-fault" insurance (in which the insured person's company rather than that of the party at fault pays the bills), caps on damages in medical malpractice suits, and comparative negligence (in which responsibility for an accident is apportioned among those involved in it). Taken together, these developments have turned what was once an almost exclusively private branch of law into one that is more and more controlled by public policy concerns.

Nowhere is the unique character of modern tort law clearer than in the broadened application of strict liability standards. In the nineteenth century, the concept applied with a very few exceptions to ultrahazardous activities, but in this century judges have increasingly applied it to a variety of consumer-related goods. Products liability rests on the assumption that with the spread of new technologies and the growing remoteness of producers from consumers, strict liability standards encourage manufacturers to give close attention to matters of safety. Such assumptions are hotly disputed, once again, by Posner, Epstein, and other Law and Economics scholars.

Greenman v. *Yuba Power Products, Inc.*
59 Cal. 2d 57 (1962)

Perhaps nowhere was the so-called death of contract more evident than in cases in which the traditional rule requiring privity between buyer and seller was set aside. This line of development began with McPherson v. Buick Motor Co. *(N.Y., 1916), a case that involved an injury caused by a defective automobile wheel. Judge Benjamin Cardozo's opinion established the notion of third-party liability when privity of contract did not exist. In* Greenman, *the California Supreme Court, which was the most important court for establishing modern tort law, further extended this doctrine. The court was asked to consider whether a manufacturer's liability for defective products was governed by the law of contract warranties or by the law of strict liability. Judge Roger Traynor, who wrote the opinion in this case, was, like Cardozo, one of the great twentieth-century state judges.*

TRAYNOR, Justice.

Plaintiff brought this action for damages against the retailer and the manufacturer of a Shopsmith, a combination power tool that could be used as a saw, drill, and wood lathe. He saw a Shopsmith demonstrated by the retailer and studied a brochure prepared by the manufacturer. He decided he wanted a Shopsmith for his home workshop, and his wife bought and gave him one for Christmas in 1955. In 1957 he bought the necessary attachments to use the Shopsmith as a lathe for turning a large piece of wood he wished to make into a chalice. After he had worked on the piece of wood several times without difficulty, it suddenly flew out of the machine and struck him on the forehead, inflicting serious injuries. About ten and a half months later, he gave the retailer and the manufacturer written notice of claimed breaches of warranties and filed a complaint against them alleging such breaches and negligence.

After a trial before a jury, the court . . . submitted to the jury only the cause of action alleging breach of implied warranties against the retailer and the causes of action alleging negligence and breach of express warranties against the manufacturer. The jury returned a verdict for the retailer against plaintiff and for plaintiff against the manufacturer in the amount of $65,000. The trial court denied the manufacturer's motion for a new trial and entered judgment on the verdict. The manufacturer . . . appeal[s].

Plaintiff introduced substantial evidence that his injuries were caused by defective design and construction of the Shopsmith. His expert witnesses testified that inadequate set screws were used to hold parts of the machine together so that normal vibration caused the tailstock of the lathe to move away from the piece of wood being turned permitting it to fly out of the lathe. They also testified that there were other more positive ways of fastening the parts of the machine together, the use of which would have prevented the accident. The jury could therefore reasonably have concluded that the manufacturer negligently constructed the Shopsmith. The jury could also reasonably have concluded that statements in the manufacturer's brochure were untrue, that they constituted express warranties, and that plaintiff's injuries were caused by their breach.

*   *   *

A manufacturer is strictly liable in tort when an article he places on the market knowing that it is to be used without inspection for defects, proves to have a defect that causes injury to a human being. Recognized first in the case of unwholesome food products, such liability has now been extended to a variety of other products that create as great or greater hazards if defective. . . .

Although . . . strict liability has usually been based on the theory of an express or implied warranty running from the manufacturer to the plaintiff, the abandonment of the requirement of a contract between them, the recognition that the liability is not assumed by agreement but imposed by law . . . , and the refusal to permit the manufacturer to define the scope of its own responsibility for defective products . . . , make clear that the liability is not one governed by the law of contract warranties but by the law of strict liability in tort.

We need not recanvass the reasons for imposing strict liability on the manufacturer. . . . The purpose of such liability is to insure that the costs of injuries resulting from defective products are borne by the manufacturers that put such products on the market rather than by the injured persons who are powerless to protect themselves. Sales warranties serve this purpose fitfully at best. . . . In the present case, for example, plaintiff was able to plead and prove an express warranty only because he read and relied on the representations of the Shopsmith's ruggedness contained in the manufacturer's brochure. Implicit in the machine's presence on the market, however, was a representation that it would safely do the jobs for which it was built. Under these circumstances, it should not be controlling whether plaintiff selected the machine because of the statements in the brochure, or because of the machine's own appearance of excellence that belied the defect lurking beneath the surface, or because he merely assumed that it would safely do the jobs it was built to do. It should not be controlling whether the details of the sales from manufacturer to retailer and from retailer to plaintiff's wife were such that one or more of the implied warranties of the sales act arose. . . . To establish the manufacturer's liability it was sufficient that plaintiff proved that he was injured while using the Shopsmith in a way it was intended to be used as a result of a defect in design and manufacture of which plaintiff was not aware that made the Shopsmith unsafe for its intended use.

The judgment is affirmed.

Fassoulas v. Ramey
450 So. 2d 822 (Fla. 1984)

Medical malpractice suits have been one of the most visible and controversial aspects of modern tort law. Nowhere else has the general expectation of justice and the idea of recompense for wrongs of every nature been more evident. In cases such as this one, issues of emotional suffering and not just physical injury add a new dimension to the meaning of damages in modern tort law.

PER CURIAM . . .

Plaintiffs, Edith and John Fassoulas, were married and had two children, both of whom had been born with severe congenital abnormalities. After much consideration, they decided not to have any more children due to the fear of having another physically deformed child and the attendant high cost of medical care. They then decided that John would undergo a vasectomy. This medical procedure was performed in January 1974 by defendant, Dr. Ramey. However, due to the negligence of the defendant in performing the operation, in giving medical advice concerning residual pockets of sperm, and in examining and judging the viability of sperm samples, Edith twice became pregnant and gave birth to two children. The first of these, Maria, was born in November 1974 and had many congenital deformities. Roussi, the second of the post-vasectomy children and the fourth Fassoulas child, was born in September 1976 with a slight physical deformity which was corrected at birth; he is now a normal, healthy child.

The plaintiffs sued Dr. Ramey and his clinic in tort based on medical malpractice for the two "wrongful births." They sought as damages Edith's past and future lost wages, her anguish and emotional distress at twice becoming pregnant, her loss of the society, companionship and consortium of her husband, John's mental anguish and emotional distress, his loss of the society, companionship and consortium of his wife, medical and hospital expenses and the expenses for the care and upbringing of the two new children until the age of twenty-one.

At trial, the jury found in favor of the plaintiffs, finding the defendant 100% negligent with reference to Maria and 50% negligent with reference to Roussi. The plaintiffs were found to be comparatively negligent as to the birth of Roussi. Damages were assessed in the amount of $250,000 for the birth of Maria and $100,000 for the birth of Roussi, the latter sum being reduced to $50,000 because of the plaintiff's comparative negligence. . . .

The rule in Florida is that "a parent cannot be said to have been damaged by the birth and rearing of a normal, healthy child." "[I]t has been imbedded in our law for centuries that the father and now both parents or legal guardians of a child have the sole obligation of providing the necessaries in raising the child, whether the child be wanted or unwanted." "The child is still the child of the parents, not the physician, and it is the parents' legal obligation, not the physician's, to support the child." For public policy reasons, we decline to allow rearing damages for the birth of a healthy child.

The same reasoning forcefully and correctly applies to the ordinary, everyday expenses associated with the care and upbringing of a physically or mentally deformed child. We likewise hold as a matter of law that ordinary rearing expenses for a defective child are not recoverable as damages in Florida.

We agree with the district court below that an exception exists in the case of special upbringing expenses associated with a deformed child. Special medical and educational expenses, beyond normal rearing costs, are often staggering and quite debilitating to a family's financial and social health; "indeed the financial and emotional drain associated with raising such a child is often overwhelming to the affected parents." There is no valid policy argument against parents being recompensed for these costs of extraordinary care in raising a deformed child to majority. We hold these special upbringing costs associated with a deformed child to be recoverable.

[The court allowed only the extraordinary rearing costs associated with Maria; it permitted nothing for the birth of Roussi.]

Note: No-Fault Insurance

Some physicians have pushed for no-fault malpractice insurance as a means of stemming the rising costs of practice in certain particularly hazardous areas, such as obstetrics, neurosurgery, and orthopedics. While this proposal has made little headway, the no-fault concept has had far greater success in automobile-related torts. In 1970, Massachusetts became the first state to adopt a no-fault automobile law, and by 1987 about one-half of the states had embraced similar schemes. At the time, Massachusetts had the highest automobile premiums in the nation, and consumer action groups sought to curtail these expenses by eliminating the need to determine fault in an accident. As the Massachusetts statute provided, however, the plan was a modified no-fault scheme, since it permitted victims, in serious cases, to still bring suits to pay for high medical costs and such. While states have failed to adopt no-fault plans for medical malpractice, some of them have embraced caps on awards for pain and suffering.

Legal Liberalism and Public Law

Post-war liberal culture transformed public as well as private law. Blacks, women, and other minorities rocked the American social order with demands for genuine equality while political dissenters, in the midst of the Cold War with the Soviet Union and China, insisted on the broadest possible scope for their civil liberties. The National Association for the Advancement of Colored People and the American Civil Liberties Union adopted increasingly bold litigation strategies designed to win through the courts that which they could not attain through the regular political process. Both groups, of course, had pressed earlier in the century for the extension of civil liberties and civil rights, but only after the constitutional revolution of 1937, in which the justices purposely turned their attention to these matters, was there significant progress.

The Court's response to these demands stirred great controversy. Conservative critics, such as Harvard professor Raoul Berger and Attorney General Edwin Meese, charged the justices with using judicial power to usurp legislative power, with distorting the meaning of federalism, and with substituting their values for the original intentions of the Framers. While most liberals applauded the work of the High Court under the chief justiceship of Earl Warren from 1954 to 1969, discordant voices in the Critical Legal Studies movement, which began at the University of Wisconsin in 1974, insisted that the justices had done too little to affect really meaningful change in American constitutionalism.

Civil Rights: Race

Brown v. Board of Education of Topeka, Kansas
347 U.S. 483 (1954)

Beginning in the 1940s, the NAACP's Legal Defense Fund mounted a litigation strategy designed to dislodge the separate-but-equal doctrine of Plessy v. Ferguson (1896). The South remained a racially divided society, with blacks and whites using different public toilets, different seats in movie theaters, and different public schools. Under the leadership of Thurgood Marshall, however, the NAACP in 1950 decided to challenge directly the separate-but-equal doctrine. Brown v. Board of Education was the result. The case was actually a class action brought not only by black elementary-school children in Topeka, Kansas, but by other school-age children in South Carolina, Virginia, and Delaware. A companion case, Bolling v. Sharpe (1954), was also decided by the Court, although it was brought in the District of Columbia under the Fifth rather than the Fourteenth Amendment.

Mr. Chief Justice WARREN delivered the opinion of the Court.

These cases came to us from the States of Kansas, South Carolina, Virginia, and Delaware. They are premised on different facts and different local conditions, but a common legal question justifies their consideration together in this consolidated opinion.

In each of the cases, minors of the Negro race . . . seek the aid of the courts in obtaining admission to the public schools of their community on a nonsegregated basis. In each instance, they have been denied admission to schools attended by white children under laws requiring of permitting segregation according to race. This segregation was alleged to deprive the plaintiffs of the equal protection of the laws under the Fourteenth Amendment. In each of the cases other than the Delaware case, a three-judge federal district court denied relief to the plaintiffs on the so-called "separate but equal" doctrine announced by this Court in *Plessy v. Ferguson* (1896). . . . Under that doctrine, equality of treatment is accorded when the races are provided substantially equal facilities, even though these facilities be separate. In the Delaware case, the Supreme Court of Delaware adhered to that doctrine, but ordered that the plaintiffs be admitted to the white schools because of their superiority to the Negro schools.

The plaintiffs contend that segregated public schools are not "equal" and cannot be made "equal," and that hence they are deprived of the equal protection of the laws. Because of the obvious importance of the question presented, the Court took jurisdiction. Argument was heard in the 1952 Term, and reargument was heard this Term on certain questions propounded by the Court.

Reargument was largely devoted to the circumstances surrounding the adoption of the Fourteenth Amendment in 1868. It covered exhaustively consideration of the Amendment in Congress, ratification by the states, then existing practices in racial segregation, and the views of proponents and opponents of the Amendment. This discussion and our own investigation convince us that, although these sources cast some light, it is not enough to resolve the problem with which we are faced. At best, they are inconclusive. The most avid proponents of the post-War Amendments undoubtedly intended them to remove all legal distinctions among "all persons born or naturalized in the United States." Their opponents, just as certainly, were antagonistic to both the letter and the spirit of the Amendments and wished them to have the most limited effect. What others in Congress and the state legislatures had in mind cannot be determined with any degree of certainty.

An additional reason for the inconclusive nature of the Amendment's history, with respect to segregated schools, is the status of public education at that time. In the South, the movement toward free common schools, supported by general taxation, had not yet taken hold. Education of white children was largely in the hands of private groups. Education of Negroes was almost nonexistent, and practically all of the race were illiterate. In fact, any education of Negroes was forbidden by law in some states. Today, in contrast, many Negroes have achieved outstanding success in the arts and sciences as well as in the business and professional world. It is true that public school education at the time of the Amendment had advanced further in the North, but the effect of the Amendment on Northern States was generally ignored in the congressional debates. Even in the North, the conditions of public education did not approximate those existing today. The curriculum was usually rudimentary; ungraded schools were common in rural areas; the school term was but three months a year in many states; and compulsory school attendance was virtually unknown. As a consequence, it is not surprising that there should be so little in the history of the Fourteenth Amendment relating to its intended effect on public education.

In the first cases in this Court construing the Fourteenth Amendment, decided shortly after its adoption, the Court interpreted it as proscribing all state-imposed discriminations against the Negro race. The doctrine of "separate but equal" did not make its appearance in this Court until 1896 in the case of *Plessy v. Ferguson*, supra, involving not education but transportation. American courts have since labored with the doctrine for over half a century. In this Court, there have been six cases involving the "separate but equal" doctrine in the field of public education. . . . [T]he validity of the doctrine itself was not challenged. In more recent cases, all on the graduate school level, inequality was found in that specific benefits enjoyed by white students were denied to Negro students of the same educational qualifications. In none of these cases was it necessary to re-examine the doctrine to grant relief to the Negro plaintiff. And in *Sweatt v. Painter*, supra, the Court expressly reserved decision on the question whether *Plessy v. Ferguson* should be held inapplicable to public education.

In the instant case, that question is directly presented. Here, unlike *Sweatt v. Painter*, there are findings below that the Negro and white schools involved have been equalized, or are being equalized, with respect to buildings, curricula, qualifications and salaries of teachers, and other "tangible" factors. Our decision, therefore, cannot turn on merely a comparison of these tangible factors in the Negro and white schools involved in each of the cases. We must look instead to the effect of segregation itself on public education.

In approaching this problem, we cannot turn the clock back to 1868 when the Amendment was adopted, or even to 1896 when *Plessy v. Ferguson* was written. We must consider public education in the light of its full development and its present place in American life throughout the Nation. Only in this way can it be determined if segregation in public schools deprives these plaintiffs of the equal protection of the laws.

Today, education is perhaps the most important function of state and local governments. Compulsory school attendance laws and the great expenditures for education both demonstrate our recognition of the importance of education to our democratic society. It is required in the performance of our most basic public responsibilities, even service in the armed forces. It is the very foundation of good citizenship. Today it is a principal instrument in awakening the child to cultural values, in preparing him for later professional training, and in helping him to adjust normally to his environment. In these days, it is doubtful that any child may reasonably be expected to succeed in life if he is denied the opportunity of an education. Such an opportunity, where the state has undertaken to provide it, is a right which must be made available to all on equal terms.

We come then to the question presented: Does segregation of children in public schools solely on the basis of race, even though the physical facilities and other "tangible" factors may be equal, deprive the children of the minority group of equal educational opportunities? We believe that it does.

In *Sweatt v. Painter* (1950), in finding that a segregated law school for Negroes could not provide them equal educational opportunities, this Court relied in large part on "those qualities which are incapable of objective measurement but which make for greatness in a law school." In *McLaurin v. Oklahoma State Regents* (1950), the Court, in requiring that a Negro admitted to a white graduate school be treated like all other students, again resorted to intangible considerations: "his ability to study, to engage in discussions and exchange views with other students, and, in general, to learn his profession." Such considerations apply with added force to children in grade and high schools. To separate them from others of similar age and qualifications solely because of their race generates a feeling of inferiority as to their status in the community that may affect their hearts and minds in a way unlikely ever to be undone. The effect of this separation on their educational opportunities was well stated by a finding in the Kansas case by a court which nevertheless felt compelled to rule against the Negro plaintiffs:

"Segregation of white and colored children in public schools has a detrimental effect upon the colored children. The impact is greater when it has the sanction of the law; for the policy of separating the races is usually interpreted as denoting the inferiority of the negro group. A sense of inferiority affects the motivation of a child to learn. Segregation with the sanction of law, therefore, has a tendency to [retard] the educational and mental development of Negro children and to deprive them of some of the benefits they would receive in a racial[ly] integrated school system."

Whatever may have been the extent of psychological knowledge at the time of *Plessy v. Ferguson*, this finding is amply supported by modern authority. Any language in *Plessy v. Ferguson* contrary to this finding is rejected.

We conclude that in the field of public education the doctrine of "separate but equal" has no place. Separate educational facilities are inherently unequal. Therefore, we hold that the plaintiffs and others similarly situated for whom the actions have been brought are, by reason of the segregation complained of, deprived of the equal protection of the laws guaranteed by the Fourteenth Amendment. This disposition makes unnecessary any discussion whether such segregation also violates the Due Process Clause of the Fourteenth Amendment.

Because these are class actions, because of the wide applicability of this decision, and because of the great variety of local conditions, the formulation of decrees in these cases presents problems of considerable complexity. On reargument, the consideration of appropriate relief was necessarily subordinated to the primary question—the constitutionality of segregation in public education. We have now announced that such segregation is a denial of the equal protection of the laws. In order that we may have the full assistance of the parties in formulating decrees, the cases will be restored to the docket, and the parties are requested to present further argument on Questions 4 and 5 previously propounded by the Court for the reargument this Term. The Attorney General of the United States is again invited to participate. The Attorneys General of the states requiring or permitting segregation in public education will also be permitted to appear as *amici curiae* upon request to do so by September 15, 1954, and submission of briefs by October 1, 1954.

It is so ordered.

"Southern Declaration on Integration"
March 12, 1956

Chief Justice Warren's opinion in Brown *ignited a fire storm of southern protest. An entire generation of white southern segregationist politicians, such as Governor George Wallace of Alabama, built their careers by claiming that the decision violated the tradition that local authorities should regulate race relations. White Citizens Councils in the South conspired to frustrate implementation of the decision, and the Ku Klux Klan, which had been moribund for a number of years, sprang back to life. Southern politicians clearly understood what their white voting constituencies wanted, and the "Southern Declaration on Integration" was the initial step in what became a program of massive southern resistance to* Brown *and to the High Court decisions that followed in its wake. It was signed by ninety-six southern congressmen, practically the entire southern delegation in the House of Representatives.*

We regard the decision of the Supreme Court in the school cases as clear abuse of judicial power. It climaxes a trend in the Federal judiciary undertaking to legislate, in derogation of the authority of Congress, and to encroach upon the reserved rights of the states and the people.

The original Constitution does not mention education. Neither does the Fourteenth Amendment nor any other amendment. The debates preceding the submission of the Fourteenth Amendment clearly show that there was no intent that it should affect the systems of education maintained by the states.

The very Congress which proposed the amendment subsequently provided for segregated schools in the District of Columbia.

When the amendment was adopted in 1868, there were thirty-seven states of the Union. Every one of the twenty-six states that had any substantial racial differences among its people either approved the operation of segregated schools already in existence or subsequently established such schools by action of the same law-making body which considered the Fourteenth Amendment.

As admitted by the Supreme Court in the public school case (*Brown v. Board of Education*), the doctrine of separate but equal schools "apparently originated in *Roberts v. City of Boston* (1849), upholding school segregation against attack as being violative of a state constitutional guarantee of equality." This constitutional doctrine began in the North—not in the South—and it was followed not only in Massachusetts but in Connecticut, New York, Illinois, Indiana, Michigan, Minnesota, New Jersey, Ohio, Pennsylvania and other northern states until they, exercising their rights as states through the constitutional processes of local self-government, changed their school systems.

In the case of *Plessy v. Ferguson* in 1896 the Supreme Court expressly declared that under the Fourteenth Amendment no person was denied any of his rights if the states provided separate but equal public facilities. This decision has been followed in many other cases. . . .

This interpretation, restated time and again, became a part of the life of the people of many of the states and confirmed their habits, customs, traditions, and way of life. It is founded on elemental humanity and common sense, for parents should not be deprived by Government of the right to direct the lives and education of their own children.

Though there has been no constitutional amendment or act of Congress changing this established legal principle almost a century old, the Supreme Court of the United States, with no legal basis for such action, undertook to exercise their naked judicial power and substituted their personal political and social ideas for the established law of the land.

This unwarranted exercise of power by the court, contrary to the Constitution, is creating chaos and confusion in the states principally affected. It is destroying the amicable relations between the white and Negro races that have been created through ninety years of patient effort by the good people of both races. It has planted hatred and suspicion where there has been heretofore friendship and understanding.

Without regard to the consent of the governed, outside agitators are threatening immediate and revolutionary changes in our public school systems. If done, this is certain to destroy the system of public education in some of the states.

With the gravest concern for the explosive and dangerous condition created by this decision and inflamed by outside meddlers:

We reaffirm our reliance on the Constitution as the fundamental law of the land.

We decry the Supreme Court's encroachments on rights reserved to the states and to the people, contrary to established law and to the Constitution.

We commend the motives of those states which have declared the intention to resist forced integration by any lawful means.

We appeal to the states and people who are not directly affected by these decisions to consider the constitutional principles involved against the time when they too, on issues vital to them, may be the victims of judicial encroachment.

Even though we constitute a minority in the present Congress, we have full faith that a majority of the American people believe in the dual system of government which has enabled us to achieve our greatness and will in time demand that the reserved rights of the states and of the people be made secure against judicial usurpation.

We pledge ourselves to use all lawful means to bring about a reversal of this decision which is contrary to the Constitution and to prevent the use of force in its implementation.

In this trying period, as we all seek to right this wrong, we appeal to our people not to be provoked by the agitators and troublemakers invading our states and to scrupulously refrain from disorder and lawless acts.

Note: Race and the Constitution

Brown v. *Board of Education* was the Court's greatest twentieth-century decision, and it was certainly one of the most important decisions in its entire history. The justices did not overturn *Plessy* v. *Ferguson*; instead, they abolished the separate-but-equal doctrine in public schools and, by implication, in all public facilities. Although two more decades of difficult litigation lay ahead, the *Brown* decision equipped the NAACP with a precedent that allowed it to attack de jure segregation throughout the nation. The decision did not mean that segregation came to an end, however; it persisted (and still persists today) on a de facto basis throughout the nation, largely as a result of residential housing patterns.

Chief Justice Earl Warren's opinion, which was the first of his tenure on the Court, owed as much to principles of equity as to strict constitutional law. The justices had originally hoped to find some guidance in either the history of the Fourteenth Amendment or the social sciences to clarify the issues. Their quest, of course, underscored the impact of Legal Realism on the Court and the infiltration of nonlegal materials into its decision-making process. In the end, however, both avenues of inquiry proved unavailing, and the Chief Justice resorted to principles of equity.

The decision in *Brown* I stated only the broad principles behind the Court's decision. It did not provide a specific remedy. The Court ordered the parties to reappear at the next term to argue what action should be taken to implement the decision. In *Brown* II, 349 U.S. 294 (1955), the Court ordered lower federal courts to require "defendants [to] make a prompt and reasonable start toward full compliance" by ensuring that the "parties to these cases" were admitted "to public schools on a racially nondiscriminatory basis with all deliberate speed." The wording was an invitation to delay that white southern segregationists readily accepted.

Change in the racial composition of public schools in the South was glacial, and school boards there openly flaunted the High Court's mandate. In 1957, for example, President Dwight D. Eisenhower finally called out federal troops to restore order in Little Rock, Arkansas, and to integrate Little Rock Central High School. The Court, in *Cooper* v. *Aaron* (1958), took the same occasion to reassert that it alone could conclusively interpret the meaning of the Constitution. Even after Little Rock, the movement toward integrated public schools staggered along, with white opponents adopting a variety of techniques, going so far in some instances as to close the public schools altogether.

Faced with these pressures, the NAACP sought and ultimately received support from increasingly frustrated federal judges in the South. The turning point came in the 1971 case of *Swann et al.* v. *Charlotte-Mecklenburg Board of Education.* Chief Justice Warren Burger, speaking for a unanimous Court, approved a lower federal court plan calling for busing of schoolchildren in order to achieve certain mathematical ratios between black and white students in each school.

The evidence suggests that despite tremendous efforts to bring about greater racial balance in public schools, de facto segregation persists. While the number of interracial schools has increased dramatically since 1954, many schools remain predominately white or black. And the busing scheme adopted in *Swann* remains a source of controversy, so much so that in many communities school boards have adopted magnet-school programs as a substitute. These programs encourage the crossing of racial lines by offering different programs of study in schools, many of whose students must be bused in order to attend.

MARTIN LUTHER KING, JR.
"Letter from Birmingham City Jail"
1963

While imprisoned in the Birmingham, Alabama, jail in 1963 for failing to file an Alabama tax return, Martin Luther King, Jr., responded to critics who complained that his tactics of civil disobedience against white racism were not only illegal but immoral. King was particularly stung by the attack made on him by white clergymen, to whom this letter was addressed, who charged that his tactics of resistance were fomenting civil discord and bloodshed. They urged a cautious and lawful approach. Like the abolitionists of the 1840s and 1850s, King had no time to wait, and he argued as well that nonviolent civil disobedience was a proper response to the immorality of southern race relations. King wrote the letter on bits and pieces of newspapers that were smuggled out by a black jail attendant.

You express a great deal of anxiety over our willingness to break laws. This is certainly a legitimate concern. Since we so diligently urge people to obey the Supreme Court's decision of 1954 outlawing segregation in the public schools, it is rather strange and paradoxical to find us consciously breaking laws. One may well ask, "How can you advocate breaking some laws and obeying others?" The answer is found in the fact that there are two types of laws: There are *just* laws and there are *unjust* laws. I would be the first to advocate obeying just laws. One has not only a legal but moral responsibility to obey just laws. Conversely, one has a moral responsibility to disobey unjust laws. I would agree with Saint Augustine that "An unjust law is no law at all."

Now what is the difference between the two? How does one determine when a law is just or unjust? A just law is a man-made code that squares with the moral law or the law of God. An unjust law is a code that is out of harmony with the moral law. To put in the terms of Saint Thomas Aquinas, an unjust law is a human law that is not rooted in eternal and natural laws. Any law that uplifts human personality is just. Any law that degrades human personality is unjust. All segregation statutes are unjust because segregation distorts the soul and damages the personality. It gives the segregator a false sense of superiority and the segregated a false sense of inferiority. To use the words of Martin Buber, the great Jewish philosopher, segregation substitutes an "I–it" relationship for the "I–thou" relationship, and ends up relegating persons to the status of things. So segregation is not only politically, economically, and sociologically unsound, but it is morally wrong and sinful. Paul Tillich has said that sin is separation. Isn't segregation an existential expression of man's tragic separation, an expression of his awful estrangement, his terrible sinfulness? So I can urge men to obey the 1954 decision of the Supreme Court because it is morally right, and I can urge them to disobey segregation ordinances because they are morally wrong.

Let us turn to a more concrete example of just and unjust laws. An unjust law is a code that a majority inflicts on a minority that is not binding on itself. This is *difference* made legal. On the other hand a just law is a code that a majority compels a minority to follow that it is willing to follow itself. This is *sameness* made legal.

Let me give another explanation. An unjust law is a code inflicted upon a minority which that minority had no part in enacting or creating because they did not have the unhampered right to vote. Who can say the legislature of Alabama which set up the segregation laws was democratically elected? Throughout the state of Alabama all types of conniving methods are used to prevent Negroes from becoming registered voters and there are some counties without a single Negro registered to vote despite the fact that the Negro constitutes a majority of the population. Can any law set up in such a state be considered democratically structured?

These are just a few examples of just and unjust laws. There are some instances when a law is just on its face but unjust in its application. For instance, I was arrested Friday on a charge of parading without a permit. Now there is nothing wrong with an ordinance which requires a permit for a parade, but when the ordinance is used to preserve segregation and to deny citizens the First Amendment privilege of peaceful assembly and peaceful protest, then it becomes unjust.

I hope you can see the distinction I am trying to point out. In no sense do I advocate evading or defying the law as the rabid segregationist would do. This would lead to anarchy. One who breaks an unjust law must do it *openly*, *lovingly* (not hatefully as the white mothers did in New Orleans when they were seen on television screaming "nigger, nigger, nigger") and with a willingness to accept the penalty. I submit that an individual who breaks a law that conscience tells him is unjust, and willingly accepts the penalty by staying in jail to arouse the conscience of the community over its injustice, is in reality expressing the very highest respect for the law.

Civil Rights: Gender and Privacy

Women learned from the civil rights movement's fight against race-based discrimination. Since the mid-nineteenth century, women had fought to achieve political and economic equality, but with little success. During the early twentieth century, Alice Paul, a leader of the National Woman's party, had urged the adoption of an Equal Rights Amendment to the federal Constitution, but her efforts came to naught.

By the 1960s, women's roles had changed dramatically, both in the home and in the job market. As the incidence of two-wage-earner families increased, so did the demands of women for greater recognition. The Civil Rights Act of 1964 was particularly important because, as a result of last-minute maneuvering in Congress, that measure included a provision banning discrimination in employment based on gender. The National Organization for Women (NOW), founded in 1966, relied on the act to press for greater rights for women. Part of NOW's energies were also expended in an ultimately unsuccessful effort to pass the Equal Rights Amendment to the Constitution. Like the NAACP and the ACLU, however, NOW organizers understood that even without such authority the federal courts offered an ideal forum in which to enhance the rights of women. The outcome has been additional new guarantees for women, although the High Court has refused to impose the same level of scrutiny on gender-based legislation as it has on race-based measures. These developments are particularly clear in three areas: privacy and procreation, sex as a suspect classification, and employment discrimination.

Griswold v. *Connecticut*
381 U.S. 479 (1965)

Estelle Griswold was the executive director of the Planned Parenthood League of Connecticut. She was arrested in November 1961 for giving information to married persons about available contraceptive devices and was fined $100 under a Connecticut law prohibiting the distribution of birth-control devices or birth-control information. Connecticut courts had twice upheld the decision. When it

reached the Supreme Court, the justices had to consider whether there was a
constitutional basis for a right to privacy, since no such right was explicitly
enumerated in the Constitution.

MR. JUSTICE DOUGLAS delivered the opinion of the Court.

Coming to the merits, we are met with a wide range of questions that implicate the Due Process Clause of the Fourteenth Amendment. Overtones of some arguments suggest that *Lochner* v. *New York* (1905) should be our guide. But we decline that invitation. . . . We do not sit as a super-legislature to determine the wisdom, need, and propriety of laws that touch economic problems, business affairs, or social conditions. This law, however, operates directly on an intimate relation of husband and wife and their physician's role in one aspect of that relation.

The association of people is not mentioned in the Constitution nor in the Bill of Rights. The right to educate a child in a school of the parents' choice—whether public or private or parochial—is also not mentioned. Nor is the right to study any particular subject or any foreign language. Yet the First Amendment has been construed to include certain of these rights.

By *Pierce* v. *Society of Sisters* (1920), the right to educate one's children as one chooses is made applicable to the States by the force of the First and Fourteenth Amendments. By *Meyer* v. *Nebraska* (1925), the same dignity is given the right to study the German language in a private school. In other words, the State may not, consistently with the spirit of the First Amendment, contract the spectrum of available knowledge. The right of freedom of speech and press includes not only the right to utter or to print, but the right to distribute, the right to receive, the right to read . . . and freedom of inquiry, freedom of thought, and freedom to teach . . . indeed the freedom of the entire university community. . . . Without those peripheral rights the specific rights would be less secure. And so we reaffirm the principle of the *Pierce* and the *Meyer* cases.

In *NAACP* v. *Alabama* (1962), we protected the "freedom to associate and privacy in one's associations," noting that freedom of association was a peripheral First Amendment right. Disclosure of membership lists of a constitutionally valid association, we held, was invalid "as entailing the likelihood of a substantial restraint upon the exercise by petitioner's members of their right to freedom of association." In other words, the First Amendment has a penumbra where privacy is protected from governmental intrusion. In like context, we have protected forms of "association" that are not political in the customary sense but pertain to the social, legal, and economic benefit of the members. . . .

Those cases involved more than the "right of assembly"—a right that extends to all irrespective of their race or ideology. . . . The right of "association" like the right of belief is more than the right to attend a meeting; it includes the right to express one's attitudes or philosophies by membership in a group or by affiliation with it or by other lawful means. Association in that context is a form of expression of opinion; and while it is not expressly included in the First Amendment its existence is necessary in making the express guarantees fully meaningful.

*   *   *

The foregoing cases suggest that specific guarantees in the Bill of Rights have penumbras, formed by emanations from those guarantees that help give them life and substance. . . . Various guarantees create zones of privacy. The right of association contained in the penumbra of the First Amendment is one, as we have seen. The Third Amendment in its prohibition against the quartering of soldiers "in any house" in time of peace without the consent of the owner is another facet of that privacy. The Fourth Amendment explicitly affirms the "right of the people to be secure in their persons, houses, papers, and effects, against unreasonable searches and seizures." The Fifth Amendment in its Self-Incrimination Clause enables the citizen to create a zone of privacy which government may not force him to surrender to his detriment. The Ninth Amendment provides: "The enumeration in the Constitution, of certain rights, shall not be construed to deny or disparage others retained by the people."

The present case, then, concerns a relationship lying within the zone of privacy created by several fundamental constitutional guarantees. And it concerns a law which, in forbidding the *use* of contraceptives rather than regulating their manufacture or sale, seeks to achieve its goals by means having a maximum destructive impact upon that relationship. Such a law cannot stand in light of the familiar principle, so often applied by this Court, that a "governmental purpose to control or prevent activities constitutionally subject to state regulation may not be achieved by means which sweep unnecessarily broadly and thereby invade the area of protected freedoms" *NAACP* v. *Alabama* (1958). Would we allow the police to search the sacred precincts of marital bedrooms for telltale signs of the use of contraceptives? The very idea is repulsive to the notions of privacy surrounding the marriage relationship.

We deal with a right of privacy older than the Bill of Rights—older than our political parties, older than our school system. Marriage is a coming together for better or for worse, hopefully enduring, and intimate to the degree of being sacred. It is an association that promotes a way of life, not causes; a harmony in living, not political faiths; a bilateral loyalty, not commercial or social projects. Yet it is an association for as noble a purpose as any involved in our prior decisions.

Reversed.

Note: The Debate in *Griswold*

The justices divided sharply over where to locate the new constitutional right of privacy. Some members of the Court (John Marshall Harlan and Byron White) believed it was rooted in the due process clause; another faction (Douglas and Tom Clark) thought it was covered by one of the "penumbras" of the Ninth Amendment; and still a third group (Arthur Goldberg, Earl Warren, and William Brennan) agreed with both groups, concluding that the Ninth Amendment provided the source of authority to infer unwritten rights into the Constitution.

The *Griswold* case also exhumed the whole substantive due process question. This concept had been discredited in matters of economic regulation, but Justices Harlan, White, Goldberg, Brennan, and Warren defended it in *Griswold* as the best approach to establishing the validity of unwritten rights. Douglas, as his opinion makes clear, explicitly disavowed such a course of action, as did Justice Hugo Black, who wrote a strong dissenting opinion. But Black not only failed to persuade in this case, but also lost the larger battle, as the decision in *Roe* v. *Wade* (1973) underscores. The Court, however, has refused to extend this right of privacy to consenting homosexual adults. In *Bowers* v. *Hardwick* (1986), the justices let stand a Georgia sodomy statute.

Roe v. Wade
410 U. S. 113 (1973)

Jane Roe was an unmarried pregnant woman who wanted an abortion. Texas law, which was like most other abortion statutes in the United States, forbade this procedure unless the life of the mother was at risk. Roe began her lawsuit in March 1970, although when the case reached the Supreme Court she had already had her child and given it up for adoption. Critics of this decision, of which there are many, claim that the Court should never have heard it because the issue that it raised had been mooted by the birth of the child. What do you think? Again, this case has implications not only for the rights of women, but for the ways in which the High Court uses its powers.

Mr. JUSTICE BLACKMUN delivered the opinion of the Court.

The principal thrust of appellant's attack on the Texas statutes is that they improperly invade a right, said to be possessed by the pregnant woman, to choose to terminate her pregnancy. Appellant would discover this right in the concept of personal "liberty" embodied in the Fourteenth Amendment's Due Process Clause; or in personal, marital, familial, and sexual privacy said to be protected by the Bill of Rights or its penumbras. . . ; or among those rights reserved to the people by the Ninth Amendment. . . . Before addressing this claim, we feel it desirable briefly to survey, in several aspects, the history of abortion, for such insight as that history may afford us, and then to examine the state purposes and interests behind the criminal abortion laws.

It perhaps is not generally appreciated that the restrictive criminal abortion laws in effect in a majority of States today are of relatively recent vintage. Those laws, generally proscribing abortion or its attempt at any time during pregnancy except when necessary to preserve that pregnant woman's life, are not of ancient or even of common-law origin. Instead, they derive from statutory changes effected, for the most part, in the latter half of the nineteenth century.

*   *   *

It is thus apparent that at common law, at the time of the adoption of our Constitution, and throughout the major portion of the nineteenth century, abortion was viewed with less disfavor than under most American statutes currently in effect. Phrasing it in another way, a woman enjoyed a substantially broader right to terminate a pregnancy than she does in most States today. At least with respect to the early stage of pregnancy, and very possibly without such a limitation, the opportunity to make this choice was present in this country well into the nineteenth century. Even later, the law continued for some time to treat less punitively an abortion procured in early pregnancy.

*   *   *

Three reasons have been advanced to explain historically the enactment of criminal abortion laws in the nineteenth century and to justify their continued existence.

It has been argued occasionally that these laws were the product of a Victorian social concern to discourage illicit sexual conduct. Texas, however, does not advance this justification in the present case. . . .

A second reason is concerned with abortion as a medical procedure. When most criminal abortion laws were first enacted, the procedure was a hazardous one for the woman. This was particularly true prior to the development of antisepsis. . . .

Modern medical techniques have altered this situation. Appellants and various *amici* refer to medical data indicating that abortion in early pregnancy, that is, prior to the end of the first trimester, although not without its risk, is now relatively safe. Mortality rates for women undergoing early abortions, where the procedure is legal, appear to be as low or lower than the rates for normal childbirth. Consequently, any interest of the State in protecting the woman from an inherently hazardous procedure, except when it would be equally dangerous for her to forgo it, has largely disappeared. Of course, important state interests in the areas of health and medical standards do remain. The State has a legitimate interest in seeing to it that abortion, like any other medical procedure, is performed under circumstances that insure maximum safety for the patient. This interest obviously extends at least to the performing physician and his staff, to the facilities involved, to the availability of after-care, and to adequate provision for any complication or emergency that might arise. . . . Moreover, the risk to the woman increases as her pregnancy continues. Thus, the State retains a definite interest in protecting the woman's own health and safety when an abortion is proposed at a late stage of pregnancy.

The third reason is the State's interest—some phrase it in terms of duty—in protecting prenatal life. Some of the arguments for this justification rests on the theory that a new human life is present from the moment of conception. The State's interest and general obligation to protect life then extends, it is argued, to prenatal life. Only when the life of the pregnant mother herself is at stake, balanced against the life she carried within her, should the interest of the embryo or fetus not prevail. Logically, of course, a legitimate state interest in this area need not stand or fall on acceptance of the belief that life begins at conception or at some other point prior to live birth. In assessing the State's interest, recognition may be given to the less rigid claim that as long as at least *potential* life is involved, the State may assert interests beyond the protection of the pregnant woman alone.

Parties challenging state abortion laws have sharply disputed in some courts the contention that a purpose of these laws, when enacted, was to protect prenatal life . . . [and] they claim that most state laws were designed solely to protect the woman. Because medical advances have lessened this concern, at least with respect to abortion in early pregnancy, they argue that with respect to such abortions the laws can no longer be justified by any state interest. There is some scholarly support for this view of original purpose. The few state courts called upon to interpret their laws in the late nineteenth and early twentieth centuries did focus on the State's interest in protecting the woman's health rather than in preserving the embryo and fetus. Proponents of this view point out that in many States, including Texas, by statute or judicial interpretation, the pregnant woman herself could not be prosecuted for self-abortion or for cooperating in an abortion performed upon her by another. They claim that adoption of the "quickening" distinction through received common law and state statutes tacitly recognizes the greater health hazards inherent in the late abortion and impliedly repudiates the theory that life begins at conception. . . .

The Constitution does not explicitly mention any right of privacy. In a line of decisions, however, . . . the Court has recognized that a right of personal privacy, or a guarantee of certain areas or zones of privacy, does exist under the Constitution. In varying contexts, the Court or individual Justices have, indeed, found at least the roots of that right.

*   *   *

This right of privacy, whether it be founded in the Fourteenth Amendment's concept of personal liberty and restrictions upon state action, as we feel it is, or, as the District Court determined, in the Ninth Amendment's reservation of rights to the people, is broad enough to encompass a woman's decision whether or not to terminate her pregnancy. The detriment that the State would impose upon the pregnant woman by denying this choice altogether is apparent. Specific and direct harm medically diagnosable even in early pregnancy may be involved. Maternity, or additional offspring, may force upon the woman a distressful life and future. Psychological harm may be imminent. Mental and physical health may be taxed by child care. There is also the distress, for all concerned, associated with the unwanted child, and there is the problem of bringing a child into a family already unable, psychologically and otherwise, to care for it. In other cases, as in this one, the additional difficulties and continuing stigma of unwed motherhood may be involved. All these are factors the woman and her responsible physician necessarily will consider in consultation.

On the basis of elements such as these, appellant and some *amici* argue that the woman's right is absolute and that she is entitled to terminate her pregnancy at whatever time, in whatever way, and for whatever reason she alone chooses. With this we do not agree. Appellant's arguments that Texas either has no valid interest at all in regulating the abortion decision, or no interest strong enough to support any limitation upon the woman's sole determination, are unpersuasive. The Court's decisions recognizing a right of privacy also acknowledge that some regulation in areas protected by that right is appropriate. As noted above, a State may properly assert important interests in safeguarding health, in maintaining medical standards, and in protecting potential life. At some point in pregnancy, these respective interests become sufficiently compelling to sustain regulation of the factors that govern the abortion decision. The privacy right involved, therefore, cannot be said to be absolute. In fact, it is not clear to us that the claim asserted by some *amici* that one has an unlimited right to do with one's body as one pleases bears a close relationship to the right of privacy previously articulated in the Court's decisions. The Court has refused to recognize an unlimited right of this kind in the past. . . .

We, therefore, conclude that the right of personal privacy includes the abortion decision, but that this right is not unqualified and must be considered against

important state interests in regulation. . . . [This] right, nonetheless, is not absolute
and is subject to some limitations; and . . . at some point the state interests as to
protection of health, medical standards, and prenatal life, become dominant. . . .

While certain "fundamental rights" are involved, the Court has held that regulation limiting these rights may be justified only by a "compelling state interest" . . . and that legislative enactments must be narrowly drawn to express only
the legitimate state interests at stake. . . .

In the recent abortion cases, . . . courts have recognized these principles. Those
striking down state laws have generally scrutinized the State's interests in protecting
health and potential life, and have concluded that neither interest justified broad
limitations on the reasons for which a physician and his pregnant patient might
decide that she should have an abortion in the early stages of pregnancy. Courts
sustaining state laws have held that the State's determinations to protect health or
prenatal life are dominant and constitutionally justifiable.

*   *   *

The appellee and certain *amici* argue that the fetus is a "person" within the
language and meaning of the Fourteenth Amendment. In support of this, they
outline at length and in detail the well-known facts of fetal development. If this
suggestion of personhood is established, the appellant's case, of course, collapses,
for the fetus' right to life would then be guaranteed specifically by the Amendment . . . [but] no case [can] be cited that holds that a fetus is a person within the
meaning of the Fourteenth Amendment.

The Constitution does not define "person" in so many words. Section 1 of the
Fourteenth Amendment contains three references to "person." The first, in defining
"citizens," speaks of "persons born or naturalized in the United States." . . . "Person"
is used in other places in the Constitution. . . . But in nearly all these instances, the
use of the word is such that it has application only postnatally. None indicates, with
any assurance, that it has any possible pre-natal application.

All this, together with our observation . . . that throughout the major portion of
the nineteenth century prevailing legal abortion practices were far freer than they are
today, persuades us that the word "person," as used in the Fourteenth Amendment,
does not include the unborn. This is in accord with the results reached in those few
cases where the issue has been squarely presented.

The pregnant woman cannot be isolated in her privacy. She carries an embryo
and, later, a fetus. . . . The situation therefore is inherently different from marital
intimacy, or bedroom possession of obscene material, or marriage, or procreation,
or education. . . . As we have intimated above, it is reasonable and appropriate for
a State to decide that at some point in time another interest, that of health of the
mother or that of potential human life, becomes significantly involved. The woman's privacy is no longer sole and any right of privacy she possesses must be
measured accordingly.

Texas urged that, apart from the Fourteenth Amendment, life begins at conception and is present throughout pregnancy, and that, therefore, the State has a compelling interest in protecting that life from and after conception. We need not resolve
the difficult question of when life begins. When those trained in the respective
disciplines of medicine, philosophy, and theology are unable to arrive at any con-

sensus, the judiciary, at this point in the development of man's knowledge, is not in a position to speculate as to the answer.

It should be sufficient to note briefly the wide divergence of thinking on this most sensitive and difficult question. There has always been strong support for the view that life does not begin until live birth. . . . Substantial problems for precise definition of this view are posed, however, by new embryological data that purpose to indicate that conception is a "process" over time, rather than an event, and by new medial techniques such as menstrual extraction, the "morning-after" pill, implantation of embryos, artificial insemination, and even artificial wombs.

*   *   *

In view of all this, we do not agree that, by adopting one theory of life, Texas may override the rights of the pregnant woman that are at stake. We repeat, however, that the State does have an important and legitimate interest in preserving and protecting the health of the pregnant woman, whether she be a resident of the State or a nonresident who seeks medical consultation and treatment there, and that it has still *another* important and legitimate interest in protecting the potentiality of human life. These interests are separate and distinct. Each grows in substantiality as the woman approaches term and, at a point during pregnancy, each becomes "compelling."

With respect to the State's important and legitimate interest in the health of the mother, the "compelling" point, in the light of present medical knowledge, is at approximately the end of the first trimester. This is so because of the now-established medical fact, referred to above, that until the end of the first trimester mortality in abortion may be less than mortality in normal childbirth. It follows that, from and after this point, a State may regulate the abortion procedure to the extent that the regulation reasonably relates to the preservation and protection of maternal health. Examples of permissible state regulation in this area are requirements as to the qualifications of the person who is to perform the abortion; as to the licensure of that person; as to the facility in which the procedure is to be performed, that is, whether it must be a hospital or may be a clinic or some other place of less-than-hospital status; as to the licensing of the facility; and the like.

This means, on the other hand, that, for the period of pregnancy prior to this "compelling" point, the attending physician, in consultation with his patient, is free to determine, without regulation by the State, that, in his medical judgment, the patient's pregnancy should be terminated. If that decision is reached, the judgment may be effectuated by an abortion free of interference by the State.

With respect to the State's important and legitimate interest in potential life, the "compelling" point is at viability. This is so because the fetus then presumably has the capability of meaningful life outside the mother's womb. State regulation protective of fetal life after viability thus has both logical and biological justifications. If the State is interested in protecting fetal life after viability, it may go so far as to proscribe abortion during that period, except when it is necessary to preserve the life or health of the mother.

Measured against these standards, Article 1196 of the Texas Penal Code, in restricting legal abortions to those "procured or attempted by medical advice for the purpose of saving the life of the mother," sweeps too broadly. The statute made no distinction between abortions performed early in pregnancy and those performed later, and it limits to a single reason, "saving" the mother's life, the legal justification for the procedure. The statute, therefore, cannot survive the constitutional attack made upon it here. . . .

Note: The Future of *Roe*

The Supreme Court has reaffirmed its *Roe* holding in several subsequent cases, but recently the justices have displayed a new willingness to reevaluate it altogether. In *Webster* v. *Reproductive Health Services* (1989), for example, a closely divided Court concluded that a statutory ban placed by the state of Missouri on the use of public employees and facilities for performance or assistance of nontherapeutic abortions did not contravene the Constitution. The opinion of the Court, which was written by Chief Justice William Rehnquist, did not reach the issue fully, however, since the disputed portion of the statute was its preamble, which provided that "the life of each human being begins at conception" and that "unborn children have protectable interests in life, health and well being." Whether the preamble was part of the statute, however, had not been settled by the Missouri or lower federal courts, and on this basis, the justices decided that the constitutional validity of the measure was mooted until such time as that issue was settled. Pro-choice activists, however, read the Court's actions as indicating a new willingness on the part of the justices to overturn *Roe*.

Civil Rights: Affirmative Action

Affirmative action programs were one of the most controversial aspects of the civil rights revolution. Such programs offered remedies meant to counter past racial and gender discrimination but they faced serious constitutional and political objections.

Johnson v. Transportation Agency, Santa Clara County
107 S. Ct. 1442 (1987)

This case began when Paul Johnson was passed over for promotion to road dispatcher for Santa Clara County, California. Instead, Diane Joyce was awarded that position, one that no female had previously occupied. Her promotion was based on a voluntary affirmative action plan adopted by the county with the purpose of bringing women into traditionally male-dominated positions. Joyce was selected even though the review committee had determined that Johnson was the more worthy candidate. He then sued in federal court, claiming that the selection procedure violated Title VII of the Civil Rights Act of 1964. He was joined in his action by President Ronald Reagan's Justice Department, which filed an amicus *brief.*

Justice BRENNAN delivered the opinion of the court.
The first issue is therefore whether consideration of the sex of applicants for

skilled craft jobs was justified by the existence of a "manifest imbalance" that reflected underrepresentation of women in "traditionally segregated job categories" [*United Steelworkers* v. *Weber* (1979)]. In determining whether an imbalance exists that would justify taking sex or race into account, a comparison of the percentage of minorities or women in the employer's work force with the percentage in the area labor market or general population is appropriate in analyzing jobs that require no special expertise, or training programs designed to provide expertise. . . . Where a job requires special training, however, the comparison should be with those in the labor force who possess the relevant qualifications. . . . The requirement that the "manifest imbalance" relate to a "traditionally segregated job category" provides assurance both that sex or race will be taken into account in a manner consistent with Title VII's purpose of eliminating the effects of employment discrimination, and that the interests of those employees not benefitting from the plan will not be unduly infringed.

A manifest imbalance need not be such that it would support a prima facie case against the employer, . . . since we do not regard as identical the constraints of Title VII and the federal constitution on voluntarily adopted affirmative action plans. Application of the "prima facie" standard in Title VII cases would be inconsistent with *Weber*'s focus on statistical imbalance, and could inappropriately create a significant disincentive for employers to adopt an affirmative action plan. . . . A corporation concerned with maximizing return on investment, for instance, is hardly likely to adopt a plan if in order to do so it must compile evidence that could be used to subject it to a colorable Title VII suit.

It is clear that the decision to hire Joyce was made pursuant to an Agency plan that directed that sex or race be taken into account for the purpose of remedying underrepresentation. The Agency Plan acknowledged the "limited opportunities that have existed in the past," App. 57, for women to find employment in certain job classifications "where women have not been traditionally employed in significant numbers." As a result, observed the Plan, women were concentrated in traditionally female jobs in the Agency, and represented a lower percentage in other job classifications than would be expected if such traditional segregation had not occurred. Specifically, 9 of the 10 Para-Professionals and 110 of the 145 Office and Clerical Workers were women. By contrast, women were only 2 of the 28 Officials and Administrators, 5 of the 58 Professionals, 12 of the 124 Technicians, none of the Skilled Craft Workers, and 1—who was Joyce—of the 110 Road Maintenance Workers. The Plan sought to remedy these imbalances through "hiring, training and promotion of . . . women throughout the Agency in all major job classifications where they are underrepresented."

*   *   *

As the Agency Plan recognized, women were most egregiously underrepresented in the Skilled Craft job category, since none of the 238 positions was occupied by a woman. In mid-1980, when Joyce was selected for the road dispatcher position, the Agency was still in the process of refining its short-term goals for Skilled Craft Workers in accordance with the directive of the Plan. This process did not reach fruition until 1982, when the Agency established a short-term goal for that year of three women for the 55 expected openings in that job category—a modest goal of about 6% for that category.

We reject petitioner's argument that, since only the long-term goal was in place for Skilled Craft positions at the time of Joyce's promotion, it was inappropriate for the Director to take into account affirmative action considerations in filling the road dispatcher position. The Agency's Plan emphasized that the long-term goals were not to be taken as guides for actual hiring decisions, but that supervisors were to consider a host of practical factors in seeking to meet affirmative action objectives, including the fact that in some job categories women were not qualified in numbers comparable to their representation in the labor force.

By contrast, had the Plan simply calculated imbalances in all categories according to the proportion of women in the area labor pool, and then directed that hiring be governed solely by those figures, its validity fairly could be called into question. This is because analysis of a more specialized labor pool normally is necessary in determining underrepresentation in some positions. If a plan failed to take distinctions in qualifications into account in providing guidance for actual employment decisions, it would dictate mere blind hiring by the numbers, for it would hold supervisors to "achievement of a particular percentage of minority employment or membership . . . regardless of circumstances such as economic conditions or the number of qualified minority applicants . . ."

Justice Scalia dissenting:

Today's decision does more, however, than merely reaffirm *Weber*, and more than merely extend it to public actors. It is impossible not to be aware that the practical effect of our holding is to accomplish de facto what the law—in language even plainer than that ignored in *Weber* . . .—forbids anyone from accomplishing *de jure*: in many contexts it effectively *requires* employers, public as well as private, to engage in intentional discrimination on the basis of race or sex. This Court's prior interpretations of Title VII, especially the decision in *Griggs* v. *Duke Power Co.* (1971), subject employers to a potential Title VII suit whenever there is a noticeable imbalance in the representation of minorities or women in the employer's work force. Even the employer who is confident of ultimately prevailing in such a suit must contemplate the expense and adverse publicity of a trial, because the extent of the imbalance, and the "job relatedness" of his selection criteria, are questions of fact to be explored through rebuttal and counter-rebuttal of a "prima facie case" consisting of no more than the showing that the employer's selection process "selects those from the protected class at a 'significantly' lesser rate than their counterparts." . . . If, however, employers are free to discriminate through affirmative action, without fear of "reverse discrimination" suits by their nonminority or male victims, they are offered a threshold defense against Title VII liability premised on numerical disparities. Thus, after today's decision the *failure* to engage in reverse discrimination is economic folly, and arguably a breach of duty to shareholders or taxpayers, wherever the cost of anticipated Title VII litigation exceeds the cost of hiring less capable (though still minimally capable) workers. (This situation is more likely to obtain, of course, with respect to the least skilled jobs—perversely creating an incentive to discriminate against precisely those members of the nonfavored groups least likely to have profited from societal discrimination in the past.) It is predictable, moreover, that this incentive will be greatly magnified by economic pressures brought to bear by government contracting agencies upon employers who refuse to discriminate in the fashion we have now approved. A statute designed to establish a color-blind and gender-blind work place has thus been converted into a powerful engine of racism and sexism, not merely *permitting* intentional race- and sex-based discrimination, but often making it, through operation of the legal system, practically compelled.

It is unlikely that today's result will be displeasing to politically elected officials, to whom it provides the means of quickly accommodating the demands of organized groups to achieve concrete, numerical improvement in the economic status of particular constituencies. Nor will it displease the world of corporate and governmental employers (many of whom have filed briefs as *amici* in the present case, all on the side of Santa Clara) for whom the cost of hiring less qualified workers is often substantially less—and infinitely more predictable—than the cost of litigating Title VII cases and of seeking to convince federal agencies by nonnumerical means that no discrimination exists. In fact, the only losers in the process are the Johnsons of the country, for whom Title VII has been not merely repealed but actually inverted. The irony is that these individuals—predominantly unknown, unaffluent, unorganized—suffer this injustice at the hands of a Court fond of thinking itself the champion of the politically impotent. I dissent.

Note: Affirmative Action

The Court in *Johnson* attempted to come to terms with one of the most controversial aspects of the modern civil rights revolution—affirmative action, or, as its critics term it, reverse discrimination. Proponents of these measures argue that they are necessary to overcome long-standing discriminatory practices, as a way of essentially providing damages to a class of persons that had been injured by previous governmental and private policies. The defenders also insist that there are certain social groups in America that have suffered discrimination and that the traditional emphasis on rights of the individual should be extended to these groups. In essence, they urge a group rather than an individual approach to matters of discrimination. Critics of affirmative action programs complain that such programs not only break with traditional constitutional values, but seriously weaken the principle of individual rights. Such class legislation, they argue, will have the long-term effect of rewarding incompetence instead of rewarding ability and talent. Such programs, of course, are not new, since they can be viewed as a logical extension of the social welfare policies embraced in the 1930s by the New Deal.

Johnson was not the first instance in which the Court had wrestled with the issue of affirmative action, as the opinion of William Brennan and the dissent of Antonin Scalia make clear. In fact, at the time the Court decided the case, it had three important precedents: *University of California Regents* v. *Bakke*, 438 U.S. 265 (1978); *United Steelworkers* v. *Weber*, 443 U.S. 193 (1979); and *Fullilove* v. *Klutznick*, 448 U.S. 448 (1980). All three cases involved race-conscious affirmative action programs. In *Bakke*, a majority of five justices held that Title VI of the Civil Rights Act of 1964 forbade fixed racial quotas in educational institutions receiving federal funds. The justices held unconstitutional a program by the University of California at Davis that set aside for blacks a certain number of positions in the entering medical school class. The justices, however, did agree that the federal law permitted taking minority racial status into account as a "plus" factor in the admissions process.

In *Weber*, the Court took a bolder step. This case involved a voluntary affirmative action plan by an employer to eliminate conspicuous racial imbalance in traditionally segregated job categories. Such programs, according to Justice Brennan's majority opinion, did not violate Title VII of the Civil Rights Act because the goal of the act was to enhance economic opportunity for those previously discriminated against. In essence, Brennan was saying that as a matter of constitutional law and public policy, a qualified white male employee would have to give way to an equally qualified black and/or female, even if there was no showing that a previous pattern of discrimination had existed. It was this matter that most disturbed Justice Scalia.

In the *Fullilove* case, the High Court sustained a federal law that had set aside at least 10 percent of contracts on each public-works project for racial minority contractors. Unlike *Weber*, the Court treated this matter as a remedial effort meant to correct past wrongs. More recently, however, the Rehnquist Court has displayed increasing impatience with such set-aside programs. For example, in *City of Richmond* v. *Croson* (1989), Justice Sandra Day O'Connor, writing for a 7 to 2 majority, held unconstitutional a city ordinance that required at least 30 percent of the dollar amount of each contract be set aside for minority businesses. Justice O'Connor found that the city had failed to tailor its plan in sufficiently narrow ways to address only the prior effects of past discsriminatory practices.

The *Johnson* case is of interest as well because it treated the issue of gender discrimination. The most important case has been *Meritor Savings* v. *Mechelle Vinson*, 477 U.S. 57 (1986). Mechelle Vinson had accused her supervisor of demanding sexual favors (including fondling and sexual intercourse) as a requirement for keeping her job. The supervisor and the bank denied this charge, and a federal district court found no violation of the law. The Supreme Court, however, concluded that Title VII of the Civil Rights Act of 1964 made sexual harassment a form of discrimination and that women could, under the law, press claims in federal courts based on the concept that an employer had created a "hostile environment."

Civil Liberties

The pre-twentieth-century Supreme Court seldom addressed issues of civil liberties. State high court judges, relying on state constitutions, addressed questions of freedom of speech, press, association, and religion—when they were addressed at all. Only during the crisis over the Alien and Sedition Acts of the late 1790s did the federal courts become involved significantly in settling the constitutional boundaries of civil liberties. During the first half of the twentieth century, however, the Court heard an increasing number of cases involving these issues. This development, as with civil rights, was part of the long-term process of intensifying centralization within the American federal system. Growing ethnic diversity and the entry of the United States into both world wars generated social tensions over the proper scope of governmental authority with regard to basic freedoms. Special-interest groups, most notably the American Civil Liberties Union, which was born in 1914 to support opponents of World War I, pressed issues of individual liberty in the federal courts as had never been done before. Moreover, following the constitutional revolution of 1937 and the demise of judicial oversight of economic regulation, the justices of the Roosevelt Court increasingly filled their dockets with civil liberties cases.

Throughout the post–World War II era, the Court has continually struggled with the tension between individual liberty and governmental authority. Much of that tension can be traced to pressures for political and social consensus stimulated by the Cold War. National security interests, for example, were regularly cited during the red scare of the early 1950s and during the great protests over the war in Vietnam as a legitimate basis for curtailing political dissent. The limits of individual liberty were also tested by minority religious groups, such as the Jehovah's Witnesses, who refused to abide by the values of the dominant Protestant religious majority.

The following materials provide only a sampling of the broad and rich contemporary history of civil liberties. As with the section on civil rights, the cases covered below speak eloquently to the Supreme Court's role in seeking a balance between the rights of the individual and the authority of government. Not surprisingly, the justices' role in settling disputes over civil liberties was as controversial as it was in the area of civil rights.

Dennis et al. v. *United States*
341 U.S. 494 (1951)

Fear of Communist subversion in the United States dated to the Russian Revolution of 1917. This paranoia of Americans intensified during the red scare of the early 1950s. Growing antagonism between the United States and the Soviet Union, the threat of nuclear war, and the Communist revolution in mainland China ushered in the darker spirits of American politics. Senator Joseph McCarthy of Wisconsin, for example, boosted his political fortunes by claiming that hundreds of Soviet agents had infiltrated the Pentagon. Eugene Dennis was the head of the American Communist party, and following a spectacular trial in New York City in 1949, he and several other party members were found guilty under the Smith Act of advocating the overthrow of the government of the United States. There was no proof that they had actually engaged in *such activity; instead, the evidence indicated that they had only* advocated *such a result. In previous First Amendment cases, the Court had held that mere advocacy was not a sufficient basis to restrict individual liberty.*

MR. CHIEF JUSTICE VINSON announced the judgment of the Court.

The obvious purpose of the [Smith Act] is to protect existing Government, not from change by peaceable, lawful and constitutional means, but from change by violence, revolution and terrorism. That it is within the *power* of the Congress to protect the Government of the United States from armed rebellion is a proposition which requires little discussion. Whatever theoretical merit there may be to the argument that there is a "right" to rebellion against dictatorial governments is without force where the existing structure of the government provides for peaceful and orderly change. We reject any principle of governmental helplessness in the face of preparation for revolution, which principle, carried to its logical conclusion, must lead to anarchy. No one could conceive that it is not within the power of Congress to prohibit acts intended to overthrow the Government by force and violence. The question with which we are concerned here is not whether Congress has such *power*, but whether the *means* which it has employed conflict with the First and Fifth Amendments to the Constitution.

One of the bases for the contention that the means which Congress has employed are invalid takes the form of an attack on the face of the statute on the grounds that by its terms it prohibits academic discussion of the merits of Marxism-Leninism, that it stifles ideas and is contrary to all concepts of a free speech and a free press.

*   *   *

The very language of the Smith Act negates the interpretation which petitioners would have us impose on that Act. It is directed at advocacy, not discussion. Thus, the trial judge properly charged the jury that they could not convict if they found that petitioners did "no more than pursue peaceful studies and discussions or teaching and advocacy in the realm of ideas." He further charged that it was not unlawful "to conduct in an American college or university a course explaining the philosophical theories set forth in the books which have been placed in evidence." Such a charge is in strict accord with the statutory language, and illustrates the meaning to be placed on those words. Congress did not intend to eradicate the free discussion of political theories, to destroy the traditional rights of Americans to discuss and evaluate ideas without fear of governmental sanction. Rather Congress was concerned with the very kind of activity in which the evidence showed these petitioners engaged.

*   *   *

In this case we are squarely presented with the application of the "clear and present danger" test, and must decide what that phrase imports.

*   *   *

Obviously, the words cannot mean that before the Government may act, it must wait until the putsch is about to be executed, the plans have been laid and the signal is awaited. If Government is aware that a group aiming at its overthrow is attempting to indoctrinate its members and to commit them to a course whereby they will strike when the leaders feel the circumstances permit, action by the Government is required. The argument that there is no need for Government to concern itself, for Government is strong, it possesses ample powers to put down a rebellion, it may defeat the revolution with ease needs no answer. For that is not the question. Certainly an attempt to overthrow the Government by force, even though doomed from the outset because of inadequate numbers or power of the revolutionists, is a sufficient evil for Congress to prevent. The damage which such attempts create both physically and politically to a nation makes it impossible to measure the validity in terms of the probability of success, or the immediacy of a successful attempt. In the instant case the trial judge charged the jury that they could not convict unless they found that petitioners intended to overthrow the Government "as speedily as circumstances would permit." This does not mean, and could not properly mean, that they would not strike until there was certainty of success. What was meant was that the revolutionists would strike when they thought the time was ripe. We must therefore reject the contention that success or probability of success is the criterion.

*   *   *

Chief Judge Learned Hand, writing for the majority below, interpreted the phrase as follows: "In each case [courts] must ask whether the gravity of the 'evil,' discounted by its improbability, justifies such invasion of free speech as is necessary to avoid the danger." 183 F2d at 212. We adopt this statement of the rule. As articulated by Chief Judge Hand, it is as succinct and inclusive as any other we might devise at this time. It takes into consideration those factors which we deem relevant, and relates their significances. More we cannot expect from words.

The mere fact that from the period 1945 to 1948 petitioners' activities did not result in an attempt to overthrow the Government by force and violence is of course no answer to the fact that there was a group that was ready to make the attempt. The formation by petitioners of such a highly organized conspiracy, with rigidly disciplined members subject to call when the leaders, these petitioners, felt that the time had come for action, coupled with the inflammable nature of world conditions, similar uprisings in other countries, and the touch-and-go nature of our relations with countries with whom petitioners were in the very least ideologically attuned, convince us that their convictions were justified on this score. And this analysis disposes of the contention that a conspiracy to advocate, as distinguished from the advocacy itself, cannot be constitutionally restrained, because it comprises only the preparation. It is the existence of the conspiracy which creates the danger. . . . If the ingredients of the reaction are present, we cannot bind the Government to wait until the catalyst is added.

*   *   *

We hold that sections 2(a) (1), 2(a) (3) and 3 of the Smith Act do not inherently, or as construed or applied in the instant case, violate the First Amendment and other provisions of the Bill of Rights, or the First and Fifth Amendments because of indefiniteness. Petitioners intended to overthrow the Government of the United States as speedily as the circumstances would permit. Their conspiracy to organize the Communist Party and to teach and advocate the overthrow of the Government of the United States by force and violence created a "clear and present danger" of an attempt to overthrow the Government by force and violence. They were properly and constitutionally convicted for violation of the Smith Act. The judgments of conviction are upheld.

*   *   *

MR. JUSTICE BLACK, dissenting.

*   *   *

At the outset I want to emphasize what the crime involved in this case is, and what it is not. These petitioners were not charged with an attempt to overthrow the Government. They were not charged with overt acts of any kind designed to overthrow the Government. They were not even charged with saying anything or writing anything designed to overthrow the Government. The charge was that they agreed to assemble and to talk and publish certain ideas at a later date: The indictment is that they conspired to organize the Communist Party and to use speech or newspapers and other publications in the future to teach and advocate the forcible overthrow of the Government. No matter how it is worded, this is a virulent from of prior censorship of speech and press, which I believe the First Amendment forbids. I would hold section 3 of the Smith Act authorizing this prior restraint unconstitutional on its face and as applied.

But let us assume, contrary to all constitutional ideas of fair criminal procedure, that petitioners although not indicted for the crime of actual advocacy, may be punished for it. Even on this radical assumption, the other opinions in this case show that the only way to affirm these convictions is to repudiate directly or indirectly the established "clear and present danger" rule. This the Court does in a way which greatly restricts the protections afforded by the First Amendment. The opinions for affirmance indicate that the chief reason for jettisoning the rule is the expressed fear that advocacy of Communist doctrine endangers the safety of the Republic. Undoubtedly, a governmental policy of unfettered communication of ideas does entail dangers. To the Founders of this Nation, however, the benefits derived from free expression were worth the risk. They embodied this philosophy in the First Amendment's command that "Congress shall make no law . . . abridging the freedom of speech, or of the press. . . ." I have always believed that the First Amendment is the keystone of our Government, that the freedoms it guarantees provide the best insurance against destruction of all freedom. At least as to speech in the realm of public matters, I believe that the "clear and present danger" test does not "mark the furthermost constitutional boundaries of protected expression" but does "no more than recognize a minimum compulsion of the Bill of Rights."

So long as this Court exercises the power of judicial review of legislation, I cannot agree that the First Amendment permits us to sustain laws suppressing freedom of speech and press on the basis of Congress' or our own notions of mere "reasonableness." Such a doctrine waters down the First Amendment so that it amounts to little more than an admonition to Congress. The Amendment as so construed is not likely to protect any but those "safe" or orthodox views which rarely need its protection. . . .

*   *   *

Public opinion being what it now is, few will protest the conviction of these Communist petitioners. There is hope, however, that in calmer times, when present pressures, passions and fears subside, this or some later Court will restore the First Amendment liberties to the high preferred place where they belong in a free society.

Note: Free Speech and Internal Security

Chief Justice Fred Vinson's opinion in *Dennis* modified the "clear and present danger" test earlier crafted by Oliver Wendell Holmes, Jr. Until *Dennis*, the Court had generally given a liberal interpretation to that test, but the Cold War climate undermined it. The Court did so by modifying the test to provide that offenders could be punished under the Smith Act for conspiring to teach and advocate revolution against the government of the United States. They did not have to take any direct, forcible action.

The federal government relied on *Dennis* to prosecute Communist party members. Over the next six years, the government obtained 128 indictments against party leaders and members, and of these more than 100 were convicted. By the early

1960s, however, as the Cold War climate eased, the Court reevaluated its position with regard to internal security and the First Amendment. First in *Yates* v. *United States* (1957) and then in *Scales* v. *United States* (1961), the justices sustained key provisions of the Smith Act but adopted much tougher evidentiary requirements to prove that an actual threat existed. The Court went even further in *Albertson* v. *S.A.C.B.* (1965), when it made virtually unenforceable a provision of the McCarran Internal Security Act of 1950 that required Communist party members to register with the government. Since being a member of the Communist party was illegal, the McCarran Act registration requirement violated the self-incrimination provision of the Fifth Amendment. In *Brandenburg* v. *Ohio*, 395 U.S. 444 (1969), the Court went even further by declaring an Ohio criminal syndicalism law unconstitutional because it inevitably punished advocacy and assembly.

Engel et al. v. Vitale et al.
370 U.S. 421 (1962)

The Warren Court rewrote much First Amendment law, especially in the area of religious freedom. The religion clause cases, of which Engel *was the most controversial, also revealed the tremendous nationalizing effect that the justices had on American culture. Traditionally, local government and officials had been left to regulate matters such as school prayer. But in* Engel, *the justices reviewed the requirement by New York State school officials that students in the public schools recite daily a nondenominational prayer.*

Mr. Justice Black delivered the opinion of the Court.

The respondent Board of Education of Union Free School District No. 9, New Hyde Park, New York, acting in its official capacity under state law, directed the School District's principal to cause the following prayer to be said aloud by each class in the presence of a teacher at the beginning of each school day:

"Almighty God, we acknowledge our dependence upon Thee, and we beg Thy blessings upon us, our parents, our teachers and our Country."

This daily procedure was adopted on the recommendation of the State Board of Regents. . . . These state officials composed the prayer which they recommended and published as a part of their "Statement on Moral and Spiritual Training in the Schools," saying: "We believe that this Statement will be subscribed to by all men and women of good will, and we call upon all of them to aid in giving life to our program."

Shortly after the practice of reciting the Regents' prayer was adopted by the School District, the parents of ten pupils brought this action in a New York State Court insisting that use of this official prayer in the public schools was contrary to the beliefs, religions, or religious practices of both themselves and their children. Among other things, these parents challenged the constitutionality of both the state law authorizing the School District to direct the use of prayer in public schools and the School District's regulation ordering the recitation of this particular prayer on the ground that these actions of official governmental agencies violate that part of the First Amendment of the Federal Constitution which commands that "Congress shall make no law respecting an establishment of religion"—a command which was "made applicable to the State of New York by the Fourteenth Amendment of the said Constitution. . . ."

We think that by using its public school system to encourage recitation of the Regents' prayer, the State of New York has adopted a practice wholly inconsistent with the Establishment Clause. There can, of course, be no doubt that New York's program of daily classroom invocation of God's blessings as prescribed in the Regents' prayer is a religious activity. It is a solemn avowal of divine faith and supplication for the blessings of the Almighty. The nature of such a prayer has always been religious, none of the respondents has denied this and the trial court expressly so found.

*   *   *

The petitioners contend among other things that the state laws requiring or permitting use of the Regents' prayer must be struck down as a violation of the Establishment Clause because that prayer was composed by governmental officials as a part of a governmental program to further religious beliefs. For this reason, petitioners argue, the State's use of the Regents' prayer in its public school system breaches the constitutional wall of separation between Church and State. We agree with that contention since we think, that the constitutional prohibition against laws respecting an establishment of religion must at least mean that in this country it is no part of the business of government to compose official prayers for any group of the American people to recite as a part of a religious program carried on by government.

It is a matter of history that this very practice of establishing governmentally composed prayers for religious services was one of the reasons which caused many of our early colonists to leave England and seek religious freedom in America.

*   *   *

The First Amendment was added to the Constitution to stand as a guarantee that neither the power nor the prestige of the Federal Government would be used to control support or influence the kinds of prayer the American people can say—that the people's religions must not be subjected to the pressures of government for change each time a new political administration is elected to office. Under that Amendment's prohibition against governmental establishment of religion, as reinforced by the provisions of the Fourteenth Amendment, government in this country, be it state or federal, is without power to prescribe by law any particular form of prayer which is to be used as an official prayer in carrying on any program of governmentally sponsored religious activity.

There can be no doubt that New York's state prayer program officially establishes the religious beliefs embodied in the Regents' prayer. The respondents' argument to the contrary, which is largely based upon the contention that the Regents' prayer is "non-denominational" and the fact that the program, as modified and approved by state courts, does not require all pupils to recite the prayer but permits those who wish to do so to remain silent or be excused from the room, ignores the essential nature of the program's constitutional defects. Neither the fact that the prayer may be denominationally neutral nor the fact that its observance on the part of the students is voluntary can serve to free it from the limitations of the Establishment Clause, as it might from the Free Exercise Clause, of the First Amendment, both of which are operative against the States by virtue of the Fourteenth Amendment. Although these two clauses may in certain instances overlap, they forbid two quite different kinds of governmental encroachment upon religious freedom. The Establishment Clause, unlike the Free Exercise Clause, does not depend upon any showing of direct governmental compulsion and is violated by the enactment of laws which establish an official religion whether those laws operate directly to coerce nonobserving individuals or not. This is not to say, of course, that laws officially prescribing a particular form of religious worship do not involve coercion of such individuals. When the power, prestige and financial support of government is placed behind a particular religious belief, the indirect coercive pressure upon religious minorities to conform to the prevailing officially approved religion is plain. But the purposes underlying the Establishment Clause go much further than that. Its first and most immediate purpose rested on the belief that a union of government and religion tends to destroy government and to degrade religion. The history of governmentally established religion both in England and in this country showed that whenever government had allied itself with one particular form of religion, the inevitable result had been that it had incurred the hatred, disrespect and even contempt of those who held contrary beliefs. That same history showed that many people had lost their respect for any religion that had relied upon the support of government to spread its faith. The Establishment Clause thus stands as an expression of principle on the part of the Founders of our Constitution that religion is too personal, too sacred, too holy, to permit its "unhallowed perversion" by a civil magistrate. Another purpose of the Establishment Clause rested upon an awareness of the historical fact that governmentally established religions and religious persecutions go hand in hand.

*   *   *

It has been argued that to apply the Constitution in such a way as to prohibit state laws respecting an establishment of religious services in public schools is to indicate a hostility toward religion or toward prayer. Nothing, of course, could be more wrong. The history of man is inseparable from the history of religion. And perhaps it is not too much to say that since the beginning of that history many people have devoutly believed that "More things are wrought by prayer than this world dreams of." It was doubtless largely due to men who believed this that there grew up a sentiment that caused men to leave the cross-currents of officially established state religions and religious persecution in Europe and come to this country filled with the hope that they could find a place in which they could pray when they pleased to the God of their faith in the language they chose. And there were men of this same faith in the power of prayer who led the fight for adoption of our Constitution and also for our Bill of Rights with the very guarantees of religious freedom that forbid the sort of governmental activity which New York has attempted here. These men knew that the First Amendment, which tried to put an end to governmental control of religion and of prayer, was not written to destroy either. They knew rather that it was not written to quiet well-justified fears which nearly all of them felt arising out of an awareness that governments of the past had shackled men's tongues to make them speak only the religious thoughts that government wanted them to speak and to pray only to the God that government wanted them to pray to. It is neither sacrilegious nor antireligious to say that each separate government in this country should stay out of the business of writing or sanctioning official prayers and leave that purely religious function to the people themselves and to those the people choose to look to for religious guidance.

*   *   *

The judgment of the Court of Appeals of New York is reversed and the cause remanded for further proceedings not inconsistent with this opinion.

Reversed and remanded.

*   *   *

MR. JUSTICE STEWART, dissenting.

With all respect, I think the Court has misapplied a great constitutional principle. I cannot see how an "official religion" is established by letting those who want to say a prayer say it. On the contrary, I think that to deny the wish of these school children to join in reciting this prayer is to deny them the opportunity of sharing in the spiritual heritage of our Nation.

*   *   *

At the opening of each day's Session of this Court we stand, while one of our officials invokes the protection of God. Since the days of John Marshall our Crier has said, "God save the United States and this Honorable Court." Both the Senate and the House of Representatives open their daily Sessions with prayer. Each of our Presidents, from George Washington to John F. Kennedy, has upon assuming his Office asked the protection and help of God.

The Court today says that the state and federal governments are without constitutional power to prescribe any particular form of words to be recited by any group of the American people on any subject touching religion. One of the stanzas of "The Star-Spangled Banner," made our National Anthem by Act of Congress in 1931, contains [the verse]:

"And this be our motto 'In God is our Trust.'"

In 1954 Congress added a phrase to the Pledge of Allegiance to the Flag so that it now contains the words "one Nation *under* God, indivisible, with liberty and justice for all." In 1952 Congress enacted legislation calling upon the President each year to proclaim a National Day of Prayer. Since 1865 the words "IN GOD WE TRUST" have been impressed on our coins.

I do not believe that this Court, or the Congress, or the President has by the actions and practices I have mentioned established an "official religion" in violation of the Constitution. And I do not believe the State of New York has done so in this case. What each has done has been to recognize and to follow the deeply entrenched and highly cherished spiritual traditions of our Nation—traditions which come down to us from those who almost two hundred years ago avowed their "firm Reliance on the Protection of divine Providence" when they proclaimed the freedom and independence of this brave new world.

I dissent.

New York Times Company v. United States
United States v. Washington Post Company
403 U.S. 713 (1971)

In 1971, President Richard M. Nixon was seeking to extricate the United States from the Vietnam War through secret talks with the North Vietnamese government. Daniel Ellsberg, a former Department of Defense employee, copied a highly classified report, "History of U.S. Decision-Making Process on Viet Nam Policy," and gave parts of it to the New York Times *and the* Washington Post. *When the newspapers began to publish these so-called Pentagon Papers, Nixon ordered government attorneys, on national security grounds, to gain a lower federal court injunction against further publication. A majority of the Court resisted this argument, holding in a per curiam decision that prior restraint on publication carried an extremely heavy burden of proof. The government's lawyers failed to meet this burden. At the same time, some of the justices objected that they were rushed to decide the case and that, under certain circumstances, such as war plans, they would embrace the government's position. These two cases, which were consolidated before the Court, presented the classic question of whether the government could exercise prior restraint over the press.*

PER CURIAM.

Mr. Justice BLACK, with whom Mr. Justice DOUGLAS joins, concurring.

*   *   *

In seeking injunctions against these newspapers and in its presentation to the Court, the Executive Branch seems to have forgotten the essential purpose and history of the First Amendment. When the Constitution was adopted, many people strongly opposed it because the document contained no Bill of Rights to safeguard certain basic freedoms. They especially feared that the new powers granted to a central government might be interpreted to permit the government to curtail freedom of religion, press, assembly, and speech. In response to an overwhelming public clamor, James Madison offered a series of amendments to satisfy citizens that these great liberties would remain safe and beyond the power of government to abridge. Madison proposed what later became the First Amendment in three parts, two of which are set out below, and one of which proclaimed: "The people shall not be deprived or abridged of their right to speak, to write, or to publish their sentiments; *and the freedom of the press, as one of the great bulwarks of liberty, shall be inviolable.*" The amendments were offered to *curtail* and *restrict* the general powers granted to the Executive, Legislative, and Judicial Branches two years before in the original Constitution. The Bill of Rights changed the original Constitution into a new charter under which no branch of government could abridge the people's freedoms of press, speech, religion, and assembly. Yet the Solicitor General argues and some members of the Court appear to agree that the general powers of the Government adopted in the original Constitution should be interpreted to limit and restrict the specific and emphatic guarantees of the Bill of Rights adopted later. I can imagine no greater perversion of history. Madison and the other Framers of the First Amendment, able men that they were, wrote in language they earnestly believed could never be misunderstood: "Congress shall make no law . . . abridging the freedom . . . of the press. . . ." Both the history and language of the First Amendment support the view that the press must be left free to publish news, whatever the source, without censorship, injunctions, or prior restraints.

In the First Amendment the Founding Fathers gave the free press the protection it must have to fulfill its essential role in our democracy. The press was to serve the governed, not the governors. The Government's power to censor the press was abolished so that the press would remain forever free to censure the Government. The press was protected so that it could bare the secrets of government and inform the people. Only a free and unrestrained press can effectively expose deception in government. And paramount among the responsibilities of a free press is the duty to prevent any part of the government from deceiving the people and sending them off to distant lands to die of foreign fevers and foreign shot and shell. In my view, far from deserving condemnation for their courageous reporting, the *New York Times*, the *Washington Post*, and other newspapers should be commended for serving the purpose that the Founding Fathers saw so clearly. In revealing the workings of government that led to the Vietnam war, the newspapers nobly did precisely that which the Founders hoped and trusted they would do.

The Government's case here is based on premises entirely different from those that guided the Framers of the First Amendment. . . .

[W]e are asked to hold that despite the First Amendment's emphatic command, the Executive Branch, the Congress, and the Judiciary can make laws enjoining publication of current news and abridging freedom of the press in the name of "national security." The Government does not even attempt to rely on any act of Congress. Instead it makes the bold and dangerously far-reaching contention that the courts should take it upon themselves to "make" a law abridging freedom of the press in the name of equity, presidential power and national security, even when the representatives of the people in Congress have adhered to the command of the First Amendment and refused to make such a law. . . . To find that the President has "inherent power" to halt the publication of news by resort to the courts would wipe out the First Amendment and destroy the fundamental liberty and security of the very people the Government hopes to make "secure." No one can read the history of the adoption of the First Amendment without being convinced beyond any doubt that it was injunctions like those sought here that Madison and his collaborators intended to outlaw in this Nation for all time.

The word "security" is a broad, vague generality whose contours should not be invoked to abrogate the fundamental law embodied in the First Amendment. The guarding of military and diplomatic secrets at the expense of informed representative government provides no real security for our Republic. The Framers of the First Amendment, fully aware of both the need to defend a new nation and the abuses of the English and Colonial Governments, sought to give this new society strength and security by providing that freedom of speech, press, religion, and assembly should not be abridged.

Rights of the Accused

The Supreme Court also nationalized the rights of the accused. Since colonial times, local authorities had administered criminal justice. The federal Bill of Rights protections for the accused (the Fourth, Fifth, and Sixth Amendments) applied against the federal and not state and local governments. The Warren Court's constitutional revolution, however, carried over into this area as well, with the justices incorporating the protections of these amendments against the states through the Fourteenth Amendment. In *Mapp* v. *Ohio* (1961), the High Court extended the exclusionary rule to the states. This rule provided that evidence seized in an illegal search could not be used in court against the accused. In *Gideon* v. *Wainwright* (1963), the Warren Court nationalized the right to counsel provided for in the Sixth Amendment, when it held that the failure to provide Clarence Earl Gideon, a small-time Florida thief, with counsel in a felony proceeding was unconstitutional. These and other cases were decided at the same time that the crime rate surged as children of the post–World War II baby boom swelled the ranks of sixteen- to twenty-seven-year-olds—the age cohort most prone to criminal activity. Thus when the Court provided more protection for criminals, the crime rate shot up. In this climate, law-and-order politicians attacked the Court and demanded get-tough measures, including restoration of the death penalty in several states.

Miranda v. Arizona
384 U.S. 436 (1966)

Of all the Warren Court decisions involving the rights of the accused, the Miranda *outcome generated the greatest controversy. This case was one of five consolidated by the Court that involved arrest, interrogation, and pretrial detention. In it, a majority of the justices extended the line of reasoning developed in* Gideon *and addressed as well in* Escobedo v. Illinois *(1964), where the justices had reversed a state murder conviction because the accused had been denied the right to counsel during interrogation and because the arresting officers had failed to advise him of his constitutional right to remain silent. In* Miranda, *the Court established, for the first time, guidelines for police officials that were designed to protect suspects against self-incrimination.*

MR. CHIEF JUSTICE WARREN delivered the opinion of the Court.

* * *

On March 13, 1963, petitioner, Ernesto Miranda, was arrested at his home and taken in custody to a Phoenix police station. He was there identified by the complaining witness. The police then took him to "Interrogation Room No. 2" of the detective bureau. There he was questioned by two police officers. The officers admitted at trial that Miranda was not advised that he had a right to have an attorney present. Two hours later, the officers emerged from the interrogation room with a written confession signed by Miranda. At the top of the statement was a typed paragraph stating that the confession was made voluntarily, without threats or promises of immunity and "with full knowledge of my legal rights, understanding any statement I make may be used against me."

At his trial before a jury, the written confession was admitted into evidence over the objection of defense counsel, and the officers testified to the prior oral confession made by Miranda during the interrogation. Miranda was found guilty of kidnapping and rape. He was sentenced to 20 to 30 years' imprisonment on each count, the sentences to run concurrently. On appeal, the Supreme Court of Arizona held that Miranda's constitutional rights were not violated in obtaining the confession and affirmed the conviction. . . . In reaching its decision the court emphasized heavily the fact that Miranda did not specifically request counsel.

                    *   *   *

An understanding of the nature and setting of . . . in-custody interrogation is essential to our decisions today. The difficulty in depicting what transpires at such interrogations stems from the fact that in this country they have largely taken place incommunicado. From extensive factual studies undertaken in the early 1930's, including the famous Wickersham Report to Congress by a Presidential Commission, it is clear that police violence and the "third degree" flourished at that time. In a series of cases decided by this Court long after these studies, the police resorted to physical brutality—beating, hanging, whipping—and to sustained and protracted questioning incommunicado in order to extort confessions. The Commission on Civil Rights in 1961 found much evidence to indicate that "some policemen still resort to physical force to obtain confessions." . . . The use of physical brutality and violence is not, unfortunately, relegated to the past or to any part of the country. Only recently in Kings County, New York, the police brutally beat, kicked and placed lighted cigarette butts on the back of a potential witness under interrogation for the purpose of securing a statement incriminating a third party. . . .

                    *   *   *

[W]e stress that the modern practice of in-custody interrogation is psychologically rather than physically oriented. . . . To be alone with the subject is essential to prevent distraction and to deprive him of any outside support. The aura of confidence in his guilt undermines his will to resist. He merely confirms the preconceived story the police seek to have him describe. Patience and persistence, at times relentless questioning, are employed. To obtain a confession, the interrogator must "patiently maneuver himself or his quarry into a position from which the desired objective may be attained." When normal procedures fail to produce the needed result, the police may resort to deceptive stratagems such as giving false legal advice. It is important to keep the subject off balance, for example, by trading on his insecurity about himself or his surroundings. The police then persuade, trick, or cajole him out of exercising his constitutional rights.

                    *   *   *

At the outset, if a person in custody is to be subjected to interrogation, he must first be informed in clear and unequivocal terms that he has the right to remain silent. For those unaware of the privilege, the warning is needed simply to make them aware of it—the threshold requirement for an intelligent decision as to its exercise. More important, such a warning is an absolute prerequisite in overcoming the inherent pressures of the interrogation atmosphere. It is not just the subnormal or woefully ignorant who succumb to an interrogator's imprecations, whether implied or expressly stated, that the interrogation will continue until a confession is obtained or that silence in the face of accusation is itself damning and will bode ill when presented to a jury. Further, the warning will show the individual that his interrogators are prepared to recognize his privilege should he choose to exercise it.

The Fifth Amendment privilege is so fundamental to our system of constitutional rule and the expedient of giving an adequate warning as to the availability of the privilege so simple, we will not pause to inquire in individual cases whether the defendant was aware of his rights without a warning being given. Assessments of the knowledge the defendant possessed, based on information as to his age, education, intelligence, or prior contact with authorities, can never be more than speculation; a warning is a clearcut fact. More important, whatever the background of the person interrogated, a warning at the time of the interrogation is indispensable to overcome its pressures and to insure that the individual knows he is free to exercise the privilege at that point in time.

The warning of the right to remain silent must be accompanied by the explanation that anything said can and will be used against the individual in court. This warning is needed in order to make him aware not only of the privilege, but also of the consequences of forgoing it. It is only through an awareness of these consequences that there can be any assurance of real understanding and intelligent exercise of the privilege. Moreover, this warning may serve to make the individual more acutely aware that he is faced with a phase of the adversary system—that he is not in the presence of persons acting solely in his interest.

The circumstances surrounding in-custody interrogation can operate very quickly to overbear the will of one merely made aware of his privilege by his interrogators. Therefore, the right to have counsel present at the interrogation is indispensable to the protection of the Fifth Amendment privilege under the system we delineate today. Our aim is to assure that the individual's right to choose between silence and speech remains unfettered throughout the interrogation process. A once-stated warning, delivered by those who will conduct the interrogation, cannot itself suffice to that end among those who most require knowledge of their rights. A mere warning given by the interrogators is not alone sufficient to accomplish that end. Prosecutors themselves claim that the admonishment of the right to remain silent without more "will benefit only the recidivist and the professional." . . . Even preliminary advice given to the accused by his own attorney can be swiftly overcome by the secret interrogation process. . . . Thus, the need for counsel to protect the Fifth Amendment privilege comprehends not merely a right to consult with counsel prior to questioning, but also to have counsel present during any questioning if the defendant so desires.

The presence of counsel at the interrogation may serve several significant subsidiary functions as well. If the accused decides to talk to his interrogators, the assistance of counsel can mitigate the dangers of untrustworthiness. With a lawyer present the likelihood that the police will practice coercion is reduced, and if coercion is nevertheless exercised the lawyer can testify to it in court. The presence of a lawyer can also help to guarantee that the accused gives a fully accurate statement to the police and that the statement is rightly reported by the prosecution at trial. . . .

An individual need not make a pre-interrogation request for a lawyer. While such request affirmatively secures his right to have one, his failure to ask for a lawyer does not constitute a waiver. No effective waiver of the right to counsel during interrogation can be recognized unless specifically made after the warnings we here delineate have been given. The accused who does not know his rights and therefore does not make a request may be the person who most needs counsel.

*   *   *

Accordingly we hold that an individual held for interrogation must be clearly informed that he has the right to consult with a lawyer and to have the lawyer with him during interrogation under the system for protecting the privilege we delineate today. As with the warnings of the right to remain silent and that anything stated can be used in evidence against him, this warning is an absolute prerequisite to interrogation. No amount of circumstantial evidence that the person may have been aware of this right will suffice to stand in its stead. Only through such a warning is there ascertainable assurance that the accused was aware of this right.

*   *   *

Once warnings have been given, the subsequent procedure is clear. If the individual indicates in any manner, at any time prior to or during questioning, that he wishes to remain silent, the interrogation must cease. At this point he has shown that he intends to exercise his Fifth Amendment privilege; any statement taken after the person invokes his privilege cannot be other than the product of compulsion, subtle or otherwise. Without the right to cut off questioning, the setting of in-custody interrogation operates on the individual to overcome free choice in producing a statement after the privilege has been once invoked. If the individual states that he wants an attorney, the interrogation must cease until an attorney is present. At that time, the individual must have an opportunity to confer with the attorney and to have him present during any subsequent questioning. If the individual cannot obtain an attorney and he indicates that he wants one before speaking to police, they must respect his decision to remain silent.

*   *   *

Our decision is not intended to hamper the traditional function of police officers in investigating crime. When an individual is in custody on probable cause, the police may, of course, seek out evidence in the field to be used at trial against him. Such investigation may include inquiry of persons not under restraint. General on-the-scene questioning as to facts surrounding a crime or other general questioning of citizens in the fact-finding process is not affected by our holding. It is an act of responsible citizenship for individuals to give whatever information they may have to aid in law enforcement. In such situations the compelling atmosphere inherent in the process of in-custody interrogation is not necessarily present.

In dealing with statements obtained through interrogation, we do not purport to find all confessions inadmissible. Confessions remain a proper element in law enforcement. Any statement given freely and voluntarily without any compelling influences is, of course, admissible in evidence. The fundamental import of the privilege while an individual is in custody is not whether he is allowed to talk to the police without the benefit of warnings and counsel, but whether he can be interrogated. There is no requirement that police stop a person who enters a police station and states that he wishes to confess to a crime, or a person who calls the police to offer a confession or any other statement he desires to make. Volunteered statements of any kind are not barred by the Fifth Amendment and their admissibility is not affected by our holding today.

Note: The Supreme Court and Criminal Justice

The Supreme Court was sharply divided over Chief Justice Warren's *Miranda* opinion, in part because the justices, especially John Marshall Harlan, believed that the new procedures weighted the criminal justice process in favor of the criminal and against the public. Harlan also argued in dissent that it was unnecessary to incorporate the self-incrimination provisions of the Fifth Amendment into the Fourteenth, since, in his view, the due process clause of the Fourteenth Amendment provided all the protection necessary against coerced confessions by police officials.

The *Miranda* warning subsequently became a standard part of police practice. Studies have shown that the warning system, contrary to fears at the time, has actually benefited police arrest and conviction records because it has forced a higher standard of conduct on police officials. Even though Presidents Nixon and Ronald Reagan blasted the decision and promised to appoint law-and-order justices to the bench who would be tough on crime, the High Court has carved out only minor exceptions to this milestone ruling. At the same time, the Court has refused to further advance the rights of the accused. Many of the highest appellate courts of the states, however, have continued to chart new and innovative paths in this and other areas of civil liberties and civil rights by invoking the authority of Bill of Rights provisions contained in their own state constitutions.

Renewed enthusiasm for the death penalty in capital crimes was one response to the crime wave of the 1960s and early 1970s. Historically, that penalty had fallen most often on blacks and poor persons, a finding that raised serious questions about whether the law was being equally applied. The NAACP Legal Defense Fund challenged a host of state laws mandating the death penalty for crimes ranging from rape to murder. They were joined by other critics, notably the ACLU, that argued that capital punishment was contrary to the prohibition against "cruel and unusual" punishment contained in the Eighth Amendment. In *Furman* v. *Georgia* (1972), the closely divided justices held that the Georgia death penalty was unconstitutional because it was capriciously imposed, but only two of the justices found that it violated per se the Eighth Amendment. In the wake of *Furman*, the vast majority of states redrew their death penalty statutes to make them comply with the Court's direction that they be rationally applied. Amid great public support for capital punishment, Justice Potter Stewart, in *Gregg* v. *Georgia* (1976), announced the Court's new position upholding the revised Georgia statute. Justices William Brennan and Thurgood Marshall vigorously dissented, claiming that the penalty of death was on its face cruel and unusual. Shortly after *Gregg*, public executions began once again.

The Modern Presidency and Separation of Powers

One of the main features of American legal and constitutional development during the post–World War II period has been the growing power of the federal government through the movement of authority from the periphery of the states to the core in Washington, D.C. Both Congress and the Supreme Court have been beneficiaries of and contributors to this development. This same pattern has also characterized the presidency. The growing strength of the presidential office results from the need for decisive leadership in protecting American national security interests in a nuclear age and administering an ever-expanding domestic bureaucracy. As Lawrence M. Friedman has observed, "Weak Presidents are still possible, but a weak Presidency is not."[2]

Throughout American history, presidential power has expanded especially rapidly during wartime. The emergency conditions associated with World Wars I and II, for example, offered Presidents Woodrow Wilson and Franklin D. Roosevelt the opportunity to stretch the constitutional boundaries of their offices. In a few instances, the Court has resisted these efforts. In *Youngstown Sheet & Tube, et al.* v. *Sawyer* (1952), the justices held by a vote of 6 to 3 that President Harry Truman had unconstitutionally usurped legislative power when he directed that strike-bound steel mills remain open during the undeclared Korean War. Most of the time, however, the Court has left Congress and the president to struggle between themselves over the scope of their wartime authority.

The result has been a cyclical pattern of Congress acceding to, in the early phases of emergencies, presidential initiatives and then attempting later on to recapture lost authority. Consider the Vietnam conflict. Presidents Lyndon B. Johnson and Richard M. Nixon believed that their office commanded sufficient constitutional authority to conduct military operations in Vietnam without a formal declaration of war. In the early years of the conflict, President Johnson wrested from a compliant Congress the Gulf of Tonkin Resolution of August 7, 1964. The resolution approved and supported "the determination of the President, as Commander in Chief, to take all necessary measures to repel any armed attack against the forces of the United States" and "to take all necessary steps, including the use of armed force, to assist any member . . . of the Southeast Asian Collective Defense Treaty requesting assistance in defense of its freedom."[3] The resolution, however, was predicated on an apparently erroneous report that two American destroyers in the Gulf of Tonkin had been fired on by North Vietnamese gunboats.

President Richard M. Nixon also claimed the Tonkin Gulf Resolution as his authority to take actions necessary to end the war in Vietnam. Nixon's progress in securing a negotiated settlement contributed to his landslide victory over liberal Democrat George McGovern in 1972. With the war winding down, Congress began the process of attempting to rein in presidential power both domestically and internationally. Its boldest measure was the War Powers Act of 1973, which placed certain restraints on presidential military actions when Congress had not declared war. Nixon vetoed the measure, but Congress overrode it. Ultimately, however, the greatest blow to the prestige of the presidential office came from the actions of Nixon and his political operatives in domestic matters.

United States v. *Nixon*
418 U.S. 683 (1974)

During the 1972 presidential campaign, supporters of President Richard M. Nixon, including Attorney General John Mitchell, authorized a break-in at Dem-

ocratic party headquarters in the Watergate office complex in Washington, D.C. The burglars were caught, but instead of bringing the participation of his staff and Republican party officials to light, President Nixon chose to cover up their role. Nixon, however, had tape-recorded his conversations with various persons about the cover-up, and he refused to provide the tapes either to Special Prosecutor Leon Jaworski, who had been appointed to investigate the affair, or to federal District Court Judge John Sirica, who subpoenaed them. Nixon claimed that as president, he had an absolute privilege to control materials generated in his office.

MR. CHIEF JUSTICE BURGER delivered the opinion of the Court.

*   *   *

In the performance of assigned constitutional duties each branch of the Government must initially interpret the Constitution, and the interpretation of its powers by any branch is due great respect from the others. The President's counsel . . . reads the Constitution as providing an absolute privilege of confidentiality for all Presidential communications. Many decisions of this Court, however, have unequivocally reaffirmed the holding of *Marbury* v. *Madison* (1803), that "[i]t is emphatically the province and duty of the judicial department to say what the law is."

*   *   *

Our system of government "requires that federal courts on occasion interpret the Constitution in a manner at variance with the construction given the document by another branch. . . ." Notwithstanding the deference each branch must accord the others, the "judicial Power of the United States" vested in the federal courts by Art. III, Section 1, of the Constitution can no more be shared with the Executive Branch than the Chief Executive, for example, can share with the Judiciary the veto power, or the Congress share with the Judiciary the power to override a Presidential veto. Any other conclusion would be contrary to the basic concept of separation of powers and the checks and balances that flow from the scheme of a tripartite government. . . .

The second ground asserted by the President's counsel in support of the claim of absolute privilege rests on the doctrine of separation of powers. Here it is argued that the independence of the Executive Branch within its own sphere . . . insulates a President from a judicial subpoena in an ongoing criminal prosecution, and thereby protects confidential Presidential communications.

However, neither the doctrine of separation of powers, nor the need for confidentiality of high-level communications, without more, can sustain an absolute, unqualified Presidential privilege of immunity from judicial process under all circumstances. The President's need for complete candor and objectivity from advisers calls for great deference from the courts. However, when the privilege depends solely on the broad, undifferentiated claim of public interest in the confidentiality of such conversations, a confrontation with other values arises. Absent a claim of need to protect military, diplomatic, or sensitive national security secrets, we find it difficult to accept the argument that even the very important interest in confidentiality of Presidential communications is significantly diminished by production of such material for *in camera* inspection with all the protection that a district court will be obliged to provide.

The impediment that an absolute, unqualified privilege would place in the way of the primary constitutional duty of the Judicial Branch to do justice in criminal prosecutions would plainly conflict with the function of the courts under Art. III. In designing the structure of our Government and dividing and allocating the sovereign power among three co-equal branches, the Framers of the Constitution sought to provide a comprehensive system, but the separate powers were not intended to operate with absolute independence.

*   *   *

To read the Art. II powers of the President as providing an absolute privilege as against a subpoena essential to enforcement of criminal statutes on no more than a generalized claim of the public interest in confidentiality of nonmilitary and non-diplomatic discussions would upset the constitutional balance of "a workable government" and gravely impair the role of the courts under Art. III.

Since we conclude that the legitimate needs of the judicial process may outweigh Presidential privilege, it is necessary to resolve those competing interests in a manner that preserves the essential functions of each branch. The right and indeed the duty to resolve that question does not free the Judiciary from according high respect to the representations made on behalf of the President. . . .

The expectation of a President to the confidentiality of his conversations and correspondence, like the claim of confidentiality of judicial deliberations, for example, has all the values to which we accord deference for the privacy of all citizens and, added to those values, is the necessity for protection of the public interest in candid, objective, and even blunt or harsh opinions in Presidential decision-making. A President and those who assist him must be free to explore alternatives in the process of shaping policies and making decisions and to do so in a way many would be unwilling to express except privately. These are the considerations justifying a presumptive privilege for Presidential communications. The privilege is fundamental to the operation of Government and inextricably rooted in the separation of powers under the Constitution. . . . We agree with Mr. Chief Justice Marshall's observation, therefore, that "[i]n no case of this kind would a court be required to proceed against the president as against an ordinary individual."

But this presumptive privilege must be considered in light of our historic commitment to the rule of law. This is nowhere more profoundly manifest than in our view that "the twofold aim [of criminal justice] is that guilt shall not escape or innocence suffer." . . . We have elected to employ an adversary system of criminal justice in which the parties contest all issues before a court of law. The need to develop all relevant facts in the adversary system is both fundamental and comprehensive. The ends of criminal justice would be defeated if judgments were to be founded on a partial or speculative presentation of the facts. The very integrity of the judicial system and public confidence in the system depend on full disclosure of all the facts, within the framework of the rules of evidence. To ensure that justice is done, it is imperative to the function of courts that compulsory process be available for the production of evidence needed either by the prosecution or by the defense.

*   *   *

In this case the President challenges a subpoena served on him as a third party requiring the production of materials for use in a criminal prosecution; he does so on the claim that he has a privilege against disclosure of confidential communications.

He does not place his claim of privilege on the ground they are military or diplomatic secrets. As to these areas of Art. II duties the courts have traditionally shown the utmost deference to Presidential responsibilities.

*   *   *

No case of the Court, however, has extended this high degree of deference to a President's generalized interest in confidentiality. Nowhere in the Constitution . . . is there any explicit reference to a privilege of confidentiality, yet to the extent this interest relates to the effective discharge of a President's powers, it is constitutionally based.

The right to the production of all evidence at a criminal trial similarly has constitutional dimensions. The Sixth Amendment explicitly confers upon every defendant in a criminal trial the right "to be confronted with the witnesses against him" and "to have compulsory process for obtaining witnesses in his favor." Moreover, the Fifth Amendment also guarantees that no person shall be deprived of liberty without due process of law. It is the manifest duty of the courts to vindicate those guarantees, and to accomplish that it is essential that all relevant and admissible evidence be produced.

In this case we must weigh the importance of the general privilege of confidentiality of Presidential communications in performance of the President's responsibilities against the inroads of such a privilege on the fair administration of criminal justice. The interest in preserving confidentiality is weighty indeed and entitled to great respect. However, we cannot conclude that advisers will be moved to temper the candor of their remarks by the infrequent occasions of disclosure because of the possibility that such conversations will be called for in the context of a criminal prosecution.

On the other hand, the allowance of the privilege to withhold evidence that is demonstrably relevant in a criminal trial would cut deeply into the guarantee of due process of law and gravely impair the basic function of the courts. A President's acknowledged need for confidentiality in the communications of his office is general in nature, whereas the constitutional need for production of relevant evidence in a criminal proceeding is specific and central to the fair adjudication of a particular criminal case in the administration of justice. Without access to specific facts a criminal prosecution may be totally frustrated. The President's broad interest in confidentiality of communications will not be vitiated by disclosure of a limited number of conversations preliminarily shown to have some bearing on the pending criminal cases.

We conclude that when the ground for asserting privilege as to subpoenaed materials sought for use in a criminal trial is based only on the generalized interest in confidentiality, it cannot prevail over the fundamental demands of due process of law in the fair administration of criminal justice. The generalized assertion of privilege must yield to the demonstrated, specific need for evidence in a pending criminal trial.

Note: The Resignation of Richard Nixon

Chief Justice Warren Burger's opinion was a powerful blow to the concept of absolute presidential privilege. Nixon clearly hoped to use the privilege as a basis for keeping the tapes that would reveal his complicity in the Watergate break-in out of the hands of prosecutors and thus enable him to maintain his office. But with the Court's decision, Nixon was faced with either repudiating the federal courts by refusing to surrender the materials or giving the materials and facing certain impeachment by the House of Representatives.

After Nixon's counsel reviewed the tape of June 23, 1972, there was no doubt of his early complicity in an effort to cover up the affair. In it, the president ordered his staff to use the Central Intelligence Agency to abort the Watergate investigation, clear evidence of the crime of obstruction of justice.

In the meantime, the House Committee on the Judiciary was preparing to impeach the president. The House committee voted three articles of impeachment against the president, doing so on the theory that Nixon had abused his constitutional power. The House Committee on the Judiciary rejected two other proposed articles of impeachment: the bombing of Cambodia and corruption in the president's personal and partisan finances. Whether the committee had adopted a proper constitutional view of the impeachment power was a matter of sharp debate, but its behavior was moot in any case because Nixon was vulnerable to impeachment by the full House and conviction before a trial in the Senate on the basis of his criminal wrongdoing. Faced with that reality, the president resigned from office on August 8, 1974.

The Contours of Modern Legal Culture
The Law Explosion and Access to Legal Services

The quest for "total justice," to use Lawrence M. Friedman's phrase, became in the minds of many postwar commentators and officials a problem in itself. More lawyers and more judges seemed to be necessary to attain that goal, and the concomitant expansion of the legal system required more funds and greater involvement by judges in the day-to-day lives of Americans. One result was a supposed new disease— hyperlexis, or excessive law. Its symptoms were too many lawyers, too many law suits, too many delays in settling disputes, and too many high dollar judgments.

An increasingly complex society, however, seemed to demand fuller delivery of legal services. Historically, the profession had functioned on the basis of referrals and disdained advertising as unprofessional. Moreover, in some instances simply knowing that counsel existed was not enough; there had to be some means, in the fee-based structure of the American legal profession, to pay for those services. The government, for many liberal reformers of the 1960s, was the obvious agency to provide that financial support.

DEREK C. BOK

"What Are American Law Schools Doing Wrong?
A Lot"
1983

Derek C. Bok, president of Harvard University and before that dean of the Harvard Law School, wrote the following in his annual report to the Harvard

Board of Overseers in 1983. Bok's perspective on both the law explosion and the purposes of law in society is one of the most important critiques of post–World War II legal culture.

The laws that govern affluent clients and large institutions are numerous, intricate, and applied by highly sophisticated practioners. In this sector of society, rules proliferate, law suits abound, and the cost of legal services grows much faster than the cost of living. For the bulk of the population, however, the situation is very different. Access to the courts may be open in principle. In practice, however, most people find their legal rights severely compromised by the cost of legal services, the baffling complications of existing rules and procedures, and the long-frustrating delays involved in bringing proceedings to a conclusion. From afar, therefore, the legal system looks grossly inequitable and inefficient. There is far too much law for those who can afford it and far too little for those who cannot.

One half of our difficulty lies in the burdens and costs of our tangle of laws and legal procedures. Contrary to popular belief, it is not clear that we are a madly litigious society. Our courts may seem crowded, since we have relatively few judges compared with many industrial nations. Nevertheless, our volume of litigated cases is not demonstrably larger in relation to our total population than that of other western nations.

At the same time, the complexity of litigation seems to be increasing. The number of federal agencies jumped from 20 to 70 in the last two decades while the pages of federal regulations tripled in the 1970's alone. Paralleling these trends, the supply of lawyers has doubled since 1960 so that the United States now boasts the largest number of attorneys per thousand population of any major industrialized nation— three times as many as in Germany, 10 times the number in Sweden, and a whopping 20 times the figure in Japan. Just what society pays for this profession of law is hard to guess. Lloyd Cutler, author of *Conflicts of Interest*, put the figure at $30 billion a year, but the truth is that nobody has bothered to find out.

*   *   *

Our legal system leads to much waste of money that could be put to better purposes. But even greater costs result from the heavy use of human talent. Not only does the law absorb many more young people in America than in any other industrialized nation; it attracts an unusually large proportion of the exceptionally gifted. The average College Board scores of the top 2,000 or 3,000 law students easily exceed those of their counterparts entering other graduate schools and occupations, with the possible exception of medicine. The share of all Rhodes scholars who go on to law school has risen to approximately 40 percent in recent years, dwarfing the figures for any other occupational group. Some readers may dismiss these statistics on the ground that lawyers often move to careers in business or public life. But the facts fail to support this rationalization, for roughly three quarters of all law school graduates are currently practicing their profession. . . .

The net result of these trends is a massive diversion of exceptional talent into pursuits that often add little to the growth of the economy, the pursuit of culture, or the enhancement of the human spirit. I cannot press this point too strongly. As I travel around the country looking at different professions and institutions, I am constantly struck by how complicated many jobs have become, how difficult many institutions are to administer, how pressing are the demands for more creativity and intelligence. However aggressive our schools and colleges are in searching out able youths and giving them a good education, the supply of exceptional people is limited. Yet far too many of these rare individuals are becoming lawyers at a time when the country cries out for more talented business executives, more enlightened public servants, more inventive engineers, more able high school principals and teachers.

These points may seem carping or conjectural, but they are not without tangible effects. A nation's values and problems are mirrored in the ways in which it uses its ablest people. In Japan, a country only half our size, 30 percent more engineers graduate each year than in all the United States. But Japan boasts a total of less than 15,000 lawyers, while American universities graduate 35,000 every year. It would be hard to claim that these differences have no practical consequences. As the Japanese put it, "Engineers make the pie grow larger; lawyers only decide how to carve it up."

The elaborateness of our laws and the complexity of our procedures absorb the energies of this giant bar, raise the cost of legal services, and help produce the other great problem of our legal system—the lack of access for the poor and middle class. The results are embarrassing to behold. . . . The blunt, inexcusable fact is that this nation, which prides itself on efficiency and justice, has developed a legal system that is the most expensive in the world, yet cannot manage to protect the rights of most of its citizens.

Contemporary Legal Thought and Theory

In the post–World War II era, legal thought moved in new and different directions. Although the ideas of the Legal Realist emerged as the consensus view of law, both Critical Legal Studies and Law and Economics offered competing visions based on trenchant analysis.

MARK TUSHNET
"Critical Legal Studies: An Introduction to Its Origins and Underpinnings" 1986

Mark Tushnet, a professor at the Georgetown University Law Center, was one of the founding members of the Critical Legal Studies (CLS) movement in 1974. CLS had direct connections to the Legal Realists, especially in its critical (i.e., skeptical or questioning) attitude toward the use of abstract concepts to order legal decisions and in its belief that lawyers and judges were the agents of their own personalities, not of some disembodied concept called law. But as this excerpt makes clear, the advocates of CLS have gone far beyond the Legal Realists.

CLS accepts the critical aspect of Legal Realism but challenges its constructive program. Because it does so by using the critical techniques developed by the

Realists, CLS is in this sense a true descendant of Realism. The way in which CLS is concerned with the political dimensions of law and domination can be explored by examining the CLS attack on policy analysis, balancing, and shared social values—that is, on the constructive program of Legal Realism.

The Legal Realists' constructive program . . . offered its method of balancing. Sensible decision makers, brought up in their society and sensitive to its present desires and its aspirations, would be able to take into account everything that policy analysis identified and could come up with the right answers. Here CLS makes a simple point. In our society the class of decision-makers is not representative enough to provide the assurance the Realists wanted. Decision-makers are an elite, demographically unrepresentative and socialized into a set of beliefs about society and technology that skew the balance that they reach. The CLS challenge to balancing, then, is the claim that balancing is a social process that needs to be examined sociologically. The concern for sociological analysis of the actual exercise of power is one part of the legacy of progressive historiography. Sociological analysis inevitably raises political questions. For example, CLS argues that the Realists did not go far enough in demanding a democratization of law and notably, that neither the New Deal nor the present Democratic Party does so either.

Concern for the politics of legal thought is even more evident in the most fundamental part of the CLS challenge to the Legal Realists' constructive program. The Realists wanted lawyers to worry about how the legal system promoted broadly shared social values. Parts of the CLS argument here are simple applications of the Realists' critical arguments: The social values are described so abstractly that they could justify any decision, and there is some disagreement even about these abstract values—consider the environmentalists' challenge to arguments for increasing a society's material wealth. But the more important part of the CLS argument goes deeper: CLS insists that the social values, on which there may well be agreement, are not valuable in some abstract and timeless sense. They are values because our society is structured to produce in its members just that set of values. But if that is so, the entire constructive enterprise collapses on itself, because you cannot think about altering legal rules to conform to a society's values when those values are constructed partly on the basis of the legal rules themselves.

Taken together, the CLS arguments are bound to be unsettling. If the argument about the social construction of values is correct, people who talk about radical changes in social organization are likely to seem at least weird and off-the-wall. CLS tries to put into question the deepest values of a society: Because there is nothing timeless about those values, we might simply decide to abandon them. CLS might not be able to make much headway with these arguments were it not aided by developments in other disciplines such as philosophy and sociology, whose important thinkers have also argued that social reality is itself socially constructed.

* * *

CLS has developed a critique of . . . social theory which draws on the legacy of Legal Realism. . . . [But instead] of having political positions flow from social theory, the dominant CLS project simply takes political positions. But not just any political positions. The politics of the dominant position is the politics of decentering, disrupting whatever understandings happen to be settled, criticizing the existing order whatever that order is. Some CLS proponents are attracted to small-scale decentralized socialism. But that attraction must be understood as the embodiment of a critique of large-scale centralized capitalism. It cannot set forth a permanent program, the realization of which would be the end of politics. In fact, in a socialist society, the critical legal scholar would criticize socialism as denying the importance of individual achievement, and decentralization as an impediment to material and spiritual achievement. Roberto Unger captured this dimension of the irrationalist project in his description of destabilization rights, "claims to the disruption of established institutions . . . that have . . . contributed to the very kind of crystallized plan of social hierarchy and division that the entire constitution wants to avoid."

*   *   *

But the most important implication of the dominant CLS analysis is that any critique of the existing order is consistent with the project of CLS. Statistical studies, casual empiricism, classical social theory, the most old-fashioned doctrinal analysis—all might be critical legal studies so long as three conditions are met. First, the work should not be defended on grounds that suggest that something more enduring than interminable critique might result from following it through. Second, it must be designed as a critique rather than as a defense of the existing order—or of a slightly modified version of the existing order that, once modified, would be the end of politics. Finally, the work should actually operate as a critique.

Perhaps the program of interminable critique swallows itself. If it is widely accepted, people may at first resign themselves to their inability to transcend critique. But they may come to see that inability is itself transcendent, creating a new form of life in which the terms on which critique must proceed today have become unintelligible.

RICHARD A. POSNER
"The Ethical and Political Basis of the Efficiency Norm in Common Law Adjudication"
1980

Richard Posner taught for many years at the University of Chicago Law School before his appointment by President Ronald Reagan to the federal court of appeals. Judge Posner, as both a teacher and a jurist, was one of the pioneers of the Law and Economics movement, which in the 1970s and 1980s mounted a strong attack on Legal Realism and was at the opposite pole from the Critical Legal Studies movement. The following selection summarizes the most salient views of the Law and Economic school.

The main ethical argument of this Article . . . is that wealth maximization, especially in the common law setting, derives support from the principle of consent. . . . [T]he political counterpart of consent—consensus—explains the role of wealth maximization in shaping the common law. The principle of consent supports the wealth-maximization norm in the common law setting precisely because common law judges deal with problems, and by methods, in which redistributive considerations are not salient. This means that consent to efficient solutions can be presumed; but it also means that politically influential groups can do no better, in general, than to support efficient policies. Such policies maximize aggregate wealth in a setting where, by hypothesis, altering the shares (redistribution) is not a feasible means by which a group can increase its wealth. . . .

*　　*　　*

I want to defend the . . . wealth-maximization approach . . . by reference to the idea of consent. . . . The notion of consent used here is what economists call ex ante compensation. I contend, I hope, uncontroversially, that if you buy a lottery ticket and lose the lottery, then, so long as there is no question of fraud or duress, you have consented to the loss. Many of the involuntary, uncompensated losses experienced in the market, or tolerated by the institutions that take the place of the market where the market cannot be made to work effectively, are fully compensated ex ante and hence are consented to. . . .

The concept of ex ante compensation provides an answer to the argument that the wealth-maximization criterion, applied unflinchingly in market settings . . . would violate the principle of consent. A more difficult question is raised, however, by the similar attempt to ground nonmarket, but arguably wealth-maximizing institutions, such as the embattled negligence system of automobile accident liability, in the principle of consent. In what sense may the driver injured by another driver in an accident in which neither was at fault be said to have consented to the injury, so as not to be entitled, under a negligence system, to compensation?

To answer this question, we must consider the effect on the costs of driving . . . under a system of strict liability. By hypothesis they would be higher; otherwise the negligence system would not be the wealth-maximizing system and no issue of justifying wealth maximization by reference to the principle of consent would arise. Would drivers be willing to incur higher costs of driving in order to preserve the principle of ex post compensation? They would not. Any driver who wanted to be assured of compensation in the event of an accident regardless of whether he was at fault need only buy first-party, or accident, insurance, by hypothesis at lower cost than he could obtain compensation ex post through a system of strict liability.

This can be most easily visualized by imagining that everyone involved in a traffic accident is identical—everyone is the same age, drives the same amount, and so on. In these circumstances everyone will pay the same rate for both liability insurance and accident insurance. The difference between negligence and strict liability will be that under negligence, liability-insurance rates will be lower and accident insurance rates higher, because fewer accidents will give rise to liability, while under strict liability the reverse will be true. But if, as I am assuming, negligence is the more efficient system, the *sum* of the liability and accident insurance premiums will be lower under negligence, and everyone will prefer this.

*　　*　　*

I have used the example of negligence versus strict liability because it has been used to argue that the wealth-maximization approach is inconsistent with an approach consistent with notions of personal autonomy or, in the terminology of this Article, consent. Other examples could be offered, but it is not the purpose of this Article to deduce the institutional structure implied by wealth maximization; it is to show that social institutions that maximize wealth without requiring ex post compensation need not on that account be viewed as inconsistent with an ethical system premised on the principle of consent.

*   *   *

The domain within which the principle of consent can supply an ethical justification for social institutions that maximize wealth is limited in at least two principal aspects.

1. Where the distributive impact of a wealth-maximizing policy is substantial and nonrandom, broad consent will be difficult to elicit or impute without actual compensation. I mentioned this possibility in connection with the choice between negligence and strict liability to govern traffic accidents but it seemed unimportant there. Suppose, however, the issue was whether to substitute a proportionate income tax for the current progressive one. The substitution would increase the wealth of society if the increase in output (counting both work and leisure as output) by upper bracket taxpayers, whose marginal-tax rate would be lowered by the substitution, exceeded the reduction in output caused by raising the marginal tax rate of lower bracket taxpayers. However, unless the net increase in output was sufficiently great to result in an increase in the after-tax incomes even of those taxpayers who would be paying higher taxes under a proportionate than under a progressive income tax—and let us assume it was not—the lower bracket taxpayers could hardly be assumed to consent to the tax change, even though it would be wealth maximizing.

I was first stimulated to investigate the ethical foundations of wealth maximization by the suggestion that it was too unappealing a value to ascribe to common law judges. Yet it is precisely in the context of common law adjudication, as contrasted with the redistributive statutory domain illustrated by my tax example, that a consensual basis for wealth maximization is most plausible. The rules that govern the acquisition and transfer of property rights, the making and enforcement of contracts, and liability for accidents and the kinds of naked aggression that were made crimes at common law are supported by a broad consensus and distribute their benefits very widely. For example, only a naive analysis of the economic consequences of refusing to enforce the leases that poor people sign with presumably wealthier landlords would conclude that the poor would be better off under such a regime. Landlords would either charge higher rentals because of the greater risk of loss or shift their property into alternative uses, so that the low-income housing supply would be smaller and its price higher. If we can generalize from this example that the choice between common law rules usually does not have systematic distributive consequences, then it is reasonable to suppose that there is—or would be, if it paid people to inform themselves in these matters—general consent to those common law rules that maximize wealth. If so, a common law judge guided by the wealth-maximization criterion will at the same time be promoting [the common good].

*   *   *

The potential for using the common law to redistribute wealth is not great even in cases involving complete strangers. Consider again the negligence system of automobile-accident liability. It is hard to see how moving to a system of strict liability would increase the wealth of a compact, readily identifiable, and easily organizable group in the society. The principal effect would simply be to increase or decrease most people's wealth a small amount, depending upon whether strict liability is more or less efficient than negligence in the automobile setting.

There is a literature that contends that the common law has been biased in favor of the rich—has served, that is, systematic and perverse redistributive ends. The above analysis makes this an implausible contention, though it would carry me too far afield to attempt to refute it in detail here. If I am correct that the common law is not an effective method of redistributing wealth, whether from rich or poor, farmers or railroads, tenants or landlords, or between any reasonably well defined, plausibly effective interest groups, then there is no reason to expect the common law to be dominated by redistributive concerns even if legislatures are.

*   *   *

This analysis implicitly treats judges simply as agents of the government and hence does not confront the difficulties that judicial independence from political control poses for any self-interest theory of judicial behavior. That is a problem in the economics of agency. The utility of the analysis is in relating the efficiency theory of the common law to the redistributive theory of the state, albeit some of the links in the chain are obscure. Notice that it is an implication of the theory that where legislatures legislate within the area of common law regulation—as with respect to rights and remedies in torts, contracts, property, and related fields—they too will be trying to promote efficiency. For, in this view, it is not the nature of the regulating institution, but the subjects and methods of regulation, that determine whether the government will promote efficiency or redistribute wealth.

The relationship of the above political analysis to the ethical discussion in the earlier parts of the Article should now be clear. The principle of consent that I extracted . . . was another name for an absence of systematic distributive effects. The probabilistic compensation discussed in connection with the negligence system of automobile accident liability made it possible to ignore ex post distributive effects in evaluating that system. By the same token, no group can hope to benefit ex ante from a change in the system, assuming the system is the most efficient one possible, and those few and scattered parties who lose out ex post are a diffuse and therefore ineffective interest group. If this example can be generalized to the common law as a whole, it provides a reason for believing that the political forces in the society will converge in seeing efficiency in common law adjudication. In this instance what is ethical is also politic.

Notes

Chapter 1

1. George L. Haskins, *Law and Authority in Early Massachusetts: A Study in Tradition and Design* (New York: Macmillan, 1960).

2. Reprinted in William F. Swindler, comp., *Sources and Documents of United States Constitutions* (New York: Oceana, 1975), 8:364.

3. Joseph Story, *Commentaries on the Constitution* (Boston: Little, Brown, 1833), sec. 148.

4. Arthur Bestor, "The American Civil War as a Constitutional Crisis," *American Historical Review* 69 (1964): 327–352.

5. Julius Goebel, Jr., "King's Law and Local Custom in Seventeenth Century New England," 31 *Colum. L. Rev.* 416 (1931), at 420.

6. Daniel J. Boorstin, *The Americans*, vol. 1, *The Colonial Experience* (New York: Random House, 1958), 27.

7. Quoted in Stephen Botein, *Early American Law and Society* (New York: Knopf 1983), 14.

8. [John Winthrop,] *Winthrop's Journal: History of New England, 1630–1649* (New York, 1908), 2:352.

9. 1678 Remonstrance, in *Records of the Governor and Company of Massachusetts Bay in New England*, comp. Nathaniel Shurtleff (Boston: W. White, 1853–54), 200–201.

10. John Adams, "Novanglus," in *Works of John Adams*, ed. Charles Francis Adams (Boston: Little, Brown, 1851), 4:122.

11. Swindler, *Sources and Documents of United States Constitutions*, 4:29–30.

12. Richard B. Morris, *Studies in the History of American Law, with Special Reference to the Seventeenth and Eighteenth Centuries* (New York, 1930), 126–127.

13. Marylynn Salmon, *Women and the Law of Property in Early America* (Chapel Hill: University of North Carolina Press, 1986), xv.

14. Pennsylvania Act of 1718, chap. xxx, in *The General Laws of Pennsylvania from 1700–1849*, comp. James Dunlop (Philadelphia, 1849), 65.

15. Letter to editor of *New York Journal*, 21 January 1733, in Morris, *Studies in the History of American Law*, 133–134.

16. 43 Eliz. 1, ch. 20.

17. Richard B. Morris, *Government and Labor in Early America* (New York: Columbia University Press, 1946), 386.

18. Shurtleff, *Records of Massachusetts Bay*, 2:180 (spelling has been slightly modernized by the editors).

19. Reprinted in Perry Miller, ed., *The American Puritans: Their Prose and Poetry* (Garden City, N.Y.: Doubleday, 1956), 79.

20. Quoted in Haskins, *Law and Authority in Early Massachusetts*, 102.

21. Shurtleff, *Records of Massachusetts Bay*, 1:111.

22. Shurtleff, *Records of Massachusetts Bay*, 5:63.

23. Shurtleff, *Records of Massachusetts Bay*, 3:243–244; "Apparrel," in *The Laws and Liberties of Massachusetts, 1641–1691*, ed. John D. Cushing (Wilmington, Del.: Scholarly Resources, 1976), 2:73.

24. Shurtleff, *Records of Massachusetts Bay*, 1:126, 274–275.

25. *Records and Files of the Quarterly Courts of Essex County, Massachusetts* (Salem, Mass.: Essex Institute, 1911), 1:303.

26. Order of 1619, in *Journals of the House of Burgesses of Virginia, 1619–1776*, ed. H. R. McIlwaine (Richmond, Va., 1905–1915), 1:10.

27. George Webb, *The Office and Authority of a Justice of the Peace* (Williamsburg, Va., 1736), 165.

28. David H. Flaherty, *Privacy in Colonial New England* (Charlottesville: University Press of Virginia, 1972), 185–186, 211.

29. Thomas Cooper and David J. McCord, eds., *The Statutes at Large of South Carolina* (Columbia, S.C., 1836–41), 7:412.

30. Kai T. Erikson, *Wayward Puritans: A Study in the Sociology of Deviance* (New York: Macmillan, 1966), 12.

Chapter 2

1. Latin: *jus dicere*, "to pronounce the law"; *jus dare*, "to give the law."

Chapter 3

1. Daniel J. Boorstin, *The Americans*, vol. 3, *The National Experience* (New York: Random House, 1965), 35.

2. R. Kent Newmyer, *Supreme Court Justice Joseph Story: Statesman of the Old Republic* (Chapel Hill: University of North Carolina Press, 1985), 204.

3. James Willard Hurst, *Law and the Conditions of Freedom in the Nineteenth Century United States* (Madison: University of Wisconsin Press, 1956), 5; Morton J. Horwitz, *The Transformation of American Law, 1780–1860* (Cambridge, Mass.: Harvard University Press, 1977), 1, 2.

4. William Blackstone, *Commentaries on the Laws of England*, 4 vols., ed. A. W. Brian Simpson (Oxford: Clarendon Press, 1765–69; reprint, Chicago: University of Chicago Press, 1979), 1:455.

5. Hurst, *Law and the Conditions of Freedom in the Nineteenth Century United States*, 3–32.

6. Tapping Reeve, *The Law of Baron and Femme, of Parent and Child, Guardian and Ward, Master and Servant, and of the Powers of Courts of Chancery*, 2nd ed., ed. L. Chittenden (Burlington, Vt.: Chauncey Goodrich, 1846), 358.

7. Leonard W. Levy, *The Law of the Commonwealth and Chief Justice Shaw* (Cambridge, Mass.: Harvard University Press, 1957), 183.

8. Blackstone, *Commentaries on the Laws of England*, 2:258, 400–401.

9. Simpson, "Introduction" to Blackstone, *Commentaries on the Laws of England*, 2:v–vi.

10. Quoted in ibid., 2:x.

11. Lawrence M. Friedman, *A History of American Law*, 2nd ed. (New York: Simon and Schuster, 1985), 275.

12. William Wetmore Story, *A Treatise on the Law of Contracts Not Under Seal* (Boston: Little, Brown, 1844), 73–74.

13. Ibid.

14. Horwitz, *Transformation of American Law,* 160.

15. Ibid., 210.

16. John Langbein, "Introduction" to Blackstone, *Commentaries on the Laws of England,* 3:iii.

17. G. Edward White, "The Intellectual Origins of Torts in America," 86 *Yale L.J.* 671 (1977) [reprinted in Kermit Hall, ed., *Tort Law in American History* (New York: Garland, 1987), 576].

18. Ibid., 678 [Hall at 583].

19. Horwitz, *Transformation of American Law*, 86.

20. Charles O. Gregory, "Trespass to Nuisance to Absolute Liability," 37 *Va. L. Rev.* 359–397 at 365 (1951) [reprinted in Hall, *Tort Law in American History*, 203–241]; Horwitz, *Transformation of American Law*, 89–90.

21. Levy, *Law of the Commonwealth and Chief Justice Shaw*, 162; Robert A. Silverman, *Law and Urban Growth: Civil Litigation in the Boston Trial Courts, 1880–1900* (Princeton, N.J.: Princeton University Press, 1981), 107.

Chapter 4

1. The complicated question of who actually owned Dred Scott is dealt with in Don Fehrenbacher, *The Dred Scott Case: Its Significance in American Law and Politics* (New York: Oxford University Press, 1978), 267–276.

2. Ibid., 3.

3. Harold M. Hyman and William M. Wiecek, *Equal Justice Under Law: Constitutional Development, 1835–1875* (New York: Harper & Row, 1982), 390.

4. Rayford Logan, *The Betrayal of the Negro*, rev. ed. (New York: Collier Books, 1965).

5. Michael Les Benedict, *The Impeachment of Andrew Johnson* (New York: Norton, 1973), 49.

6. Herman Belz, *Emancipation and Equal Rights* (New York: Norton, 1978), 110, 114.

7. Hyman and Wiecek, *Equal Justice Under Law,* 477.

Chapter 5

1. C. Vann Woodward, *The Strange Career of Jim Crow* (New York: Oxford University Press, 1955), 50–51.

2. John P. Reid, *Law for the Elephant: Property and Social Behavior on the Overland Trail* (San Marino, Calif.: Henry E. Huntington Library, 1980), 359, 363–364.

3. William E. Nelson, *The Americanization of the Common Law: The Impact of Legal Change on Massachusetts Society, 1760–1830* (Cambridge, Mass.: Harvard University Press, 1975), 117–120.

Chapter 6

1. John Locke, *Fundamental Constitutions of Carolina* (1669), in *The Federal and State Constitutions, Colonial Charters, and Other Organic Laws . . .* , ed. Francis N. Thorpe (Washington, D.C.: Government Printing Office, 1909), 5:2772–2786.

2. Quoted in Francis R. Aumann, *The Changing American Legal System: Some Selected Phases* (1940; reprint, New York: Da Capo Press, 1969), 13.

3. Colden Letter Books, 1765–1775, in *Collections of the New-York Historical Society* 2 (1877): 71.

4. Laws of New York 1848, chap. 379, Part II, Tit. I, § 62.

5. *Reubens* v. *Joel*, 13 N.Y. 488, 493 (1856), quoted in Lawrence M. Friedman, *A History of American Law*, 2nd ed. (New York: Simon and Schuster, 1985), 393–394.

6. Charles M. Hepburn, *The Historical Development of Code Pleading in America and England* (Cincinnati, 1897), 130.

7. Henry M. Ingersoll, "Some Anomalies of Practice," 1 *Yale L.J.* 89 (1891), at 92.

8. 36–37 Vict., ch. 66.

9. *Sharon* v. *Sharon*, 75 Cal. 1, 28 (1888).

10. William E. Nelson, *The Americanization of the Common Law: The Impact of Legal Change on Massachusetts Society, 1760–1830* (Cambridge, Mass.: Harvard University Press, 1975), 175.

11. Zephaniah Swift, *A System of the Laws of the State of Connecticut* (Windham, Conn., 1795), 1:410.

12. Lysander Spooner, "An Essay on the Trial by Jury" (1852), in [Spooner,] *Let's Abolish Government* (1898; reprint, New York, 1972), 5–11.

13. Quoted in Oliver Wendell Holmes, Jr., *The Common Law*, ed. Mark De Wolfe Howe (Cambridge, Mass.: Harvard University Press, 1963), xii.

14. [Oliver Wendell Holmes, Jr.,] Book review, 14 *Am. L. Rev.* 233 (1880) (reviewing the second edition of Langdell, *Contracts* casebook).

Chapter 7

1. Michael Les Benedict, "Laissez Faire and Liberty: A Re-evaluation of the Origins of Laissez-Faire Constitutionalism," 3 *Law & Hist. Rev.* 293 (1985), at 298.

2. Thomas K. McCraw, *Prophets of Regulation: Charles Francis Adams, Louis D. Brandeis, James M. Landis, Alfred E. Kahn* (Cambridge, Mass.: Harvard University Press, 1984), 23.

3. 7 Cush. (61 Mass.) 53 (1851).

4. 4 Met. (45 Mass.) 564 at 566.

5. *Wabash, St. Louis and Pacific Ry. Co.* v. *Illinois*, 118 U.S. 557 (1886) at 577.

6. *Cincinnati, New Orleans and Texas Pacific Ry. Co.* v. *I.C.C.*, 162 U.S. 184 (1896), and *I.C.C.* v. *Alabama Midlands Ry.*, 168 U.S. 144 (1897), respectively.

7. *People* v. *Budd*, 117 N.Y. 1 (1889) (Peckham, J. Dissenting).

8. *Santa Clara County* v. *Southern Pacific R.R. Co.*, 118 U.S. 394 (1886).

9. 247 U.S. 251 (1918).

10. 259 U.S. 20 (1922).

Chapter 8

1. The case, *United States* v. *McWilliams*, 54 F. Supp. (1944), which ended in a mistrial, is discussed in Leo Ribuffo, "*United States* v. *McWilliams*: The Roosevelt Administration and the Far Right," in *American Political Trials*, ed. Michal R. Belknap (Westport, Conn.: Greenwood Press, 1981), 201–232.

2. Quotations in Roger Daniels, *The Decision to Relocate the Japanese-Americans* (Philadelphia: Lippincott, 1975), 12–29, 47.

3. Ibid., 87.

4. Mark Haller, "Urban Crime and Criminal Justice: The Chicago Case," in *American*

Law and the Constitutional Order: Historical Perspectives, ed. Lawrence M. Friedman and Harry N. Scheiber (Cambridge, Mass.: Harvard University Press, 1978), 305.

5. Richard Kluger, *Simple Justice* (New York: Knopf, 1976), 138.

6. National Association for the Advancement of Colored People, *Thirty Years of Lynchings in the United States, 1889–1919* (New York: NAACP, 1919), 41–105.

Chapter 9

1. Edward A. Purcell, Jr., "American Jurisprudence Between the Wars: Legal Realism and the Crisis of Democratic Theory," in *American Law and the Constitutional Order: Historical Perspectives*, ed. Lawrence M. Friedman and Harry N. Scheiber (Cambridge, Mass.: Harvard University Press, 1978), 360.

2. Quoted in Peter H. Irons, *The New Deal Lawyers* (Princeton, N.J.: Princeton University Press, 1982), 120.

3. Melvin I. Urofsky, *A March of Liberty: A Constitutional History of the United States* (New York: Knopf, 1988), 698–699.

Chapter 10

1. Lawrence M. Friedman, *Total Justice* (New York: Russell Sage Foundation, 1985), 5.

2. Lawrence M. Friedman, *A History of American Law*, 2nd ed. (New York: Simon and Schuster, 1985), 656.

3. Gulf of Tonkin Resolution (1964), Public Law 88–408, August 10, 1964.

Appendix
The Constitution of
the United States

WE THE PEOPLE OF THE UNITED STATES, in order to form a more perfect Union, establish Justice, insure domestic Tranquility, provide for the common defence, promote the general Welfare, and secure the Blessings of Liberty to ourselves and our Posterity, do ordain and establish this Constitution for the United States of America.

Article. I

Section. 1. All legislative Powers herein granted shall be vested in a Congress of the United States, which shall consist of a Senate and House of Representatives.

Section. 2. The House of Representatives shall be composed of Members chosen every second Year by the People of the several States, and the Electors in each State shall have the Qualifications requisite for Electors of the most numerous Branch of the State Legislature.

No Person shall be a Representative who shall not have attained to the Age of twenty five Years, and been seven Years a Citizen of the United States, and who shall not, when elected, be an Inhabitant of that State in which he shall be chosen.

Representatives and direct Taxes shall be apportioned among the several States which may be included within this Union, according to their respective Numbers, which shall be determined by adding to the whole Number of free Persons, including those bound to Service for a Term of Years, and excluding Indians not taxed, three fifths of all other Persons. The actual Enumeration shall be made within three Years after the first Meeting of the Congress of the United States, and within every subsequent Term of ten Years, in such Manner as they shall by Law direct. The Number of Representatives shall not exceed one for every thirty Thousand, but each State shall have at Least one Representative; and until such enumeration shall be made, the State of New Hampshire shall be entitled to chuse three, Massachusetts eight, Rhode-Island and Providence Plantations one, Connecticut five, New-York six, New Jersey four, Pennsylvania eight, Delaware one, Maryland six, Virginia ten, North Carolina five, South Carolina five, and Georgia three.

When vacancies happen in the Representation from any State, the Executive Authority thereof shall issue Writs of Election to fill such Vacancies.

The House of Representatives shall chuse their Speaker and other Officers; and shall have the sole Power of Impeachment.

Section. 3. The Senate of the United States shall be composed of two Senators from each State, chosen by the Legislature thereof, for six Years; and each Senator shall have one Vote.

Immediately after they shall be assembled in Consequence of the first Election, they shall be divided as equally as may be into three Classes. The Seats of the Senators of the first Class shall be vacated at the Expiration of the second Year, of the second Class at the Expiration of the fourth Year, and of the third Class at the Expiration of the sixth Year, so that one third may be chosen every second Year; and if Vacancies happen by Resignation, or otherwise, during the Recess of the Legislature of any State, the Executive thereof may make temporary Appointments until the next Meeting of the Legislature, which shall then fill such Vacancies.

No Person shall be a Senator who shall not have attained to the Age of thirty Years, and been nine Years a Citizen of the United States, and who shall not, when elected, be an Inhabitant of that State for which he shall be chosen.

The Vice President of the United States shall be President of the Senate, but shall have no Vote, unless they be equally divided.

The Senate shall chuse their other Officers, and also a President pro tempore, in the Absence of the Vice President, or when he shall exercise the Office of President of the United States.

The Senate shall have the sole Power to try all Impeachments. When sitting for that Purpose, they shall be on Oath or Affirmation. When the President of the United States is tried, the Chief Justice shall preside: And no Person shall be convicted without the Concurrence of two thirds of the Members present.

Judgment in Cases of Impeachment shall not extend further than to removal from Office, and disqualification to hold and enjoy any Office of honor, Trust or Profit under the United States: but the Party convicted shall nevertheless be liable and subject to Indictment, Trial, Judgment and Punishment, according to Law.

Section. 4. The Times, Places and Manner of holding Elections for Senators and Representatives, shall be prescribed in each State by the Legislature thereof, but the Congress may at any time by Law make or alter such Regulations, except as to the Places of chusing Senators.

The Congress shall assemble at least once in every Year, and such Meeting shall be on the first Monday in December, unless they shall by Law appoint a different Day.

Section. 5. Each House shall be the Judge of the Elections, Returns and Qualifications of its own Members, and Majority of each shall constitute a Quorum to do Business; but a smaller Number may adjourn from day to day, and may be authorized to compel the Attendance of absent Members, in such Manner, and under such Penalties as each House may provide.

Each House may determine the Rules of its Proceedings, punish its Members for disorderly Behaviour, and, with the Concurrence of two thirds, expel a Member.

Each House shall keep a Journal of its Proceedings, and from time to time publish the same, excepting such Parts as may in their Judgment require Secrecy; and the Yeas and Nays of the Members of either House on any question shall, at the Desire of one fifth of those Present, be entered on the Journal.

Neither House, during the Session of Congress, shall, without the Consent of the other, adjourn for more than three days, nor to any other Place than that in which the two Houses shall be sitting.

Section. 6. The Senators and Representatives shall receive a Compensation for their Services, to be ascertained by Law, and paid out of the Treasury of the United States. They shall in all Cases, except Treason, Felony and Breach of the Peace, be privileged from Arrest during their Attendance at the Session of their respective Houses, and in going to and returning from the same; and for any Speech or Debate in either House, they shall not be questioned in any other Place.

No Senator or Representative shall, during the Time for which he was elected, be appointed to any civil Office under the Authority of the United States, which shall have been created, or the Emoluments whereof shall have been encreased during such time; and no Person holding any Office under the United States, shall be a Member of either House during his Continuance in Office.

Section. 7. All Bills for raising Revenue shall originate in the House of Representatives; but the Senate may propose or concur with Amendments as on other Bills.

Every Bill which shall have passed the House of Representatives and the Senate shall, before it become a Law, be presented to the President of the United States; If he approve he shall sign it, but if not he shall return it, with his Objections to that House in which it shall have originated, who shall enter the Objections at large on their Journal, and proceed to reconsider it. If after such Reconsideration two thirds of that House shall agree to pass the Bill, it shall be sent, together with the Objections, to the other House, by which it shall likewise be reconsidered, and if approved by two thirds of that House, it shall become a Law. But in all such Cases the Votes of both Houses shall be determined by yeas and Nays, and the Names of the Persons voting for and against the Bill shall be entered on the Journal of each House respectively. If any Bill shall not be returned by the President within ten Days (Sundays excepted) after it shall have been presented to him, the Same shall be a Law, in like Manner as if he had signed it, unless the Congress by their Adjournment prevent its Return, in which Case it shall not be a Law.

Every Order, Resolution, or Vote to which the Concurrence of the Senate and House of Representatives may be necessary (except on a question of Adjournment) shall be presented to the President of the United States; and before the Same shall take Effect, shall be approved by him, or being disapproved by him, shall be repassed by two thirds of the Senate and House or Representatives, according to the Rules and Limitations prescribed in the Case of a Bill.

Section. 8. The Congress shall have Power To lay and collect Taxes, Duties,

Imposts and Excises, to pay the Debts and provide for the common Defence and general Welfare of the United States; but all Duties, Imposts and Excises shall be uniform throughout the United States.

To borrow Money on the credit of the United States;

To regulate Commerce with foreign Nations, and among the several States, and with the Indian Tribes;

To establish an uniform Rule of Naturalization, and uniform Laws on the subject of Bankruptcies throughout the United States;

To coin Money, regulate the Value thereof, and of foreign Coin, and fix the Standard of Weights and Measures;

To provide for the Punishment of counterfeiting the Securities and current Coin of the United States;

To establish Post Offices and Post Roads;

To promote the Progress of Science and useful Arts, by securing for limited Times to Authors and Inventors the exclusive Right to their respective Writings and Discoveries;

To constitute Tribunals inferior to the supreme Court;

To define and punish Piracies and Felonies committed on the high Seas, and Offences against the Law of Nations;

To declare War, grant Letters of Marque and Reprisal, and make Rules concerning Captures on Land and Water;

To raise and support Armies, but no Appropriation of Money to that Use shall be for a longer Term than two Years;

To provide and maintain a Navy;

To make Rules for the Government and Regulation of the land and naval Forces;

To provide for calling forth the Militia to execute the Laws of the Union, suppress Insurrections and repel Invasions;

To provide for organizing, arming, and disciplining, the Militia, and for governing such Part of them as may be employed in the Service of the United States, reserving to the States respectively, the Appointment of the Officers, and the Authority of training the Militia according to the discipline prescribed by Congress;

To exercise exclusive Legislation in all Cases whatsoever, over such District (not exceeding ten Miles square) as may, by Cession of particular States, and the Acceptance of Congress, become the Seat of the Government of the United States, and to exercise like Authority over all Places purchased by the Consent of the Legislature of the State in which the Same shall be, for the Erection of Forts, Magazines, Arsenals, dock-Yards, and other needful Buildings;—And

To make all Laws which shall be necessary and proper for carrying into Execution the foregoing Powers, and all other Powers vested by this Constitution in the Government of the United States, or in any Department or Officer thereof.

Section. 9. The Migration or Importation of such Persons as any of the States now existing shall think proper to admit, shall not be prohibited by the Congress prior to the Year one thousand eight hundred and eight, but a Tax or duty may be imposed on such Importation, not exceeding ten dollars for each Person.

The Privilege of the Writ of Habeas Corpus shall not be suspended, unless when in Cases of Rebellion or Invasion the public Safety may require it.

No Bill of Attainder or ex post facto Law shall be passed.

No Capitation, or other direct, Tax shall be laid, unless in Proportion to the Census or Enumeration herein before directed to be taken.

No Tax or Duty shall be laid on Articles exported from any State.

No Preference shall be given by any Regulation of Commerce or Revenue to the Ports of one State over those of another: nor shall Vessels bound to, or from, one State, be obliged to enter, clear, or pay Duties in another.

No Money shall be drawn from the Treasury, but in Consequence of Appropriations made by Law, and a regular Statement and Account of the Receipts and Expenditures of all public Money shall be published from time to time.

No Title of Nobility shall be granted by the United States: And no Person holding any Office of Profit or trust under them, shall, without the Consent of the Congress, accept of any present, Emolument, Office, or Title, of any kind whatever, from any King, Prince, or foreign State.

Section. 10. No State shall enter into any Treaty, Alliance, or Confederation; grant Letters of Marque and Reprisal; coin Money; emit Bills of Credit; make any Thing but gold and silver Coin a Tender in Payment of Debts; pass any Bill of Attainder, ex post facto Law, or Law impairing the Obligation of Contracts, or grant any Title of Nobility.

No State shall, without the Consent of the Congress, lay any Imposts or Duties on Imports or Exports, except what may be absolutely necessary for executing it's inspection Laws: and the net Produce of all Duties and Imposts, laid by any State on Imports or Exports, shall be for the Use of the Treasury of the United States; and all such Laws shall be subject to the Revision and Controul of the Congress.

No State shall, without the Consent of Congress, lay any Duty of Tonnage, keep Troops, or Ships of War in time of Peace, enter into any Agreement or Compact with another State, or with a foreign Power, or engage in War, unless actually invaded, or in such imminent Danger as will not admit of delay.

Article. II.

Section. 1. The executive Power shall be vested in a President of the United States of America. He shall hold his Office during the term of four Years, and, together with the Vice President, chosen for the same Term, be elected, as follows

Each State shall appoint, in such Manner as the Legislature thereof may direct, a Number of Electors, equal to the whole Number of Senators and Representatives to which the State may be entitled in the Congress: but no Senator or Representative, or Person holding an Office of Trust or Profit under the United States, shall be appointed an Elector.

The Electors shall meet in their respective States, and vote by Ballot for two Persons, of whom one at least shall not be an Inhabitant of the same State with themselves. And they shall make a List of all the Persons voted for, and of the

Number of Votes for each; which List they shall sign and certify, and transmit sealed to the Seat of the Government of the United States, directed to the President of the Senate. The President of the Senate shall, in the Presence of the Senate and House of Representatives, open all the Certificates, and the Votes shall then be counted. The Person having the greatest Number of Votes shall be the President, if such Number be a Majority of the whole Number of Electors appointed; and if there be more than one who have such Majority, and have an equal Number of Votes, then the House of Representatives shall immediately chuse by Ballot one of them for President; and if no Person have a Majority, then from the five highest on the List the said House shall in like Manner chuse the President. But in chusing the President, the Votes shall be taken by States, the Representation from each State having one Vote; A quorum for this Purpose shall consist of a Member or Members from two thirds of the States, and a Majority all the States shall be necessary to a Choice. In every Case, after the Choice of the President, the Person having the greatest Number of Votes of the Electors shall be the Vice President. But if there should remain two or more who have equal Votes, the Senate shall chuse from them by Ballot the Vice President.

The Congress may determine the Time of chusing the Electors, and the Day on which they shall give their Votes; which Day shall be the same throughout the United States.

No Person except a natural born Citizen, or a Citizen of the United States, at the time of the Adoption of this Constitution, shall be eligible to the Office of President, neither shall any Person be eligible to that Office who shall not have attained the Age of thirty five Years, and been fourteen Years a Resident within the United States.

In Case of the Removal of the President from Office, or of his Death, Resignation, or Inability to discharge the Powers and Duties of the said Office, the Same shall devolve on the Vice President, and the Congress may by Law provide for the Case of Removal, Death, Resignation or Inability, both of the President and Vice President, declaring what Officer shall then act as President, and such Officer shall act accordingly, until the Disability be removed, or a President shall be elected.

The President shall, at stated Times, receive for his Services, a Compensation, which shall neither be encreased or diminished during the Period for which he shall have been elected, and he shall not receive within that Period any other Emolument from the United States, or any of them.

Before he enters on the Execution of his Office, he shall take the following Oath or Affirmation:—"I do solemnly swear (or affirm) that I will faithfully execute the Office of President of the United States, and will to the best of my Ability, preserve, protect and defend the Constitution of the United States."

Section. 2. The President shall be Commander in Chief of the Army and Navy of the United States, and of the Militia of the several States, when called into the actual Service of the United States; he may require the Opinion, in writing, of the principal Officer in each of the executive Departments, upon any Subject relating to the

Duties of their respective Offices, and he shall have Power to grant Reprieves and Pardons for Offences against the United States, except in Cases of Impeachment.

He shall have Power, by and with the Advice and Consent of the Senate, to make Treaties, provided two thirds of the Senators present concur; and he shall nominate, and by and with the Advice and Consent of the Senate, shall appoint Ambassadors, other public Ministers and Consuls, Judges of the supreme Court, and all other Officers of the United States, whose Appointments are not herein otherwise provided for, and which shall be established by Law; but the Congress may by Law vest the Appointment of such inferior Officers, as they think proper, in the President alone, in the Courts of Law, or in the Heads of Departments.

The President shall have Power to fill up all Vacancies that may happen during the Recess of the Senate, by granting Commissions which shall expire at the End of their next Session.

Section. 3. He shall from time to time give to the Congress Information of the State of the Union, and recommend to their Consideration such Measures as he shall judge necessary and expedient; he may, on extraordinary Occasions, convene both Houses, or either of them, and in Case of Disagreement between them, with Respect to the Time of Adjournment, he may adjourn them to such Time as he shall think proper; he shall receive Ambassadors and other public Ministers; he shall take Care that the Laws be faithfully executed, and shall Commission all the Officers of the United States.

Section. 4. The President, Vice President and all civil Officers of the United States, shall be removed from Office on Impeachment for, and Conviction of, Treason, Bribery, or other high Crimes and Misdemeanors.

Article. III.

Section. 1. The judicial Power of the United States, shall be vested in one supreme Court, and in such inferior Courts as the Congress may from time to time ordain and establish. The Judges, both of the supreme and inferior Courts, shall hold their Offices during good Behaviour, and shall, at stated Times, receive for their Services, a Compensation, which shall not be diminished during their Continuance in Office.

Section. 2. The judicial Power shall extend to all Cases, in Law and Equity, arising under this Constitution, the Laws of the United States, and Treaties made, or which shall be made, under their Authority;—to all Cases affecting Ambassadors, other public Ministers and Consuls;—to all Cases of admiralty and maritime Jurisdiction;—to Controversies to which the United States shall be a Party;—to Controversies between two or more States;—between a State and Citizens of another State;—between Citizens of different States,—between Citizens of the same State claiming Lands under Grants of different States, and between a State, or the Citizens thereof, and foreign States, Citizens of Subjects.

In all cases affecting Ambassadors, other public Ministers and Consuls, and those in which a State shall be Party, the supreme Court shall have original Jurisdiction. In all the other Cases before mentioned, the supreme Court shall have appellate Jurisdiction, both as to Law and Fact, with such Exceptions, and under such Regulations as the Congress shall make.

The Trial of all Crimes, except in Cases of Impeachment, shall be by Jury; and such Trial shall be held in the State where the said Crimes shall have been committed; but when not committed within any State, the Trial shall be at such Place or Places as the Congress may by Law have directed.

Section. 3. Treason against the United States, shall consist only in levying War against them, or in adhering to their Enemies, giving them Aid and Comfort. No Person shall be convicted of Treason unless on the Testimony of two Witnesses to the same overt Act, or on Confession in open Court.

The Congress shall have Power to declare the Punishment of Treason, but no Attainder of Treason shall work Corruption of Blood, or Forfeiture except during the Life of the Person attainted.

Article. IV.

Section. 1. Full Faith and Credit shall by given in each State to the public Acts, Records, and judicial Proceedings of every other State. And the Congress may be general Laws prescribe the Manner in which such Acts, Records and Proceedings shall be proved, and the Effect thereof.

Section. 2. The Citizens of each State shall be entitled to all Privileges and Immunities of Citizens in the several States.

A Person charged in any State with Treason, Felony, or other Crime, who shall flee from Justice, and be found in another State, shall on Demand of the executive Authority of the State from which he fled, be delivered up, to be removed to the State having Jurisdiction of the Crime.

No Person held to Service or Labour in one State, under the Laws thereof, escaping into another, shall, in Consequence of any Law or Regulation therein, be discharged from such Service or Labour, but shall be delivered up on Claim of the Party to whom such Service or Labour may be due.

Section. 3. New States may be admitted by the Congress into this Union; but no new State shall be formed or erected within the Jurisdiction of any other State; nor any State be formed by the Junction of two or more States, or Parts of States, without the consent of the Legislatures of the States concerned as well as of the Congress.

The Congress shall have Power to dispose of and make all needful Rules and Regulations respecting the Territory or other Property belonging to the United States; and nothing in this Constitution shall be so construed as to Prejudice any Claims of the United States, or of any particular States.

Section. 4. The United States shall guarantee to every State in this Union a Republican Form of Government, and shall protect each of them against Invasion; and on Application of the Legislature, or of the Executive (when the Legislature cannot be convened) against domestic Violence.

Article. V.

The Congress, whenever two thirds of both Houses shall deem it necessary, shall propose Amendments to this Constitution, or, on the Application of the Legislatures of two thirds of the several States shall call a Convention for proposing Amendments, which, in either Case, shall be valid to all Intents and Purposes, as Part of this Constitution, when ratified by the Legislatures of three fourths of the several States, or by Conventions in three fourths thereof, as the one or the other Mode of Ratification may be proposed by the Congress; Provided that no Amendment which may be made prior to the Year One thousand eight hundred and eight shall in any Manner affect the first and fourth Clauses in the Ninth Section of the first Article; and that no State, without its Consent, shall be deprived of it's equal Suffrage in the Senate.

Article. VI.

All Debts contracted and Engagements entered into, before the Adoption of this Constitution, shall be as valid against the United States under this Constitution, as under the Confederation.

This Constitution, and the Laws of the United States which shall be made in Pursuance thereof; and all Treaties made, or which shall be made, under the Authority of the United States, shall be the supreme Law of the Land; and the Judges in every State shall be bound thereby, any Thing in the Constitution or Laws of any State to the Contrary notwithstanding.

The Senators and Representatives before mentioned, and the Members of the several State Legislatures, and all executive and judicial Officers, both of the United States and of the several States, shall be bound by Oath or Affirmation, to support this Constitution; but no religious Test shall ever be required as a Qualification to any Office or public Trust under the United States.

Article. VII.

The Ratification of the Conventions of nine States, shall be sufficient for the Establishment of this Constitution between the States so ratifying the Same.

Done in Convention by the Unanimous Consent of the States present the Seventeenth Day of September in the Year of our Lord one thousand seven hundred and Eighty seven and of the Independence of the United States of America the Twelfth. In witness thereof We have hereunto subscribed our Names,

G°: WASHINGTON—Presid^t
and deputy from Virginia

New Hampshire	{ John Langdon Nicholas Gilman	Delaware	Geo: Read Gunning Bedford jun John Dickinson Richard Bassett Jaco: Broom
Massachusetts	{ Nathaniel Gorham Rufus King		
Connecticut	{ Wm Saml Johnson Roger Sherman	Maryland	James McHenry Dan of St Thos Jenifer Danl Carroll
New York	{ Alexander Hamilton		
New Jersey	Wil: Livingston David A. Brearley. Wm Paterson. Jona: Dayton	Virginia	{ John Blair— James Madison Jr.
Pennsylvania	B. Franklin Thomas Mifflin Robt Morris Geo. Clymer Thos. FitzSimons Jared Ingersoll James Wilson Gouv Morris	North Carolina	W^m. Blount Richd Dobbs Spaight. Hu Williamson
		South Carolina	J. Rutledge Charles Cotesworth Pinckney Charles Pinckney Pierce Butler.
		Georgia	{ William Few Abr Baldwin

Amendments to the Constitution

ARTICLES IN ADDITION TO, and Amendment of the Constitution of the United States of America, proposed by Congress, and ratified by the Legislatures of the several States, pursuant to the fifth Article of the original Constitution.

Article I.

Congress shall make no law respecting an establishment of religion, or prohibiting the free exercise thereof; or abridging the freedom of speech, or of the press; or the right of the people peaceably to assemble, and to petition the Government for a redress of grievances.

Article II.

A well regulated Militia, being necessary to the security of a free State, the right of the people to keep and bear Arms, shall not be infringed.

Article III.

No Soldier shall, in time of peace be quartered in any house, without the consent of the Owner, nor in time of war, but in a manner to be prescribed by law.

Article IV.

The right of the people to be secure in their persons, houses, papers, and effects, against unreasonable searches and seizures, shall not be violated, and no Warrants shall issue, but upon probable cause, supported by Oath or affirmation, and particularly describing the place to be searched, and the persons or things to be seized.

Article V.

No person shall be held to answer for a capital, or otherwise infamous crime, unless on a presentment or indictment of a Grand Jury, except in cases arising in the land or naval forces, or in the Militia, when in actual service in time of War or public danger; nor shall any person be subject for the same offence to be twice put in jeopardy of life or limb; nor shall be compelled in any criminal case to be a witness against himself, nor be deprived of life, liberty, or property, without due process of law; nor shall private property be taken for public use, without just compensation.

Article VI.

In all criminal prosecutions, the accused shall enjoy the right to a speedy and public trial, by an impartial jury of the State and district wherein the crime shall have been committed, which district shall have been previously ascertained by law, and to be informed of the nature and cause of the accusation; so be confronted with the witnesses against him; to have compulsory process for obtaining witnesses in his favor, and to have the Assistance of Counsel for his defence.

Article VII.

In Suits at common law, where the value in controversy shall exceed twenty dollars, the right of trial by jury shall be preserved, and no fact tried by a jury, shall be otherwise re-examined in any Court of the United States, than according to the rules of the common law.

Article VIII.

Excessive bail shall not be required, nor excessive fines imposed, nor cruel and unusual punishments inflicted.

Article IX.

The enumeration in the Constitution, of certain rights, shall not be construed to deny or disparage others retained by the people.

Article X.

The powers not delegated to the United States by the Constitution, nor prohibited by it to the States, are reserved to the States respectively, or to the people. [The first ten amendments went into effect December 15, 1791]

Article XI.

The Judicial power of the United States shall not be construed to extend to any suit in law or equity, commenced or prosecuted against one of the United States by Citizens of another State, or by Citizens or Subjects of any Foreign State. [January 8, 1798]

Article XII.

The Electors shall meet in their respective states, and vote by ballot for President and Vice-President, one of whom, at least, shall not be an inhabitant of the same state with themselves; they shall name in their ballots the person voted for as President, and in distinct ballots the person voted for as Vice-President, and they shall make distinct lists of all persons voted for as President, and of all persons voted for as Vice-President, and of the number of votes for each, which lists they shall sign and certify, and transmit sealed to the seat of the government of the United States, directed to the President of the Senate;—The President of the Senate shall, in the presence of the Senate and House of Representatives, open all the certificates and the votes shall then be counted;—The person having the greatest number of votes for President, shall be the President, if such number be a majority of the whole number of Electors appointed; and if no person have such majority, then from the persons having the highest numbers not exceeding three on the list of those voted for as President, the House of Representatives shall choose immediately, by ballot, the President. But in choosing the President, the votes shall be taken by states, the representation from each state having one vote; a quorum for this purpose shall consist of a member or members from two-thirds of the states, and a majority of all the states shall be necessary to a choice. And if the House of Representatives shall not choose a President whenever the right of choice shall devolve upon them, before the fourth day of March next following, then the Vice-President shall act as President, as in the case of the death or other constitutional disability of the President.— The person having the greatest number of votes as Vice-President, shall be the Vice-President, if such number be a majority of the whole number of Electors appointed, and if no person have a majority, then from the two highest numbers on the list, the Senate shall choose the Vice-President; a quorum for the purpose shall consist of two-thirds of the whole number of Senators, and a majority of the whole number shall be necessary to a choice. But no person constitutionally ineligible to the office of President shall be eligible to that of Vice-President of the United States. [September 25, 1804]

Article XIII.

Section 1. Neither slavery nor involuntary servitude, except as a punishment for crime whereof the party shall have been duly convicted, shall exist within the United States, or any place subject to their jurisdiction.

Section 2. Congress shall have power to enforce this article by appropriate legislation. [December 18, 1865]

Article XIV.

Section 1. All persons born or naturalized in the United States, and subject to the jurisdiction thereof, are citizens of the United States and of the State wherein they reside. No State shall make or enforce any law which shall abridge the privileges or immunities of citizens of the United States; nor shall any State deprive any person of life, liberty, or property, without due process of law; nor deny to any person within its jurisdiction the equal protection of the laws.

Section 2. Representatives shall be apportioned among the several States according to their respective numbers, counting the whole number of persons in each State, excluding Indians not taxed. But when the right to vote at any election for the choice of electors for President and Vice President of the United States, Representatives in Congress, the Executive and Judicial officers of a State, or the members of the Legislature thereof, is denied to any of the male inhabitants of such State, being twenty-one years of age, and citizens of the United States, or in any way abridged, except for participation in rebellion, or other crime, the basis of representation therein shall be reduced in the proportion which the number of such male citizens shall bear to the whole number of male citizens twenty-one years of age in such State.

Section 3. No person shall be a Senator or Representative in Congress, or elector of President and Vice President, or hold any office, civil or military, under the United States, or under any State, who, having previously taken an oath, as a member of Congress, or as an officer of the United States, or as a member of any State legislature, or as an executive or judicial officer of any State, to support the Constitution of the United States, shall have engaged in insurrection or rebellion against the same, or given aid or comfort to the enemies thereof. But Congress may by a vote of two-thirds of each House, remove such disability.

Section 4. The validity of the public debt of the United States, authorized by law, including debts incurred for payment of pensions and bounties for services in suppressing insurrection or rebellion, shall not be questioned. But neither the

United States nor any State shall assume or pay any debt or obligation incurred in aid of insurrection or rebellion against the United States, or any claim for the loss or emancipation of any slave; but all such debts, obligations and claims shall be held illegal and void.

Section 5. The Congress shall have power to enforce, by appropriate legislation, the provisions of this article. [July 28, 1868]

Article XV.

Section 1. The right of citizens of the United States to vote shall not be denied or abridged by the United States or by any State on account of race, color, or previous condition of servitude—

Section 2. The Congress shall have power to enforce this article by appropriate legislation.—[March 30, 1870]

Article XVI.

The Congress shall have power to lay and collect taxes on incomes, from whatever source derived, without apportionment among the several States, and without regard to any census or enumeration. [February 25, 1913]

Article XVII.

The Senate of the United States shall be composed of two senators from each State, elected by the people thereof, for six years; and each Senator shall have one vote. The electors in each State shall have the qualifications requisite for electors of the most numerous branch of the State legislature.

When vacancies happen in the representation of any State in the Senate, the executive authority of such State shall issue writs of election to fill such vacancies: *Provided,* That the legislature of any State may empower the executive thereof to make temporary appointments until the people fill the vacancies by election as the legislature may direct.

This amendment shall not be so construed as to affect the election or term of any senator chosen before it becomes valid as part of the Constitution. [May 31, 1913]

Article XVIII.

After one year from the ratification of this article, the manufacture, sale, or transportation of intoxicating liquors within, the importation thereof into, or the exportation thereof from the United States and all territory subject to the jurisdiction thereof for beverage purposes is hereby prohibited.

The Congress and the several States shall have concurrent power to enforce this article by appropriate legislation.

This article shall be inoperative unless it shall have been ratified as an amendment to the Constitution by the legislatures of the several States, as provided in the Constitution, within seven years from the date of the submission thereof to the States by Congress. [January 29, 1919]

Article XIX.

The right of citizens of the United States to vote shall not be denied or abridged by the United States or by any State on account of sex.

The Congress shall have power by appropriate legislation to enforce the provisions of this article. [August 26, 1920]

Article XX.

Section 1. The terms of the President and Vice-President shall end at noon on the twentieth day of January, and the terms of Senators and Representatives at noon on the third day of January, of the years in which such terms would have ended if this article had not been ratified; and the terms of their successors shall then begin.

Section 2. The Congress shall assemble at least once in every year, and such meeting shall begin at noon on the third day of January, unless they shall by law appoint a different day.

Section 3. If, at the time fixed for the beginning of the term of the President, the President-elect shall have died, the Vice-President-elect shall become President. If a President shall not have been chosen before the time fixed for the beginning of his term, or if the President-elect shall have failed to qualify, then the Vice-President-elect shall act as President until a President shall have qualified; and the Congress may by law provide for the case wherein neither a President-elect nor a Vice-President-elect shall have qualified, declaring who shall then act as President, or the manner in which one who is to act shall be selected, and such person shall act accordingly until a President or Vice-President shall have qualified.

Section 4. The Congress may by law provide for the case of the death of any of the persons from whom the House of Representatives may choose a President whenever the right of choice shall have devolved upon them, and for the case of the death of any of the persons from whom the Senate may choose a Vice-President whenever the right of choice shall have devolved upon them.

Section 5. Sections 1 and 2 shall take effect on the 15th day of October following the ratification of this article.

Section 6. This article shall be inoperative unless it shall have been ratified as an amendment to the Constitution by the legislatures of three-fourths of the several States within seven years from the date of its submission. [February 6, 1933]

Article XXI.

Section 1. The eighteenth article of amendment to the Constitution of the United States is hereby repealed.

Section 2. The transportation or importation into any State, Territory or possession of the United States for delivery or use therein of intoxicating liquors, in violation of the laws thereof, is hereby prohibited.

Section 3. The article shall be inoperative unless it shall have been ratified as an amendment to the Constitution by convention in the several States, as provided in the Constitution, within seven years from the date of the submission thereof to the States by the Congress. [December 5, 1933]

Article XXII.

Section 1. No person shall be elected to the office of the President more than twice, and no person who has held the office of President, or acted as President, for more than two years of a term to which some other person was elected President shall be elected to the office of the President more than once. But this Article shall not apply to any person holding the office of President when this Article was proposed by the Congress, and shall not prevent any person who may be holding the office of President, or acting as President, during the term within which this Article becomes operative from holding the office of President or acting as President during the remainder of such term.

Section 2. This article shall be inoperative unless it shall have been ratified as an amendment to the Constitution by the legislatures of three-fourths of the several States within seven years from the date of its submission to the States by the Congress. [February 27, 1951]

Article XXIII.

Section 1. The District constituting the seat of government of the United States shall appoint in such manner as the Congress may direct:

A number of electors of President and Vice-President equal to the whole number of Senators and Representatives in Congress to which the District would be entitled if it were a State, but in no event more than the least populous State; they shall be in addition to those appointed by the States, but they shall be considered, for the purposes of the election of President and Vice-President, to be electors appointed by a State; and they shall meet in the District and perform such duties as provided by the twelfth article of amendment.

Section 2. The Congress shall have the power to enforce this article by appropriate legislation. [March 29, 1961]

Article XXIV.

Section 1. The right of citizens of the United States to vote in any primary or other election for President or Vice President, for electors for President or Vice President, or for Senator or Representative in Congress, shall not be denied or abridged by the United States or any State by reason of failure to pay any poll tax or other tax.

Section 2. The Congress shall have power to enforce this article by appropriate legislation. [January 23, 1964]

Article XXV.

Section 1. In case of the removal of the President from office or of his death or resignation, the Vice President shall become President.

Section 2. Whenever there is a vacancy in the office of Vice President, the President shall nominate a Vice President who shall take office upon confirmation by a majority vote of both Houses of Congress.

Section 3. Whenever the President transmits to the President pro tempore of the Senate and the Speaker of the House of Representatives his written declaration that he is unable to discharge the powers and duties of his office, and until he transmits to them a written declaration to the contrary, such powers and duties shall be discharged by the Vice President as Acting President.

Section 4. Whenever the Vice President and a majority of either the principal officers of the executive departments or of such other body as Congress may by law provide, transmit to the President pro tempore of the Senate and the Speaker of the House of Representatives their written declaration that the President is unable to discharge the powers and duties of his office, the Vice President shall immediately assume the powers and duties of the office as Acting President.

Thereafter, when the President transmits to the President pro tempore of the Senate and the Speaker of the House of Representatives his written declaration that no inability exists, he shall resume the powers and duties of his office unless the Vice President and a majority of either the principal officers of the executive departments or of such other body as Congress may by law provide, transmit within four days to the President pro tempore of the Senate and the Speaker of the House of Representatives their written declaration that the President is unable to discharge the powers and duties of his office. Thereupon Congress shall decide the issue, assembling within forty-eight hours for that purpose if not in session. If the Congress, within twenty-one days after receipt of the latter written declaration, or, if Congress is not in session, within twenty-one days after Congress is required to assemble, determines by two-thirds vote of both Houses that the President is unable to discharge the powers and duties of his office, the Vice President shall continue to discharge the same as Acting President; otherwise, the President shall resume the powers and duties of his office. [February 10, 1967]

Article XXVI.

Section 1. The right of citizens of the United States, who are eighteen years of age or older, to vote shall not be denied or abridged by the United States or by any State on account of age.

Section 2. The Congress shall have power to enforce this article by appropriate legislation [June 30, 1971]

Sources and Credits

Chapter 1

p. 5, Carl Stephenson and Frederick George Marcham, eds., *Sources of English Constitutional History* (New York, 1972), 1:121; **6,** Carl Stephenson and Frederick George Marcham, eds., *Sources of English Constitutional History* (New York, 1972), 2:586; **7,** William F. Swindler, ed., *Sources and Documents of United States Constitutions,* 2nd ser. (London, 1982), 1:133–134, 137; **8,** John Locke, *Two Treatises of Government,* ed. Peter Laslett (Cambridge, 1967), 341–388 (italics omitted); **11,** William F. Swindler, ed., *Sources and Documents of United States Constitutions* (New York, 1975), 5:15; **12,** Perry Miller, ed., *The American Puritans: Their Prose and Poetry* (Garden City, N.Y., 1956), 79–83; **13,** *The Complete Writings of Roger Williams,* ed. Samuel L. Caldwell (New York, 1963), 3:3–4, 247–250 (italics omitted); **15,** Max Farrand, ed., *The Laws and Liberties of Massachusetts* (1648; rpt., Cambridge, Mass., 1929) (italics omitted); **17,** William F. Swindler, ed., *Sources and Documents of United States Constitutions* (New York, 1979), 8:359–361; **18,** Mattie E. E. Parker, ed., *The Colonial Records of North Carolina: North Carolina Charters and Constitutions, 1578–1698* (Raleigh, N.C., 1963), 165–183; **20,** William F. Swindler, ed., *Sources and Documents of United States Constitutions* (New York, 1979), 8:253, 254; **21,** *The Colonial Laws of New York from 1664–1719* (Albany, N.Y., 1894), 1:111–116; **24,** William Blackstone, *Commentaries on the Laws of England* (Oxford, 1765), 1:106–108; **25,** Mark D. Howe, *Readings in American Legal History* (Cambridge, Mass., 1949), 233–235; **27,** Stanley N. Katz, ed., *A Brief Narrative of the Case and Trial of John Peter Zenger* (Cambridge, Mass., 1972), 65, 67–68, 69–70, 74–75, 78–79, 99; **30,** William Blackstone, *Commentaries on the Laws of England* (Oxford, 1765), 1:430–434; **33,** William W. Hening, comp., *Virginia Statutes at Large, 1619–1660* (New York, 1823), 1:336–337; **34,** *The Book of the General Laws of . . . New Plimouth (1685),* reprinted in facsimile in *The Laws of the Pilgrims,* ed. John D. Cushing (Wilmington, Del., 1977), 12–13 (original pagination); **35,** Henry Steele Commager, ed., *Documents of American History,* 9th ed. (Englewood Cliffs, N.J., 1973), 37–38; **36,** John D. Cushing, comp., *The First Laws of the State of South Carolina* (Wilmington, Del., 1981), 163–175; **41,** [Daniel Horsmanden], *A Journal of . . . the Conspiracy Formed by Some White People, in Conjunction with Negro and Other Slaves, for Burning the City of New-York in America, and Murdering the Inhabitants,* ed. Thomas J. Davis (1744; rpt., Boston, 1971), 37–43; **43,** William Simpson, *The Practical Justice of the Peace and Parish-Officer of His Majesty's Province of South Carolina* (Charlestown, S.C., 1761), 227–239; **45,** John D. Cushing, ed., *The Earliest Printed Laws of Delaware, 1704–1741* (Wilmington, Del., 1978), 216–223; **48,** *The Diary of Samuel Sewall,* ed. Thomas M. Halsey (New York, 1973), 1:533–534; **49,** Max Farrand, ed., *The Laws and Liberties of Massachusetts* (1648; rpt., Cambridge, Mass., 1929); **50,** Nicholas Trott, comp., *The Laws of the Province of South Carolina* (Charleston, S.C., 1734), reprinted in facsimile in *The Earliest Printed Laws of South Carolina, 1692–1794,* ed. John D. Cushing (Wilmington, Del., 1978), 1:287–288; **51,** W. Elliot Woodward, ed., *Records of the Salem Witchcraft Copied from the Original Documents* (Roxbury, Mass., 1864), 1:109–126; **54,** Samuel G. Drake, ed., *The Witchcraft Delusion in New England* (1866; rpt., New York, 1970), 1:35–42.

Chapter 2

p. 58, John Wingate Thornton, ed., *The Pulpit of the American Revolution: or the Political Sermons of the Period of 1776* (Boston, 1860), 78–79; **60,** Bernard Bailyn, ed., *Pamphlets of the American Revolution, 1750–1776* (Cambridge, Mass., 1965), 1:424–425, 438–439, 442–446, 448, 454–470; **61,** William Blackstone, *Commentaries on the Laws of England* (Oxford, 1765), 1:106–109, 160–162; **63,** William F. Swindler, ed., *Sources and Documents of United States Constitutions,* 2nd ser. (London, 1982), 1:234–235; **64,** William F. Swindler, ed., *Sources and Documents of United States Constitutions,* 2nd ser. (London, 1982), 1:292–295; **65,** *The Complete Writings of Thomas Paine,* ed. Philip S. Foner (New York, 1945), 1:13–16, 29; **66,** William F. Swindler, ed., *Sources and Documents of United States Constitutions,* 2nd ser. (London, 1982), 1:321–322; **69,** William F. Swindler, ed., *Sources and Documents of United States Constitutions* (New York, 1979), 10:48–50; **71,** Jack P. Greene, ed., *Colonies to Nation, 1763–1789: A Documentary History of the American Revolution* (New York, 1967), 2:325–328, 331–332; **73,** John P. Cushing, ed., *The First Laws of the Commonwealth of Pennsylvania* (Wilmington, Del., 1984), 282–287; **74,** William W. Hening, ed., *The Statutes at Large of Virginia* (Richmond, Va., 1823), 12:84–86; **75,** Thomas P. Abernathy, ed. (rpt., New York, 1964), 111–115, 131–143; **78,** William F. Swindler, ed., *Sources and Documents of United States Constitutions,* 2nd ser. (London, 1982), 1:384, 385, 387–388, 389–390; **80,** William F. Swindler, ed., *Sources and Documents of United States Constitutions,* 2nd ser. (London, 1982), 1:335–336, 337, 338, 339, 342, 343; **81,** Max Farrand, ed., *The Records of the Federal Convention of 1787* (1911; rpt., New Haven, Conn., 1937), 1:18–23, 132–136, 250–255, 446–448; **85,** Herbert J. Storing, ed., *The Complete Antifederalist* (Chicago, 1981), 2:6–8; **86,** *The Federalist,* ed. Jacob E. Cooke (Cleveland, 1961); **94,** *The Papers of Alexander Hamilton,* ed. Howard C. Syrett (New York, 1969), 15:38–39. *The Papers of James Madison.* ed. Thomas Mason et al. (Charlottesville, Va., 1985), 15:67, 68–69; **96,** James D. Richardson, comp., *A Compilation of the Messages and Papers of the Presidents* (New York, 1897–1917), 1:205–216; **97,** Sedition Act of 1798, ch. 74, 1 Stat. 596; **98,** Philip B. Kurland and Ralph Lerner, eds., *The Founders' Constitution* (Chicago, 1987), 5:131–136; **101,** Davis N. Lott, ed., *The Presidents Speak: The Inaugural Addresses of the American Presidents from Washington to Kennedy* (New York, 1961), 15–17; **104,** Judiciary Act of 1789, ch. 20, secs. 25, 34, 1 Stat. 73; **105,** Thomas Jefferson, "Opinion on the Constitutionality of the Bill for Establishing a National Bank," in *The Papers of Thomas Jefferson,* ed. Julian Boyd (Princeton, N.J., 1974), 19:275–281. Alexander Hamilton, "Opinion on the Constitutionality of an Act to Establish a Bank," in *The Papers of Alexander Hamilton,* ed. Harold C. Syrett (New York, 1964), 8:97–134.

Chapter 3

p. 132, James D. Richardson, ed., *A Compilation of the Messages and Papers of the Presidents* (Washington, D.C., 1897), 1139–1154; **163,** Joseph Angell, *A Treatise on the Law of Watercourses,* 5th ed. (Boston, 1854), 531–565; **167,** Walter Prescott Webb, *The Great Plains* (Boston, 1931), 431–434.

Chapter 4

p. 190, Thomas R. R. Cobb, *An Inquiry into the Law of Negro Slavery* (Savannah, Ga., 1858), 17, 21–28, 35–37, 67–70, 84–85; **213,** Paul M. Angle, *Created Equal? The Complete Lincoln–Douglas Debates of 1858* (Chicago, 1958), 1–9; **219,** *The Collected Works of Abraham Lincoln,* ed. Roy B. Basler (New Brunswick, N.J., 1953), 4:262–271; **224,** *The Collected Works of Abraham Lincoln,* ed. Roy B. Basler (New Brunswick, N.J., 1953), 6:28–30; **225,** *The Collected Works of Abraham Lincoln,* ed. Roy B. Basler (New Brunswick, N.J., 1953), 8:332; **228,** James D. Richardson, ed., *The Messages and Papers of the Presidents of the United States* (Washington, D.C., 1897), 3907–3916; **231,** Laws of Mississippi 1865, 83–86, 90–93; **234,** Act of April 9, 1866, 14 Stat. 27 (1866).

Chapter 5

p. 255, Quoted in C. Vann Woodward, *The Strange Career of Jim Crow* (New York, 1955), 50–51; **264,** Elizabeth Cady Stanton, Susan B. Anthony, and Matilda Joslyn Gage, eds., *History of Woman Suffrage,* 2nd ed. (Rochester, N.Y., 1889), 1:70–73; **271,** Joel P. Bishop, *Commentaries on the Law of Marriage and Divorce* (Boston, 1881), 1–5; **285,** Cesare Beccaria, *On Crimes and Punishments,* trans. Henry Paolucci (1764; rpt., New York, 1986), 66–67, 93–95; **286,** Charles Loring Brace, *The Dangerous Classes of New York and Twenty Years Work Among Them* (New York, 1880), 25, 35–37, 42–47.

Chapter 6

p. 305, Lemuel Shaw, "Profession of the Law in the United States," 7 *Am. Jurist & Law Mag.* 56 (1832); **307,** Alexis de Tocqueville, *Democracy in America,* trans. Henry Reeve (New York, 1945), 1:104–107, 118–119, 155–157, 247–249, 255–257, 283–286, 288–290; **312,** Perry Miller, ed., *The Legal Mind in America: From Independence to the Civil War* (Ithaca, N.Y., 1962), 192–199; **313,** Perry Miller, ed., *The Legal Mind in America: From Independence to the Civil War* (Ithaca, N.Y., 1962), 260–272; **317,** Perry Miller, ed., *The Legal Mind in America: From Independence to the Civil War* (Ithaca, N.Y., 1962), 222–225; **319,** *The Miscellaneous Writings of Joseph Story,* ed. William W. Story (Boston, 1852), 715–726; **322,** *Speeches, Arguments and Miscellaneous Papers of David Dudley Field,* ed. A. P. Sprague (New York, 1884), 1:226–260; **326,** *Report of the Debates and Proceedings of the Convention for the Revision of the Constitution of the State of Ohio, 1850–1851* (Columbus, Ohio, 1851), 1:697–700; **328,** James D. Richardson, ed., *A Compilation of the Messages and Papers of the Presidents* (New York, 1907), 18:8016–8024; **333,** Dennis R. Nolan, ed., *Readings in the History of the American Legal Professions* (Indianapolis, 1980), 204–205; **334,** Perry Miller, ed., *The Legal Mind in America: From Independence to the Civil War* (Ithaca, N.Y., 1962), 84–91; **337,** Christopher C. Langdell, *A Selection of Cases on the Law of Contracts* (Boston, 1871); **340,** Thomas M. Cooley, *A Treatise on the Constitutional Limitations which Rest upon the Legislative Power of the States of the American Union* (1868; rpt., New York, 1972), 351–357, 393, 594–596; **343,** Christopher G. Tiedemann, *A Treatise on the Limitations of Police Power in the United States* (St. Louis, 1886), vi–viii; **344,** Kirk H. Porter and Donald B. Johnson, eds., *National Party Platforms, 1840–1960* (Urbana, Ill., 1961), 89–91; **347,** Oliver Wendell Holmes, Jr., *The Common Law* (1881; rpt., Cambridge, Mass., 1963); **350,** Julius J. Marke, ed., *The Holmes Reader* (Dobbs Ferry, N.Y., 1964), 41–56.

Chapter 7

p. 357, New Jersey Laws 1851, 321–322; **357,** Utah Laws 1896, chs. 28, 72; **358,** Illinois Laws 1887, ch. 168; **359,** Laws of New York 1910, ch. 674, secs. 215, 217, 219; **361,** *Proceedings of the Constitutional Convention . . . of 1875–1876 . . . for the State of Colorado* (Denver, 1907), 665, 698, 700; **363,** Interstate Commerce Act, ch. 104, secs. 1–5, 24 Stat. 379; **365,** Olney Papers, Manuscripts Division, Library of Congress, in *Liberty and Justice: The Modern Constitution: American Constitutional Development Since 1865,* ed. James M. Smith and Paul L. Murphy (New York, 1967), 292–293; **366,** Sherman Anti-Trust Act of 1890, ch. 647, secs. 1–2, 26 Stat. 209.

Chapter 8

p. 402, Louis D. Brandeis and Samuel D. Warren, "The Right to Privacy," 4 *Harv. L. Rev.* 193 (1890); **409,** Reprinted from *World War I and the Origins of Civil Liberties in the United States* by Paul L. Murphy, 127–132, by permission of W. W. Norton & Company, Inc. Copyright © 1979 by W. W. Norton & Company, Inc.; **443,** Roscoe Pound and Felix Frankfurter, *Criminal Justice in Cleveland* (Cleveland, 1922), 3–5; **451,** From *Lynching and the Law* by James H. Chadbourn, 1–12. Copyright © 1933 by The University of North Carolina Press. Reprinted by permission.

Chapter 9

p. 457, Oliver Wendell Holmes, *Collected Legal Papers* (New York, 1920), 291–297; **460,** Phillip B. Kurland and Gerhard Casper, eds., *Landmark Briefs and Arguments of the Supreme Court of the United States: Constitutional Law* (Arlington, Va., 1975), 16:18–20, 22–23, 104–106, 110–111; **464,** *Proceedings of the American Law Institute* (Philadelphia, 1923), 1:48–52; **467,** *Law and the Modern Mind* by Jerome Frank, 148–153. Copyright 1930 by Brentano's, Inc. Copyright 1930, 1933, 1949 by Coward-McCann, Inc. Copyright renewed in 1958 by Florence K. Frank. Excerpts from Anchor Books Edition, 1963. Reprinted by arrangement with the estate of Barbara Frank Kristein; **483,** *Franklin D. Roosevelt: Selected Speeches, Messages, Press Conferences, and Letters,* ed. Basil Rauch (New York, 1957), 170–181.

Chapter 10

p. 516, Excerpt from "Letter from Birmingham Jail" from *Why We Can't Wait* by Martin Luther King, Jr., 84–86. Copyright © 1963, 1964 by Martin Luther King, Jr. Reprinted by permission of HarperCollins Publishers; **550,** 12 *Student Lawyer* 46–51 (September 1983). Reprinted by permission; **552,** Mark Tushnet, "Critical Legal Studies: An Introduction to Its Origins and Underpinnings," 36 *Journal of Legal Education* 505–517 (1986). Reprinted by permission; **554,** Richard Posner, "The Ethical and Political Basis of the Efficiency Norm in Common Law Adjudication," 8 *Hofstra L. Rev.* 487–507 (1980). Reprinted by permission.

Index of Cases